# CONCISE DICTIONARY OF MUSIC

First published 1982

Reprinted 1984

This edition 1986, reprinted 1992



HarperCollins Publishers,
77-85 Fulham Palace Road,
Hammersmith, London W6 8JB.

ISBN 1 85501 248 0
Printed and bound in Great Britain by
HarperCollins Manufacturing, Glasgow

# PREFACE

The major composers naturally claim a prominent place in the Dictionary; their entries include a biographical outline and a critical evaluation, followed by a list of their principal compositions. However, a host of less well known composers are also included, as are performers, critics, musicologists, theoreticians, librettists, instrument-makers, orchestras and opera companies. A particular effort has been made to add the more prominent members of the generation of performers and composers to have emerged in the 1970s and 1980s.

The numerous articles on musical theory and notation, carefully cross-referenced, are clarified by the use of music examples, and the appendix of signs and symbols will prove useful to the reader ignorant of the basic elements of notation, and guide them to more detailed articles in the main text of the Dictionary. The articles on styles, forms, periods and movements, together with the bibliography given under the entry entitled *history of music*, will help the reader to build up an overall picture of the history of Western music, and extensive articles have been devoted to such topics as the history of opera, ballet, film music, and musical criticism. The growing interest in medieval and Renaissance music is reflected in the coverage of the Dictionary, which also caters for the jazz enthusiast in its inclusion of some of the leading figures from the history of jazz.

Ian Crofton

# ABBREVIATIONS USED IN THE DICTIONARY

| | |
|---|---|
| adj. | adjective |
| anon. | anonymous |
| approx. | approximate, approximately |
| attrib. | attributed |
| b. | born |
| B.B.C. | British Broadcasting Corporation |
| *c* | about |
| cent. | century |
| cm. | centimetres |
| Cz. | Czech |
| Dan. | Danish |
| E | east |
| *eg* | for example |
| Eng. | English |
| estab. | established |
| *etc* | etcetera |
| Fin. | Finnish |
| *fl* | flourished |
| ft | foot, feet |
| Fr. | French |
| Gael. | Gaelic |
| Ger. | German |
| govt. | government |
| Gr. | Greek |
| Hung. | Hungarian |
| *ie* | in other words |
| incl. | including |
| It. | Italian |
| Lat. | Latin |
| misattrib. | misattributed |
| mm | millimetres |
| movt. | movement |
| Ms, Mss | manuscript, manuscripts |
| Norw. | Norwegian |
| N | north |
| obs. | obsolete |
| op | opus |
| opp | plural of opus |
| op posth | opus posthumous |
| orig. | originally |
| perf. | performed, performance |
| pl. | plural |
| Port. | Portuguese |
| poss. | possibly, possible |
| prob. | probably, probable |
| pseud. | pseudonym |
| rev. | revised |
| Rom. | Romanian |
| Russ. | Russian |
| S | south |
| sing. | singular |
| Sp. | Spanish |
| St | Saint |
| trans. | translated by |
| US | American |
| vol., vols. | volume, volumes |
| W | west |
| WW | World War |
| yr., yrs. | year, years |

# A

**A** (Eng., Ger.; It., Fr., *la*), (1) sixth note (or submediant) of scale of C major. Practice of using letters A to G for successive octaves dates from 10th cent. A in middle of treble clef is note (normally played by oboe) to which orchestra tunes. International agreement fixes pitch at 440 cycles per second. *See* KEY, NOTATION, PITCH, SCALE;
(2) As abbrev. *A.* = alto, associate.

**Aaron, Pietro** (*c* 1490–1545), Italian theorist. A progressive, he rejected many surviving medieval conventions. Best known for *Thoscanella de la musica* (1523).

**Abaco, Evaristo Felice Dall'** (1625–1742), Italian composer, violinist. Wrote trio sonatas, violin sonatas, orchestral concertos.

**Abba-Cornaglia, Pietro** (1851–94), Italian composer, historian. Works incl. operas, Requiem, chamber music.

**Abbado, Claudio** (1933– ), Italian conductor. In 1970s became musical director of La Scala, Milan, and conductor of Vienna Philharmonic. Conductor of London Symphony Orchestra from 1979. Noted for interpretations of Verdi, Rossini.

**Abbatini, Antonio Maria** (*c* 1597–1680), Italian composer. Works incl. Masses, psalms, motets, antiphons. With Marazzoli wrote one of earliest known comic operas, *Dal male il bene* (1653).

**Abbé, Joseph Barnabé Saint-Sevin l'** (1721–1803), French virtuoso violinist. Wrote music for violin, and *Les Principes du violon* (1761).

**Abbey, John** (1785–1859), English organ-builder, active in France from 1826.

**abbellimenti** (It.), ornaments.

**Abduction from the Seraglio,** *see* ENTFÜHRUNG.

**ABEGG Variations,** work for piano, op 1, by Schumann (1830). Dedicated to friend, Meta von Abegg, from whose name he derived theme, using notes A–B flat–E–G–G.

**Abel, Carl Friedrich** (1723–87), German composer, bass viol player. Works incl. symphonies, chamber music.

**Abell, John** (1653–1724), Scottish counter-tenor. In service of Charles II and James II. Publications incl. 3 song collections.

**Abendmusiken** (Ger.), evening musical performances, esp. those given every autumn in Marienkirche, Lübeck. First mentioned 1673, with Buxtehude as organist. In 1705, young Bach travelled 230 miles to hear the *Abendmusiken* under Buxtehude.

**Abert, Hermann** (1871–1927), German historian, musicologist. Wrote studies of Greek and medieval music, biography of Schumann, study of Mozart.

**Abgesang** (Ger.), 'aftersong'. Concluding portion of stanza of Minnesinger or Meistersinger song.

**Abraham, Gerald Ernest** (1904– ), English musicologist. A specialist in Russian music, his works incl. *Masters of Russian Music* (with M.D. Calvocoressi, 1936), *Eight Soviet Composers* (1943).

**Abschiedssymphonie,** *see* FAREWELL SYMPHONY.

**Absil, Jean** (1893– ), Belgian composer. Compositions, unconventional in rhythm and harmony, incl. 5 symphonies, concertos for violin, viola, cello, piano, choral and chamber music.

**absolute music,** term denoting music that has no admitted associations with anything outside itself. Most music is in this category. Also called abstract music. Opposite is PROGRAMME MUSIC.

**absolute pitch** or **perfect pitch,** gift of recognizing pitch of any note heard, or of singing note at any pitch without help from instrument.

**abstract music,** same as ABSOLUTE MUSIC.

**Academic Festival Overture,** orchestral piece, op 80, by Brahms (1880). Written after receiving honorary Ph.D. from University of Breslau (1879). Overture contains number of German students' songs, incl. 'Gaudeamus igitur'. First perf. Breslau, 1881.

**Academy of St Martin-in-the-Fields,** chamber orchestra founded 1956. Directed by Neville Marriner to 1978, then by Iona Brown. Named after London church in which it gave concerts.

**a cappella** (It.), 'in the church style'. Term applied to choral music without accompaniment.

**accelerando** (It.), 'quickening (the time)'. Abbrev. is *accel.*

**accent,** (1) the rhythm of music is made clear by accent. On the whole, accent recurs at regular intervals, *eg* in 4/4 time on 1st beat of bar, and with less force on 3rd; in 3/4 on 1st beat of bar. However, this is by no means universal; there is no reason why accent should coincide with 'strong' beats.

Accent signs:

| | |
|---|---|
| > | normally indicates strong accent; |
| — | stress or pressure; |
| ∧ ∨ | heavy pressure; |

Other abbreviations indicating strong emphasis: *sf, sfz* (*sforzando,* 'forcing'), *sfp* or *fp* (*sforzando piano* or *forte piano,* an accent followed immediately by *piano*), *rf* or *rfz* (*rinforzando,* 'reinforcing');

(2) French term for NACHSCHLAG.

**acciaccatura** (It.), a 'crushing' (implying violent pressure). (1) Keyboard ornament in 17th, 18th cents; dissonant note of shortest poss. duration struck at the same time as chord it decorates;

(2) name is now applied to short APPOGGIATURA, an ornamental note of minimum duration, sounded immediately before, or simultaneously with, main note. Notated by auxiliary note in smaller type with stroke through stem.

**accidental,** comprehensive term for SHARP, DOUBLE SHARP, FLAT, DOUBLE FLAT or NATURAL prefixed to note. Accidental before note applies to all subsequent repetitions of that note (if any) in same bar, unless cancelled by another accidental.

**accompaniment,** subordinate part(s), usually instrumental added to principal part(s). May be mere duplication, but more often independent though incorporating details of principal part(s). Where a piece is scored for equal partners, *eg* sonata for violin and piano, piano part should not be considered an accompaniment.

*See* ADDITIONAL ACCOMPANIMENTS, OBBLIGATO.

**accordion, piano-accordion,** portable reed organ, invented by Friedrich Buschmann of Berlin, 1822. Sounds are produced by metal reeds freely vibrating within frames, air being supplied by bellows operated by player pushing and pulling instrument – hence nickname, 'squeeze-box'. In accordion both hands press studs, producing single notes or chords; in piano-accordion, right hand plays on keyboard. Largely confined to popular music, though Chaikovsky, Shostakovich, Gerhard and Roy Harris have used it.

**Achtel** (Ger.), quaver.

**Acis and Galatea,** masque or pastoral opera by Handel, first perf. 1718/20. Libretto by John Gay (based on Ovid) with additions by Dryden, Hughes, Pope. In 1708 Handel had written Italian cantata on same subject.

**Acis et Galatée,** opera by Lully, first perf. 1686. Libretto by J. G. de Campistron. Haydn wrote opera on same subject (1790).

**acoustic bass,** organ stop in which pipes of sixteen foot pedal stop sound with rank a fifth above, producing RESULTANT TONE an octave below sixteen foot pipes.

**acoustics,** the science of sound. Sound consists of impact on ear of air vibrations set in motion by (1) vibration of elastic material, (2) vibration of air column in pipe, or (3) vibrations electrically produced or transmitted. Elastic material may be (a) gut string or wire (string instruments, keyboard instruments except organ family), (b) reed(s) (oboe, clarinet), (c) membrane (vocal chords in voice, lips in brass instruments, skin of drum), (d) solid body (bells, triangle, xylophone *etc*).

*Intensity* of note is determined by amplitude of vibration; greater amplitude gives louder sound.

*Pitch* of note is determined by frequency of vibration: low frequency gives low note *etc*. On the whole short strings or pipes produce higher frequency.

*Resonance* of note depends on presence of auxiliary material (*eg* belly of violin) or air column (*eg* in woodwind instruments) that vibrates in sympathy or by direct contact with original vibrations (*eg* of string or reed).

*Quality* of note depends on complex character of vibrations. Most instruments, when single note is played, in fact produce very faint 'overtones' of the HARMONIC SERIES; richness of quality depends on number and selection of these overtones.

**action,** (1) mechanism of keyboard instrument, esp. pressure required to sound note;

(2) distance between strings and fingerboard in stringed instrument, dictated by height of bridge.

**act tune,** 17th, 18th-cent. term for instrumental music played between acts of play. Many examples by Purcell. Modern term is *entr'acte.*

**acute,** ornament in 17th cent. English music.

**acute mixture,** organ stop giving overtones tuned slightly sharp.

**adagietto** (It.), slightly faster than *adagio.*

**adagio** (It.), 'at ease', *ie* slow. Often used to describe slow movt.

**Adagio for Strings,** short, popular orchestral piece by Samuel Barber, orig. movt. from string quartet. First perf. 1938.

**adagissimo** (It.), very slow.

**Adam, Adolphe Charles** (1803–56), French composer, teacher, critic. Most successful as composer of *opéra comique, eg Le Postillon de Longjumeau* (1836); best remembered for ballet *Giselle* (1841).

**Adam de la Hale** or **Halle** (*c* 1230–88), nicknamed 'le Bossu' ('the hunchback'), French *trouvère,* composer. Wrote songs, polyphonic motets, rondeaux. Most famous work is dramatic pastoral *Le Jeu de Robin et Marion,* regarded as precursor of *opéra comique.*

**added sixth,** the addition of a sixth to major or minor triad, *eg* in C major, A is added above triad of C–E–G. *See* CHORD, FIGURED BASS, HARMONY.

**additional accompaniments,** parts for extra instruments added to 17th, 18th cent. works considered by later interpreters to lack fullness. Handel (esp. his *Messiah*) has been chief victim of this unfortunate practice, though Bach and Mozart have also suffered.

**à deux cordes** (Fr.; It., *a due cordes*), on two strings.

**Addinsell, Richard** (1904–77), British composer. Best known for *Warsaw Concerto,* written for film *Dangerous Moonlight* (1941).

**Adieux, l'absence et le retour, L',** *see* LEBEWOHL.

**Adler, Larry** (1914– ), American mouth-organist. Has inspired works by Milhaud, Vaughan Williams, Malcolm Arnold.

**ad libitum** (Lat.), 'at pleasure'; abbrev., *ad lib.* Grants freedom to performer as to (1) rhythm, tempo, *etc,* (2) use of alternative passage by composer, (3) improvization of cadenza, (4) inclusion or omission of some part or passage.

**Adlung, Jacob** (1699–1762), German organist, teacher. Wrote *Musica mechanica organoedi* (1768), treatise on manufacture and care of keyboard instruments.

**Admeto, Re di Tessaglia** (It., *Admetus, King of Thessaly*), opera by Handel, libretto by N.F. Haym or P.A. Rolli. First perf. London, 1727.

**a due** (It.), 'in two parts'. Generally written *a 2:* (1) in wind parts indicates that single melodic line is to be played by two instruments in unison; (2) in string parts indicates that passage in two parts is to be played *divisi* (term normally used now). So also *a 3, a 4.*

**Aeolian harp,** zither-like instrument with strings of different thickness all tuned to same note. Not played, but placed outside to catch wind; wind makes strings vibrate with various harmonies depending on speed, producing series of chords. Known in ancient times; name derives from Aeolus, god of winds.

**Aeolian mode,** MODE which, on piano, uses white notes from A to A.

**aeolina, aeoline,** soft organ stop, resembling sound of Aeolian harp.

**aerophone,** any instrument in which movement of air causes sound production. *See* INSTRUMENTS.

**aerophore,** device enabling wind instrumentalists to play continuously without pausing for breath. Air from bellows operated by player's foot is pumped through tube to player's mouth and then to his instrument while he breathes through his nose.

**Affektenlehre** (Ger.), system of musical aesthetics formulated in Germany in 18th cent. and widely accepted. Maintained compositions should be judged by extent to which they portrayed and aroused certain emotions.

**affetto** (It.), 'affection'.

**affettuoso** (It.), 'affectionate', *ie* with tender emotion.

**affrettando** (It.) 'hurrying', *ie* increasing the speed.

**Africaine, L'** (Fr., *The African Girl*), opera by Meyerbeer, libretto by A. E. Scribe. First perf. Paris, 1865. Story concerns Vasco da Gama and his love for African girl.

**agitato** (It.), 'agitated', *ie* restless and wild.

**Agnus Dei** (Lat.), 'Lamb of God'. Concluding portion of musical setting of Roman Mass. In Requiem Mass, is followed by *Lux aeterna.*

**agogic,** term describing deviations from strict tempo and rhythm necessary for subtle performance of musical phrase.

**Agon,** ballet score by Stravinsky, written for George Balanchine. First perf. New York, 1957.

**Agostini, Paolo** (1583–1629), Italian composer, organist. Wrote much church music, some of it for several choirs.

**agréments** (Fr.), ornaments.

**Agricola, Alexander,** orig. Alexander Ackermann (*c* 1446–*c* 1506), Flemish composer. Patrons incl. Lorenzo de' Medici. Composed church and instrumental music, chansons.

**Agricola, Johann Friedrich** (1720–74), German organist, composer. Pupil of J.S. Bach and Quantz. Became court composer to Frederick the Great. Works incl. operas and choral and instrumental music.

**Agricola, Martin,** orig. name Sore (1486–1556), Flemish writer on music, composer. Most notable work is *Musica instrumentalis deudsch.* Also composed hymns, motets and instrumental music.

**Agrippina,** opera by Handel, libretto by V. Grimani. First perf. Venice, 1709.

**Aguiari** or **Agujari, Lucrezia** (1743–83), Italian soprano, nicknamed 'La Bastardella'. Admired by Mozart, her range spanned 3 octaves above middle C.

**Aguilera de Heredia, Sebastian** (b. 1560–70), Spanish composer. Works incl. Magnificats and organ music.

**Ahle, Johann Rudolph** (1625–73), German organist, composer.

Wrote many works for voices and instruments. His tune for hymn 'Beloved Jesu, we are here' became very popular.

**Aichinger, Gregor** (1564–1628), German composer. Wrote church music strongly influenced by Venetian school of Gabrieli.

**Aida,** opera by Verdi, libretto by A. Ghislanzoni and composer. Story concerns war between Egypt and Ethiopia; Aida, daughter of Ethiopian king and slave at Egyptian court, loves Radames, Egyptian commander-in-chief. Conflict between love and patriotism ends in death of both. First perf. Cairo, 1871.

**air,** simple tune for voice or instrument. In 17th cent. England 'ayre' was song for one or several voices. *See* also ARIA.

**Air on the G String,** name given to arrangement for violin and accompaniment by August Wilhemj of 2nd movt. of Bach's Suite no. 3 in D major for orchestra. Violin part (transposed down) played on lowest (G) string.

**Ais** and **Aisis** (Ger.), A sharp and A double sharp respectively.

**Akademische Festouvertüre,** *see* ACADEMIC FESTIVAL OVERTURE.

**Akhron** or **Achron, Joseph** (1886–1943), Lithuanian-born composer, violinist, teacher. Moved to US, 1925. Works incl. 3 violin concertos, chamber music.

**Akimenko, Feodor Stepanovich** (1876–1945), Ukrainian composer. Pupil of Balakirev and Rimsky-Korsakov; became Stravinsky's first composition teacher. Long resident in France. Works incl. symphony, violin concerto, opera, chamber and piano music, and songs.

**à la hongroise,** *see* ALL' ONGARESE.

**Alain, Jean,** *see* ALEYN.

**Alain, Jehan Ariste** (1911–40), French composer. Pupil of Dukas and Roger-Ducasse. Killed in action in WWII. Works, original in idiom and distinguished in execution, incl. choral, organ, piano and chamber music, and songs.

**alalá** (Sp.), type of Galician folk melody, sung in free rhythm and often ornamented with grace notes. Appears to have melodic affinities with plainsong.

**Alanus, Johannes,** *see* ALEYN.

**Alayrac, D',** *see* DALAYRAC.

**Albanesi, Licia** (1913– ), American soprano, b. Italy. One of Toscanini's favourite singers.

**Albéniz, Isaac** (1860–1909), Catalan composer, pianist. Wrote operas, but mainly remembered for later piano works esp. suite *Iberia* (1909), influenced by Spanish popular music.

**Albert, Eugène Francis Charles d'** (1864–1932), Franco-English composer, pianist, b. Scotland; settled in Germany. Studied with Liszt. Wrote 21 operas, concertos, symphony, chamber and piano music.

**Albert, Heinrich** (1604–51), German composer, poet. Cousin and pupil of Schütz. Published 8 collections of *Arien* – sacred and secular songs with German words for one or more voices with accompaniment. Adaptation of melody of his 'Gott des Himmels' was used by Bach in his *Christmas Oratorio*.

**Albert Herring,** comic opera by Britten, libretto by Eric Crozier after Maupassant's short story *Madame Husson's May King*. First perf. Glyndebourne, 1947. Story concerns the virtuous Albert, an East Anglian shopkeeper; he is elected King of the May, becomes drunk and frees himself from his mother and other local puritans.

**Alberti, Domenico** (1710–40), Italian singer, harpsichordist, composer. In his keyboard sonatas, was addicted to using 'Alberti bass' (not actually invented by him), conventional figuration for left hand consisting of 'broken chords', *ie* simple arpeggio treatment of series of chords; much used by 18th, early 19th-cent. composers incl. Mozart.

**Albertini, Giovacchino** (1751–1812), Italian composer. Director of music at Polish court. Operas incl. *Don Juan* (1783) to Polish text.

**Alberto de ripa, Alberto Mantovano,** *see* RIPPE.

**Albicastro, Henrico,** orig. Weyssenburg (*fl* late 17th cent.), Swiss violinist, composer. Wrote sonatas and orchestral concertos.

**Albinoni, Tommaso** (1671–1750), Italian composer, violinist. One of 1st composers to write concertos for solo violin. Prolific output incl. *c* 50 operas. Much admired by Bach.

**Alboni, Marietta** (1826–94), Italian contralto, one of greatest in operatic history. Esp. associated with Rossini's operas.

**alborada** (Sp.; Fr. *aubade*), 'morning song'. Form of music for bagpipes and side-drum popular in Galicia. Used in Ravel's *Miroirs* for piano (1905).

**Albrechtsberger, Johann Georg** (1736–1809). Austrian organist, composer, teacher. Taught Beethoven counterpoint (1794–5) but did not regard him as promising pupil. Wrote many religious and instrumental works.

**Albumblatt** (Ger.), 'album leaf'. Title frequently given by 19th-cent. composers to short, intimate piece. Wagner's was esp. popular.

**Alceste,** (1) opera by Gluck, libretto by R. Calzabigi (It. version), F. du Roullet (revised Fr. version). First perf. Vienna, 1767. Plot borrowed from Greek legend of wife who offers to die in place of her husband, Admetus, and is subsequently restored to life;

(2) opera by Lully, libretto by P. Quinault. First perf. Paris, 1764.

**Alcestis,** *see* ALKESTIS.

**Alchemist, The** (Ger., *Der Alchymist*), opera by Spohr, libretto by 'Fr. Georg Schmidt' (pseud. of K. Pfeiffer), based on story by Washington Irving. First perf. Cassel, 1830.

**Alcina,** opera by Handel, libretto by A. Marchi (from Ariosto's *Orlando Furioso*). First perf. London, 1735.

**Alcock, John** (1715–1806), English organist, composer. Wrote glees and instrumental and church music. His son, **John Alcock** (*c* 1740–91), was also organist and composer.

**Aldeburgh Festival,** annual music festival held at Aldeburgh, Suffolk. Founded 1948. Long associated with Britten, some of whose operas were first perf. there.

**Aldrich, Richard** (1863–1937), American music critic. Music editor of *New York Times* (1902–23). Works incl. volume of essays and 2 books on Wagner.

**aleatory** or **aleatoric music,** music containing chance or random elements – a trend in many compositions since 1945. Aleatory elements may be fairly closely controlled (*eg* in some works of Lutoslawski) or highly indeterminate (*eg* in some works of Stockhausen). The choice of chance elements may be variously decided, *eg* John Cage used *I-Ching* for *Music of Changes* (1951).

**Alembert, Jean le Rond d'** (1717–83), French philosopher, mathematician, writer on music. Advocated operatic reform along lines practised by Gluck.

**Alessandri, Felice** (1742–98), Italian composer, conductor. Wrote *c* 35 operas incl. comic *Il vecchio geloso* (1781), and instrumental music.

**Alessandro,** opera by Handel, libretto by P.A. Rolli. First perf. London, 1726.

**Alessandro Stradella,** opera by Flotow, libretto by 'W. Friedrich' (pseud. of F.W. Riese). First perf. Hamburg, 1844. Opera is based on life of 17th-cent. composer, Stradella.

**Alexander Balus,** oratorio by Handel, libretto by T. Morell. First perf. London, 1748.

**Alexander Nevsky,** cantata by Prokofiev for soprano, chorus, orchestra. First perf. 1939, using material from composer's score for Eisenstein's film.

**Alexander's Feast,** ode for soloists, chorus and orchestra by Handel, to words by Dryden. First perf. London, 1736.

**Alexandrov, Anatol Nikolayevich** (1888–1946), Russian composer. Compositions, rather conservative in style, incl. 2 operas, orchestral suites, film and piano music, songs.

**Aleyn, John, John Alain** or **Johannes Alanus,** (d. *c* 1373), English composer, theorist. Member of Chapel Royal. Only known works are Gloria in *Old Hall Manuscript,* and motet 'Sub Arthuro plebs vallata'.

**Alfano, Franco** (1876–1954), Italian opera composer. Operas incl. *Risurrezione* (1904), *La leggenda de Sakuntala* (1921), but best remembered for completion of Puccini's *Turandot.*

**al fine** (It.), 'to the end'. Usually in phrases *da capa al fine* (from the beginning to the end), *dal segno al fine* (from the sign to the end). *See* DA CAPO and DAL SEGNO.

**Alfonso and Estrella,** opera by Schubert, libretto by Franz von Schober. First perf. Weimar, 1854.

**Alfonso el Sabio,** Alfonso X, nicknamed 'the Wise' (1221–84), king of Castile and Leon (1252–84). A patron of music and poetry, he compiled collection of *c* 400 *Cantigas de Santa Maria* (hymns to the Virgin). Music shows influence of Provençal troubadours, but also has specifically Spanish characteristics.

**Alfvén, Hugo** (1872–1960), Swedish composer. Works incl. 5 symphonies, choral, chamber and piano music, songs. Best known for Swedish rhapsody for orchestra *Midsommarvaka*.

**Algarotti, Francesco** (1712–64), Italian scholar. Advocated abandonment of outworn conventions of early 18th-cent. opera along lines similar to Gluck.

**Alkan, Charles Henri Valentin,** real name Morhange (1813–88), French composer, pianist. Friend of Liszt, Chopin, George Sand; one of leading piano teachers in Paris. Wrote piano pieces of daunting technical complexity and adventurousness, using 'Lisztian' and 'Brahmsian' ideas before Liszt or Brahms.

**Alkestis,** (1), opera by Rutland Boughton, libretto from Gilbert Murray's version of Euripedes. First perf. Glastonbury, 1922.

(2) opera by Wellesz, libretto by Hugo von Hofmannsthal (based on Euripides). First perf. Mannheim, 1924.

**alla breve** (It.), term meaning that BREVE is to be taken as standard of mensuration instead of SEMIBREVE, *ie* that music is to be performed twice as fast as notation would suggest. In 18th cent.,

¢

is normal time-signature for piece marked *alla breve*.

**allargando** (It.), 'getting broader', and, in consequence, slower.

**alla tedesca** (It.), short for *alla danza tedesca*, *ie* in style of German dance or ALLEMANDE of either type.

**alla turca** (It.), 'in the Turkish style'. *See* JANISSARY MUSIC.

**alla zingarese** (It.), in style of gypsy music (from *zingaro*, a gypsy).

**alla zoppa** (It.), 'in a limping manner', *ie* syncopated. Applied particularly to rhythm known as SCOTCH SNAP.

**allegretto** (It.), diminutive of allegro, indicating moderately quick movt., somewhat slower than allegro.

**Allegri, Gregorio** (1582–1652), Italian priest, composer, papal singer. Composed church music, incl. nine-part *Miserere*, sung annually in Holy Week in Sistine Chapel.

**allegro** (It.), 'lively'. Used to indicate a brisk movement, often in association with other adjectives or qualifying expressions, *eg allegro moderato, allegro con brio.*

**Allegro, il Penseroso ed il Moderato, L'** (It., The lively man, the thoughtful man, and the moderate man), cantata for soloists, chorus and orchestra by Handel, libretto compiled from Milton by C. Jennens, with addition of *Il Moderato.*

**allemande** (Fr.), short for *danse allemande*, 'German dance':

(1) moderately slow dance of German origin in duple time, adopted in 16th cent. by French, then by English (Eng., almain, almen, almand; It., *allemanda, tedesca*). In 17th, early 18th cents., was normally 1st of 4 contrasted dances in suite; composers did not always adhere to slow tempo;

(2) brisk dance in triple time, current in late 18th, early 19th cents.; still popular in Swabia, Switzerland (Ger., *deutscher Tanz;* It., *danza tedesca*). Prototype of waltz.

**Allen, Hugh Percy** (1869–1946), English musical scholar. Director of Royal College of Music, London, and professor of music at Oxford. Esp. active in spreading enthusiasm for the works of Bach.

**allentando** (It.), 'slowing down'.

**Allison, Richard** (*fl* 16th–17th cent.), English composer. Published harmonization of metrical psalms for voice(s) and instruments, and collection of madrigals. Also wrote music for mixed consort.

**allmählich** (Ger.), 'gradual, gradually'.

**all' ongarese** (It.; Fr., *à la hongroise*), in style of Hungarian (gypsy) music.

**all' ottava** (It.), 'at the octave' (above or below). *See* OTTAVA.

**all' unisono** (It.), 'in unison', *ie* 2 or more instruments are to play the same notes.

**almain, alman, almand,** *see* ALLEMANDE.

**Almeida, Francisco Antonio d'** (*fl* 1740), Portuguese composer. His comic opera *La Spinalba* (1739) is earliest surviving Italian opera by a Portuguese. Also composed church music.

**Almenräder, Karl** (1786–1843), German bassoonist. Made considerable improvements in structure of bassoon.

**Almira,** opera by Handel (his first), libretto by F.C. Feustking (based on Italian of G. Pancieri). First perf. Hamburg, 1705.

**Alphorn** (Ger.), 'alpine horn'. Primitive instrument still used by herdsmen in Switzerland and other mountainous countries. Made of wood, bound by bark; either straight or slightly curved, with upturned bell; may be up to 3m (10ft) long. Produces notes of HARMONIC SERIES.

**Alpine Symphony** (Ger., *Eine Alpensinfonie*), symphony by Richard Strauss, depicting events in course of mountain climb. First perf. Berlin, 1915.

**Also sprach Zarathustra** (Ger., *Thus Spake Zarathustra*), symphonic poem by Richard Strauss, op 30, inspired by Nietzsche's work of same name. First perf. Frankfurt, 1896.

**alt,** (1) in phrase *in alt* (from Lat., *in alto,* in the height), applied to notes from G above treble stave to F above that; notes in octave above are said to be *in altissimo;*

(2) (Ger.), ALTO.

**Altenburg, Johann Ernst** (1734–1801), German trumpeter, organist. Author of *Versuch einer Anleitung zur heroisch-musikalischen Trompeter-und-Pauker-Kunst* (1795).

**alteration,** (1) conventional augmentation of value of breve, semibreve or minim in mensural notation before 1600. *See* RHYTHMIC MODES, MENSURAL NOTATION;

(2) chromatic alteration is raising or lowering of note of scale by means of ACCIDENTAL.

**Althorn** (Ger.), brass instrument of SAXHORN family.

**Altnikol, Johann Christoph** (1719–59), German harpsichordist, organist, composer. Pupil and son-in-law of J.S. Bach, whose last composition – choral prelude 'Vor deinen Thron' – was dictated to Altnikol from the composer's death-bed.

**alto** (It.), lit. 'high', (1) highest adult male voice, now employed mainly in church or male-voice choirs. Range of voice is roughly 2 octaves, from D in middle of bass clef to D near top of treble clef, though lower notes lack resonance; upper part of range made poss. by cultivation of FALSETTO voice. In 17th-cent. England, alto (known as counter-tenor) was popular as solo voice;

(2) low female voice (properly called contralto), covering slightly higher range than male alto, which it has supplanted in music for mixed voices;

(3) (Fr.), viola;

(4) prefixed to name of instrument; indicates one size larger than treble (or soprano) member of family, *eg* alto saxophone;

(5) alto clef is the C clef, in which middle C falls on third line of stave; now only used for viola:

**alto basso,** *see* TAMBOURIN DE BÉARN.

**Alto Rhapsody,** work by Brahms, op 53, for solo contralto, male-voice chorus and orchestra. Based on Goethe's philosophical poem, 'Harzreise im Winter'. First perf. Jena, 1870.

**Alwyn, William** (1905– ), English composer. Pupil of McEwan. Works, in traditional style, incl. opera *Miss Julie*, 5 symphonies, symphonic prelude (*The Magic Island*, after Shakespeare's *Tempest*), impressive piano sonata, film and chamber music, and 4 song cycles.

**Amadeus Quartet,** British string quartet. Founded 1948, since when it has acquired international reputation, esp. in performances of Beethoven. Members are Norbert Brainin, Sigmund Nissel (violins), Peter Schidlof (viola), Martin Lovett (cello).

**Amadigi di Gaula** (It., *Amadis of Gaul*), opera by Handel, libretto prob. by J.J. Heidegger. First perf. London, 1715.

**Amadis,** opera by Lully, libretto by P. Quinault. First perf. Paris, 1684.

**Amahl and the Night Visitors,** first opera designed for TV. Written by Menotti, text by composer. Broadcast by NBC, 1951. Sentimental story (of Magi and crippled child they meet on way to Bethlehem) has ensured world-wide popularity.

**Amati,** famous family of violin-makers at Cremona, Italy, in 16th, 17th cents. Earliest known is **Andrea Amati** (*c* 1500–*c* 1575); most famous is **Nicolo Amati** (1596–1684), who was master of Antonio Stradivari.

**Ambros, August Wilhelm** (1816–76), musical historian, composer, pianist, civil servant. His *Geschichte der Musik* (1862–81) is standard work. Compositions incl. opera *Bratislav and Jitka* and overture to *Othello*.

**Ambrose** (340–97), bishop of Milan. Appears to have introduced into Western Church Syrian practice of antiphonal singing; also encouraged hymn singing. No melodies of so-called Ambrosian chant (or plainsong) can be attributed to him with certainty.

**America,** symphony by Bloch; 'epic rhapsody' of impressions of his life in US, quoting Indian, Negro music, Civil War songs *etc.*

**American in Paris, An,** descriptive piece for orchestra by Gershwin (1928). Basis of music for film of same name (1951).

**American organ,** free-reed keyboard instrument, orig. known as Melodeon, introduced by Mason and Hamlin of Boston, Mass. *c.* 1860. Differs from harmonium in that in latter air is forced through reeds, whereas in former it is drawn through by suction. American organ is nearer in tone-quality to organ, but is less expressive than harmonium.

**American Quartet,** Dvořák's string quartet in F, op 96 (1893). Written in US, partly inspired by Negro tunes.

**Amico Fritz, L'** (It., *Friend Fritz*), opera by Mascagni, libretto by 'P. Suardon' (pseud. of N. Daspuro), based on novel by Erckmann-Chatrian. First perf. Rome, 1891. Opera is light pastoral comedy, rarely performed outside Italy.

**Amner, John** (1579–1641), English organist. Composed services, anthems and hymns for voices and instruments.

**Amor Brujo, El,** *see* LOVE, THE MAGICIAN.

**amore** (It.), 'love'. *Con amore,* lovingly.

**Amore dei Tre Re, L'** (It., *The Love of the Three Kings*), opera by Montemezzi, libretto by S. Benelli. First perf. La Scala, Milan, 1913 (conducted by Toscanini).

**amoroso** (It.), lovingly.

**Amour des Trois Oranges,** *see* LOVE FOR THREE ORANGES.

**Amphion Anglicus,** volume of songs by John Blow, published 1700.

**Amy, Gilbert** (1936– ), French composer, conductor. Pupil of Milhaud, Messiaen, Boulez. Director since 1967 of concerts of the Domaine Musical (founded 1954 for promotion of new music). Complex orchestral pieces incl. *Antiphonies* (1963), *Trajectories* (1966), *Adagio et Stretto* (1977–8); has also written chamber and piano music.

**Anacréon,** opera-ballet by Cherubini, libretto by R. Mendouze. First perf. Paris, 1803. Now known mainly for overture.

**anche** (Fr.), reed, reed instrument, reed pipe (in organ).

**ancient cymbals** or **antique cymbals,** small cymbals, usually found in pairs, producing definite notes. Much used by dancing girls in Ancient World. Produce soft, delicate sounds. Use revived by Berlioz; also used by Debussy, Ravel.

**andamento** (It.), (1) 'movement'; (2) 18th-cent. term for fugue subject of substantial length, often falling naturally into 2 contrasted sections; (3) episode in fugue; (4) movt. in suite.

**andante** (It.), 'going, moving'. Now generally used of a moderate tempo, inclining to slowness ('at a walking pace') rather than actually slow. Hence used as title of piece or movt. in this tempo. *Piu andante* means 'moving more', *ie* slightly faster.

**andantino** (It.), diminutive of ANDANTE. Ambiguous, but generally interpreted as 'slightly faster' (rather than slower) than andante.

**Anderson, Marian** (1902– ), American contralto. First black singer to appear at New York Metropolitan (1955). Much admired by Toscanini. Mostly sung in concert hall rather than opera house.

**An die ferne Geliebte** (Ger.), 'to the distant beloved'. Song-cycle of 6 songs by Beethoven, op 98 (1816), to words by A. Jeitteles.

**André,** German publishing firm. Family incl. **Johann André** (1741–99), composer of many operas. His son **Johann Anton André** (1775–1842), was also composer, and wrote books on harmony, counterpoint and composition.

**Andreae, Volkmar** (1879–1962), Swiss composer, conductor, principal of Zurich Conservatoire (1914–39). Works incl. 2 operas, 2 symphonies, chamber and choral music, songs.

**Andriessen, Hendrik** (1892– ), Dutch composer, organist. Wrote religious works, 3 symphonies, chamber music, songs. His son, **Juriaan Andriessen** (1925– ), is composer, pianist, conductor. Has written orchestral and chamber music.

**Andriessen, Willem** (1887–1964), Dutch composer, pianist. Wrote piano concerto, orchestral scherzo, and choral music.

**Anerio, Felice** (*c* 1560–1614), Italian composer to Papal Chapel, 1594–1602. His brother, **Giovanni Francesco Anerio** (*c* 1567–1630) was also composer. Both wrote much sacred music, madrigals.

**Anet, Jean-Baptiste** (*c* 1661–1755), French violinist. A pupil of Corelli, he was greatly admired by his contemporaries.

**Anfossi, Pasquale** (1727–97), Italian opera composer. Influenced young Mozart, esp. through *La finta giardiniera* (1774); Mozart reset libretto following year.

**Angeles, Victoria de los** (1923– ), Spanish soprano. Active in opera and on concert platform. Has done much to popularize Spanish songs.

**angelica** (Fr., *angélique*), type of lute in use during late 17th, early 18th cents.

**Angel of Fire, The** (also known as **The Fiery Angel**), opera by Prokofiev, libretto based on story by V. Bryusov. Controversial subject is diabolical possession, sorcery, exorcism. Composed 1925, but first staged Venice, 1955.

**anglaise** (Fr.), short for *danse anglaise,* English dance: dance in quick duple time, one of dances of foreign origin (cf. POLONAISE) introduced in 17th cent. and so incorporated in suite as one of *Galanterien* or optional dances added to normal *allemande, courante, sarabande, gigue.* Term also applied to other dances of English origin.

**Anglebert, Jean Henri d'** (*c* 1628–91), French harpsichordist, organist, composer. His *Pièces de clavessin* (1689) incl. both original pieces and transcriptions of Lully, and is a valuable record of contemporary ornamentation.

**Anglès, Higini** (1888–1969), Catalan musicologist. Edited several collections of Spanish music.

**Anglican chant,** harmonized setting, designed to be used for successive verses of canticles and psalms in English Prayer Book. *Single chant* consists normally of 7 bars, unequally divided into 3 and

4, caesura in middle corresponding to colon in text. This is repeated for each verse. *Double, triple* or *quadruple chant* serve for groups of 2, 3 or 4 verses respectively. If double chant is used for psalm with odd no. of verses, 2nd half of chant is repeated for odd verse. Difficulty of accommodating verses of different length to same tune is solved by treating specified bars as reciting notes of indefinite length; uniform interpretation of rhythm is ensured by system of 'pointing'. The Anglican chant is basically imitation of Gregorian tones.

**anima** (It.), 'spirit'. *Con anima,* with spirit.

**animando** (It.), becoming animated.

**animato** (It.), 'animated'.

**Animuccia, Giovanni** (*c* 1500–71), Italian composer. *Maestro di cappella* at St Peter's, Rome (1555–71). Composed *Laudi spirituali* for Oratory of St Philip Neri (*see* LAUDA, ORATORIO). Also wrote church music and madrigals.

**Annibale Padovano** (1527–75), Italian organist, composer. Works incl. 4-part *ricercari* and other instrumental music, church music and madrigals.

**Anschlag** (Ger.), (1) lit. 'touch', *ie* either way in which player depresses keys of keyboard instrument or way in which they respond; (2) an ornament, sometimes known as double APPOGGIATURA, consisting of 2 successive grace notes, one lower than principal note, the other a second above it. Notated by 2 small notes, first played on beat. First note is normally either repetition of preceding note or second below principal note.

**Ansermet, Ernest** (1883–1969), Swiss conductor. Conductor with Diaghilev's Russian ballet from 1915, conducting many first perfs. of works by Stravinsky. In 1918 founded Orchestre de la Suisse Romande.

**answer,** in exposition of FUGUE, answer is 2nd entry of subject, presented while 1st entry continues in counterpoint to it. In 4-part fugue, 2nd and 4th entries of subject will normally be transposed, so answering respectively 1st and 3rd entries. If transposition of subject is exact, answer is called 'real' answer. If transposition is modified in some way, answer is called 'tonal'.

**Antarctic Symphony** (*Sinfonia Antartica*), Vaughan Williams' 7th symphony (1953), based on his music for film *Scott of the Antarctic.*

**Antheil, George** (1900–59), American composer, pianist. Pupil of Bloch. Works incl. *Ballet mécanique* (1925; score used aeroplane propellers, motor-horns and other mechanical devices), operas *eg Volpone* (after Jonson), piano sonatas, symphonies, film music.

**anthem,** (Eng. corruption of ANTIPHON), setting of non-liturgical English words used in Anglican services, placed after third collect. Derives from Latin MOTET of Roman church, but has since developed on independent lines.

**anticipation,** sounding of note(s) before chord to which it or they belong.

**antiphon,** plainsong setting of sacred words, sung before and after psalm or canticle in Latin church service, with intention of emphasizing its significance. Term ANTIPHONAL derives from practice of alternating performance between 2 sets of singers.

**antiphonal,** (1) book containing music sung by choir in Office of Roman Church *ie* in all services other than Mass (music for Mass is contained in GRADUAL);

(2) now word is applied to musical effects brought about by groups of performers being positioned in different places in auditorium or on platform – one group 'responding' to other group(s) (*eg* between 1st and 2nd violins in many 18th, 19th-cent. symphonies).

**anvil** (Fr., *enclume*; Ger., *Amboss*; It., *ancudine*), instrument composed of steel bars struck with hard wooden or metal beater. Intended to sound like blacksmith's anvil. Used by several 19th-cent. composers incl. Verdi, Wagner.

**Apel, Willi** (1893– ), American musicologist, b. Germany. Books incl. *The Notation of Polyphonic Music 800–1600, Harvard Dictionary of Music,* and *Masters of the Keyboard.*

**apertum,** *see* OUVERT.

**a piacere** (It.), 'at pleasure', same as AD LIBITUM.

**Apollonicon,** elaborate type of BARREL ORGAN, with keyboards for 6 performers and stops imitating orchestral instruments. Made by Flight and Robson, organ-builders; first exhibited, London, 1817.

**Apostles, The,** oratorio by Elgar, op 49. First perf. Birmingham, 1903. Intended as first part of trilogy: second part is *The Kingdom* (1906), third never completed.

**Appalachia,** orchestral piece with final chorus by Delius consisting of variations on old slave song. Written 1896, revised 1902; first perf. Elberfeld, Germany, 1904.

**Appalachian Spring,** ballet by Copland, inspired by Hart Crane's poem about rural marriage. First perf. by Martha Graham company, New York, 1945.

**appassionato** (It.), 'impassioned'. *Sonata appassionata*, title given (not by composer) to Beethoven's piano sonata in F minor, op 57.

**Appia, Adolphe** (1862–1928), Swiss operatic designer. A disciple of Wagner, his pioneering reforms paved the way for the more abstract presentation of Wagnerian (and other) opera today.

**appoggiatura** (It.; Ger., *Vorschlag*), lit. a 'leaning'. There are 3 principal forms (1) the *long appoggiatura*, now known simply as appoggiatura, is note of varying length, alien to harmony note. Notated by auxiliary note in smaller type indicating length (*eg* if appoggiatura is written as small quaver tied to crotchet, both notes should be played as quavers). Many 18th-cent. composers left appoggiaturas unwritten, relying on taste and knowledge of conventions of performers to supply them in appropriate places;

(2) the *short appoggiatura,* now known inaccurately as the ACCIACCATURA, is very short note of indefinite length, orig. played on beat (like long appoggiatura) and indicated by same signs. In mid 18th-cent. music appoggiatura is short in following cases: (i) when it precedes short notes, (ii) when it decorates repetitions of same note,

(iii) when it resolves on to note dissonant with bass, so that it is itself consonant with bass.

In latter part of 18th cent. short appoggiatura began to be distinguished by oblique stroke across small note. In 19th cent. short appoggiatura began to be played before beat; this is now normal except when playing older music;

(3) the *passing appoggiatura,* current in 18th cent., normally occurred when principal notes of melody formed sequence of thirds. Indicated in same way as ordinary appoggiatura, but played before beat.

The name *double appoggiatura* is sometimes given to ornament normally called ANSCHLAG.

**Apprenti sorcier, L',** *see* SORCERER'S APPRENTICE, THE.

**Après-midi d'un faune, L',** *see* PRÉLUDE À L'APRÈS-MIDI D'UN FAUNE.

**a punta d'arco** (It.), with the point of the bow.

**Aquin, D',** *see* DAQUIN.

**Arabella,** opera by Richard Strauss, libretto by Hugo von Hofmannsthal. First perf. Dresden, 1933. This Viennese comedy of love and complications concerns Arabella, the daughter of an impoverished count who wants her to make a profitable marriage.

**arabesque** (Fr., Eng.; Ger., *Arabeske*), in architecture, ornament in Arabic style. Hence in music: (1) decorative treatment of thematic material; (2) lyrical piece of fanciful style. In latter sense first used by Schumann (op 18) and subsequently by others incl. Debussy.

**Araja,** or **Araia, Francesco** (1709–70), Italian opera composer, resident in Russia (1735–1759). Operas incl. *La clemenza di Tito* (1751), first opera with Russian libretto.

**Arbeau, Thoinot** (1519–95), French priest. Wrote treatise on dancing (1589) which incl. a number of dance tunes, some of which were used by Warlock in his *Capriol Suite.*

**Arbós, Enrique Fernandez** (1863–1939), Spanish violinist, conductor. Orchestrated music by Albéniz, incl. *Iberia.*

**Arcadelt, Jacob** (*c* 1504–after 1567), composer, prob. of Flemish origin. Famous as composer of Italian madrigals; also wrote French *chansons,* motets, masses.

**Archduke Trio,** nickname for piano trio in B flat major by Beethoven, op 97 (1811), dedicated to Archduke Rudolph.

**archet** (Fr.), bow.

**archi** (It.), lit. 'bows'; refers to any group of stringed instruments played with bows.

**archlute** (Fr., *archiluth;* Ger., *Erzlaute;* It., *arciliuto*), large bass lute, with 2 necks, one for stopped strings running over fingerboard, other for independent bass strings (*see* LUTE). Much used in 17th cent. for playing bass part in concerted compositions.

**arch viol,** 17th-cent. keyboard instrument designed to resemble several viols played with one bow; not successful.

**arciliuto** (It.), ARCHLUTE.

**arco** (It.; Fr., *archet*; Ger., *Bogen*), bow (of string instrument);

*coll'arco*, with the bow (usually abbrev. to *arco*), as opposed to *pizzicato*, plucked with the finger; *strumenti d'arco* (or plural *archi* alone), string instruments; *arcata*, stroke of the bow; *arcato*, bowed.

**Arditi, Luigi** (1822–1903), Italian composer, conductor. His waltz-song 'Il baccio' (the kiss) achieved extraordinary popularity.

**Arensky, Anton Stepanovich** (1861–1906), Russian composer. Studied under Rimsky-Korsakov. Compositions, nearer to mainstream of Western European music than to ideals of Russian nationalists, incl. 3 operas, ballet, incidental music to Shakespeare's *Tempest,* 2 symphonies, violin concerto, cantatas, church, chamber and piano music, songs. Best known works are piano trio in D minor (op 32) and variations on Chaikovsky's 'Legend' from 2nd string quartet in A minor (op 35).

**Arezzo, Guido d',** *see* GUIDO D'AREZZO.

**Argento, Dominick** (1927– ), American composer. Pupil of Nabokov, Cowell and Dallapiccola. Operas incl. *The Boor* (1957), *The Shoemaker's Holiday* (1967), *Miss Havisham's Fire* (1978–9). Has also written ballets, song cycles, and choral and orchestral music.

**Argyll Rooms,** name of 3 successive buildings in London used for musical performance in the early 19th cent. First was first home of the Philharmonic Society (now the Royal Philharmonic Society). Second, designed by John Nash, was principal concert hall in London until destroyed by fire (1830). Third failed to achieve same success.

**aria** (It.; Eng., Fr., *air*; Ger., *Arie*), (1) song for one or more voices, now used exclusively of solo song. Came into current use in early 17th cent., when used in opera and chamber CANTATA to describe symmetrical piece of vocal music, as opposed to declamatory recitative. By early 18th cent., aria completely dominated opera. There were large number of accepted types, designed to exploit capabilities of singers and to afford contrast within work. Symmetrical structure had also become stereotyped: contrasted middle section followed by repetition of first section; hence this form became known as the *da capo* aria. *Da capo* aria was transferred naturally to oratorio; in both, singers added improvised ornaments. Modern habit of shortening *da capo* by playing only instrumental introduction is indefensible, as it destroys symmetry.

Over-rigid musical structure of *da capo* often failed to harmonize with words; by later 18th cent. protests were made against dominance of *da capo* aria, these protests taking practical form in work of Gluck. However, principle of using lyrical pieces to intensify dramatic situations was not challenged until Wagner demonstrated possibility of new continuity, in which set vocal pieces are abandoned and function of establishing symmetry is assigned to orchestra;

(2) instrumental piece of song-like character, *eg* the theme of Bach's *Goldberg Variations.*

**Ariadne auf Naxos** (Ger., *Ariadne on Naxos*), opera by Richard Strauss, libretto by Hugo von Hofmannsthal. First (unsuccessful) version, without prologue, designed to follow perf. of Molière's *Le Bourgeois gentilhomme;* first perf. Stuttgart, 1912. In second version, the Molière was replaced by operatic prologue in which idealist composer learns that his opera is to be performed simultaneously with a *commedia dell'arte* entertainment. His opera follows, consisting of story of Ariadne abandoned on Naxos by Theseus and delivered by Bacchus; but this suffers comic interruptions from *commedia dell'arte* players. First perf. Vienna, 1916, with Lotte Lehmann as composer.

**Ariane et Barbe-Bleue** (Fr., *Ariadne and Bluebeard*), opera by Paul Dukas, almost literal setting of Maeterlinck's play. Rarely staged, but considered one of great operas of 20th cent. First perf. Paris, 1907.

**Arianna, L',** opera by Monteverdi, libretto by O. Rinuccini. First perf. Mantua, 1608. Only a fragment survives.

**Arie** (Ger.), air, ARIA.

**arietta** (It.), diminutive of ARIA. Short song (or instrumental piece), simpler in character and structure than aria.

**ariette** (Fr.), (1) short ARIA;
(2) in early 18th-cent. opera, brilliant aria in Italian style;
(3) in late 18th-cent. *opéra comique,* song introduced into dialogue scene.

**arioso** (It.), 'like an aria', (1) piece of recitative with characteristics (*eg* expressive melodic line, rhythmical definition) demanding more song-like interpretation than declamatory style proper to recitative. Much used by Bach, also by modern composers;
(2) short vocal solo in lyrical style;
(3) instrumental piece similar in style to vocal *arioso.*

**Ariosti, Attilio** (1666–*c* 1740), Italian opera composer. Involved with Handel and Bononcini in producing Italian opera in London (1720–28). His own operas incl. *Cajo Marzio Coriolano* (1723) and *Il Muzio Scevola* (1727).

**Arlecchino** (It., *Harlequin*), opera by Busoni, libretto by composer. First perf. Zurich, 1917.

**Arlésienne, L'** (Fr., *The Girl from Arles*), play of Provençal life by Alphonse Daudet (1840–97), with incidental music for small orchestra by Bizet. First perf. Paris, 1872. Music now known in form of 2 orchestral suites (2nd arranged by Guiraud).

**Armida** (It.; Fr., *Armide*), name of operas by several composers, inspired by Tasso's poem of Crusades, *La Gerusalemme liberata* (Jerusalem Delivered). Operas incl.;
(1) by Lully, libretto by Quinault, first perf. Paris, 1686;
(2) by Gluck, using Quinault's libretto, Paris, 1777;
(3) by Haydn, libretto by Durandi (in Italian), Esterházy, 1784;
(4) by Rossini, libretto by Schmidt, Naples, 1817;
(5) by Dvořák, libretto by 'Jaroslav Vrchlický' (pseud. of E.B. Frida), Prague, 1904. Handel's *Rinaldo* was also inspired by characters in Tasso's poem.

**armonica,** *see* HARMONICA (1).

**Armstrong, Louis** (1900–71), black American jazz trumpeter. One of greatest and most ebullient figures in jazz history. Spent childhood in New Orleans. Reached peak in 1920's in Chicago with Hot Five and Hot Seven. Retained immense popularity, but later became superb entertainer rather than important jazz figure. His great performances incl. *Willie the Weeper, West End Blues, Weather Bird, Tight Like This.*

**arm viol,** *see* VIOLA DA BRACCIO.

**Arne, Thomas Augustine** (1710–78), English composer. His many operas incl. ambitious *Artaxerxes* (1762), comic *Thomas and Sally* (1760). Also wrote 2 oratorios, instrumental music. His masque *Alfred* (1740) contains patriotic song 'Rule Britannia'; also wrote songs for Shakespeare plays.

His illegitimate son, **Michael Arne** (1740–86), was a singer and composer of dramatic music, *eg* for Garrick's *Cymon* (1767).

Thomas Arne's sister, **Susanna Maria Arne** (1714–66), was a singer and actress. Sang in first perf. of Handel's *Messiah.*

**Arnell, Richard Anthony Sayer** (1917– ), English composer. Pupil of John Ireland. Compositions incl. 3 ballets (*eg Punch and the Child*), 5 symphonies, violin concertos, symphonic poem (*Lord Byron*), chamber and piano music.

**Arnold, Madeleine Sophie** (1740–1802), French singer, actress. Known esp. for roles in Gluck's operas.

**Arnold, Malcolm Henry** (1921– ), English composer. Pupil of Gordon Jacob. Compositions, mainly in straightforwardly melodious, often humorous style, incl. 7 symphonies, concertos for horn, clarinet, piano duet, symphony for strings, orchestral *Beckus the Dandipratt* and *Tam O'Shanter*, chamber and film music.

**Arnold, Samuel** (1740–1802), English organist, composer, editor. Organist at Chapel Royal (1783), Westminster Abbey (1793). Wrote several oratorios, and much music for stage. Edited first collected edition (though incomplete and inaccurate) of Handel's works.

**Aronowitz, Cecil** (1916–78), English viola player, born South Africa of Russo-Lithuanian parentage. Pupil of Vaughan Williams. Founder member of Melos Ensemble.

**arpa** (It.), harp.

**arpeggio** (It., *arpeggiare,* 'to play the harp'), (1) notes of chord played not simultaneously but in rapid succession – 'broken' or 'spread out' – as on the harp. Modern practice is to play all arpeggios ascending, using one of following signs:

Question whether arpeggio begins before or on beat depends on context. In piano music following distinction should be made between chords in which right and left hands play arpeggios simultaneously (a) and those in which single arpeggio is divided between two hands (b):

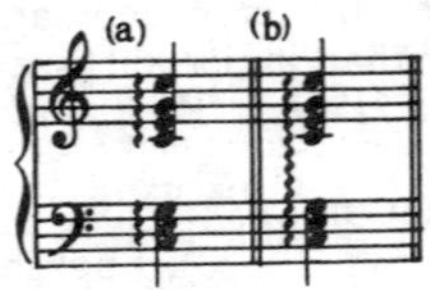


(2) term is also applied to successive notes of chord, ascending and descending, written out in full and performed in strict time as part of technical training of every singer and instrumentalist.

**arpeggione** (It.), instrument, invented by Staufer of Vienna (1823), with 6 strings tuned as for guitar but played with bow.

**arpicordo** (It.), early name for HARPSICHORD.

**arpo** (It.), harp.

**arrangement,** (1) adaptation of a piece of music to make it suitable for perf. by forces other than those for which it was originally composed. Purpose of arrangement may be (a) to facilitate study or domestic performance; (b) to enlarge repertory of particular medium; (c) to enable work written for large number of performers to be given with more limited resources. Degree of modification required varies; composer may go beyond necessary modification to elaborate and add to original text. Bach, Beethoven, Brahms all made noted arrangements;

(2) harmonized setting, for voices or instruments, of existing melody. Folk song provides obvious material for such treatment.

**Arrau, Claudio** (1903– ), Chilean pianist. Studied under Krause, Liszt's pupil. Taught in Berlin, 1925–40. Opened piano school in Santiago, Chile. One of greatest 20th-cent. interpreters of Beethoven, Schumann, Chopin, Brahms, Liszt.

**Arriaga, Juan Crisóstomo Antonio** (1806–26), Spanish composer (full name Arriaga y Balzola). Would have become major figure but for his early death. His opera was performed when he was 13. String quartets show eloquent maturity of expression and fine sense of proportion. Also wrote symphony and 8-part *Et Vitam Venturi*, described by Cherubini as masterpiece.

**Arrieta y Corera, Emilio** (1823–94), Spanish opera composer. Works incl. light opera *Marina* (1855, enlarged 1871).

**Ars antiqua** (Lat.), 'the old art'; music of late 12th, 13th cents., in contrast with *Ars nova,* music of 14th cent.

**arsis** (Ger.), (1) lit. 'a raising' (of hand or foot), hence an up-beat, in contrast to *thesis,* a down-beat. Romans, medieval theorists and many modern writers use *arsis* of a strong accent. Hence there is some confusion, though there is now a tendency to accept Greek meaning;

(2) expression *per arsin et thesin* was formerly applied to imitation by contrary motion, since one part goes up where other goes down, and vice versa.

**Ars nova** (Lat.), 'the new art'. *See* ARS ANTIQUA.

**Artaria,** Vienna music-publishing firm, of Italian origin. Publications began 1778, and incl. works by Haydn, Mozart and Beethoven.

**Artaxerxes,** opera by Arne, libretto adapted by composer from Metastasio's *Artaserse*. First perf. London, 1762.

**Art of Fugue, The** (Ger., *Die Kunst der Fuge*), work by J.S. Bach, written 1749, published 1750. Consists of 13 fugues and 4 canons demonstrating almost every possible kind of contrapuntal treatment of the one theme. Text also includes choral prelude and unfinished fugue. Bach did not indicate instruments for which work is intended, but whole work can be played by one player on keyboard. Transcriptions have been made by Wolfgang Graeser (for orchestra), Roy Harris (for string quartet).

**Artusi, Giovanni Maria** (*c* 1540–1613), Italian theorist, composer. Most celebrated work was *Delle imperfettioni della musica moderna* (1600–3), attacking music of more advanced contemporaries, esp. Monteverdi.

**As** (Ger.), A flat.

**Asafiev, Boris** (1884–1949), Russian composer, musicologist. Works incl. operas, ballets.

**Ases** (Ger.), A double flat.

**Ashkenazy, Vladimir** (1937– ), Russian pianist, conductor, settled in West in 1963. One of leading pianists of his generation, with special flair for Mozart, Beethoven, Chopin.

**Aspelmayr, Franz** (1728–86), German composer. Works incl. opera *Die Kinder der Natur* (1778). One of first Viennese composers to practise new instrumental style of Mannheim school.

**aspiration** (Fr.), ornament current in 17th, 18th cents. Equivalent of English *springer* and German *Nachschlag.*

**assai** (It.), 'very', *eg allegro assai,* very fast.

**Aston** or **Ashton, Hugh** (*c* 1485–after 1549), English composer. Works incl. hornpipe for virginals, which anticipates later developments, and some church music.

**Astorga, Emanuele Gioacchino Cesare Ricon, Baron d'** (1680–1757), Sicilian nobleman, composer, of Spanish descent. Works incl. opera *Dafni* (1709), *Stabat Mater* (1707), and chamber cantatas. J.J. Albert (1832–1915) wrote opera based on his life (1866).

**Atalanta,** opera by Handel, librettist unknown. First perf. London, 1736. Work ends with firework display.

**a tempo** (It.; Fr., *au mouvement)*; 'in time'. Used to restore normal tempo of piece after *rallentando, allargando, a piacere, etc,* or after section marked at faster or slower speed than that indicated at beginning of piece.

**Athaliah,** oratorio by Handel, libretto by S. Humphreys. First perf. Oxford, 1733.

**Athalie,** incidental music by Mendelssohn, op 74, written for Racine's tragedy. First perf. Berlin, 1845.

**atonality,** term often used loosely of music whose harmony appears unfamiliar, but properly applied to music which rejects traditional tonality, *ie* which abandons use of tonic or key-centre to which all notes and chords of piece are related.

Breakdown of tonality began during second half of 19th cent., esp. in works of Wagner (where modulation sometimes disguises true tonal centre of music) and Debussy. Schoenberg's *Transfigured Night* was only short step from Wagner's *Tristan;* though it does not now sound exceptionally atonal. Schoenberg was central figure in evolution of atonality, but preferred to talk of *pantonality* (*ie* synthesis of all keys rather than absence of any). His suspension of tonality ultimately led to his conscious systemization of atonality in form of 12-note music.

**attacca** (It.), 'attack', *ie* start next movt. or section without any break. So also *attacca subito,* begin suddenly.

**attacco** (It.), short figure used as subject for imitation in fugue or other polyphonic composition.

**Attaingnant, Pierre** (d. *c* 1551), French music publisher, first in Paris to print from movable types. Publications incl. works by Sermisy, Certon and Janequin.

**Attaque du moulin, L'** (Fr. *The Attack on the Mill*), opera by Bruneau, libretto by L. Gallet (based on story by Zola). First perf. Paris, 1893.

**Atterberg, Kurt** (1887–1974), Swedish composer, conductor, critic. Works incl. 9 symphonies, concertos for violin, cello, horn and piano, 5 operas, choral, orchestral and chamber music.

**Attey, John** (d. *c* 1640), last of English lutenist songwriters. Only published work was *The First Booke of Ayres* (1622), incl. well-known 'Sweet was the song the virgin sang'. Songs are designed to be sung by 4 voices with lute, or as solos with accompaniment for lute and bass viol.

**At the Boar's Head,** opera by Holst, libretto by composer. Text drawn from Shakespeare's *Henry IV,* much of music from English folk song. First perf. Manchester, 1925.

**Attwood, Thomas** (1765–1838), English composer, organist at St Paul's Cathedral, London. Numerous compositions incl. anthems for coronations of George IV, William IV, and many works for stage. Favourite pupil of Mozart, close friend of Mendelssohn.

**Atys,** opera by Lully, libretto by P. Quinault. First perf. St Germain, 1676.

**aubade** (Fr.; Sp., *alborada*), morning music, as opposed to serenade (evening music). Often used as title of short instrumental pieces.

**Auber, Daniel François Esprit** (1782–1871), French opera composer. From 1823, collaborated with librettist Augustin Eugène Scribe. Wrote 45 operas in all, incl.: *La Muette de Portici* (1828, known in England as *Masaniello*), first of French romantic 'grand operas'; *Fra Diavolo* (1830), his best work in *opéra comique; Les Diamants de la couronne* (1841), *Manon Lescaut* (1856). Director of Paris Conservatoire from 1842, and of Imperial Chapel from 1857.

**Aubert, Jacques** (1689–1753), French violinist, composer. Member of king's band of 24 violins and of Opéra orchestra. Wrote violin concertos, ballets, instrumental and theatre music.

**Aubert, Louis François Marie** (1877–1968), French composer. Pupil of Fauré. Known for opera *La Forêt bleue* (1913), orchestral work *Habañera* (1919).

**Aubry, Pierre** (1874–1910), French musicologist. Advocated interpretation of troubadour melodies in accordance with rhythm of words, *ie* that music should be transcribed in one of the RHYTHMIC MODES.

**au chevalet,** *see* BOWING.

**Audran, Edmond** (1840–1901), French composer. Known for large number of comic operas esp. *La Mascotte* (1880), *La Poupée* (1896).

**Auer, Leopold** (1845–1930), Hungarian-born violinist, teacher. Pupil of Joachim. Taught in St Petersburg, then in 1918 settled in New York. Pupils incl. Jascha Heifetz.

**Auf dem Anstand** (Ger.), 'at the hunting station', nickname for Haydn's symphony no 31 in D major (1765), also known as *Mit dem Hornsignal,* 'with the horn call'.

**Aufstieg und Fall der Stadt Mahagonny,** *see* RISE AND FALL OF THE CITY OF MAHAGONNY.

**Augener,** London music-publishing and printing firm, founded 1853 by George Augener (d. 1915).

**augmentation,** presentation of theme in notes double the value of those originally assigned to it (*see* CANON); opposite is DIMINUTION.

**augmented interval,** the following intervals can be augmented by sharpening upper, or flattening lower, note: major second, major third, fourth, fifth, major sixth, major seventh, octave. Augmented fourth occurs between 4th and 7th notes of every major scale; other augmented intervals necessitate notes foreign to key.

**augmented sixth,** *see* AUGMENTED INTERVAL. So-called chord of augmented sixth has 3 forms hallowed by tradition, known respectively (for no good reason) as Italian, French, German: A flat, C, F sharp; A flat, C, D, F sharp; A flat, C, E flat, F sharp. Since on keyboard it is impossible to distinguish between F sharp and G flat, last of 3 may also be treated as DOMINANT SEVENTH chord (in this case in key of D flat): A flat, C, E flat, G flat.

**augmented triad,** chord composed, in simplest form, of 2 major thirds, *eg* C, E, G sharp. Notes of chord can also be arranged as follows: E, G sharp, C; or, G sharp, C, E. *See* CHORD, INVERSION.

**Augustine** (real name Aurelius Augustinus) (354–430), one of the fathers of the Latin church, who also wrote about music. His *De musica* (*c* 387–89) deals principally with metre.

**aulos,** generic term used by ancient Greeks for any wind instrument (Lat., *tibia*). Term used more particularly for double-reed instrument, most important wind instrument of ancient Greeks. Played in pairs, with reeds held inside mouth. Shown on numerous painted vases.

**au mouvement,** *see* A TEMPO.

**aural training,** purpose of aural training is to teach pupils to recognize sounds and rhythms they hear and to write them down on paper. Ability to do this is indispensable for study of harmony and counterpoint, and essential for any musician.

**Auric, Georges** (1899– ), French composer. Influenced by Erik Satie, became member of *Les Six* (*see* SIX). Compositions, notable for wit and charm, pay tribute to popular music, Stravinsky, Ravel; incl. songs, chamber and piano music, ballets (*eg Les Matelots*), music for films (*eg* René Clair's *A Nous la liberté*).

**Aus Italien** (Ger., *From Italy*), symphony by Richard Strauss, op 16 (1886), inspired by visit to Italy.

**Austin, Frederic** (1872–1952), English baritone, composer. Director of British National Opera Company from 1924. Had great success with his version of *The Beggar's Opera* (1920).

**au talon,** *see* BOWING.

**authentic mode,** *see* MODE.

**autoharp,** kind of zither in which chords are obtained by pressing keys that stop or damp strings. Invented in late 19th cent.

**Ave Maria** (Lat.), 'Hail, Mary', prayer to Virgin used in RC Church, often set to music, *eg* by Liszt, Schubert, Gounod.

**Avison, Charles** (1709–70), English organist, composer. Mainly known for treatise *An Essay on Musical Expression* (2nd ed., 1753), giving valuable evidence on contemporary taste and practice.

**ayre,** *see* AIR (2).

# B

**B** (Eng.; Fr., It., *si*; Ger., *H*), (1) seventh (or leading) note of scale of C major. In German nomenclature, *B* is B flat and *H* is B natural; (2) as abbrev., *B* = Bass, Bachelor (*B. Mus.* or *Mus. B.* = Bachelor of Music).

**Babbitt, Milton** (1916– ), American composer. Early work influenced by Webern, later turned to electronic music. Works incl. chamber music, composition for synthesizer, *Vision and Prayer* (words by Dylan Thomas to electronic tape accompaniment).

**Babell, William** (*c* 1690–1723), English composer, harpsichordist, violinist. Made showy transcriptions for harpsichord of popular operatic arias; also wrote sonatas for violin and oboe.

**Babin, Victor** (1908–72), Russian-born pianist, composer. Pupil of Schnabel. Often played in 2-piano pieces with wife, Vitya Vronsky. Compositions are mainly instrumental. Directed Cleveland Conservatory in US from 1961.

**Baborák,** Bohemian national dance, consisting of alternating sections of 3/4 and 2/4 time.

**baby grand,** smallest size of grand piano.

**Baccusi, Ippolito** (*c* 1545–1609), Italian composer. Wrote Masses, motets and madrigals.

**Bach, Carl Philipp Emanuel** (1714–88), German composer. Second son and pupil of J.S. Bach. In 1740 became harpsichordist to Frederick the Great in Berlin and Potsdam. In 1767 became director of music at 5 principal churches in Hamburg. Music is characteristic of mid 18th cent., reacting against father's polyphony and counterpoint. Essence of work is taste and refinement, esp. understanding of expressive possibilities of keyboard. Had remarkable skill in improvisation. Works incl. 2 oratorios, 50 keyboard concertos, several collections of keyboard sonatas. Sonatas show growth of thematic treatment of contrasted keys, from which classical SONATA FORM developed. His *Essay on the proper method of playing keyboard instruments* (2 parts, 1753, 1762) is valuable guide to contemporary style, esp. to interpretation of ornaments.

**Bach, Johann** (later **John**) **Christian** (1735–82), German composer. Youngest son of J.S. Bach by second wife; studied under father, then brother C.P.E. Bach. Moved to Italy in (1756), then to London (1762) where he remained – hence nickname 'English' or 'London' Bach. Became music-master to George III's wife, Queen Charlotte. Showed much kindness to Mozart (aged 8) when he visited London, and was early influence on Mozart's style, esp. in piano concertos. Works incl. 11 operas, an oratorio, *c* 40 piano concertos, *c* 90 symphonies and other orchestral works, chamber and piano music, songs. Pioneered use of piano as solo instrument in Britain.

**Bach, Johann Christoph** (1642–1703), German organist, composer. Cousin of J.S. Bach's father. Wrote motet *Ich lasse dich nicht* ('I wrestle and pray') among other vocal and instrumental works.

**Bach, Johann Christoph Friedrich** (1732–95), German composer. Eldest surviving son of J.S. Bach's second marriage. Taught music by father. From 1750 spent life in service of Count Wilhelm of Schaumberg-Lippe at Bückeberg. Wrote oratorios, cantatas, motets, keyboard concertos and sonatas, chamber music, songs.

**Bach, Johann Michael** (1648–94), German organist, composer, son of J.S. Bach's great-uncle, and father of J.S. Bach's first wife, Maria Barbara. He composed motets and organ music.

**Bach, Johann Sebastian** (1685–1750), German composer. Born at Eisenach, became pupil of brother (Johann Christoph), then choirboy at Lüneburg, where he possibly had organ lessons from Böhm. In 1703 became violinist in Weimar court orchestra, then organist at Arnstadt. In 1707 became organist at Mühlhausen and married cousin, Maria Barbara. In 1708 moved back to Weimar as court organist (where he wrote bulk of organ music), then in 1717 to Anhalt-Köthen as Prince Leopold's director of music (where he concentrated on secular instrumental works). Wife died in 1720; married Anna Magdalena Wicken following year. In 1723 became cantor of St Thomas's, Leipzig, where he remained for the rest of his life, composing mainly church music. Became blind just before he died. Of 20 children, only 10 survived infancy.

Chief influences in Bach's music are Lutheran chorale, church and organ music of predecessors, and contemporary French and Italian styles in instrumental music. In his lifetime he had great reputation as organist, but music was considered over-elaborate and old-fashioned. He combined extraordinary contrapuntal skill with mastery of picturesque and passionate expression. His music was always written for a practical purpose – for church services, patrons, or instruction of his sons. Bach was a universal musician, and his music, though steeped in the flavour of its period, has a universal appeal.

Principal compositions:

(1) Church music: Magnificat; *St John Passion* (1723); *St Matthew Passion* (1729); *Christmas Oratorio* (1734); *Mass in B minor;* 198 cantatas; 6 motets;

(2) Secular choral music: 23 cantatas;

(3) Orchestra: 6 Brandenburg Concertos (1721); 4 overtures (or suites); 2 violin concertos; concerto for 2 violins; concertos for one or more harpsichords; concerto for harpsichord, flute, violin;

(4) Chamber music: 3 sonatas and 3 partitas for violin solo; 6 suites for solo cello; flute sonatas; violin sonatas; *viola da gamba* sonatas; *Musical Offering* (1747);

(5) Harpsichord or clavichord: 7 toccatas; chromatic fantasia and fugue; 15 two-part inventions; 15 three-part inventions (symphonies); 6 French suites; 6 English suites; *The Well-Tempered Clavier* (1722, 1744); 6 partitas (1731); Italian concerto (1735);

Goldberg variations (1742); *The Art of the Fugue* (prob. intended for keyboard);

(6) Organ: 6 sonatas; 143 chorale preludes; fantasias, preludes, fugues, toccatas.

**Bach, Wilhelm Friedemann** (1710–84), German composer, organist. Eldest and one of most distinguished of J. S. Bach's sons. Studied under father. Organist at Dresden, then Halle, then went freelance, but despite being outstanding organist, he died in poverty. Numerous compositions incl. works for harpsichord and organ, trio sonatas, symphonies, cantatas.

**Bach Gesellschaft** (Ger., 'Bach Society'), organization formed 1850 to publish complete edition of works of J.S. Bach. Last of 46 vols. was issued in 1900. The *Neue Bach Gesellschaft* (New Bach Society), founded 1900, has issued performing editions of many of Bach's works. A new complete edition was initiated by the Johann-Sebastian-Bach-Institut, Göttingen, in 1954.

**Bachianas Brasileiras,** name of series of works by Villa-Lobos combining Bachian procedures with elements of Brazilian traditional music.

**Bach trumpet,** modern instrument designed to make practicable the playing of high, florid trumpet parts in works of Bach and contemporaries.

**Backer-Gröndahl, Agathe Ursula** (1847–1907), Norwegian pianist, composer. Studied with von Bülow, who admired her gifts. Composed songs and piano pieces.

**backfall,** term current in 17th-cent. England for short APPOGGIATURA. where ornamental note is one degree of scale above principal note. *Double backfall* was equivalent to SLIDE taken from above, *ie* with 2 ornamental notes above principal note.

**Backhaus, Wilhelm** (1884–1969), German pianist. Achieved world fame as exponent of German classics, esp. sonatas of Beethoven.

**Bacon, Ernst** (1898– ), American pianist, conductor, composer. Compositions incl. 2 symphonies, musical play *The Tree on the Plains,* piano quintet, choral works.

**badinage** or **badinerie** (Fr.), 'frolic', term used in 18th cent. for quick, frivolous movt. in duple time, *eg* in Bach's suite in B minor for flute and strings. Is one of optional dances or *Galanterien* in SUITE.

**Badings, Henk** (1907– ), Dutch composer, teacher, b. in East Indies. Orig. a mining engineer, has become one of best established of modern Dutch composers. Has written opera *The Night Watch,* ballets, 10 symphonies, concertos for violin, two violins, cello, and chamber, piano and vocal music; has also experimented with electronic music.

**bagatelle** (Fr.), 'trifle'. Short piece, usually (but not necessarily) written for piano, and usually of light, humorous or whimsical character. Beethoven composed 3 sets of *Bagatellen* for piano (op 33, op 119, op 126 – 26 pieces in all).

**bagpipe** (Fr., *cornemuse;* Ger., *Sackpfeife;* It., *cornamusa*), reed instrument, with one or more pipes, to which air is supplied from skin reservoir or bag inflated by player. Prob. of Asiatic origin; introduced to Europe in 1st cent. AD by Romans, and in time became popular in every European country. Various forms exist: (1) bag may be inflated by player's breath through pipe or by bellows under arm: (2) pipes may have single or double reeds: (3) bagpipe normally has not only one (or two) pipes with finger holes (the 'chanter' or 'chaunter') on which melody is played, but also one or more 'drone' pipes, each tuned to single note, providing simple, monotonous accompaniment. In past bagpipe has been used as military instrument and for popular music-making. These two functions survive in Scotland, where art has reached highest form in PIBROCH. Apart from fashionable craze in France in reigns of Louis XIV and Louis XV, bagpipe disappeared from polite society. Has occasionally been used by composers for pastoral or bucolic effects (*eg* by Verdi in *Otello*).

**baguette** (Fr.), drumstick.

**Baird, Tadeusz** (1928– ), Polish composer of Scottish ancestry. Works, mostly orchestral, incl. 3 symphonies, piano concerto (1949), *Expressions* for violin and orchestra (1959), *Psychodram* (1972).

**Baker, Janet** (1933– ), English mezzo-soprano, formerly contralto. One of Britain's most sensitive operatic and concert-hall singers. Excels in tragic roles, but range extends through character parts to comedy. In concert-hall, associated esp. with Mahler, Schumann, songs and cantatas of 17th, 18th cents. DBE, 1976.

**Bakfark, Balint** or **Valentin** (1507–76), Hungarian lutenist, composer. Travelled widely in Europe and served in Polish court (1549–66). Wrote both original works and transcriptions for lute.

**Balakirev, Mily Alexeyevich** (1837–1910), Russian composer. Leader of group of Russian nationalist composers known as 'The Five' or 'The Mighty Handful' (consisting of Balakirev, Borodin, Cui, Mussorgsky, Rimsky-Korsakov). Arrived in St Petersburg in 1855, making name as pianist, but preferred to teach. Instructed and encouraged other members of 'The Five'. Became first director of Free School of Music in St Petersburg, but venture was not financially successful. After nervous breakdown in 1872 became railway clerk, and later school inspector; then director of Court Chapel (1883-95). Compositions, influenced both by Russian folk music and Western romantic composers (esp. Liszt), incl. 2 symphonies, 2 symphonic poems *(Russia, Tamara)*, overture *King Lear,* piano sonata, Oriental fantasy *Islamey* for piano solo, songs.

**balalaika** (Russ.), triangular guitar of Tartar origin, very popular among Russian peasantry. Normally has 3 strings, and is made in several sizes.

**Balfe, Michael William** (1808–70), Irish composer, baritone, violinist. Started career in London, later studied in Italy. *The Bohemian Girl* (1843) is best known of his 29 operas.

**Ball, George Thomas Thalben** (1896– ), Australian-born organist. Held various posts in England, and established himself as world famous recitalist.

**ballabile** (It.), in a dancing manner.

**ballad,** (1) narrative song, either traditional or (as in the 19th cent.) written in imitation of traditional forms. From 16th to 19th cents. words of ballads, frequently dealing with contemporary events, were printed on sheets and sold at fairs *etc*;

(2) sentimental drawing-room song of late 19th, early 20th cents.

(3) instrumental piece = BALLADE (2).

**ballade** (Fr.), (1) type of medieval French verse with refrain at end of stanza, frequently set to music by *trouvères*, or, with more complexity, by polyphonic composers;

(2) in 19th, 20th cents., instrumental piece, sometimes of considerable length, of lyrical, romantic character. Chopin pioneered this type of *ballade.*

**ballad opera,** type of opera popular in Britain in mid 18th cent., in which dialogue was interspersed with songs set to popular tunes (often actually taken from works of well-known composers). Best-known is John Gay's *The Beggar's Opera* (1728).

**Ballard,** French publishing firm, active from mid 16th to late 18th cents. Published Lully's operas.

**ballata** (It.), 14th-cent. Italian verse form with refrain at beginning and end of stanza, frequently set to music.

**ballet,** dramatic entertainment presented by dancers in costume with musical accompaniment. Existed in ancient world, Middle Ages, Renaissance. Landmark was French production of *Circe* (1581) which combined dancing with dramatic plot to form organic whole; it also had spoken declamation and singing. Form was popular in 17th-cent. French court, and led to development of English masque. Lully wrote many such ballets, often collaborating with Molière to combine spoken drama and ballet; when he turned to opera, he incorporated ballet in new form.

Association of ballet and opera continued through 18th cent., but ballet also maintained separate existence. Jean Georges Noverre (1727–1810) was leading virtuoso and innovator of 18th cent. – Mozart wrote *Les petits riens* (1778) for him. French ballet spread to other countries, incl. Russia, where Imperial School of Ballet was founded in 18th cent. Chaikovsky's famous scores are evidence of popularity of ballet in 19th-cent. Russia. Reform came with Sergei Diaghilev (1872–1929), who encouraged many young composers, esp. Stravinsky, Ravel. British revival led to ballet-scores by Vaughan Williams, Bliss, Britten. Leading choreographers such as Sir Frederick Ashton and Kenneth Macmillan have created ballets out of established concert-hall pieces (*eg* Elgar's *Enigma Variations*). In US, George Balanchine has been leading creative force, inspiring Stravinsky (*eg Agon,* 1957); Copland and Bernstein have also composed well-known scores. Russia's great tradition was enriched by Prokofiev's masterpieces (*eg Romeo and Juliet,* 1935).

**ballett** (It., *balletto*), composition for several voices, mainly homophonic in character, generally with refrain to words *fa la.* Originated in Italy at end of 16th cent., and imitated in other countries (*eg* by Thomas Morley in England). Music was generally in lively, square-cut rhythm, suitable for dancing.

**balletto** (It.), (1) *see* BALLETT; (2) dance movt. in suite; (3) ballet.

**Balliff, Claude** (1924– ), French composer. Pupil of Messiaen. Works incl. orchestral *Poème de la felicité* (1978), and instrumental, chamber and piano music.

**Balling, Michael** (1866–1925), German conductor. Associated with Bayreuth Festival (1906–14); conductor with Hallé Orchestra (1912–14). Edited complete works of Wagner.

**ballo** (It.), dance. *Tempo di ballo,* in dance time.

**Ballo in Maschera, Un,** *see* MASKED BALL.

**Baltzar, Thomas** (*c* 1630–63), German violinist. In service of Queen Christina of Sweden and later of Charles II in England, where his virtuosity created a sensation.

**bamboo pipe,** simple wooden pipe resembling recorder. Rear thumb-hole and 6 front fingerholes.

**Banchieri, Adriano** (1568–1634), Italian composer, theorist, poet. Founder of Accademia de' floridi in Bologna. Works incl. madrigal dramas, concerted instrumental music, and organ and church music. One of first writers to give instruction in playing from *figured bass* in treatise *L'organo suonario.*

**band,** term once applied to any large-scale group of instrumentalists but now reserved for ensembles other than concert orchestra. *See* BRASS BAND, JAZZ BAND, MILITARY BAND, ORCHESTRA.

**bandora,** bass instrument very similar to CITTERN.

**bandurria** (Sp.), Spanish instrument of guitar family, similar to English CITHER, with 6 double strings generally played with plectrum.

**Banister, John** (d. 1679), English violinist. Played in service of Charles II. Began series of public concerts (1672), among first of their kind.

**banjo,** American Negro instrument of guitar family. Body consists of shallow metal drum covered with parchment on top side and open at bottom. Strings (between 5 and 9) are played with fingers or plectrum. Supposedly brought to US by slaves from West Africa, origin being attributed to Arab traders. Introduction into jazz bands led to development of 4-string tenor model, tuned like viola.

**banjolin,** kind of BANJO with short neck and 4 strings.

**Banks, Don** (1923– ), Australian composer. Has also worked in London. Works incl. concertos for violin and horn, chamber and electronic music.

**Bantock, Granville** (1868–1946), English composer. Professor at Birmingham University (1908–34). As conductor encouraged young British composers. As composer was prolific, attracted by local colour of many countries, from Scotland to China. Works, in romantic tradition, incl. *Fifine at the Fair, Dante and Beatrice* and other symphonic poems, *Hebridean Symphony,* opera, choral works. Knighted 1930.

**bar,** (1) properly, vertical line drawn across one or more staves of music, now generally known in Britain as 'bar-line' (Fr., *barre*; Ger., *Taktstrich*; It., *barra*). Orig. purpose was to guide eye when music was presented simultaneously on several staves or in TABLATURE. Increasing rhythmical symmetry of 17th cent., which became stereotyped in 18th, 19th cents., led to false association between bar-line and ACCENT. It is more logical and practical to regard bar-line as convenient sign of subdivision, which may or may not coincide with rhythmical accent. This does not exclude use of bars of different lengths where change is appropriate. The most important thing is that composer's intentions should be clear to performer;

(2) space between 2 bar-lines, known in US as 'measure' (Fr., *mesure;* Ger., *Takt;* It., *battuta*). In US bar-line is known simply as 'bar'.

**Barber, Samuel** (1910-81), American composer, former singer. Compositions are original, yet show respect for romantic tradition; incl. 2 major operas *(Vanessa, Anthony and Cleopatra)*, ballets for Martha Graham, 2 symphonies, symphony in one movt., overture *(School for Scandal)*, violin, piano and cello concertos, 2 *Essays* for orchestra, *Capricorn Concerto,* choral, chamber and piano music. Wrote *Dover Beach* (1931), setting for string quartet and voice of Matthew Arnold's poem, for himself to sing. Most famous work is *Adagio for Strings* (1936), adapted from slow movt. of string quartet.

**Barber of Baghdad, The,** comic opera by Cornelius, libretto by composer (based on *Arabian Nights*). First perf. Weimar, 1858.

**Barber of Seville, The** (It., *Il Barbiere di Siviglia*), comic opera by Rossini, libretto by C. Sterbini (based on Beaumarchais's play of same name). Story tells how Count Almaviva loves Rosina, ward of Dr Bartolo, and succeeds with help of Figaro (the barber of Seville) in defeating Bartolo's attempts to separate them. First perf. (Rome, 1816) had violent reception due to presence of supporters of Paisiello's rival version (libretto by G. Petrosellini, first perf. St Petersburg, 1782). Work later came to be recognized as high-water mark of Rossini's comic genius. Mozart's *Marriage of Figaro* (1786) is based on Beaumarchais' play of the same name, sequel to *The Barber of Seville.*

**barber-shop quartet,** quartet of amateur male singers specializing in close-harmony arrangements of popular songs. Developed from informal music-making found in barber shops in Britain and Europe in 16th, 17th cents. Declined in 18th cent., but tradition maintained in US, where annual contests are held.

**Barbiere di Siviglia, Il,** *see* BARBER OF SEVILLE.

**Barbieri, Francisco A.** (1823-94), Spanish composer, musicologist. Wrote comic operas of characteristically Spanish type, *eg Pan y Toros* (1864).

**Barbingant,** 15th-cent. composer of a Mass and some *chansons,* whose identity was for long confused with that of Jacques BARBIREAU.

**Barbireau, Jacques** (*c* 1408–91), Flemish composer. Wrote church music and *chansons.*

**Barbirolli, Sir John** (1899–1970), English conductor of Italian origin, real name Giovanni Battista Barbirolli. Succeeded Toscanini as conductor of New York Philharmonic (1937). In 1943 returned to Britain to rebuild Hallé Orchestra of Manchester, and stayed with them for rest of his life, imposing his stamp very strongly. Repertory based mainly on romantic, late-romantic music, esp. Elgar, Mahler, Vaughan Williams, Brahms, Delius, Sibelius, but also gave memorable performances of opera, and conducted Haydn superbly. Knighted 1949.

**barcarola** (It.), BARCAROLLE.

**barcarolle** (Fr.; Ger., *Barkarole*; It., *barcarola*), from It., *barca,* 'boat'. Properly a boating-song sung by Venice gondoliers, but also applied to any piece of music in same rhythm (6/8 or 12/8).

**bard,** orig. Celtic minstrel, whose duties incl. composition of extempore songs in honour of patron. Had considerable political influence in medieval Wales. Practice of bardic gatherings revived in 19th cent. at annual Welsh *Eisteddfod* ('session'), now largely musical competition festivals.

**Bardi, Giovanni** (1534–1612), Count of Vernio. A Florentine nobleman, himself a composer, his house was a meeting-place of poets, musicians and scholars interested in creating a music-drama on lines of Greek tragedy. First operas originated from these gatherings.

**Barenboim, Daniel** (1942– ), Argentine-born pianist, conductor. Began European career in 1954; soon established himself as important exponent of music of Mozart, Beethoven. As conductor, his interpretations of 19th, early 20th-cent. repertory, esp. Beethoven, Berlioz, Brahms, Bruckner, Elgar, reveal exceptional talent.

**Bärenreiter,** firm of music-publishers founded in Augsburg in 1924 by Karl Vötterle.

**Bargiel, Woldemar** (1828–97), German teacher, composer, stepbrother of Clara Schumann. Works, strongly influenced by Schumann, incl. symphony, 3 orchestral overtures, chamber, piano and choral music.

**baritone,** (1) high bass voice, midway between bass and tenor, with range of *c* 2 octaves, from G on bottom line of bass clef to G above middle C;

(2) brass instrument of *saxhorn* family (Fr., *bugle ténor*; Ger., *Tenorhorn*; It., *flicorno tenore*). Built in B flat at same pitch as EUPHONIUM, but has smaller bore and only 3 valves. Used only in wind bands, and written for as transposing instrument: written compass is from F sharp below middle C to C above treble clef, but sounding from E below bass clef to B flat in middle of treble clef;

(3) the baritone clef is the F clef on the 3rd line (now obsolete); *see* CLEF;

(4) baritone oboe, *see* HECKELPHONE;

(5) baritone saxophone, *see* SAXOPHONE.

**Barkarole** (Ger.), BARCAROLLE.

**bar-line,** *see* BAR (1).

**Bärmann, Heinrich Joseph** (1784–1847), German clarinettist, for whom Weber and Mendelssohn wrote pieces.

**Barnard, John** (*fl* early 17th cent.), minor canon of St Paul's Cathedral, London. Published first printed collection of English cathedral music under title *The First Book of Selected Church Musick* (1641). A second collection survives in manuscript.

**Barnby, Joseph** (1838–96), English composer, conductor, organist. Pioneered Bach's passions with English audiences.

**Barnett, John** (1802–90), English opera composer, son of German and Hungarian parents, and a second cousin of Meyerbeer. Most important work was *The Mountain Sylph* (1834), one of first English romantic operas.

**Barnett, John Francis** (1837–1916), English pianist, composer. Nephew of John Barnett. Works incl. symphony, chamber, choral and piano music. Completed Schubert's symphony no. 7 in E major from composer's sketches.

**baroque** (Port., *barroco,* 'rough pearl'), orig. 'grotesque', but now used as a technical term for lavish architectural style of 17th, early 18th cents. Borrowed by musicians as general description of music of same period. Usual to distinguish between early baroque (Gabrieli, Monteverdi, Frescobaldi, *etc*) and late baroque (Alessandro Scarlatti, Bach, Handel, *etc*). Pre-baroque period (late 15th, 16th cents.) generally called RENAISSANCE, post-baroque (late 18th cent.), ROCOCO. 'Baroque' applied to music has no pejorative overtones.

**Baron, Ernst Gottlieb** (1696–1760), German lutenist, who published several theoretical works.

**Baroni, Leonora** (b. 1611), famous Mantuan singer and gamba player. Said to have been mistress of Cardinal Mazarin, who brought her to Paris in 1644.

**Barraqué, Jean** (1928–73), French composer. Worked in experimental laboratories of Radiodiffusion Française, Paris. Works incl. piano sonata, *Sequence* for soprano and chamber ensemble, *Le Temps restitué* for voices and orchestra, *Audelà du hasard* for voices and instrumental groups, and *Chant après chant* for percussion.

**barrel organ,** mechanical organ in which air is admitted to pipes by means of pins on rotating barrel. Very common in England in late 18th, early 19th cents. (*eg* in village churches). Term applied (incorrectly) to 19th-cent. street piano, also operated by barrel-and-pin mechanism; currently used in this sense.

**Bartered Bride, The** (Czech, *Prodaná Nevěsta*), comic opera by Smetana, libretto by K. Sabini. First perf. Prague, 1866. This Bohemian rustic comedy, concerning love intrigue, is most internationally popular of Czech operas.

**Barthélemon, François Hippolyte** (1741–1808), French violinist, composer. Active in England, Ireland and France. Associated with Haydn when latter visited London. Own works incl. stage music, violin sonatas and concertos, and hymn-tune 'Awake my soul'.

**Bartók, Béla** (1881–1945), Hungarian composer, pianist. Received early encouragement from Dohnányi. Collaborated with Kodály in study and collection of genuine Hungarian folk music (as opposed to international gypsy music known as 'Hungarian'). This helped to free him from earlier influences (incl. Liszt and Strauss). Compositions are product of highly original mind, sometimes finding expression in almost aggressive objectivity. Music was 'modern' not in obedience to any fashionable creed or artificial system but in its new and sincere attempts to solve problems of composition. Result may sometimes be forbidding, but is always impressive. His authority and intensity have established him as one of major figures of 20th-cent. music. In 1940 he moved to US, teaching at Columbia and Harvard; he died in poverty in New York.

Bartók's toughest, most dissonant music was written in his middle years, *eg* first piano concerto (1926). Second piano concerto (1931) is just as energetic but has greater tonal beauty. Style grew more lyrical, developing bitter-sweet quality, with *Music for Strings, Percussion and Celesta* (1937) and second violin concerto (1938). His 6 string quartets (spanning his career) contain purest expression of his musical ideas. Like those of Haydn and Beethoven they are receptacles for his most experimental thoughts and as important in the progress of music in their century. His piano works also repay study: his *Mikrokosmos* is the best keyboard teaching music since Bach, and contains the essentials of his style.

Principal compositions:

(1) Orchestra: rhapsody for piano and orchestra; 2 suites; 3 piano concertos; 2 rhapsodies for violin and orchestra; *Music for Strings, Percussion and Celesta*; *Divertimento* for strings; concerto for orchestra; 2 violin concertos; viola concerto (unfinished);

(2) Stage: *Duke Bluebeard's Castle* (opera); *The Wooden Prince* (ballet); *The Miraculous Mandarin* (pantomime);

(3) Chamber music: 6 string quartets; 2 violin sonatas; rhapsody for cello and piano; sonata for 2 pianos and percussion;

(4) Piano: sonatina; sonata; *Allegro barbaro*; *Mikrokosmos*; bagatelles, sketches, études *etc*;

(5) Choral: *Cantata profana*. Also numerous arrangements of folk songs for voices and instruments.

**baryton** (Ger.; It., *viola di bordone*), bowed string instrument used in Germany in 18th cent. Basically a bass viol with 6 bowed strings, with large number of additional strings vibrating in sympathy (as on *viola d'amore*).

**bass** (Fr., *basse*; Ger., *Bass*; It., *basso*), in general, 'low', as opposed to 'high'. Term is particularly used of lowest part of a composition, foundation on which harmony is built. Also used in following senses:

(1) lowest adult male voice, with range of *c* 2 octaves, from E below bass clef to E above middle C;

(2) prefixed to name of instrument, indicates either largest member of family or (where contrabass instrument occurs) second largest;

(3) short for double bass, and (in military bands) for bass tuba;

(4) bass clef is F clef on 4th line (*see* CLEF).

*See* FIGURED BASS.

**bassadanza** (It.), *see* BASSE DANSE.

**Bassani, Giovanni Battista** (1657–1716), Italian composer, organist. Works incl. oratorios, operas, church and instrumental music.

**bass-bar,** strip of wood glued inside belly of members of violin and viol families immediately under left foot of bridge.

**bass-baritone,** term used to indicate bass voice with good command of upper register.

**bass clarinet** (Fr., *clarinette basse*; Ger., *Bassklarinette*; It., *clarinetto basso, clarone*), single-reed instrument, built an octave lower than clarinet, with metal bell turned upwards for convenience. Formerly made in B flat and A but now only in B flat. Compass is from E flat below middle C to G 2 octaves above G on 2nd line of treble clef, sounding from D flat below bass clef to F at top of treble clef. *See* TRANSPOSING INSTRUMENTS.

**bass drum** (Fr., *grosse caisse*; Ger., *grosse Trommel*; It., *gran cassa*), percussion instrument of indeterminate pitch. Consists of large wooden shell, cylindrical in shape, covered on one or both sides with vellum. Normally beaten with stick having large felt-covered knob, but can be played with timpani sticks if roll is required.

**basse chiffrée** (Fr.), figured bass.

**basse danse** (Fr.), lit. 'low dance', so called because feet were kept close to ground, in contrast to leaping dances such as GALLIARD. *Basse danse* was court dance current in France in 15th, early 16th cents., later superseded by stately PAVANE. Earlier music consisted of melody (or 'tenor') in long notes of equal duration, around which one or more instruments improvised in style featuring rapid figuration and frequent syncopations. In early 16th cent. musical style changed; surviving examples in triple time are scored for *eg* solo lute, 4-part instrumental ensemble.

Some examples of similar Italian *bassadanza* survive, with written-out parts embellishing tenors.

**basse fondamentale,** *see* FUNDAMENTAL BASS.

**basset horn** (Fr., *cor de basset*; Ger., *Bassethorn*; It., *corno di bassetto*), alto clarinet, invented in late 18th cent. Generally built in key of F, and notes are written a fifth higher than they sound. Compass is from C below middle C to G octave above G on top of treble clef, sounding from F at bottom of bass clef to C above treble clef. Name prob. due to fact that shape was orig. curved.

**bass flute** (Fr., *flûte alto*; Ger., *Altflöte*; It., *flautone*), instrument built a fourth lower than normal FLUTE, more properly called alto flute. Compass is from middle C to C two octaves above, sounding from G below middle C to G octave above G on top of treble clef. *See* TRANSPOSING INSTRUMENTS.

**bass horn** (Fr., *serpent droit*; Ger., *Basshorn*), obsolete instrument, dating from late 18th cent. Consists of SERPENT of wood or brass made in shape of bassoon. Also known as RUSSIAN BASSOON.

**Bassklarinette** (Ger.), bass clarinet.

**basso** (It.), bass. *Basso continuo* (lit. 'continuous bass'), FIGURED BASS, *ie* bass line of composition marked with figures to indicate harmonies to be played on keyboard. *Basso ostinato* (lit. 'obstinate bass'), GROUND BASS, *ie* figure repeated in bass throughout composition or part of composition, while upper parts change.

**basso continuo,** *see* BASSO.

**basson** (Fr.), bassoon. *Basson russe,* Russian bassoon.

**bassoon** (Fr., *basson*; Ger., *Fagott*; It., *fagotto*), double-reed instrument dating from 16th cent., with compass from B flat below bass clef to D on 4th line of treble clef. Made of wooden tube doubled back on itself, hence name *fagotto,* 'bundle of sticks'. Double bassoon (Fr., *contrebasson*; Ger., *Kontrafagott*; It., *contrafagotto*) is built an octave lower, and made of wood or metal.

**basso ostinato,** *see* BASSO.

**Bassposaune** (Ger.), bass trombone.

**bass trombone,** *see* TROMBONE.

**Basstrompete** (Ger.), bass trumpet.

**bass trumpet,** *see* TRUMPET.

**bass tuba,** *see* TUBA.

**bass viol,** *see* VIOL.

**Bastien et Bastienne,** *Singspiel* by Mozart, libretto by F.W. Weiskern from C.S. Favart's parody of Rousseau's *Le Devin du village*. Written by Mozart at age of 12. First perf. Vienna, 1768.

**Bataille, Gabriel** (*c* 1575–1630), lutenist at French court. Known for *Airs de différents autheurs mis en tablature de luth* (1608–18).

**Bate, Stanley** (1913–59), English composer, pianist. Studied with Nadia Boulanger, Hindemith. Substantial output incl. 4 symphonies, 3 piano concertos, 3 violin concertos, harpsichord concerto, cello concerto, piano works, several ballets.

**Bateson, Thomas** (*c* 1570–1630), English organist. Apparently first B.Mus. of Trinity College, Dublin. Composed 2 sets of madrigals (1604–18).

**Bathe, William** (1564–1614), English writer. At first in service of Queen Elizabeth, he later became Jesuit priest. His *Briefe Introduction to the True Art of Musicke* (1584) was first book on music theory printed in England. Also wrote *A Briefe Introduction to the Skill of Song* (1600).

**baton,** stick with which conductor gives directions to performers. *See* CONDUCTING.

**Batten, Adrian** (1591–1637), English organist (at St Paul's), composer of church music. Thought to have compiled Batten Organ Book, large collection of 16th-cent. church music.

**batterie** (Fr.), BATTERY. Also, percussion section of orchestra.

**battery,** 17th, 18th-cent. term for ARPEGGIO.

**Battle of Vitoria, The,** *see* WELLINGTON'S VICTORY.

**battuta** (It.), (1) 'beat'. *A battuta,* in strict time. *Senza battuta,* without any regular beat, *ie* in free time (*eg* in recitative);

(2) particularly 1st beat in bar, hence 'bar'. *Ritmo di tre battute,*

3-bar rhythm, *ie* with main accent falling at beginning of every 3 bars.

**Bauer, Harold** (1873–1951), pianist, of German and English parentage. Pupil of Paderewski. Played in piano trios with Thibaud and Casals. Early devotee of Debussy.

**Bäurl, Bäwerl,** *see* PEUERL.

**Bax, Arnold Edward Trevor** (1883–1953), English composer. Knighted 1937, Master of the King's Musick from 1942. Romantic style powerfully influenced by affection for Ireland, Irish folklore. Compositions incl. 7 symphonies, 4 symphonic poems *(The Garden of Fand, Tintagel, November Woods, Overture to a Picaresque Comedy)*, concertos for violin, much chamber music, songs, folksong arrangements.

**Bayreuth,** town in Germany where Wagner built festival theatre, provided by public subscription, for perf. of own operas. With hooded orchestra pit, 1800-seat auditorium resembling classical amphitheatre, the Festspielhaus has acoustics ideal for Wagner's operas. First production was *Der Ring des Nibelungen* (1876). After Wagner's death (1883), control of theatre passed in turn to widow Cosima, son Siegfried, daughter-in-law Winifred. New era began in 1951 under auspices of grandsons Wieland and Wolfgang. Former created whole new style of Wagner production; when he died (1966), artistic control was left to Wolfgang.

**B.B.C. Symphony Orchestra,** founded 1930 by British Broadcasting Association. Principally involved in studio broadcasts, but also appears at public concerts, incl. Promenade Concerts. First conductor was Adrian Boult (1930–49), followed by Sir Malcolm Sargent, Rudolf Schwarz, Antal Dorati, Colin Davis, Pierre Boulez, Rudolf Kempe, Gennadi Rozhdestvensky.

**be** (Ger.), flat.

**Beach, Amy Marcy** (1867–1944), generally known as Mrs H.H. Beach (née Cheney), American pianist, composer. Works incl. Mass, piano concerto, *Gaelic Symphony* (1896) – first symphonic work by US woman.

**Bear, The,** nickname of Haydn's symphony no. 82 in C major (1786) – one of the *Paris* series, thus also known as *L'Ours*. Name derives from last movt., said to sound like bear dancing to bagpipe tune.

**Bearbeitung** (Ger.), arrangement.

**beat,** (1) unit of measurement in music, indicated in choral and orchestral works by motion of conductor's stick (Fr., *temps*; Ger., *Taktschlag, Zählzeit*; It., *battuta*). Number of beats in bar depends on TIME-SIGNATURE and on speed of movt. Movt. in 4/4 time may have 8 beats if very slow, 4 if speed is moderate, 2 if very fast. In exceptional cases may only be 1 beat in bar; this occurs most frequently in very quick movts. in 3/4 or 3/8 time. *See also* DOWN-BEAT;

(2) early English name for various ornaments.

**Beatles, The,** group of 4 young British pop singers and poet-composers: John Lennon (1940–80), Paul McCartney (1942– ),

George Harrison (1943– ), and Ringo Starr (1940– ). Made sensational series of recordings during 1960s, attracting attention from professors as well as pop enthusiasts. Disbanded *c* 1970. Recordings, full of feeling, sharpness, inventiveness, incl. *Revolver*, *Rubber Soul*, *Help!*, *Sergeant Pepper*, *Abbey Road*, *Let It Be*.

**Béatrice et Bénédict,** opera by Berlioz, libretto by composer based on Shakespeare's *Much Ado About Nothing*. First perf. Baden-Baden, 1862.

**bebop,** *see* BOP.

**Bebung** (Ger.), form of VIBRATO used on CLAVICHORD. Finger repeatedly presses key without releasing it, varying tension of string, so producing minute variations of pitch. Indicated by following sign:

or

**bécarre** (Fr.), natural.

**Bechstein,** firm of piano-makers founded in Berlin, 1856.

**Beck, Conrad** (1901– ), Swiss composer. Friend of Roussel, Honegger. Works incl. 7 symphonies, concertos, *Der Tod des Oedipus* (chorus and orchestra), *Angelus Silesius* (oratorio), *La Grande ourse* (ballet), 4 string quartets.

**Beck, Franz** (1723–1809), German composer. Pupil of J. Stamitz. Lived in Bordeaux from 1761. His many symphonies are important in early history of the form.

**Becken** (Ger.), cymbals.

**Bedford, David** (1937– ), English composer. Pupil of Berkeley and Nono. Prolific output incl. *Star's End* for rock instruments and orchestra (1974), *Star Clusters, Nebulae, and Places in Devon* for double chorus and brass (1971).

**Bédos de Celles, Dom François** (1709–79), Benedictine monk, author of *L'Art du facteur d'orgues* (1766–78), work on organ-building which also contains valuable information about interpretation and tempo of music of period.

**Bedyngham, John** (*fl* early 15th cent.), English composer of church music. Some of his works are in TRENT CODICES.

**Beecham, Thomas** (1879–1961), English conductor. First appeared as conductor in London in 1905. Knighted 1914, succeeded to father's baronetcy, 1916. Founder and conductor of London Philharmonic (1932), Royal Philharmonic (1946). Active in promoting opera in Britain, introducing many unfamiliar works *eg* Strauss's operas. Sympathies lay with romantics (esp. Berlioz, Bizet), but had special predilection for works of Mozart, Handel, Delius (whose works he championed).

**Bee's Wedding, The,** name given (though not by composer) to Mendelssohn's *Song without Words*, no 34 in C major. Known in Germany as *Spinnerlied*.

**Beethoven, Ludwig van** (1770–1827), German composer of Flemish descent. Born in Bonn. His grandfather and father were also musicians. He left school aged 11, and took various posts as harpsichord player, organist, and viola player. He met Haydn and went to Vienna (where he stayed for the rest of his life) to study with him in 1792. They did not get on; Beethoven then took lessons from Albrechtsberger, Salieri and Schenk. He made his first public appearance in Vienna in 1795, playing the B flat major piano concerto, op 19. He rejected the 18th-cent. system of patronage, whereby the musician was tied to the service of an employer. His increasing deafness, which he knew to be incurable, led him, in 1802, to contemplate suicide. His battle with deafness is waged in the *Eroica* symphony (1804), the biggest and most powerful symphony written up to that time. His failure to find a wife (despite being constantly in love with one or other of his pupils) increased his isolation; his temper was not improved by the cares of acting as guardian to his feckless nephew, Karl. By 1819 he was completely deaf, but went on to produce some of his greatest, most thoughtful works, rising above the agonies of his private life and reaching into the future of his art. These works were of course misunderstood at the time, but were enormously influential on later composers. He became very ill in 1826, and died the following year, having sketched a 10th symphony.

Beethoven did not find composition easy; he repeatedly revised his original sketches until satisfied. His sympathy with liberal ideas (he was brought up as a Catholic but later adopted his own deistic views) found expression in works like *Egmont,* and the 9th symphony, and esp. in his only opera, *Fidelio,* which has become a universal symbol of love and liberty. He was the first great 'subjective' composer: the C minor piano concerto, written in 1800, marks the dawn of a new attitude to music, very different from classical objectivity. Many of his works, esp. those of middle period (*eg* the *Appassionata* sonata) reflect his tempestuousness and dissatisfaction with convention, yet there is also a deep sincerity and native simplicity. He was impatient with technical restrictions, and could be merciless to voices and instruments. On the other hand, some of his slow movements have a sense of calm contemplation that show a different facet of his personality – *eg* the slow movements of the 9th symphony and the A minor string quartet, op 132.

Principal compositions:

(1) Orchestra: 9 symphonies (last with vocal soloists and chorus); violin concerto; 5 piano concertos; concerto for piano, violin and cello; overtures – *Coriolan, Leonore* nos 1, 2, 3, *Namensfeier* (Name-Day), *The Consecration of the House;* overtures to works in (3); fantasia for piano, orchestra and chorus; 2 romances for violin and orchestra;

(2) Choral works: 2 Masses (C major and D major); oratorio – *Christus am Ölberg* (The Mount of Olives); also 9th symphony;

(3) Stage works: opera – *Fidelio;* incidental music to *Egmont, King Stephen, The Ruins of Athens;* ballet – *The Creatures of Prometheus;*

(4) Chamber music: septet; quintet for piano and wind; string quintet; 16 string quartets and *Grosse Fuge;* 4 string trios; serenade

for flute, violin and viola; 6 piano trios; trio for clarinet, cello and piano; 10 violin sonatas; 5 cello sonatas; horn sonata;

(5) Piano: 32 sonatas; 21 sets of variations; *Bagatellen;*

(6) Songs: *An die ferne Geliebte* (To the Distant Beloved – song cycle); *Ah, perfido* (Ah, faithless one – *scena* for soprano and orchestra); other songs for voice and piano.

**Beggar's Opera, The,** ballad opera by John Gay. First perf. London, 1728. Consists of play interspersed with *c* 70 songs set to popular tunes of time, some by Purcell and Handel. Satirizes both urban vices and conventions of Italian opera. Songs arranged by John Christopher Pepusch. New additions have been made by Frederic Austen, Edward Dent, Benjamin Britten.

**Begleitung** (Ger.), accompaniment.

**Beinum, Eduard van** (1901–59), Dutch conductor. Conducted Concertgebouw Orchestra, Amsterdam, from 1945.

**Bekker, Paul** (1882–1937), German writer on music, critic. Most important works are *Beethoven* (1925) and *Wagner* (1931).

**Belaiev, Mitrophane Petrovich** (1836–1904), Russian publisher. Founded firm in Leipzig in 1885, publishing many works by Russian composers.

**bel canto** (It.), lit., beautiful song or singing. Usually applied to fine, sustained singing in Italian manner, with emphasis on beauty of tone, phrasing, agility, and ability to take high notes without strain. Work of Bellini, Donizetti, Rossini (among others) depended on such singing.

**bell,** most public bells are made of bell metal (bronze consisting of 4 parts copper to 1 part tin), cast to produce characteristic mix of harmonics. Largest bell (now cracked) is Tsar Kolokol (Emperor Bell) in Moscow, cast in 1733 and weighing 193 tons. Bells are chimed by moving clapper (or swinging bell so clapper strikes sides) or by hitting with mallet. CARILLON of bells can produce tune. Changes of bells are rung by many churches (also possible on hand bells): ringers attempt to progress through possible permutations of ringing order (for 5 bells, 120 changes; for 6 bells, 720, and so on).

In orchestras, tubular bells made of long tubes of brass are struck with mallet to simulate sound of bells. Set is tuned chromatically; suspended in same arrangement as keyboard.

**Bell Anthem,** name given to 'Rejoice in the Lord alway', anthem for voices and strings by Purcell; beginning suggests tolling of bells.

**Belle Hélène, La,** operetta by Offenbach, libretto by H. Meilhac and L. Halévy. First perf. Paris, 1864.

**Bellérophon,** opera by Lully, libretto by Corneille. First perf. Paris, 1679.

**bell harp,** kind of zither invented in England in early 18th cent. Gripped by fingers and swung through air (hence 'bell') while plucking strings with plectrums attached to thumbs.

**Bellini, Vincenzo** (1801–1835), Italian composer, b. Sicily. Studied with Zingarelli in Naples, where came into contact with Donizetti. First opera, *Adelson e Salvina* (1825), led to many commissions. His lyrical gifts quickly reached maturity. Subsequent operas incl. *Bianca e Fernando* (1826), *Il Pirata* (1827), *La Straniera* (1829), *Zaira* (1829), *I Capuletti ed i Montecchi* (1830, based on story of Romeo and Juliet), *La Sonnambula* (1831), *Norma* (1831). Last opera was *I Puritani* (1835, inspired by Scott's *Old Mortality*). Died in Paris of dysentery.

**bell lyra** or **bell lyre,** portable glockenspiel played in military bands. Consists of metal bars attached to lyre-shaped frame with handle. Player holds handle in one hand, mallet in other.

**Bell Rondo** (It., *Rondo alla campanella*), finale of Paganini's violin concerto in B minor (*c* 1824), imitating sound of bells. On it Liszt based 'La Campanella' for piano (1838, rev. 1851).

**bell tree,** set of small bells mounted vertically on long rod. Usually played by running stick along set, producing arpeggio.

**belly** (Fr., *table*), upper part of soundbox of string instrument, often known as 'table'.

**Belshazzar,** oratorio by Handel, libretto by C. Jennens. First perf. London, 1745.

**Belshazzar's Feast,** oratorio by Walton, words selected (mainly from Bible) by Sacheverell Sitwell. First perf. at Leeds Festival, 1931. Abrasive score gave English choral tradition much-needed injection of vitality. Sibelius wrote orchestral suite on same subject.

**bémol** (Fr.), **bemolle** (It.), flat.

**ben, bene** (It.), well, very.

**Benda, Jiři Antonin** or **George** (1722–95), Czech composer, pianist, oboist. Wrote church, orchestral and chamber music, operettas, and instrumental music for 3 MELODRAMAS.

**Benedicite** (Lat.), canticle known as 'Song of the Three Children'; alternative to Te Deum in Anglican Morning Service.

**Benedict, Julius** (1804–85), English composer, conductor, b. Germany. Pupil of Hummel, Weber. Wrote many instrumental works, oratorios, operas, but remembered only for *The Lily of Killarney* (1862). Knighted 1871.

**Benedictus** (Lat.), (1) second part of *Sanctus* of Roman Mass; (2) canticle *Benedictus Dominus Israel* ('Blessed be the Lord God of Israel'), alternative to Jubilate in Anglican Morning Service.

**Benet, John** (*fl* 15th cent.), English composer. Wrote Mass, motets and Mass movements.

**Benevoli, Orazio** (1605–72), Italian composer. Worked in Archduke's court in Vienna (1643–45), and was *maestro di cappella* at Vatican (1645–72). Composed large-scale church music, some of it for several choirs; one Mass is in 53 vocal and instrumental parts.

**Benjamin, Arthur** (1893–1960), Australian composer, pianist. Works, showing lively sense of humour combined with accomplished technique, incl. operas *The Devil Take Her* (1931), *Prima Donna, A Tale of Two Cities, Tartuffe,* concertino for piano and orchestra, violin concerto, *Overture to an Italian Comedy,* symphony, chamber and film music, songs, and widely popular *Jamaican Rumba.*

**Bennet, John** (*c* 1575–after 1614), English composer. Wrote some hymn-tunes, many madrigals incl. famous 'All creatures now are merry minded'.

**Bennett, Richard Rodney** (1936– ), English composer, pianist. Studied under Lennox Berkeley, Howard Ferguson, Boulez. Prolific writing employs serialism with polish and vigour. Most important pieces are operas, employing considerable theatrical talent: *The Mines of Sulphur* (1965, a spook story), *A Penny for a Song* (comedy), *Victory* (inspired by Conrad). Piano concerto, first symphony and *Aubade* for orchestra have all been very successful. Has also written 4 string quartets, *Calendar* for chamber ensemble, piano and film music.

**Bennett, Robert Russell** (1894–1981), American composer. Pupil of Carl Busch, Nadia Boulanger. Works incl. opera *Maria Malibran* (1935), *Abraham Lincoln Symphony, Symphony in D for the Dodgers* (title referring to Brooklyn baseball team), film, chamber and choral music.

**Bennett, William Sterndale** (1816–75), English composer, pianist. Friend of Mendelssohn, Schumann. Founded Bach Society (1849), giving first perf. in England of Bach's *St. Matthew Passion* (1854). Works, strongly influenced by Mendelssohn, incl. symphony, 4 piano concertos, overtures *(The Naiads, The Woodnymphs)*, *The Woman of Samaria* (oratorio), choral and piano music, songs. Knighted 1871.

**Benoît, Pierre** (or **Peter**) **Léopold Léonard** (1834–1901), Belgian composer. Promoted national movement which led to foundation of L'Ecole Flamande de Musique, Antwerp (1867), of which he became director. Works incl. 3 operas, 3 oratorios, and several choral cantatas.

**Bentzon, Jørgen** (1897–1948), Danish composer. Pupil of Nielsen. Works incl. 2 symphonies (1st on Dickens), orchestral variations, 5 string quartets, chamber music.

**Bentzon, Niels Viggo** (1919– ), Danish composer, pianist. Cousin of above. Uses 12-note technique. Works incl. 14 symphonies (4th, *Metamorphoses*, is milestone), 7 concertos and 11 sonatas for piano, opera *(Faust III)*, 2 violin concertos, 9 string quartets, chamber music, cantana *(Bonjour Max Ernst)*.

**Benvenuto Cellini,** opera by Berlioz, libretto by L. de Wailly and A. Barbier. First perf. Paris, 1838. Berlioz's first opera, based on life of Italian sculptor, was not initially a success, and was known only for concert overture, *Roman Carnival* (1844), using material from opera. Opera has since been recognized as masterpiece.

**bequadro** (It.), natural.

**berceuse** (Fr.; Ger., *Wiegenlied*), 'cradle song'.

**Berenice,** opera by Handel, libretto by A. Salvi. First perf. London, 1737. Remembered for minuet.

**Berg, Alban** (1885–1935), Austrian composer. Studied with and greatly influenced by Schoenberg, esp. in development of atonality and serialism. Reputation estab. by first opera, *Wozzeck* (1917–21), a free-atonal work. Adopted TWELVE-NOTE SYSTEM soon after, using it distinctively *eg* in violin concerto (1935) and unfinished opera *Lulu* (1929–35). Violin concerto is one of most important 20th-cent. concertos. Berg was slow, careful, sensitive composer, whose few works reveal great intelligence and technical mastery, combined with greater warmth of imagination than his master. Berg was gifted and devoted teacher himself.

Principal works:

(1) Operas: *Wozzeck* (1921), *Lulu* (1929–35);

(2) Orchestra: 3 orchestral pieces, chamber concerto for piano, violin and 13 instruments, violin concerto;

(3) Chamber music: string quartet, *Lyric Suite* for string quartet;

(4) Piano: sonata.

Also several songs, with piano and orchestra.

**bergamasca** (It.; Fr., *bergamasque*), (1) popular dance, named after Bergamo in N. Italy, current in 16th, early 17th cents. Orig. constructed on recurring pattern of tonic-subdominant-dominant-tonic harmonies. By early 17th cent., dance became associated with particular tune;

(2) 19th-cent. dance in quick 6/8 time, similar to tarantella;

(3) in Debussy's *Suite bergamasque* for piano, adjective seems to have no special significance.

**bergerette** (Fr., *berger,* 'shepherd'), (1) 16th-cent. dance in brisk triple time; (2) 18th-cent. French song dealing with shepherds and shepherdesses.

**bergomask,** *see* BERGAMASCA.

**Berio, Luciano** (1925– ), Italian composer, conductor. Pupil of Ghedini and Dallapiccola. Though siding with avant-garde, and employing advanced techniques, has managed to achieve world-wide popularity with succession of colourful, dramatic works, nearly always containing underlying element of Italian lyricism. Made name in early 1960s with *Circles* (text by E.E. Cummings) for woman's voice, harp and percussion, using spatial effects. Subsequent works incl. series of *Sequenze* for various solo instruments, *Tempi Concertanti* for flute and chamber ensemble, large-scale *Sinfonia,* concerto for 2 pianos, *Nones* for orchestra, *Allelujah* (series of pieces for different ensembles), *Bewegung* for orchestra, electronic works (*Mutations, Chants parallèles*). Music for stage incl. *Allez, Hop!*

**Bériot, Charles Auguste de** (1802–70), Belgian violinist, teacher, composer. His first wife was the singer Maria Malibran. His brilliant playing was influential. Compositions incl. concertos, studies and instruction books. Pupils incl. Henri Vieuxtemps.

**Berkeley, Lennox Randal Francis** (1903– ), English composer. Pupil of Nadia Boulanger. Works, orig. influenced by Stravinsky and showing French regard for clarity, precision and deep sympathy for human voice, incl. oratorio *Jonah,* operas *Nelson, A Dinner Engagement, Ruth,* ballet *The Judgement of Paris, Stabat Mater,* 4 symphonies, concertos for piano, 2 pianos, violin, cello and flute, witty orchestral divertimento, and chamber and piano music.

**Berkshire Festival,** annual festival of music founded 1937 at

Tanglewood, Mass., by Koussevitsky, with Boston Symphony as regular orchestra. From 1940 courses also held in composition, conducting and performance.

**Berlin, Irving,** orig. Israel Baline (1888– ), American composer, b. Russia. Wrote some of America's finest pop songs. First international success was 'Alexander's Ragtime Band' (1911); most famous song is prob. 'White Christmas' (1942). Musicals incl. *Top Hat* (1935), *Call Me Madam* (1950).

**Berlin Philharmonic Orchestra,** founded 1882, with Franz Wüllner as first conductor, followed by Joseph Joachim, Karl Klindworth, Hans von Bülow, Arthur Nikisch, Wilhelm Furtwängler and, since 1955, Herbert von Karajan.

**Berlioz, [Louis] Hector** (1803–69), French composer. Son of doctor, born near Grenoble. Father sent him to Paris to study medicine (1821), which Berlioz disliked. Eventually entered Paris Conservatoire (1826) to study composition; progressive views made him enemy of Cherubini. Eventually won *Prix de Rome* (1830) with cantata, *Sardanapale.* Fell in love with Irish actress, Harriet Smithson, who inspired *Symphonie fantastique* (1830). Before meeting her, became engaged to pianist Marie Moke, who, however, married Camille Pleyel instead. Married Harriet Smithson in 1833, but separated by 1842. Married singer Marie Recio (1854). To finance composition worked as music critic; in 1838 Paganini gave him 20,000 francs. First official appointment came in 1859, as librarian of Conservatoire, though French govt. had subsidized composition of *Symphonie funèbre et triomphale,* performed on 10th anniversary of 1830 revolution.

With this money, he travelled extensively, conducting his works and causing a sensation; he was particularly successful in Germany (visited Liszt in 1855). By 1858 had completed greatest masterpiece, opera *The Trojans,* based on Virgil's *Aeneid,* but work never had complete performance in his lifetime. Failure of *The Trojans* so dispirited Berlioz that he practically ceased composition. His last years were dogged by loneliness and a serious nervous affliction.

Old-fashioned objections to Berlioz's work have died away, partly because conductors and orchestras have learnt how to master the music's phrasing, and its swerving rhythms, delicacy of orchestration and passionate melancholy. Berlioz was once thought of as a composer of brassy brilliance, but even some of his grandest works achieve their most memorable effects by stealth. Not till *L'Enfance du Christ* did public realize restraint and purity of his music, and it took them long to recognize the classical masterpiece lying behind the romantic programme of the *Symphonie fantastique.*

Though renowned as orchestrator, Berlioz was not proficient on any instrument. Nearest thing to concerto he wrote was poetic *Harold in Italy* (based on Byron), but solo viola part was so unostentatious that Paganini (who commissioned it) declined to perform it. Poetry also marks Berlioz's vocal music; *Nuits d'été* (1841–56), settings of Gautier, was first important song cycle written for voice and orchestra.

Principal works:

(1) Operas: *Benvenuto Cellini* (1838), *The Trojans* (1865–9), *Béatrice et Bénédict* (1862);

(2) Orchestra: *Symphonie fantastique, Harold in Italy* (for viola and orchestra), overtures – *King Lear, Le Corsaire, Roman Carnival, Les Francs-Juges, Waverley, Rob Roy*;

(3) Choral works: *Sara la baigneuse, Lélio ou le retour à la vie* (sequel to *Symphonie fantastique*), *Roméo et Juliette* (dramatic symphony), *Symphonie funèbre et triomphale, La Damnation de Faust, Grande Messe des Morts* (Requiem Mass), *L'Enfance du Christ, Te Deum, L'Impériale*;

(4) Song cycle *Les Nuits d'été,* 2 scenas for voice and orchestra (*Herminie, Cléopâtre*), songs and works for small vocal ensembles.

**Bermudo, Juan** (*fl* 16th cent.), Spanish author of instruction book on music and musical instruments, *Libro llamado declaración de instrumentos* (1555).

**Bernardi, Steffano** (d. before 1638), Italian composer. *Kapellmeister* at Salzburg Cathedral (1628–34). Composed madrigals, and church and instrumental music; also published successful primer of counterpoint (1615).

**Berners, Lord,** orig. Gerald Hugh Tyrwhitt-Wilson (1883–1950), English composer, painter, author, diplomat. Music is often ironic, parodying romantic conventions; Gallic leanings evident in titles. Works incl. many ballets *eg The Triumph of Neptune* (1926), *A Wedding Bouquet* (1937), opera *Le Carosse du Saint-Sacrement* (1924), *Fantaisie espagnole,* Fugue in C minor for orchestra, songs, piano music *eg Valses bourgeoises.*

**Bernhard, Christoph** (1627–92), German tenor singer, composer. Held various church posts in Germany. Works incl. Mass and Protestant church music.

**Bernstein, Leonard** (1918– ), American conductor, composer, pianist. Studied under Walter Piston (composition), Koussevitsky and Fritz Reiner (conducting). Started conducting at Berkshire Music Center, went on to New York Philharmonic. Specializes in Mahler, Ravel, Sibelius, early Stravinsky. Also conducts opera. As composer, has been most successful with musicals, *On the Town* (1944), *Wonderful Town* (1952), *Candide* (1956), *West Side Story* (1957). Concert pieces more controversial: 3 symphonies *(Jeremiah, The Age of Anxiety, Kaddish)* sometimes seem excessively ambitious. Other works incl. ballets *Fancy Free* and *Facsimile, Chichester Psalms* for chorus and orchestra, modern Mass, opera *Trouble in Tahiti,* music for film *On the Waterfront.*

**Berton, Henri Montan** (1767–1844), French composer, violinist. Numerous works incl. *c* 50 operas, of which *Aline, Reine de Golconde* (1803) was the most successful.

**Bertoni, Ferdinando Giuseppe** (1725–1813), Italian composer.

Pupil of Martini. Works incl. operas (*eg Orfeo,* 1776), oratorios and instrumental works.

**Berwald, Franz Adolf** (1796–1868), Swedish composer, violinist. Distinctive music not appreciated during lifetime, but now more frequently performed. Works incl. 4 symphonies, several symphonic poems, concertos, chamber music, several operas *eg A Rustic Betrothal in Sweden* (given with Jenny Lind), *Estrella di Soria.*

**Bes** (Ger.), B double flat.

**Besard, Jean Baptiste** (b. *c* 1567), French doctor of law, lutenist, composer. Published 2 anthologies of lute music, which incl. his own compositions: *Thesaurus harmonicus* (1603), *Novus partus sive concertationes musicae* (1617).

**Besseler, Heinrich** (1900–69), German musicologist, specializing in study of medieval music.

**Besson, Gustave Auguste** (1820–75), French manufacturer of brass instruments, in which he introduced several improvements. Also constructed a contrabass clarinet.

**bestimmt** (Ger.), decisively.

**Betz, Franz** (1835–1900), German baritone. Sang Hans Sachs in first perf. of *Die Meistersinger* (1868) and Wotan in first perf. of *Der Ring des Nibelungen* (1876).

**Beurlin,** *see* PEUERL.

**Bevin, Elway** (1554–1639), English organist. Wrote instruction book on music, and Service in the Dorian mode which is still sung.

**bewegt** (Ger.), 'moved', *ie* with animation (It., *mosso*). *Bewegter,* faster (It., *più mosso*). *Mässig bewegt,* at moderate speed.

**bezifferter Bass** (Ger.), figured bass.

**Bianchi, Francesco** (1752–1810), Italian opera composer, conductor. Worked in Paris, Milan, Venice, London and Dublin. Most popular of numerous operas was *La Villanella rapita* (1783). Committed suicide.

**Biber, Heinrich Ignaz Franz von** (1644–1704), German composer, violinist. Works, often of considerable technical difficulty, consist of chamber compositions for various groupings, incl. sonatas for violin and figured bass (15 of these are associated with incidents in life of Christ and Virgin Mary), and Passacaglia for unaccompanied violin. Made considerable use of *scordatura* (modifications of accepted tuning of violin).

**bicinium** (Lat.; *bis,* twice, and *canere,* to sing), term used in 16th, 17th cents. for composition for 2 voices or (later) 2 instruments.

**Biggs, Edward George Power** (1906–77), American organist, b. Britain. Known for performances of Bach.

**Bigot de Morogues, Maria,** née **Kiene** (1786–1820), Alsatian pianist. Met Haydn and Beethoven in Vienna; latter seems to have become very much attached to her. Gave lessons to 7-year-old Mendelssohn in Paris.

**Billington, Elizabeth,** née **Weichsel** (1765–1818), English operatic soprano. Pupil of J.C. Bach. Had great reputation both in England and in Europe.

**Billy Budd,** (1) opera by Britten, libretto by E.M. Forster and Eric Crozier, based on Herman Melville's story. First perf. London, 1951 (rev. 1961); (2) opera by Ghedini, libretto by Salvatore Quasimodo. First perf. Venice, 1949.

**binary form,** term indicating that piece of music can be divided into 2 sections. Characteristic of much early dance music, and transferred to other kinds of music by 17th cent. In 17th-cent. music, 1st section may end (a) in tonic key, (b) on half close, (c) in related key, *ie* dominant or (if minor key) relative major; 2nd section naturally ends in tonic. Of possible endings to 1st section, tonic suggested premature ending, and half close tended to sound indefinite, hence use of related key became standard. This resulted in modulation in 1st part to establish related key, then 2nd section consisted of modulation back to tonic. This latter modulation offered much opportunity for development, and 2nd section tended to be longer than 1st, often passing through several keys before reaching tonic. This became standard procedure by early 18th cent.

Recapitulation, which was feature of *da capo* aria, was introduced into pieces in binary form, *ie* 1st section would be repeated at end of 2nd section, but modified so that what was in related key would now be in tonic. Further development (mid 18th cent.) was to make contrast between 2 key centres of 1st section more vivid by contrast of thematic material. This procedure was basis of SONATA FORM as practised in second half of 18th cent.; practice of repeating long 2nd section soon died out, though 1st section was repeated till end of 19th cent.

**Binchois** or **de Binche, Gilles** (*c* 1400–60), Flemish composer. Fame as song-writer rivalled that of Dufay. Also wrote sacred music.

**Bindungszeichen** (Ger.), *see* SLUR (1).

**bird organ** or **serinette,** miniature forerunner of barrel organ, invented in 17th cent., orig. made to teach songbirds to sing tunes. Later versions imitated bird song and were built into cages of mechanical birds.

**Bird Quartet** (Ger., *Vogelquartett*), one of Haydn's 'Russian Quartets', op 33, no 3.

**Birds, The** (It., *Gli Uccelli*), orchestral suite by Respighi (1927), based on bird pieces by 17th, 18th-cent. masters.

**Birmingham Symphony Orchestra, City of,** founded 1920, orig. City of Birmingham Orchestra. Earliest conductor was Appleby Matthews (1920–4); successors incl. Sir Adrian Boult, Leslie Heward, George Weldon, Rudolf Schwarz, Andrzej Panufnik, Hugo Rignold, Louis Frémaux, Simon Rattle.

**Birtwistle, Harrison** (1934– ), English composer. Member of 'Manchester School' with Alexander Goehr, Peter Maxwell Davies, John Ogden. Works, often offering uncompromisingly tough sonorities, incl. opera *Punch and Judy,* abrasive chamber piece *Tragoedia, Refrains and Choruses* for wind quintet, *Monody for Corpus Christi* for soprano, flute, violin and horn, and *The Triumph of Time* for orchestra.

**bis** (Fr.), 'twice' (Lat., *bis*). Indicates that passage over which word is written is to be played twice.

**bisbigliando** (It.), 'whispering'.

**biscroma** (It.), demisemiquaver.

**Bishop, Henry Rowley** (1786–1855), English composer, conductor. First British musician to be knighted (1842). Wrote and adapted large number of works for stage, vandalizing operas by Mozart, Rossini, Beethoven *etc.* Now chiefly remembered for song 'Home, sweet home' (from opera *Clari, or the Maid of Milan,* 1823).

**bitonality,** use of 2 keys simultaneously, whether indicated by different key signatures or not. However clear distinction is between 2 keys, ear instinctively seizes on any points they may have in common. Famous examples in Stravinsky's *Petrushka,* pieces by Milhaud. *See also* POLYTONALITY.

**biwa,** Japanese LUTE.

**Bizet, Georges,** orig. Alexandre César Léopold Bizet (1838–75), French composer. Sent to Paris Conservatoire at age of 10; studied under Marmontel, Gounod, Halévy (whose daughter he later married). Wrote sparkling Symphony in C at age of 17, won prize offered by Offenbach with operetta *Le Docteur Miracle,* and in 1857 won *Prix de Rome.* After 3 years in Rome, returned to Paris, but early operas (*The Pearl Fishers, Ivan the Terrible*) were not successful. The conductor Pasdeloup encouraged him with orchestral *Roma* suite and *Patrie* overture. In 1872 was commissioned to write incidental music to Daudet's Provençal play, *L'Arlésienne;* play was failure, but lively music lives on in 2 exquisitely coloured suites that contain essence of Bizet's musical personality. That essence also appears in last work, opera *Carmen;* it ran for 37 performances during which Bizet died (1875). Like Berlioz, Bizet was plagued by lack of public recognition, resulting in lack of self-confidence which in turn sometimes resulted in failure to exploit his musical gifts. Nevertheless, he is one of the greatest of French composers. His other works incl. operas *Don Procopio, The Fair Maid of Perth, Djamileh,* piano pieces *eg Jeux d'enfants,* and songs.

**Björling, Jussi** (1911–60), Swedish tenor. Known internationally, esp. for roles in Italian opera.

**Blacher, Boris** (1903–75), German composer, b. China. Music, freely contrapuntal in style and involving ingenious system of variable rhythmic metres, has been very influential. Works incl. 'scenic oratorio' on *Romeo and Juliet,* oratorio *The Grand Inquisitor* (after Dostoevsky), 2 piano concertos, orchestral variations on theme by Paganini, string quartets, piano music, songs.

**black pudding,** another name for SERPENT.

**bladder and string,** folk instrument consisting of inflated bladder attached to pole. Taut string is fastened to each end of pole, passing over bladder, and is bowed to give sound.

**Blake, David** (1936– ), English composer. Works, some using serial techniques, incl. opera *Toussaint L'Ouverture* (1977), romantic violin concerto (1976), and orchestral, vocal and chamber music.

**Blamont, François Colin de** (1690–1760), French composer. Pupil of Lalande. Worked in service of French court. Works incl. ballets, pastorales, cantatas, motets and *divertissement* for marriage of Louis XV in 1725.

**blanche** (Fr.), minim.

**Blangini, Giuseppe Marco Maria Felice** (1781–1841), Italian singer, teacher, composer. Director of music to King Jerome of Westphalia (Napoleon's brother) at Cassel (1809–14). Numerous operas incl. *Nephtali ou Les Ammonites* (1806).

**Bläser, Blasinstrumente** (Ger.), wind instruments. *Blasmusik*, music for wind.

**Blavet, Michel** (1700–68), French flautist, composer. Wrote one of earliest French *opéras-comiques, Le Jaloux corrigé* (1752), mainly compiled from arias in Italian comic operas.

**Blech, Harry** (1910– ), English conductor, violinist. Leader of Blech Quartet (1936–50), and from 1949 director of London Mozart Players.

**Blech, Leo** (1871–1958), German conductor, composer. Pupil of Humperdinck. Held posts in Prague, Berlin and Vienna. Compositions incl. symphonic poems, choral works, songs and several operas, incl. *Versiegellt* (1908).

**Blechinstrumente** (Ger.), brass instruments.

**Bliss, Arthur** (1891–1975), English composer. Pupil of Stanford, Vaughan Williams, Holst. After WWI, works like *Rout* for soprano and 10 instruments (1919), *Conversations* (1919), and *Colour Symphony* (1922) revealed daringly experimental talent. Changed direction in later works, his vigour and independence becoming related to English romantic tradition. Knighthood (1950) and appointment as Master of the Queen's Musick (1953) seemed to consolidate his conservatism, though work was often impressive. Compositions incl. *Music for Strings*, piano concerto, orchestral *Variations on a theme by John Blow*, clarinet and oboe quintets, and choral *Pastoral (Lie strewn the white flocks)*. Stage works incl. opera *The Olympians* (1949, libretto by J.B. Priestley), ballets *Checkmate, Miracle in the Gorbals, Adam Zero.*

**Blitheman, William** (d. 1591), English composer, organist at Chapel Royal. Wrote church and keyboard music. Teacher of John Bull.

**Blitzstein, Marc** (1905–64), American composer, pianist. Pupil of Nadia Boulanger, Schoenberg. Works, often politically motivated, incl. operas *eg The Cradle will Rock* (1937), *No for an Answer* (1940), symphonic poem *Freedom Morning* (dedicated to Negro troops of WWII), choral work *The Airborne* (for US Air Force). Also wrote piano concerto, string quartet, piano sonata.

**Bloch, Ernest** (1880–1959), American composer, b. Switzerland. Studied in Europe (pupil of Jaques-Dalcroze), then settled in US (though returned to Switzerland 1930–8). Music has been called typically Jewish in its intensity, conscious pathos, and love of orchestral colour. Works incl. well-known Jewish rhapsody, *Shelomo* (Solomon), for cello and orchestra, opera *Macbeth* (1910), *Avodath*

*Hakdesh* (Sacred Service) for baritone, chorus and orchestra, *Israel Symphony* for voices and orchestra, violin concerto, Concerto Symphonique for piano and orchestra, *American Symphony*, concerto grosso for piano and strings, 4 string quartets, *Baal Shem* and other works for violin and piano, piano quintet, piano sonata, songs.

**block chords,** harmonic procedure whereby notes of chords move simultaneously in 'blocks', instead of different contrapuntal directions. Debussy used device in piano pieces; subsequently adopted by many modern jazz pianists.

**Blockflöte** (Ger.; Fr., *flûte-à-bec*), recorder or beaked flute.

**Blockx, Jan** (1851–1912), Belgian composer. Supported Flemish nationalism. Works incl. symphony, symphonic triptych, cantatas, operas *eg Bruid der Zee* (*La Fiancée de la mer*, 1901).

**Blodek, Vilem** (1834–74), Czech flautist, composer. Numerous works incl. comic opera *V Studni* (In the Well, 1867).

**Blom, Eric Walter** (1888–1959), English critic. Worked as music critic of *The Birmingham Post* and *The Observer*, and as editor of *Music and Letters*. Books incl. *Mozart* (1930) and *Beethoven's Sonatas Discussed* (1938). Edited 5th edition of Grove's *Dictionary of Music and musicians*.

**Blomdahl, Karl-Birger** (1916–68), Swedish composer. Most famous work is opera *Aniara* (set on space-ship); also wrote 3 symphonies, concertos for violin and viola, chamber music, piano pieces.

**Blow, John** (1649–1708), English composer, organist. Held various posts in Chapel Royal, Westminster Abbey, St. Paul's Cathedral. Teacher of Purcell. Music, though in general less vivid than Purcell's, has similar independence of convention; incl. numerous court odes, anthems, songs (collected under title *Amphion Anglicus*, 1700), harpsichord solos and masque *Venus and Adonis* (virtually a miniature opera).

**Bluebeard's Castle** (Hung., *A Kékszakállú Herceg Vára*), opera by Bartók, libretto by B. Balázs. First perf. Budapest, 1918.

**Blue Danube, The** (Ger., *An der Schönen blauen Donau*), waltz by Johann Strauss the younger (1867).

**blues, the,** the 'classical' Negro basis of American jazz. Often sad, but can be exuberant and joyous. Evolved partly from spirituals, but emphasis is on solo voice rather than choral settings. Quickly estab. own musical form: strictly, 12 bars long, each verse consisting of 3 lines of 4 bars each (2nd line usually repeating 1st), with unvarying chord sequence as ground bass. Other characteristics are occurence of 'blue notes' (minor 3rd and 7th), and 'break' at end of lines. The discipline of the blues has not proved limiting: has greatly inspired jazz musicians from Bessie Smith to Charlie Parker and beyond.

**Blume, Friedrich** (1893–1975), German musicologist. Edited complete works of Praetorius, and collection of old choral music. Most important work is his history of Protestant church music (1931).

**Blüthner,** firm of piano manufacturers, founded at Leipzig in 1853 by Julius Ferdinand Blüthner (1824–1910).

**B Minor Mass,** setting of Latin text of Mass by Bach for soloists, chorus and orchestra. Only 5 of 24 numbers are in B minor. *Kyrie* and *Gloria* were written in 1733 to support Bach's application for title of court composer to Frederick Augustus II, Elector of Saxony. Bach subsequently completed work by adding new settings and adapting numbers from earlier works.

**Boatswain's Mate, The,** comic opera by Ethel Smythe, libretto by composer (based on story by W.W. Jacobs). First perf. London, 1916.

**bocca chiusa** (It.; Fr., *bouche fermée*), singing with closed lips.

**Boccherini, Luigi** (1743–1805), Italian composer, cellist. Toured widely as cellist, winning great reputation. Settled (1769) in Madrid, where Infante Don Luis became his patron. Chamber composer to Friedrich Wilhelm II of Prussia (1786–97). Subsequently neglected; died in poverty in Madrid. Prolific composer: works incl. 125 string quintets (one contains famous minuet), 102 string quartets, 60 string trios, 27 violin sonatas, much other chamber music, 4 cello concertos (one in B flat major is standard of repertory), oratorios, cantatas, church music and opera *Clementina.*

**Bodansky, Arthur** (1877–1939), Austrian conductor. Became assistant to Mahler at Imperial Opera, Vienna. After various posts in Europe, became conductor at New York Metropolitan in 1915, and then of New York Society of the Friends of Music (1918–1931).

**Boehm,** *see also* BÖHM.

**Boehm, Theobald** (1794–1881), German flautist. Invented Boehm system, improved key mechanism for flute, applied to other instruments *eg* clarinet.

**Boethius, Anicius Manlius Severinus** (*c* 480–524), Roman philosopher, statesman, executed by Theodoric. Best known for *De consolatione philosophiae.* His treatise *De institutione musica,* based on Greek sources, was standard textbook throughout Middle Ages.

**Bogen** (Ger.; It., *arco*), 'bow' – in string parts used, like *arco,* to contradict preceding *pizzicato.*

**Bohème, La** (Fr., *Bohemian Life*), opera by Puccini, libretto by G. Giacosa and L. Illica (based on Henri Murger's *Scènes de la vie de Bohème*). First perf. Turin, 1896 (conducted by Toscanini). Story deals with life in Latin Quarter in Paris, esp. love affairs of Rodolfo and Mimi, and Marcello and Musetta. Rodolfo and Mimi separate; when finally reunited Mimi dies of consumption. Also title of opera by Leoncavallo (Venice, 1897).

**Böhm,** *see also* BOEHM.

**Böhm, Georg** (1661–1733), German organist, composer. Wrote church music and many works for organ and harpsichord.

**Böhm, Karl** (1894–1981), Austrian conductor. Held appointments at Graz (1918), Munich (1921), Darmstadt (1927), Hamburg (1931), Dresden (1934), Vienna State Opera (1954). Became *éminence grise* of Salzburg Festival. Long regarded as leading conductor of Mozart and Richard Strauss.

**Boïeldieu, François A.** (1775–1834), French opera composer. Most successful operas were *Le Calife de Bagdad* (1800), *La Dame blanche* (1825).

**bois** (Fr.), wood. *Instruments de bois* (or *bois* alone), woodwind instruments.

**Boito, Arrigo** (1842–1918), Italian composer, poet, librettist. Wrote operas incl. *Mefistofele* (1868). Chiefly remembered for brilliant librettos for Verdi's *Otello* and *Falstaff*.

**Bolero,** Spanish dance in moderate triple time. Characteristic rhythm marked on castanets, *eg*

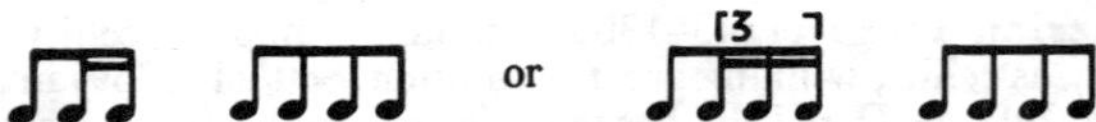


Ravel's *Bolero* for orchestra (1928) made dance esp. popular.

**bombard,** double-reed instrument, now obsolete; bass of SHAWM family.

**bombarde,** organ reed stop of great power made at 8ft, 16ft and 32ft pitches.

**bombardon,** term used in military bands for bass TUBA.

**bones,** pairs of small sticks held in each hand and clicked together rhythmically, like castanets. Orig. made of ox rib; known since medieval times.

**bongo** (pl. **bongos**), small Cuban drum usually played in pairs with fingers.

**Bonno, Giuseppe** (1710–88), Austrian composer. Studied in Naples, then worked for Imperial court in Vienna. Numerous compositions incl. 20 works for stage, and 3 oratorios.

**Bononcini, Giovanni** (1670–*c* 1747), Italian composer, cellist. Moved to London (1720) where rivalry grew up between Handel and himself; left in 1732. Wrote many operas, oratorios, cantatas, *etc.* His father, **Giovanni Maria Bononcini** (1642–78), was composer and theorist. Works incl. chamber sonatas, solo cantatas, and treatise on counterpoint. His brother, **Antonio Maria Bononcini** (1674–1726), was also composer. Works incl. 20 operas and 3 oratorios. His *Il trionfo di Camilla* (1696) was one of first Italian operas to be given in London, albeit at first in English (1706).

**Bonporti, Francesco Antonio** (1672–1749), Italian composer. Pupil of Corelli. His chamber music incl. trio and solo sonatas.

**boogie-woogie** (sometimes just 'boogie'), JAZZ style, special type of piano BLUES. Became popular in late 1930s, early 1940s. Characterized by continuous sharply rhythmic *ostinato* bass played by left hand, while right hand provides melody, adhering to 12 bar period, though with great rhythmic variety and improvisation within that framework.

**Boosey,** London firm of music-publishers and manufacturers of musical instruments, founded 1816 by Thomas Boosey, and since

1930 amalgamated with Hawkes and Son as Boosey and Hawkes, Ltd.

**bop, bebop** or **rebop,** JAZZ style. Developed in New York at end of WWII. Distinguished by solos using dissonant chords, complex rhythms, and continuous mainly improvised melodic line. Through charismatic playing of Dizzy Gillespie, Miles Davis and Charlie 'Bird' Parker, bop revolutionized jazz.

**Bordoni, Faustina** (1700–81), Italian soprano. Appeared in Venice, Naples, Florence and Vienna. Taken to London in 1726 by Handel, where her notorious rivalry with Francesca Cuzzoni was satirized in *The Beggar's Opera* (1728).

**bore** (It.), **boree** (Eng.), *see* BOURRÉE.

**bore,** diameter of tube of wind instrument.

**Boris Godunov,** opera by Mussorgsky, libretto by composer (after Pushkin's *Boris Godunov* and Karamzin's History of the Russian Empire). Initially rejected by St Petersburg Opera in 1870, subsequently much revised by composer and others; now established as greatest Russian opera. Several versions exist (by *eg* Rimsky-Korsakov, Shostakovich).

**Borodin, Alexander Porfirevich** (1833–87), Russian composer, scientist. Member of The FIVE. Illegitimate son of prince. In 1864 became professor of organic chemistry at Academy of Medicine, St Petersburg. Began composing as boy; stimulated by meeting with Balakirev in 1862, who conducted first perf. of his first symphony (1869). Other works (not numerous) incl. 2 more symphonies (3rd unfinished), *In the Steppes of Central Asia* for orchestra, 2 string quartets, 2 operas – parody *Bogatyri* (1867), and *Prince Igor* (completed after his death by Rimsky-Korsakov and Glazunov), which incl. famous *Polovtsian Dances*; also wrote songs. One of most strongly national of the 19th-century Russian composers, drawing inspiration from folksong and Oriental sources.

**borre, borree, borry,** old English spellings of BOURRÉE.

**Borren, Charles Jean Eugène van den** (1874–1966), Belgian musicologist. Works incl. books on Franck, Lassus, Dufay, and on early keyboard music in England and the Low Countries. Also prepared editions of 15th and 16th-cent. music.

**Boschot, Adolphe** (1871–1955), French music critic. Specialized in study of Berlioz, whose life he wrote (*Histoire d'un romantique,* 1906–13).

**Bösendorfer,** firm of piano manufacturers, founded in Vienna (1828) by Ignaz Bösendorfer (1796–1859).

**Bossi, Marco Enrico** (1861–1925), Italian organist, composer. Wrote organ, choral, orchestral and chamber music and operas.
His son, **Renzo Bossi** (1883–1965), was also a composer. Works incl. operas *eg Rosa Rossa* (after Oscar Wilde), and another based on Shakespeare's *The Taming of the Shrew,* and orchestral and chamber music.

**Bostiber, Hugo** (1875–1942), Austrian musicologist. Completed C.F.

Pohl's biography of Haydn by adding third vol. (1927), and also wrote history of the overture (1913).

**Boston Symphony Orchestra,** founded by H.L. Higginson in 1881. First conductor was Sir George Henschel, succeeded by Wilhelm Gericke, Artur Nikisch, Emil Paur, Karl Muck, Max Fiedler, Henri Rabaud, Pierre Monteux, Serge Koussevitsky, Charles Münch, Erich Leinsdorf, Seiji Ozawa.

**Bote and Bock,** Berlin firm of music-publishers, founded 1838 by Edouard Bote and Gustav Bock.

**Bottesini, Giovanni** (1821–89), Italian double-bass virtuoso, conductor, composer. Compositions incl. several operas *eg Ero e Leandro* (1879), and oratorio *The Garden of Olivet* (1887).

**Bottrigari, Ercole** (1531–1612), Italian author. Wrote dialogue *Il desiderio, overo de' concerti di varii strumenti musicali* (1594), which gives valuable picture of musical life and practice in late 16th-cent. Italian court.

**bouche fermée,** *see* BOCCA CHIUSA.

**bouchés,** *see* SONS BOUCHÉS.

**bouffe,** *see* OPÉRA-BOUFFE.

**Boughton, Rutland** (1878–1960), English opera composer. Studied under Stanford and Walford Davies. Settled in Glastonbury, Somerset, intending to write series of operas on Arthurian legends and to establish home for their performance. Scheme never completed, but opera *The Immortal Hour* was given there (1914), followed by other productions. *The Immortal Hour* proved far more successful than later operas *eg Alkestis* (1922), *The Lily Maid* (1934).

**Boulanger, Juliette Nadia** (1887–1979), French composer, teacher. Famous for having taught many distinguished musicians. Studied at Paris Conservatoire, where later became professor. Active in reviving old music, incl. Monteverdi. Her sister, **Lili Juliette Marie Olga Boulanger** (1893–1918), was also composer. First woman to win *Grand Prix de Rome* (1913). Works incl. symphonic poems, cantata *Faust and Helen,* chamber music and songs.

**Boulez, Pierre** (1925– ), French composer, conductor, pianist. One of most important figures of modern music. Abandoned career as mathematician to study music under Messiaen. Learnt serial technique from René Leibowitz. With Madeleine Renaud and Jean-Louis Barrault founded Domaine Musical in Paris (1953), specializing in promotion and performance of new music. Has continued to promote new music *eg* in concerts with New York Philharmonic and B.B.C. Symphony Orchestra. From 1977 has presided over IRCAM, vanguard music institute in Paris. Has composed less recently, but his compositions make him one of the most challenging and widely discussed of contemporary composers. *Le Marteau sans maître,* for voice and chamber orchestra, and *Pli selon pli* (Fold upon fold), for soprano and orchestra, are classics. Other works incl. *Le Soleil des eaux* for voices, chorus and orchestra,

3 piano sonatas, *Structures I* and *II* for 2 pianos, and *Livre* for string quartet.

**Boult, Adrian Cedric** (1889– ), English conductor. Conducted first perf. of Holst's *The Planets* (1918). Became conductor of City of Birmingham Orchestra (1922). Musical director of B.B.C. (1930–42), conductor of B.B.C. Symphony Orchestra (1930–49). Conducted many other orchestras. Until his retirement, excelled in performance of classics and music of Elgar, Vaughan Williams and Walton. Knighted 1937.

**bourdon** (Fr.), lit. 'burden':
(1) drone bass, *eg* that produced on lowest strings of HURDY-GURDY;
(2) soft organ stop, using stopped pipes generally of 16ft tone.

**Bourgault-Ducourray, Louis Albert** (1840–1910), French composer. Won *Grand Prix de Rome* (1862). One of first composers to draw attention to possibilities of modal and non-European scales. Numerous compositions incl. 5 operas, choral and orchestral music. Also published collections of Greek, Breton, Welsh and Scottish folksongs.

**bourrée** (Fr.; Eng., borry, boree, borree, borre; It., *bore*), (1) French dance in brisk duple time, starting in third quarter of bar. Prob. originated in early 17th cent. In 18th-cent. suite was one of *Galanterien* or optional dances inserted between SARABANDE and GIGUE. Two bourrées were often written to form contrasted pair (as was done with MINUET and GAVOTTE);
(2) dance in triple time, still current in Auvergne.

**bouzouki,** fretted string instrument of Greece. Played by plucking strings with much use of tremolo to prolong notes. Enjoyed great revival in 1960s, *eg* in music of Mikis Theodorakis.

**bow** (Fr., *archet*; Ger., *Bogen*; It., *arco*), instruments of viol and violin families are played with bow, consisting of horse-hair strung on wooden stick. Name derives from fact that orig. shape of stick was convex. Tension of hair can be varied by adjustable nut at one end of stick. Shape of bow has varied: modern bow came in at end of 18th cent. Longer than earlier bows; stick tapers towards point (*ie* end furthest from hand, as opposed to heel) and is slightly curved towards hair. Bows used for viola, cello and double-bass are similar to violin bow, but progressively heavier; cello and double-bass bows are progressively shorter.

**bowed harp,** primitive violin, first depicted in 12th-cent. Norwegian carving. Held vertically on knee; its 2 to 4 strings were played simultaneously to give drone beneath melody. Very similar to CRWTH.

**bowing,** in general, technique of playing string instrument with bow. In particular, method of playing notes or passages, indicated by conventional signs: ⊓ indicates down-bow, *ie* arm moves from left to right, and V indicates up-bow, *ie* arm moves from right to left. Strong down-bow ensures good attack. Increased pressure possible with up-bow, after bow has already touched string, helps produce steady crescendo. If two or more notes are to be played without changing direction of bow, slur is placed over them. Normally no perceptible break between 2 consecutive notes on up- and down-bows; if note is to be detached, horizontal stroke is placed above it. Also poss. to detach notes slightly without changing direction of bow (indicated by combining slur and horizontal stroke). Notes can also be played staccato without changing direction of bow (slur combined with dots above notes). Within section of orchestra, bowing must be consistent.

Following terms indicate particular method of using bow: (a) *col legno,* lit. 'with the wood', *ie* bouncing stick on strings; (b) *a punta d'arco,* with point of bow; (c) *am Frosch* (Ger.), *au talon* (Fr.), with nut or heel of bow (*ie* end nearest hand); (d) *sul tasto* or *sulla tastiera* (It.), *sur la touche* (Fr.), *am Griffbrett* (Ger.), on the fingerboard, *ie* play near, or above fingerboard producing rather colourless tone; (e) *sul ponticello* (It.), *au chevalet* (Fr.), *am Steg* (Ger.), on the bridge, *ie* play near bridge, producing glassy, brittle tone; (f) *martellato* (It.), *martelé* (Fr.), lit. 'hammered', heavy, detached up-and-down strokes, played with point of bow without taking bow from string; (g) *flautando* or *flautato,* played like flute, *ie* producing light, rather colourless tone by playing gently near end of fingerboard; (h) *spiccato,* lit. 'clearly articulated', *ie* light staccato played with middle of bow and loose wrist; (i) *saltando* (It.), *sautillé* (Fr.), allowing bow to bounce lightly on string.

**Bowman, James** (1941– ), English counter-tenor. Known both for performances in opera and in concert hall.

**Boyce, William** (1711–79), English composer, organist. Pupil of Maurice Greene. Held various posts incl. composer (1736) and organist (1758) to Chapel Royal, Master of the King's Musick (1755). Suffered from increasing deafness. Works incl. church music, cantatas, odes, 20 symphonies, chamber music, and works for stage. Music for play *Harlequin's Invasion* (1759) incl. song 'Heart of Oak', commemorating British victories of that year.

**Brabançonne, La,** Belgian national anthem, written in 1830, when Belgium was struggling free from Holland.

**brace,** vertical line, generally accompanied by bracket, used to join 2 or more staves together.

**Brade, William** (*c* 1560–1630), English viol player, composer. Held several court appointments in Denmark and Germany. Published on the Continent several vols. of concerted instrumental music, mostly dance movements.

**Braham, John,** orig. Abraham (1777–1856), English tenor, of Jewish birth. He was original Sir Huon in Weber's *Oberon,* and was admired esp. for performances of Handel.

**Brahms, Johannes** (1833–97), German composer. Born in Hamburg, son of double-bass player, who gave him first music lessons. Home life was happy, if humble. Parents' ambition to make him piano prodigy were thwarted by his teacher, Cossel. Played in sailors' taverns *etc.* Career advanced by tour with Hungarian gypsy violinist, Eduard Reményi (1853). Met Joachim, Liszt and Schumann, who encouraged him. Deeply disturbed by Schumann's attempted suicide (1854) and subsequent madness, and by his suppressed love for Clara Schumann (he never married); this turmoil can be heard in D minor piano concerto (1858). Became director of music to Prince of Lippe-Detmold (1857), giving him time to compose. Went to Vienna (1863) and remained there holding various posts. Death of mother (1865) inspired part of *German Requiem* (1857–68), which uses texts from Luther's translation of Bible. Brahms took responsibilities as post-Beethoven symphonist very seriously; started 1st symphony in early 20s, but did not complete it till he was 43. After première in Karlsruhe (1876), symphony was hailed as 'Beethoven's Tenth'. Brahms went on to complete 2nd symphony (1877), violin concerto (1879), 2nd piano concerto (1881), 3rd symphony (1833) and 4th symphony (1885), gaining him reputation as one of greatest composers of the day. Later years were uneventful, though his music gained touching autumnal beauty and new intimacy of expression, *eg* in clarinet quintet and trio (1891). Died year after travelling to Clara Schumann's funeral.

Brahms's music reflects both the austerity of his N German home and the sensuous charm of Vienna. He was also influenced by early experience of Hungarian gypsy music, not only in his so-called Hungarian Dances but also in passages of such works as the clarinet quintet. Another influence was German folksong, detectable in many works and the subject of his collection of *Volkslieder* for voice and piano. Brahms was most successful of all romantic composers in reconciling conflicting claims of lyricism and classical form. His unwillingness to join musical 'progressives' of the period, and his early stand against Liszt's 'New German' school, resulted in his being disparaged by some musicians (*eg* Hugo Wolf) and admired by others (*eg* Hanslick), who used him as principal weapon against 'unhealthy' Wagnerism. However, modern listeners are now able to accept both figures as major 19th-cent. composers.

Principal compositions

(1) Orchestra: 2 serenades, 4 symphonies, 2 piano concertos, violin concerto, concerto for violin and cello, *Variations on the St Anthony Chorale,* (formerly known as *Variations on a theme of Haydn*), *Academic Festival Overture, Tragic Overture*;

(2) Choral works: *A German Requiem, Rinaldo,* Rhapsody for alto solo, male chorus and orchestra, *Song of Destiny, Song of Triumph, Song of the Fates*;

(3) Chamber music: 2 string sextets, 2 string quintets, 3 string quartets, clarinet quintet, piano quintet, 3 piano quartets, 3 piano trios, trio for clarinet, cello and piano, trio for violin, horn and piano, 3 violin sonatas, 2 cello sonatas, 2 clarinet sonatas;

(4) Piano solos: 3 sonatas, variations on (a) theme of Schumann, (b) original theme, (c) Hungarian theme, (d) theme of Paganini (2 sets), variations and fugue on theme of Handel, 3 rhapsodies, intermezzi, capriccios, ballades, *etc*;

(5) Piano duet: variations on (a) theme of Schumann, (b) theme of

Haydn (for 2 pianos), sonata for 2 pianos (= the piano quintet), *Liebeslieder* waltzes and *Neue Liebeslieder* waltzes (with optional voice parts), Hungarian dances;

(6) Organ: 11 chorale preludes;

(7) Songs: nearly 200 solo songs, duets, folksong arrangements.

Brahms also edited Couperin's keyboard music.

**Brain, Dennis** (1921–57), English horn player. Became most famous horn player of his day; played in Royal Philharmonic and Philharmonia Orchestras. Works written for him incl. Britten's *Serenade* and Hindemith's concerto.

**Branco, Luis Freita** (1890–1955), Portuguese composer, teacher. Pupil of Humperdinck. Works incl. 5 symphonies, 5 symphonic poems, violin concerto, oratorio, chamber, piano and organ music, and songs.

**Brandenburg Concertos,** 6 orchestral concertos written by Bach (1721) for Christian Ludwig, Margrave of Brandenburg. Scoring is as follows:

no 1 in F major for 2 horns, 3 oboes, bassoon, *violino piccolo,* strings and continuo;

no 2 in F major for trumpet, recorder, oboe, violin, strings and continuo;

no 3 in G major for 3 violins, 3 violas, 3 cellos, double-bass and continuo;

no 4 in G major for violin, 2 recorders, strings and continuo;

no 5 in D major for flute, violin, harpsichord, strings (without 2nd violin) and continuo;

no 6 in B flat major for 2 violas, 2 bass viols, cello, double-bass and continuo.

**Brandenburgers in Bohemia, The** (Czech, *Branibori v Cecḥách*), opera by Smetana, libretto by K. Sabina. First perf. Prague, 1866.

**branle** (Fr.; It., *brando*; Eng., brawl, brangill), orig. (15th cent.) step in BASSE DANSE (from *branler,* to sway), hence dance with swaying movement, current in France in 16th, 17th cents. Could also be sung. Existed in variety of forms, *eg branle simple* (in duple time), *branle gai* (in triple time).

**brass band,** band consisting of brass instruments and drums, as opposed to MILITARY BAND, which incl. woodwind. Standard organization in England is: 1 E flat cornet, 8 B flat cornets, 1 B flat flugelhorn (treble saxhorn), 3 E flat saxhorns, 2 B flat baritones, 2 euphoniums, 2 tenor trombones, 1 bass trombone, 2 E flat bombardons (bass tubas), 2 B flat bombardons. With exception of bass trombone, all instruments are treated as transposing instruments, parts being written in treble clef.

Popularity of brass band in England dates from early 19th cent. Standards of performance are extremely high, and are maintained by competition festivals dating from early 19th cent. More recently, distinguished composers have written test pieces for these. There being little music of quality written for brass bands, normal repertory largely depends on arrangement.

**brass instruments** (Fr., *instruments de cuivre*; Ger., *Blechinstrumente*; It., *strumenti d'ottone*), instruments made of metal, in which sound is produced by vibration of lips, transmitted to tube by cup- or funnel-shaped mouthpiece. Successive notes of harmonic series are produced by increased tension of lips. Intervening notes are produced by lengthening sounding tube, either with movable slide (trombone) or with valves which open extra lengths of tubing (all other brass instruments). *See* BARITONE CORNET, EUPHONIUM, FLUGELHORN, HORN, SAXHORN, TROMBONE, TRUMPET, TUBA.

**Bratsche** (Ger.), viola.

**Brautwahl, Die** (Ger., *The Choice of a Bride*), opera by Busoni, libretto by composer (after story by E.T.A. Hoffmann). First perf. Hamburg, 1912.

**bravura** (It.), lit. 'bravery', 'swagger'. In music, term implies display; *bravura* passage requires some feat of virtuosity by performer.

**brawl,** *see* BRANLE.

**Bream, Julian [Alexander]** (1933– ), English guitarist, lutenist. Britten and others have written works for him.

**break,** (1) in jazz, short solo passage;

(2) change in tone-quality sometimes occurring in movements between REGISTERS;

(3) verb, describing deepening of male voice in puberty.

**Bream, Julian** (1933– ), English guitarist, lutenist. Pupil of Segovia. Has revived much early music. Britten and Walton have written works for him.

**breit** (Ger.), grandly, broadly – used to describe manner, not tempo, of performance.

**Breitkopf und Härtel,** Leipzig firm of music-publishers. Bernhardt Christoph Breitkopf (1695–1777) founded printing business in 1719, which was enlarged to incl. music-printing by his son Johann Gottlob Breitkopf (1719–94). Johann's son Christoph assigned the business to Gottfried Christoph Härtel (1763–1827). Firm's outstanding achievement is publication of complete editions of works of great composers from Palestrina to Wagner.

**Brendel, Alfred** (1931– ), Austrian pianist, resident in London from 1974. Has acquired international reputation as soloist. Has also composed works for piano.

**Brenet, Michel,** pseud. of Antoinette Christine Marie Bobillier (1858–1918), French musicologist. Published large number of historical works, incl. biographies of Grétry, Palestrina, Handel and Haydn, and history of symphony before Beethoven.

**Bretón, Tomás** (1850–1923), Spanish composer. Director of Madrid Conservatory from 1903. Enthusiast for Spanish national music; wrote large number of *zarzuelas* (operettas), *eg La Verbena de la Paloma* (1894). Other works incl. 9 operas, oratorio *El Apocalipsis,* violin concerto and chamber music.

**Bréval, Jean Baptiste** (1756–1825), French cellist, composer. Works incl. orchestral and chamber music, comic opera, and instruction book for cello.

**breve** (Lat., *brevis,* 'short'), orig. short note. Introduced in early 13th cent.; as notes of still shorter value were introduced it became longer. Now longest note, still occasionally used; equal to 8 minims. Written

||O|| or |=|

*See* ALLA BREVE, NOTATION.

**Bréville, Pierre Onfroy De** (1861–1949), French composer, teacher, critic. Pupil of Franck. Works, notable for sensitive lyricism, incl. opera *Éros vainqueur* (1910), choral and chamber music, and many songs.

**Brian, William Havergal** (1876–1972), English composer, b. Dresden. Mainly self-taught. Compositions, some demanding very large forces and suffering from early 20th-cent. extravagance, incl. *A Gothic Symphony* (2nd of 32), opera *The Tigers,* comedy overtures *Dr Merryheart, By the waters of Babylon* for chorus and orchestra, piano music, songs.

**bridge,** (1) (Fr., *chevalet*; Ger., *Steg*; It., *ponticello*), piece of wood standing on belly of string instruments, supporting strings. In viol and violin families, not fixed to belly, but held by tension of strings. Has 2 feet: right foot (on side of highest string) stands almost over soundpost; left foot is free to vibrate. Transmission of vibrations to belly assisted by bass-bar glued inside belly underneath left foot of bridge. *See* VIOLIN;

(2) passage in composition linking 2 important statements of thematic material; often consists of modulation or series of modulations from one key to another.

**Bridge, Frank** (1879–1941), English composer, viola player, conductor. Member of English String Quartet for several years. Works incl. symphonic poems, *A Prayer* for chorus and orchestra, 4 string quartets, string sextet, piano quintet, phantasy quartet for piano and strings, 2 piano trios, violin sonata, cello sonata, works for piano and organ, songs. Earlier works in romantic tradition; later works (incl. 3rd and 4th string quartets) turn aside from traditional tonality. Taught Britten composition.

**Bridgetower, George Augustus Polgreen** (1780–1860), Polish-born violinist, son of African father and European mother. Lived partly in England and partly on the Continent. Gave first performance of Beethoven's *Kreutzer Sonata* (Vienna, 1803).

**Brigg Fair,** 'English rhapsody' on Lincolnshire folksong by Delius (1907).

**brillant** (Fr.), **brillante** (It.), brilliant (direction for performance).

**brindisi** (It.), drinking song, toast.

**brio** (It.), vigour; *con brio,* vigorously.

**brisé** (Fr.), 'broken' – used of arpeggio in keyboard and harp music, and of détaché bowing in string music.

**British National Opera Company,** company formed 1922 to perform operas throughout Britain. Disbanded 1929. Productions incl. Holst's *At the Boar's Head* and *The Perfect Fool,* and Vaughan Williams's *Hugh the Drover.*

**Britten, [Edward] Benjamin** (1913–77), English composer, conductor, pianist. Born at Lowestoft. Received first piano lessons from mother; started composing at age of 5. During school holidays took composition lessons from Frank Bridge. Later studied under Harold Samuel, Arthur Benjamin and John Ireland. Earliest published work was sinfonietta for chamber orchestra (1932). Worked with G.P.O. film unit (1935–7), writing music for famous documentary, *Night Mail.* As pacifist, went to US at start of WWII, but returned 1942, having won Coolidge Medal. Had written several brilliant works (some in collaboration with W.H. Auden), but opera *Peter Grimes* (1945) really established his reputation. Consolidated position as leading British opera writer with *The Rape of Lucretia* (1946), *Albert Herring* (1947), *Billy Budd* (1951), *Gloriana* (1953), *The Turn of the Screw* (1954) and *A Midsummer Night's Dream* (1960). Flair for setting words to music also revealed in many concert works, from song cycles (*eg Winter Words* based on poems by Hardy) to *War Requiem* (combining bitter war poems by Wilfred Owen with Latin words of RC Requiem). Subsequent output incl. 3 church parables, inspired by plainsong, operas *Owen Wingrave* (1970, for TV), *Death in Venice* (1973). After serious operation, resumed composing with setting of T. S. Eliot to add to series of vocal canticles, 3rd string quartet, and revision of operetta *Paul Bunyan* (1941, to words by Auden). Britten wrote most of his works for specific performers, esp. tenor Peter Pears, who certainly influenced his style, and cellist Rostropovich (cello symphony, cello suites). Throughout his life the little coastal town of Aldeburgh and the North Sea continued to be major sources of inspiration. Founded Aldeburgh Festival in 1948.

Principal works:

(1) Operas: *Paul Bunyan* (1941), *Peter Grimes* (1945), *The Rape of Lucretia* (1946), *Albert Herring* (1947), *Billy Budd* (1951), *Gloriana* (1953), *The Turn of the Screw* (1954), *A Midsummer Night's Dream* (1960), *Owen Wingrave* (1970), *Death in Venice* (1973).

Also *Let's Make an Opera, Noye's Fludde*; 3 church parables: *Curlew River* (1964), *The Burning Fiery Furnace* (1966), *The Prodigal Son* (1968); arrangement of *The Beggar's Opera;*

(2) Choral works: *A boy was born, Ballad of Heroes, Hymn to St Cecilia, A Ceremony of Carols, Rejoice in the Lamb, Saint Nicholas, Spring Symphony, Cantata Academica, Cantata Misericordium, War Requiem, Voices for Today*;

(3) Orchestra: *Sinfonietta, Simple Symphony, Variations on a theme of Frank Bridge* (strings), piano concerto, violin concerto, *Sinfonia da Requiem, Young Person's Guide to the Orchestra* (Variations and fugue on a theme by Purcell), cello symphony, overture *The Building of the House*;

(4) Chamber music: 3 string quartets, *Phantasy Quartet*, 2 suites for solo cello;

(5) Song cycles and songs: *Our Hunting Fathers, On This Island, Les Illuminations, Serenade for tenor, horn and strings, Nocturne, Seven Sonnets of Michelangelo, The Holy Sonnets of John Donne, A Charm of Lullabies, Winter Words,* six *Holderlin Fragments, Songs and Proverbs of William Blake, The Poet's Echo,* canticles, folk song arrangements and other songs.

**Broadwood,** firm of piano manufacturers, founded (*c* 1728) in London by Burkat Shudi for manufacture of harpsichords. John Broadwood became partner in 1770. Started making pianos in 1773 (grand pianos from 1781), patenting several improvements.

**broken chord,** chord in which notes are sounded one after the other, not simultaneously. Term used in preference to Italian *arpeggio*.

**broken consort,** *see* CONSORT.

**broken octaves,** passage of octaves performed not simultaneously but alternating between 2 registers – much used in piano music.

**Brossard, Sebastien de** (*c* 1654–1730), French composer. Works incl. church and chamber music, and songs. Also published important *Dictionnaire de musique* (1703).

**Brown, Christopher** (1943– ), English composer. Pupil of Berkeley and Blacher. Works incl. orchestral *Triptych* (1978), cantata *David* (1970) and other religious choral works, and chamber music.

**Brown, Earle** (1926– ), American composer. Collaborated with Cage in 1950s on electronic music. Works, sometimes employing aleatory effects, incl. *Pages*, orchestral *Modules*, and choral, chamber and instrumental music.

**Browne, John** (*fl* 15th cent.), English composer. Little is known of his life. Surviving works incl. antiphons and incomplete Magnificat (all in *Eton Choirbook*), and 3 carols.

**Bruch, Max** (1838–1920), German composer of Jewish birth. Director of Liverpool Philharmonic Society (1880–3); held various posts in Germany. Works incl. 3 symphonies, 3 violin concertos (1st, in G minor, is one of the most popular works in repertory), operas, operetta, choral works, chamber music and well-known setting of Hebrew melody *Kol Nidrei* for cello and orchestra (op 47).

**Bruckner, Anton** (1824–96), Austrian composer. Son of village schoolmaster. Received scanty musical education till father's death (1837); then went as choirboy to monastery of St Florian, where he became organist in 1845. Ambitious to compose, he moved to Vienna (1855) to study counterpoint with Simon Sechter. Became organist at Linz Cathedral (1856–68); during this period visited Munich and saw and was profoundly influenced by Wagner's *Tristan*. From 1868 he taught organ and theory at Vienna Conservatory. By then had composed symphonies nos 0 and 1. Work as organist and admiration for Wagner helped him to forge very individual symphonic style. Detractors said his symphonies were like organ works writ large, or like Wagner without drama; latter accusation is perhaps true – his music can sound like Wagner purged of conflict and eroticism. At heart his symphonies, as well as his choral and organ music, are religious works, proclaiming his simple RC faith. Their size, spaciousness and originality of form resulted in their being misunderstood during the composer's lifetime. Bruckner allowed well-intentioned friends to make cuts in them, and to alter the orchestration, with the result that their magnificent cathedral-like structure was weakened: paradoxically, the cut version can sound longer than the original, as the natural proportions and logic of its thought have been disturbed. Today, as appreciation of Bruckner has developed, his original ideas are generally preferred.

Principal works:
(1) Symphonies:
no 0 in D minor (1863–4),
no 1 in C minor (1865–6),
no 2 in C minor (1871–2),
no 3 in D minor (1873),
no 4 in E flat major (Romantic) (1874),
no 5 in B flat major (1875–6),
no 6 in A major (1879–81),
no 7 in E major (1881–3),
no 8 in C minor (1884–5),
no 9 in D minor (unfinished) (1887–94).
(All dates for original versions);

(2) Choral music: Mass in D minor (1864), Mass in E minor (1866), Mass in F minor (*Grosse Messe*) (1867–8), Te Deum in C major (1881), Psalm CL (1892), numerous smaller sacred works;

(3) Chamber music: string quartet in C minor (1862), string quintet in F major (1878–9).

Also organ music, male-voice choruses and songs.

**Brüll, Ignaz** (1846–1907), Austrian pianist, composer. Toured Europe as soloist. Works incl. symphony, 2 piano concertos, violin concerto, and several operas.

**Brumel, Antoine** (*c* 1450–*c* 1520), Flemish composer. Held posts at Chartres Cathedral, Notre Dame, Paris, and at ducal court at Ferrara. Composed numerous Masses, and polyphonic *chansons*.

**Bruneau, Alfred,** orig. Louis Charles Bonaventure (1857–1934), French composer, critic. Pupil of Massenet. Mainly wrote operas, some with libretti by Zola (*eg L'Ouragan,* 1901), some based on Zola's works (*eg Naïs Miscoulin,* 1907). Also wrote *Requiem Mass.*

**brunette** (Fr.), amorous pastoral song; current in late 17th, 18th cents.

**Brustwerk** (Ger.), one of manuals in old German organs, with stops of quieter tone than those on Great organ *(Hauptwerk)*. Also known as *Brustpositiv.* No exact English equivalent.

**buffo** (It.; fem., *buffa*), comic; *opera buffa,* comic opera. As noun, means comic actor or singer.

**bugle,** brass instrument with conical tube and cup-shaped mouthpiece, used for giving military signals. Regulation bugle of

British Army is in B flat; has no pistons or keys so can only sound notes of HARMONIC SERIES; working compass is B flat (below middle C), F, B flat, D, F. Bugles also built in G and occasionally in F. *See* KEY BUGLE.

**bugle à clefs** (Fr.), key bugle.

**Bühne** (Ger.), stage or theatre. Wagner called *Parsifal* a *Bühnenweihfestspiel, ie* sacred festival drama.

**Bull, John** (1563–1628), English organist, composer. Organist at Hereford Cathedral, gentleman of Chapel Royal (1586), first professor of music at Gresham College (1596–1607). Left England (1613) to work as organist in Brussels, then Antwerp. Compositions incl. church music and many works for keyboard; latter require considerable virtuosity and show individuality in treatment of harmonic progression.

**Bull, Ole Børneman** (1810–80), Norwegian violinist. Largely self-taught, inspired by hearing Paganini. Displayed great virtuosity in performance of own compositions. Interest in Norwegian folk music influenced Grieg.

**bull roarer,** *see* THUNDER STICK.

**Bülow, Hans Guido von** (1830–94), German pianist, conductor, composer. Orig. law student at Leipzig. Became devoted adherent of Wagner after hearing *Lohengrin* (1850). Studied piano with Liszt (1851). Married Cosima, Liszt's daughter in 1857, but divorced her (1870) after she left him for Wagner. Bülow is usually considered first virtuoso conductor (esp. with Meiningen Orchestra). Gave first performances of Wagner's *Tristan und Isolde* and *Die Meistersinger von Nürnberg.* As pianist had remarkable repertory and extraordinary memory.

**Bumbry, Grace** (1937– ), American mezzo-soprano. Made debut in 1960. In 1961 became first black singer to appear at Bayreuth. Know esp. for interpretations of Carmen and Salome.

**Bund** (Ger.), fret (on viol, lute, *etc*). *Bundfrei,* 'unfretted', term applied to CLAVICHORD in which each note has separate string.

**burden, burthen,** refrain line (sometimes nonsense) at end of ballad verse.

**Burgon, Geoffrey** (1941– ), English composer. Employs wide range of modern styles and techniques. Pieces for music theatre incl. *Joan of Arc* (1970). Has also written ballets, orchestral music, and pieces for various combinations of voices and instruments.

**Burgundian school,** name given to number of composers of first half of 15th cent., esp. Dufay and Binchois. Court of dukes of Burgundy at Dijon was important cultural centre; their territories embraced Netherlands and E France.

**Burkhard, Willy** (1900–55), Swiss composer, pianist, conductor. Works, inclining to austere simplicity (reminiscent of Hindemith) and showing respect for traditional forms, incl. 2 symphonies, *Ulenspiegel Variations* for orchestra, concerto for string orchestra, 2 string quartets, chamber and choral music.

**burla, burlesca** (It.; Fr., *burlesque*; Ger., *Burleske*), lit. 'jest'. Short piece of lively and frolicsome character. Also applied to extended composition in playful style.

**Burney, Charles** (1726–1814), English historian, organist, composer. Studied with Arne. Wrote *A General History of Music* (4 vols., 1776–89), and books on state of music in Europe.

**Busch, Fritz** (1890–1951), German conductor. As anti-Nazi, settled in Denmark. Known as conductor at Glyndebourne. His brother, **Adolf Georg Wilhelm Busch** (1891–1952), was violinist, composer. Leader of Busch Quartet. Also anti-Nazi; took Swiss nationality (1935). Numerous compositions incl. choral symphony, concertos, orchestral and chamber works, songs.

**Bush, Alan Dudley** (1900– ), English composer, teacher, writer. Studied with John Ireland. Works, in approachable style and often reflecting Communist sympathies, incl. operas, *(eg Wat Tyler, Men of Blackmoor)*, 3 symphonies, piano concerto (with male voice declaiming left-wing text), violin concerto, incidental music, chamber music (*eg Dialectic* for string quartet), choral work *(The Winter Journey)*, and songs.

**Busnois, Antoine** (d. 1492), Flemish composer. Worked at Burgundian court. Works incl. church music and part-songs.

**Busoni, Ferruccio Benvenuto** (1866–1924), Italian composer, pianist, teacher. Lived mostly in Germany, but also in Italy, Austria, Finland, US, Switzerland. Started as child prodigy in Vienna; as pianist, noted both for virtuosity and intellectual approach to interpretation. Greatly admired Liszt, but large repertory incl. Alkan, Bach, Beethoven, Chopin, Mozart, Schumann and Weber. Recognized as great musical teacher. As composer, still has dedicated admirers, though wider public has failed to find his musical personality strong enough to hold them. Works, which show his intellectual stature, incl. operas *Die Brautwahl* (1912), *Turandot* (1917), *Arlecchino* (1917) and masterpiece *Doktor Faust* (1925, completed by Philipp Jarnach), orchestral suites, piano concerto with male-voice chorus, 6 piano sonatinas, *Fantasia contrappuntistica* for 2 pianos (inspired by Bach's *Art of Fugue*) chamber music, songs, and many arrangements and transcriptions. Wrote libretti for own operas, and also published essay on aesthetics.

**Busser, Henri Paul** (1872–1973), French composer, conductor. Director of Paris Opéra and Opéra-Comique. Wrote operas *(eg Daphnis et Chloé)*, orchestral and church music, and songs.

**Bussotti, Sylvano** (1931– ), Italian composer. Works, of avant-garde nature, incl. *Torso* for voice and piano, *Pour clavier* for piano, and *Five Piano Pieces for David Tudor*.

**Butterworth, George Sainton Kaye** (1885–1916), English composer. Works incl. 2 song-cycles on poems from Houseman's *A Shropshire Lad,* orchestral rhapsody with same title, and idyll for small orchestra, *The Banks of Green Willow*. Killed in WWI.

**Buus, Jachet** or **Jacques de** (d. 1565), Flemish composer. Organist at St Mark's, Venice (1541–50), and organist to Ferdinand I in

Vienna (1553–64). Published important works (incl. *ricercari*) both for organ and for instrumental ensembles.

**Buxtehude, Dietrich** (1637–1707), Danish composer, organist. Organist at Helsingborg (1657), Helsingör (1660), and at Marienkirche, Lübeck (1668), where became famous as player and as director of ABENDMUSIKEN (from 1673). At age of 19, Bach walked 200 miles to hear Buxtehude play, and was greatly influenced by him in composing for organ. Works incl. church cantatas, sonatas for instrumental ensembles, and organ music.

**BWV,** *see* SCHMIEDER.

**Byrd, William** (1543–1623), English composer, organist. Organist at Lincoln Cathedral (1563–72), gentleman (1570) then joint organist (with Tallis) of Chapel Royal. In 1575, he and Tallis obtained monopoly of printing and selling music. Despite his RC faith, managed to remain in Elizabeth I's favour. Works incl. 3 Masses, Latin church music (esp. 2 vols. of *Gradualia,* 1605–7), English church music, consort songs and part-songs, music for viols, and pieces for virginals. Byrd was one of great masters of 16th-cent. polyphony. Excelled in composition of church music, esp. for RC church, where combined supreme technical mastery with intimate understanding of texts. Songs grew out of indigenous English tradition, showing little Italian influence.

**Byzantine music,** *ie* music of Christian church in Eastern Roman Empire. Music of Byzantine liturgy survives in notation of ancient origin. Correspondences between Byzantine and Gregorian music show early influence of Eastern Church on Western; further contribution to West was organ, though used in Byzantium only for secular purposes.

# C

**C** (Eng., Ger.; Fr., *ut, do*; It., *do*), (1) key-note or tonic of scale of C major;

(2) as abbrev. = *cantus* (It., *canto*), contralto, *con* (with), *col* or *colla* (with the); *c.B.* = *col Basso,* indicating cellos are to play with double-basses; *C.B.* = contrabasso (double-bass); *C.F.* = CANTUS FIRMUS;

(3) C clef, ornamental form of letter C, indicates middle C or

May be placed on any line of stave, but only following 3 are used in recent scores:

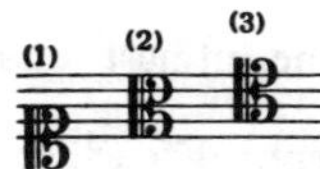


These are (1) soprano clef, still used in late 19th-cent. German scores; (2) alto clef, once used for alto voice and alto trombone, but now only for viola; (3) tenor clef, once used for tenor voice, now used for tenor trombone and upper register of bassoon, cello and double-bass;

(4) the sign

is time signature, indicating 4 crotchets (quarter-notes) in the bar (4/4). If vertical stroke is drawn through C, thus:

it generally indicates that minim is to be taken as unit of measurement (2/2) instead of crotchet. *See* ALLA BREVE, MENSURAL NOTATION, TIME-SIGNATURE.

**C.A.,** abbrev for *coll' arco* (with the bow).

**cabaletta** (It.), formerly, simple operatic aria, with incisive and continuously repeated rhythm, often found in Rossini. In later 19th-cent. opera, term came to be used for showy concluding section of aria, with emphasis on incisive and reiterated rhythm.

**Caballé, Montserrat** (1933– ), Spanish soprano. Made opera debut in 1956. Noted esp. in Italian opera.

**Cabanilles, Juan** (1644–1712), Spanish composer of organ music. Organist at Valencia Cathedral from 1665.

**Cabezón, Antonio de** (1510–66), Spanish organist, composer. Blind from birth. Organist to Charles V and Philip II. Compositions, mainly for keyboard, incl. liturgical pieces and variations on secular songs.

**cabinet organ** (US), AMERICAN ORGAN.

**caccia** (It.), lit, 'chase' or 'hunt':

(1) 14th-cent. Italian hunting poem set to music for 2 voices in canon, generally with instrumental accompaniment;

(2) *corno da caccia, oboe da caccia, see* HORN, OBOE.

**Caccini, Giulio** (*c* 1550–1618), Italian singer, composer. Member of circle in Florence who wished to recreate music and drama of ancient Greece. This led to composition of solo songs with figured bass accompaniment, designed to reproduce accents and emotions of poetry; Caccini published several of these under title *Le Nuove Musiche* (1602, lit. 'new music(s)'). Also wrote early opera, *L'Euridice* (1600), following same principles.

**cachucha,** Spanish solo dance in 3/4 time, with rhythm somewhat like bolero.

**cacophony,** sounds of the utmost dissonance, usually used in derogatory sense.

**Cadéac, Pierre** (*fl* 16th cent.), French composer. Known for church music and *chansons.*

**cadence,** lit. 'a falling' (Lat., *cadere,* to fall). Term is applied to concluding phrase (or phrase suggesting conclusion) at end of section or end of complete melody, and to harmonization of such phrases. A number of conventional formulae for such harmonization have developed, though there are innumerable possible variations, esp. as composers often enhance effect of final close by interpolating something unexpected at last moment.

Conventional names have been given to certain simple types of cadential formulae current in classical and romantic periods:

(1) perfect cadence (or full close) – dominant to tonic;

(2) imperfect cadence (or half close) – tonic to dominant (normally occurs in middle of composition, not end);

(3) plagal cadence – subdominant to tonic;

(4) interrupted cadence – dominant to some chord other than tonic (strictly not a cadence, but so-called because ear expects tonic chord).

Names given above are those most commonly used in Britain, but there is no absolute uniformity of nomenclature; *eg* nos (1) and (3) are often referred to as 'perfect (authentic)' and 'perfect (plagal)'.

Among many possible modifications of these basic formulae, one of commonest is substitution of minor chord for major, or vice versa, in plagal cadence, *eg* (1) subdominant minor in major key, (2) tonic major in minor key (the so-called *tierce de Picardie*). Substitution of tonic major in perfect cadence in minor key is also very common. Approach to these simple cadences can be varied by use of chords extraneous to key.

**cadenza** (It.), lit. 'cadence', though has come to have different, but related meaning. First used to describe improvisation introduced by 18th-cent. opera singers before final cadence of aria. Practice was borrowed by soloists in instrumental concertos. Instrumental *ritornello* normally followed final cadence for soloist. Convention was to pause on 6/4 chord on dominant then embark on improvisation and conclude with cadence previously deferred. In classical concerto, cadenza most frequently occurs in 1st movt., though additional cadenzas occur later in work. Player was not only expected to display virtuosity, but also to make allusions to thematic material of movt. Although cadenzas were normally improvised, Mozart wrote several cadenzas for his piano concertos. Beethoven wrote cadenzas (often more than one) for all his piano concertos; the one in 1st movt. of *Emperor Concerto* is integral part of work. Post-Beethoven composers have tended to write built-in cadenzas for their concertos (Brahms's violin concerto being an exception). Cadenza in modern works has become anachronism, since conditions to which it orig. owed existence no longer exist. Practice of improvising to classical concertos has now completely disappeared; players either write their own beforehand or use published examples by others. In such cases, disparity of style between cadenza and rest of work can be very marked, *eg* Britten's cadenza for Haydn's C major cello concerto.

**Cadman, Charles Wakefield** (1881–1946), American composer, organist, critic. Made use of American Indian themes. Works incl. *Pennsylvania Symphony* (in which iron plate is banged), operas, piano and organ music, songs.

**Cadmus et Hermione** (Fr., *Cadmus and Hermione*), opera by Lully, libretto by P. Quinault. First perf. Paris, 1673.

**Caffarelli,** stage name of Gaetano Majorano (1710–83), Italian castrato singer. Pupil of Porpora. Had enormous reputation in Italy, and also appeared in London and Paris.

**Cage, John** (1912– ), American composer, pianist, mycologist. Pupil of Adolph Weiss, Henry Cowell, Schoenberg and Varèse. Invented prepared piano, in which various objects are placed on or between strings of piano, thus changing tone and sound. Tireless experimenter and musical nonconformist; has explored aleatory music, electronic music and silent music, all of which reduce or do away with role of composer. Created first 'happening' (Black Mountain College, 1952). Works incl. *Winter Music* for 1 to 20 performers, *Radio Music* and *Imaginary Landscape* for various numbers of radios, piano concerto, *Music of Changes* for prepared piano. His *4' 33"* is most famous silent piece ever written, and *0' 0"* has been designed 'to be performed in any way to anyone'.

**caisse** (Fr.), drum; *grosse caisse,* bass drum.

**Caix d'Hervelois, Louis de** (*c* 1670–1760), French viola da gamba player. In service of Duke of Orleans. Wrote pieces for flute and for viola da gamba.

**calando** (It.), giving way, both in volume and speed; *ie* combination of *diminuendo* and *ritardando.*

**Caldara, Antonio** (1670–1736), Italian cellist, composer. Wrote *c* 100 operas and oratorios, church and chamber music.

**Caletti-Bruni,** *see* CAVALLI.

**Caliph of Baghdad, The,** opera by Boïeldieu, libretto by C.G. d'A. de Saint-Just. First perf. Paris, 1880.

**Callas, Maria,** orig. Maria Kalogeropoulou (1923–77), soprano, b. in US of Greek parentage. Sang regularly at La Scala, Milan, through 1950s, early 1960s, establishing reputation as finest dramatic soprano of the day. Excelled in *bel canto* works, *eg* operas of Bellini, Donizetti, Cherubini, doing much to revive public interest in them. Though vocal technique was not unflawed, qualities as operatic actress more than compensated for this. In later 1960s, realizing voice was failing, withdrew from operatic stage.

**Callcott, John Wall** (1766–1821), English composer, organist. Famous as writer of glees.

**calliope,** organ powered by steam instead of air. Can be played manually or operated mechanically. Its very loud sound makes it suitable for use in fairgrounds. Invented in US in 1856.

**Calvé, Emma** (1858–1942), French soprano. Sang in opera internationally until 1910, when she retired from stage and appeared only on concert platform. Esp. known for interpretation of role of Carmen.

**Calvocoressi, Michael D.** (1877–1944), English critic, of Greek parentage. Works incl. *Masters of Russian Music* (with G. Abraham, 1936), *A Survey of Russian Music* (1944), and 2 studies of Mussorgsky.

**calypso,** song from Trinidad, originating in plantations in 18th cent. Words are often topical or satirical, with syncopated rhythm, accompanied by primitive instruments (*eg* bottle and spoon).

**Calzabigi, Raniero da** (1714–95), Italian critic, author. Lived partly in Paris and Vienna. He was the force behind a number of Gluck's operatic reforms, and wrote librettos for Gluck's *Orfeo, Alceste* and *Paride ed Elena.*

**Cambert, Robert** (*c* 1628–77), French composer, organist. Pupil of Chambonnières. With poet Pierre Perrin produced *La Pastorale d'Issy* (1659), and *Pomone* (1671), both pioneer works in history of French opera. Cambert also set *Les Peines et Plaisirs d'Amour* (1672) to libretto by G. Gilbert. Lived in London after 1672.

**cambiata** (It.), short for *nota cambiata,* changed note. Used mainly of 16th-cent. counterpoint, term implies use of dissonant note where one would expect consonant note. Currently used in 2 senses:

(1) of an accented passing dissonance. Palestrina's music occurs on even beats of bar in descending passage; other composers show greater freedom in its use;

(2) of a sequence of notes, also known as 'changing note group', which occurs most frequently in following forms:

(a)

(b)

Second note is dissonant with one or more of other parts, but instead of moving step by step to third note (as is usual with passing dissonance) it leaps.

**camera** (It.), 'room'. Used in 17th, early 18th cents. to distinguish music suitable for performance in secular surroundings from that suitable for performance in church, *eg sonata da camera.* Eng. term 'chamber music' is literal translation of *musica da camera. See* SONATA.

**Cameron, Basil** (1884–1974), English conductor. In 1940 became assistant conductor of Henry Wood Promenade Concerts, London.

**campana** (It.), bell. Diminutive, *campanella.*

**campanelli** (It.), glockenspiel.

**campanology,** study of bells or art of bell ringing.

**Campion** or **Campian, Thomas** (1567–1620), English poet, song-writer, physician. Educated at Cambridge. Published 4 books on lute songs, and 5th in association with Philip Rosseter, and treatise on counterpoint. Also wrote music for several court masques.

**Campra, André** (1660–1744), French composer. Composed distinguished church music, but best known for *divertissements* and operas, *eg L'Europe galante* (1697), *Tancrède* (1702).

**canarie** (Fr.), French dance of 17th cent. Takes name from Canary Islands. Very similar to gigue: in 3/8 or 6/8 time, with persistent dotted rhythm.

**cancan,** French (esp. Parisian) dance of late 19th cent., in quick 2/4 time. Grew out of quadrille; famed for lasciviousness.

**cancrizans,** 'crab-like' (Lat., *cancer,* 'crab'). *See* CANON (5), RETROGRADE MOTION.

**Cannabich, Christian** (1731–98), German violinist, composer, conductor. Pupil of Johann Stamitz. Much praised as conductor.

**canon** (Gr., rule), polyphonic composition in which one part is imitated by one or more other parts, entering subsequently in such a way that successive statements of melody overlap.

If imitation is exact in every detail, canon is 'strict'; if modified by introduction or omission of accidentals, it is 'free'. Common practice is to end with short coda, in which imitation is abandoned, to make satisfactory conclusion. If on other hand each part, on coming to end of melody, goes back to beginning again and repeats, result is 'perpetual' or 'infinite' canon, popularly known as a 'round' (*eg* 'Three blind mice'). Canons are often accompanied by one or more independent parts and have also been written on ground bass.

Problems to be solved in canonic writing have fascinated composers of all ages. Part which imitates may begin at same pitch as original melody or at interval above or below it; hence terms 'canon at the unison', 'canon at the fifth' *etc.*

Among possible varieties of canon are:

(1) canon by inversion, or contrary motion (*canon per arsin et thesin*). Part which imitates is same as original melody, but upside down;

(2) canon by augmentation. Part which imitates is in longer notes than original;

(3) canon by diminution. Part which imitates is in shorter notes than original;

(4) combination of (1) and (2) or (1) and (3);

(5) crab canon *(canon cancrizans)* or retrograde canon. Part which imitates is written backwards, beginning with end;

(6) crab canon by inversion. Part which imitates is written backwards and upside down.

Two or more canons may be combined. Simple canon between two parts is called 'canon two in one', because both parts sing same melody. If two two-part canons are combined, result will be 'canon four in two'.

**cantabile** (It.), 'singable'. Applied to instrumental piece, which indicates that player should make music sing.

**cantando** (It.), 'singing'. Same as CANTABILE.

**cantata** (It., *cantare,* 'to sing'), properly, piece which is sung, as opposed to 'sonata', piece which is played. In early 17th cent. word was used of extended pieces of secular music, for one or two voices with accompaniment, normally consisting of contrasting sections of declamatory recitative and aria. Style was similar to opera, but intended for concert performance. In course of 17th cent., cantata was imitated by French, German and English composers; was extended to include settings of religious texts and became increasingly elaborate. In Germany, Lutheran chorale was introduced into cantata as basis for extended treatment. This type of cantata, scored for soloists, chorus and orchestra and owing much to example of opera, was model adopted by Bach. Since late 18th cent., term 'cantata' has generally been used for secular or sacred choral works, with or without soloists, accompanied by orchestra, which are similar in conception to oratorio but less extended.

**cantatrice** (It.), woman singer.

**Cantelli, Guido** (1920–56), Italian conductor. Protégé of Toscanini. Regarded as one of the most exciting conductors of his generation. Killed in air-crash.

**Canteloupe, Marie-Joseph** (1879–1957), French composer, collector of folk songs. Compositions incl. instrumental works, songs, and operas *Le Mas* (1929) and *Vercingétorix* (1933). Best known today for delightful collection of *Songs of the Auvergne.*

**canti carnascialeschi** (It.), 'carnival songs': part-songs of popular character of early 16th cent. performed at court festivals during annual carnival.

**canticle,** hymn using words from Bible, other than psalm, used in Christian liturgy. Also used of concert piece with religious text.

**cantiga,** Spanish or Portuguese folk song. Over 400 *Cantigas de Santa*

*Maria* (hymns of the virgin) were collected by Alfonso the Wise (1221–84), king of Castile and Leon (1252–84).

**cantilena** (It.), sustained, flowing melodic line.

**cantillation,** unaccompanied chanting in free rhythm and plainsong style. Used esp. of Jewish liturgical music.

**canto** (It.), song, melody; *col canto,* indicates that accompanist takes tempo from singer.

**canto fermo,** *see* CANTUS FIRMUS.

**cantor** (Lat.), 'singer'. Chief singer in choir; or director of music in cathedrals, collegiate churches and similar establishments (Eng. 'chanter' or 'precentor'). Though office of precentor still exists in English cathedrals, actual work of training choir is normally undertaken by organist. In England, genitive *cantoris* indicates half of choir sitting on side of precentor; other half, on dean's side, is called *decani.* This division is regularly used in antiphonal chanting of psalms, and frequently in anthems and services.

**cantus firmus** (Lat.; It., *canto fermo*), 'fixed song'; pre-existing melody used, often in long notes, as foundation of polyphonic composition. Plainsong melodies were widely used in Middle Ages and later. Other materials drawn upon were secular songs, Lutheran chorals, scales, and solmization syllables representing vowels in verbal text. *See* COUNTERPOINT, TENOR.

**cantus planus** (Lat.), PLAINSONG.

**canzona, canzone,** or **canzon** (It.; Fr., *chanson*) 'song'. Used of vocal piece or instrumental piece modelled on vocal form. In particular:

(1) in 16th cent., polyphonic setting of secular poem, simpler and more popular in style than madrigal;

(2) name used in Italy at same period for polyphonic French chanson *(canzon francese)*;

(3) from 17th cent., solo song with keyboard accompaniment;

(4) in opera, song of simple type, in contrast to elaborate aria;

(5) 16th-cent. transcription for lute or keyboard of French *chanson*;

(6) instrumental piece in same style written for keyboard or instrumental ensemble (late 16th, early 17th cents.), sometimes described as *canzon per sonar* (for playing) or *da sonar.* From contrasted sections introduced into such pieces developed separate movts. of sonata;

(7) instrumental piece (or movt. in sonata) of polyphonic character (17th, early 18th cents.);

(8) instrumental piece or movt. in style of song.

**canzonetta** (It.; Eng., canzonet), diminutive of CANZONA:

(1) short piece of secular vocal music, light in character, for 2 or more voices, with or without instrumental accompaniment. In 16th cent., normally in form AABCC;

(2) solo song of similar character;

(3) instrumental piece, in same style as CANZONA (6).

**Caplet, André** (1878–1925), French composer, conductor. Close friend of Debussy, whose *Children's Corner* he arranged for orchestra. Works incl. symphonic poem on Poe's *Mask of the Red Death,* church and chamber music, and songs.

**capotasto** (It.), 'head *(capo)* of finger-board *(tasto)*' of string instrument. Also, mechanical device, consisting of cross bar of wood, metal or ivory (Fr., *barre*), for shortening all strings simultaneously and hence raising pitch; simplifies performance of pieces in extreme keys, but only practical on instruments with FRETS.

**cappella,** *see* A CAPPELLA, MAESTRO DI CAPPELLA.

**capriccio** (It.; Fr., *caprice*), in general, piece in which composer follows his fancy. In particular:

(1) in late 16th, 17th cents., instrumental piece, fugal in character, similar to *ricercar, fantasia* and *canzona,* though sometimes more fanciful in choice of themes;

(2) piece which does not fall into one of conventional forms of its period;

(3) technical study;

(4) original piece of lively character;

(5) potpourri or rhapsody.

**Capriccio,** opera by Richard Strauss, libretto by C. Krauss and composer. First perf. Munich, 1942. Strauss's last opera, in which poet and composer are rival suitors.

**Capriol,** suite for strings by Warlock (1926) based on old French dances.

**Cardew, Cornelius** (1936–81), English composer, pianist, guitarist. Disciple of Stockhausen. Music, shunning conventions and leaving final decisions to performers, incl. *Octet 1961.*

**Cardillac,** opera by Hindemith, libretto by F. Lion (based on story by Hoffmann), later replaced by composer. First perf. Dresden, 1926.

**Cardus, Neville** (1889–1975), English critic. Joined *Manchester Guardian* in 1917, ultimately becoming senior London music critic. Books incl. study of Mahler's first 5 symphonies.

**Carestini, Giovanni** (*c* 1705–*c* 1760), Italian castrato singer, with remarkable contralto voice. Sang in several of Handel's operas in London, and also in Rome, Prague, Berlin and St Petersburg.

**Carey, Henry** (*c* 1690–1743), English composer, dramatist. Works incl. operettas (often satires and burlesques), songs, cantatas. Wrote words and tune (though not famous one) of 'Sally in our alley'.

**carillon,** (1) set of bells hung in bell tower, struck by hammers connected to keyboard and pedalboard, or to automatic mechanism powered by clockwork or electricity, so producing tune;

(2) organ stop with bell-like sound.

**Carissimi, Giacomo** (1605-74), Italian composer. Active in direction of church music in Rome. Played important part in cultivation of solo cantata. Was one of first to break from 17th-cent. practice of opera on sacred subjects. Oratorios *(eg Jonas Baltazar)*, though often dramatic in treatment, were intended for church not stage, and so include narrator, who sings in recitative.

**Carl Rosa Opera Company,** founded in 1873 by Carl Rosa (orig.

Karl Rose), German violinist. Active as touring company in Britain until 1958 when it was superseded by Sadler's Wells.

**Carlton, Nicholas** (*fl* early 17th cent.), English composer. Wrote one of earliest known keyboard duets, entitled 'A Verse for two to play on one Virginal or Organ'.

**Carlton, Richard** (*c* 1558–*c* 1638), English composer. Published set of 5-part madrigals, remarkable for their free use of dissonance, and contributed to *The Triumphes of Oriana* (1601).

**Carmen,** opera by Bizet, libretto by H. Meilhac and L. Halévy (after story by Prosper Mérimée). First perf. Paris, 1875. Story concerns fatal love of Don José, sergeant of the guard, for gypsy girl Carmen, who works in cigarette factory.

**Carmina Burana** (Lat., 'songs from Beuron'), scenic oratorio or cantata by Carl Orff. First perf. Frankfurt, 1937. Based on 13th-cent. Latin poems (with interpolations in old French and old German) on subjects of love, drink and kindred pleasures.

**Carnaval,** set of 20 piano pieces by Schumann, op 9 (1835), with subtitle *Scènes mignonnes sur quatre notes* (dainty scenes on four notes). Four notes are derived from Asch, home town of girl Schumann was in love with at time. Letters ASCH can represent either A, E flat (Ger., Es), C, B (Ger., H) or A flat (Ger., As), C, B; letters are also only 'musical' notes in Schumann's name. Music depicts ball attended by composer and friends and various *commedia dell'arte* figures.

**Carnaval romain, Le** *(The Roman Carnival)*, concert overture by Berlioz, op 9 (1844), based on material from opera *Benvenuto Cellini*, op 23 (1834–8).

**Carnival,** concert overture by Dvořák, op 92 (1891).

**Carnival Jest from Vienna** (Ger., *Faschingsschwank aus Wien*), set of 5 piano pieces by Schumann, op 26 (1839).

**Carnival of the Animals** (Fr., *Le Carnaval des animaux*), satirical suite by Saint-Saëns for 2 pianos, string quintet, flute, clarinet and xylophone (though often played by full orchestra), described as *fantaisie zoologique*. Composed 1886, but not published till 1922.

**carol** (Fr., *noël*; Ger., *Weihnachtslied*), though now used of a song for Christmas, in medieval English it meant any song with a burden (or refrain).

**Caron, Philippe** (*fl* later 15th cent.), Flemish composer. Prob. pupil of Dufay. Composed *chansons* and Masses.

**Carpani, Giusseppe Antonio** (1752–1825), Italian-born writer. Wrote several opera libretti, and study of Haydn's music entitled *Le Haydine* (1812), subsequently pirated by Henri Beyle.

**Carpenter, John Alden** (1876–1951), American businessman, composer. Works incl. jazz pantomime *Krazy Kat* (1922), ballets *The Birthday of the Infanta* (1919), *Skyscrapers* (1926).

**Carreras, José** (1946– ), Spanish tenor. Has sung at Covent Garden, New York Metropolitan and La Scala.

**Carse, Adam** (1878–1958), English composer, writer on music. Works incl. 2 symphonies, but best known for arrangements of old music (esp. early classical symphonies), text-books on music theory and books on history of orchestra and orchestral instruments.

**Carter, Elliot** (1908– ), American composer. Pupil of Walter Piston and Nadia Boulanger in Paris; has held various teaching posts. As composer, has emerged as one of major figures of US musical life, admired as much abroad as at home. Uses traditional forms as receptacles for ideas of remarkable freshness and power. Works incl. *Variations for Orchestra* (1955), double concerto for harpsichord and piano (1956), piano concerto (1965), *Concerto for Orchestra* (1970), *Symphony of 3 Orchestras* (1976–7) and 3 string quartets. Chamber music is of quality unsurpassed by that of any contemporary composer. Has also written ballets *Pocahontas* (1939) and *The Minotaur* (1947).

**Caruso, Enrico** (1873–1921), Italian tenor. Most famous in history. Made first public appearance in Naples (his home town) in 1894. In 1902 reached Covent Garden, and in 1903 New York Metropolitan, where he subsequently made more than 600 appearances. His beauty of tone and perfection of phrasing can be heard on his many recordings – from which he made a fortune.

**Casals, Pau** or **Pablo** (1876–1973), Catalan cellist, conductor, composer. Made first solo appearance in Paris (1898). In 1905 joined piano trio founded by Alfred Cortot. Formed orchestra in Barcelona (1919). In 1940 left Spain in protest against Franco's Government. Lived at Prades in French Pyrenees, where founded Casals Festival (1950); settled in Puerto Rico in 1956.

His remarkable gifts of execution and interpretation (esp. of Bach's unaccompanied suites) did more than anything else to raise prestige of solo cello in 20th cent. Also a remarkable accompanist. Compositions incl. works for cello and choral works *eg The Manger*.

**Casella, Alfredo** (1883–1947), Italian composer, conductor, pianist, critic. Pupil of Fauré. Took active part in furthering cause of modern Italian music and in organizing Venice *Biennale* festivals. Music, eclectic in style, incl. 3 operas *eg Il deserto tentato* (1937, glorifying Abyssinian war), ballets *eg La giara* (after Pirandello), 3 symphonies, concertos and other orchestral works, cello and piano music, songs.

**Casimiri, Raffaele** (1880–1943), Italian choral conductor, composer, musicologist. Director of music at St John Lateran, Rome, from 1911. Edited much old music, incl. new edition of Palestrina, and wrote studies of Palestrina and Lassus.

**cassa** (It.), drum.

**Cassadó, Gaspar** (1897–1966), Catalan cellist, composer. Pupil of Casals. Works incl. 3 string quartets, piano trio, and *Rapsodia catalonia* for orchestra.

**cassation** (It., *cassazione*), term used in 18th cent. for instrumental suite suitable for open-air performance, thus similar to serenade or divertimento.

**Casse-Noisette,** *see* NUTCRACKER.

**castanets** (Fr., *castagnettes*; Ger., *Kastagnetten*; It., *castagnette*), percussion instrument, characteristic of Spain, consisting of 2 shell-shaped pieces of hard wood joined by cord passing over thumbs, and struck together by fingers. In orchestra, modified form is normally used, in which clappers are attached to stick. Word derives from diminutive of Spanish word for 'chestnut'.

**Castelnuovo-Tedesco, Mario** (1895–1968), Italian composer. As Jew, fled to US in 1939. Works incl. 2 piano concertos, 2 violin concertos, very popular guitar concerto, several overtures to Shakespeare's plays, chamber and piano music, and songs.

**Castile-Blaze, François Henri Joseph** (1784–1857), French writer on music, composer. Adapted large number of Italian and German operas for French stage.

**Castor et Pollux,** opera by Rameau, libretto by P.J.J. Bernard. First perf. Paris, 1737.

**castrato** (It.), adult male singer – now defunct – with soprano or contralto voice, produced by castration before puberty. This has effect of preventing voice from 'breaking'; in consequence, castrato combined boy's range with man's power and capacity. Principle field of activity was in Italian *opera seria* in 17th, 18th cents.; many were famous for virtuosity and beauty of voice. Castrati often took male parts, which has become one difficulty in revival of operas of period. Their parts are either transposed down octave (damaging musical texture) or taken by female soprano or mezzo-soprano (damaging dramatic credibility).

**Castro, Jean de** (*fl* 16th cent.), composer prob. Walloon. Wrote church music, madrigals, and *chansons* (incl. settings of Ronsard).

**Castro, Juan José** (1895-1968), Argentinian composer. Pupil of d'Indy in Paris. Works incl. *Sinfonía Argentina, Sinfonía biblica,* ballet music and operas, *eg Proserpina y el extranjero* (1952).

**Castrucci, Pietro** (1679–1752), Italian violinist. Pupil of Corelli. Moved to England in 1715, and led orchestra in Handel's opera performances for several years. Compositions incl. 12 *concerti grossi* and 30 violin sonatas. His brother **Prospero Castrucci** (d. 1760), also a violinist, was original of Hogarth's picture 'The Enraged Musician'.

**catalán,** Spanish dance from Catalonia.

**Catalani, Alfredo** (1854–93), Italian composer. Known for opera *La Wally* (1892).

**Catalani, Angelica** (1780–1849), Italian soprano. Travelled widely. Singing said to have been remarkable for its execution and beauty of tone, but extravagant in the liberties she took with the music.

**catch,** round for 3 or more voices. Popularity began in 17th cent.; became remarkable for ingenuity of composition and coarseness of words. Purcell wrote more than 50. By late 18th cent., became custom to introduce puns *etc* into catch. Word prob. derived from Italian CACCIA.

**Catel, Charles-Simon** (1773–1830), French composer. During Revolution wrote much military music and works in celebration of the new régime. Also wrote 10 operas incl. *Les Bayadères* (1810), and standard textbook on harmony.

**Caurroy, François Eustache du** (1549–1609), French composer. Became master of music in royal chapel. One of group of French composers who experimented in writing music in longs and shorts in imitation of classical scansion. Works incl. polyphonic vocal music, both sacred and secular, and instrumental fantasias.

**Caustun, Thomas** (d. 1569), English composer. One of earliest composers to write services for Anglican church. Also wrote anthems and settings of the metrical psalms.

**Cavaillé-Col, Aristide** (1811–99), member of French firm of organ-builders, influential in improving technique of organ-building in France in 19th cent.

**Cavalieri, Emilio de'** (*c* 1550–1602), amateur Italian composer. One of Florentine *camerata* who tried to recreate spirit of Greek drama, and one of first to write the new declamatory solo song with figured bass accompaniment. Works incl. *La rappresentazione di anima e di corpo* (1600), morality play set to music.

**Cavalleria Rusticana** (It., Rustic Chivalry), opera by Mascagni, libretto by G. Menasci and G. Targioni-Tozzetti (based on play by G. Verga). First perf. Rome, 1890. In Italian *verismo* style, it is fierce story of love and revenge in Sicilian village. Traditionally staged with Leoncavallo's *I Pagliacci* (1892).

**Cavalli, Pietro Francesco,** orig. Caletti-Bruni (1602–76), Italian composer. Wrote more than 40 operas, *eg Le nozze di Teti e di Peleo* (1639), *Ercole amante* (1662, written for Paris). Style of operas shows growing importance of song (as opposed to recitative) in Italian opera of period. Also wrote church music.

**cavata** (It.), lit. 'carving' or 'engraving'. Used in 18th cent. of epigrammatic ariosos sometimes found at end of long recitative, *eg* in Bach's cantatas.

**cavatina** (It.), diminutive of *cavata* (lit. 'extraction') – term used in 18th cent. for *arioso* section occurring in recitative:

(1) orig. song in opera or oratorio, less elaborate in structure and treatment (though not necessarily less important) than *da capo* aria;

(2) instrumental piece or movt. of similar character.

**Cavazzoni, Marco Antonio** (before 1490–after 1559), Italian composer, known as Marcantonio Cavazzoni da Bologna, *detto* d'Urbino. Published *Recerchari, Motetti, Canzoni* (1523) for organ.

His son, **Girolamo Cavazzoni** (*c* 1509–after 1577), was also a composer. Published *Intavolatura cioè Recercari Canzoni Himni Magnificati* (1543).

**Cavendish, Michael** (1565-1628), English composer. Wrote lute songs and madrigals, *eg* 'Come gentle swains' which was first work by English composer to incl. refrain 'Long live fair Oriana' (rewritten for Morley's anthology *The Triumphes of Oriana,* 1601).

**Cazzati, Maurizio** (*c* 1620–77), Italian composer. Taught G.B. Vitali. Works incl. much secular and sacred vocal music, and sonatas for various instrumental combinations, important in the early history of the form.

**CB,** abbrev. of contrabassi (double basses).

**cebell,** gavotte-like dance, found in England in 17th cent.

**cédez** (Fr.), 'give way', *ie* go a little slower.

**Cecilia, St,** patron saint of music. Martyred in Sicily in 2nd or 3rd cent. Her association with music did not arise till early 15th cent. Her saint day, 22 Nov., is widely celebrated.

**celere** (It.), quick. *Celerità,* speed; *celeramente,* quickly.

**celesta,** keyboard instrument invented (1886) by Auguste Mustel in Paris. Hammers strike steel bars, underneath which are series of wooden resonators. Ethereal tone heard to best advantage in higher register. Written compass is from C on 2nd line of bass clef to octave above C above treble clef, but actual sound is octave higher.

**cello,** *see* VIOLONCELLO.

**cembalo** (It.), (1) dulcimer; (2) abbrev. of *clavicembalo* (*see* HARPSICHORD).

**Cenerentola, La** *(Cinderella)*, opera by Rossini, libretto by J. Ferretti. First perf. Rome, 1817. Greatest and most human of stage works based on Perrault's fairytale. Others incl. Massenet's opera *Cendrillon* (1899) and Prokofiev's ballet (1945).

**cents,** units by which musical intervals are measured. Cent is 100th of semitone in well-tempered scale; octave contains 1200 cents.

**Ceòl beag** (Gaelic, 'little music'), class of music for Scottish bagpipes, consisting of marches, strathspeys and reels. **Ceòl meadhonach** ('middle music'), consists of folk songs, lullabies, laments, slow marches *etc.* **Ceòl mór** ('big music'), consists of salutes, gatherings, laments and commemorative tunes; also known as PIBROCH.

**Céphale et Procris** (Fr., *Cephalus and Procris*), opera by Grétry, libretto by J.F. Marmontel. First perf. Versailles, 1773.

**Cerha, Friedrich** (1926– ), Austrian composer, violinist. Teaches electronic composition. Completed orchestration of 3rd act of Berg's *Lulu* (first perf. Paris, 1979). Own works incl. series of *Spiegel* for orchestra (1960–71).

**Cerone, Domenico Pietro** (1566–1625), Italian singer, writer on music. In service of Philip II and Philip III of Spain (1592–1603). Principal theoretical work, written in Spanish, was *El Melopeo y Maestro* (The Musician and Master, 1613), which also contains much information about contemporary music and musicians.

**Certon, Pierre** (d. 1572), French composer. Pupil of Josquin des Prés. Wrote Masses, motets, psalm settings (preserved in arrangements by G. Morlaye for voice and lute, published 1554), and *chansons.*

**cervelas,** *see* RACKET.

**Ces** (Ger.), C flat.

**Ceses** (Ger.), C double flat.

**Cesti, Marc' Antonio** (1623-69), Italian opera composer. Became Franciscan monk. Operas, *eg Orontea* (1649), *La Dori* (1661), *Il* *pomo d'oro* (1667), are important contribution to development of *aria* in music-drama.

**cetera** (It.), CITTERN.

**ceterone** (It.), large CITTERN.

**Chabrier, Alexis Emmanuel** (1841–94), French composer. Took music lessons while studying law; worked as civil servant for 18 yrs. before taking up composition full-time. Enthusiastic admirer of Wagner, whose influence is seen in *eg* opera *Gwendoline* (1866). He is most himself in comic operas, *L'Etoile* (1877), *Une Education manquée* (1879), *Le Roi malgré lui* (1887), which combine Gallic wit with charm of melody and deft orchestration. These are now rarely performed. Best known for vivacious orchestral rhapsody *España* (1883) and *Marche Joyeuse*. Songs and piano pieces are also of high quality.

**chace,** *see* CACCIA.

**chaconne** (Fr.; It., *ciaccona*), stately dance in triple time, prob. imported into Spain from Mexico in late 16th cent. Like PASSACAGLIA (from which it is often indistinguishable), was habitually written in form of series of variations on (a) ground bass *(basso ostinato)* or (b) stereotyped harmonic progression. Esp. popular in 17th cent. in operas and keyboard music. Most famous example of type (b) is chaconne in Bach's Partita in D minor for solo violin.

**chacony,** 17th-cent. English version of CHACONNE.

**Chadwick, George Whitefield** (1854–1931), American composer. Works, in romantic tradition but with American quality, incl. several operas and choral pieces, 3 symphonies, symphonic poems, chamber and keyboard music, songs.

**Chaikovsky, Piotr Ilyich** (1840–93), Russian composer. Born at Votkinsk; son of chief inspector of mines, who encouraged his piano playing. Moved to St Petersburg at age of 8. Mother died when he was 14, and in same year he started composing. At 19 became clerk in Ministry of Justice, but continued private study of music, taking lessons from Zaremba and Anton Rubinstein at St Petersburg Conservatory. By 1866 was professor of harmony at new Moscow Conservatory, directed by Anton Rubinstein's brother Nicolai. In same year wrote 1st symphony *(Winter Dreams)*, though stress of composition led to nervous breakdown. In 1868 came into contact with Rimsky-Korsakov, Balakirev and others of Russian nationalist school, but regarded them (except for Rimsky) as talented, rather presumptuous amateurs, while they thought him a somewhat dull eclectic (though he was already writing music as profoundly Russian as any of them).

While working on his greatest opera, *Eugene Onegin*, married infatuated admirer, Antonina Ivanovna Milyukova (1877). But his by now definite homosexuality meant marriage was doomed, and in despair he attempted to drown himself in Volga. However, about same time he acquired sympathetic admirer and patroness, Nadezhda von Meck, with whom he corresponded but never talked. In 1890,

Mme von Meck abruptly terminated his allowance, which upset him, but he was by now financially secure. In 1891 he made conducting tour of US. Wrote 6th symphony *(Pathétique)* in 1893, but died of cholera soon after its première.

Though Chaikovsky's works have been accused of structural weakness, their warm, open-hearted melodies, dramatic sweep, and brilliant and picturesque orchestration dictate their own form, and they have proved immensely popular. He himself considered opera *Eugene Onegin* his finest work, and posterity has generally agreed with him.

Principal compositions:

(1) Stage works: 11 operas incl. *Vakula the Smith* (1876; revived as *The Little Shoes,* 1887; published as *Les Caprices d'Oxane*), *Eugene Onegin* (1879), *Joan of Arc* (1881), *Mazeppa* (1884), *The Enchantress* (1887), *The Queen of Spades* (1890), *Iolanthe* (1892); 3 ballets – *Swan Lake* (1876), *Sleeping Beauty* (1889), *Nutcracker* (1891–2); incidental music for *Snow Maiden* (1873) and *Hamlet* (1891);

(2) Orchestra: 6 symphonies; *Manfred* symphony (1885); overture-fantasia *Romeo and Juliet* (1869; final revision 1880); fantasias: *The Tempest* (1873), *Francesca da Rimini* (1876); overtures: *The Storm* (1864), *The Year 1812* (1880); 3 suites (1879, 1883, 1884); symphonic poem *Faet* (1868); symphonic ballad *The Voyevoda* (1891); *Capriccio Italien* (1880); serenade in C for string orchestra;

(3) Orchestra and solo instrument: 3 piano concertos; concert-fantasia for piano and orchestra (1884); violin concerto in D (1878); *Variations on a Rococo Theme* for cello and orchestra (1876);

(4) Chamber music: 3 string quartets; piano trio in A minor (1882); string sextet *Souvenir de Florence* (begun 1887, rev. 1892); *Souvenir d'un lieu cher* for violin and piano;

(5) Piano: sonata in C sharp minor (1865); *The Seasons* (1876); sonata in G (1878); *Children's Album* (1878); *Dumka* (1886);

Also several sets of songs; church music, cantatas and other choral works; books on musical theory.

**chair organ,** term used in England in 17th, 18th cents. for small organ (Fr., *positif*) used in conjunction with larger instrument, 'great organ'. Two orig. separate, but became incorporated, being played on different manuals. *See* CHOIR ORGAN.

**chaleur** (Fr.), warmth. *Chaleureux, chaleureusement,* warmly.

**Chaliapin, Fedor Ivanovich** (1873–1933), Russian bass. Best known for role in Mussorgsky's *Boris Godunov.* Had remarkable voice and great stage sense.

**chalumeau** (Fr.), (1) generic term for rustic reed-pipe (Lat., *calamellus;* Eng., shawm) in use up to 18th cent.;

(2) in first half of 18th cent. also applied to clarinet;

(3) now applied to lower register of clarinet. *See* CLARINET; SHAWM.

**chamber music** (Fr., *musique de chambre*; Ger., *Kammermusik*; It., *musica da camera*), properly music suitable for performance in room of house, as opposed to church or theatre. Orig. incl. vocal as well as instrumental music; now generally applied to instrumental works for limited number of performers, with only one player to each part. Such music is necessarily intimate in character, though now usually played in concert halls. Characteristic forms incl. fantasia or ricercar for viols (16th, early 17th cents.), trio sonata for 2 violins and bass with organ or harpsichord (17th, early 18th cents.), string quartet for 2 violins, viola and cello, (late 18th cent. to present day). Pieces have been written for many other combinations of string, wind and keyboard instruments (*eg* clarinet quintet, for clarinet and string quartet, and piano trio, for piano, violin and cello).

*See* DUO, TRIO, QUARTET, QUINTET, SEXTET, SEPTET, OCTET, NONET.

**chamber opera,** opera written for reduced forces, suitable for performance in more intimate theatre than grand opera house.

**chamber orchestra,** small orchestra (not necessarily consisting only of strings), performing CHAMBER MUSIC.

**Chambonnières, Jacques Champion de** (*c* 1602–*c* 1672), French harpsichordist, composer. Harpsichordist to court of Louis XIII and XIV. Works for harpsichord rank high among 17th-cent. keyboard music, and had great influence. Taught d'Anglebert and Louis Couperin.

**Chaminade, Cécile** (1857–1944), French pianist, composer. Works incl. orchestral, choral and chamber music, but best known for songs and piano pieces.

**champêtre** (Fr.), rural, rustic.

**Chandos Anthems,** series of anthems by Handel, composed (1716–20) for Earl of Carnarvon, later Duke of Chandos.

**change ringing,** *see* BELL.

**changing note,** *see* CAMBIATA (2).

**Chanler, Theodore** (1902–61), American composer. Pupil of Bloch and Nadia Boulanger. Works incl. chamber opera *The Pot of Fat* (1955), violin sonata and other chamber music, song cycles (*Epitaphs* and *The Children*) and other songs.

**chanson** (Fr.), song, for either single voice or vocal ensemble. Also applied, like AIR, to instrumental piece of vocal character. Normal word in modern French for solo song with piano accompaniment is *mélodie*.

**chant,** (1) in general, music which is sung in accordance with prescribed ritual or tradition;

(2) in particular, unaccompanied vocal music used for services of Christian church, *eg* Ambrosian chant, Gregorian chant (also called 'plainchant' or 'plainsong');

(3) in Anglican church, used only of singing of psalms and canticles;

(4) (Fr.), song, singing, voice.

**chanter** or **chaunter,** (1) part of BAGPIPE: pipe with finger holes on which melody is played, as opposed to 'drone' pipes, which merely sustain single notes;

(2) obsolete term for 'precentor' in cathedral.

**chanterelle** (Fr.), highest (E) string of violin, or highest string of similar instruments.

**Chapel Royal,** corporate body of clergy and musicians making up English court chapel. Records go back to 1135. Has played major part in development of English music and musicianship.

**Chappell,** London firm of music-publishers, founded 1812 by Samuel Chappell (d. 1834), in association with J.B. Cramer and F.T. Latour.

**character piece** (Ger., *Charakterstück*), instrumental piece, esp. for piano, portraying specific mood, attitude, place, literary conception *etc.*

**charleston,** kind of fox-trot, orig. dance of S US Negroes. Characteristic rhythm divides 4/4 bar into dotted crotchet followed by quaver tied to minim.

**Charpentier, Gustave** (1860–1956), French composer. Studied under Massenet. Works incl. instrumental music and songs, but fame rests on opera *Louise* (1900), concerning life and loves of working-class people in Paris. By 1931 it had received 800 performances in Paris alone. After 2nd opera, *Julien, ou la vie du poète* (1913), failed to achieve same success, Charpentier virtually gave up composition.

**Charpentier, Marc-Antoine** (1634–1704), French composer. Pupil of Carissimi. Works incl. operas *Les Amours d'Acis et de Galatée* (1678) and *Médée* (1693), other stage music, oratorios (unique in France at time) and much church music.

**Chasse, La** (Fr., *The Hunt*), title of 2 works by Haydn, containing hunting-call themes: (1) string quartet in B flat major, op 1, no 1 (*c* 1755); (2) Symphony no 73 in D major (1781).

**chaunter,** *see* CHANTER.

**Chausson, Ernest** (1855–99), French composer. Pupil of Massenet and Franck. Works, sensitive and romantic in style, incl. opera *Le Roi Arthus* (1903), symphony, well-known *Poème* for violin and orchestra, *Poème de l'amour et de la mer* for voice and orchestra, concerto for piano, violin and string quartet, and songs.

**Chávez, Carlos** (1899–1978), Mexican composer, conductor. Works, often based on Indian folk music, incl. symphonies, piano concerto, violin concerto, chamber, choral, piano and ballet music, and songs.

**chef d'attaque** (Fr.), leader of orchestra.

**chef d'orchestre** (Fr.), conductor.

**chekker** (Old Fr., *éschaquier*), keyboard instrument with strings, used in 14th, 15th cents. Exact nature unknown, though said to be like organ in appearance, though sounding with strings.

**Cherepnin, Nicolai** (1873–1945), Russian composer, pianist, conductor. Studied under Rimsky-Korsakov. Conductor of Diaghilev Ballets (1909–14). Wrote orchestral works, piano concerto, 2 Masses, piano pieces and songs, and completed Mussorgsky's *Sorochintsi Fair*. His son, **Alexander Cherepnin** (1899–1977), was composer and pianist. Toured extensively as pianist. Published collections of modern oriental music.

**Cherubini, [Maria] Luigi [Carlo Zenobia Salvatore]** (1760–1842), Italian composer. Visited London (1784–6); appointed composer to king. Settled in Paris (1788), becoming director of Conservatoire (1822). In operas written for Paris he showed, *eg* in *Médée* (1797), that old traditions of *opéra comique* with spoken dialogue were not inconsistent with tragic subject. His *Les Deux Journées* (1800, known in English as *The Water-Carrier*) is classic example of 'rescue' opera. Cherubini was much admired by Beethoven, who used 'rescue' idea for his opera *Fidelio*. On the other hand, Berlioz regarded him as obstacle in his progress at Paris Conservatoire. After 1813, devoted himself mostly to church music. Also wrote 6 string quartets, 6 piano sonatas, and book on counterpoint and fugue.

**chest voice,** lower 'register' of voice, as distinct from higher register ('head voice').

**Chester,** firm of music-publishers, founded at Brighton in 1860 and transferred to London in 1915.

**Cheval de Bronze, Le** (Fr., *The Bronze Horse*), opera by Auber, libretto by A.E. Scribe. First perf. Paris, 1835.

**chevalet** (Fr.; Ger., *Steg*; It., *ponticello*), bridge of string instrument. *Au chevalet, see* BOWING.

**chiaro, chiara** (It.), clear. *Chiaramente,* clearly, distinctly, *chiarezza,* clarity, distinctness.

**chiavette** (It.), plural of diminutive of *chiave* (key, clef). First used in 18th cent. to indicate use of clefs other than those normal for voices in music of 16th, early 17th cent., *eg* use of tenor clef for bass part (thus avoiding necessity for leger-lines).

**Chicago Symphony Orchestra,** one of leading orchestras of US. Founded 1891 by Theodore Thomas. Successors have incl. Artur Rodzinski, Rafael Kubelick, Fritz Reiner and Sir Georg Solti.

**chiesa** (It.), 'church'. Used in 17th, early 18th cents. to distinguish music suitable for performance in church *(eg Sonata da Chiesa)* from that suited to secular surroundings. *See* SONATA.

**Child, William** (*c* 1606–97), English organist, composer. Organist at Windsor and Chapel Royal. Compositions, mainly church music, show adherence to traditional styles, but also accept new manner of Restoration music.

**Childhood of Christ,** *see* ENFANCE DU CHRIST.

**Child of Our Time, A,** oratorio by Tippett. First perf. London, 1944. Work concerns persecution of Jews in Germany under Nazis. Incorporates Negro spirituals in score.

**Children's Corner,** suite of piano pieces by Debussy (1908), dedicated to his infant daughter. Incl. *Gradus ad Parnassum* (satire on technical exercises) and *Golliwog's Cakewalk*. Orchestrated by Caplet, 1911.

**chimes,** small set of bells. Stone chimes known since ancient times; orchestral equivalent is tubular bells. Wind chimes or aeolian bells are hung in open air to strike against each other and sound as wind blows.

**Chinese block,** hollowed block of wood struck with drum-stick to give hard resonant tap. Also known as wood block, clog box, tap box.

**Chinese temple block,** *see* TEMPLE BLOCK.

**Chisholm, Erik** (1904–65), Scottish composer, conductor. Conducted British premières (in Glasgow) of Mozart's *Idomeneo* and *La Clemenza di Tito* and Berlioz's *Trojans* and *Beatrice and Benedick*. Professor of music at Cape Town from 1946. Compositions incl. opera trilogy *Murder in Three Keys,* orchestral and piano music.

**chitarra** (It.), guitar.

**chitarrone** (It.), large LUTE.

**chiuso,** *see* CLOS.

**choir,** (1) place in cathedral where singers are stationed;
(2) body of singers;
(3) in US, particular section of orchestra, *eg* 'brass choir';
(4) short for CHOIR ORGAN.

**choirbook,** large medieval manuscript volume designed so that separate parts of choral composition could be read by number of singers standing in front of lectern. Music not written in score: parts written separately on 2 facing pages (thus saving space). Use inevitably declined in favour of more practical system of separate PART-BOOKS.

**choir organ** (Fr., *positif*; Ger., *Unterwerk*; It., *organo di coro*), in modern use, section of organ played from lowest of 3 or more manuals. Generally consists of quieter stops, suitable for solo work; frequently enclosed in box with movable shutters (like SWELL ORGAN), enabling player to make *crescendo* or *diminuendo.* If organ has no SOLO ORGAN, choir organ may incl. powerful reed stop (trumpet or tuba), or alternatively trumpet stop on GREAT ORGAN may also be available on choir organ, making possible trumpet solo with heavy accompaniment on great organ. *See* MANUAL, ORGAN.

**choke cymbal,** *see* HI-HAT CYMBAL.

**Chopin, Frédéric François,** orig. Fryderyk Franciszek Chopin (1810–49), Polish-born composer, son of French father and Polish mother. Born near Warsaw, received first piano lessons at age of 6. Composed first polonaise at age of 7 and played in public at age of 8, playing before Czar Alexander I at 15. At 16, entered Warsaw Conservatory, studying composition under Joseph Elsner. In 1829 composed F minor piano concerto (usually known as 2nd, but in fact written before E minor concerto, published as no 1). Same year visited Vienna, Dresden and Prague, and revealed love for Konstancja Gladkowska. Following year left Warsaw, and in 1831 settled in Paris, giving lessons and playing in concerts. Also met Liszt, Mendelssohn, Berlioz and Bellini, and began his association with novelist George Sand in 1837. His secret engagement to Marya Wodzinska had just ended. Began to suffer from steadily worsening tuberculosis. Continued (till 1847) to live with George Sand, who (6 years older than he) looked after him devotedly and helped his genius to flower. Many of his finest works were written during period of their liaison. When relationship broke up, Chopin's inspiration and health deteriorated. Tour in 1848 of England and Scotland exhausted him, and he died following year.

Chopin's compositions are almost entirely for piano. Though owed something to Field and Hummel (and study of Bach), was hardly influenced at all by major composers of own period. Created individual art of keyboard-writing, making virtue of evanescent tone of piano and using melodic decoration as enrichment of harmonic texture. Master of art of suggestion; explored harmonic territory far beyond conventional boundaries of period. Other influences incl. Polish folk music (esp. in mazurkas), and melodic style (often requiring considerable virtuosity) of Italian opera. Made mazurka, as pianistic form, peculiarly his own; did same with ballade and keyboard scherzo, whose sharp, sardonic quality made them very different from Beethoven's. His 24 preludes, one in each key, are his tribute to Bach. Though recognizing that his genius lay in short, perfectly proportioned piano pieces, full of poetic intensity, he proved in sonatas that he could sustain large design without losing grip on his material. Same applies to concertos, where orchestration is apt and sensitive.

Principal compositions:

(1) Piano and orchestra: 2 concertos; *Andante spianato* and *Polonaise*; fantasia on Polish airs; *Rondo à la Krakowiak*; variations on 'Là ci darem';

(2) Piano solo: 4 *Ballades*; 3 *Ecossaises*; 27 *Etudes*; 3 impromptus; 51 Mazurkas; 19 Nocturnes; 12 *Polonaises*; 25 preludes; 4 scherzos; 3 sonatas; 17 waltzes; *Barcarolle*; *Berceuse*; *Fantaisie* in A minor; *Fantaisie-Impromptu*;

(3) Chamber music: piano trio; cello sonata; Introduction and *Polonaise* for cello and piano;

(4) Songs: 17 Polish songs.

**Chor** (Ger.), choir, chorus.

**choral,** (1) adj. used in music involving chorus, *eg* choral symphony; (2) (Ger.), (a) plainsong (Gregorian chant); (b) hymn-tune of Lutheran church (see CHORALE).

**chorale** (Eng. phonetic spelling of Ger. *Choral*), hymn-tune of Lutheran church. Earliest publications date from 1524. Materials used in 16th cent. incl. (1) adaptations of Latin hymns of RC church, (2) adaptations of pre-Reformation popular hymns in Germany, (3) adaptations of secular songs, (4) original hymns *(eg Ein' feste Burg)*. In 16th cent. melodies showed considerable rhythmical freedom, but by 18th cent. shape acquired 4-square symmetry, as in Bach's harmonizations. Bach made no attempt to preserve original flavour of tunes; they became virtually 18th-cent. compositions. Bach revival in 19th cent. led to incorporation of several Lutheran chorales in English hymn-books (sometimes modified). *See also* CHORALE CANTATA, CHORALE PRELUDE.

**chorale cantata,** type of church cantata which makes use of text, and prob. melody, of Lutheran hymn or chorale. Bach wrote greatest examples, sometimes simple but sometimes grand and complex like *Ein' feste Burg.*

**chorale fantasia** or **fantasy,** organ piece in which chorale melody is freely treated.

**chorale prelude,** generic term for piece of organ music based on hymn-tune. Originated in Lutheran church in Germany in 17th cent., with custom of playing introduction to hymn (or chorale) on organ. Various types of treatment were employed; melody might be used *eg* as basis for fugue or variations.

**Chorale Fantasia,** (1) work by Beethoven for piano solo, chorus and orchestra, op 80 (1808), consisting of theme and variations, with improvisatory introduction for piano. Words of choral section are poem in praise of music by Christoph Kuffner. Work is prophetic of Choral Symphony;

(2) setting by Gustav Holst, op 51 (1930), of words by Robert Bridges for chorus, organ, brass, strings and percussion.

**Choral Symphony,** (1) popular name for Beethoven's symphony no 9 in D minor, op 125 (1823); last movt. is setting of Schiller's ode *An die Freude* (To joy) for soloists, chorus and orchestra. Orig. title was 'Symphony with final chorus';

(2) setting of poems by Keats for soprano solo, chorus and orchestra by Gustav Holst, op 41 (1924);

(3) symphonies written for chorus and orchestra (though not entitled 'choral') incl. Mahler's 8th symphony (1907), Vaughan Williams *A Sea Symphony* (1910); those with choral finales incl. Mendelssohn's *Hymn of Praise* ('symphony-cantata'), op 52 (1840), Liszt's *Faust Symphony* (1857), Mahler's 2nd symphony (1884-94).

**chord,** term normally used of 3 or more chords sounded simultaneously. Chord may be represented by only 2 different notes, but in that case 3rd note is implied. Classification of chords and their relation to each other forms part of study of harmony. *Diatonic chord* is one that uses only notes proper to key. Distinction between consonant and dissonant chords is arbitrary, since different standards of consonance and dissonance have prevailed at different times.

Chord of 3 notes in which lowest note is accompanied by third and fifth above it is known as *triad, eg*:

major triad:

minor triad:

augmented triad:

diminished triad:

Of diatonic triads in key of C major, 3 are major, 3 are minor and 1 is diminished:

All other triads in this key are chromatic. Range of diatonic triads in minor key is wider, as minor key incl. both flat and sharp sixths, and both flat and sharp sevenths (*see* MINOR). There are therefore 13 diatonic triads in minor key – 5 major, 4 minor, 1 augmented, and 3 diminished:

Chords in above examples are generally said to be in *root position*. Major and minor triads in root position are called *common chords*. Disposition of notes above bass does not affect nature of chord. Following are possible versions of triad of C major in root position:

Where harmony is in more than 3 parts it is obviously necessary to double one or more notes of triad, either at unison or octave. In 3-part harmony, and in 4-part harmony if movement of parts makes it desirable, fifth of major or minor triad is often omitted and bass note doubled.

If notes of chord in root position are rearranged so that one of upper notes becomes lowest, result is generally known as *inversion*. There are only 2 possible inversions of triad, *eg* root position: C–E–G; first inversion: E–G–C; second inversion: G–C–E. On keyboard instrument it is not possible to tell, without context, whether augmented triad is in root position or inverted, *eg* root position of augmented triad on C: C–E–G sharp; first inversion of augmented triad on A flat: C–E–A flat; second inversion of augmented triad on E: B sharp–E–G sharp.

In FIGURED BASS, first inversion of triad is called 6/3 chord (or *chord of the sixth*), since 2 upper notes are respectively sixth and third above lowest note. Similarly second inversion of triad is called 6/4 chord. If sixth in minor 6/3 chord is sharpened, result is called AUGMENTED SIXTH chord. Major 6/3 chord on fourth degree of scale is called NEAPOLITAN SIXTH chord.

If additional third is added above triad in root position, thus producing chord of 4 notes, result is called *chord of the seventh,* because highest note is seventh above lowest. Seventh chords in key of C major may be classified as:

(1) major triad with major third superimposed:

(2) major triad with minor third superimposed:

(3) minor triad with minor third superimposed:

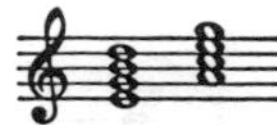

(also the seventh on D);

(4) diminished triad with major third superimposed:

All these are *diatonic sevenths,* because they do not involve any note foreign to key. (2) is called *dominant seventh* chord, because lowest note is *dominant* of key. Introduction of chromatic notes makes possible further combinations, *eg*:

diminished triad with minor third superimposed:

This is known as *diminished seventh* chord.

In 3-part harmony it is necessary to omit one of notes of seventh chord. Since seventh cannot be omitted, either fifth or, less frequently, third will be omitted. Thus dominant seventh chord in C major may be represented by one of the following:

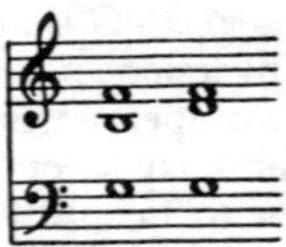

Same thing may happen in 4-part harmony if movement of parts makes it desirable, in which case bass note is usually doubled.

Theory of inversions is also applied to 4-note chords. There are 3 possible inversions of these, *eg*:

root position:

first inversion:

second inversion:

third inversion:

On keyboard instruments, inversions of diminished seventh chord are indistinguishable from transpositions of same chord in root position, *eg*:

This makes it possible to use any diminished seventh chord as means of modulating to (and so from) any major or minor key.

Superimposition of third on seventh chord produces *chord of the ninth.* Ninth chord with third added becomes *chord of the eleventh.* Eleventh chord with third added becomes *chord of the thirteenth, eg*:

These can be inverted. Third added to thirteenth chord does not produce new chord, since note added is bass note doubled 2 octaves higher.

Inversion and superimposition of thirds makes it possible to build up chords described above, but does not explain their origin or function. Chord did not arise from conscious rearrangement of triad, but arose naturally in middle ages from use of passing note in 3-part writing. Chords other than triads also arose from practice of using suspensions or passing notes, *eg* seventh could be treated as dissonance to be resolved or one merely occurring in passing. Familiarity with sound of chords produced and of chords in 5 or more parts and their inversions led to their use as normal elements in harmonic progression. Use of chromatic notes as suspended dissonances, appoggiaturas or passing notes led to further extension of harmonic vocabulary. Chords once regarded as dissonant came to be accepted as concords on to which more strongly dissonant chords could resolve.

*See* HARMONY, INVERSION.

**chording,** 'bad chording' refers to singing in which parts are out of tune with each other.

**chordophone,** any instrument in which string vibrates to produce sound. Basically 4 groups: (1) zithers, in which string is stretched between 2 ends of board and plucked or struck to produce sound (group incl. piano, harpsichord); (2) lutes, in which strings are strung from neck over bridge to body and may be plucked (*eg* guitar) or bowed (*eg* violin); (3) lyres; (4) harps.

**chord symbol,** simple notation for harmonic progressions often used in popular music. Each symbol consists of letter that may be followed by number. Letter indicates root note of basic triad and number indicates interval between added note and root note. For example, C indicates C major triad (C–E–G), and Cm or C– indicates minor triad (C–E flat–G). C6: sixth (A) is added; C7: minor seventh (B flat); C maj, C maj 7 or C△: major seventh (B); C9: ninth (D); C11: eleventh (F); C13: thirteenth (A). Added notes may be sharpened

♯ or +

or flattened

♭ or –

*eg*

C major 13 ♯ 11

indicates C–E–G–B–D–F sharp–A. Abbrev. 'sus' means suspension; C sus is C–F–G. Chords may be played in any inversion.

**choreographic poem,** symphonic poem intended as score of ballet.

**Chorton** (Ger.), 'choir pitch', *ie* pitch to which organs in Germany were formerly tuned. Pitch was neither constant nor universal.

**chorus** (Fr., *choeur*; Ger., *Chor*; It., *coro*), (1) body of singers in which there are several performers to each part, as opposed to soloists in choral work. *Semi-chorus* is smaller body of singers used in association with, or contrast to, large chorus;

(2) music written for body of singers of this kind;

(3) in solo song, refrain intended for number of singers;

(4) medieval Latin name for CRWTH.

**Chou, Wen-chung** (1923– ), Chinese composer. Went to USA in 1946 and became US citizen in 1958. Pupil of Varèse. Works, in which his Chinese origins are prominent, incl. *Metaphors* for wind and symphony orchestra, *The Dark and the Light* for piano, percussion and strings, *To a Wayfarer* for clarinet and strings, *Cursive* for flute and piano, and *Yu Ko* for 9 players.

**Christmas Concerto,** *concerto grosso* by Corelli, op 6, no 8 (1712).

**Christmas Oratorio** (Ger., *Weihnachtsoratorium*), (1) series of 6 church cantatas by Bach (1734);

(2) name sometimes given to Schütz's *Historia der freudenund gnadenreichen Geburth Gottes und Mariens Sohnes Jesu Christi* (1664).

**'Christmas' Symphony,** alternative nickname for Hadyn's 'LAMENTATION' SYMPHONY.

**Christoff, Boris** (1919– ), Bulgarian bass. Made opera debut in 1945. Known esp. for interpretation of Boris Godunov.

**Christ on the Mount of Olives** (Ger., *Christus am Ölberge*), oratorio by Beethoven, op 85 (1802), text by F.X. Huber.

**Christophe Colomb,** opera by Milhaud, libretto by P. Claudel. First perf. (with German text by R.S. Hoffman), Berlin, 1930.

**chromatic** (Gr. *chromatikos*), lit. 'coloured', hence 'embellished'. In particular:

(1) in ancient Greek music used to describe modification of diatonic tetrachord (or descending scale of 4 notes), by which 2nd note from top was flattened a semitone;

(2) by natural transference applied in Western European music to notes foreign to mode or key, produced by use of accidentals, whereas 'diatonic' refers to notes forming part of ordinary scale of mode or key. Sharpened sixth and seventh used in minor key were orig. chromatic notes, but became so firmly established as regular alternatives to sixth and seventh of diatonic scale that they ceased to be regarded as chromatic;

(3) chromatic chord: chord which includes one or more notes foreign to key. Chord which is chromatic in one key may be diatonic in another, *eg* chord of D flat major is chromatic in key of C major, where it needs accidentals, but not in key of A flat major, where it needs none. This means that chord which is merely embellishment of one key may be integral part of another, so that after using such a chord it is equally possible to remain in first key or to modulate to second (*see* CHORD, HARMONY);

(4) chromatic harmony: harmony which makes substantial use of chromatic chords. Use of chromatic notes for melodic purposes does not necessarily produce chromatic harmony, since they may merely be decoration of diatonic harmony (*see* HARMONY);

(5) chromatic instrument: instrument whose normal compass includes all notes of chromatic scale (*see* below). Chromatic compass is now normal on all instruments. Before invention of valves for horn and trumpet in early 19th cent., these instruments were incapable of playing chromatic scale;

(6) chromatic scale: scale proceeding entirely by semitones. In general, written with sharps if it ascends, and with flats if it descends, though application of this principle depends on key;

(7) in 16th-cent. Italy *cromatico* was also used of black notes, *ie* notes of smaller time value (It., *croma,* 'quaver').

**Chromatic Fantasia and Fugue,** keyboard work in D minor by Bach (*c* 1720–3). Chromatic harmony much used in fantasia.

**chromatic harp,** *see* HARP.

**chrotta,** *see* CRWTH.

**Chrysander, Karl Franz Friedrich** (1826–1901), German historian, musicologist. Edited complete edition of Handel's works, and wrote biography of Handel.

**church modes,** *see* MODE.

**Chybinski, Adolf** (1880–1952), Polish historian. Took active part in publication of old Polish music, and wrote extensively on history of Polish music and on Polish folksong.

**ciaccona** (It.), chaconne.

**cialamello** (It.), shawm.

**Cibber, Susanna Maria,** *see* ARNE.

**cibell** or **cebell,** dance form in gavotte rhythm, current in England in late 17th, early 18th cents.

**Ciconia, Johannes** (*c* 1335–1411), Walloon composer, theorist. Lived in Padua from 1402. Works incl. Mass movements, motets, and songs in Italian and French.

**Cid, Le** (Fr., *The Cid*), opera by Massenet, libretto by A.P. d'Ennery,

L. Gallot, E. Blau (based on Corneille's tragedy). First perf. Paris, 1885. Farinelli, Pacini and Cornelius also wrote operas on same subject.

**Cifra, Antonio** (1584–1629), Italian composer. Prolific compositions incl. much church music.

**Cigány** (Hungarian), 'Gypsy'.

**Cilèa, Francesco** (1866–1950), Italian composer. Wrote several operas incl. successful *Adriana Lecouvreur* (1902).

**Cimarosa, Domenico** (1749–1801), Italian opera composer. Rapidly became one of foremost opera composers of his time. Worked mainly in Rome and Naples, but was also in service of Catherine II of Russia, then Emperor Leopold II in Vienna. Of *c* 60 operas, most famous is comic opera in Mozartian idiom, *Il matrimonio segreto* (*The Secret Marriage,* 1792). Also wrote Masses, oratorios, cantatas, songs and piano sonatas.

**cimbalom,** form of DULCIMER used in Hungary. Consists of series of metal strings strung on pegs fixed onto wooden box. Strings are struck with sticks held in player's hands.

**cimbasso** (It.), bass tuba.

**Cinderella,** *see* CENERENTOLA, LA.

**cinelli** (It.), cymbals. More usual term is *piatti.*

**cinque-pace** (from Fr., *cinq pas,* 'five steps'), term used for GALLIARD by Elizabethan writers.

**cipher, ciphering,** continuous sounding of organ note due to mechanical fault.

**circle of fifths** (Ger., *Quintenzirkel*), clockwise arrangement of the 12 keys in order of ascending fifths. Thus, beginning with C, order of major keys would be C, G, D, A, E, B (or C flat), F sharp (or G flat), C sharp (or D flat), A flat, E flat, B flat, and F. After 12 such steps, orig. key is reached again. Composers have sometimes used circle of fifths as source of inspiration.

**circular breathing,** technique of sustaining note on wind instrument by breathing in while playing note.

**cis** (Ger.), C sharp. *Cis cis,* C double sharp.

**cistre** (Fr.), CITTERN.

**cittern, cither, cithern** (Fr., *cistre*; Ger., *Zither*; It., *cetra*), plucked string instrument similar to LUTE, but with flat back and wire strings, popular in 16th, 17th cents. Played with plectrum or fingers. Music was written in TABLATURE. In 18th-cent. England known as English guitar. Modern German ZITHER is different instrument.

**civettescamente,** coquettishly.

**Claire de lune** (Fr., *Moonlight*), popular piano piece by Debussy, 3rd movt. of *Suite bergamasque.*

**clairon** (Fr.), bugle. Also 4ft trumpet stop on organ.

**clairseach,** Irish HARP. Portable gut-strung type was developed in Ireland in 19th cent.; has finger levers instead of pedals.

**clarinet** (Fr., *clarinette*; Ger., *klarinette*; It., *clarinetto*), single-reed instrument, dating from late 17th cent. As tube is cylindrical, lowest octave is reproduced twelfth (not octave) higher by 'overblowing', *ie* series from G (below middle C) to F sharp on treble clef becomes series from D on treble clef to C sharp above. Notes between 2 series are produced by opening thumbhole and using keys, which also extend compass down minor third. Complete compass is from E below middle C to octave above C above treble clef.

Clarinets were orig. made in several sizes in order to facilitate playing in different keys. To save player trouble of learning different fingering, each instrument was treated as TRANSPOSING INSTRUMENT. By late 18th, early 19th cent. only 3 sizes were in normal use: in C (sounding as written), in B flat (sounding tone lower), and in A (sounding minor third lower). Clarinet in C is now obsolete in orchestra, though occasionally revived for old music. Other 2 are in regular use, though some prefer to use only B flat clarinet, with extra key to obtain extra semitone at bottom. Sounding compass of B flat clarinet is from D in middle of bass clef to octave above B flat above treble clef; and of A clarinet, from C sharp in middle of bass clef to octave above A above treble clef. Smaller clarinet in E flat (sounding minor third higher than written) is used in military bands and occasionally in orchestra: similar instrument in D has been made for orchestral use. Larger members of family are BASSET HORN, BASS CLARINET, and CONTRABASS or PEDAL CLARINET.

**clarinet quintet,** chamber work for clarinet and string quartet, *eg* those by Mozart (K 581), and Brahms (op 115).

**clarinette** (Fr.), clarinet.

**clarinette d'amour** (Fr.), alto clarinet in A flat or G with bulb-shaped bell (like *oboe d'amore*), current in late 18th cent.

**clarinetto** (It.), clarinet (diminutive of *clarino,* 'trumpet').

**clarino** (It.), (1) trumpet. Esp. applied, in 17th, early 18th cent., to high register of trumpet;

(2) clarinet, on account of similarity of tone in early 18th cent. Diminutive *clarinetto* is normal term.

**clarion,** (1) *see* TRUMPET; (2) 4ft trumpet stop on organ.

**Clarke, Jeremiah** (*c* 1673-1707), English composer, organist. Pupil of Blow. Organist at Winchester College, St Paul's Cathedral and Chapel Royal. Compositions incl. anthems, odes, music for stage, and harpsichord pieces. Among latter is 'The Prince of Denmark's March' (falsely attrib. to Purcell), widely known as 'Trumpet Voluntary'.

**clarone** (It.), bass clarinet.

**clarsach,** Scottish CLAIRSEACH.

**classical music,** term 'classical' is used by historians to distinguish music which accepts certain basic conventions of form and structure, and uses them as natural framework for expression of ideas, from music which is more concerned with expression of individual emotions than with achievement of formal unity, *ie* ROMANTIC MUSIC. In practice, term is generally restricted to 18th, early 19th-cent. music, *ie* roughly from Bach to Beethoven. As works of masters of this period are constantly performed and have stood test of time, they are also 'classical' in sense in which one speaks of 'classics' of literature.

This meaning of term is applied to any well-established work, *eg* Berg's *Wozzeck* is said to be 'modern classic'. Historical distinction, however, is not strictly valid, since many works of romantic period (roughly 1830–1910) show considerable preoccupation with formal design, while equally romantic elements are apparent in much 17th and 18th-cent. music. Probably truer to say that romantic composers of 18th cent. were often selfconscious, whereas 'classical' composers of 18th cent. were not. Beethoven's works, with their marked struggle between formal unity and intensely individual expression, may be said to stand at juncture of two periods. In present cent., 'classical music' is often applied to serious, as opposed to popular music. *See also* NEO-CLASSICISM.

**Classical Symphony,** title given by Prokofiev to his 1st symphony (1918). Piece is witty pastiche.

**Claudio da Correggio,** *see* MERULO, CLAUDIO.

**clausula** (Lat.), lit. (1) 'close', (2) 'clause' or 'section'. Hence (1) CADENCE, in music in 2 or more parts (cf. Eng., full close, half close);
(2) in ORGANA or polyphonic compositions of late 12th, early 13th cents., clearly defined section, complete in itself (also known as PUNCTUM).

**clausum** (Lat.), *see* CLOS.

**clavecin** (Fr.), harpsichord.

**claves,** short wooden cylindrical sticks held in hands and clicked together to emphasize beat. Orig. Cuban.

**clavicembalo** (It.), harpsichord; abbrev., *cembalo*.

**clavichord** (Fr., *clavicorde*; Ger., *Clavichord, Klavichord*; It., *clavicordio*), keyboard instrument. First mentioned at beginning of 15th cent. Prob. developed from MONOCHORD. In clavichord, which is oblong in shape, there is series of stretched strings running roughly parallel with front of instrument. Depression of key presses small blade of brass (called 'tangent') against string. This divides string into 2 lengths, one of which is free to vibrate while other is damped by piece of cloth. Since tone is produced by pressure, it can to some extent be controlled by player, who by repeated pressure on key can produce minute variations of pitch, similar to violinist's *vibrato* (*see* BEBUNG).

In pre-18th-cent. clavichords, single string may do duty for more than 1 note, thus reducing number of strings necessary. Clavichord of this type was called *fretted* (Ger., *gebunden*); clavichord with separate string for each note (Ger., *bundfrei*) was introduced in early 18th cent. Clavichords with pedals (like organ) were also made in 18th cent. With increasing use of piano, clavichord came to be neglected. Has been successfully revived in 20th cent., though small tone makes it ineffective in concert hall.

**clavicymbal,** Eng. for It. *clavicembalo,* harpsichord.

**clavicytherium,** upright type of harpsichord or spinet.

**clavier,** (1) (Fr.), keyboard;
(2) (Ger., also *Klavier*), (a) keyboard (cf. CLAVIERÜBUNG); (b)

keyboard instrument with strings, *ie* clavichord, harpsichord or piano;

(3) (Eng.), (a) often used by modern writers, esp. US, as equivalent of German word; (b) keyboard designed for finger practice; makes no sound except for clicks.

**Clavierübung** (Ger.), lit., 'keyboard practice'. Title of collection of keyboard music by Bach. Published in 4 parts: Part I (1731): 6 partitas; Part II (1735): ITALIAN CONCERTO and overture in French style (partita in B minor); Part III (1739): organ prelude in E flat major, 21 chorale preludes, 4 *duetti* for harpsichord, organ fugue in E flat major (known in England as 'St Anne's'); Part IV (1742): GOLDBERG VARIATIONS.

**clef** (Fr. *clef,* 'key'; Ger., *Schlüssel*; It., *chiave*), sign used to determine pitch of particular line on stave, from which pitch of remaining lines and of spaces can be deduced. Three clefs now in use:

are ornamental forms of letters g, c and f, and represent respectively notes *g*' (octave above 4th string of violin), *c*' (called middle C, fifth below *g*') and *f* (fifth below *c*'). All 3 clefs were used in variety of positions until latter half of 18th cent. Since then position of G (treble) clef has been on 2nd line of stave:

and position of F (bass) clef has been on 4th line:

C clef is placed either on 3rd line (alto clef) or on 4th line (tenor clef):

Alto clef, formerly used for alto voice and alto trombone, is now used only for viola. Tenor clef, formerly used for tenor voice, is now used only for tenor trombone and upper register of bassoon, cello and double bass.

C clef on 1st line (soprano clef):

is now obsolete.

In modern vocal scores, G clef is also used for tenor voice, though music will sound octave lower than written pitch; this transposition is sometimes indicated by following signs:

For transposition in instrumental notation *see* TRANSPOSING INSTRUMENTS.

Though old practice of changing position of clef in course of composition has been abandoned, there are many occasions when change of clef is necessary to avoid excessive use of LEGER LINES.

**Clemens non Papa, Jacobus,** orig. Jacques Clément (*c* 1510–57), Flemish composer. One of most distinguished of his time. Works, remarkable for expressive quality, incl. polyphonic Masses, motets, *chansons* and Flemish psalms.

**Clément, Jacques,** *see* CLEMENS NON PAPA.

**Clementi, Muzio** (1752–1832), Italian composer, pianist. Born in Rome; son of silversmith. At age of 14, having shown considerable talent as composer, was taken to England and continued studies there. Also won outstanding success as performer. Though lived much in England, also travelled widely on Continent. Personally knew Haydn, Mozart and Beethoven, among many other musicians.

Influence on other pianists and composers for piano was considerable. John Field was his pupil. Did more than anyone to develop style of writing which exploited characteristics of piano, as opposed to harpsichord. Numerous compositions incl. symphonies, *c* 60 piano sonatas (sometimes descriptive, *eg Didone abbandonata*), and *Gradus ad Parnassum,* series of piano studies which achieve remarkable union of technical instruction and artistic expression.

**Clemenza di Tito, La** (It., *The Clemency of Titus*), opera by Mozart, libretto adapted from Metastasio by C. Mazzolà. First perf. Prague, 1791. Mozart's last opera; written in haste for coronation of Leopold II as King of Bohemia. Reverted to *opera seria* form. At time of revolutionary turmoil, Mozart diplomatically chose story of Roman emperor who forgave conspiring subjects.

**Clérambault, Louis Nicolas** (1676–1749), French organist, composer. Compositions incl. cantatas, harpsichord and organ music.

**Cleveland Orchestra, The,** one of leading orchestras of US. Founded 1918. Conductors have incl. Sokoloff, Rodzinski, Leinsdorf, George Szell, Boulez and Lorin Maazel.

**Cliquot, François Henri** (1728–91), French organ-builder, member of family of organ-builders. Built organs for a number of Paris churches incl. Sainte-Chapelle, St Sulpice and Notre Dame. Much of his work still survives.

**cloches** (Fr.), bells.

**clochette** (Fr.) *see* GLOCKENSPIEL.

**'Clock' Symphony,** nickname of Haydn's Symphony no 101 in D major. In slow movt., accompanying instruments suggest ticking of clock.

**clos** (Fr.; Lat., *clausum*; It., *chiuso*), 'closed', medieval term used in dance music, and similarly structured vocal pieces, to indicate final cadence at end of repeated section, in contrast to intermediate cadence (Fr., *ouvert*; Lat., *apertum*; It., *verto*) used when section is performed first time. *Ouvert* and *clos* thus correspond to what is now called 'first time' (or 'first ending') and 'second time'.

**close,** CADENCE. *Half close*, imperfect cadence. *Full close*, perfect cadence.

**close harmony,** harmony in which notes of chords are kept close together – often as close as octave.

**cluster,** *see* NOTE CLUSTER.

**coach horn,** straight horn, 3 to 4ft long, comprising conical wide-bore tube of copper and funnel-shaped bell. Played with cup mouthpiece.

**Coates, Albert** (1882–1953), English conductor, composer, b. Russia. Compositions incl. operas *Samuel Pepys* (1929) and *Pickwick* (1936).

**Coates, Edith Mary** (1908– ), English mezzo-soprano. Sang with Sadler's Wells from 1931 and at Covent Garden from 1946. Created role of Auntie in Britten's *Peter Grimes*.

**Coates, Eric** (1886–1957), English composer, viola player. Orchestral compositions are light but impeccable.

**Cobbett, Walter Willson** (1847–1937), English businessman, amateur violinist. Rendered considerable service to cause of chamber music by (1) offering prizes for new works by English composers (*see* PHANTASY), (2) founding the Chamber Music Association, which is connected with the British Federation of Music Festivals, and (3) editing *Cyclopedia of Chamber Music* (2 vols., 1929).

**Cobbold, William** (1560–1639), English composer, organist. Harmonized 5 tunes from Thomas East's *The Whole Booke of Psalmes* (1592), wrote several consort songs, and contributed madrigal to *The Triumphes of Oriana* (1601).

**Cockaigne,** concert overture by Elgar, op 40 (1901), subtitled *In London Town*.

**Coclicus, Adrianus Petit** or **Adrian Coclico** (*c* 1500–*c* 1563), Flemish composer, singer. Pupil of Josquin des Prés. Moved to Wittenberg (1545) and became Protestant. Member of Chapel Royal, Copenhagen, in 1556. His *Compendium musices* (1552) is valuable exposition of current musical practice. His collection of psalms, *Consolationes Piae* (1552), contains first known use of term MUSICA RESERVATA.

**coda** (It.), lit. 'tail'; passage (long or short) at end of piece or movt., which extends ideas that have already received logical or symmetrical expression and brings work to satisfying conclusion, *eg*:

(1) in CANON, short concluding passage in which strict imitation is abandoned in order to construct convincing cadence;

(2) in FUGUE, similar passage, often based on PEDAL POINT, which sums up and clinches arguments already presented by polyphonic treatment of subject;

(3) in movt. in SONATA FORM, passage added to end of recapitula-

tion. In 18th cent. was usually short, but often greatly expanded by Beethoven, *eg* in 1st movt. of *Eroica*.

**codetta** (It.), dimin. of CODA. Esp. applied to (1) short passage forming tail-piece to particular section of composition, and (2) extension of fugue subject which serves to delay next entry.

**col, coll', colla, colle** (It.), 'with the'. *Cogli*, *coi* are plural forms.

**Colasse, Pascal** (1649–1709), French composer. Wrote operas and church music. Said to have written inner parts (*ie* those between treble and bass) of Lully's music.

**Colbran, Isabella Angela** (1785–1845), Spanish dramatic soprano. Had European reputation. In 1822 married Rossini. Sang leading soprano roles in premières of several of Rossini's operas.

**Coleman,** *see* COLMAN.

**Coleridge-Taylor, Samuel** (1875–1912), English composer. Father was native of Sierra Leone; mother was English. Made reputation with choral setting of Longfellow's *Hiawatha's Wedding Feast* (1898) – still popular – followed by *The Death of Minnehaha* (1899) and *Hiawatha's Departure* (1900). Other works incl. oratorio *The Atonement* (1903), cantata *A Tale of Old Japan* (1911), orchestral, chamber and stage music.

**colla parte** (It.), 'with the part', *ie* accompaniment is to follow any modifications of tempo made by soloist.

**colla punta dell' arco** (It.), with the point of the bow.

**coll' arco** (It.), 'with the bow'; abbrev. *arco*. Used in string music to contradict previous *pizzicato* (plucked with finger).

**Collard,** London firm of piano manufacturers, orig. founded by Clementi. F.W. Collard was one of 5 partners of firm in 1802. After Clementi's death in 1832 firm was known as Collard and Collard.

**colla voce** (It.), 'with the voice'. Same as *colla parte*, but applied only to accompaniment of vocal solo.

**collegium musicum** (Lat.), society for practice and study of (esp. old) music, generally associated with university. Term used in Germany in 17th, 18th cents., and revived in 20th.

**col legno,** *see* BOWING.

**Colles, Henry Cope** (1879–1943), English critic, historian. Became principal music critic of *The Times* in 1911. Edited 3rd (1927) and 4th (1940) editions of Grove's *Dictionary of Music and Musicians*. Books incl. *Brahms* (1908), *The Growth of Music* (3 vols. 1912–16), *Voice and Verse* (1928).

**Collingwood, Lawrence Arthur** (1887– ), English conductor, composer. Conductor of Sadler's Wells Opera (1931–47). Compositions incl. opera *Macbeth* (1934).

**coll' ottava** (It.), doubled at the octave (above and below). *See* OTTAVA.

**Colman** or **Coleman, Charles** (d. 1664), English composer. Court musician to Charles II and James II. One of composers of instrumental music in first English opera, *The Siege of Rhodes* (1656). Also wrote songs.

He had two musical sons, **Charles Colman** (d. *c* 1694), and

**Edward Colman** (d. 1669), both of whom were also court musicians.

**Colonne, Edouard** (orig. Judas) (1838–1910), French violinist, conductor. Founded Concerts Colonne (orig. known as Concert National) in 1873, at which many works by French composers (esp. Berlioz) were given.

**colophony,** same as ROSIN.

**color,** *see* ISORHYTHM.

**coloratura** (It.; Ger., *Koloratur*), elaborate ornamentation of melodic line in music for solo instruments or (esp.) voices. Word does not solely apply to high soprano. Arias incl. such ornamentation occur constantly in 18th, 19th-cent. (esp. Italian) opera.

**colour,** word used, by analogy with painting, to describe individual tone-quality of instruments and voices, or their association together, *eg* orchestral colour.

**Colour Symphony, A,** symphony by Bliss (1922). Movts. are headed Purple, Red, Blue and Green.

**colpo** (It.), stroke; *colpo d'arco*, stroke of the bow.

**combination pedals,** (1) properly, device for bringing into action several rows of organ pipes by admitting air to soundboard on which they are placed;
(2) also used in same sense as COMPOSITION PEDALS.

**combination tone** or **resultant tone,** faint note resulting from sounding two notes simultaneously. Two different kinds: (1) *difference tones*, resulting from difference between frequencies of notes sounded, (2) *summation tones* (fainter than difference tones), resulting from sum of their frequencies. Two notes orig. sounded also combine with combination tone to produce further combination tones. If three or more notes are sounded together, number of combination tones will be proportionately increased.

**come** (It.), as; *come prima*, as at first; *come sopra*, as above; *come sta*, as it stands, *ie* without any modification of text.

**comes** (It.), 'companion'. Name given by older theorists to second part to enter CANON or FUGUE; first part known as *dux* (leader).

**commodo,** obs. form of COMODO.

**common chord,** major or minor CHORD in root position.

**common time,** 4 crotchets in bar, indicated by time signature 4/4 or C. *See* C, TIME.

**communion** (Lat., *communio*), antiphon sung after communion at Mass.

**comodo** (It.), 'convenient', *ie* at convenient speed, neither too fast nor too slow. Often combined with *allegro*.

**compass,** complete range of pitch of voice or instrument.

**Compenius,** firm of organ-builders active in late 16th, early 17th cent. Compenius organ of 1612 still survives in Frederiksborg, Denmark.

**Compère, Loyset** (*c* 1450–1518), Flemish composer. Poss. pupil of Ockeghem. Works incl. Masses, motets, and *chansons*.

**competition festivals,** meetings for competitive performance (with or without prizes) of choral music, songs, chamber music and solo instrumental music. First organized in Britain by J.S. Curwen at Stratford, East London (1882), and by Mary Wakefield in Westmorland (1885). Welsh EISTEDDFOD (in modern form) and brass band festivals both date from late 19th cent. Similar festivals are also held in USA and Commonwealth.

**composition,** (1) individually created musical piece, thus not applied to folk songs or arrangements; (2) act of writing music.

**composition pedals,** set of metal pedals, or buttons operated by feet, used in organ to bring stops into action without having to draw them by hand. Each pedal also puts out of action any other stops that happen to be drawn.

**composition pistons,** similar in action to composition pedals, but are placed below manuals and controlled by fingers or thumbs.

**compound time,** time in which each beat in bar is divisible into 3, *eg* in 6/8, 9/8 and 12/8 there are respectively 2, 3 and 4 dotted crotchet beats, each divisible into 3 quavers. Opposite is simple time, *eg* 2/4, 3/4, 4/4, where each beat is crotchet, divisible into 2 quavers.

**Comte Ory, Le,** opera by Rossini, libretto by A.E. Scribe and C.G. Delestre-Poirson. First perf. Paris, 1828.

**Comus,** masque by Milton, with music by Henry Lawes. First perf. Ludlow Castle, 1634. Later adapted by John Dalton, with music by Arne (London, 1738).

**con** (It.), 'with'; *con affeto*, with tender emotion; *con amore*, lovingly; *con anima*, with spirit; *con brio*, vigorously; *con fuoco*, with fire.

**concert,** (1) public performance of music other than opera or church music; esp. performance by group, as opposed to RECITAL by soloist. Until late 17th cent., such performances were heard only at courts of kings or houses of wealthy patrons. Pioneer of public concerts was John Banister, who organized series at Whitefriars, London, in 1672. First specially designed concert hall is prob. Holywell Music Room, Oxford (1748). *See* CONCERT SPIRITUEL, PROMENADE CONCERTS;

(2) Fr. word *concert* means 'concerto' as well as 'concert'.

**concertant** (Fr.), **concertante** (It.), (1) as adj., used to describe work, either for orchestra or for 2 or more instruments, in which one or more solo parts are prominent;

(2) It. word *concertante*, as noun, = *sinfonia concertante*.

**concertato** (It.), CONCERTANTE. *Coro concertato*, group of solo singers forming contrast to full choir (17th cent.). *Stile concertato, see* STILE.

**concert band** (US), band of wind and percussion instruments.

**concerted,** adj. applied to piece in which parts all have more or less equal importance.

**Concertgebouw** (Dutch), lit. 'concert building'; Amsterdam's main concert hall. Society of same name was founded in 1883. Concertgebouw Orchestra was directed (1895–1945) by William Mengelberg, succeeded by Eduard van Beinum (to 1959) and Bernard Haitink; famed esp. for performances of Bruckner and Mahler.

**concertina,** form of ACCORDION, patented by Sir Charles Wheatstone (1829). Hexagonal in shape. Small pistons or studs, placed at each end of instrument, take place of keyboard.

**concertino** (It.), dimin. of CONCERTO:

(1) group of soloists in *concerto grosso* (17th, 18th cents.);

(2) work of one or more solo instruments with orchestra, less formal in structure than ordinary concerto (Ger., *Konzertstück, Concertstück*).

**concert instruments,** instruments (incl. all string and keyboard instruments) whose notation is at same pitch as music sounds (also called instruments in C). Others are called TRANSPOSING INSTRUMENTS.

**concert-master** (US; Ger., *Konzertmeister*), first violin (Eng., leader) of orchestra.

**concerto** (It.; Fr., *concert*; Ger., *Konzert*),

(1) orig. (late 16th to early 18th cents.), work for one or more voices with instrumental accompaniment, either for figured bass or with addition of other instruments. Bach used word for several of his church cantatas;

(2) work for several instruments, supported by figured bass and offering opportunities for contrast (17th, early 18th cents.), esp.:

(3) *concerto grosso*, orchestral work in several movts., with passages for group of solo instruments (*concertino*) as contrast to *tutti* for main body (*concerto grosso*). Favourite solo group consisted of 2 violins and cello (accompanied, like *tutti*, by figured bass), but many other combinations are found;

(4) solo concerto (*ie* for one instrument with orchestra) dates from early 18th cent., when violin was most favoured solo instrument. Keyboard instruments, being used to play figured bass accompaniment, were not at first thought of as suitable for playing solos in concertos. By late 18th cent., solo concerto had become normal type, and many keyboard concertos were written. Works of same character for more than one solo instrument were also written. By Mozart's time, figured bass for keyboard instrument had ceased to be indispensable, but harpsichord or piano normally played with orchestra, even in concertos for keyboard instrument.

Solo concerto had obvious similarities with operatic aria. Hence contrasts between *ritornelli* for full orchestra and solo sections were normal, and opportunities for improvised display were offered at cadence before final *ritornello* (*see* CADENZA). Mozart, however, achieved much closer integration of soloist and orchestra, and his example has been followed by many subsequent composers;

(5) word *concerto* has also been used by modern composers in sense similar to (2) above, *ie* composition for instrumental ensemble, though without implication of figured bass;

(6) Bach's *Concerto in the Italian Style* is for solo harpsichord, which imitates style of solo concerto with orchestra by contrasting between soloist and *tutti*.

**concerto grosso,** *see* CONCERTO (3).

**concert overture,** form originating in 19th cent., consisting of orchestral piece similar to overture to opera or play but intended purely for concert room. Often have title and programme, *eg* Mendelssohn's *The Hebrides*, Chaikovsky's *Romeo and Juliet*.

**concert pitch,** conventional term for standard international pitch, according to which A in middle of treble clef is fixed at 440 cycles per second. Brass bands in Britain use higher pitch (*see* PITCH).

**Concert spirituel** (Fr.), lit. 'sacred concert'. Organization founded in Paris (1725) by A.D. Philidor to give concerts on religious festivals when Opéra was closed. Secular works were soon introduced. Concerts ended 1791.

**Concertstück,** *see* CONCERTINO (2).

**concitato** (It.), agitated.

**concord,** combination of sounds agreeable to ear – opposite of DISCORD. However, as interpretations of what is agreeable have varied widely, any precise definition or list of concords is arbitrary and has no absolute validity. *See* CONSONANCE.

**Concord Sonata,** piano sonata no 2 by Ives. Inscribed 'Concord, Mass., 1840–60' and written in experimental style, incl. note-clusters produced by laying strip of wood along keyboard. Movts. are entitled *Emerson*, *Hawthorne*, *The Alcotts* and *Thoreau*.

**concrete music,** *see* MUSIQUE CONCRÈTE.

**conducting,** direction of performance given by group of singers or players or both. Involves not only precise indications of speed, dynamics and phrasing, but also careful preparation to ensure balance is correct and that intentions of composer are adequately represented.

Use of baton, though goes back at least to 15th cent., did not become general till later 19th cent. Before that, methods used incl. hand, roll of paper, or violin bow. Stick was sometimes used to beat time audibly, *eg* at Paris Opéra in 17th, 18th cents. Elsewhere in 18th cent. opera was normally directed from harpsichord, and symphonies by principal 1st violin. When baton was introduced to London by Spohr (1820) and to Leipzig by Mendelssohn (1835), it was regarded as novelty. Increasing complication of orchestral writing and growth of forces employed made clear and visible direction indispensable, and use of baton soon became general (though not universal). Normal conducting practice is to use right hand for beating time with baton and left to indicate entries, dynamics and expression in general.

**conductus** (Lat.), in 12th, 13th cents., metrical Latin song, sacred or secular, usually for between one and three voices.

**Conforto** or **Conforti, Giovanni Luca** (b. *c* 1560), Italian singer in Papal choir. Author of instruction book giving valuable information about late 16th-cent. practice of improvised ornamentation in vocal music.

**conga,** (1) tall narrow drum, usually single handed and played with fingers, often in pairs;

(2) dance in which people form long winding line.

**conjunct,** opposite of disjunct. Both terms refer to succession of notes of different pitch. Melody is said to move by conjunct motion if notes proceed to adjacent degrees of scale (*eg* opening of 'Three Blind Mice'), and by disjunct motion if notes form intervals larger than a second.

**Consecration of the House, The** (Ger., *Die Weihe des Hauses*), overture in C major by Beethoven, op 124, written for opening of Josephstadt Theatre, Vienna, in 1822.

**consecutive intervals,** if any interval between 2 parts is followed immediately by same interval between same 2 parts, 2 intervals are described as 'consecutive' or 'parallel', *eg* C played with E above followed by G played with B above are consecutive thirds; C played with F above followed by E played with A above are consecutive fourths, and so on. Consecutive fifths and octaves came to be avoided in 15th cent. (presumably because they were felt to prejudice independence of parts), and this ban continued to late 19th cent., and is still incorporated in teaching of elementary harmony.

**conservatory** (Fr., *conservatoire*; Ger., *Konservatorium*; It. and Sp., *conservatorio*), school specializing in musical training.

**console,** part of organ from which player controls instrument, *ie* keyboards, pedals, stops, music desk, *etc*.

**consonance,** consonance and dissonance provide valuable contrast in music, one suggesting repose, the other stress. However, interpretations have always varied as to which intervals or chords are consonant and which dissonant. Traditionally major and minor thirds, perfect fourth, perfect fifth, major and minor sixths and octave are classed as consonant, and all other intervals (*eg* second, diminished fifth) as dissonant. Only unison and octave are mathematically consonant (octave above given note having twice its frequency); all other intervals are dissonant to greater or lesser degree.

**con sordino** (It.), 'with mute' (abbrev. *con sord*). Countermanded by *senza sordino* (abbrev. *senza sord*).

**consort,** in 16th, 17th cents., chamber ensemble, esp. of instruments alone, *eg* consort of viols. Ensemble of instruments from different families is now often incorrectly called 'broken consort' as distinct from 'whole consort' of like instruments.

**Consul, The,** opera by Menotti, libretto by composer. First perf. New York, 1950. Story deals with attempt to escape from totalitarian state, frustrated by bureaucratic consul who never appears.

**Contes d'Hoffmann, Les,** *see* TALES OF HOFFMANN.

**continuo** (It.), abbrev. of *basso continuo* (lit. 'continuous bass'), *ie* bass line of composition marked with figures to indicate harmonies to be played on keyboard (*see* FIGURED BASS). In 17th, 18th cents., *continuo* is played throughout work (not, as sometimes thought, just during recitative), unless otherwise indicated.

**contrabass,** (1) as prefix, indicates instrument built octave lower than normal bass of family, *eg* contrabass trombone;
(2) as noun = DOUBLE BASS.

**contrabass** or **pedal clarinet,** 19th-cent. invention; present form dates from 1890. Built in B flat, octave below bass clarinet. Written compass is from E below bass clef to E at top of treble clef, sounding from octave below D below bass clef to D above bass clef. Has not become normal member of orchestra.

**contrabasso** (It.), double bass.

**contrabass trombone, contrabass tuba** *etc*, *see* TROMBONE, TUBA, *etc*.

**contradanza** (It.), contredanse.

**contrafactum,** in medieval music, vocal composition in which orig. words are replaced by others of different character (*eg* sacred by secular and vice versa).

**contrafagotto** (It.), double BASSOON.

**contralto,** (1) lowest female voice, with compass of roughly 2 octaves from F below middle C to G above treble clef;
(2) in 16th, 17th cents., male alto or countertenor.

**contrapunctus** (Lat.), (1) counterpoint; (2) piece of contrapuntal style.

**contrapuntal,** adj. derived from counterpoint.

**contrary motion,** *see* INVERSION (2).

**contratenor,** in 14th, early 15th cents., name for part with roughly same range as tenor, which it often crosses. In 18th cent., distinction developed between *contratenor altus* (high contratenor) and *contratenor bassus* (low contratenor), with prevailing range respectively above and below tenor. Terms were subsequently reduced to *altus* (alto) and *bassus* (bass).

**contrebasse** (Fr.), double bass.

**contrebasson** (Fr.), double BASSOON.

**contredanse** (Fr.; Ger., *Kontretanz*; It. *contradanza*), corruption of Eng. 'country dance'. Lively dance popular in France and Germany in 18th cent. Mozart and Beethoven wrote several.

**Converse, Frederick Shepherd** (1871–1940), American composer. Works incl. 6 symphonies, symphonic poems, chamber music, and several operas *eg The Pipe of Desire*.

**Conzert** (Ger.), *see* KONZERT.

**Cooke, Arnold** (1906– ), English composer. Pupil of Hindemith. Works incl. opera *Mary Barton* (after Mrs Gaskell), concertos for oboe, clarinet, violin and cello, 4 string quartets, piano and chamber music.

**Cooke, Deryck** (1919–76), English musicologist. Wrote successful 'performing version' of Mahler's unfinished 10th symphony.

**coperto** (It.), 'covered'. *Timpani coperto*, *see* TIMPANI.

**Copland, Aaron** (1900– ), American composer, conductor, pianist, lecturer, author. Born in Brooklyn, New York. Studied piano with Paul Wittgenstein, and composition with Rubin Goldmark and Nadia Boulanger. Has held various academic posts. Has worked tirelessly as champion of US and modern music. Though some works (*eg* piano sonata) are written in international abstract idiom, much of his music is identifiably 'American' *eg* in folk opera *The Tender Land* (1954) and ballets *Billy the Kid* (1938), *Rodeo* (1942) and

*Appalachian Spring* (1944). Other elements in work incl. Latin-American, in *El Salon Mexico* (1936), and jazz, in *Music for the Theatre* (1925). Orchestral works, containing his own special vein of poetry, incl. *Dance Symphony* (1925), piano concerto (1926), *Statements* (1935), *Outdoor Overture* (1938), *Quiet City* (1940), *Connotations* (1963) and *Music for a Great City* (1965). Author of several books on music.

**Coppélia,** ballet with music by Delibes, from story by Hoffmann. First perf. Paris, 1870.

**Coq d'or, Le,** *see* GOLDEN COCKEREL.

**cor** (Fr.), French horn, generally known simply as HORN.

**cor anglais,** *see* OBOE.

**coranto** (It.), *see* COURANTE.

**corda** (It.), string. *Una corda* (in piano music), 'one string', *ie* use left-hand pedal, which on grand piano normally shifts whole keyboard slightly to right, so that hammers can strike only 1 or 2 of 3 strings assigned to each note – thus reducing volume. On upright piano left-hand pedal produces similar result by bringing hammers nearer keys. Another system (now obsolete) damped strings with strip of felt. *Tre corde* (3 strings) or *tutte le corde* (all the strings) is indication that left-hand pedal is to be released. *See* MUTE.

**corda vuota** (It.), open string.

**corde** (Fr.), string. *Instruments à cordes* (or *cordes* alone), string instruments. *Quatuor à cordes*, string quartet. *Corde à jour*, *corde à vide*, open string. *À la corde*, play with bow kept on string, so playing *legato*.

**cor de basset** (Fr.), basset horn.

**cor de chasse** (Fr.), lit. 'hunting horn', 18th cent. name for French HORN.

**Corelli, Arcangelo** (1653–1713), Italian violinist, composer. Studied at Bologna and travelled as young man in Germany. Returned to Rome at around age of 30, and there enjoyed patronage of Cardinal Pietro Ottoboni. Had European reputation as violinist and composer. In trio sonatas *(sonate da chiesa* and *sonate da camera)*, solo violin sonatas and *concerti grossi* he not only showed talent for vivacious and intimate expression but also helped to establish characteristic style for violin both as solo instrument and in orchestra.

**Coriolan** *(Coriolanus)*, play by H.J. von Collin, with overture by Beethoven (op 62, 1807).

**cori spezzati** (It.), 'divided choirs'. Term used of antiphonal choruses which are characteristic feature of Venetian church music of 16th, 17th cents.

**Corkine, William** (*fl* 15th–16th cents.), English composer. Wrote lute-songs and instrumental pieces.

**cornamusa** (It.), bagpipe.

**cornamuto torto** (It.), Krummhorn.

**Cornelius, Peter** (1824–74), German composer, writer on music. Close friend of Liszt and Wagner, chief representatives of the 'new music' which he championed in his literary works. Compositions incl. songs and part-songs, and 3 operas *The Barber of Baghdad* (1858), *The Cid* (1865) and *Gunlöd* (completed by Carl Hoffbauer, 1891).

**cornemuse** (Fr.), bagpipe.

**cornet,** (1) brass instrument with 3 valves (Fr., *cornet à pistons*, *piston*; Ger., *Kornett*; It., *cornetta*), dating from early 19th cent. Written compass is from F sharp below middle C to C above treble clef. Normally built in B flat (*see* TRANSPOSING INSTRUMENTS), in which case sounding compass is tone lower than written compass. By using larger CROOK or by turning switch on instrument its pitch can be lowered semitone, and it becomes cornet in A. Cornet in E flat is used in brass bands, with sounding compass 3 semitones higher than written compass.

Cornet is standard instrument in brass band and military band, where its flexibility makes it esp. suitable for light and rapid passages. Not normal member of symphony orchestra outside France. Capable of producing very expressive tone in *cantabile* passages;

(2) organ stop with several ranks (*ie* with several pipes of different pitches for each note, cf. MIXTURE), very popular in 18th cent. for florid solos;

(3) = CORNETT.

**cornet à bouquin** (Fr.), obsolete cornett.

**cornet à pistons** (Fr.), modern cornet.

**cornett** (Fr., *cornet à bouquin*; Ger., *Zink*; It., *cornetto*), wind instrument, entirely different from modern CORNET. Now obsolete, was used from Middle Ages up to 18th cent. Normal type was slightly curved and made of wood or ivory, with holes stopped by fingers, and cup-shaped mouthpiece. Made in several sizes, commonest having compass of 2 octaves from A below middle C, with possible extension upwards. Served as treble to trombone family, with which it was frequently associated. Seems to have had wide range of expression.

**cornetta** (It.), modern CORNET; *cornetta a chiavi*, key bugle; *cornetto*, obsolete CORNETT.

**Cornett-ton** (Ger.), pitch used by German *Stadtpfeifer* in early 18th cent. Prob. same as CHORTON.

**Cornish, William** *see* Cornyshe.

**corno** (It.), HORN.

**corno di bassetto** (It.), basset horn.

**Cornyshe** or **Cornish, William** (*c* 1468–1523), English playwright, composer. Wrote secular part-songs and antiphons.

**coro** (It.), choir, chorus; also used of body of instrumental players. *See also* CORI SPEZZATI.

**corona** (It., Lat., crown), PAUSE sign placed above note, so called because it resembles crown.

**Coronation Anthems,** 4 anthems written by Handel for coronation of George II in Westminster Abbey (1727). Most famous is *Zadok the Priest*.

**Coronation Concerto** (Ger., *Krönungskonzert*), name given to

Mozart's piano concerto in D major, K 537 (1788); he is said to have performed it at Frankfurt in 1790 on occasion of coronation of Leopold II.

**Coronation Mass** (Ger., *Krönungsmesse*), Mozart's Mass in C major, K 317 (1779); said to have been composed in commemoration of crowning of miraculous image of Virgin near Salzburg, *c* 1744.

**Coronation of Poppaea, The,** *see* INCORONAZIONE DI POPPEA, L'.

**Correa de Arauxo, Francisco** (*c* 1576–1663), Spanish organist, composer. His *Facultad orgánica* (1626) contains 69 compositions for organ.

**Corregidor, Der** (Ger., *The Corregidor*), opera by Hugo Wolf, libretto by R. Mayreder (based on Alarcón's story *The Three-cornered Hat*). First perf. Mannheim, 1896. Wolf's only completed opera.

**corrente** (It.), *see* COURANTE.

**Corrette, Michel** (1709–95), French organist, composer. Works incl. instrumental, church and stage music. Also published instrumental and singing tutors, and anthology of violin solos.

**cortamente,** 'shortly'.

**Cortot, Alfred Denis** (1877–1962), Swiss-born pianist, conductor, resident in France. Conducted early performances of Wagner in France. On piano, famed for performances of Chopin. Played piano trios with Thibaud and Casals for many years.

**Così fan tutte** ('Thus do all women') opera by Mozart, libretto by L. da Ponte. First perf. Vienna 1790. Subtitle is *La scuola degli amante* ('The School for Lovers'). Story concerns woman's fickleness, subject of wager between 2 enamoured officers and philosopher Don Alfonso.

**Costa, Michael Andrew Agnus** (orig. Michele Andreas Agnus) (1808–84), Italian-born conductor, composer. Works incl. several operas. Came to Britain in 1829, rapidly establishing reputation as conductor. Knighted 1869.

**Costeley, Guillaume** (*c* 1531–1606), French composer, organist. Worked at French court. Reputation rests on *c* 100 polyphonic *chansons*; also wrote some keyboard music.

**Cosyn, Benjamin** (*fl* 17th cent), English organist, composer. His Ms collection of virginal music contains mostly music by Bull, Gibbons and himself.

**Cotton, John** or **Johannes Cotto** (*fl* early 12th cent.), theorist, poss. an English monk in Normandy, or a monk known as Johannes Affligemensis at a monastery near Brussels. His treatise *De musica cum tonario* contains a section on organum.

**coulé** (Fr.), *see* SLIDE (1).

**counterpoint** (adj., *contrapuntal*), combination of 2 or more independent parts in harmonious texture. Hence word also refers to contrapuntal part added to existing part, *ie* part B is said to be counterpoint to part A. Independence is of 2 kinds, melodic and rhythmic. Second is more forceful than first, though rhythmic independence without melodic characterization is not sufficient to produce counterpoint.

Combination of 2 or more melodic lines results in series of related chords. Relationship between notes of each individual chord and relationship between chords themselves constitutes HARMONY. Counterpoint is therefore inseparable from harmony; but as it is poss. to write series of chords without melodic or rhythmic interest in every individual part, harmony can exist without counterpoint. Conventions of harmony, however, are historically product of counterpoint (*see* CHORD), *ie* certain conventions of contrapuntal writing resulted in harmonic relationships which became so familiar that they were stereotyped and came to exist in own right. Harmony is therefore crystallization of counterpoint.

In earliest known music in parts (late 9th cent.) there is no rhythmic and hardly any melodic independence (*see* ORGANUM). By 13th cent., art of counterpoint had fully matured (*see* MOTET), though music without independence in parts still survived. In 14th cent., new rhythmic freedom was established (following abandonment of RHYTHMIC MODES), and in 15th, use of IMITATION developed (already familiar in CANON), which became integral part of 16th-cent. writing and formed basis of 17th-cent. fugue. By 18th cent., conception of tonality (or key relationships) as vital element in structure of piece of music influenced contrapuntal writing, without weakening its basic principles. This is also true of 19th-cent. music. Present cent. has seen marked tendency to free counterpoint from dependence on traditional harmony, allowing it to develop on own lines, so creating new harmonic relationships and establishing new harmonic conventions.

Some forms of composition, *eg* canon and fugue, are by their very nature contrapuntal. Others, such as 16th-cent. motet and madrigal, may be wholly contrapuntal in conception; but it is very common to find contrasts between truly contrapuntal sections (called polyphonic, *see* POLYPHONY) and others virtually without melodic or rhythmic independence in parts (called homophonic, *see* HOMOPHONY). Counterpoint is not in fact a musical form, but a way of organizing musical material, to be used when desired.

Whatever style or idiom is being employed, contrapuntal thinking is necessity for any serious composer. Teaching of counterpoint was systematized in 16th cent., and developed notably by Fux in *Gradus ad Parnassum* (1725) which established 5 'species' of 'strict' counterpoint. Later practice ('free' counterpoint) has been to study methods of great masters rather than to obey arbitrary rules (terms 'strict' and 'free' being relative).

If counterpoint is so written that parts can be interchanged, *eg* bass becomes treble and vice versa, it is called invertible. Invertible counterpoint between 2 parts is called DOUBLE COUNTERPOINT. Where 3 parts can be so interchanged, each making suitable bass for other 2, result is triple counterpoint. Similarly with 4 or more interchangeable parts (quadruple, quintuple counterpoint, *etc*), possible permutations increasing rapidly according to number of parts.

**countersubject,** melody designed as counterpoint to subject (principal theme) of FUGUE. First appears as continuation (in same part) of first statement of subject, thus normally occurring in association with ANSWER (second statement of subject, in different part); thus it is both continuation of subject and contrast to it. Association continues regularly until EXPOSITION is complete. Later appearances of countersubject in association with subject are not determined by any hard or fast principle but depend on inclination of composer. Countersubject may also supply thematic material for episodes or intermediate passages which occur between recurrent appearances of subject. Generally designed to make DOUBLE COUNTERPOINT with subject.

Countersubject is not essential in fugue; several of Bach's are without one. Equally there may be more than one countersubject. Cases occur where countersubject enters simultaneously with subject at beginning of fugue; here countersubject has characteristics of subject, so that fugue of this kind may be described as fugue with 2 subjects.

**counter-tenor,** highest male voice (also known as alto), produced by using head register. Used widely in late 17th cent.; use revived in 20th.

**country dance,** name given to traditional English dance of popular origin. *See also* CONTREDANSE.

**coup d'archet** (Fr.), stroke of bow, bowing.

**coup de langue** (Fr.), tonguing.

**Couperin,** French family of musicians whose talent stretched over 5 generations, from 17th to 19th cent. All worked in Paris, and at least 9 were organists at Church of St Gervais. Most famous was 2nd generation's François, known as 'Couperin le Grand'.

**Louis Couperin** (*c* 1626–61), viol player, organist. Pupil of Chambonnières. One of most accomplished keyboard composers of his time; also one of first French composers to write solo and trio sonatas for strings. His brothers Charles (1638–78/9) and François (1630–*c* 1700) were organists, and François was also violinist.

**François Couperin ['le Grand']** (1668–1733) was, like father Charles, organist at St Gervais, and in 1693 became organist to king at Versailles. Excelled as composer of keyboard music, works for instrumental ensemble, secular songs and church music. Harpsichord music, arranged in *ordres* (or suites) is model of refinement, skill and charm; many pieces bear fanciful titles (Couperin called them portraits) which suggest romantic imagination, disciplined, however, by scrupulous regard for formal symmetry.

Music also shows great talent for description, irony and imitation. Church music is noble, dignified and profoundly impressive. Also published *L'Art de toucher le clavecin* (1716), valuable both for evidence of contemporary practice and its grace and humour.

Other notable members of family incl. **Armand-Louis Couperin** (1725–89), who had great reputation as organist, playing at St Gervais, and for king at Versailles; and **Gervais-Francois**

**Couperin** (1759–1826), who was also organist at St Gervais, and wrote variations on Revolutionary song 'Ah, ça ira' (1790).

**coupler,** device used to augment resources of organ. Couplers, which are controlled by stops or tabs, are of 3 kinds:

(1) octave and sub-octave couplers, which automatically double in octave above or below any note played;

(2) manual couplers, which enable player to combine resources of 2 manuals. These couplers also exist as octave and sub-octave couplers;

(3) pedal couplers (Fr., *tirasses*), which operate in similar way to manual couplers, *eg* Choir to Pedal coupler makes available on pedals any stops drawn on Choir manual.

**couplet,** (1) same as DUPLET;

(2) two-note slur, *ie* 2 notes of equal value slurred together; 2nd note should be slightly curtailed in playing;

(3) precursor of episode in RONDO (found esp. in works by Couperin).

**courante** (Fr.; It., *coranto, corrente*), short for *danse courante*, running dance. Lively dance in triple time. Originated in 16th cent.; immensely popular in 17th, 18th cents., becoming regular member of SUITE.

**Courvoisier, Walter** (1875–1931), Swiss composer, orig. a surgeon. Works incl. operas *Lancelot und Elaine* (1917) and *Die Krähen* (1921), choral, orchestral, chamber and piano music, and songs.

**Coussemaker, Charles Edmond Henri de** (1805–76), French musicologist, lawyer. His historical works and transcriptions of medieval music have long since been superseded, though his collection of *Scriptores* is still useful.

**Cousser, Johann Sigmund,** *see* KUSSER.

**Covent Garden,** London opera house, properly, The Royal Opera House, Covent Garden. Before 1892, called Royal Italian Opera House. Has own opera and ballet companies. Musical directors of Opera have incl. Solti and Colin Davis. Two previous theatres on site (first estab. 1732).

**cow bell,** as used in orchestra, square bell struck with stick to emphasize beat.

**Cowell, Henry Dixon** (1897–1965), American composer, pianist, teacher, writer on music. One of 20th cent.'s great experimenters. As teenager, developed technique employing NOTE-CLUSTERS, played by striking keyboard with fist, forearm, or elbow. Also pioneer of sounds produced by plucking or stroking strings inside piano. Invented RHYTHMICON (with Lev Thérémin). Had very broad variety of sources and methods, and composed prolifically. Works incl. 19 symphonies, piano concerto (1929) and other experimental piano works, series of pieces for various instrumental groupings called *Hymn and Fuguing Tune*, pieces with bizarre or synthesized titles (*Continuations, Synchrony, Tocanta, etc*), 2 ballets (*The Building of Banba, Atlantis*), opera *O'Higgins of Chile*, 5 string quartets, and other chamber music.

**Cowen, Frederic Hymen** (1852–1935), English composer,

conductor, b. Jamaica. Compositions incl. 4 operas, 7 oratorios, several cantatas, 6 symphonies, 4 overtures, piano concerto, orchestral suites, and nearly 300 songs.

**Cox and Box,** opera by Sullivan, libretto by F.C. Burnand (from J.M. Morton's farce, *Box and Cox*). First perf. London, 1867.

**crab canon,** *see* CANON, RETROGRADE MOTION.

**Cracovienne** (Fr.), *see* KRAKOWIAK.

**Craft, Robert** (1923– ), American conductor, writer. Closely associated with Stravinsky during composer's latter years. Published conversations and journal of his travels with Stravinsky, which give many valuable insights.

**crash cymbal,** suspended cymbal struck with stick to produce brilliant crash.

**Creation, The** (Ger., *Die Schöpfung*), oratorio by Haydn (1798). German text by Baron van Swieten is translation of English libretto selected from Book of Genesis and Milton's *Paradise Lost*.

**'Creation' Mass** (Ger., *Schöpfungsmesse*), mass in B flat major by Haydn (1801), no 11 in complete ed., no 4 in Novello's ed. Nickname derives from resemblance of passage to one in *The Creation*.

**Creatures of Prometheus, The,** *see* PROMETHEUS.

**crécelle** (Fr.), rattle.

**Crecquillon, Thomas** (*c* 1490–1557), Flemish composer. Worked for a time in service of Charles V. Prolific composer of *chansons*, 4-part motets, and other church music.

**credo** (Lat.), initial word of Creed in RC Mass – in full, 'Credo in unum' (I believe in one God).

**crescendo** (It.), 'increasing', *ie* getting louder. Abbrev. is *cresc.* Opposite is *decrescendo* or *diminuendo*.

**crescendo pedal,** pedal on organ which when applied adds successively more and more stops.

**Creston, Paul,** orig. Joseph Guttoveggio (1906– ), American composer, of Italian origin. Works incl. 5 symphonies, concertos and other works for variety of unusual instruments (*eg* marimba, accordion, trombone and harp), choral works, piano pieces and songs.

**Cries of London,** some of the traditional melodies to which itinerant traders in London proclaimed their wares were arranged as rounds or catches by early 17th-cent. composers. More elaborate settings, in form of fantasias for voices and instruments, were made by Weelkes, Gibbons, Dering, and others.

**Cristofori, Bartolomeo** (1655–1731), *see* PIANOFORTE.

**criticism, musical,** the reasoned discussion, in a periodical or book, of public performances or compositions, new or old. Published criticism first appeared in Germany in the early 18th cent. with Mattheson's periodical *Critica Musica* (1722–5), which was followed by musical periodicals in various other countries, their number and variety increasing throughout the 19th cent.; a surviving example is the *Musical Times* (1844) in Britain. Musical criticism in daily newspapers did not start until the 19th cent.; in Britain, *The Times* seems to have been the first newspaper to have employed a music critic. In Vienna Eduard Hanslick, active as a critic from 1848, came to exercise a strong influence on opinion, particularly through his support of Brahms and opposition to Wagner.

The function of the critic is to assess value, to maintain standards, to sift, define and educate, and to say, simply, what it was like to be listening to music at a certain time. The assessment of performance, however valuable to the performers and however instructive for the public, is clearly less important than the assessment of compositions, since creative art endures and performances do not. In both, the essential requisites are the widest possible knowledge, a cultivated taste, and complete sincerity. Attempts have been made to reduce criticism to an exact science. In so far as every critic is an individual human being, with his own private reactions to what he hears, this is clearly an impossibility. Even though there is often general agreement about the value of particular compositions or particular composers, there have been, and still are, many cases of individual critics taking a markedly different line from their colleagues; and there are also plenty of examples of judgements almost universally accepted in one age and rejected in the next.

Criticism is also part of the function of the historian. This has often been denied, on the ground that history is an objective science, concerned with what has happened and not with its value. On the other hand, since all history is of necessity selective, there must be some criterion for selection; and it is difficult to see how selection can operate without an assessment of values.

From the early 19th cent. musical criticism has been a profession in itself. However, several composers have also been active as critics, including Weber, Schumann, Berlioz, Liszt, Wagner, Wolf, and Debussy. At the same time composers rarely make the best critics, probably because their affinities with certain kinds of music, however unconscious, are particularly strong.

**Croce, Giovanni** (*c* 1557–1609), Italian composer. Wrote Masses, motets and other church music, and several books of madrigals.

**Croche, Monsieur,** imaginary person invented by Debussy as mouthpiece for his own critical opinions: see *Monsieur Croche the Dilettante Hater* (1927).

**croche** (Fr.), quaver (word for crotchet is *noire*). *Double croche*, semiquaver.

**Croft, William** (1678–1727), English composer. Organist of Chapel Royal (1704), Westminster Abbey (1708). Wrote keyboard music, music for stage, odes, anthems, setting of Burial Service (still used), and famous hymn-tune 'St Anne' ('O God our Help in Ages Past').

**croma** (It.), quaver. Hence adj. *cromatico* not only means 'chromatic', but in 16th cent. was applied to composition making liberal use of black notes.

**cromorne** (Fr.), Krummhorn.

**crook,** piece of tubing inserted into brass instrument between mouthpiece and body of instrument. Pitch of instrument varies according to size of crook. Thus horn with A crook will sound major third higher than with F crook. In 18th, early 19th cents., before introduction of valves or pistons on horns and trumpets, use of crooks was necessary in order to enable these instruments to be played in variety of keys. Crooks are still necessary in certain circumstances. *See* TRANSPOSING INSTRUMENTS.

**crooning,** soft, sentimental style of singing through microphone, supported by dance band. Popular in 1930s and 1940s.

**Cross, Joan** (1900– ), English soprano. Sang at Sadler's Wells and Covent Garden and was founder member of English Opera Group. One of leading British opera singers of 20th cent. Created roles in several of Britten's operas.

**cross-fingering,** use of fingering (on woodwind instruments) other than that using successive fingers while playing scale.

**Crosse, Gordon** (1937– ), English composer. Works incl. works for children (*eg Meet my Folks!* and *Ahmet the Woodseller*), *Changes* (inspired by bell-ringing), *Symphonies* for chamber orchestra, and 3 operas, *Purgatory*, *The Grace of Todd* and *The Story of Vasco*.

**cross relation,** US equivalent of FALSE RELATION.

**cross rhythms,** conflicting rhythmic patterns performed simultaneously.

**crot,** *see* CRWTH.

**crotales,** (1) set of small bells tuned to chromatic scale and played with sticks;
(2) *cymbales antiques*; *see* CYMBALS (3).

**Crotch, William** (1775–1847), English composer, organist. Child prodigy. Professor at Oxford from 1797. Works incl. oratorios, anthems and keyboard works.

**crotchet** (US, quarter-note; Fr., *noire*; *Ger*., *Viertel*; It., *semiminima*), time-value, fourth part of semibreve and twice value of quaver. Represented by sign

♩

Crotchet rest is indicated by 2 different signs:

𝄽 𝄾

**crowd,** *see* CRWTH.

**Crüger, Johannes** (1598–1662), German composer, theorist. Published theoretical works and several collections of Lutheran hymns with music. Many of his settings are still in use, *eg* 'Nun danket alle Gott' ('Now thank we all our God') and 'Jesu, meine Freude' ('Jesu, joy and treasure').

**cruit,** *see* CRWTH.

**Crumb, George** (1929– ), American composer. Works incl. *Ancient Voices of Children* for soprano and instrumental ensemble, and series of piano pieces entitled *Makrokosmos* in tribute to Bartók.

**crwth** (Welsh; Irish, *crot*, *cruit*; Eng., crowd; Lat., *chorus*), bowed lyre. Popular in Middle Ages, and survived in Wales up to 19th cent.

Later form had 4 strings passing over fingerboard (like violin), with 2 additional unstopped strings at side.

**csárdás,** Hungarian dance, consisting of slow, melancholy section *(lassú)* followed by fast, vivacious section *(friss)*.

**cuckoo,** short pipe with single finger-hole, giving 2 notes a major third apart in imitation of cuckoo's call.

**Cui, César Antonovich** (1835–1918), Russian-born composer, son of French father and Lithuanian mother. Army engineer by profession. Friend of Balakirev, and member of The FIVE, though own compositions were neither strongly nationalist nor particularly distinguished. Wrote several operas, *eg The Captive in the Caucasus*, *Mam'zelle Fifi*; completed Dargomizhsky's *The Stone Guest* and made one of several completions of Mussorgsky's *Sorochintsy Fair*.

**cuivre** (Fr.), brass. *Instruments de cuivre* (or *cuivres* alone), brass instruments.

**cuivré** (Fr.; Ger., *schmetternd*), 'brassy'. Indication to brass players to play with harsh, blaring tone.

**Cunning Little Vixen, The** (Czech, *Přihody Lišky Bystrousky*), opera by Janáček, libretto by R. Těsnohlídeck. First perf. Brno, 1924. Story mingles animals and humans; vixen is heroine.

**Cupid and Death,** masque by James Shirley, with music by Matthew Locke and Christopher Gibbons. First perf. London, 1653.

**cupo** (It.), dark, sombre.

**Curlew River,** first of Britten's 3 parables for church performance others being *The Burning Fiery Furnace* and *The Prodigal Son*. The work is based on Japanese Noh play, which W. Plomer's libretto transfers to English Fens. Story concerns search of mother (played by tenor) for her lost child. First perf. Orford church, Suffolk, 1964.

**curtain music** or **curtain tune,** same as ACT TUNE.

**curtall,** name given in 16th, 17th cents. to small bassoon. Larger form, roughly corresponding to modern bassoon, was called *double curtall*.

**Curwen, John** (1816–80), *see* TONIC SOL-FA.

**Curzon, Clifford** (1907– ), English pianist. Pupil of Schnabel, Wanda Landowska and Nadia Boulanger. Esp. notable for performances of Mozart, Beethoven, Schubert and Brahms. Knighted 1977.

**custos,** *see* DIRECT.

**Cuzzoni, Francesca** (1700–70), Italian operatic soprano. Sang in Handel's operas in London, where she achieved great popularity. Involved in notorious rivalry with Faustina Bordoni.

**cyclic,** adj. implying some unity between various sections or movts. of extended work, esp. unity arising from thematic connection. Cyclic Masses began to be written in 15th cent.; thematic association also occurs in 16th, 17th-cent. dance suites. Beethoven introduced it into symphonic music (in 5th symphony), and it was later developed by romantic composers.

**cymbals,** (1) early English name for chime-bells (Fr., *cymbales*; Ger., *Zimbeln*; It., *cymbala*);

(2) percussion instruments of great antiquity, still used in orchestra and military bands (Fr., *cymbales*; Ger., *Becken*; It., *piatti*, *cinelli*). Consist of 2 metal plates, held in hands and clashed together. There are 2 ways of using single cymbal: (a) hitting it with stick, hard or soft, in manner of gong, (b) performing roll on it with timpani or side-drum sticks. Cymbals can also be clashed rapidly together to produce persistent vibration. Range of dynamics is considerable, and can be further modified by using different sizes;

(3) small cymbals were used like castanets by dancers in ancient world (Fr., *cymbales antiques*); use revived by Berlioz in 'Queen Mab' scherzo of his *Roméo et Juliette* symphony.

**cymbalum, cymbalom, cymbalon,** alternative forms of CIMBALOM.

**Czar and Carpenter** (Ger., *Zar und Zimmermann*), opera by Lortzing, libretto by composer. Story concerns complications that ensue when Peter the Great disguises himself as carpenter. First perf. Leipzig, 1837.

**czardas,** *see* CSÁRDÁS.

**Czerny, Karl** (1791–1857), Austrian-born composer, son of Czech piano teacher. Taught by father and Beethoven. Earned great reputation as teacher (Liszt was his pupil). Prolific composer in every form, and arranged many works by others, but is now known only for technical studies, still in use.

# D

**d,** in TONIC SOL-FA d = *doh*, first note (or tonic) of major scale.

**D,** second note (or supertonic) of scale of C major (Eng., Ger.; Fr., *ré*; It., *re*). As abbrev. D. = discantus, doctor, dominant. D. Mus. or Mus. D. = Doctor of Music. *D.C.* = DA CAPO; *D.S.* = DAL SEGNO; *m.d.* = *mano destra, main droite* (right hand). D. is also symbol applied to Deutsch's numerical catalogue of Schubert's works.

**da** (It), of, from.

**da capo** (It.), lit. 'from the head', *ie* go back again to beginning of piece. Abbrev. is *D.C.* For *da capo* aria *see* ARIA.

**Daffner, Hugo** (1882–1941), German composer. Pupil of Reger. Works incl. 3 operas and 2 symphonies.

**Dafne,** the first known opera, music (not extant) by Peri, libretto by Rinuccini. First perf. Florence, 1597.

**Dahl, Viking** (1895– ), Swedish composer, critic. Works incl. opera *Sjömansvisa*, ballets, orchestral, chamber and piano music, and songs.

**Dalayrac, Nicolas,** orig. d'Alayrac (1753–1809), French composer. Wrote nearly 60 *opéras comiques*, *eg Tout pour l'amour* (based on *Romeo and Juliet*), *Deux Mots*. Also wrote set of string quartets.

**D'Albert,** *see* ALBERT.

**Dalby, Martin** (1942– ), Scottish composer. Works incl. symphony and other orchestral works, *Almost a Madrigal* (1977) for wind and percussion, and music for various combinations of voices and instruments.

**Dale, Benjamin James** (1885–1943), English composer. Made reputation with piano sonata in D minor (1902). Other works, romantic in style and finely crafted, incl. suite for viola and piano (1907) and cantata *Before the Paling of the Stars* (1912).

**Dalibor,** opera by Smetana, libretto by Joseph Wenzig (in German), translated into Czech by E. Spindler. First perf. Prague, 1868. One of Czechoslovakia's great national operas, story tells how Dalibor has been imprisoned as revolutionary, and how his beloved, Milada, tries to rescue him and is killed in the process.

**Dall'Abaco,** *see* ABACO.

**Dallam, Ralph** (d. 1673), English organ-builder. Built organs after Restoration, incl. St George's, Windsor.

**Dallam, Robert** (1602–65), English organ-builder. Built several organs before Civil War, incl. York Minster, St Paul's Cathedral and Durham Cathedral. He was prob. son of Thomas Dallam.

**Dallam, Thomas** (*fl* early 17th cent.), English organ-builder. Built organs for King's College, Cambridge (1606) and Worcester Cathedral (1613). Also built mechanical organ which Queen

Elizabeth sent as present (with Dallam as escort) to Sultan of Turkey.

**Dallapiccola, Luigi** (1904–75), Italian composer. Studied at Florence Conservatory, where later became professor. Profoundly impressed by music of Schoenberg, Berg and Webern. First Italian composer to adopt serial techniques, applying them to his fundamental Italian lyricism, which find outlet esp. in operas. Only received recognition he deserved after fall of fascist regime.

Works incl. anti-fascist *Canti di prigionia* (Songs of Captivity, 1941), *Sex Carmina Alcaei* (Six Songs of Alcaeus, 1944), dedicated to Webern, and operas *Il Prigioniero* (The Prisoner, 1950), expressing compassion for political prisoners, and *Ulisse* (1968). Though much of his music was written for voice, also wrote orchestral and instrumental works *eg Piccola musica notturna* (Little Night Music, 1944), *Dialoghi* for cello (1960), and canonic sonatina for piano.

**Dallery,** family of French organ-builders active in 18th cent.

**dal segno** (It.) 'from the sign', *ie* go back to point in music marked by sign 𝄋.

Abbrev. is *D.S.*

**Daman,** *see* DAMON.

**Dame Blanche, La** (Fr., *The White Lady*), opera by Boïeldieu, libretto by A.E. Scribe (adapted from Walter Scott's *Guy Mannering* and *The Monastery*). First perf. Paris, 1825.

**Damnation of Faust, The,** 'dramatic legend' or 'concert opera' for soloists, chorus and orchestra by Berlioz. Text is adaptation of Gérard de Nerval's French translation of Goethe's *Faust*, with additions by composer and A. Gandonnière. First perf. Paris, 1846. Sometimes staged as opera.

**Damoiselle élue, La** (*The Blessed Damozel*), cantata by Debussy (1887–8), based on French translation of Rossetti's poem.

**Damon** or **Daman, William** (*c* 1540–91), Walloon composer. Went to England *c* 1564, and was later in service of Queen Elizabeth. Published harmonizations of metrical psalm-tunes, and also wrote other church music.

**Damoreau, Laure Cynthie** (1801–63), French operatic soprano, known as La Cinti. First appeared at Paris Opéra in 1826. Taught singing at Paris Conservatoire (1834–56), and published *Méthode de chant*.

**damper,** piece of felt, glued to strip of wood, which covers piano string and prevents it from vibrating. *See* PIANOFORTE.

**Dämpfer** (Ger.), mute. *Mit Dämpfer*, with mute. *Dämpfer weg*, without mute.

**Damrosch, Leopold** (1832-85), German conductor, violinist, composer. Intimate friend of Wagner and Liszt. Moved to New York, where was active as conductor. Wrote many vocal and instrumental works. His sons, **Frank Heino Damrosch** (1859–1937) and **Walter Johannes Damrosch** (1862–1950), were also prominent conductors in New York; latter gave several US premières of Wagner, and wrote 5 operas himself.

**dance band,** band that plays for strict tempo dancing. Usually consists of brass section of trumpets and trombones, reed section of saxophones doubling clarinets, and rhythm section of piano, bass and drums.

**Dandrieu, Jean François** (1682–1738), French organist, composer. Wrote harpsichord, organ and chamber music.

**D'Anglebert,** *see* ANGLEBERT.

**Danican, François André,** *see* PHILIDOR.

**Daniel** or **Danyel, John** (1564–after 1625), English composer, brother of poet Samuel Daniel. Musician to Queen Anne (consort of James I) and to Charles I. Published *Songs for the Lute, Viol and Voice* (1606), incl. elaborate and pathetic setting, with chromatic harmonies, of 'Can doleful notes'.

**Danse macabre,** orchestral piece, op 40, by Saint-Saëns (1874), based on verses by Henri Cazalis, and quoting Dies Irae. Represents traditional idea of Death playing violin for dance of skeletons.

**Dante Sonata,** abbrev. of title of Liszt's one-movt. piano work, 'After a reading of Dante' (1837–9, rev. 1849).

**Dante Symphony,** orchestral work by Liszt (1857), with female chorus in final section. There are 2 movts., *Inferno* and *Purgatorio*, leading to *Magnificat*. Dedicated to Wagner.

**danza tedesca** (It.), 'German dance'; *see* TEDESCA, ALLEMANDE, DEUTSCHER TANZ.

**Danyel,** *see* DANIEL.

**Daphnis et Chloé,** ballet by Ravel, with choreography by Fokine and décor by Bakst. First perf. Paris, 1912. Work calls for chorus as well as orchestra. Two suites were subsequently arranged by composer for concert performance.

**Daphne,** opera by Richard Strauss, libretto by J. Gregor (based on classical legend). First perf. Dresden, 1938.

**Da Ponte,** *see* PONTE.

**Daquin, Louis Claude** (1694–1792), French organist, composer. Began as child prodigy; became organist at French Chapel Royal (1739). Wrote harpsichord music, incl. well known 'The Cuckoo'.

**Dardanus,** opera by Rameau, libretto by C.A.L. de La Bruère. First perf. Paris, 1739.

**D'Arezzo,** *see* GUIDO D'AREZZO.

**Dargomizhsky, Alexander Sergeievich** (1813–69), Russian composer. Largely self-taught, though encouraged by Glinka. Operas incl. *The Russalka* (1856) and *The Stone Guest* (1872, completed by Cui and orchestrated by Rimsky-Korsakov). Had considerable influence on nationalist school and Chaikovsky. Also wrote songs and 3 orchestral fantasias.

**Dart, Thurston** (1921–71), English harpsichordist, organist, conductor, scholar. Professor of music at Cambridge, then at London University. Travelled widely as solo harpsichordist, and was outstanding continuo player.

**Das,** for German titles beginning thus, see second word of title.

**Dauer** (Ger.), duration. *Dauernd*, 'enduring', *ie* lasting, continuing.

**Daughter of the Regiment, The** (Fr., *Fille du régiment*), opera by Donizetti, libretto by J.H.V. de Saint-Georges and J.F.A. Bayard. First perf. Paris, 1840.

**Dauprat, Louis François** (1781–1868), French hornist, composer. Wrote 5 horn concertos and other pieces for horn, and standard instruction book for horn.

**Dauvergne, Antoine** (1713–97), French violinist, composer. Master of king's chamber music, manager of Paris Opéra, and one of directors of Concert Spirituel. After writing much chamber music, turned to opera in 1752. His *Les Troqueurs* (1753) was said to be first French comic opera in style of Italian intermezzo, with recitative instead of dialogue.

**Davenant, William** (1606–68), English poet, dramatist. Wrote libretto of first English opera, *The Siege of Rhodes* (1656).

**David, Félicien César** (1810–76), French composer. Works incl. 2 symphonies, 24 string quintets and several operas. Made reputation with *Le Désert* for chorus and orchestra (1844), notable for oriental colouring.

**David, Ferdinand** (1810–73), German composer, violinist. Pupil of Spohr and friend of Mendelssohn. Pupils incl. Joachim. Compositions incl. 5 violin concertos. Wrote standard violin tutors.

**David, Johann Nepomuk** (1895–1977), Austrian composer, organist, writer. Works incl. 8 symphonies and other orchestral pieces, 2 violin concertos, *Requiem Chorale* for soloists, chorus and orchestra, and chamber and organ music.

**Davidov, Karl** (1838–89), Russian composer, cellist. Director of St Petersburg Conservatoire (1876–86). Works incl. 4 cello concertos.

**Davidovsky, Mario** (1934– ), Argentinian composer. Pupil of Copland. Noted for electronic music, incl. series of studies called *Synchronisms* (or *Sincronismi*). Has also written works for chamber ensemble.

**Davidsbündler** (Ger., Members of the League of David), imaginary association invented by Schumann to fight against Philistines in music. 'Marche des Davidsbündler contre les Philistins' occurs in *Carnaval*, op 9, and he also wrote 18 dances entitled *Davidsbündlertänze*, op 6 (1837).

**Davies, Fanny** (1861–1934), English pianist. Pupil of Clara Schumann. Excelled in music of Schumann and Brahms, latter of whom she knew well, but also played much early keyboard music.

**Davies, Henry Walford** (1869–1941), English organist, composer. Held various academic and organist's posts. Master of the King's Musick (1934–41); knighted 1922. Works incl. several for chorus and orchestra written for festivals, *eg Everyman* (1904), and *Solemn Melody* for organ and strings (1908).

**Davies, Peter Maxwell** (1934– ), English composer. With Birtwistle, Goehr and others, became one of 'Manchester School'. Also studied in Italy (with Petrassi) and US (with Roger Sessions). Taught at Cirencester Grammar School (1959–62), writing *O Magnum Mysterium* for school choir and orchestra. Formed own ensemble. Pierrot Players, later renamed Fires of London. Music is greatly influenced by medieval and Renaissance techniques, which he employs in modern context, often with keen sense of parody. Works incl. opera *Taverner* (based on life of 16th-cent. composer and heretic), 2 symphonies, 2 fantasies on Taverner's *In Nomine*, *Prolation* and *Worldes Blis* for orchestra, *St Michael Sonata* for wind ensemble, *St Thomas Wake* (foxtrot for orchestra). Many works contain strong elements of music theatre, *eg Eight Songs for a Mad King* for voice and chamber ensemble. Latterly has been inspired by Orkney islands, resulting in works such as *From Stone to Thorn* for soprano and chamber ensemble, and operas *The Martyrdom of St Magnus* and *The Lighthouse* (to texts by Orkney poet George Mackay Brown).

**Davis, Colin** (1927– ), English conductor. Musical director of Sadler's Wells (1961–5), chief conductor of B.B.C. Symphony Orchestra (1967–71), musical director of Royal Opera House, Covent Garden (from 1971). Esp. associated with music of Mozart, Berlioz and Tippett. Knighted 1978.

**Davis, Miles** (1926– ), black American jazz trumpeter, flugelhorn player. Began as disciple of Charlie Parker and soon developed into one of major and most individual figures in modern jazz. Much of his playing is cool, melancholy and muted, though not exclusively so. Recordings incl. *Sketches of Spain*.

**Davison, Archibald Thomson** (1883–1961), American conductor, musicologist. Professor of music at Harvard (1940–54). Publications incl. *Choral Conducting* (1940), *The Technique of Choral Composition* (1945), and *Historical Anthology of Music* (with W. Apel, 2 vols., 1946, 1950).

**Davy, Richard** (*fl* late 15th, early 16th cents.), English composer. Church music incl. Passion, Magnificat and antiphons.

**Daza, Esteban** (*fl* 16th cent.), Spanish lutenist. Published collection (1576) of fantasies for *vihuela*, arrangements of motets, madrigals and *villancicos* for voice and *vihuela*.

**D.C.,** abbrev. of DA CAPO.

**dead march,** funeral march, esp. that in Handel's oratorio *Saul*.

**Death and the Maiden** (Ger., *Der Tod und das Mädchen*), song by Schubert (1817) to words by M. Claudins. Also nickname of Schubert's D minor string quartet: slow movt. uses song as subject for variations.

**Death and Transfiguration** (Ger., *Tod und Verklärung*), symphonic poem by Richard Strauss, op 24 (1889).

**Death in Venice,** opera by Benjamin Britten, libretto by M. Piper (based on story by Thomas Mann). First perf. Aldeburgh Festival, 1973.

**De Bériot,** *see* BÉRIOT.

**debile, debole** (It.), **débile** (Fr.), weak.

**Debora e Jaele** (It., *Deborah and Jael*), opera by Pizzetti, libretto by composer. First perf. Milan, 1922. Considered the finest of Pizzetti's music dramas.

**Debussy, Claude Achille** (1862–1918), French composer. Born near Paris. Received piano lessons from age of 8. Entered Paris Conservatoire (1873). Worked in Russia for 2 years. Won *Prix de Rome* (1884) with 'lyric scene' *L'Enfant prodigue*, which, with *La Damoiselle élue* (1888), shows influence of Massenet. More individual style developed through *Printemps* (1886), string quartet (1893) and orchestral *Prélude à l'après-midi d'un faune* (1894, illustrating Mallarmé's poem). Married dressmaker Rosalie (Lili) Texier (1899), but left her 5 years later. Became music critic for *Revue Blanche* (1901); his criticism, though sometimes prejudiced, is frank and witty.

Kaleidoscopic harmonies and shifting tone-colours of Debussy's music, *eg* in 3 orchestral *Nocturnes* (1899), are counterpart of elusive style of impressionist painters and symbolist poets. Impressionism became ruling principle of his music, *eg La Mer* (1905) and *Images* (1906–12) for orchestra, and opera *Pelléas et Mélisande* (1902). Latter is setting of Maeterlinck's play and represents reaction to Wagnerism. Same style is found in songs and piano music (usually with picturesque titles), in which he discovered sonorities disregarded by previous composers. Despite its power of suggestion, his music is not vague but shows precise and methodical workmanship and responds to absolute clarity of performance. His late chamber works show laconic style, and suggest beginning of new phase. Died of cancer in 1918.

Principal compositions:

(1) Orchestra: *Printemps* (1886); *Prélude à l'après-midi d'un faune* (1894); *Nocturnes* (1899); *La Mer* (1905); *Images* (1912);

(2) Chamber music: string quartet (1893); cello sonata (1915); sonata for flute, viola and harp (1915); violin sonata (1916–17);

(3) Piano: *Suite bergamasque* (1905); *Pour le piano* (1901); *Estampes* (1903); *Images* (1905 and 1907); *Children's Corner* (1908); *Preludes* (book i, 1910; book ii, 1913); *Études* (1915); *En blanc et noir* for 2 pianos (1915);

(4) Choral works: *L'Enfant prodigue* (1884); *La Damoiselle élue* (1888); *Le Martyre de Saint Sébastien* (1911);

(5) Opera: *Pelléas et Mélisande* (1902);

(6) Songs: more than 50.

**decani** (Lat.), lit. 'of the dean'; *see* CANTOR.

**deceptive cadence,** same as interrupted CADENCE.

**déchant** (Fr.), descant.

**décidé** (Fr.), lit. 'decided', *ie* with decision, firmly.

**decimette,** piece for 10 instruments or voices.

**deciso** (It.), same as DÉCIDÉ.

**declamando, declamato** (It.), lit. 'declaiming', 'declaimed', *ie* in declamatory style.

**decrescendo** (It.), 'decreasing', *ie* getting softer, opposite of *crescendo*. Abbrev. is *decresc.*

**Dedekind, Constantin Christian** (1628–1715), German poet, composer. Wrote many sacred and secular songs, and sacred oratorios for voice and continuo.

**Deering,** *see* DERING.

**De Falla,** *see* FALLA.

**Defesch, William** (1687–1761), Flemish composer. Dismissed from post in Antwerp, came to London *c* 1732. Works incl. oratorio, concertos, chamber music, and cello sonatas.

**degree,** position of note in given scale (major or minor) is classified by its degree, *eg* in scale of C major, C is 1st degree, D 2nd degree, E 3rd degree *(etc)* of scale, until 1st degree (C above) is reached. Alternative terms for 1st to 7th degrees are TONIC, SUPERTONIC, MEDIANT, SUBDOMINANT, DOMINANT, SUBMEDIANT, LEADING-NOTE. *See also* TONIC SOL-FA.

**Dehn, Siegfried Wilhelm** (1799–1858), German musicologist, teacher. Edited many works of 16th and 17th cents., as well as several works of Bach. Theoretical works incl. books on harmony and counterpoint. Pupils incl. Glinka, Cornelius, and Anton Rubinstein.

**dehors, en** (Fr.), lit. 'outside'. Instruction to emphasize melody or some other aspect of piece, so that it stands out from surroundings.

**Deidamia,** opera by Handel, libretto by P.A. Rolli. First perf. London, 1741. Handel's last opera, apparently intended to deflate ironically the tradition of *opera seria* that had served Handel throughout his career.

**Deiters, Hermann** (1883–1907), German writer of music. Edited 3rd and 4th editions of Jahn's life of Mozart, and translated and revised Thayer's life of Beethoven.

**De Koven,** *see* KOVEN.

**Delannoy, Marcel François Georges** (1898–1962), French composer. Mainly self-taught. Works incl. several ballets and operas incl. *Le Poirier de misère* (1927), *Puck* (1949) and ballet-cantata *Le fou de la dame*.

**Delibes, Clément Philibert Léo** (1836–91), French composer. Pupil of Adam. Held various opera and organist posts; professor of composition at Paris Conservatoire from 1881. Works incl. operas *Le Roi l'a dit* (1873) and *Lakmé* (1883), and ballets *Coppélia* (1870) and *Sylvia* (1876), containing charming light music and colouring.

**delicato** (It.), delicate; *delicatamente*, delicately.

**délié** (Fr.), lit. 'untied', *ie* (1) staccato; (2) lightly, easily.

**Delius, Frederick** (1862-1934), English composer of German parentage. Born in Bradford; son of wool-merchant. Migrated to Florida as orange-planter (1884) but soon gave it up for music.

In 1886 went to study in Leipzig, where met Grieg and Sinding. Settled permanently in France in 1889. In Paris met Strindberg, Gaugin, Florent Schmitt and Ravel, and married artist Jelka Rosen. Many of his compositions were first performed in Germany. Took some time to become known in Britain; growth of popularity there was very largely due to Sir Thomas Beecham's enthusiasm. In later years Delius became blind and paralysed, but with assistance of Eric

Fenby managed to dictate several compositions before his death at home at Grez-sur-Loing near Fontainebleau.

Though early works were influenced by Grieg, music falls into no ready-made category. Marked esp. by luscious use of shifting chromatic harmonies and by style which prefers rhapsody to calculated construction; basis of melodic style is, however, diatonic, and often shows affinity with folk song. Like many romantic composers of period, he demands extravagantly large orchestra, which he used often with deeply poetic feeling for nature, as in *A Mass of Life* (text from Nietzsche's *Also Sprach Zarathustra*) and orchestral interludes of opera *A Village Romeo and Juliet*, though some of the climaxes are coarse and overloaded. Music is perhaps most characteristic when intimate, but is also frequently marked by robust vigour.

Principal compositions:

(1) Orchestra: *Over the hills and far away* (1895); piano concerto (1897, rev. 1906); *Paris* (1899); *Appalachia* (1896, rev. with chorus 1902); *Brigg Fair* (1907); *In a Summer Garden* (1908); *On Hearing the First Cuckoo in Spring* and *Summer Night on the River* (1913); *North Country Sketches* (1914); concerto for violin and cello (1916); violin concerto (1916); *Eventyr* (1917); cello concerto (1921);

(2) Choral works: *Sea-Drift* (1903); *A Mass of Life* (1905); *Songs of Sunset* (1907); *Song of the High Hills* (1912); *Requiem* (1916, on words by Nietzsche); *Songs of Farewell* (1930);

(3) Operas: *Irmelin* (1892); *Koanga* (1897); *A Village Romeo and Juliet* (1901); *Fennimore and Gerda* (1910);

(4) Chamber music: 3 violin sonatas; cello sonata; 2 string quartets.

**Deller, Alfred George** (1912–79), English counter-tenor. Has done much for revival of late 17th-cent. English music, and use of counter-tenor voice. Has also specialized in early 17th-cent. lute-songs, and works of Handel. Britten wrote role of Oberon for him in *A Midsummer Night's Dream*.

**Dello Joio, Norman** (1913– ), American composer, pianist, organist. Pupil of Hindemith. Works incl. operas (2 on St Joan), ballets, incidental music, *New York Profiles* (1949) and *Colonial Variations* (1976) for orchestra, clarinet concerto, *Proud Music of the Storm* (1967) for organ, brass and chorus, choral, chamber and piano music, and songs.

**Del Mar, Norman** (1919– ), English conductor. Founded Chelsea Symphony Orchestra (1944). Has held various posts incl. conductor of B.B.C. Scottish Symphony Orchestra (1960–65). Now guest conductor of leading orchestras.

**Delvincourt, Claude** (1888–1954), French composer. Director of Paris Conservatoire from 1941. Works, notable for capacity for humour and vivid colouring, incl. oriental ballet *L'Offrande à Siva*, comic opera *La femme à barbe*, chamber music and songs.

**démancher** (Fr.), lit. 'to un-neck', *ie* to SHIFT (Fr., *manche* = neck of stringed instrument).

**Demeur, Anne Arsène** (1824–92), French operatic soprano. Created role of Dido in Berlioz's *The Trojans*.

**demi-cadence,** imperfect CADENCE.

**demi-jeu** (Fr.), lit 'half-play', *ie* play at half power on organ, harmonium, *etc*.

**demi-pause** (Fr.), 'half-rest', *ie* minim rest.

**demisemiquaver** (Fr., *triple croche*; Ger., *Zweiunddreissigstel*; It., *biscroma*; US, thirty-second note), half a semiquaver, or 1/32 of semibreve. Single demisemiquaver is written

group of four

demisemiquaver rest

**demi-ton** (Fr.), semitone.

**De Monte,** *see* MONTE.

**Denkmäler der Tonkunst in Bayern** (Ger., *Monuments of Music in Bavaria*), series supplementary to DENKMÄLER DEUTSCHER TONKUNST. First vol. appeared 1900.

**Denkmäler der Tonkunst in Österreich** (Ger., *Monuments of Music in Austria*), series of publications of old music analogous to DENKMÄLER DEUTSCHER TONKUNST, incl. works by foreign composers written in Austria or found in Austrian libraries. Incl. 6 vols. of 16th-cent. music from so-called TRENT CODICES, operas by Monteverdi, Cesti and Gluck, and 2 vols. of early 18th-cent. Viennese instrumental music. First vol. published 1894.

**Denkmäler deutscher Tonkunst** (Ger., *Monuments of German Music*), series of publications of old music by German composers, as well as works by foreign composers resident in Germany. First vol. published 1892. Supplementary series DENKMÄLER DER TONKUNST IN BAYERN started in 1900. Nazi government replaced two series in 1935 with *Das Erbe deutscher Musik (The Heritage of German Music)*, subdivided into (1) *Reichsdenkmale* (national monuments), (2) *Landschaftsdenkmale* (regional monuments); latter ceased publication in 1942.

**Denner, Johann Christoph** (1655–1707), German maker of woodwind instruments at Nurenberg. Said to have invented clarinet *c* 1700, poss. by improving instrument already in existence.

**Dent, Edward Joseph** (1876–1957), English musical historian, teacher and opera translator. Professor of music at Cambridge. Principal research was in field of opera. Wrote many translations of opera libretti.

**Denza, Luigi** (1846–1922), Italian composer. Wrote opera

*Wallenstein* (1876) and more than 500 songs, though only remembered for song 'Funiculi funicula' (1880).

**déploration** (Fr.), lament.

**Deprez,** *see* JOSQUIN DES PRÉS.

**Der,** for German titles beginning thus *see* second word of title.

**Dering** or **Deering, Richard** (*c* 1580–1630), English composer. Studied in Italy. Organist to Charles I's consort Queen Henrietta Maria. Works incl. motets, Italian madrigals and music for viols.

**Dernesch, Helga** (1939– ), Austrian mezzo-soprano, formerly soprano. Has sung at Bayreuth, Salzburg, and since 1968 with Scottish Opera. Known for Strauss and Wagner roles.

**Des** (Ger.), D flat.

**De Sabata,** *see* SABATA.

**descant** (Fr., *déchant*), translation of medieval Latin *discantus*, lit. 'a different song':

(1) melodic line, or counterpoint, added to existing melodic line *(cantus prius factus)*, whether extempore or on paper;

(2) in 13th, 14th cents. '*discantus*' (usually translated as 'discant') referred esp. to note-against-note style of one discanting voice against tenor, predominantly in contrary motion. In England, style persisted into 15th cent;

(3) in 16th, 17th cents., upper part of polyphonic composition (Ger., *Diskant*); hence instrument which plays upper part *eg* descant recorder;

(4) in modern English practice, contrasted melody to be sung simultaneously with one which is already familiar, such as hymn or folksong.

*See* COUNTERPOINT, FABURDEN, FAUXBOURDON, SIGHT, RECORDER.

**Déserteur, Le** (Fr., *The Deserter*), opera by Monsigny, libretto by J.M. Sedaine. First perf. Paris, 1769. Opera looks forward to 19th cent. in its grandeur and intensity.

**Deses** (Ger.), D double flat.

**Désir, Le,** *see* TRAUERWALZER.

**desk,** pair of players in orchestra sharing music stand.

**Des Prés,** *see* JOSQUIN DES PRÉS.

**Dessau, Paul** (1894–1979), German conductor, composer. Lived in France and US during Nazi era. Works incl. *The Trial of Lucullus* (libretto by Brecht), incidental music to plays by Brecht, children's operas, orchestral, chamber and film music, and songs.

**dessous** (Fr.), lit. 'below', 'under', *ie* lower part.

**dessus** (Fr.), lit. 'above', 'over', so (1) upper part, (2) treble; *dessus de viole*, treble viol.

**Destinn, Emmy,** stage name of Emmy Kittl (1878–1930), Czech operatic soprano. Pupil of Marie Loewe-Destinn, whose surname she borrowed for professional purposes. Sang in Europe and USA. Sang Minnie in first perf. of Puccini's *La Fanciulla del West* (New York, 1910). Also known as dramatist, poet and novelist. Changed name to Destinova after WWI.

**Destouches, André Cardinal** (1662–1749), French opera composer. Became pupil of Campra after life as soldier and sailor. Held various posts under Louis XIV. First work, *Issé* (1697), a *pastorale héroique*, was very successful. Later wrote several operas, *eg Omphale*, ballets, *eg Les Eléments*, solo cantatas with orchestra, and church music.

**détaché,** style of playing string instrument so that noticeable bow change is made on every note – though not necessarily so detached as to be staccato.

**Dett, Robert Nathaniel** (1882–1943), black American composer, pianist. Pupil of Nadia Boulanger. Works incl. several choral compositions. Active in study of Negro music.

**Dettingen Te Deum,** setting by Handel for soloists, chorus and orchestra, written to commemorate victory at Dettingen in 1743. Much of music is borrowed or adapted from Te Deum by Antonio Urio, though has been said that Urio's work is actually by Handel.

**deutlich** (Ger.), distinct.

**Deutsch,** *see* DEUTSCHER TANZ.

**Deutsch, Otto Erich** (1883–1967), Austrian bibliographer. Made special study of Schubert. His thematic catalogue resulted in replacement of old and often misleading opus numbers with 'Deutsch' (or 'D') numbers.

**Deutscher Tanz** (Ger.; It., *danza tedesca*), 'German dance'. Also known as *Deutsch* or *Teutsch*. In late 18th, early 19th cents., brisk dance in waltz time. Examples occur in works of Mozart, Beethoven and Schubert. *See also* ALLEMANDE, LÄNDLER, WALTZ.

**Deutsches Requiem, Ein,** *see* GERMAN REQUIEM.

**Deutschland über alles,** German national anthem, written just before upheavals of 1848 and sung to tune Haydn wrote for Austrian national hymn.

**deux** (Fr.), two; *à deux* indicates 2 separate parts merge, or single part divides into 2.

**Deux Journées, Les** (Fr., *The Two Days*), opera by Cherubini, libretto by J.N. Bouilly. First perf. Paris, 1800. Much admired by Beethoven. Known in Britain as *The Water Carrier*.

**deux temps** (Fr.), (1) in 2/2 time; (2) *valse à deux temps* indicates quick waltz with only 2 steps to 3 beats of bar.

**development** (Fr., *développement*; Ger., *Durchführung*; It., *svolgimento*), exploitation of possibilities of thematic material by means of contrapuntal elaboration, modulation, rhythmical variation, *etc.* In movt. in SONATA FORM development section follows exposition (in which principal themes are stated). Compositions devoted to development of one simple theme are called 'monothematic'.

**Devienne, François** (1759–1803), French flautist, bassoonist, composer. Played prominent part in music of Revolution, and was member of band of Garde Nationale. Wrote several operas, music for *fêtes nationales*, concertos for flute, bassoon and horn, *sinfonies concertantes* for various wind instruments and orchestra, and much chamber music. Also wrote flute tutor.

**Devil and Kate, The** (Czech, *Cert a Káča*), opera by Dvořák, libretto by A. Wenig. First perf. Prague, 1899. Kate is garrulous country wench who, failing to win dancing partner at fair, offers to dance with the Devil. Latter at first thinks her a suitable victim to take to the Underworld, but later is more than happy to return her to earth.

**Devil's Trill, The** (It., *Il Trillo del Diavolo*), violin sonata in G minor by Tartini, said to be based on music Devil played to him in dream. Title alludes to famous trill in last movt.

**Devin du Village, Le** (Fr., *The Village Soothsayer*), opera by Rousseau, libretto by composer. First perf. Fontainebleau, 1752. Rousseau's most important stage work, it was parodied by C.S. Favart in *Les Amours de Bastien et Bastienne.* Mozart used German version of parody in his *Bastien und Bastienne* (1768).

**Devrient, Eduard** (1801–77), German operatic baritone, theatre director. Wrote libretto of Marschner's opera *Hans Heiling* (1833), in which he sang title role. His memoirs of Mendelssohn incl. account of revival of Bach's *St Matthew Passion* in 1829, in which he sang part of Jesus.

**Devrient, Wilhelmine,** *see* SCHRÖDER-DEVRIENT.

**Diabelli, Anton** (1781–1858), Austrian composer. Pupil of Michael Haydn. Founded firm of music publishers. Published piano variations on waltz-theme (of his own composition) by 50 composers, to which Beethoven added 33 (*Diabelli Variations*, op 120); contributors incl. Czerny, Hummel, Liszt (aged 12) and Schubert.

**diabolus in musica** (Lat.), lit. 'the devil in music'. Term originated in Middle Ages as warning against use of TRITONE, which was regarded as 'dangerous' progression.

**Dialogues des Carmélites, Les** (Fr., *The Carmelites*), opera by Poulenc, libretto by G. Bernanos. First perf. La Scala, Milan, 1957.

**Diamants de la Couronne, Les** (Fr., *The Crown Diamonds*), opera by Auber, libretto by A.E. Scribe and J.H.V. de Saint-Georges. First perf. Paris, 1841.

**Diamond, David Leo** (1915– ), American composer. Studied with Nadia Boulanger. Works incl. 8 symphonies, concertos for piano, violin and cello, *Rounds* for string orchestra, *A Night Litany* (to text by Ezra Pound) for chorus, chamber and piano music, and songs.

**diapason,** (1) in Greek and medieval theory, OCTAVE interval;

(2) (Fr.), tuning-fork. *Diapason normal*, concert PITCH;

(3) generic term for family of flue-pipes on organ, which provide substantial foundation of organ tone. *Open Diapason* (Fr., *principal, montre*; Ger., *Prinzipal*): (1) on manuals normally of 8ft pitch, with metal pipes; (2) on pedals normally of 16ft pitch, with wood or metal pipes. Corresponding stop of 4ft pitch is generally called Principal or Octave (Fr., *prestant*; Ger., *Oktave, Prinzipal 4 Fuss, Kleinprinzipal*). *Double diapason*: manual stop of 16ft pitch, similar to Bourdon. *Stopped diapason*: manual stop of 8ft pitch and mellow flute-like tone; pipes are same length as those of 4ft stop, but being closed at one end sound octave lower (*see* ORGAN).

**diapente** (Gr.), perfect fifth interval.

**diaphony,** (1) orig. Gr. word means dissonance, and was used in this sense by some medieval writers;
(2) used generally by early medieval theorists to describe ORGANUM. By 13th cent., Lat. word *discantus* was generally preferred (*see* DESCANT).

**diatonic,** in strict sense used of notes proper to key, *eg* in key of D major, following notes are diatonic and constitute diatonic scale: D–E–F sharp– G–A–B–C sharp–D. Any other notes involve accidentals and are CHROMATIC. In minor keys sharpened sixth and seventh are in such common use, though not strictly proper to key, that they are also regarded as diatonic, *eg* in key of D minor, notes B natural and C sharp are added to proper diatonic scale: D–E–F–G–A–B flat–C–D.

**Diatonic chord,** chord composed of notes proper to key.

**Diatonic harmony,** strictly harmony which employs only diatonic chords; more generally, harmony which is predominantly based on diatonic chords and their association. *Diatonic tetrachord*, *see* TETRACHORD. *See* CHROMATIC (1), ENHARMONIC (1).

**Dichterliebe** (Ger., *Poet's Love*), cycle of 16 songs by Schumann, op 48 (1840), to words by Heinrich Heine.

**Dichtung** (Ger.), poetry; *symphonische Dichtung*, symphonic poem.

**Dickinson, Peter** (1934– ), English composer. Works incl. *The Judas Tree* (piece of theatre with music), organ concerto and other orchestral works, *Late Afternoon in November* for 16 solo voices, choral, church, chamber, piano and organ music, and songs.

**dictionaries of music,** *see* HISTORY OF MUSIC.

**Dido and Aeneas,** opera by Purcell, libretto by Nahum Tate (inspired by Virgil). First perf. London, 1689. Usually described as Purcell's 'only opera', his other stage works being masques.

**Die,** for German titles beginning thus, *see* second word of title.

**Diepenbrock, Alphons** (1862–1921), Dutch composer. Greatly influenced contemporaries. Works incl. church music, incidental music for plays, and songs.

**Dieren, Bernard van** (1884–1936), Dutch-born composer, resident in England after 1909. Compositions, admired by limited circle, incl. *Chinese Symphony* for soloists, chorus and orchestra (1914), comic opera *The Tailor* (1917), chamber music, and songs.

**dièse** (Fr.), sharp.

**Dies Irae** (Lat., 'day of wrath'), early 13th-cent. SEQUENCE, forming part of Requiem Mass. Traditional plainsong melody has been used by more modern composers, *eg* Berlioz (*Symphonie fantastique* 1830), Liszt (*Totentanz* 1849), Rakhmaninov (*Rhapsody on a Theme of Paganini* 1936).

**diesis** (Gr.), (1) in Pythagorean theory, difference between fourth and 2 'major' tones (*see* TONE), *ie* semitone slightly smaller than that of scale based on harmonic series. Also known as *limma*;
(2) in Aristotelian theory, quarter-tone of ENHARMONIC tetrachord;
(3) in modern acoustics, theoretical interval between B sharp and

C, C sharp and D flat *etc*; *great diesis* is interval between 4 minor thirds (*eg* E–G–B flat–D flat–F flat) and octave (E–E); for *enharmonic diesis*, *see* ENHARMONIC (2). *See also* HARMONIC SERIES, TEMPERAMENT;

(4) (It.), sharp.

**Dietrich, Albert Hermann** (1829–1908), German composer. Pupil and friend of Schumann. Collaborated with Schumann and Brahms in writing violin sonata for Joachim (1853). Other works incl. operas *Robin Hood* (1879) and *Das Sonntagskind* (1886), symphony, concertos for horn, violin and cello, choral and piano music, and songs.

**Dietrich, Sixt** (*c* 1492–1548), German composer. Prominent adherent of Reformation. Wrote much church music, incl. antiphons and Latin hymns, and songs.

**Dieupart, Charles** (d. *c* 1740), French composer, violinist, harpsichordist. Settled in London and took active part in introduction of Italian opera to England. Wrote *Six suites de clavessin* for harpsichord, clear traces of which appear in Bach's English Suites.

**diferencia** (Sp.), in 16th cent., VARIATION or DIVISION.

**difference tone,** *see* COMBINATION TONE.

**diluendo** (It.), 'dissolving', *ie* fading away.

**dilungando** (It.), lengthening.

**diminished interval,** perfect or minor interval reduced by flattening upper note or sharpening lower, *eg*: perfect fifth, C to G; diminished fifth, C to G flat, or C sharp to G; minor seventh, C to B flat; diminished seventh, C to B double flat, or C sharp to B flat. On keyboard instruments diminished intervals are indistinguishable from augmented or major interval below, *eg*: diminished fifth, C to G flat sounds same as augmented fourth, C to F sharp; harmonic function of intervals, however, remains distinct.

**diminished seventh chord,** chord composed of 3 minor thirds, or diminished triad with diminished seventh superimposed, *eg* B–D–F–A flat. By means of enharmonic changes, *eg* writing G sharp for A flat, chord of this kind can be used as transition to any major or minor triad, *eg*: B–D–F–A flat to C–E–G or C–E flat–A; B–D–E sharp–G sharp to A–D–F sharp–A, *etc*.

**diminished triad,** minor triad with fifth flattened, *eg*: minor triad, C–E flat–G; diminished triad, C–E flat–G flat. Triad on seventh note of major scale (*eg* in key of C major, B–D–F) is only diminished triad proper to key; all others require accidentals. In minor keys, same triad occurs if seventh note is sharpened, and triad on second note of scale is also diminished (*eg* in key of C minor, D–F–A flat).

**diminuendo** (It.), 'diminishing the tone', *ie* getting softer. Opposite of *crescendo*; same as *decrescendo*. Abbrev. is *dim.* or *dimin.*

**diminution,** (1) presentation of theme in notes of smaller time-value than original presentation. *See* AUGMENTATION, CANON;

(2) in 16th, 17th-cent. music, ornamentation (often improvised) of simple melodic line by breaking it up into notes of smaller value. *See* DIVISION.

**di molto** (It.), 'extremely'. *Allegro di molto*, extremely fast.

**D'Indy,** *see* INDY.

**di nuovo** (It.), 'again'. *Poi a poi di nuovo vivente*, gradually getting lively again.

**Dioclesian** (full title, *The Prophetess, or the History of Dioclesian*) opera with dialogue, adapted from Beaumont and Fletcher by Thomas Betterton, with music by Purcell. First perf. London, 1690.

**direct,** sign rather like ornamental W, formerly used in manuscripts and printed music, (1) at end of line or page, positioned on staff to indicate in advance pitch of next note, (2) in middle of line, to draw attention to change of clef (Lat., *custos*).

**dirge,** vocal or instrumental composition intended for use at funerary rites.

**Dirigent** (Ger.), conductor.

**Diruta, Girolamo** (b. *c* 1560), Italian organist, teacher. One of foremost players of his time; known today for *Il Transilvano* (2 vols., 1593, 1609), elaborate treatise on organ-playing.

**Dis** (Ger.), D sharp.

**discant,** *see* DESCANT.

**discantus** (Lat.), descant. *Discantus supra librum*, 'descant on the book', *ie* improvisation of counterpoint to existing melody – common practice from Middle Ages to end of 16th cent. *See* SIGHT.

**discord,** combination of notes which incl. at least one dissonant interval. In popular use applied to music in which relationship between series of dissonances is not intelligible to listener. *See* CONSONANCE, DISSONANCE.

**Disis** (Ger.), D double sharp.

**disjunct,** opposite of CONJUNCT.

**Diskant** (Ger.), soprano, treble. *Diskantmesse*, modern term for 15th-cent. Mass in which plainsong, generally freely embroidered, appears not in tenor but in upper part. *Diskantschlüssel*, soprano CLEF.

**Dissoluto Punito, Il** (It., *The Rake Punished*), subtitle of DON GIOVANNI.

**dissonance,** etymologically a jarring sound, or 'discord'. Term is incapable of precise definition, since ear is inevitably subjective. Ways in which dissonance can occur in music, however, remain constant: (1) by introducing passing note which is dissonant with rest of chord, (2) by tying over, or suspending, from one chord, note which is dissonant with next chord, (3) as essential note of chord. Historically type (3) is result of other two, *ie* dissonances which are familiar as passing notes or suspensions come in time to be accepted without preparation. *See* CONSONANCE.

**'Dissonance' Quartet,** nickname for Mozart's string quartet in C major, K 465 (1785), whose slow introduction makes remarkable use of dissonance.

**distinto** (It.), distinct, clear.

**Distler, Hugo** (1908–42), German composer, organist. Committed suicide during WWII. Works, mainly religious, incl. *c* 50 motets, Passion, oratorio *Nativity*, harpsichord concerto, and organ music.

**Distratto, Il** (It., *The Absent-minded Man*), nickname for Haydn's Symphony no 60 in C major (1774–5), used as incidental music for comedy of that title produced in Vienna.

**dital harp,** another name for HARP-GUITAR.

**Ditson,** American firm of music-publishers in Boston, Mass. Orig. Parker & Ditson (1832), then Oliver Ditson & Co. (1857), after its founder, Oliver Ditson (1811–88).

**Dittersdorf, Karl Ditters von** (1739–99), Austrian violinist, composer. Orig. Karl Ditters but ennobled in 1773. One of most prolific composers of his time. Wrote *c* 40 operas, *eg Doktor und Apotheker* (1786) and version of *The Marriage of Figaro* (poss. predating Mozart's). Other works incl. oratorios, Masses, over 100 concertos, chamber music and piano sonatas. Symphonies incl. 12 on subjects from Ovid's *Metamorphoses*.

**diversion,** same as VARIATION.

**divertimento** (It.), term originating in late 18th cent. for suite of movts. for chamber ensemble or orchestra, designed primarily for entertainment. Some of greatest were written by Mozart. Title still used in 20th cent. *eg* by Bartók.

**divertissement** (Fr.), (1) entertainment in form of ballet, with or without songs, interpolated in opera or play for sake of variety;

(2) fantasia on well-known tunes;

(3) divertimento.

**Divine Poem, The,** symphonic poem by Skryabin, also known as Symphony no 3. Describes soul's struggle to achieve divinity. First perf. Paris, 1905.

**divisi,** *see* A DUE (2).

**division,** (1) term current in England in 17th, 18th cents. for ornamental elaboration of simple melodic line;

(2) in particular, variation on GROUND BASS, written or improvised. Favourite medium for divisions of this kind in 17th-cent. England was solo bass viol, accompanied by harpsichord or organ, with 2nd bass viol playing bass line. *See* DIMINUTION.

**division viol,** bass VIOL slightly smaller than normal size, suitable for DIVISIONS.

**Dixie,** song by Daniel Emmett written in 1859 for Negro minstrel shows. Later became associated with Confederate Army during Civil War.

**Dixieland,** style of 'classical' jazz derived from music that originated in New Orleans at start of 20th cent. Simple and cheerful; usually performed by small groups.

**Dixon, Dean** (1915–76), black American conductor. Worked mainly outside US, in Goteborg, Frankfurt, Sydney and the Netherlands.

**do** (It.), C. *See* DOH.

**Dobrowen, Issay Alexandrovich** (1894–1953), Russian conductor, composer. Conducted internationally. Compositions incl. piano concerto, violin concerto, piano music and songs.

**Dodecachordon** (Gr.), book published 1547 by Heinrich Loriti under pseud. of Glareanus. It is so-called because it upholds theory that there were 12, not 8, church modes. The 4 additional modes were Aeolian and Hypoaeolian (with final on A) and Ionian and Hypoionian (with final on C). *See* MODE.

**dodecaphonic** or **dodecuple,** terms referring to TWELVE-NOTE SYSTEM of composition.

**'Dog' Waltz,** *see* MINUTE WALTZ.

**doh,** Eng. form of It., *do* (C). In TONIC SOL-FA, first note (or tonic) of major scale.

**Dohnányi, Ernö** or **Ernst von** (1877–1960), Hungarian composer, pianist. In 1897 made début as pianist; in same year 1st symphony was performed. Was exceptionally able pianist; frequently toured Europe and US. In 1931 became general director with Hungarian Radio. In 1949 settled in US. Principal compositions are in German (esp. Brahmsian) tradition rather than Hungarian national idiom favoured by Bartók and Kódaly. Now remembered more for *Variations on a Nursery Theme* for piano and orchestra than for other works, which incl. 3 operas (*eg The Tenor*), 3 symphonies, orchestral suite, violin concerto, *Ruralia Hungarica* for orchestra, and chamber, instrumental and piano music.

**doigté** (Fr.), fingering.

**Doktor Faust,** opera by Busoni, completed after his death by Philipp Jarnach, libretto by composer. First perf. Dresden, 1925. Based on orig. Faust legend, not Goethe's drama.

**Doktor und Apotheker** (Ger., *Doctor and Apothecary*), opera by Dittersdorf, libretto by G. Stephanie. First perf. Vienna, 1786.

**dolce** (It.), sweet, gentle. *Dolcissimo*, very sweet.

**dolcian, dulcian** or **dulzian,** 16th, 17th-cent. names for bassoon.

**Dolega-Kamienski** *see* KAMIEŃSKI.

**dolente** (It.), sorrowful.

**Doles, Johann Friedrich** (1715–97), German composer, organist. Pupil of Bach, and one of his successors at Leipzig. Wrote Masses, Passions, cantatas, motets *etc*.

**Dolly,** suite of 6 children's pieces for piano duet by Fauré, op 56 (1893). Later orchestrated as ballet by Rabaud.

**Dolmetsch, Arnold** (1858–1940), Swiss-born musicologist, instrument-maker and violinist, son of Swiss father and French mother. Studied in Brussels with Vieuxtemps, settled in Britain (1914) where founded Haslemere Festival of old music (1925) in which members of his family took part. Made many old instruments, *eg* viols, harpsichords and esp. recorder, which he made immensely popular. His younger son **Carl Dolmetsch** (1911– ) has become foremost exponent of recorder.

**doloroso** (It.), sorrowful.

**Dolzflöte** (Ger.), soft flute-like organ stop.

**Domaine Musical,** society founded by Pierre Boulez, Jean-Louis Barrault and Madeleine Renaud in Paris in 1954 to promote concerts of new music. In 1967 Gilbert Amy succeeded Boulez as director.

**dombra,** *see* DOMRA.

**Domestic Symphony** (*Symphonia Domestica)*, by Richard Strauss (1904), autobiographical symphonic poem in several movts.

**dominant,** (1) fifth degree of major or minor scale. In key of C, dominant is therefore G. *Dominant chord* or *dominant triad*, triad on dominant, *ie* in C major, notes G, B, D. *Dominant seventh chord*, dominant triad (G,B,D) with addition of seventh (F) from bass. Convention of harmonizing melodic cadence:

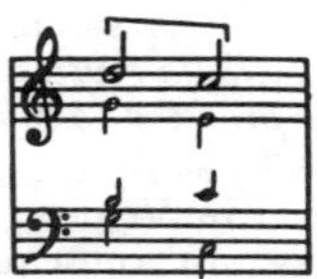

with dominant and tonic triads dates from latter half of 15th cent. This is so-called perfect cadence or full close. This close relationship between dominant and tonic triads plays important part in establishing new key (*see* MODULATION). Substitution of dominant seventh chord for dominant triad in perfect cadence:

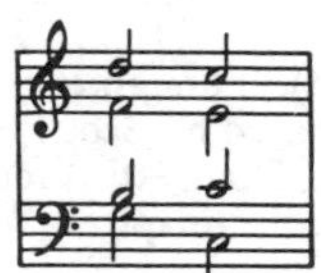

originated in introduction of seventh as passing or ornamental note; (2) name given to reciting note (properly *repercussio*, tenor or *tuba*) of each of Gregorian psalm-tones, and hence to a degree of scale in each mode on which this note falls. *See* MODE, TONE.

**Domingo, Placido** (1941– ), Spanish tenor. Made opera debut in 1961. Has international reputation, esp. for roles in Italian opera.

**dompe,** *see* DUMP.

**domra** or **dombra,** kind of balalaika. In Russia, usually has round body with 3 (sometimes 2) metal strings tuned fourth apart and played with plectrum.

**Donato, Baldessare** (*c* 1530–1603), Italian organist, composer, singer. Held various positions at St Mark's, Venice. Published volume of motets and several books of madrigals.

**Donatoni, Franco** (1927– ), Italian composer. Has used most of progressive musical forms (*eg* serialism and aleatory techniques). Works incl. *Per Orchestra, Strophes* and *Sezioni* for orchestra, concerto for kettledrums with strings and brass, chamber music, and *Black and White* for 2 pianos.

**Don Carlos,** opera by Verdi, libretto in French by F.J. Méry and C. du Locle (after Schiller's play). First perf. Paris, 1867 (rev. 1884 for La Scala, Milan, with Italian libretto). Story concerns love of Don Carlos, son of Philip II of Spain, for Elisabeth de Valois, whom his father wishes to marry.

**Don Giovanni,** comic opera (*dramma giocoso*) by Mozart, libretto by L. da Ponte. Full title is *Il dissoluto punito, ossia Don Giovanni* (The Rake Punished, or Don Juan). First perf. Prague, 1787 (conducted by composer). Inspired by Don Juan legend and esp. by play by Bertati.

**Doni, Giovanni Battista** (1594–1647), Italian writer on music. Made special study of Greek music and published *Compendio del trattato de' generi e de modi della musica* (1635), *Annotationi sopra il compendio* (1640) and *De praestantia musicae veteris* (1647).

**Donizetti, Gaetano** (1797-1848), Italian composer, b. Bergamo. First opera was performed in Venice in 1818. Wrote *c* 75 operas with remarkable rapidity. In consequence, work, though often charming, is generally superficial, depending to a large extent on virtuosity of soloists. Wrote for all leading Italian opera houses, and many abroad. Best known works are serious operas *Anna Bolena* (1830), *Il Furioso all'isola di San Domingo* (1833), *Lucrezia Borgia* (1833), *Torquato Tasso* (1833), *Maria Stuarda* (1834), *Marino Faliero* (1835), *Lucia di Lammermoor* (1835), *Roberto Devereux* (1837), *La Favorita* (1840) and *Linda di Chamounix* (1842), and comic operas *L'Elisir d'amore* (1832), *La Fille du régiment* (1840) and *Don Pasquale* (1843). Though it is for his comedies – and for *Lucia di Lammermoor* (based on Scott), with its dramatic sextet and famous Mad Scene – that Donizetti is most widely loved, some of his serious works (esp. Schiller-inspired *Maria Stuarda*) are coming back into favour.

**Don Juan,** (1) *see* DON GIOVANNI; (2) symphonic poem by Richard Strauss, op 20 (1884).

**'Donkey' Quartet,** another nickname for Haydn's QUINTENQUARTETT.

**Donna Diana,** opera by Rezniček, libretto by composer (after Moreto's comedy, *El Lindo Don Diego*, 1654). First perf. Prague, 1894.

**Don Pasquale,** comic opera by Donizetti, libretto by composer and unknown collaborator, after A. Anelli's *Ser Marc'Antonio*. First perf. Paris, 1843. Donizetti's greatest comedy deals with gulling of Don Pasquale, an elderly bachelor, into false marriage contract.

**Don Quixote,** (1) opera by Massenet (Fr., *Don Quichotte*), libretto by H. Cain. First perf. Monte Carlo, 1910;

(2) symphonic poem by Richard Strauss, op 35 (1898), based on Cervantes' novel. Described as 'Fantastic variations on a theme of knightly character'.

**doppel** (Ger.), double. *Doppel-B*, double flat; *Doppelkreuz*, double sharp; *Doppelfagott*, double bassoon; *Doppelschlag*, TURN; *Doppeltaktnote*, breve.

**doppio** (It.), double. *Doppio diesis*, double sharp; *doppio bemolle*, double flat; *doppio movimento*, twice as fast; *doppio pedale*, 'double pedal', *ie* indication in organ music that 2 feet play simultaneously.

**Dorati, Antal** (1906– ), American conductor, b. Hungary. Pupil of Bartók and Kodály. Has conducted several orchestras in US and Europe, incl. B.B.C. Symphony Orchestra (1963–7), Royal Philharmonic Orchestra (from 1976) and Detroit Symphony Orchestra (from 1977).

**Dorian mode,** (1) in ancient Greek music, descending scale E–D–C–B–A–G–F–E;

(2) from Middle Ages onwards applied to ascending scale D–E–F–G–A–B–C–D. *See* GREEK MUSIC, MODE.

**Dorian Toccata and Fugue,** name given to organ toccata and fugue in D minor by Bach (not famous one); orig. written without key signature, so giving appearance that it was in DORIAN MODE.

**Doric,** same as DORIAN.

**Dorn, Heinrich Ludwig Egmont** (1804–92), German composer, conductor, teacher, critic. Taught Schumann counterpoint (1830–2). Numerous operas incl. *Die Nibelungen* (1854).

**dot,** (1) written above or below note, *eg*:

(a) normally indicates STACCATO, *ie* (in this instance) crotchets are played approximately as quavers followed by quaver rests;

(b) in 18th-cent. violin music, series of dots with slur, *eg*:

indicates that notes are to be detached but without changing bow. Normal notation today is:

(c) in 18th-cent. clavichord music, series of dots with slur, placed over or under single note:

indicates BEBUNG, *ie* gently repeated movement of finger on key giving effect similar to vibrato on guitar;

(d) in 18th-cent. French music, often has rhythmical significance: *see* 2 (iv) below;

(2) written after note, dot indicates prolongation of normal length by one-half. Hence:

In older music, dot was used to indicate such prolongation not only within bar but also beyond barline.

Double dot, first suggested by Leopold Mozart in 1756, indicates prolongation of normal length by three-quarters, *eg*:

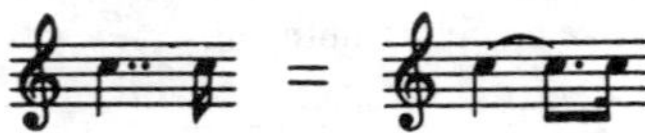

Dot and double dot are also used after rests, indicating that value of rest is prolonged by half and three-quarters respectively.

In music of 17th, early 18th cents., use of dot was neither precise nor consistent. Various theorists gave advice on interpretation; following points should be noted:

(i) in passages of following kind:

dot is assumed after rest, and first note loses half its written value;

(ii) in general, in movts. where triplets occur consistently, rhythm

(iii) in general, however, value of dotted note is to be prolonged, and value of subsequent note or notes reduced accordingly. This applies esp. to dotted quavers and dotted semiquavers, but may also apply to dotted crotchets. Much depends on character and tempo of piece. Leopold Mozart's invention of double dot gave precise notation for this convention;

(iv) in French music, and music in French style, it became fashion to play successions of quavers or semiquavers (sometimes also crotchets) unevenly, *ie* alternately long and short (normally no instruction was given). In certain cases this would mean that

would be played

but lengthening was not always so considerable, and cannot be exactly represented in notation. Notes which were altered in this way were called *notes inégales*, and rhythm was termed *pointé*. Where alteration was not required, notes often had dots over them (*not* indicating *staccato*) or were marked *notes égales*.

**double,** (1) (Eng.), octave lower, *eg* double bassoon, built octave lower than bassoon;

(2) (Eng.), prefixed to instrument, may also signify one that combines two instruments in one, *eg* double horn, which combines essential features of horn in F and horn in B flat alto (*see* HORN);

(3) (Eng.), 18th-cent. term for variation (of air or dance movt.), consisting primarily of melodic ornamentation of new figuration.

**doublé** (Fr.), turn.

**double bar,** sign used to indicate end of composition or section:

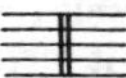

It is not necessarily equivalent to barline, as it may occur in any part of bar. Often accompanied by dots indicating that preceding or succeeding section or both are to be repeated:

**double bass** (Fr., *contrebasse*; Ger., *Kontrabass*; It., *contrabasso*), largest bowed stringed instrument and foundation of string ensemble. Differs in shape from other members of violin family, being modelled on old double-bass viol (or *violone*) – sloping shoulders are characteristic feature. Music for it is written octave higher than real sounds, to avoid constant use of leger lines. Modern instrument has 4, sometimes 5, strings. With 4 strings, normally tuned as follows: E below bass clef, A, D, G (sounding octave lower), though some players prefer: D below bass clef, G, D, G. With 5 strings, tuned as follows: C below bass clef (or even B), E, A, D, G.

In orchestral music extended passages for double basses alone are rare. In chamber music, double bass has rarely been used, except in large ensembles; some notable exceptions incl. Schubert's 'Trout' quintet and Dvořák's quintet in G major. Double bass (played *pizzi-*

*cato*) is, however, fundamental to many jazz ensembles (esp. in association with piano and drums).

**double bassoon** (Fr., *contrebasson*; Ger., *Kontrafagott*; It., *contrafagotto*), double-reed instrument, of wood or metal, built octave lower than BASSOON.

**double cadence** (Fr.), TURN.

**double chant,** Anglican CHANT consisting of 4 sections, to which 2 verses of psalm or canticle are to be sung.

**double concerto,** concerto for 2 solo instruments and orchestra.

**double counterpoint,** name given to invertible counterpoint in 2 parts. Consists in adding to existing melody second melody which will fit equally well above or below first. In theory, added melody can move up or down any interval to its new position, but in practice commonest intervals are those of octave, tenth and twelfth. It is not uncommon for 1st melody to move octave at same time, or even 2 octaves, in opposite direction, either to prevent crossing of parts or to make room for additional parts in between. Double counterpoint occurs frequently in fugues since COUNTERSUBJECT may be required to enter above subject in one place and below it in another.

**double croche** (Fr.), semi-quaver.

**double diapason,** *see* DIAPASON (3).

**double dot,** *see* DOT (2).

**double flat,** the sign ♭♭ indicating that pitch of note to which it is prefixed is to be lowered 2 semitones, *eg* on keyboard instrument B double flat will sound same as A.

**double fugue,** (1) properly, FUGUE in which new theme is introduced in course of piece and being itself treated fugally is finally combined with original subject, to which it forms countersubject;

(2) name sometimes given to fugue in which subject and countersubject appear simultaneously at beginning and are regularly associated throughout piece.

**double reed,** 2 pieces of cane, lower, thicker ends being bound round metal tube, while upper ends, which are very thin, practically meet, leaving, however, small aperture through which player's breath is forced. This method of tone production is used in oboe, cor anglais, heckelphone, bassoon, double bassoon and sarrusophone.

**double sharp,** the sign × indicating that pitch of note to which it is prefixed is to be raised 2 semitones, *eg* on keyboard instrument F double sharp will sound same as G.

**double stop,** chord of 2 notes played on bowed string instrument (*eg* violin) by using 2 adjacent strings. Term incl. chords where open string is used.

**double tonguing,** means of achieving rapid articulation of successive notes (esp. repeated notes) on flute and brass instruments. Consists in alternately articulating consonants T and K. Not possible on reed instruments where mouthpiece is held inside mouth. *See* TRIPLE TONGUING.

**double touch,** system employed by some modern organ-builders, by which heavier pressure on keys can be used to bring into action new registration, without necessity of changing stops. In this way it is possible for solo and accompaniment to be played on same manual in 2 contrasted tone-colours. Common on cinema organs.

**doucement** (Fr.), sweetly, gently.

**Dowland, John** (1563–1626), English composer, lutenist. In service of English Ambassador in Paris (1580–4), where became RC. As RC, failed to get post at English court (1594); travelled widely on Continent. Subsequently in service of Christian IV of Denmark, and James I and Charles I of England. Had great reputation both as performer and composer. His 4 books of ayres are most important English contribution to literature of solo song with lute accompaniment. Also published collection of instrumental ensemble music entitled *Lachrimae, or Seaven Teares figured in seaven passionate Pavans* (1605). His son, **Robert Dowland** (*c* 1585–1641), was also lutenist and composer. Succeeded father as lutenist to Charles I (1626).

**down-beat,** downward movement of conductor's stick or hand, marking first beat of bar. Term also applied simply to first beat of bar.

**down-bow,** drawing of bow across strings of string instrument. Opposite is up-bow, *ie* pushing of bow in other direction.

**D'Oyly Carte, Richard** (1844–1901), English impresario. Instigated (1875) long-standing collaboration of Gilbert and Sullivan, and founded D'Oyly Carte Opera Company to perform their works.

**Draghi, Antonio** (1635–1700), Italian composer. In service of Imperial Court at Vienna from 1658. One of most prolific composers of his time. Wrote enormous number of operas and oratorios.

**Draghi, Giovanni Battista** (*c* 1640–*c* 1710), Italian musician. Resident in London; in service of Charles II, Catherine of Braganza and James II. Compositions incl. setting of Dryden's Ode for St Cecilia's Day.

**Dragonetti, Domenico** (1763–1846), Italian double-bass virtuoso, composer. Moved to London (1794). Had great reputation. Acquainted with Haydn and Beethoven.

**drame lyrique** (Fr.), one of French names for opera.

**dramma lirico** (It.), same as DRAME LYRIQUE.

**dramma per musica** (It.), lit. 'drama by (or through) music', *ie* opera. Term much used in Italy in 17th, 18th cents.

**drängend** (Ger.), hurrying.

**Drdla, František** or **Franz** (1868–1944), Czech violinist, composer. Wrote 2 operas but best known for violin solos, *eg Souvenir*.

**Dream of Gerontius, The,** oratorio by Elgar, op 38, to text taken from poem by Cardinal Newman. First perf. Birmingham Festival, 1910.

**Dreigroschenoper, Die,** *see* THREEPENNY OPERA.

**Dreiklang** (Ger.), triad.

**dringend** (Ger.), pressing onwards, urgent.

**driving note,** obs. term applied to suspended note (*see* SUSPENSION) or any note causing SYNCOPATION.

**drohend** (Ger.), threatening.

**drone,** lower pipes of bagpipe, each producing single persistent note.

**droit(e)** (Fr.), right. *Main droite* (*m.d.*), with the right hand (*eg* in keyboard music).

**drone bass,** bass part which imitates drone of bagpipe by remaining on same note.

**Druckman, Jacob** (1928– ), American composer. Associated (like Gunther Schuller) with so-called 'third stream' movement, in which post-serial techniques are combined with elements of modern jazz.

**drum,** for various kinds of drum used in orchestra *see* BASS DRUM, SIDE DRUM, TABOR, TENOR DRUM, TIMPANI.

**drum kit,** set of drums and cymbals arranged so that they may all be played by one person. Drummer sits behind snare drum around which are arranged tenor drum, bass drum operated by foot pedal, and hi-hat cymbal operated by other foot. Crash cymbals are fixed to drums or supported on stands, and all are played by sticks, mallets or wire brushes. May incl. other drums and accessories (*eg* temple blocks).

**Drum Mass,** *see* PAUKENMESSE.

**Drum Roll Symphony** (Ger., *Symphonie mit dem Paukenwirbel*), nickname for Haydn's Symphony no 103 in E flat major (1795). Opens with kettledrum roll.

**d.s.,** abbrev. of DAL SEGNO.

**Düben,** family of musicians of German origin who settled in Sweden in 17th cent.

**Andreas Düben** (*c* 1590–1662) was organist at Leipzig and then at Swedish court from 1621, later becoming *Kapellmeister* (1640). Works incl. 8-part motet for burial of Gustavus Adolphus.

His son, **Gustaf Düben** (1624–90), succeeded father as *Kapellmeister* in 1663. In addition to own compositions, made collection of contemporary music preserved in library at Uppsala.

**Ducasse,** *see* ROGER-DUCASSE.

**Du Caurroy,** *see* CAURROY.

**Dudelsack** (Ger.), bagpipe.

**due corde** (It.), 'two strings': (1) in violin music, indicates that passage playable on 1 string is to be played on 2, so producing undulating effect;

(2) in piano music, occasionally used to countermand *una corda* (*see* CORDA).

**duet,** composition for 2 singers or players, with or without accompaniment. Term 'duo' is more generally used for instrumental music, with exception of PIANO DUET.

**Dufay, Guillaume** (*c* 1400–74), Flemish composer. Prob. took degree at University of Bologna, before becoming priest. Worked at Cambrai, Rimini, Papal Chapel and court of Savoy. Later became canon at Cambrai, Bruges and Mons. Dufay was most important composer of his time, master both of church music and secular song. During long creative life he absorbed impressive range of styles and made them his own. Earliest works stand at end of Middle Ages, while mature compositions signify flowering of the Renaissance.

**Dukas, Paul** (1865–1935), French composer, critic. Studied at Paris Conservatoire. Severely self-critical; published very little. Strongly influenced by impressionism, but without sacrificing distinctive clarity of his style. Best-known works are orchestral scherzo *The Sorcerer's Apprentice* (1897), opera *Ariadne and Bluebeard* (1907, setting of Maeterlinck play) and ballet *La Peri* (1912). Also wrote remarkable piano sonata in E flat minor. *Ariadne and Bluebeard*, though rarely staged, is one of outstanding operas of 20th cent.

**dulcet,** dulciana of 4ft length and pitch.

**dulcian** *see* DOLCIAN.

**dulciana,** soft, open metal diapason stop on organ. Usually of 8ft length and pitch, but can be 4 or 16ft.

**dulcimer** (Fr., *tympanon*; Ger., *Hackbrett*; It., *cembalo, salterio tedesco*), instrument of eastern origin which came to Europe in Middle Ages. Like psaltery, consists of strings stretched over wooden frame, but these, instead of being plucked, are struck with hammers held in hands. Pianoforte is adaptation of this principle, hammers being controlled by keyboard. Enlarged form of dulcimer called PANTALEON was popular in 18th cent. Dulcimer is still popular in Hungary where it is called CIMBALOM. Name dulcimer is also used in US for instrument of ZITHER type.

**dulcitone,** keyboard instrument, in which tuning-forks are struck by hammers.

**Dulichius, Philipp** (1562–1631), German teacher, composer of church music. Published *Centuria octonum et septenum vocum harmonias sacras....continens* (1607–12).

**dulzian,** *see* DOLCIAN.

**Dumbarton Oaks Concerto,** concerto in E flat major for 15 instruments by Stravinsky (1938), in style of modern *concerto grosso*. Title refers to residence of R.W. Bliss near Washington D.C., where work was first performed.

**dumb** or **dummy keyboard,** silent keyboard (often portable), used by some pianists for finger practice.

**dumka,** (1) Slavonic term for folk ballad, generally of sentimental or melancholy character (pl., *dumky*).

**Dumky Trio,** piano trio by Dvořák, op 96 (1891), consisting of 6 movts., each in form of DUMKA.

**Dumont, Henry** (1610–84), Walloon composer. Worked in Paris. Published 5 Masses, numerous motets, chansons and instrumental music.

**dump** or **dompe,** 16th, 17th-cent. musical and literary term, prob. denoting elegy or lament. Musical examples often carry name of person in title. All are instrumental, and most are constructed over simple GROUND BASS.

**Dunhill, Thomas Frederick** (1877–1946), English composer, teacher. Pupil of Stanford. Works incl. symphony, chamber music, songs and operas *eg Tantivy Towers* (1931, to libretto by A.P. Herbert).

**Duni** or **Duny, Egidio Romoaldo** (1709–75), Italian-born composer. Settled in Paris (1757), where became leading composer of *opéra comique*, *eg Les Moissonneurs* (1768).

**Dunstable, John** (d. 1453), English musician, mathematician. One of most important composers of 15th cent., with considerable reputation on Continent. In service of Duke of Bedford (regent of France, 1422–35). Compositions are almost entirely for church. Also wrote treatises on astronomy.

**Duny,** *see* DUNI.

**duo,** duet.

**duodecuple,** same as DODECAPHONIC.

**duodrama,** *see* MELODRAMA.

**Duparc, Henri** (full name Marie Eugène Henri Foucques-Duparc) (1848–1933), French composer, pupil of Franck. Abandoned composition after 1885 for health reasons. Reputation rests on 15 songs, among finest products of 19th-cent. lyricism. Other works incl. symphonic poem *Lénore* (1875).

**duplet,** group of 2 notes occupying time normally taken by 3, *eg*:

**duple time,** TIME in which number of beats in bar is multiple of 2, *eg* 2/4, 4/4, 2/2. (Time with 4 beats in bar is also known as 'common' or 'quadruple' time.) If beats are divisible by 2, time is 'simple'; if divisible by 3, it is 'compound', *eg* in simple duple time of 2/4, minim is divisible into 2 crotchets or 4 quavers; in compound duple time of 6/8, dotted minim is divisible into 3 quavers or crotchet and quaver.

**duplex instruments,** instruments (esp. brass) that combine two instruments in one, *eg double euphonium*, which can play through wide euphonium bell or narrow saxtromba bell, and double horn; *see* DOUBLE (2).

**duplum** (Lat.), part immediately above tenor in 12th-cent. organum. Third part above these was called *triplum*. In 13th-cent. motet, *duplum* was called *motetus*.

**Duport, Jean Louis** (1749–1819), French cellist. At outbreak of Revolution moved to Berlin. Founded modern technique of cello playing. It was with him (or his brother) that Beethoven played his 2 cello sonatas, op 5.

His brother, **Jean Pierre Duport** (1741–1818), was also cellist. Worked in Paris and Berlin. Mozart composed piano variations on a minuet by him (K 573).

**Du Pré, Jacqueline** (1945– ), English cellist. Outstanding interpreter of cello concertos (esp. Elgar's) and many works in duo and trio repertory. Career cut short by ill-health.

**Dupré, Marcel** (1886–1971), French organist, composer. Widor's pupil and successor at St Sulpice. Director of Paris Conservatoire (1954–6). Noted recitalist and improviser. Compositions incl. organ, chamber and choral music, and songs.

**Duprez, Gilbert** (1806–96), French operatic tenor. Sang Edgardo in first perf. of *Lucia di Lammermoor* (Naples, 1835), and created title role in Berlioz's *Benvenuto Cellini* (1838). Numerous compositions, which had little success, incl. 8 operas, oratorio, and other choral works.

**Dur** (Ger.), major (as applied to key).

**duramente** (It.), 'with hardness', *ie* sternly, harshly.

**Durand,** French firm of music-publishers, founded Paris, 1869.

**Durante, Francesco** (1684–1755), Italian composer. One of most important figures of 'Neapolitan' school. Works are mostly Church music, but also wrote 6 harpsichord sonatas. Famous teacher; pupils incl. Pergolesi.

**Durchführung** (Ger.), lit. 'through-leading', *ie* development section of sonata movt. Also applied to exposition of fugue.

**Durchgangsnote** (Ger.), PASSING NOTE.

**durchkomponiert** (Ger.), lit. 'composed throughout' or 'through-composed'. Term applied to songs with fresh music for each verse.

**Durey, Louis Edmond** (1888–1979), French composer. Member of 'Les Six'. Best work is found in chamber music and songs, showing both individuality and refinement.

**Duruflé, Maurice** (1902– ), French organist, composer. Pupil of Dukas. Brilliant recitalist. Compositions incl. organ and chamber music.

**Dušek,** *see* DUSSEK.

**Dušek, Josepha** (1754–1824), Bohemian soprano, wife of pianist and composer F.X. Dušek (1731–99). Mozart composed for her the concert aria 'Bella mia fiamma' (K 528, 1787). Also gave first perf. of Beethoven's *scena* 'Ah perfido' (1796).

**Dushkin, Samuel** (1891–1976), Polish-Russian violinist, later a US citizen. Pupil of Auer and Kreisler. Gave recitals with Stravinsky, and gave first perf. of latter's violin concerto (1931) and *Duo concertant* (1932).

**Dussek, Jan Ladislav,** orig. Dušek (1760–1812), Czech pianist, composer. Pupil of C.P.E. Bach in Hamburg. Travelled widely in Europe as soloist; noted for beauty of touch. Compositions incl. piano concertos and sonatas, and chamber music. Piano sonatas, some having programme titles, foreshadow characteristics of romantic piano music, esp. in use of pathetic chromaticism.

**Dutilleux, Henri** (1916– ), French composer. Works, dissonant but not 'advanced', and notable for technical brilliance, incl. 2 symphonies, *Métaboles* for orchestra, popular cello concerto, and piano sonata.

**Duval, François** (*c* 1673–1728), French violinist, composer. Member of orchestra of Louis XIV. First French composer to publish sonatas for violin and continuo.

**dux,** *see* COMES.

**Dvořák, Antonin** (1841–1904), Czech composer. Born near Prague; son of village innkeeper and butcher. Learnt rudiments of violin, viola and organ at village school. Studied at Prague organ school for

3 years. Became viola player with Prague National Theatre (1862) for 11 years, during which time he was active as composer. Success as composer enabled him to devote himself entirely to composition and teaching from 1873. Received government grant in 1875 on recommendation of Brahms and Hanslick. Brahms continued to encourage him thereafter and helped to get his works published. In 1884, made first of several visits to England; subsequently composed various works for English musical societies, *eg* D minor symphony (1885). In 1891 made honorary doctor of music by Cambridge University, and appointed professor at Prague University, then director of National Conservatory of Music in New York (1892–5). Experiences in US, esp. of music of Indians and Negroes, reflected in last symphony (*From the New World*, 1893) and *American Quartet* (1893). Director of Prague Conservatory from 1901 till his death.

All Dvořák's music has natural freshness which sometimes conceals skill of construction and scrupulous care in shaping of themes. Principal influences were Smetana, Brahms, Wagner and Czech folk song. Appreciation of folk song made it easier for him to welcome idioms of US Indian and Negro music. None of these influences dominated him; rather he assimilated them into his own musical personality. Dvořák could be discursive and had exasperating habit of saying same thing twice (*eg* in G minor and *New World* symphonies and cello concerto). This fault is not found in great D minor symphony (no 7), tautest and most powerful of his works, and one of outstanding symphonic masterpieces of later 19th cent. Lyrical side of his personality found outlet in operas, though only *Rusalka* has proved popular outside Czechoslovakia.

Re-numbering of Dvořák's symphonies to incorporate 4 early works has caused some confusion. Correct chronological numbering of 9 works now runs:

No 1 in C minor (*The Bells of Zlonice*) (formerly unnumbered)
No 2 in B flat (formerly unnumbered)
No 3 in E flat (formerly unnumbered)
No 4 in D minor (formerly unnumbered)
No 5 in F major (formerly no 3)
No 6 in D major (formerly no 1)
No 7 in D minor (formerly no 2)
No 8 in G major (formerly no 4)
No 9 in E minor (*From the New World*, formerly no 5)

Principal compositions:

(1) Operas: *King and Collier* (1874), *The Pigheaded Peasants* (1874), *Vanda* (1875), *The Peasant a Rogue* (1877), *Dimitrij* (1882), *Jakobin* (1888, rev. 1897), *The Devil and Kate* (1899), *Rusalka* (1900), *Armida* (1904);

(2) Choral works: *Hymnus* (1872), *Stabat Mater* (1877), *The Spectre's Bride* (1884), *St Ludmilla* (1886), Mass in D (1887), Requiem Mass (1890), *Te Deum* (1892);

(3) Orchestra: 9 symphonies, *Symphonic Variations* (1887), 6 overtures, incl. *Carnival* (1891), 5 symphonic poems, 3 Slavonic

rhapsodies, 2 cello concertos (1865, 1895), piano concerto (1876), violin concerto (1880);

(4) Chamber music: 4 piano trios (last is *Dumky* trio), string trio, 2 piano quartets, 13 string quartets, piano quintet, 2 string quintets, string sextet.

Also many songs and duets, piano solos and piano duets.

**dynamics,** (1) degrees of loudness or softness in musical performance; (2) signs by which these are indicated in score. Those in ordinary use, with abbrevs., are: *pianissimo (pp)*, very soft; *piano (p)*, soft; *mezzo piano (mp)*, moderately soft; *mezzo forte (mf)*, moderately loud; *forte (f)*, loud; *fortissimo (ff)*, very loud; *poco forte (pf)*, moderately loud; *forte piano (fp)*, loud and immediately soft; *sforzato* and *sforzando (sf, sfz)*, heavily accented; *crescendo (cres.*, or < *)*, getting louder; *decrescendo* and *diminuendo (decresc.* and *dim.*, or > *)*, getting softer. For signs used for accentuation, *see* ACCENT.

**Dyson, George** (1883–1964), English composer, teacher. Director of Royal College of Music in London (1937–52). Knighted in 1941. Compositions incl. symphony and several choral works *eg The Canterbury Pilgrims*.

**Dzerjinsky, Ivan** (1909–78), Russian composer. Best known for opera *Quiet Flows the Don* (1923–4), inspired by Sholokhov's novel; first perf. Leningrad, 1935.

# E

**E** (Eng., Ger.; Fr., It., *mi*), third note (or mediant) of scale of C major.

**Eagles,** *see* ECCLES.

**ear training,** same as AURAL TRAINING.

**East, Michael** (*c* 1580–1648), English composer, organist. Works incl. madrigals, music for viols, church music.

**East, Est** or **Este, Thomas** (d. *c* 1608), English music-publisher. Issued some of most important works by late 16th, early 17th-cent. English composers, incl. Byrd's *Psalmes, Sonets and Songs* (1588), *Musica Transalpina* (1588, 1597), *The Triumphes of Oriana* (1601), Byrd's *Gradualia,* part i (1605), and madrigals by Morley, Wilbye, Weelkes and Bateson.

**Eberl, Anton** (1765–1807), Austrian pianist, composer. Travelled widely as soloist. Compositions, much admired in his day, incl. 5 operas, symphonies, concertos, chamber music and piano sonatas. Close friend of Mozart, under whose name some of his piano works were orig. published.

**Eberlin, Johann Ernst** (1702–62), German composer, organist. Works incl. church and keyboard music.

**Ebony Concerto,** work written by Stravinsky for jazz clarinettist, Woody Herman, and his band. First perf. 1946.

**Eccard, Johann** (1553–1611), German composer. Pupil of Lassus. Mostly wrote Lutheran church music, incl. settings of chorales; also wrote secular part-songs.

**Eccles** or **Eagles, Solomon** (1618–83), English musician. Taught virginals and viol. Became Quaker and migrated to West Indies and America. His son, **Solomon Eccles,** was violinist, composer, in service of Charles II, James II and William III. His sons, **Henry** (*c* 1670–*c* 1742) and **John Eccles** (1668–1735), were both violinists and composers. Latter became Master of King's Musick (1700), and wrote music for many plays.

**échappée** (Fr.), abbrev. of *note échappée, ie* 'escaped note'. Term used in theory of harmony to describe progression between 2 adjacent notes which first takes step in 'wrong' direction, then reverts to note orig. aimed at by interval of third.

**échelle** (Fr.), scale. *Gamme* is more usual term.

**Echo et Narcisse** (Fr., *Echo and Narcissus*), opera by Gluck, libretto by L.T. de Tschudy. First perf. Paris, 1779.

**echo attachment,** electronic device that adds artificial echo to sound of electric instrument. For higher quality echo, *echo chamber* is used, consisting of sealed chamber with loudspeaker, microphones and acoustic delay line.

**echo organ,** set of pipes placed further away than main body of organ and designed to suggest echo.

**éclatant** (Fr.), (1) brilliant; (2) blaring.

**École d'Arcueil,** group of French musicians, disciples of Satie, taking name from Paris suburb where he lived. Group (founded 1923) incl. Henri Sauguet, Maxime Jacob and Roger Désormière.

**écossaise** (Fr.), short for *danse écossaise,* 'Scottish dance'. Quick dance in 2/4 time, popular in Britain and on Continent in late 18th, early 19th cents. Examples occur in works of Beethoven and Schubert. There is no evidence of any Scottish connection. Not to be confused with SCHOTTISCHE.

**Edinburgh Festival,** summer festival of music and drama held in Scotland, one of largest in world. Founded 1947. Features orchestras and soloists of world class, and several important works have been commissioned.

**Egdon Heath,** symphonic poem by Holst (1928), inspired by Thomas Hardy.

**Egge, Klaus** (1906–79), Norwegian composer. Pupil of Valen. Works, strongly influenced by folk music, incl. 5 symphonies, 2 piano concertos, oratorio, chamber and piano music, songs.

**Egk, Werner** (1901– ), German composer, conductor. Operas incl. *Die Zaubergeige* (1934), *Peer Gynt* (1938, based on Ibsen), *Irish Legend* (1954, inspired by Yeats) and *The Government Inspector* (1957, based on Gogol), *Abraxas* (1979). Other works incl. oratorio *Columbus,* violin concerto, and French suite (after Rameau) for orchestra.

**Egmont,** tragedy by Goethe, dealing with revolt of Netherlands against Spanish domination, for which Beethoven wrote overture and incidental music (op 84, 1810), incorporating *entr'actes* and songs.

**Ehrling, Sixten** (1918– ), Swedish conductor. Chief conductor of Swedish National Opera (1953–1960), musical director of Detroit Symphony Orchestra (1963–73).

**Eichheim, Henry** (1870–1942), American composer, violinist. Works, heavily influenced by Eastern music, incl. 3 ballets (*Chinese Legend, Burmese Pwe* and *The Moon, My Shadow and I*), and orchestral works employing oriental instruments.

**Eighteen Twelve** *(The Year 1812)*, concert overture by Chaikovsky, written in 1882 for commemoration of 70th anniversary of Napoleon's retreat from Moscow. Score incorporates optional parts for canon and military band.

**eighth-note** (US), quaver.

**eilen** (Ger.), to hurry. *Nicht eilen,* do not hurry.

**Eine Kleine Nachtmusik,** *see* KLEINE NACHTMUSIK.

**Einem, Gottfried von** (1918– ), Austrian composer, b. Switzerland. Pupil of Blacher. Works incl. operas *Danton's Death* (1947), *The Old Lady's Visit* (after Dürrenmatt, 1971), *Jesu Hochzeit* (1980), ballet *Princess Turandot* (after Gozzi), *Philadelphia Symphony* and other orchestral works.

**einfach** (Ger.), simply.

**Einleitung** (Ger.), introduction.

**Einstein, Alfred** (1880–1952), German-born historian, critic. Music critic on various newspapers until 1933, when he went into exile, settling in US in 1939. Editor of 3 editions of Riemann's *Musik-Lexikon* (1919, 1922, 1929). Numerous publications incl. 3rd edition of Köchel's catalogue of Mozart's works (1937), books on Gluck, Mozart and Schumann, *Music in the Romantic Era* (1947), and *The Italian Madrigal* (1949).

**Eis** (Ger.), E sharp.

**Eisis** (Ger.), E double sharp.

**Eisler, Hanns** (1898–1962), German composer, of Austrian parentage. Pupil of Schoenberg. Friend of Brecht. Fled to US from Nazis; persecuted for leftist views after WWII and returned to East Germany, 1950. Works incl. 2 operas (*Goliath* and *Johannes Faustus*), *German Symphony* for solo voices, chorus and orchestra, *Lenin Requiem*, instrumental quintet entitled *14 Ways of Describing Rain* and other chamber music, film and theatre music, and many songs, often in collaboration with Brecht.

**Eisteddfod** (Welsh), lit. 'assembly' or 'session'. Esp. applied to gathering of Welsh bards. Held in very early times. Now a competition festival, not necessarily confined to music. Most important is National Eisteddfod, revival dating from 19th cent.

**Eitner, Robert** (1832–1905), German lexicographer, musicologist. Founded Gesellschaft für Musikgeschichte (Society for Musical Research), 1868, and edited its journal, as well as series of musical and theoretical works of the past. Also produced invaluable biographical and bibliographical reference works.

**Ek, Gunnar** (1900– ), Swedish composer. Works incl. symphonies and *Swedish Fantasy* for orchestra.

**electronde,** electronic instrument similar to THÉRÉMIN, but incorporating mechanism to interrupt *glissando* and to control amplification. Tone is produced by utilizing difference between 2 frequencies. Invented by Martin Taubmann (1929).

**electrone,** electric organ, first produced in 1939 by John Compton Organ Co. Provided with stops and couplers like ordinary organ, but sound is produced by amplifying electrically generated vibrations.

**electronic instruments,** there are 3 principal ways in which electricity is used to produce (as distinct from merely reproducing) musical sounds:

(1) by amplifying existing vibrations, *eg* in Everett Orgatron (1934);

(2) by generating frequencies corresponding to vibrations of notes and converting them into sound, *eg* in Hammond organ (1934), where system of intensifying or suppressing individual members of limited harmonic series makes possible the artificial representation of tone of large number of different instruments;

(3) by utilizing difference between 2 frequencies, *eg* in Thérémin (1924), where difference is controlled by movement of hand through air.

**electronic music,** general term embracing any type of music where composers work with sounds electronically produced and/or treated, usually in special studios. Huge amount has been produced since 1950s, varying from commercial jingles to most rigorous *avant garde* music. Using technical criteria, 3 main types may be distinguished:

(1) prerecorded tape music, (a) of purely electronic production and treatment; (b) of MUSIQUE CONCRÈTE, *ie* taped compositions of 'naturally' produced sounds electronically treated;

(2) live electronic music either (a) combining use of performers and tapes, or (b) using simultaneous modulation of 'live' (instrumental) and/or electronic sounds;

(3) computer music incl. (a) digitally synthesized compositions; (b) compositions created as in (1), but in studio where computer is used to control various electronic components and to sequence work; (c) instrumental compositions, scores of which are prepared with aid of computer.

First purpose-designed studio was founded in Paris by Pierre Schaeffer (1951). Since then many more have emerged in Europe, US and Japan. Techniques have developed with introduction of *eg* multi-track recorders, voltage control, SYNTHESIZERS, and digital synthesis. Notable composers who have worked with electronic music incl. Boulez, Berio, Stockhausen, Bruno Maderna, Penderecki, Harrison Birtwistle, Henri Pousseur, Edgard Varèse, and Takemitsu.

**elegy** (Fr., *élégie*; It., *elegia*), lament, esp. for dead.

**Elegy for Young Lovers,** opera by Henze, libretto by W.H. Auden and C. Kallman. First perf. (in German translation), Schwetzingen, 1961. Story concerns egotistical poet.

**Elektra,** opera by Richard Strauss, libretto by Hugo von Hofmannsthal (after Sophocles). First perf. Dresden, 1909. Story concerns revenge of Elektra and brother Orestes on mother Clytemnestra and lover Aegisthus for murder of father Agamemnon. Avenged, Elektra dances herself to death.

**eleventh,** interval of octave and fourth, *eg* from D below treble clef to G above treble clef. For 'chord of the eleventh' *see* CHORD.

**Elgar, Edward William** (1857–1934), English composer. Son of Worcester music-dealer and organist. Had no formal musical training, but learned organ, violin and bassoon. Abandoned early idea of becoming solo violinist. Held various minor posts in Worcester as conductor and organist. Married Caroline Alice Roberts and went to live in London, but failed to make career there, and settled in Malvern (1891). First important perf. was concert overture *Froissart* (1890), followed by various choral works *eg The Light of Life* (1896) and *Caractacus* (1898). Reputation as leading composer was estab. by *Enigma Variations* for orchestra (1899) and oratorio *The Dream of Gerontius* (1900), one of several works inspired by his Catholicism. Next 20 years (until death of wife in 1920) were notable for composition of 2 more oratorios, several large-scale orchestral works and some chamber music. After 1920, wrote little of importance: 3rd symphony, commissioned by B.B.C., and opera *The Spanish Lady* survive only in sketches. Professor of music at Birmingham University (1905–8) and Master of the King's Musick (1924). Knighted in 1904; became baronet, 1931.

Elgar began career as romantic and remained one, though exuberance of maturity was superseded by wistful nostalgia of old age. Delighted in colour and showed great mastery of orchestra. His generous display of emotion repelled some who felt that English music should be reserved, but many others awoke to discovery of his rich humanity, conveyed in intensely personal style. Oratorios are confession of his faith: *The Dream of Gerontius* is traditionally regarded as finest, but some think *The Kingdom* is structurally superior.

Principal compositions:

(1) Oratorios: *The Light of Life* (1896), *The Dream of Gerontius* (1900), *The Apostles* (1903), *The Kingdom* (1906);

(2) Other choral works: *The Black Knight* (1893), *Scenes from the Bavarian Highlands* (1896), *King Olaf* (1896), *The Banner of St George* (1897), *Caractacus* (1898), *Coronation Ode* (1902), *The Music Makers* (1912), *The Spirit of England* (1916);

(3) Orchestra: *Froissart* (1890), *Serenade for strings* (1893), *Enigma Variations* (1899), *Cockaigne* (1901), *In the South* (1904), *Introduction and Allegro* for strings (1905), *Pomp and Circumstance* (nos 1–4, 1901–7, no 5, 1930), *The Wand of Youth* (1907–8), 2 symphonies (1908, 1911), violin concerto (1910), *Falstaff* (1913), cello concerto (1919), *Nursery Suite* (1933);

(4) Brass band: *Severn Suite* (1930; also arranged for orchestra and solo organ);

(5) Chamber music: Piano quintet (1919), string quartet (1919), violin sonata (1919);

(6) Organ: 2 sonatas (1896, 1933; 2nd arranged from *Severn Suite*);

(7) Songs: *Sea Pictures,* with orchestra (1899), songs with piano, part-songs.

**Elijah,** oratorio by Mendelssohn, op 70, with words from Bible. First perf. Birmingham, 1846.

**Elisir d'amore, L'** (It., *The Elixir of Love*), opera by Donizetti, libretto by F. Romani (based on Scribe's *Le Philtre*). Story tells how bashful young man buys 'elixir' from quack doctor which turns out to be cheap wine, but he nevertheless wins heroine.

**Elizalde, Federico** (1907– ), Spanish composer, conductor, b. Philippines. Studied under Bloch. Works incl. opera *Paul Gauguin,* sinfonia concertante for piano and orchestra, and violin concerto.

**Elkin,** London firm of music-publishers, founded 1903 by W.W.A. Elkin.

**Ellington, 'Duke',** orig. Edward Kennedy Ellington (1899–1974), black American jazz composer, pianist and band leader. Greatest musical 'colourist' in jazz history. Nickname 'Duke' refers to aristocracy of his style and personality. Career straddled several eras of jazz history and Ellington produced great jazz to match style of each phase, from grittiness of output in 1920s to experiments with Shakespeare (*Such Sweet Thunder* suite) in 1950s, and subsequent jazz impressions of 'classical' works, *eg* Chaikovsky's *Nutcracker* suite. Among his masterpieces are *Black and Tan Fantasy, Mood Indigo, Creole love call, Creole Rhapsody* and *Concerto for Cootie.*

**Ellinwood, Leonard** (1905– ), American musicologist. Special field is medieval music. Edited *Musica Hermanni Contracti* (1936) with English translation, and works of Francesco Landini.

**Ellis, David** (1933– ), English composer. Works incl. opera *Crito* (1963), symphony, violin and piano concertos and other orchestral works, and choral, chamber and piano music.

**Elman, Mischa** (1891–1967), Russian violinist. Became US citizen in 1923. Toured internationally.

**Elmendorff, Karl** (1891–1962), German conductor. Active as opera conductor in many German cities, and appeared regularly at Bayreuth (1927–42).

**Elsner, Joseph Xaver** (1769–1854), Polish composer, b. Germany. Works incl. operas, church music, symphonies, concertos, chamber music and ballets. First director of Warsaw Conservatory (1821–30), which he helped to found; pupils incl. Chopin.

**embellishments,** *see* ORNAMENTS.

**embouchure,** (1) mouthpiece of wind instrument;

(2) correct shaping of lips necessary to produce accurate intonation and good tone. Only acquired by persistent practice. Known colloquially as 'lip'.

**Emmanuel, Marie François Maurice** (1862–1938), French composer, musicologist. Works incl. 2 symphonies, and operas *Prométhée enchaîné* (1918) and *Salamine* (1929), both after Aeschylus. Historical studies incl. important *Histoire de la langue musicale* (1911).

**Emperor Concerto,** nickname given in Britain and US to Beethoven's piano Concerto no 5 in E flat, op 73 (1808).

**Emperor Quartet** (Ger., *Kaiserquartett*), nickname of Haydn's quartet in C, op 76, no 3 (*c* 1799), slow variations of which consist of variations on EMPEROR'S HYMN.

**Emperor's Hymn** (Ger., *Kaiserlied*), patriotic hymn by Haydn (1797). Haydn used it in EMPEROR QUARTET. Adopted as national anthem of Austria and later of Germany. Used in Britain as hymn tune.

**Empfindung** (Ger.), 'feeling'. *Mit Empfindung*, with feeling. *Empfindungsvoll,* full of feeling.

**empfindsamer Stil** (Ger.), sensitive style. Term refers to 18th-cent. style of C.P.E. Bach, Quantz and others who tried to make their music expressive of 'true and natural' feeling, thereby paving way for 19th-cent. romanticism.

**enchaînez** (Fr.), 'link up', *ie* go straight to next movement or section.

**Encina,** *see* ENZINA.

**enclume** (Fr.), anvil.

**encore** (Fr.), again. Cry of English-speaking audiences (though not of

French ones) who want to hear more music than they paid for. If performer complies, additional music is called an 'encore'.

**Enesco, Georges,** orig. George Enescu (1881–1955), Romanian composer, conductor, violinist. Studied in Vienna and Paris. Toured widely as conductor and violinist. Yehudi Menuhin was his pupil. Compositions incl. opera *Oedipe* (1936), 3 symphonies, 2 Romanian rhapsodies and chamber music.

**Enfance du Christ, L'** (Fr., *The Childhood of Christ*), oratorio by Berlioz, op 25, words by composer. First perf. Paris, 1854.

**Enfant et les sortilèges, L'** (Fr., *The Child and the Magic Spells*), opera (*fantaisie lyrique*) by Ravel, libretto by Colette. First perf. Monte Carlo, 1925.

**Engel, Carl** (1818–82), German writer on musical instruments. Came to England as young man, and soon turned to historical research and collection of instruments, many of which are now in South Kensington Museum.

**Engel, Carl** (1883–1944), American musicologist, of German origin. Chief of Music Division, Library of Congress, Washington (1922–34), editor of *The Musical Quarterly* (1929–44). Active in promoting musical research.

**Engführung,** *see* STRETTO (1).

**English Chamber Orchestra,** founded as Goldsbrough Orchestra (1948), adopted present name in 1960. Involved in Aldeburgh Festival since 1961. Has no permanent conductor.

**English fingering,** *see* FINGERING.

**English flute,** *see* FLUTE.

**English Folk Dance and Song Society,** amalgamation (1932) of Folk Song Society (founded 1898) and English Folk Dance Society (founded 1911). Arranges lectures, meetings, festivals, and publishes journal.

**English guitar,** same as CITTERN.

**English horn,** *see* OBOE (3).

**English Madrigal School, The,** edition by E.H. Fellowes of all English madrigals published in reigns of Elizabeth I and James I. 36 vols. published (1913–24); many subsequently revised by Thurston Dart.

**English Music Theatre,** *see* ENGLISH OPERA GROUP.

**English Opera Group,** organization founded in 1947 by Benjamin Britten, Eric Crozier and John Piper with object of producing small-scale operas. Britten, Berkeley and Birtwistle all wrote operas specially for group, which also revived older works, *eg* by Blow and Purcell. Had no permanent theatre, but closely linked with Covent Garden and Aldeburgh Festival. Reconstituted as English Music Theatre (1976).

**English School of Lutenist Song-Writers, The,** edition by E.H. Fellowes of songs for solo voice (or duet) with lute accompanist published by English composers between 1597–1622. Orig. edition published 1920–32; revision and additions commenced 1959.

**English Suites,** name given to set of 6 keyboard suites by Bach. On larger scale than FRENCH SUITES, and unlike latter they have preludes for first movts. Origin of title is not clear.

**enharmonic,** (1) in Greek music, enharmonic *genus* was oldest of 3 ways of sub-dividing tetrachord, other 2 being diatonic and chromatic. Orig. seems to have consisted simply of major third with semitone below (*eg* A, F, E), but in quite early times, semitone was divided into 2 quarter-tones so that there were 4 notes, not 3: A, F, quarter-tone above E, and E. Existence of these small intervals (in use until Hellenistic times) shows close association between Greek and Oriental music;

(2) in modern acoustics, enharmonic *diesis* is interval between octave (*eg* C–C), *ie* 2/1, and 3 major thirds (C–E–G sharp–B sharp), *ie* 125/64. B is therefore flatter than C, and interval is 2 ÷ 125/64 = 128/125. On keyboard instruments, however, B sharp and C are identical, and this has encouraged composers to use harmonic changes which exploit this identity; where, for example, B sharp is substituted for C, this is known as *enharmonic change*. *Enharmonic modulation* is one which makes use of such a change to facilitate progress from one key to another.

**Enigma Variations,** work by Elgar, op 36, first perf. 1899. Described on title page as 'variations on an original theme for orchestra'; word 'enigma' appears only on first page of music. Each variation is description of character or habits of individual (incl. himself), indicated by initials or nickname. Further 'enigma' lies in fact that theme and variations are closely associated with another theme which is never heard – thought by some to be 'Auld lang syne'.

**Enoch,** London firm of music-publishers. Founded 1869 by Emile Enoch. Bought by Edwin Ashdown (1927) and incorporated with his firm in 1936.

**ensemble** (Fr.), lit. 'together': (1) group of singers and players, *eg* instrumental ensemble, vocal ensemble;

(2) in opera, movt. for several singers, with or without chorus;

(3) artistic cooperation of individual members of group.

**Entführung aus dem Serail, Die** (Ger., *The Abduction from the Seraglio* or *Harem*), comic *Singspiel* (opera with dialogue) by Mozart, libretto by C.F. Bretzner, adapted by G. Stephanie. First perf. Vienna, 1782. First important opera to be written in German. Story concerns imprisonment of Constanze and her maid Blonde in palace of Pasha, attempt of Belmonte and Pedrillo to rescue them, and eventual release of all by magnanimous Pasha.

**entr'acte** (Fr.), music played between acts of play or opera.

**entrée** (Fr.), term used mainly in 17th-cent. French music:

(1) introductory piece in ballet or opera, for entry of characters on stage;

(2) independent piece of instrumental music, similar in character to (1);

(3) section of ballet or opera, equivalent of 'scene' or even 'act'.

**entry,** in fugue, 'entrance' of theme, not only at beginning but also on later appearances; also, 17th-cent. term for prelude.

**Enzina** or **Encina, Juan Del** (1468–1529), Spanish poet, dramatist, composer. Although a priest, known only by his secular compositions.

**epidiapente** (Gr.), term referring to 'CANON at the fifth'.

**Epine, L',** *see* L'EPINE.

**épinette** (Fr.), (1) spinet; (2) virginals.

**episode,** (1) in FUGUE, passage forming contrast to entries of subject and serving as link between one entry and next, often modulating to related key. Thematic material may be derived from subject or countersubject, or may be independent. First episode normally occurs after EXPOSITION; however, it is poss. to have fugue without any episodes;

(2) in RONDO, section separating entries of principal theme or section and contrasted with it.

**episodical form,** same as RONDO form.

**epithalamium,** marriage song.

**equale** (Old It.), 'equal'. As noun, piece for EQUAL VOICES or instruments of same kind, esp. trombones.

**equal temperament,** tuning of keyboard instrument in such a way that all semitones are equal. This has effect of putting all intervals except octave slightly out of tune. Advantage of system is that intervals have same value in all keys. Any other system of tuning favours some keys at expense of others and makes modulation difficult outside restricted range.

Though equal temperament was advocated by 16th-cent. theorists, it was not until 18th cent. that development of modulation and use of wide range of keys made it practical necessity (*eg* in Bach's *The Well-Tempered Clavier*). System was not universally adopted until *c* 1850.

**equal voices,** voices of same range (*eg* all basses) or same kind (*eg* all male).

**Erard, Sébastien** (1752–1831), inventor of various improvements in PIANOFORTE.

**Erbach, Christian** (*c* 1570–1635), German organist, composer. Principal works are motets; also wrote secular part-songs and keyboard music.

**Erbe deutscher Musik, Das,** *see* DENKMÄLER DEUTSCHER TONKUNST.

**Erkel, Ferencz** (1810–93), Hungarian opera composer. Conductor, then director of National Theatre, Budapest. Operas, in strongly marked national vein, were enthusiastically received in Hungary; most successful was *Hunyady László* (1844). Also wrote music for Hungarian national anthem, 'Ysten áldd meg a Magyart' (1845).

**Erlebach, Philipp** (1657–1714), German composer. Works incl. vocal cantatas, instrumental suites, and sacred and secular songs.

**Erlkönig** (Ger., *Alder King*), song by Schubert, setting of words of Goethe's ballad. Written in 1815, when Schubert was only 18.

**Ernani,** opera by Verdi, libretto by F.M. Piave (based on Victor Hugo's drama *Hernani*). First perf. Venice, 1844. Story, set in

Aragon, concerns outlaw Ernani's love for Donna Elvira, who is betrothed to elderly Spanish grandee. First of Verdi's operas to bring him fame outside Italy, though Hugo thought it a travesty of his play.

**Eroica** (It.), popular abbrev. of title of Beethoven's symphony no 3 in E flat major, op 55 (1804) – *Sinfonia eroica, composa per festeggiare il souvenire d'un grand' uomo* (heroic symphony, composed to celebrate the memory of a great man). Orig. title was *Sinfonia grande Napoleon Bonaparte,* but Beethoven angrily changed it when he heard Napoleon had taken title of emperor. Thematic material on which last movt. is built comes from no 7 of Beethoven's 12 *Kontretänze* (*c* 1800). Beethoven also used this theme and bass (1) in finale of ballet *The Creatures of Prometheus* op 43 (1801), and (2) as basis of 15 variations and fugue in E flat major for piano, op 35 (1802), sometimes known as *Eroica Variations.*

**Erwartung** (Ger., *Expectation*), monodrama (for soprano and orchestra) by Schoenberg, libretto by M. Pappenheim. Composed 1909; first perf. 1924 (Prague).

**Erzlaute** (Ger.), archlute.

**Es** (Ger.), E flat.

**escapement,** mechanism in piano which enables hammer to 'escape' after string has been struck, so leaving string free to vibrate. *Double escapement,* invented by Erard, makes it poss. to strike string second time without waiting for key to rise to normal position of rest.

**Eschig,** Paris firm of music-publishers, founded by Czech-born Maximilian Eschig (1872–1927) in 1907.

**Esercizi** (It., *Exercises*), title under which 30 of D. Scarlatti's harpsichord sonatas were published (1738).

**Eses** (Ger.), E double flat.

**España** (Sp., *Spain*), rhapsody for orchestra by Chabrier. First perf. 1883.

**espressivo** (It.), expressively. Abbrev. is *espresso.*

**essential note,** note forming part of chord, as opposed to passing note, suspension, appoggiatura *etc.*

**Est,** *see* EAST.

**Estampes** (Fr., *Engravings*), set of 3 piano pieces by Debussy (1903): *Pagodes* (pagodas), *Soirée dans Grenade* (evening in Granada), *Jardins sous la pluie* (gardens in the rain).

**estampie** (Fr.; Provençal, *estampida*), dance form current in 13th, 14th cents. Consists of several sections *(puncta)*, each of which has 1st ending (OUVERT) and 2nd ending (CLOS).

**Este,** *see* EAST.

**Esther,** oratorio by Handel. Orig. called *Haman and Mordecai* and given as masque, with libretto attrib. to Alexander Pope (after Racine); first perf. London, 1720. Later revised and enlarged; first perf. as oratorio, London, 1732.

**estinto** (It.), lit. 'extinct', *ie* so soft that music can hardly be heard.

**ethnomusicology,** study of different kinds of music to be found in any particular area, in relation to their cultural or racial context.

**Etoile du Nord, L'** (Fr., *The Star of the North*), opera by Meyerbeer, libretto by A.E. Scribe. First perf. Paris, 1854. Story concerns relationship between Tsar Peter and village girl, Katherine, who becomes his Tsarina. Some of music later incorporated by Constant Lambert in ballet *Les Patineurs*.

**Eton Choirbook,** manuscript of polyphonic music compiled *c* 1500 for use of chapel choir at Eton College.

**étouffez** (Fr.), 'damp' (imperative). Indication to player of harp, cymbals *etc.* that sound must be immediately damped (opposite of *laissez vibrer*). So also *sons étouffés,* 'damped notes'.

**Etranger, L'** (Fr., *The Stranger*), opera by d'Indy, libretto by composer. First perf. Brussels, 1903.

**Etudes Symphoniques** (Fr., *Symphonic Studies*), set of 12 variations for piano by Schumann, op 13 (1834, rev. 1852); 5 additional variations are published in modern editions.

**etwas** (Ger.), somewhat, rather.

**eude** (Fr.), STUDY.

**Eugene Onegin** (Russ., *Evgeny Onegin*), opera by Chaikovsky, op 24, libretto by composer and K. Shilovsky (based on Pushkin). First perf. (by students) Moscow, 1879; professional première, 1881. Story concerns love of Tatyana, sensitive young girl, for Onegin, cold and selfish man of the world. Onegin rejects her until, years later, she is married to another; he declares his love but she will not go with him.

**Eulenburg,** firm of music-publishers, founded in Leipzig by Ernst Eulenburg (1847–1926) in 1874. In 1892 took over series of miniature scores published by Albert Payne. Firm is now owned by Schott.

**eunuch flute,** *see* MIRLITON.

**euphonium,** brass instrument of saxhorn type, generally with 4 valves and compass of 3 octaves from B flat below bass clef. Normal instrument of military and brass bands. Used occasionally in orchestra, generally for parts marked 'tenor tuba'. *See* TUBA.

**eurhythmics,** system of rhythmic education through bodily movement, invented by JAQUES-DALCROZE.

**Euridice, L'** (It., *Eurydice*), (1) opera by Caccini, libretto by O. Rinuccini. Published in 1600, before Peri's opera, but first perf. Florence, 1602.

(2) opera by Peri, with same libretto as Caccini's opera. First perf. Florence, 1600, and published same year.

**Euryanthe,** opera by Weber, libretto by H. von Chézy. First perf. Vienna, 1823. Complex story concerns vindication of heroine's faithfulness to husband.

**Evans, Geraint** (1922– ), Welsh baritone. Made Covent Garden début in 1948, and has sung with that company ever since. Most famous roles incl. Falstaff, Figaro, Leporello in *Don Giovanni,* and Wozzeck. Well-known in US and at Salzburg Festival and Vienna Opera. Knighted 1969.

**Evans, Gil** (1912– ), Canadian jazz arranger and band leader. Famous for work with trumpeter Miles Davies. Arrangements, *eg* suite of numbers from Gershwin's *Porgy and Bess,* have richness surpassed only by Ellington.

**Ewer,** London firm of music-publishers, founded early 19th cent, by John Ewer. Acquired 1867 by Novello, who published under name Novello, Ewer & Co. until 1888.

**exercise,** (1) instrumental piece intended for technical practice rather than artistic value;
(2) in 18th cent., name applied to keyboard suite;
(3) composition written for university degrees in music.

**Expert, Henri** (1863–1952), French musicologist. Principal achievement was publication of 2 series of old French music: *Les Maîtres musiciens de la Renaissance française* (23 vols., 1894–1908), and *Monuments de la musique au temps de la Renaissance* (10 vols., 1924–9).

**exposition,** initial statement of musical material on which movt. is based:
(1) in FUGUE, consists in introducing subject to each part in turn; exposition is complete when all parts have announced subject for first time;
(2) in movt. in SONATA FORM it is more extended and traditionally consists of presentation of principal thematic material, partly in tonic key and partly in subsidiary key(s). It is convention (continuing far into 19th cent.) to repeat exposition in works in sonata form; this convention should be observed in modern performance.

**expression marks,** indications provided by composer as aid to accurate interpretation of his text. They are concerned primarily with:
(1) DYNAMICS – *eg forte* (loud),
(2) TEMPO – *eg lento* (slow),
(3) mood – *eg appassionato* (passionate).
Vogue of Italian music in 17th cent. led to adoption of Italian terms as international music language, though practice was not universal, *eg* many French composers preferred to use own language.

**expressionism,** name orig. given to movement in visual arts (*eg* to works of Kirchner, Nolde, Kokoschka), prevalent esp. in Germany, *c* 1905–30; came to be applied to literature, theatre, film and music. Term implies reaction against impressionism, which claimed objective representation of outside world; expressionism on the other hand eschews everything but the highly subjective expression of inner emotions, often using distortion and symbolism. In music, term is esp. applied to works of Schoenberg and Berg and to some works of Hindemith, but here its meaning is vague; such works can be seen as final phase of romantic tradition, in which artist turns away from world, and in upon himself.

**extension organ,** sometimes called unit organ: organ in which pipes are constructed to give more than one note each, thus saving space.

# F

**f,** in TONIC SOL-FA, fourth note (or subdominant) of major scale.

**F,** fourth note (or subdominant) of scale of C major (Eng., Ger.; Fr., It., *fa*). As abbrev., *f* = *forte* (loud), *ff* = *fortissimo* (very loud), *fp* = *forte piano* (loud and immediately soft again), *fz* = *forzando* (lit. 'forcing', *ie* accenting), *mf* = *mezzo forte* (moderately loud), *pf* = *poco forte* (moderately loud), *sf* or *sfz* = *sforzando* (same as *forzando*).

F clef originated as ornamental form of letter F and indicates note a fifth below middle C (*see* CLEF).

**fa** (Fr., It.), the note F; also fourth note of Guidonian hexachord (*see* SOLMIZATION).

**Fabri, Annibale Pio** (1697–1760), Italian tenor. Came to Britain in 1729, and sang in several of Handel's operas with great success. Subsequently appointed to Chapel Royal in Lisbon, where he died.

**faburden,** Eng. term for 15th-cent. technique of improvising 2 parts on a plainsong. Using SIGHT method, 'faburdener' sang third below plainsong melody, except for certain isolated notes at fifth below incl. first note and final notes at cadences. Treble part doubled plainsong throughout at fourth above. Origin of term and relationship with Continental FAUXBOURDON is disputed.

**Façade,** series of poems by Edith Sitwell, recited to music for flute, clarinet, saxophone, trumpet, cello and percussion by Walton. First perf. London, 1923 (rev. 1926). Some pieces later issued in 2 suites for orchestra.

**Faccio, Franco** (1840–1891), Italian composer, conductor. Close friend of Boito, who wrote libretto of his opera *Amleto* (1865). Became conductor at La Scala, where directed first perf. of Verdi's *Otello* (1887).

**facilmente** (It.), 'easily' *ie* play fluently.

**Fagott** (Ger.), **fagotto** (It.), bassoon.

**fah,** anglicized form of Italian *fa* (F). In TONIC SOL-FA, fourth note (or subdominant) of major scale.

**Fairfax,** *see* FAYRFAX.

**Fair Maid of Perth, The** (Fr., *La Jolie Fille de Perth*), opera by Bizet, libretto by J.H. Vernoy de Saint-Georges and J. Adenis (after Scott's novel). First perf. Paris, 1867.

**Fair Maid of the Mill, The,** *see* SCHÖNE MÜLLERIN, DIE.

**Fair Melusina, The,** *see* SCHÖNE MELUSINE.

**Fairy Queen, The,** operatic masque with dialogue, adapted from Shakespeare's *A Midsummer Night's Dream*, with music by Purcell. First perf. London, 1692.

**fa-la,** popular type of part-song current in late 16th, early 17th cents., known as *balletto* (It.) or BALLETT (Eng.). Name derives from use of refrain using syllables 'fa la la'.

**Falcon, Marie Cornélie** (1812–97), French operatic soprano. First appeared at Paris Opéra in 1832, and subsequently sang leading roles in first perfs. of several operas, until she lost her voice 6 years later and had to abandon the stage. Term 'falcon' still survives to describe her kind of voice.

**fall,** cadence.

**Falla, Manuel de** (1876–1946), Spanish composer, pianist. Made reputation with opera *La vida breve* (1905). Lived in Paris (1907–14), then in Spain till Civil War, when he moved to South America. Died in Argentina. Falla was outstanding Spanish composer of his time, skilful in adoption of Andalusian rhythms without becoming their slave. Acquaintance with Debussy in Paris inclined him towards impressionism, but later turned to neoclassical idiom. Severely selfcritical; published little. Orchestration is vivid and precise.

Principal works:

(1) Operas: *La vida breve* (*Life is short*, 1905), *El retablo de Maese Pedro* (*Master Peter's Puppet Show*, 1923), *La Atlántida* (completed after his death by E. Halffter);

(2) Ballets: *El amor brujo* (*Love the Magician*, 1915), *El sombrero de tres picos* (*The Three-cornered Hat*, 1919);

(3) Orchestra: *Noches en los jardines de España* (*Nights in the Gardens of Spain*, 1916) for piano and orchestra, harpsichord concerto (1926);

(4) Piano: *Fantasia bética* (1919).

**falsa musica,** *see* MUSICA FALSA.

**false relation** (US, cross relation), name given in classical harmony (*ie* late 18th, early 19th cent.) to (1) progression in which note in one part of first chord is followed by chromatic alteration of same note in another part of second chord;

(2) simultaneous sounding in single chord of note and its chromatic alteration.

**falsetto** (It.), adult male voice, used not in normal range but in higher register. If seriously cultivated, voice becomes male alto (or countertenor). Falsetto singing is used occasionally by tenors for notes which lie above normal range, and sometimes also for comic effect. Compass can range up to E at top of treble clef.

**falso bordone,** *see* FAUXBOURDON.

**Falstaff,** (1) comic opera by Verdi, to libretto by A. Boito (after Shakespeare's *The Merry Wives of Windsor* and *Henry IV*, part 1). First perf. Milan, 1893. Action is substantially the same as that of plays. Verdi's last opera, and his first comedy for 44 years;

(2) symphonic study for orchestra by Elgar, op 68 (after Shakespeare's *Henry IV* and *Henry V*), first perf. 1913.

**Fanciulla del West, La,** *see* GIRL OF THE GOLDEN WEST.

**fancy,** *see* FANTASIA (1).

**fandango,** lively Spanish dance in triple time, accompanied by guitar and castanets.

**fanfare,** flourish for trumpets, or other instruments emulating character of trumpets. Fanfares are often used as ceremonial preludes, and are sometimes incorporated in extended compositions. In French form, term also applies to brass band.

**fantasia**(It.; Fr., *fantaisie*; Ger., *Phantasie*, *Fantasie*), in general, piece in which composer follows his fancy rather than any conventional form. In particular:

(1) in 16th, 17th cents., name was frequently used of composition for string or keyboard, in which composer, instead of adopting dance form or writing variations, lets imagination play freely in contrapuntal development of theme. Eng. term was 'fancy';

(2) work for keyboard or lute of improvisatory character;

(3) extended work, freer in form than normal sonata;

(4) short piece similar to intermezzo, capriccio *etc*;

(5) work based on existing theme or themes;

(6) development section of movt. in sonata form is sometimes known as 'free fantasia'.

**Fantasiestück** (Ger.), same as FANTASIA (4).

**Fantastic Symphony,** *see* SYMPHONIE FANTASTIQUE.

**Faramondo,** opera by Handel, libretto by A. Zeno (with alterations). First perf. London, 1738.

**farandole** (Fr.), dance of ancient origin still current in Provence. Dancers advance in long chain preceded by player(s) on pipe and tabor. Usually in 6/8 time.

**farce** (Eng., Fr., from Lat. *farcire*, to stuff), (1) orig. practice of interpolating TROPES into plainsong or polyphonic settings of liturgy;

(2) in 18th-cent. opera, comic scene introduced into serious work; Italian comic operas in one act were called *farsa* (*c* 1800).

**Farewell Sonata,** *see* LEBEWOHL.

**Farewell Symphony** (Ger., *Abschiedssymphonie*), symphony no 45 in F sharp minor by Haydn (1772). Finale emphasizes desire of Prince Esterházy's musicians for a holiday: instruments stopped playing in turn, and players left room until only 2 violins were left.

**Farina, Carlo** (*fl* early 17th cent.), Mantuan violinist, composer. Held posts in Dresden and Danzig. One of first composers to exploit virtuosity in solo violin music. His 'Capriccio stravagante' (1627) incl. double stops, *pizzicato, col legno* and harmonics.

**Farinel, Michel** (b. 1649), French violinist, composer. One of earliest of many composers to write chaconnes or variations on theme known as FOLIES D'ESPAGNE, which was hence known in England as 'Farinel's Ground'.

**Farinelli,** stage name of Carlo Broschi (1705–82), Italian castrato singer. Pupil of Porpora, in whose opera *Eumene* he had great success in Rome (1721). Subsequently appeared in several European cities, and sang for Philip V and Ferdinand VI of Spain (1737–59).

**Farmer, John** (*fl* 16th–17th cents.), English composer. Published set of canons on plainsong (1591) and set of madrigals (1599).

**Farnaby, Giles** (*c* 1566–1640), English composer. Published set of canzonets for 4 voices. Keyboard pieces show equally individual imagination.

**Farrant, Richard** (d. 1581), English composer. Mostly wrote church music, incl. anthems that are still sung.

**Farrar, Geraldine** (1882–1967), American soprano. Pupil of Lilli Lehmann. Played leads opposite Caruso. Sang at New York Metropolitan (1906–22).

**Fasch, Johann Friedrich** (1688–1758), German organist, composer. Numerous works incl. church cantatas, Masses, overtures (suites), concertos and chamber music.

His son, **Karl Friedrich Christian Fasch** (1736–1800), was a harpsichordist and composer. Worked as accompanist to Frederick the Great in 1756 (in conjunction with C.P.E. Bach).

**Faschingsschwank aus Wien,** *see* CARNIVAL JEST FROM VIENNA.

**fasola,** form of SOLMIZATION, used in Britain and colonial America during 17th, early 18th cents.

**Fastes de la Grande et Ancienne Ménestrandise, Les** (Fr., *Annals of the Great and Ancient Order of Minstrelsy*), satirical suite for harpsichord published by François Couperin (le grand) in 2nd vol. of his *Pièces de clavecin* (1717). Suite refers to dispute between organists of Paris and corporation of minstrels, settled in 1707.

**Fauré, Gabriel Urbain,** (1845–1924), French composer, organist, teacher. Born in Pamiers. Son of schoolmaster. Pupil of Saint-Saëns. After holding various organist's posts, became *maître de chapelle* at the Madeleine in Paris in 1877, and organist in 1896. Teacher of composition at Paris Conservatoire from 1896, and later its director (1905–20). Last 20 years marred by deafness.

As composer he was one of the most original minds of his time. Began as romantic, but refined and clarified idioms of Schumann and Mendelssohn till they took on typically French aspect. His harmony is constantly surprising, and in handling it he showed highly sensitive ear. His zest for experiment remained throughout his life. His operas, in spite of Wagnerian overtones, have distinctive personality, though now neglected. Excelled in writing songs, but was less at home with orchestra – much of his orchestral music was scored by others. Greatly influential teacher: pupils incl. Nadia Boulanger, Enesco, Roger-Ducasse and Ravel.

Principal compositions:

(1) Operas: *Promethée* (1900), *Pénélope* (1913);

(2) Incidental music: *Shylock* (1889), *Pelléas et Mélisande* (1898);

(3) Orchestra: *Pavane* (1887), *Dolly* suite (1893–96), *Masques et bergamasques* suite (1920), *Ballade* for piano and orchestra (1881), *Fantaisie* for piano and orchestra (1919);

(4) Chamber music: 2 piano quartets (1879, 1886), 2 piano quintets (1906, 1921), piano trio (1923), string quartet (1924), 2 violin sonatas (1876, 1917), 2 cello sonatas (1918, 1922);

(5) Piano: 5 impromptus, 13 nocturnes, 13 barcarolles, 9 preludes;

(6) Church music: Requiem Mass (1887);

(7) Songs: 3 song-cycles – *La Bonne Chanson* (1891–2), *La Chanson d'Eve* (1907–10), *Le Jardin clos* (1915–18); *Mirages* (4 songs, 1919), *L'Horizon chimérique* (4 songs, 1922); numerous single songs.

**fausset** (Fr.), falsetto.

**Faust,** opera by Gounod, libretto by J. Barbier and M. Carré (after Goethe). First perf. Paris, 1859. Recitatives added 1860. One of most popular operas ever, though hardly achieves grandeur of original. Other works inspired by Goethe's drama incl. Berlioz's *The Damnation of Faust*, Schumann's *Scenes from Faust*, Liszt's *Faust Symphony*, Mahler's 8th symphony, Wagner's *Faust Overture* and Pousseur's opera, *Votre Faust*. Spohr's opera *Faust* and Busoni's *Doktor Faust* are based on original Faust legend. Hervé's operetta *Le Petit Faust* parodies both Goethe's drama and Gounod's opera.

**Faust Overture, A** (Ger., *Eine Faust – Ouvertüre*), orchestral piece by Wagner, based on Goethe (1840). Not intended as overture to opera.

**Faust Symphony, A** (Ger., *Eine Faust – Symphonie*), orchestral work by Liszt (with chorus in final movt.), based on Goethe. First perf. 1857. Movts. are portraits of Faust, Gretchen and Mephistopheles.

**Fauvel,** *see* ROMAN DE FAUVEL.

**fauxbourdon** (Fr., It., *folso bordone*), lit. 'false bass':

(1) in 15th cent. term was used to indicate simple form of 3-part harmony in which plainsong melody in treble is accompanied by 2 lower parts, one moving in parallel sixths, the other, supplied by singer, a fourth below melody. Origin and interrelation of *fauxbourdon* and English FABURDEN is uncertain;

(2) Italian name *falso bordone* came to be applied to simple 4-part harmonization of plainsong, without polyphonic elaboration;

(3) in modern English hymnody, name *fauxbourdon* is often given to counterpoint (or descant) for trebles superimposed on melody sung by congregation.

**Favart, Charles Simon** (1710–92), French librettist. Pioneer of French *opéra-comique,* writing librettos for *eg* Gluck and Grétry. Director of Opéra-Comique in Paris (1758–69).

**Favorite, La** (Fr., *The Favourite*), opera by Donizetti, libretto by A. Royer, G. Vaëz and A.E. Scribe. First perf. Paris, 1840. Story tells how novice in 14th-cent. Spanish monastery falls in love with mistress of king of Castile.

**Fayrfax, Robert** (1464–1521), English composer. Had great reputation in his lifetime. Works incl. Masses, Magnificat and motets, which show considerable dignity and feeling for sonority. Also wrote secular songs.

**Fedra** (It., *Phaedra*), opera by Pizzetti, libretto by Gabriele d'Annunzio (published as play, 1909). First perf. Milan, 1915.

**Feen, Die** (Ger., *The Fairies*), opera by Wagner, libretto by composer after Gozzi's comedy *La Donna Serpente*. First perf. Munich, 1888, 54 years after Wagner had written this, his first completed opera.

**feierlich** (Ger.), solemn, exalted.

**Feldman, Morton** (1926– ), American composer. Disciple of John Cage. Pioneer of ALEATORY and minimal music. Works incl. *Projections*, *Vertical Thoughts I–V*.

**Feldmusik** (Ger.), lit. 'field music', *ie* music to be played in open air by wind instruments; hence *Feldpartie* or *Feldpartita*, suite of pieces for open-air performance.

**Fellerer, Karl Gustav** (1902– ), German musicologist. Has written extensively on RC church music.

**Fellowes, Edmund Horace** (1870–1951), English musicologist. Publications of old English music incl. THE ENGLISH MADRIGAL SCHOOL, THE ENGLISH SCHOOL OF LUTENIST SONG-WRITERS, complete vocal and instrumental works of Byrd. Also wrote books on Byrd, Gibbons, the English madrigal, and English cathedral music.

**feminine cadence** or **feminine ending,** cadence, or ending, in which final chord is reached on weak beat of bar instead of more usual strong beat.

**Fenby, Eric** (1906– ), English composer, writer. Acted as amanuensis to blind and paralysed Delius (1928–34), helping him to complete his last works. Wrote *Delius as I Knew Him* (1936, rev. 1966). Own compositions incl. parody overture, *Rossini on Ilkla Moor*.

**Fennimore and Gerda,** opera by Delius, libretto by composer (orig. in German), after J.P. Jacobsen's novel *Niels Lyhne*. First perf. Frankfurt, 1919, though completed in 1910.

**Feo, Francesco** (1691–1761), Italian composer of so-called Neapolitan school. Wrote many operas and much church music.

**Ferguson, Howard** (1908– ), Northern Irish composer, teacher. Works incl. ballet *Chaunteclear*, partita and 4 *Diversions on Ulster Airs* for orchestra, concerto for piano and strings, chamber and piano music, and songs.

**fermata** (It.), PAUSE.

**Fernandez, Oscar Lorenzo** (1897–1948), Brazilian composer, teacher. Works, in nationalistic tradition, incl. opera *Malazarte*, symphonic suite on popular themes, *Trio brasiliero*, and piano music.

**Ferneyhough, Brian** (1943– ), English composer, resident in Switzerland from 1969. Works, of great complexity, incl. *Time and Motion Studies I–III* (1971–77) for various combinations of voices and both conventional and electronic instruments, and *La Terre est un homme* (1977–78) for orchestra.

**Ferrabosco, Alfonso** (1543–88), Italian composer. Came to England at early age and entered service of Queen Elizabeth. Left England in 1578. Published 2 vols. of Italian madrigals; also wrote motets and pieces for viols, which influenced Byrd.

His son (prob. illegitimate), **Alfonso Ferrabosco** (*c* 1575–1628), was composer and viol player. In service of James I and Charles I. Works incl. book of lute songs, music for viols, and music for several of Ben Jonson's masques.

**Ferrari, Benedetto** (1597–1681), Italian poet, composer. Librettos incl. *L'Andromeda,* set by Francesco Manelli (Venice, 1637) – first opera to be given in public theatre. Music of operas for which he wrote music is lost. Surviving compositions incl. oratorio *Sansone,* and 3 books of solo cantatas.

**Ferrier, Kathleen** (1912–53), English contralto. Most famous of her generation. Noted opera roles incl. Lucretia in Britten's *The Rape of Lucretia* (written esp. for her) and Orpheus in Gluck's *Orfeo*, but principal activity was in concert hall, where was renowned as exponent of Brahms and Mahler. Accompanied by Bruno Walter in recitals. Awarded C.B.E. (1953). Died of cancer.

**Ferroud, Pierre Octave** (1900–36), French composer, critic. Pupil of Florent Schmitt. Works incl. opera *Chirurgie* (after Chekhov), ballets, symphony and other orchestral pieces, chamber music and songs. Killed in car accident.

**Fervaal,** opera by d'Indy, libretto by composer. First perf. Brussels, 1897.

**Fes** (Ger.), F flat.

**Festa, Constanza** (after 1490–1545), Italian composer. Composed Masses, motets and hymns. His madrigal 'Quando ritrovo la mia pastorella' is known in Britain as 'Down in a flowery vale'.

**Fêtes,** 2nd of Debussy's 3 *Nocturnes* for orchestra. First perf. as set, 1901.

**Fétis, François Joseph** (1784–1871), Belgian teacher, musicologist, composer. Director of Brussels Conservatoire from 1833. Published many theoretical works, *Biographie universelle des musiciens* (8 vols., 1835–44), and *Histoire générale de la musique* (5 vols., 1869–76).

**Feuermann, Emanuel** (1902–42), Austrian cellist. Made reputation at early age. Taught at Cologne and Berlin.

**Feuersnot** (Ger., *No Fire in the City*), opera by Richard Strauss, libretto by E. von Wolzogen (based on Flemish legend). First perf. Dresden, 1901.

**Fevin, Antoine de** (d. 1512), French composer of school of Josquin des Prés. A number of his Masses and motets survive.

**Février, Henri** (1875–1957), French composer. Pupil of Massenet and Fauré. Operas incl. *Monna Vanna* and *Carmosine.*

**Ffrangcon-Davies, David Thomas** (1855–1918), Welsh baritone. Sang in concerts and oratorio in Britain, US and Europe.

**fiato** (It.), 'breath'. *Strumenti a fiato*, wind instruments.

**Fibich, Zdeněk** (1850–1900), Czech composer. Works, in romantic style, incl. 7 operas, *eg The Tempest* (after Shakespeare), MELODRAMA trilogy *Hippodamia*, 3 symphonies, symphonic poems, overtures, chamber and piano music, and songs.

**fiddle,** colloquial term for violin or similar string instrument, esp. when used in folk music. Hence 'bass fiddle', 'bull fiddle', terms for double bass.

**Fidelio,** opera by Beethoven. Full title: *Fidelio, oder Die Eheliche Liebe (Fidelio, or Wedded Love)*. Libretto orig. by J. Sonnleithner (after play by Bouilly), reduced to 2 acts by S. von Breuning (1806), and further revised by G.F. Treitschke (1814). Orig. version first perf. Vienna, 1805; second version, 1806; final version, 1814. Story concerns rescue of Florestan, political prisoner of Pizarro, by his wife Leonora, disguised as young man called Fidelio. For 4 overtures written for opera, *see* LEONORE.

**Fiedler, Arthur** (1894–1979), American conductor. In charge of 'Boston Pops' Orchestra from 1930; great popularizer.

**Field, John** (1782–1837), Irish pianist, composer. Son of violinist. Apprenticed at age of 11 to Clementi, whom he accompanied to France, Germany and Russia, demonstrating pianos that Clementi sold. Lived in Russia as teacher (pupils incl. Glinka) and soloist until 1832, when returned to Britain, followed by tour on Continent. After long illness in Naples, returned to Russia to die. Had high reputation as performer. Compositions incl. 7 piano concertos, 4 sonatas and other piano music, esp. 20 nocturnes (whose name and form he invented). Nocturnes had unmistakable influence on Chopin's: common factor is *cantabile* melody with unobtrusive accompaniment.

**Fiery Angel, The** (Russ., *Ognenny Angel*), also known as *The Angel of Fire*, opera by Prokofiev, libretto by composer (after story by V. Bryusov). Written 1919–27; first concert perf., Paris, 1954; first stage perf., Venice, 1955. Story deals with diabolical possession and exorcism in 16th cent.

**fifara** or **fiffaro** (It.), 17th cent. name for transverse FLUTE.

**fife,** small flute still used, as for many centuries, in 'drum and fife' band. In modern form, built tone lower than orchestral piccolo and has one or more keys.

**fiffaro,** *see* FIFARA.

**fifteenth,** (1) interval of 2 octaves;

(2) 2ft organ stop pitched 2 octaves higher than normal (8ft) pitch.

**fifth,** interval reached by ascending 4 steps in diatonic scale, *eg* from C to G above; also called *perfect fifth*. *Augmented fifth* is fifth in which upper note is sharpened or lower note flattened. *Diminished fifth* is fifth of which upper note is flattened or lower note sharpened. *See also* CONSECUTIVE INTERVALS.

**'Fifths' Quartet,** *see* QUINTENQUARTETT.

**figuration,** consistent use of particular melodic or harmonic FIGURE.

**figure,** short musical phrase – too short to be genuine 'theme' – but achieving, through repetition, distinctive character in course of composition.

**figured bass** (Fr., *basse chiffrée*; Ger., *bezifferter Bass*; It., *basso continuo*), formerly called 'thorough bass' (lit. translation of *basso continuo*). Bass part (intended primarily for keyboard instrument) with figures written below notes to indicate harmonies to be played above it. Figure indicates interval above written note to be played, though choice of octave in which this note is played is left to discretion of performer. System originated at beginning of 17th cent. and was universally employed until about middle of 18th cent., after which it was little used outside church music; most modern editions of old music incl. written out part. It was designed to facilitate (a) accompaniment of solo voices or instruments, *eg* in solo cantata or trio sonata, (b) enrichment of texture provided by chorus or instrumental ensemble or both (*see* CONTINUO).

Practice was not always consistent, but following principles were generally observed:

(1) note without figures implies fifth and third above;

(2) figure 3 by itself implies 5 as well;

(3) figure 4 by itself implies 5 as well;

(4) figure 6 by itself implies 3 as well;

(5) figure 7 by itself implies 3 as well;

(6) accidentals are indicated either by normal signs placed next to figures, or by diagonal strokes through figures. Accidental without any figure refers to third of chord;

(7) horizontal stroke indicates that harmony used above preceding note is to be continued above changing bass. The stroke, however, is often omitted where it is obvious that notes in bass are passing notes.

**figured chorale,** setting of chorale melody for organ, in which particular figuration is employed throughout.

**filar la voce** (It.; Fr., *filer la voix*, *filer le son*), lit. 'to draw out the voice', *ie* sustain note, in one long drawn-out breath, with or without crescendo and decrescendo.

**Fille du Régiment, La,** *see* DAUGHTER OF THE REGIMENT.

**film music,** the use of music to accompany films dates from the early part of the 20th cent. Silent films needed music, normally that of a piano, to accentuate the action, and to drown the noise of the projector; often 'special effects', such as gunfire, birdsong, thunder, etc., were provided by a percussionist. By about 1920 the practice began of employing other instruments, even complete orchestras in larger cities. With the building of large cinemas, organs were also installed, either to bear the whole burden of accompaniment or to alternate with the orchestra. Piano or organ accompaniment was often improvised. For instrumental ensembles (as well as for pianists and organists) there was available a whole library of short extracts, suitable for every conceivable emotion or situation (*eg* 'Help, help', 'Love's Response', or 'Broken Vows'). The accompaniment to a silent film was a sort of potpourri, in the compilation of which considerable ingenuity was often shown. The practice, however, was inartistic, and dissatisfaction with it led, after World War I, to the occasional composition of original music for a complete film, or to the adaptation of existing music – as in the case of the film version of Strauss's *Der Rosenkavalier,* for which the composer made a special arrangement of his own score (1925). Other composers of this period who wrote for films include Satie and Honegger.

The opportunity for a more complete association of film and music came with the development of the sound film in 1926–27, but it was only gradually realized that music could be used as an integral part of the film and only gradually that reputable composers were commissioned to provide it. Among British composers who have written film music of this kind are Bax, Bliss, Walton and Vaughan Williams. In the US, important film scores have been composed by

Copland, Virgil Thomson and Bernstein. Russia's musical contribution to the cinema has included three masterly scores by Prokofiev – *Alexander Nevsky, Lieutenant Kizhe* and *Ivan the Terrible*. Several of these works have proved capable of standing on their own feet in concert-hall versions – *eg* Vaughan Williams's *Sinfonia Antartica* (drawn from *Scott of the Antarctic*), Walton's *Spitfire Prelude and Fugue* (from *The First of the Few*) and Bernstein's *On the Waterfront* suite (from the film of the same title). Schoenberg's *Music for a Film Scene* (1930) was not written for an actual film, but it is a fascinating exercise in the genre.

Some films have used already existing works to creative effect – *eg* the music of Vivaldi in Cocteau's *Les Enfants Terribles*, of Strauss and Ligeti in *2001, A Space Odyssey*, and of Bach in Bergman's *The Silence*. Recent film scores have made increasing use of electronic music, often very effectively, as in Kagel's witty *Ludwig van* (1970).

In the great majority of commercial US and British films, however, the music tends to be imitative of such late romantics as Rakhmaninov, Strauss, and Delius. It describes a scene or mood, tends to repeat certain phrases, and is often a constant background to the film, only noticed at climactic moments.

**Filtz, Anton** (*c* 1730–60), cellist, composer, prob. of Bohemian origin. Joined Mannheim orchestra in 1754, and became one of symphonists of Mannheim school. Wrote *c* 40 symphonies, and choral and chamber music.

**final,** in church modes, note on which melody ends, *ie* the tonic. In authentic modes, final is first degree of scale, in plagal modes it is fourth degree.

**finale** (It., but now used in English), (1) last movt. of work in several movts. Were generally brisk and cheerful in 18th cent., but Beethoven challenged this convention, so opening up freedom of treatment to subsequent composers;

(2) concluding section of act of opera, often of considerable length and subdivided into smaller sections, with contrasts of tempo and key. Generally involves several singers, and often chorus as well.

**Finck, Heinrich** (1445–1527), German composer. Worked in Poland, Stuttgart, and Salzburg. Works incl. Masses, motets and secular part-songs.

His great-nephew, **Hermann Finck** (1527–58), was a composer and theorist. Best known for treatise *Practica Musica* (1556), which incl. substantial section on canon.

**fine** (It.), 'end'. In *da capo* aria and similar compositions, where recapitulation of opening section is not written in full but indicated by sign to go back to beginning, direction *fine* indicates point at which piece comes to an end.

**Fine, Irving** (1915–62), American composer. Pupil of Walter Piston and Nadia Boulanger. Works incl. symphony, orchestral 'diversion' entitled *Blue Towers*, 3 choruses from *Alice in Wonderland*, chamber music and songs.

**Fingal's Cave,** *see* HEBRIDES.

**Finger, Gottfried** or **Godfrey** (*c* 1660–after 1723), Moravian composer. Came to England *c* 1685 and became instrumentalist in James II's Catholic Chapel. Subsequently in service of Queen Sophia Charlotte of Prussia, then of Elector Palatine. Compositions incl. chamber music and music for plays.

**finger-board** (Fr., *touche*; Ger., *Griffbrett*; It., *tasto*), long strip of wood on string instrument on which fingers of left hand press down strings at any chosen point and so shorten their vibrating length and raise pitch.

**finger cymbals,** pair of tiny cymbals strapped to thumb and finger; they give high bell note of definite pitch.

**fingering,** any notation that indicates which fingers should be used in playing piece of music. In piano playing, 1 usually indicates thumb, 2 the index finger and so on up to 5 for little finger ('Continental' fingering. 'English' fingering (now obsolete), indicated thumb by +, and index to little fingers by 1 to 4. In string playing, 0 indicates open string, and 1 to 4 the index to little fingers.

**Finke, Fidelio** (1891–1968), Sudeten composer. Pupil of Novák. Director of German Academy of Music, Prague (1927–45). As composer, began as romantic and developed into disciple of Schoenberg. Works incl. opera *Die Jakobsfahrt,* and orchestral, chamber, choral and piano music.

**Finlandia,** orchestral tone-poem by Sibelius, op 26. Composed 1894. Though patriotic in character, melodies are original, not folk tunes.

**Finnissy, Michael** (1946– ), English composer. Works incl. several pieces of music theatre *eg Mr Punch* (1976–77), and vocal, instrumental and piano music.

**fino al segno** (It.), as far as the sign 𝄋

**Finot,** *see* PHINOT.

**Finta Giardiniera, La** (It., *The Girl in Gardener's Disguise*), opera by Mozart, libretto by R. De' Calzabigi, altered by M. Coltellini. First perf. Munich, 1775.

**Finta Semplice, La** (It., *The Pretended Simpleton*), opera by Mozart, libretto by M. Coltellini (after Goldoni). Mozart's first opera, written in 1768 and first perf. Salzburg in 1769 when composer was 13.

**Finzi, Gerald** (1901–56), English composer. Works, mainly in smaller forms, incl. settings for voice and piano of poems by Thomas Hardy, and cello concerto. Lyrical, pastoral style heard at best in *Dies Natalis* for voice and strings (1940).

**fioritura** (It.), lit. 'flowering' (plural *fioriture*), *ie* embellishment or ornamentation, whether improvised or written down.

**fipple flute,** *see* FLAGEOLET, RECORDER.

**Firebird, The** (Russ. *Zhar Ptitsa*), ballet with music by Stravinsky and choreography by Fokine. First perf. Paris, 1910. Concert suite from ballet made in 1911 (rev. 1919, 1947).

**Fires of London,** *see* DAVIES, PETER MAXWELL.

**Fire Symphony,** nickname for Haydn's symphony no 59 in A major (*c* 1766–8). May have been used as overture to play *The Conflagration*, hence title.

**Fireworks Music,** familiar title for Handel's *Music for the Royal Fireworks*, orig. written for wind band and first perf. London, 1749, as accompaniment to fireworks display celebrating Peace of Aix-la-Chapelle. String parts subsequently added by composer for concert performances.

**Firkušny, Rudolf** (1912– ), Czech pianist, composer. Pupil of Janáček, Schnabel and Suk. Excels in performance of Janáček. Has composed piano concerto and solo piano pieces.

**first-movement form,** *see* SONATA FORM.

**Fis** (Ger.), F sharp.

**Fischer, Carl** (1849–1923), founder of New York publishing firm which bears his name.

**Fischer, Edwin** (1886–1960), Swiss pianist, composer. Known internationally as performer, esp. of Mozart and Bach.

**Fischer, Johann Kaspar Ferdinand** (*c* 1665–1746), German composer. Keyboard works incl. harpsichord suites in French style, and *Ariadne musica neo-organoedum* (1715) – collection of 20 preludes and fugues, each in different key – looking forward to Bach's *Well-tempered Clavier*. Also wrote *Journal du printemps* for orchestra with *ad lib.* trumpets.

**Fischer-Dieskau, Dietrich** (1925– ), German baritone, conductor. Most famous German baritone of his generation. In opera, repertory ranges from Mozart to Henze. His *Lieder* repertory incl. more or less complete songs of Beethoven, Schubert, Mendelssohn, Brahms, Wolf and Strauss; also noted exponent of Bach and of Mahler's orchestral songs.

**fisarmonica** (It.), accordion.

**Fisher, F. E.,** 18th-cent. English composer, poss. of German origin (precise name and dates unknown). Worked in London (1748–1773), composing trio sonatas and other instrumental music. May be same as Friedrich Ernst Fischer, itinerant German composer of period.

**Fisis** (Ger.), F double sharp.

**Fitelberg, Grzegorz** (1879–1953), Polish composer, conductor. Associated with Polish nationalist movement. Compositions incl. 2 symphonies, and *Polish Rhapsody* for orchestra.

His son, **Jerzy Fitelberg** (1903–51), was also composer. Moved to Paris (1933), then New York (1940). Works incl. sinfonietta, 2 piano concertos, 2 violin concertos, cello concerto, 2 suites for orchestra, 5 string quartets, and other chamber music.

**Fitzwilliam Virginal Book,** most extensive manuscript collection of keyboard music (almost entirely English) of late 16th, early 17th cents., containing 297 pieces. Copied by Francis Tregian (*c* 1574–1619), prob. during his imprisonment for RC beliefs (*c* 1609–19). Incl. works by Bull, Byrd, Farnaby and Morley. Published 1899.

**Five, The,** name sometimes given to group of 19th-cent. Russian nationalist composers, also known as 'The Mighty Handful'. Term was coined by Stasov and applied to Balakirev, Borodin, Cui, Mussorgsky and Rimsky-Korsakov, whose works were thought to differ from those of 'westernized' composers such as Chaikovsky and Anton Rubinstein.

**five-three chord,** basic, or common, triad. In figured bass, denoted by figures 5/3, referring to third and fifth above root, *eg* C–E–G.

**flageolet,** small beaked flute (or recorder), with 6 holes – 4 in front and 2 at back, latter covered by player's thumbs. Dates from late 16th cent.; much in vogue in 17th cent.

**flageolet-notes** (Eng.; Fr., *flageolets*; Ger., *Flageolett-Töne*; It., *flautato, flautando*), harmonics on string instruments.

**Flagstad, Kirsten** (1895–1962), Norwegian soprano. Known internationally for outstanding purity and strength of voice, esp. in Wagner roles and Norwegian songs.

**flam,** drum stroke used to mark accent. Consists of 2 notes played very closely together.

**flamenco** or **cante flamenco** (Sp.), species of Spanish song, from Andalusia, performed with guitar accompaniment; often accompanies dance. Various sub-species named after different areas of Andalusia incl. malagueña, sevillana. Mood of music is often (though not necessarily) sad. Solo guitarists often play in 'flamenco style' as opposed to 'classical style'.

**Flanagan, William** (1923–69), American composer. Pupil of Honegger, Copland and David Diamond. Works, noted for lyricism, incl. opera *Bartleby* (after Melville's short story, 1957), *Song for a Winter Child* (1950) and *The Lady of Tearful Regret* (1958) for coloratura soprano and chamber ensemble, both to words by Edward Albee, and *The Weeping Pleiades* (1953), song cycle based on poems by A.E. Housman. Orchestral works incl. *A Concert Ode* (1951), *Notations* (1960), and *Narrative for Orchestra* (1964). Wrote incidental music for Albee's plays *The Sandbox, The Ballad of the Sad Café* and *The Death of Bessie Smith.*

**flat** (Fr., *bémol*; Ger., *Be*; It., *bemolle*), (1) the sign ♭ indicating that note to which it is prefixed is to be lowered by one semitone. Holds good for rest of bar, unless contradicted. If forms part of KEY SIGNATURE, holds good, unless contradicted, until there is new key signature which omits it. *See also* DOUBLE FLAT.

(1) In French and Italian, flattened notes are referred to by name of note followed by word for flat; in German, suffix '-s' or '-es' is added to name of note, *eg* E flat = Fr. *mi bémol*, Ger. *Es*, It. *mi bemolle*. Exception to rule is that Ger. *B* (without any suffix) = B flat (B natural is represented by H; B double flat is *Bes*);

(2) applied to an interval = minor, *eg* flat seventh = minor seventh, flat third = minor third. This use of word, though not obsolete, is old-fashioned;

(3) 'flat key' is now one which has one or more flats in the key signature, *eg* F (1 flat), B flat (2 flats), E flat (3 flats), *etc*. 'Flat key' formerly meant minor key, just as 'flat third' meant minor third;

(4) an instrument or voice is flat if the notes produced are lower than normal pitch. A single note can also be flat, as a result of faulty tuning or careless performance.

**flatté,** *see* SLIDE (1).

**Flatterzunge** (Ger.), lit. 'flutter tongue'. Method of tone production sometimes used in wind instruments: consists in rolling tongue as if saying *drrr*. Result, if applied to single note, is rapid tremolo.

**flautando** or **flautato** (It.), 'playing like a flute'. Direction to string players (1) to play harmonics, (2) to play gently near end of fingerboard.

**flauto** (It.), flute. *Flauto piccolo*, piccolo. Up to mid 18th cent., *flauto* = *flauto dolce*, *flauto d'éco*, beaked flute or recorder; *flauto traverso* or simply *traverso* = transverse FLUTE; *flauto d'amore*, transverse flute built minor third lower than normal size, now obsolete.

**flautone** (It.), bass flute.

**Flavio, Re de' Longobardi** (It., *Flavio, King of the Lombards*), opera by Handel, libretto by N.F. Haym (partly founded on Corneille's *Le Cid* and altered from S. Ghigi's earlier Italian libretto). First perf. London, 1723.

**flebile** (It.), mournful.

**Fledermaus, Die** (Ger., The Bat), operetta by Johann Strauss the younger, libretto by C. Haffner and R. Genée. First perf. Vienna, 1874. One of most popular operettas ever.

**Flesch, Carl** (1873–1944), Hungarian violinist. First appeared as soloist in Vienna, 1895, and subsequently toured widely. Taught in Bucharest, Amsterdam, Philadelphia and Berlin. His *Art of Violin-playing* is standard work.

**flexatone,** simple instrument consisting of steel blade and small clapper mounted on flexible strip. On shaking, clapper strikes blade to produce bell sound; pitch is varied by pressing blade.

**flicorno,** Italian equivalent of SAXHORN.

**Fliegende Holländer, Der,** *see* FLYING DUTCHMAN, THE.

**fliessend** (Ger.), flowing.

**Flight of the Bumble-Bee, The,** orchestral interlude in Rimsky-Korsakov's opera *The Legend of the Czar Saltan* (1900), often performed out of context, and in arrangements for all kinds of instruments.

**Flonzaley Quartet,** string quartet founded by American banker of Swiss origin, Edward de Coppet (1885–1916), in 1902, and maintained by him and his son André. So-called from name of de Coppet's summer residence in Switzerland. Disbanded 1928.

**Floridante, Il** (It., *Prince Floridantes*), opera by Handel, libretto by P.A. Rolli. First perf. London, 1721.

**Florimo, Francesco** (1800–88), Italian historian, composer. Friend of Bellini and Wagner, writing studies of both composers, and funeral symphony on death of Bellini. More important than his compositions are his historical works, which incl. a study of Neapolitan school.

**Flos Campi** (Lat., flower of the field), suite by Vaughan Williams for viola, chamber orchestra and (wordless) chorus. First perf. London, 1925.

**Flöte** (Ger.), flute. *Kleine Flöte,* piccolo.

**Flothuis, Marius** (1914– ), Dutch composer, critic. Works incl. concertos for clarinet, flute, horn, piano and violin, sinfonia concertante for clarinet, saxophone and chamber orchestra, string quartet, cello sonata, and songs.

**Flotow, Friedrich von** (1812–83), German opera composer, son of nobleman. Operas incl. *Le Naufrage de la Méduse* (1839, in collaboration with Grisar and Pilati, later rewritten by Flotow as *Die Matrosen,* 1845), *Alessandro Stradella* (1844), and *Martha* (1847).

**flourish,** (1) fanfare; (2) decorative musical figure, either written or improvised.

**Floyd, Carlisle** (1926– ), American composer, teacher. Noted mainly for operas (to own libretto), *eg Susannah* (1955), *The Passion of Jonathan Wade* (1962), *Of Mice and Men* (1970).

**flue pipes,** in ORGAN, all pipes other than reed pipes, so called because air passes through narrow aperture, or flue. Principle is similar to that of tin whistle.

**Flügel** (Ger.), lit. 'wing', *ie* harpsichord or grand piano, both of which are wing-shaped.

**Flügelhorn** (Ger.), (1) usually Anglicized as 'flugelhorn', soprano saxhorn in B flat, similar in shape to bugle, but with 3 pistons. Has same compass as B flat cornet, but fuller tone. Used in brass bands and jazz;

(2) in general, German equivalent of SAXHORN family.

**flute** (Fr., *flûte*; Ger., *Flöte*; It., *flauto*), (1) beaked flute or English flute (Fr., *flûte à bec, flûte douce*; Ger., *Blockflöte*; It., *flauto dolce, flauto d'eco*), now known exclusively as recorder;

(2) transverse or German flute (Fr., *flûte traversière, flûte allemande;* Ger., *Querflöte*; It., *flauto traverso*), now known simply as flute. 'Woodwind' instrument, generally made of either wood or silver. One end of tube is stopped, and sound is produced by blowing across aperture cut in side at that end; pitch is controlled by finger-operated key system. Compass is normally from middle C to 3 octaves above, though sometimes has extra semitone at bottom. Modern flute owes much to work of Theobald BOEHM in 19th cent. In addition to normal-sized flute there are also (a) piccolo, built octave higher, (b) *bass flute* or *alto flute* (Fr., *flûte alto*; Ger., *Altflöte*; It., *flautone*), built fourth lower. *Flûte d'amour* (Ger., *Liebesflöte*; It., *flauto d'amore*), built minor third lower, is obsolete. Flutes built minor third or semitone above normal pitch were at one time used in military bands and treated as transposing instruments (*see* TIERCE FLUTE). Though of great antiquity, flute did not come into general use in chamber and orchestral music till early 18th cent. (Note that at this time *flauto* = recorder, *flauto traverso* or *traverso* = transverse flute.)

**flûte** (Fr.), FLUTE.

**flûte-eunuque,** *see* MIRLITON.

**flutter tongue,** *see* FLATTERZUNGE.

**Flying Dutchman, The** (Ger., *Die Fliegende Holländer*), opera by Wagner, libretto by composer (after Heine's *Memoiren des Herrn von Schnabelewopski*). First perf. Dresden, 1843. Dutchman, for act of defiance, has been condemned by Satan to sail seas for ever; eventually redeemed by self-sacrifice of woman he loves.

**Foerster, Josef Bohuslav** (1859–1951), Czech composer, teacher, critic. Worked for time in Hamburg and Vienna. Friend of Mahler. Works incl. operas, *eg Jessica* (after Shakespeare's *The Merchant of Venice*), *Stabat Mater*, symphonies, violin concertos and other orchestral works, chamber music and songs.

**Foldes, Andor** (1913– ), Hungarian pianist. Pupil of Dohnányi. Settled in US, 1939. Has written piano pieces and book on piano technique.

**folía** (Sp.; It., *follia*), Portuguese dance – 'the folly' – which was origin of FOLIES D'ESPAGNE. As name implies, was orig. wild in character.

**folies d'Espagne** (Fr.), musical form in dance rhythm, current in 17th cent. and derived from FOLIA. Wild character of orig. dance gave way to stately tempo more in accordance with 17th-cent. conventions. Basic tune was used as subject for variations by many composers, most notably Corelli in violin sonata, op 5 no 12 (1700). In Britain, piece acquired name 'Farinel's Ground' from version by French composer, Michel Farinel.

**folk song** (Fr., *chanson populaire*; Ger., *Volkslied*; It., *canto popularé*), term implying song of no known authorship which has been preserved in a community by oral tradition. Folk songs have often been introduced into serious music or used as theme for variations. Use of them in 19th cent. became identified with nationalist sentiment; composers not only used them but imitated their idioms, *eg* in Russia, Bohemia and Norway. In Britain, Folk Song Society was formed in 1898, and extensive collecting was undertaken by Cecil SHARP. Study of folk song has developed into separate discipline of ETHNOMUSICOLOGY. Composers who have been esp. interested in collecting, using and imitating folk songs incl. Bartók in Hungary and Vaughan Williams in England.

**follia,** *see* FOLIA.

**foot,** in organ pipes, measure of pitch: 2ft pipe sounds middle C, and 4ft, 8ft, 16ft and 32ft pipes respectively sound C octave lower than pipe before.

**Foote, Arthur William** (1853–1937), American composer, organist. Works incl. cantatas on Longfellow's *The Farewell of Hiawatha* and *The Wreck of the Hesperus*, orchestral, chamber, organ and piano music, and songs.

**Force of Destiny, The** (It., *La Forza del Destino*), opera by Verdi, libretto by F.M. Piave. First perf. St Petersburg, 1862. Story of love, war and revenge.

**Ford, Thomas** (d. 1648), English composer, lutenist. In service of Charles I. Only published work was *Musicke of Sundrie Kindes* (1607), incl. well-known lute-song, 'Since first I saw your face'.

**Forellenquintett,** *see* TROUT QUINTET.

**Forkel, Johann Nikolaus** (1749–1818), German historian. Numerous publications incl. books on German music, but best known for biography of Bach, the first written (1802), and at a time when Bach's music had been forgotten.

**forlana, furlana** (It.; Fr. *forlane*), (1) lively dance in 6/8 or 6/4 time, originating in Friulu, NE Italy;

(2) in late 16th cent., name *ballo furlano* was applied to dance in 4/4 time and moderate tempo.

**form,** in music, as in other arts, this means intelligible shape. Basic elements used in musical form are (1) repetition, (2) variation, (3) contrast (of material, speed or dynamics). Repetition is essential because stuff of music is transient. Variation is necessary as unvaried repetition would be intolerable. Contrast is necessary because even varied repetition of some material would become monotonous. These 3 principles operate in field of (a) melody, (b) harmony, (c) rhythm, (d) tone-colour, and therefore can operate simultaneously. Particular form of melodic repetition which has no equivalent in poetry is over-lapping repetition or imitation, found in CANON and FUGUE.

Among influences which have helped to shape musical forms are (1) dance, (2) words, (3) improvisation. Many dances fall into contrasted sections and exhibit simple symmetry. These characteristics naturally appear in music written for them, and in turn influence music not specifically written for dancing but organized on same principle. Very characteristic of dance is practice of varying repetition by turning inconclusive ending into final one: *see* CLOS.

In course of time these melodic conventions were matched by harmonic ones, *eg* use of intermediate and final CADENCE. This naturally developed into BINARY FORM, which in turn gave rise to SONATA FORM.

Influence of words leads to contrasts in mood in vocal music, and this in turn affects instrumental music. If such contrasts are pursued for any length of time they become independent sections. These provide one of origins of separate 'movements' of sonatas, symphonies *etc* in 18th, 19th cents.; other origin is in contrasted dances of SUITE. Such movements are often distinguished not only by contrast of tempo and material but also by contrast of key. Influence of improvisation also results in contrasts, since no performer will wish to persist in same mood; also results in love of elaboration of simple idea.

Desire for intelligibility and infinite variety possible in music has led composers of all periods to use limited number of basic forms as skeletons for their ideas, just as poets have used sonnet or ballad. They are not conventions to which composer has to submit; on the contrary, they are servants of his invention.

In addition to forms mentioned above, *see also* CANTUS FIRMUS, CHACONNE, CHORALE, DA CAPO ARIA, FANTASIA, FUGUE, MADRIGAL, MOTET, OVERTURE, PRELUDE, RICERCAR, RONDO, SYMPHONIC POEM, TOCCATA. For works in several movts. or parts which exhibit principles of form on large scale *see* CANTATA, CONCERTO, MASS, OPERA, ORATORIO, SONATA, SYMPHONY.

**formes fixes** (Fr.), collective name for ballade, virelai and rondeau, 3 main forms of late medieval French poetry and music.

**Förster, Emanuel Aloys** (1748–1823), Silesian composer. Works incl. chamber and keyboard music – Beethoven acknowledged value of his example in writing string quartets.

**Forster, Georg** (*c* 1514–68), German doctor. Edited collection of songs entitled *Ein Ausszug guter alter und newer teutscher Liedlein* (5 sets, 1539–56).

**Förster, Josef Bohuslav** (1859–1951), Czech composer. Director of Prague Conservatory (1922–31). Works incl. operas and symphonies.

**forte** (It.), loud; usually abbrev. to *f*. *Forte piano*, loud and immediately soft again (*fp*); *fortissimo*, very loud (*ff*); *mezzo forte*, moderately loud (*mf*); *piu forte*, louder (*piu f*); *poco forte*, moderately loud (*pf*).

**fortepiano,** early Italian name for PIANOFORTE. Use in English for late 18th-cent. piano is affectation.

**fortissimo** (It.), very loud; usually abbrev. to *ff*.

**Fortner, Wolfgang** (1907– ), German composer. Initially influenced by Reger and Hindemith, but later used serial techniques. Works incl. symphony, concertos for harpsichord, piano, organ, violin and cello, and chamber, choral and stage music. Two of his operas, *The Wood* and *Blood Wedding*, were inspired by Lorca, and ballet *The White Rose* by Oscar Wilde.

**Fortspinnung** (Ger.), 'continuation'. Term for process of continuation or development of musical material in symphonies *etc*, as opposed to symmetrical repetition of that material.

**Forty-Eight, The,** common name for Bach's THE WELL-TEMPERED CLAVIER.

**forza** (It.), 'force'. *Con forza*, emphatically, vigorously.

**Forza del Destino, La,** *see* FORCE OF DESTINY, THE.

**forzando** (It.), 'forcing', *ie* strongly accented. Usually abbrev. to *fz*.

**Foss, Hubert James** (1899–1953), English critic. Music editor of Oxford University Press (1924–41). Books incl. *Music in my Time* (1933), *Ralph Vaughan Williams*; edited *The Heritage of Music* (3 vols., 1927–51).

**Foss, Lukas,** orig. Fuchs (1922– ), composer of German parentage, settled in US in 1937. Pupil of Hindemith. Works, widely performed in US, incl. opera *The Jumping Frog of Calaveras County* (based on Mark Twain's short story, 1950), symphony, 2 piano concertos, orchestral *Recordare* (after Gandhi's assassination), and oratorio *A Parable of Death* (words by Rilke).

**Foster, Stephen Collins** (1826–64), American composer. Self-taught. Composer of widely popular songs incl. 'The Old Folks at Home' ('Swanee River'), 'My Old Kentucky Home', 'Camptown Races', 'Jeannie with the Light Brown Hair' and 'Beautiful Dreamer'.

**foundation stops,** on organ, all stops except MUTATION STOPS.
**foundation tone,** tone of more dignified stops, *eg* diapasons.
**Fountains of Rome, The** (It., *Fontane di Roma*), orchestral work by Respighi. First perf. 1917.
**four in two,** *see* CANON.
**Four Last Songs** (Ger., *Vier letzte Lieder*), work by Richard Strauss for soprano and orchestra (1948), consisting of settings of poems by Hesse and Eichendorff.
**Fournier, Pierre** (1906– ), French cellist. One of most distinguished of 20th cent. Esp. noted for performances of Bach, Beethoven, Brahms, Debussy and Elgar.
**Four Saints in Three Acts,** opera by Virgil Thomson, libretto by Gertrude Stein. First perf. (by all-black cast) Hartford, Connecticut, 1934. There are 4 acts and more than 4 saints.
**Four Seasons, The** (It., *Le Quattro Stagioni*), set of 4 violin concertos by Vivaldi (1725), usually performed together.
**Four Temperaments, The,** (1) title of Carl Nielsen's 2nd symphony (1902);
(2) title of work for piano and strings by Hindemith (1940). In both works 'temperament' is used not in musical sense, but in sense of mood, *ie* choleric, phlegmatic, melancholic and sanguine.
**fourth,** interval reached by ascending 3 steps in diatonic scale, *eg* G to C above; also called *perfect fourth*. In HARMONIC SERIES, interval between third and fourth notes of series, thus having ratio 4/3.
Following terms are in use: *augmented fourth*, fourth in which upper note is sharpened or lower note flattened; *diminished fourth*, fourth in which upper note is flattened or lower note sharpened.
**fourth chord,** chord consisting of superimposed fourths, or of fourths in combination with other intervals.
**Fox Strangeways, Arthur Henry** (1859–1948), English critic. Worked for *The Times* and *The Observer*, founder and editor of *Music and Letters* (1920). Wrote *The Music of Hindustan* (1914), biography of Cecil Sharp, and English translations of many German songs.
**foxtrot,** dance of US origin in duple time; first became popular 1912. Several variants appeared, and word came to lose limited application to particular dance. Two main types – fast and slow.
**Fra Diavolo, ou L'Hôtellerie de Terracine** (Fr., *Brother Devil, or The Inn at Terracina*), comic opera by Auber, libretto by A. E. Scribe. First perf. Paris, 1830. Story concerns foiling of brigand leader, Fra Diavolo.
**Fra Gherardo,** opera by Pizzetti, libretto by composer. First perf. Milan, 1928, under Toscanini. Work is based on 13th-cent. *Chronicles of Salimbene of Parma.*
**Françaix, Jean** (1912– ), French composer. Pupil of Nadia Boulanger. Works, in neo-classical style and often succinctly written, incl. symphony, operas, oratorio, several ballets, concertino for piano and orchestra (1934), piano concerto (1936) and chamber music.
**Francesca da Rimini,** symphonic fantasy by Chaikovsky, op 32,

inspired by Dante. First perf. 1877. Chaikovsky orig. intended to write opera on subject. Operas on same subject were written by Generali, Goetz, Napravnik, Rakhmaninov and Zandonai.

**Franchetti, Alberto** (1860–1942), Italian composer of noble birth. Spectacular operas earned him nickname of 'the Meyerbeer of modern Italy'. Operas incl. *Asrael* (1888), *Cristoforo Colombo* (1892), *Germania* (1902), and *Giove a Pompei* (1921, in collaboration with Giordano).

**Franck, César Auguste** (1822–1890), Belgian composer, organist. Studied at Liège and Paris Conservatoires. Lived in Paris from 1844, becoming choirmaster at St Clotilde (1853), organist (1859) and teacher of organ at Paris Conservatoire (1872). Music is romantic in style and expansive in manner, with characteristic chromatic harmony and much emphasis on CYCLIC form. Orchestral and chamber music sometimes betrays influence of organ in use of colour contrasts and fondness for repetition and short-breathed phrases. Awarded Légion d'Honneur (for organ playing, not composition) at age of 63.

Principal compositions:

(1) Oratorios: *Ruth* (1846), *La Tour de Babel* (1865), *Rédemption* (1872), *Les Béatitudes* (1880), *Rebecca* (1881);

(2) Church music: Mass for 3 voices, motets, offertories, *Psalm 150*;

(3) Operas: *Hulda* (1894), *Ghiselle* (1896);

(4) Orchestra: Symphony in D minor, *Variations symphoniques* for piano and orchestra, symphonic poems – *Les Eolides*, *Le Chasseur maudit*, *Les Djinns* (piano and orchestra), *Psyche* (chorus and orchestra);

(5) Chamber music: string quartet, piano quintet, 4 piano trios, violin sonata;

(6) Piano: *Prelude, choral et fugue*, *Prelude, aria et final*;

(7) Organ: 3 chorales, miscellaneous pieces.

Also songs, miscellaneous piano solos, and pieces for harmonium.

**Franck, Johann Wolfgang** (b. 1644), German composer. Gave concerts in London (1690–95). Works incl. opera *Die drey Töchter Cecrops* (1679), *Geistliche Lieder* (sacred songs, 1681), and *Remedium Melancholiae* (secular songs, published in London, 1690).

**Franck, Melchior** (*c* 1573–1639), German composer. Wrote church and instrumental music, and songs.

**Franco de Colonia** or *Franco of Cologne* (*fl* 13th cent.), theorist. Systematized notation of mensural music in treatise *Ars cantus mensurabilis*.

**Frankel, Benjamin** (1906–73), English composer, teacher. Active as instrumentalist, conductor and arranger in field of popular music for several years. Serious compositions, mostly post-WWII, incl. opera *Marching Song* (1972–73), violin and viola concertos, 8 symphonies, 5 string quartets, unaccompanied sonatas for violin and viola, and much film music.

**Frankl, Peter** (1935– ), Hungarian-born pianist, UK citizen from

1967. Concert-hall soloist, and pianist in trio with György Pauk and Ralph Kirshbaum.

**Franz, Robert** (1815–92), German composer. Deafness and nervous troubles compelled him to retire in 1868. Composed over 250 songs, whose quality was quickly recognized by Schumann and Liszt.

**Fraser, Marjorie Kennedy,** *see* KENNEDY-FRASER.

**Frauenliebe und Leben** (Ger., *Woman's Love and Life*), cycle of 8 songs by Schumann, op 42 (1840), words by A. von Chamisso.

**Frau ohne Schatten, Die** (Ger., *The Woman without a Shadow*), opera by Richard Strauss, libretto by Hugo von Hofmannsthal (based on his story of same title). First perf. Vienna, 1919. Story is long and complex allegory on subject of unselfishness. Hailed by some as Strauss's masterpiece.

**Frauenlob** (Ger., praise of ladies), name given to Heinrich von Meissen (*c* 1260–1318), one of last of *Minne-singer.*

**Frederick [II] the Great** (1712–86), king of Prussia (1740–86). Keen flautist and prolific composer, esp. for flute. Employees incl. C.P.E. Bach and Quantz. J.S. Bach visited him (1747), and subsequently dedicated *Musical Offering* to him.

**Freischütz, Der** (Ger., *The Marksman*), *Singspiel* (opera with dialogue) by Weber, libretto by F. Kind. Opened up new world of romanticism to German opera.

**French harp** (US), mouth organ.

**French horn,** *see* HORN.

**French overture,** *see* OVERTURE.

**French sixth,** *see* AUGMENTED SIXTH.

**French Suites,** set of 6 keyboard suites by Bach (*c* 1722). Some say they were so-called because of supposedly characteristic French style. On smaller scale than ENGLISH SUITES.

**frequency,** rate of vibration of air-column or resonating body, expressed as number of vibrations per second. Frequency determines pitch; A above middle C has frequency of 440. *See* ACOUSTICS.

**Frere, Walter Howard** (1863–1938), English liturgiologist. Published 2 vols. of facsimiles – *Graduale Sarisburiense* (1894) and *Antiphonale Sarisburiense* (1901–24) – and catalogue of liturgical Mss, *Bibliotheca Musico-liturgica* (2 vols., 1901–32).

**Frescobaldi, Girolamo** (1583–1643), Italian composer, organist. One of outstanding organists of his time; held posts at Mantua, Florence and St Peter's, Rome. Pupils incl. Froberger. Keyboard compositions incl. *ricercari*, *canzoni francesi*, toccatas, capriccios, and collection entitled *Fiori musicali* ('musical flowers'). Also published *canzoni* for instrumental ensemble, arias for one or more voices, and set of madrigals.

**fret** (Fr., *touche*; Ger., *Bund*; It., *tasto*), thin piece of material fitted to finger-board of string instrument to facilitate stopping of string. Each fret marks position of specific note on scale, and effect of stopping on fret is to produce quality similar to that of open string. Frets are used on viol, lute, guitar and similar instruments, but not on members of violin family. Formerly made of pieces of gut tied firmly round finger-board, but now generally made of wood or metal fixed permanently in position.

**Fricker, Peter Racine** (1920– ), English composer. Works, highly concentrated and individual in idiom, incl. 5 symphonies, violin concerto, *Rapsodia Concertante* for violin and orchestra, concertos for violin, cor anglais, piano, 3 pianos, choral, chamber, organ and piano music, and songs.

**Fricsay, Ferenc** (1914–63), Hungarian conductor. Pupil of Kodály and Bartók, and a gifted exponent of their music. Worked principally in Germany.

**Friedenstag** (Ger., *Peace Day*), opera by Richard Strauss, libretto by J. Gregor. First perf. Munich, 1938. Based on Calderón's *La redención de Breda* (1625), work deals with besieged city during Thirty Years' War, and culminates in hymn to peace.

**Friedheim, Arthur** (1859–1932), Russian pianist. Pupil of Liszt, in interpretation of whose works he excelled. Lived in Germany, US and England.

**Friedländer, Max** (1852–1934), German baritone, writer on music. Edited songs of Schubert, Schumann and Mendelssohn, and wrote books on 18th-cent. German song and on songs of Brahms.

**Friedmann, Ignacy** (1882–1948), Polish pianist. Pupil of Leschetizky. Edited piano works of Chopin, Schumann and Liszt. His compositions are mainly for piano.

**Friml, Rudolf** (1879–1972), Czech composer, pianist. Settled in US (1906). Wrote series of popular operettas incl. *Rose Marie* and *The Vagabond King*.

**friska, friss** (Hung.), *see* CSÁRDAS.

**Froberger, Johann Jakob** (1616–67), German composer, organist. Pupil of Frescobaldi. Worked as organist in Vienna and also travelled extensively. Keyboard works incl. toccatas, fantasias, *canzoni*, capriccios, *ricercari and suites.*

**frog** (US), *nut* of violin or violin bow.

**Frog Galliard,** name given to popular Elizabethan tune, poss. by Dowland, who set it as lute solo and adapted it to words 'Now, oh now I needs must part'.

**'Frog' Quartet** (Ger., *Froschquartett*), nickname given to Haydn's string quartet in D major, op 50, no 6 supposedly because of 'croaking' theme in finale.

**From Bohemia's Fields and Groves,** *see* MÁ VLAST.

**From My Life** (Cz., *Z mého zivota*), title of Smetana's string quartet no 1 in E minor (1876).

**From the House of the Dead,** opera by Janáček, libretto by composer (based on Dostoyevski's *Memoirs from the House of the Dead*). Opera was completed by Bretislav Bakala and O. Zitek, and first perf. Brno, 1930. Work gives powerful and human picture of life in Siberian prison camp.

**From the New World,** title of Dvořák's symphony no 9 in E minor, op 95. Composed in US, 1893. Contains allusions to idioms of US Negro music.

**Frosch, am,** *see* BOWING.

**Froschquartett,** *see* 'FROG' QUARTET.

**frottola** (It.), lit. 'little mixture'. Type of strophic song of popular character current in aristocratic circles in late 15th, early 16th-cent. Italy. Forerunner of MADRIGAL.

**Frühlingssonate,** *see* SPRING SONATA.

**Frühlingssymphonie,** *see* SPRING SYMPHONY.

**Fuenllana, Miguel** (*fl* early 16th cent.), blind Spanish lutenist, composer. His collection *Orphenica Lyra* (1554) incl. his own lute songs and instrumental pieces, and transcriptions of madrigals and motets by his contemporaries.

**fuga,** (1) (Lat.), in 15th, 16th cents. = CANON;
(2) (It.), fugue.

**fugato** (It.), lit. 'fugued'. Term applied to section of composition which is treated fugally, though composition as whole is not fugue.

**Fuge** (Ger.), fugue.

**fughetta** (It.), short fugue.

**fugue** (Fr., *fugue*; It., *fuga*; Ger., *Fuge*), contrapuntal composition in 2 or more parts or 'voices', built on SUBJECT *ie* theme which is introduced at beginning in imitation and recurs frequently in course of composition. Second entry of subject (generally fifth higher or fourth lower, but sometimes fourth higher or fifth lower) is called ANSWER: often slightly modified to preserve tonality of piece or to facilitate third entry of subject, which will be identical with first, though in higher or lower octave. Third entry is often deferred for one or more bars, intervening space being occupied by CODETTA. When answer enters, subject continues with counterpoint to it, which if used in rest of fugue is called COUNTERSUBJECT. Countersubject is generally so designed that it can be treated in DOUBLE COUNTERPOINT with subject. Initial entries of subject are generally as many as number of parts in fugue, though sometimes there is additional entry ('redundant' entry). When all parts have made their entries, EXPOSITION of fugue is complete.

Rest of fugue consists of further entries of subject, several in related keys for sake of modulation, normally interspersed with contrapuntal EPISODES. Among devices which may be used in presentation of subject in course of fugue are AUGMENTATION, DIMINUTION, INVERSION and STRETTO. None is essential for fugue, nor are countersubjects.

Sometimes one or more countersubjects appear at beginning of fugue simultaneously with subject, in which case subject and countersubject(s) form unity and fugue is said to have subject in 2 (or more) parts. Such a fugue is often described as double (or triple, quadruple *etc*) fugue, though term 'double fugue' is more properly applied to one in which second, independent subject appears in course of fugue and is subsequently combined with first subject (and similarly with triple fugue, quadruple fugue *etc*).

Fugue may be written for voices or instruments, separately or combined. May occur as independent piece, or in association with prelude, or as movt. in larger composition, or as accompaniment to CANTUS FIRMUS. Origin of fugue is found in imitative entries in late 15th-cent. polyphonic vocal music, imitated in instrumental *ricercar* and subsequently in *canzona* and capriccio. As independent form, dates from 17th cent.

**full anthem,** ANTHEM in which voices supply all necessary harmony, without need for independent accompaniment, in contrast to VERSE ANTHEM.

**full close,** another name for perfect CADENCE.

**Fuller-Maitland, John Alexander** (1856–1936), English critic, editor. Music critic of *The Times* (1889–1911). Edited 2nd edition of Grove's *Dictionary of Music and Musicians* (1904–10), *The Fitzwilliam Virginal Book* (with W.B. Squire, 1899), and 2 vols. in Purcell Society's edition.

**full score,** orchestral SCORE, in which part for each instrument appears on separate stave, (usually) arranged in conventional order.

**fundamental,** first, or lowest, note of HARMONIC SERIES.

**fundamental bass** (Fr., *basse fondamentale*), term employed by Rameau to indicate 'root' of any chord, or 'roots' of series of chords. Any 2 chords composed of same notes, in whatever vertical order, are considered to have same fundamental bass. Foundation of theory of INVERSIONS.

**funebre** (It.), **funèbre** (Fr.), funeral (as adj.). *Marche funèbre*, funeral march.

**Funeral Ode,** *see* TRAUER-ODE.

**fuoco** (It.), 'fire'. *Con fuoco*, with fire.

**Für Elise** (Ger., For Elise), bagatelle in A minor for piano by Beethoven (*c* 1810; published 1867). It has been suggested that 'Elise' may be copyist's mistaken transcription of Therese, *ie* Therese von Brunswick, with whom Beethoven was in love.

**furiant,** Czech dance, in quick triple time with syncopation.

**furlana,** *see* FORLANA.

**Furtwängler, Wilhelm** (1886–1954), German conductor, composer. Conductor of Leipzig Gewandhaus concerts (1922–8), and Berlin Philharmonic (1922–45). Conducted frequently at Bayreuth and Salzburg festivals. Noted esp. for interpretations of Wagner, Beethoven, Brahms and Bruckner. Highly influential. Compositions incl. 2 symphonies.

**Future, Music of the,** *see* MUSIC OF THE FUTURE.

**futurism** (It., *futurismo*), movement started by Italian writer F.T. Marinetti in 1911. First concert of futurist music given by him and composer Luigi Rossolo in Milan (1914), consisting of 'networks of voices' employing thunderers, whistlers *etc*; caused riot. Futurist music defined by Marinetti as 'synthetic expression of great economic, erotic, heroic, aviational, mechanical dynamism'.

**Fux, Johann Joseph** (1660–1741), Austrian composer, theorist. Compositions incl. much church music, 10 oratorios, 18 operas and instrumental music. Treatise on counterpoint, *Gradus ad Parnassum* (1725) was long a standard work.

# G

**G** (Eng., Ger.; Fr., It., *sol*), fifth note (or dominant of scale of C major). As abbrev. *m.g.* = *main gauche* (left hand), *G.P.* = *Generalpause* (rest for complete orchestra).

G clef, now invariably placed on 2nd line of stave, is treble clef, marking G above middle C (*see* CLEF).

**Gabrieli, Andrea** (*c* 1515–86), Italian composer, organist. Pupil of Willaert. Organist at St Mark's, Venice. Compositions incl. madrigals, motets, Masses, and instrumental works.

His nephew, **Giovanni Gabrieli** (?1557–1612), was also composer and organist. Organist at St Mark's, Venice. Pupils incl. Schütz. Compositions incl. elaborate motets with instrumental accompaniment, ensemble works for 22 instruments (showing lively appreciation of colour), and organ works.

**Gabrielli, Caterina** (1730–96), Italian soprano. Pupil of Porpora. Sang in Venice, Vienna, St Petersburg and London. A brilliant coloratura.

**Gabrilovich, Ossip Salomonovich** (1878–1936), Russian-born pianist, composer. Pupil of Anton Rubinstein, Liadov, Glazunov and Leschetizky. Conducted in Munich, Detroit and Philadelphia. His wife was the singer, Clara Clemens, daughter of Mark Twain.

**Gaburo, Kenneth** (1926– ), American composer. Works incl. 2 tape operas (concrete and electronic) as well as more conventional ones (*The Snow Queen*, 1952, *The Widow*, 1959), series of works entitled *Antiphony* for mixture of instrumental and electronic forces, series of *Ideas and Transformations* for string duo, string quartet (1956), and *Line Studies* for flute, clarinet, trombone and viola (1957).

**Gade, Niels Wilhelm** (1817–90), Danish composer. Spent some years in Leipzig, where encouraged by Mendelssohn. Compositions show influence of Mendelssohn and Schumann, but also have traces of national colour. Works incl. 8 symphonies, 6 overtures, violin concerto, several cantatas, chamber and piano music, and songs.

**Gafori, Franchino** or **Franchinus Gafurius** (1451–1522), Italian theorist, composer. Most important works are *Theorica musicae* and *Practica musicae*. Compositions incl. Masses, Magnificats, and motets.

**Gagliano, Marco da** (*c* 1575–1642), Italian composer, Best known as one of first opera composers; his *Dafne* (libretto by Rinuccini) was given at Mantua in 1608. Also published 6 books of madrigals, Mass and motets.

**Gagliano,** firm of violin-makers active in Naples in late 17th and 18th cents.

**gagliarda, gaillarde,** *see* GALLIARD.

**Gál, Hans** (1890– ), Austrian composer, teacher. Resident in Edinburgh from 1938. Works incl. operas, 2 symphonies, choral and orchestral works, violin concerto and chamber music.

**galant,** *see* STYLE GALANT.

**Galanterien** (Ger.), name given in 18th cent. to dances in suite added optionally to regular allemande, courante, sarabande and gigue. Normally placed between sarabande and gigue.

**galanter Stil,** *see* STYLE GALLANT.

**Galilei, Vincenzo** (*c* 1520–91), Italian lutenist, composer. Father of astronomer Galileo Galilei. Prominent among Florentines who wished to revive Greek drama, and so gave birth to first operas. Works incl. madrigals, lute music, and instrumental duos. Also wrote theoretical works.

**gallant style,** *see* STYLE GALLANT.

**galliard** (Fr., *gaillarde*; It., *gagliarda*), lively dance, generally in triple time. Takes name from Fr., *gaillard,* 'merry'. From later 16th cent., regularly used to provide contrast to slow PAVANE, which it followed, and with which it was often thematically connected.

**Galliard, John Ernest** or **Johann Ernst** (*c* 1680–1749), oboist, composer, of German origin. Came to England in early 18th cent. as musician to Prince George of Denmark (consort of Queen Anne). In addition to numerous compositions, translated P.F. Tosi's *Opinioni de' cantori....* (1723) as *Observations on the Florid Song* (1742).

**Galli-Curci, Amelita** (1882–1963), Italian coloratura soprano. Performed internationally.

**Gallus,** *see* HANDL.

**galop,** quick dance in 2/4 time, popular in 19th cent. Originated in Germany.

**galoubet** (Fr.), 3-hole whistle flute, played with left hand while right hand beats tabor (TAMBOURIN).

**Galpin, Francis William** (1858–1945), English musicologist, collector of musical instruments, parish priest. His several books on instruments ranged from the Sumerians to latest developments in electronic sound-production. Galpin Society continues his work.

**Galuppi, Baldassare,** also called 'Il Buranello' (1706–85), Italian composer. Comic operas are notable contribution to history of the form. Also wrote oratorios, symphonies, concertos and keyboard sonatas. Browning's poem, 'A Toccata of Galuppi', refers to imaginary work.

**Galway, James** (1939– ), Northern Irish flautist. Principal flautist with leading orchestras until 1975, since when has followed highly successful solo career.

**gamba,** abbrev. of VIOLA DA GAMBA. Also organ stop imitating that instrument.

**Gambler, The,** opera by Prokofiev, libretto by composer (based on Dostoyevski's story). Composed 1915–16. First perf. Brussels, 1927, after projected Leningrad première was cancelled because of Revolution.

**gamelan orchestra,** Indonesian instrumental ensemble. Principally composed of xylophones, marimbas, gongs and drums. Music based on simple 5-note scales, but highly sophisticated in texture and rhythmically very complex.

**gamme** (Fr.), scale.

**gamut,** (1) in medieval theory, G on bottom line of bass clef; combination of *gamma* (letter G in Greek) and *ut,* 1st note of HEXACHORD;

(2) scale beginning on note *gamma ut*; hence range or compass of voice or instrument;

(3) key of G.

**Ganassi, Silvestro di** (*fl* 16th cent.), Italian theorist. Published tutors for recorder and viols.

**Ganz, Rudolph** (1877–1972), American pianist, conductor, composer, b. Switzerland. Pupil of Busoni. President of Chicago Musical College from 1934, and conducted St Louis Symphony Orchestra (1921–27).

**Ganz, Wilhelm** (1833–1914), German pianist, conductor, singing teacher. Resident in Britain from 1850. Accompanied Jenny Lind and many other famous singers. As conductor introduced Berlioz's *Symphonie fantastique* and Liszt's *Dante Symphony* to Britain.

**Ganze, Ganze Note, Ganzetaknote** (Ger.), semibreve.

**Ganzton** (Ger.), whole TONE.

**gapped scale,** scale with some intervals larger than whole tone, *eg* PENTATONIC SCALE.

**garbato** (It.), graceful.

**Garcia, Manuel del Popolo Vincente** (1775–1832), Spanish tenor, composer, conductor. Performed in opera in Paris, Italy, US and Mexico. Estab. school of singing in London. Part of Almaviva in Rossini's *The Barber of Seville* was written for him. His numerous operas had considerable success. Pupils incl. his children, Maria (Malibran), Pauline (Viardot), and Manuel II.

His son, **Manuel Patricio Rodriguez Garcia** (1805–1906), invented laryngoscope, and published *Mémoire sur la voix humaine* (1840) and *Traité complet de l'art du chant* (1847), both works of outstanding importance. Pupils incl. Jenny Lind and Julius Stockhausen.

**Gardano,** Venetian music-publishing firm, founded by Antonio Gardano. Published numerous sacred and secular works (1538–1619).

**Garden, Mary** (1877–1967), Scottish operatic soprano. Went to US as child, and moved to Paris in 1895. Roles she created incl. Debussy's Mélisande, Massenet's Sapho and Saint-Saëns's Hélène. Director of Chicago Opera (1919–20).

**Garden of Fand, The,** symphonic poem by Bax. First perf. 1920.

**Gardiner, Henry Balfour** (1877–1950), English composer. Best known work is *Shepherd Fennel's Dance* for orchestra (1911). Also promoted concerts of contemporary British music.

**Gardiner, William** (1770–1853), English writer on music, stocking-manufacturer. Adapted music by various European composers to sacred words under title *Sacred Melodies* (6 vols.).

**Gardner, John** (1917– ), English composer. Works incl. symphony, operas *The Moon and Sixpence* (inspired by Somerset Maugham's novel), *The Visitors* and *Tobermory*, ballet *Reflection*, piano concerto, orchestral, choral and chamber music, and songs.

**Garlande, Jean de** or **Johannes de Garlandia** (*fl* 13th cent.), French theorist. Wrote *De mensurabili musica*, oldest extant treatise on mensural notation. Not to be confused with grammarian Johannes de Garlandia (b. *c* 1195).

**Gaspard de la Nuit** (Fr., Gaspard of the Night), set of 3 piano pieces by Ravel (1908) inspired by prose-poems by Aloysius Bertrand.

**Gasparini, Francesco** (1668-1727), Italian composer. Pupil of Corelli. Wrote several oratorios and operas, and treatise on accompaniment from figured bass.

**Gasparo da Salò**, *see* SALÒ.

**Gassmann, Florion Leopold** (1729–74), Sudeten composer. Works incl. 54 symphonies, chamber and church music, and *c* 25 operas, *eg L'Amore Artigiano* (1769) and *La Contessina* (1770).

**Gast, Peter,** pseud. of Johann Heinrich Köselitz (1854–1918), German composer. Friend and secretary of Nietzsche, whose letters he subsequently helped to edit. Best-known work is opera *Die heimliche Ehe* (1891), founded on libretto of Cimarosa's *Il matrimonio segreto*; revived in 1933 as *Der Löwe von Venedig*. Other works incl. symphony, chamber music and songs.

**Gastein Symphony,** supposed symphony of Schubert, now lost, said to have been written in Gastein (Austria). Some think sonata in C for piano duet is arrangement of it.

**Gastoldi, Giovanni Giacomo** (*c* 1550–1622), Italian composer. Works incl. church music, madrigals and balletts. Most popular work was *Balletti a cinque voci....* (1591), collection of cheerful part-songs which was very influential, esp. in England. Morley's *First Booke of Balletts to Five Voyces* (1595) is very close imitation of the style.

**Gastoué, Amédée** (1873–1943), French writer on music. Wrote many books on Gregorian chant.

**Gatti, Guido Maria** (1892–1973), Italian writer on music. Books incl. studies of Schumann, Bizet, Pizzetti, French music, and modern Italian music.

**Gatty, Nicholas Comyn** (1874–1946), English composer, critic. Pupil of Stanford. Numerous compositions incl. several operas, *eg The Tempest*.

**Gaubert, Philippe** (1879–1941), French flautist, conductor, composer. Conductor of Société des Concerts du Conservatoire (1919–38). Compositions incl. operas, ballets, oratorio, orchestral and chamber music, and songs.

**Gaultier, Denis** (d. 1672), French lutenist, composer. Works incl. Ms *La Rhétorique des dieux,* collection of dance tunes for lute arranged in groups or suites. This method of arrangement influenced

French harpsichord composers, as did Gaultier's technique of broken chords and his use of fanciful titles.

**Jacques Gaultier** (*fl* 17th cent.) was relative of Denis, and was a lutenist and composer. Fled to England in 1618 after having killed French nobleman. Entered service of Marquess (later Duke) of Buckingham, and later of Charles I.

**Gaveaux, Pierre** (1761–1825), French composer. Numerous operas incl. *Léonore, ou l'Amour conjugal* (1798), a setting of J.N. Bouilly's libretto, which was also used (in Italian) for Paer's *Leonora* and (in German) for Beethoven's *Fidelio*.

**gavotte,** French dance in fairly quick 4/4 time, generally starting on 3rd beat of bar. Popularity began with its introduction by Lully into ballets and operas in late 17th cent., and continued in 18th cent. Where 2 gavottes occur together, 2nd is often in form of MUSETTE.

**Gay, John** (1685–1732), English poet, playwright. Wrote words of *The Beggar's Opera* (1728).

**Gazza Ladra, La,** *see* THIEVING MAGPIE, THE.

**Gazzaniga, Guiseppe** (1743–1818), Italian composer. Pupil of Porpora and Piccinni. Numerous operas incl. *Don Giovanni* (1787); libretto, by G. Bertati, was plainly familiar to Da Ponte, librettist of Mozart's *Don Giovanni,* first perf. later in same year.

**Gebrauchsmusik** (Ger.), UTILITY MUSIC.

**gebunden** (Ger.), lit. 'bound', *ie* (1) tied or slurred, (2) *see* CLAVICHORD.

**Gédalge, André** (1856–1926), French composer, teacher. Pupils incl. Ravel, Milhaud, Honegger and Schmitt. Wrote *Traité de la fugue* (1901), standard work in France. Also wrote instrumental music and works for stage.

**gedämpft** (Ger.), muted.

**gedehnt** (Ger.), 'stretched out', *ie* sustained.

**gehalten** (Ger.), sustained. *Gut gehalten,* well sustained.

**gehend** (Ger.), 'going', *ie* moving at moderate speed – same as *andante*.

**Geige** (Ger.), fiddle, violin.

**Geiringer, Karl** (1899– ), American writer on music, b. Austria. Books incl. studies of Haydn, Brahms and Bach family.

**Geistertrio** (Ger.), 'Ghost' Trio, nickname of Beethoven's piano trio in D major, op 70, no 1; name derives from mysterious character of slow movt.

**geistlich** (Ger.), religious, sacred. *Geistlicher Leider,* sacred songs.

**gemächlich** (Ger.), comfortable – equivalent of *commodo*.

**gemessen** (Ger.), lit. 'measured', hence held back, sustained in tempo.

**Geminiani, Francesco** (*c* 1679–1762), Italian violinist, composer. Pupil of Corelli. Very successful as soloist, esp. in England, where he arrived in 1714. Lived in Dublin, Paris and London. Compositions incl. sonatas, trios, concertos and harpsichord solos. Wrote treatises on musical practice and instrumental tutors.

**gemütlich** (Ger.), comfortable, easy-going.

**Generalbass** (Ger.), figured bass.

**Generalpause** (Ger.), general pause, rest of one or more bars for complete orchestra. Indicated by abbrev. G.P.

**Genoveva,** opera by Schumann, libretto by R. Reinick (based on tragedies by Tieck and Hebbel). Schumann's only opera, first perf. Leipzig, 1850. Story tells how Siegfried goes off to war, leaving his wife Genoveva in care of treacherous friend Golo. Golo tries to seduce her, fails, tries to bring about her destruction, but is himself destroyed.

**Gerber, Ernst Ludwig** (1746–1819), German author of 6-vol. biographical dictionary of music (1790–1814), for long a standard work.

**Gerbert (von Hornau), Martin** (1720–93), German historian, priest. Published history of church music, and collection of medieval treatises on music.

**Gerhard, Roberto** (1896–1970), Catalan composer, son of Swiss father and French mother. Pupil of Pedrell and Schoenberg. Settled in Britain after Spanish Civil War, where, along with Britten and Tippett, became one of most vital forces in British music. Used twelve-note technique and electronic music in constructive and picturesque fashion. Works incl. opera *The Duenna* (1948), ballets (*eg Don Quixote*), 4 symphonies, violin concerto, concerto for orchestra, concerto for 8 instruments, setting of Edward Lear's *The Akond of Swat* for singer and 2 percussionists, and chamber music.

**Gerhardt, Elena** (1883–1961), German concert soprano. Frequently accompanied by Arthur Nikisch. Excelled in performance of Schubert, Schumann, Brahms and Wolf.

**Gerle, Hans** (d. 1570), German lute-maker, lutenist. Published *Musica Teusch, auf die Instrument der grossen unnd kleinen Geygen, auch Lautten,* 1st edition of which (1532) contains transcriptions of German songs and dances; 2nd edition (1546) substitutes French *chansons* for German songs. Also published *Tabulatur auff die Laudten* (1533), containing both German and foreign pieces, and *Eyn newes sehr künstlichs Lautenbuch* (1552), which incl. many Italian pieces.

**German, Edward,** orig. Edward German Jones (1862–1936), English composer. Works incl. incidental music for plays *eg Henry VIII* (1892) and *Nell Gwyn* (1900), operettas *eg Merrie England* (1902) and *Tom Jones* (1907), 2 symphonies, symphonic poem *Hamlet, Welsh Rhapsody,* and *Theme and Six Diversions*. Knighted 1928.

**German flute,** *see* FLUTE (2).

**Germani, Fernando** (1906– ). Italian organist. Organist at St Peter's, Rome (1948–59). Internationally known as recitalist.

**German Requiem, A** (Ger., *Ein deutsches Requiem*), memorial cantata in 7 movts. by Brahms, op 45 (1866–8), with words from Luther's translation of Bible. Written in memory of composer's mother.

**German sixth,** *see* AUGMENTED SIXTH.

**Gérold, Théodore** (1866–1956), French historian, musicologist.

Numerous books incl. studies of early music, 17th-cent. French song, Bach and Schubert.

**Gershwin, George** (1898–1937), American composer, pianist. Within limited field, had delightful melodic talent, beautifully matched to polished lyrics of brother Ira. Wrote songs for shows incl. *Lady, Be Good!* (1924), *Funny Face* (1927), *Girl Crazy* (1927) and *Strike up the Band* (1930). Concert works incl. *Rhapsody in Blue* for piano and jazz orchestra (1924), piano concerto (1925) and *An American in Paris* (1928). Also wrote opera *Porgy and Bess* (1935).

**Gervaise, Claude** (*fl* 16th cent.), French violinist, composer. Works incl. dance tunes for instrumental ensemble, and *chansons*.

**Ges** (Ger.), G flat.

**gesangvoll** (Ger.), songful – same as *cantabile*.

**geschleift** (Ger.), lit. 'slurred' – same as *legato*.

**Geschöpfe des Prometheus, Die,** *see* PROMETHEUS.

**geschwind** (Ger.), quick.

**Geses** (Ger.), G double flat.

**Gesius, Bartholomaus** (*c* 1560–1613), German composer. Works incl. Masses, Magnificats, motets, Lutheran hymns, and Passion according to St John (1588).

**gestopft** (Ger.), stopped. *See* HORN.

**gestossen** (Ger.), lit. 'detached' – same as *staccato*.

**Gesualdo, Carlo** (*c* 1560–1613), Italian composer, nobleman. Friend of Tasso, several of whose poems he set to music. Wrote madrigals, motets and *responsoria*. Madrigals remarkable for degree to which they expressed mood of text, often using chromatic harmony and abrupt modulation. Notorious for murder of wife on account of her infidelity.

**getragen** (Ger.), slow and sustained – same as *sostenuto*.

**Gevaert, François Auguste** (1828–1908), Belgian historian, musicologist, composer. Won *Prix de Rome* (1847). Several of his operas were performed successfully in Paris (1853–64). Director of music at Paris Opéra (1867–70); director of Brussels Conservatoire (1871–1908). Publications incl. works on instrumentation and harmony, and editions of old music.

**Gewandhauskonzerte** (Ger.), series of concerts at Leipzig, first given 1743. Later held at Gewandhaus (Cloth Hall). Conductors have incl. Mendelssohn, Nikisch, Furtwängler and Bruno Walter.

**Ghedini, Giorgio Federico** (1892–1965), Italian composer. Works incl. operas *eg La pulce d'oro* (1940), *Billy Budd* (1949) and *L'ipocrita felice* (1956), orchestral, chamber, and choral music, piano pieces, film scores, and songs. Also made numerous transcriptions.

**Gherardello da Firenze** or **Ghirardellus da Florentia** (d. *c* 1363), Italian composer. Surviving works consist of a *Gloria* and *Agnus Dei,* and several madrigals, *ballate* and *cacce*.

**Ghiselin-Verbonnet, Johannes** (*c* 1458–after 1508), Flemish composer, apparently known as both Ghiselin and Verbonnet. Worked in Ferrara, at French court, and in Flanders. Works consist of Masses, motets, and songs to French, Dutch, Italian and Latin texts.

**Ghisi, Federico** (1901– ), Italian musicologist, composer. Books incl. *I canti carnascialeschi nelle fonte musicali del XV e XVI secoli* (1937) and *Feste musicali della Firenze Medicea* (1939). Compositions incl. chamber music and *Sinfonia italiana.*

**'Ghost' Trio,** *see* GEISTERTRIO.

**Giannini, Vittorio** (1903–66), American composer. Works incl. concertos for piano and organ, symphony, *Frescobaldiana* for orchestra, Requiem, *Stabat Mater,* chamber music, and operas *eg The Scarlet Letter* (1938) and *The Taming of the Shrew* (1953).

**Gianni Schicchi,** *see* TRITTICO.

**'Giant' Fugue,** nickname of chorale prelude for organ by Bach, from *Clavierübung,* part 3 - so called because of recurrence on pedals of imposing figure symbolizing unshakeable faith.

**Giardini, Felice de** (1716–96), Italian violinist, composer. Played in Germany and London. Emigrated to Russia (1790). Compositions incl. operas and string music. Collaborated with Avison on oratorio *Ruth.*

**Gibbons, Orlando** (1583–1625), composer and organist. Most famous of family of musicians. Chorister at King's College, Cambridge, organist at Chapel Royal (1605–19) and at Westminster Abbey (1623–5). Compositions incl. madrigals, motets, anthems, chamber pieces for strings, and keyboard works. Music has certain reserve, but does not exclude emotion. Secular songs have austerity uncommon among madrigalists of period. Several of his verse anthems have accompaniments for strings. Instrumental music, of fine quality, forms substantial and important part of his output.

His son, **Christopher Gibbons** (1615–76), was also organist and composer. Organist at Chapel Royal and Westminster Abbey. Compositions incl. anthems, fantasies for strings, and keyboard music. Collaborated with Matthew Locke on music for Shirley's masque *Cupid and Death.*

Orlando's eldest brother, **Ellis Gibbons** (1573–1603), was also a composer. Contributed 2 madrigals to *The Triumphes of Oriana* (1601).

**Gibbs, Cecil Armstrong** (1889–1960), English composer. Best known for sensitive and imaginative songs. Also wrote large-scale choral works *eg Deborah and Barak* (1937) and choral symphony *Odysseus* (1938).

**Gibson, Alexander** (1926– ), Scottish conductor. Musical director of Scottish National Orchestra from 1959. Founded Scottish Opera (1962). Knighted 1977.

**Gieseking, Walter Wilhelm** (1895–1956), German pianist, composer, b. France. Excelled in works of Debussy and Ravel. Compositions incl. chamber music and songs.

**giga,** *see* GIGUE.

**Gigault, Nicolas** (*c* 1625–1707), French composer, organist.

Published collection of *nöels* arranged for instruments, and book of organ music.

**Gigli, Beniamino** (1880–1957), Italian tenor. One of outstanding singers of 20th cent. Known internationally in opera house and concert hall.

**gigue,** (1) (Fr.) medieval name for bowed string instrument;

(2) lively dance (It., *giga*). Word apparently adapted from Eng., 'jig'. Found in English sources from *c* 1600, but not on Continent till mid 17th cent. As standardized in late 17th, early 18th cents., dance was in 6/8 rhythm, though music might be noted in variety of ways.

Gigue was last of 4 regular dances in SUITE, following allemande, courante and sarabande. When optional dances (GALANTERIEN) were added, they were generally placed between sarabande and gigue. Like other dances in suite, gigue was in BINARY FORM. There were 2 main types: (1) generally straightforward in character and simple in texture; (2) more elaborate, with fugal imitation; it was convention in this type to invert subject at beginning of 2nd section.

**'Gigue' Fugue** or **'Jig' Fugue,** nickname given to fugue in G for 2 manuals and pedal in 12/8 time, generally regarded as early work of Bach.

**Gigues** (Fr.), first of Debussy's IMAGES for orchestra.

**Gilbert, Anthony** (1934– ), English composer. Works incl. opera *The Scene Machine* (1970), symphony (1973), *Regions* for 2 chamber orchestras (1966), *Treatment of Silence* for violins and tape (1978).

**Gilbert, Henry Franklin Belknap** (1868–1928), American composer. Pupil of MacDowell. Works, often using idioms of Negro folk music, incl. ballet *The Dance in Place Congo* (1918).

**Gilbert, William Schwenk** (1836–1911), *see* SULLIVAN.

**Gillis, Don** (1912– ), American composer, conductor, brass player, teacher. Compositions, in popular idiom, incl. Symphony no 5½ ('Symphony for Fun').

**Gilman, Lawrence** (1878–1939), American critic. Wrote for *New York Herald Tribune* (1923–39). Books incl. studies of MacDowell, Wagner and Toscanini.

**Ginastera, Alberto** (1916– ), Argentinian composer. Works, often in nationalistic idiom but later in more avant-garde style, incl. 3 operas (*Don Rodrigo*, *Bomarzo* and *Beatrix Cenci*), 3 ballets (*Panambi*, *Estancia* and *Variaciones Concertantes*), concertos for piano, violin, harp and cello, psalms for chorus and orchestra, chamber and instrumental music, and songs.

**giocoso** (It.), merry.

**gioioso** (It.), joyful.

**Giordani, Guiseppe,** also known as 'Giordanello' (1753–98), Italian composer. Works incl. numerous operas, oratorios, and church and instrumental music. Aria 'Caro mio ben' is attrib. to him.

**Giordani, Tommaso** (*c* 1730–1806), Italian composer. Chiefly active in London and Dublin. Composed *c* 50 works for stage, incl. songs for Sheridan's *The Critic*. Also wrote instrumental pieces.

**Giordano, Umberto** (1867–1948), Italian composer. Wrote operas of VERISMO type, *eg Mala vita* (1892), *Andrea Chénier* (1896) and *Fedora* (1898).

**Giovanelli, Ruggiero** (*c* 1560–1625), Italian composer. Succeeded Palestrina as *maestro di cappella* at St Peter's, Rome. Works incl. church music, and many madrigals, 4 of which were published by Morley with English translations.

**Giovanni da Cascia** or **da Firenze** or **Johannes de Florentia** (*fl* early 14th cent.), Italian composer. Wrote secular vocal music, mainly madrigals.

**giraffe piano,** early 19th-cent. piano, somewhat like grand, but with upright body.

**Girl of the Golden West, The** (It., *La Fanciulla del West*), opera by Puccini, libretto by G. Civinini and C. Zangarini (after David Belasco's play). First perf. New York, 1910. Story is set in Californian gold rush.

**Gis** (Ger.), G sharp.

**Giselle,** ballet (based on story by Heine) with music by Adolphe Adam. First perf. Paris, 1841.

**Gisis** (Ger.), G double sharp.

**gittern,** medieval English name for 4-stringed instrument of *guitar* family, played with plectrum. In Tudor and Stuart times, term used loosely to refer to more than one kind of instrument, incl. Spanish guitar. Not necessarily identical with CITTERN.

**Giulini, Carlo Maria** (1914– ), Italian conductor. Principal conductor at La Scala, Milan (1953–5). Has also worked with Chicago Symphony Orchestra, Vienna Symphony Orchestra. Conductor of Los Angeles Philharmonic Orchestra since 1978. Interpretations remarkable for expressiveness and absolute integrity.

**Giulio Cesare in Egitto,** *see* JULIUS CAESAR.

**giustiniana** (It.), popular 3-part song current in Italy in 16th cent. A kind of VILLANELLA.

**giusto** (It.), proper, reasonable, exact. *A tempogiusto* or *tempo giusto,* (1) in the proper time, at a reasonable speed, (2) in strict time.

**Glagolitic Mass,** Mass by Janáček (1926) for chorus, organ and orchestra.

**Glanville-Hicks, Peggy** (1912– ), Australian-born composer, US citizen from 1948, resident in Greece from 1959. Pupil of Vaughan Williams, Wellesz and Nadia Boulanger. Works incl. operas *Caedmon, The Transposed Heads* and *Nausicaa,* ballets, *Etruscan Concerto* for piano and chamber orchestra, orchestral, chamber and film music, and songs.

**Glareanus, Henricus,** pseud. of Heinrich Loriti (1488–1563), Swiss theorist. Chiefly known for treatise, DODECACHORDON (1547).

**Glasharmonika,** *see* HARMONICA.

**Glazunov, Alexander Konstantinovich** (1865–1936), Russian composer. Taught by Rimsky-Korsakov. Teacher (1900) then director (1906) of St Petersburg Conservatory. Settled in Paris in 1928. Although associated with nationalist composers of The FIVE, most of his work belongs to main stream of European music. Never developed really individual voice, though music is characterized by brilliance, charm and technical skill.

Principal compositions:

(1) Orchestra: 8 symphonies, 2 piano concertos, violin concerto, cello concerto, concerto for saxophone, flute and strings, 6 suites (incl. *Chopiniana* and *The Seasons*), 6 overtures, symphonic poem *(Stenka Razin)*, serenades, fantasias *etc*;

(2) Chamber music: 7 string quartets, string quintet, quartet for brass;

(3) Choral works: *Memorial Cantata, Hymn to Pushkin* (female voices).

Also works for piano and organ, songs, and incidental music. Helped Rimsky-Korsakov to complete Borodin's opera *Prince Igor*.

**glee,** simple part-song, generally for male voices. Popular in England in 18th, early 19th cents.

**glee club,** society for singing glees. Orig. society founded 1787, dissolved 1857. Name subsequently adopted by other societies, *eg* male-voice choral societies at US universities.

**Glière, Reinhold Moritzovich** (1875–1956), Russian composer, of Belgian origin. Works incl. opera *Shah Senem* (incorporating Azerbaijan melodies), ballet *Red Poppy* (on Russian Revolution), 3 symphonies, violin concerto, harp concerto, *March of the Red Army, Victory Overture,* 4 string quartets, chamber and piano music, and songs.

**Glinka, Mikhail Ivanovich** (1804–57), Russian composer. Studied music privately in St Petersburg. Briefly worked as civil servant before devoting himself to music. Travelled widely in Europe, though returned to St Petersburg to produce his 2 operas. Died in Berlin.

First opera, *A Life for the Tsar* (1836), now known as *Ivan Sussanin* (orig. title), is not esp. Russian in character; its strength is its simplicity – a reaction to conventions of Italian opera. Second opera, *Russlan and Ludmilla* (1842), created characteristically Russian style, incl. oriental elements so prominent in later Russian music. In orchestral fantasia *Karaminskaya* showed how folk song could be used as basis of instrumental composition. His *Jota Aragonesa* was inspired by visit to Spain. Also wrote chamber and piano music (he was pupil of John Field), and songs.

**Gli Scherzi,** *see* RUSSIAN QUARTETS.

**glissando** (It.), lit. 'sliding' (from Fr., *glisser*), *ie* execution of rapid continuous movement up or down scale. Glissando is often abbrev. *gliss.* or indicated by oblique stroke (straight or wavy) between highest and lowest notes.

**Globokar, Vinko** (1934– ), French-born Yugoslav trombonist, composer. Pupil of Leibowitz and Berio. Latter composed for him *Sequenza* for solo trombone. Own compositions incl. *Plan, Voie, Accord, Traumdeutung, Fluide* and *Etude pour Folkora I and II,* using various combinations of voices and instruments.

**Glocke,** (Ger., pl. *Glocken*), bell.

**Glockenspiel** (Ger.; Fr., *carillon, jeu de clochettes, jeu de timbres*; It., *campanelli*), percussion instrument (various sizes) consisting of series of steel plates of different sizes, arranged like keyboard of piano so as to provide complete chromatic compass. Steel plates are struck with wooden hammers held in hands, though at one time instrument was fitted with keyboard (like CELESTA). German name has become virtually international.

**Glogauer Liederbuch** (Ger.), 15th-cent. German collection of songs and dances, arranged for vocal or instrumental ensemble.

**Gloria** (Lat.), (1) initial word of 'Gloria in excelsis Deo' (Glory to God in the highest), second part of Ordinary of Mass;

(2) *Gloria Patri* (or doxology) sung at end of psalm or canticle.

**Gloriana,** opera by Britten, libretto by W. Plomer. First perf. London, 1953. Story concerns relationship between Elizabeth I and Earl of Essex. Commissioned by Covent Garden for coronation of Elizabeth II.

**Gluck, Christoph Willibald (von)** (1714–87), German composer. Studied in Prague and Italy (under Sammartini), spent time in London and Paris, and eventually settled in Vienna.

In *Orfeo* (1762) created new style of Italian opera which incorporated choruses and ballets of French opera and abandoned conventional virtuosity for dramatic truth and moving simplicity of expression. Adoption of this style was largely due to his librettist, Raniero de' Calzabigi. Principles of their 'reform' were set out in prefaces to *Alceste* (1767) and *Paride ed Elena* (1770), and were pursued in operas Gluck wrote for Paris. Influence of French traditions is strongly marked in Paris operas: in controversy between merits of Italian and French opera, he came to be regarded as champion of latter.

Though had no immediate imitators, his work came to have considerable influence on operas of Mozart, Cherubini, Beethoven and Berlioz. Now regarded as one of major figures in operatic history. In addition to more than 100 operas (many now lost), also wrote ballets, 11 symphonies, 7 trios, flute concerto, *De profundis* for choir and orchestra, and 7 odes by Klopstock for voice and keyboard.

Italian operas incl.:

*Artaserse* (1741), *Demetrio* (1742), *Demofoonte* (1742), *Il Tigrane* (1743), *La Sofonisba* (1744), *Ipermestra* (1744), *La caduta de'giganti* (1746), *Artamene* (1746), *La Nozze d'Ercole e d'Ebe* (1747), *Semiramide Riconosciuta* (1748), *La Contesa de' Numi* (1749), *Ezio* (1750), *La clemenza de Tito* (1752), *Le Cinesi* (1754), *Antigono* (1756), *Il rè pastore* (1756), *Il Telemacco* (1765);

French *opéras-comiques* incl.: *L'Isle de Merlin* (1758), *La Cythère assiégée* (1759, Paris version 1777), *L'Arbre enchanté* (1759, Versailles version 1777), *L'Ivrogne corrigé* (1760), *La Cadi dupé* (1761), *La Rencontre imprévue* (1764);

French operas for Paris: *Iphigénie en Aulide* (1744), *Orphée et Eurydice* (1774, Vienna version 1762), *Alceste* (1776, Italian version

1767), *Armide* (1777), *Iphigénie en Tauride* (1779), *Echo et Narcisse* (1779);

'Reform' operas: *Orfeo* (1762), *Alceste* (1767), *Paride ed Elena* (1770).

**Glückliche Hand, Die** (Ger., *The Fortunate Hand*), monodrama by Schoenberg, libretto by composer. Published in 1913, first perf. Vienna, 1924. Work, for baritone and chorus, concerns artist's quest for happiness.

**Glyndebourne,** small opera house near Lewes, Sussex, built by John Christie (1882–1962). Has held annual summer seasons of opera since 1934.

**Gobbi, Tito** (1915– ), Italian baritone. One of world's great singing actors, particularly impressive in works such as *Tosca, Gianni Schicchi* and *Falstaff.*

**Godard, Benjamin Louis Paul** (1849–95), French composer, violinist. Works incl. several operas (*eg Jocelyn*), *Le Tasse* for soloists, chorus and orchestra, symphony, symphonic poems, 2 violin concertos, piano concerto, chamber, piano and incidental music, and songs.

**Godfrey, Dan(iel) Eyers** (1868–1939), English conductor. Created Bournemouth Symphony Orchestra (1893). Introduced hundreds of new works by British composers.

**Godowsky, Leopold** (1870–1938), Polish-born pianist, composer. American by naturalization. Toured widely from 1884. Published works incl. transcriptions, studies on études by Chopin, and many smaller pieces *eg Triakontameron* (30 piano pieces composed on different days).

**God save the King/Queen,** earliest known version of British national anthem is tune in galliard rhythm of uncertain origin, which appeared in collection *Thesaurus Musicus* (*c* 1744). Popularity dates from 1745 Jacobite Rebellion. Tune also adopted on Continent and started fashion for national anthems. Used for US national song 'My Country, 'tis of thee' (1831).

**Goehr, Alexander** (1932– ), English composer of German origin. Father was conductor Walter Goehr. Studied at Manchester (member of so-called Manchester School) and in Paris (under Messiaen). One of leading English composers of his generation. Works incl. opera *Arden Must Die,* several pieces of music theatre (*eg Naboth's Vineyard*), *Little Symphony,* violin concerto, several cantatas (*eg The Deluge, Sutter's Gold, Hecuba's Lament* and *A Little Cantata of Proverbs*), chamber music, and songs.

**Goetz, Hermann** (1840–76), German composer. Settled in Switzerland. Works incl. 2 operas *(eg The Taming of the Shrew)*, symphony, overture, piano concerto, violin concerto, choral works with orchestra, chamber and piano music, songs, and part songs.

**Goldberg, Szymon** (1909– ), Polish-born violinist, conductor. Played in trio with Hindemith and Feuermann (1930–34), and in duo with Lili Kraus (1935–40). Followed solo career from 1955. Conducted Netherlands Chamber Orchestra from 1955.

**Goldberg Variations,** 4th part of Bach's *Clavierübung* (1742), for 2-manual harpsichord. Written for pupil, J.T. Goldberg, to play to Count Kaiserling, who suffered from insomnia. Theme is 'aria' in chaconne rhythm, with highly ornamented melody.

**Golden Cockerel, The** (Russ., *Zolotoy Petushok;* Fr., *Le Coq d'or*), opera by Rimsky-Korsakov, libretto by V.I. Bielsky (after Pushkin). First perf. Moscow, 1909. Banned during composer's lifetime because of vein of political satire.

**Goldmark, Karl** (1830–1915), Hungarian composer, teacher, critic. Studied in Vienna, where he spent much of his life. Works incl. 6 operas (*eg The Queen of Sheba*), 2 symphonies (one called *Rustic Wedding*), overtures *Sakuntala* and *In Spring,* 2 violin concertos, choral, chamber and piano music, and songs.

His nephew, **Rubin Goldmark** (1872–1936), was also composer and teacher, resident in US. Pupil of Dvořák. Teacher of Copland and Gershwin.

**Golliwog's Cakewalk,** *see* CHILDREN'S CORNER.

**Gombert, Nicolas** (*c* 1500–60), Flemish composer. In service of emperor Charles V (1526–40). In polyphonic writing, adopted method of continuous imitation (as Palestrina was to do), and avoided both homophonic writing and use of alternating pairs of voices (characteristic of Josquin's style). Composed *c* 160 motets, 10 Masses, 8 Magnificats, and *c* 60 *chansons.*

**Gombosi, Otto** (1902–55), Hungarian musicologist. Music critic in Berlin (1929–35). Went to US in 1939. Published study of Obrecht, and edited hymns and psalms of Thomas Stoltzer (with H. Albrecht).

**Gomez, Jill** (1942– ), British soprano, b. Guyana. Has sung with leading British opera companies, and in many concert recitals. Created role of Flora in Tippett's *The Knot Garden.*

**Gondoliers, The,** operetta by Gilbert and Sullivan. First perf. London, 1889.

**gong,** percussion instrument of oriental origin. As used in orchestra, consists of piece of circular metal with rim, and is hit with leather or felt-covered wooden mallet, or bass-drum stick. Of indeterminate pitch.

**Goodall, Reginald** (1901– ), English Conductor. Conducted first perf. of *Peter Grimes* (1945). Has acquired reputation as leading interpreter of Wagner, conducting at Sadler's Wells and Covent Garden.

**Goodman, Benny** (1909– ), American jazz clarinettist. Led own band from 1933. Also known as soloist with orchestra; commissioned works from Copland, Bartók and Hindemith.

**Goossens, Eugene** (1893–1962), English conductor, composer. Worked in England, US and Australia. Champion of new music. Compositions incl. 2 operas (*Judith* and *Don Juan de Manara*), ballet, 2 symphonies, oboe concerto, orchestral, incidental, chamber and piano music, and songs.

His brother, **Léon Goossens** (1897– ), is oboist. Noted as soloist and influential teacher.

**gopack** or **hopak,** Russian folk dance in lively 2/4 time.

**gorgheggio** (It.), in singing, term used of fast, extended passage where vowel is continued over many notes.

**gorgia** (It.), lit. 'throat'. Name given to improvised embellishments used by singers in 16th, 17th cents.

**Gossec, François Joseph** (1734–1829), Belgian composer. Moved to Paris, 1751. Sympathy for ideals of French Revolution shown in compositions, which incl. symphonies, oratorios, and choral works celebrating Revolution. Long before Berlioz, experimented with instrumentation in *Messe des morts,* and generally stimulated orchestral composition in Paris.

**Gothic music,** term applied to music in N Europe contemporary with Gothic architecture (*c* 13th–early 15th cents.).

**Götterdämmerung,** *see* RING DES NIBELUNGEN.

**Gottschalk, Louis Moreau** (1829–69), American composer, pianist. Toured world as virtuoso. Compositions incl. piano pieces *(eg The Aeolian Harp* and *The Dying Poet)*, 2 operas, and orchestral works.

**Goudimel, Claude** (*c* 1514–72), French composer. Orig. RC, turned Protestant and made settings of Huguenot melodies. Also wrote *chansons*. Died in St Bartholomew massacres.

**Gould, Glenn** (1932– ), Canadian pianist. One of few performers to have 'made a case' for playing Bach on piano; though many of his interpretations have been deemed eccentric, they are often remarkably convincing. Repertory extends from 16th cent. to serial compositions. Now performs almost exclusively in recording studio.

**Gould, Morton** (1913– ), American composer, conductor, pianist. Works, often in popular idiom, incl. concerto for tap dancer and orchestra, 3 symphonies, 4 *American Symphonettes,* ballet *Fall River Legend,* and several Broadway musicals.

**Gounod, Charles François** (1818–93), French composer. Studied at Paris Conservatoire and won *Prix de Rome* in 1839. Orig. intended to become priest. Lived in Britain (1870–5) forming choir that later became Royal Choral Society. Work is uneven in quality; even in *Faust,* most famous of his operas, level is not maintained. Primarily a lyrical composer, he was most successful when light touch was required (*eg* in opera *Mireille*). When he attempted to be impressive, as in oratorio *La Rédemption,* he merely became self-conscious.

Principal compositions:

(1) Operas: *Sappho* (1851), *La Nonne sanglante* (1854), *Le Médecin malgré lui* (1895), *Faust* (1859), *Philémon et Baucis* (1860), *La Reine de Saba* (1862), *Mireille* (1864), *La Colombe* (1866), *Roméo et Juliette* (1967), *Cinq-Mars* (1877), *Polyeucte* (1878), *Le Tribut de Zamora* (1881);

(2) Oratorios: *La Rédemption* (1882), *Mars et Vita* (1885);

(3) Cantatas: *Marie Stuart* (1837), *Gallia* (1871);

(4) Church music: 9 Masses (incl. *Messe solenelle,* 1849), 3 Requiems, *Stabat Mater, Te Deum,* motets, *etc*;

(5) Orchestra: 3 symphonies.

**Gow, Neil** (1727–1807), Scottish violinist. Most famous exponent of traditional Scottish fiddle music. Added many collections of reels and strathspeys to published repertoire.

**Goyescas,** (1) 2 sets of piano pieces by Granados (1911), inspired by Goya's pictures;

(2) opera by same composer, libretto by Periquet, incorporating material from piano pieces. First perf. New York, 1916.

**G.P.,** abbrev. of GENERALPAUSE.

**Grabu, Louis** (*fl* late 17th cent.), French violinist, composer. Spent some time in London: Master of the King's Musick (1666–74) under Charles II. Composed music for Dryden's patriotic opera *Albion and Albanius* (1685) and other works for stage.

**grace note,** ornamental note used to decorate or embellish melody. Normally printed in smaller type.

**gradevole** (It.), pleasing.

**gradual** (Lat., *graduale*), (1) responsorial chant forming part of Proper of RC Mass;

(2) orig. book containing graduals, hence book containing all music of Mass to be sung by choir.

**Gradualia** (Lat.), title of 2 sets of Latin motets by Byrd (1605, 1607). Motets form complete cycle of Mass propers for principal festivals of RC church year.

**Gradus ad Parnassum** (Lat.), lit. 'steps to Parnassus' (home of the Muses):

(1) treatise on counterpoint by Fux (1725);

(2) collection of piano studies by Clementi (1817);

(3) *Doctor Gradus ad Parnassum, see* CHILDREN'S CORNER.

**Graener, Paul** (1872–1944), German composer, conductor, teacher. Works, romantic in style, incl. opera about W. F. Bach, orchestral, choral and chamber music, and songs.

**Grainger, Percy Aldridge,** orig. George Percy (1882–1961), Australian-born composer, pianist. Had international reputation as recitalist. Meeting with Grieg (1907) led to interest in folk songs, which he actively collected. Settled in US (1914). His arrangements of traditional tunes for wide variety of resources have proved greatly popular. His music contains much rhythmical energy and simple delight in sentiment and jollity. Most famous pieces are *Country Gardens* and *Handel in the Strand.*

**Granados, Enrique** (1867–1916), Spanish composer, pianist, conductor. Pupil of Pedrell. Works, in Spanish 'nationalist' idiom, incl. 7 operas, 2 symphonic poems, 3 suites and other orchestral works, choral work with organ and piano accompaniment, chamber music, songs and collection of *tonadillas.*

**Grand Duke, The,** operetta by Gilbert and Sullivan. First perf. London, 1896. Last work on which they collaborated; it was failure.

**Grand Duo,** name given to Schubert's sonata in C for piano duet. Some think it is arrangement of lost GASTEIN SYMPHONY.

**Grande Messe des Morts** (Fr.), setting of Requiem Mass by Berlioz, op 5 (1837). Commissioned by French govt. as memorial service for French soldiers killed at siege of Constantine in Algeria. Scored for exceptionally large orchestra, incl. 4 brass bands.

**grandezza** (It.), grandeur. *Con grandezza,* with grandeur.

**Grandi, Alessandro** (d. 1630), Italian composer. One of most important composers of solo cantatas, and church music in *stile concertato,* with considerable influence in his day. Also wrote madrigals (with accompaniment).

**grandioso** (It.), in an imposing manner.

**grand jeu** (Fr.), full organ.

**grand opera,** term that arose in France in 19th cent. to distinguish serious operas set to music throughout from *opéra-comique,* which had dialogue. Term came to be used not simply of form but of lavish scale of performances.

**grand piano,** *see* PIANO.

**Graner Messe** (Ger.), Mass for soloists, chorus and orchestra by Liszt. Composed for dedication of Cathedral at Esztergom (in Ger., Gran) in Hungary (1856).

**Grassineau, James** (*c* 1715–67), London-born secretary to Pepusch, and author of *A Musical Dictionary ... of Terms and Characters* (1740), largely a translation of Brossard's *Dictionnaire de musique* (1703).

**Grassini, Josephina** (1773–1850), Italian operatic contralto. Sang in Italy, Paris and London, where she was rival of Mrs Billington. Renowned both for her singing and her dramatic ability.

**Graun, Karl Heinrich** (1704–59), German composer, singer. Works incl. 30 operas (*eg Montezuma*), dramatic cantatas, Passion Cantata (*Der Tod Jesu*) and other church music, piano concertos and trios.

His brother, **Johann Gottlieb** (*c* 1702/3–71), was composer and violinist. Pupil of Tartini. Composed *c* 100 symphonies, 20 violin concertos, church cantatas, string quartets and other chamber music.

**Graupner, Christoph** (1683–1760), German composer. Works incl. operas, and much church and instrumental music.

**grave** (It.), solemn, slow.

**gravicembela** (It.), harpsichord.

**grazioso** (It.), graceful.

**great,** abbrev. of great ORGAN.

**Great C Major Symphony,** name given to Schubert's symphony no 9 (1828), to distinguish it from shorter 6th symphony in same key.

**Great Fugue,** *see* GROSSE FUGE.

**great organ,** *see* ORGAN.

**Great Organ Mass,** *see* GROSSE ORGELMESSE.

**Grechaninov, Alexander Tikhonovich** (1864–1956), Russian composer. Pupil of Rimsky-Korsakov. Lived in Paris from 1925; settled in New York in 1941. Works incl. music for Russian Orthodox and RC churches, *Missa Oecumenica* (Ecumenical Mass), 5 symphonies, orchestral, chamber and piano music, songs and music for children.

**Greek music,** surviving fragments of ancient Greek music are very few and widely scattered in time. Much theoretical writing exists, but there were frequent disagreements, and much modification obviously took place as time went on. Modal patterns were used, though names of these sometimes changed. Intervals smaller than semitone were also used (*see* ENHARMONIC) – evidence of Asiatic influence. Prob. did not use harmony (word *harmonia* was used of consistent pattern of melodic material). Modes had non-musical associations (according to Plato): one was considered martial, another languorous *etc*.

Roman theorist Boethius derived much from Greek writers, but did not understand them clearly. Medieval theorists who used Boethius added further misunderstandings, *eg*, Greek names were assigned to medieval modes, but medieval nomenclature did not correspond with the Greek. However, Greek theory made 2 important contributions: (1) it supplied a terminology (*eg* tonic, diatonic, melody, harmony); (2) it provided basis for medieval and modern acoustics by establishing mathematical basis of musical sounds.

**Greenberg, Noah** (1919–66), American choral conductor. Founded New York Pro Musica in 1952, and did much to develop interest in medieval and Renaissance music in America.

**Greene, Harry Plunket** (1865–1936), Irish-born baritone. Excelled in interpretation of English songs; also made a few appearances in opera. His book, *Interpretation of Song* (1912), is standard work.

**Greene, Maurice** (1695–1755), English composer, organist. Master of the King's Musick from 1735. Friend of Handel. Works incl. opera, oratorios, duets, trios, catches and canons.

**Greensleeves,** traditional English tune, at least as old as Shakespeare (who refers to it). Vaughan Williams wrote *Fantasia on Greensleeves*.

**Greeting, Thomas** (*fl* 17th cent.), English violinist, flageolet player. In service of Charles II. Published flageolet tutor, *The Pleasant Companion* (1673), and taught flageolet to Samuel Pepys and his wife.

**Gregorian Chant,** term referring to large collection of ancient monophonic melodies, preserved, and until recently widely performed, within RC church. Most chants belong either to MASS or OFFICE. Earliest manuscripts are of Frankish provenance and were written in 9th–11th cents. Before 9th cent., chants were prob. disseminated orally. Modern knowledge of origins of Gregorian chant, and poss. connections with Pope Gregory (590–604), is therefore sketchy, and theories are controversial, though it prob. originated in Rome. *See* BYZANTINE MUSIC, PLAINSONG.

**Grenon, Nicolas** (*fl* 15th cent.), French singer, composer.

**Grétry, André Ernest Modeste** (1741–1831), Belgian composer. Produced operas in Paris from 1768. Works incl. many operas (mostly comic), 6 small symphonies (1758), Requiem, motets and other church music, 2 piano quartets with flute, and piano sonatas. Most successful opera was *Richard Coeur-de-Lion* (1784) excellent example of late 19th-cent. *opéra-comique*.

**Grieg, Edvard Hagerup** (1843–1907) Norwegian composer. Began composing at age of 9. Encouraged by Ole Bull, went to study in Leipzig (1858). Later studied under Niels Gade in Copenhagen. On return to Norway became involved in nationalist movement in music. Married cousin Nina Hagerup (1867), who sang many of his songs. Made two visits to Italy (where met Liszt) and several to Britain.

Individual charm of his music lies in combination of national idioms and romanticism he imbibed at Leipzig. Evolved very individual practice of modulation and use of dissonance, bold for its time. Primarily a lyrical composer, he was most successful in short pieces of tender and lively character. Longer works, *eg* piano concerto, are marred by tendency to repeat short phrases, and attempt to create formal structure in German tradition results in artificiality. Nevertheless, Liszt admired his piano concerto, and it continues to be enormously popular. Popularity of *Peer Gynt* is due to qualities which won success for his works in shorter forms – though music shows little understanding of irony and bitter characterization of Ibsen's play.

Principal compositions:

(1) Orchestra: overture *In Autumn* (1866), piano concerto (1868, rev. 1907), 2 suites from *Peer Gynt* (1888, 1891), 3 pieces from *Sigurd Jorsalfar* (1898), *Holberg Suite* for strings (1885);

(2) Chamber music: string quartet, 3 violin sonatas, cello sonata;

(3) Piano: Sonata in E minor, *Lyric Pieces* (10 books), *Ballads*, many collections of folk songs and dances;

(4) Choral works: *At a Southern Convent Gate* (1871), *Recognition of Land* (1872, rev. 1881);

(5) Incidental music: *Sigurd Jorsalfar* (1872), *Peer Gynt* (1875, rev. orchestration, 1886).

Also melodrama *Bergljot*, numerous songs (incl. *Haugtussa* cycle) and part-songs.

**Griffbrett** (Ger.), lit. 'grip board', *ie* finger-board of violin *etc. Am Griffbrett, see* BOWING.

**Griffes, Charles Tomlinson** (1884–1920), American composer. Though studied in Berlin (under Humperdinck), inclined towards French impressionism. Works incl. symphonic poem *The Pleasure Dome of Kubla Khan*, dance drama *The Kairn of Koridwen*, and string quartet *(Sketches on Indian Themes)*.

**Grigny, Nicolas de** (1672–1703), French composer, organist. Bach made copy of his *Livre d'orgue* (1711).

**Grisi, Giulia** (1811–69), Italian operatic soprano. Had outstanding success in London and Paris. Sang Adalgisa in first perf. of Bellini's *Norma* (1831), and Norina in first perf. of Donizetti's *Don Pasquale* (1843). Frequently sang with second husband, tenor Giovanni Matteo Mario.

Her elder sister, Giuditta, was a mezzo-soprano. Appeared together in first perf. of Bellini's *I Capuletti ed i Montecchi*, Giudetta singing Romeo to Giulia's Juliet.

**Grocheo, Johannes de** (*fl c* 1300), theorist, active in Paris. Treatise

*De musica* gives valuable information on musical forms and instruments of his time.

**groppo,** *see* GRUPPO.

**grosse caisse** (Fr.), bass drum.

**Grosse Fuge** (Ger., *Great Fugue*), fugue by Beethoven for string quartet, orig. intended as finale of B flat quartet, op 130. Due to its length and complexity, however, Beethoven published it separately as op 133 (1825) and wrote new finale for B flat quartet.

**Grosse Orgelmesse** (Ger., *Great Organ Mass*), name given to Haydn's *Missa in honorem Beatissimae Virginis Mariae* in E flat (*c* 1766). Has prominent part for organ. *See* KLEINE ORGELMESSE.

**Grossen Quartette, Die** (Ger., The Great Quartets), alternative name for SUN QUARTETS.

**grosse Trommel** (Ger.), bass drum.

**Grossi, Ludovico,** *see* VIADANA.

**ground,** (1) = GROUND BASS;
(2) composition built on ground bass.

**ground bass** (It., *basso ostinato*), bass line constantly repeated throughout composition, forming foundation for varied melodic, harmonic or contrapuntal treatment. Widely cultivated in 17th, early 18th cents. Effect was to substitute formal and unifying symmetry for polyphonic development characteristic of 16th-cent. music. Instrumental improvisation above ground bass was also common, esp. in Britain, for bass viol; *see* DIVISION (2), DIVISION VIOL. Among forms related to use of ground bass are CHACONNE, FOLIO, PASSACAGLIA.

**Grove, George** (1820–1900), English scholar, editor, writer on music. Best known as founder and first editor of *Dictionary of Music and Musicians* (1879–89). Also first director of Royal College of Music (1882–94). Knighted 1883.

**Groves, Charles** (1915– ), English conductor. Conducted B.B.C. Northern Orchestra (1944–51), Bournemouth Symphony Orchestra (1951–61), Welsh National Opera (1961–63), Royal Liverpool Philharmonic Orchestra (1963–77), English National Opera (1977–79). Knighted 1973.

**Grovlez, Gabriel** (1879–1944), French conductor, composer. Conducted at Paris Opéra (1914–33). Compositions incl. symphonic poems, ballets, and comic opera *Le Marquis de Carabas*. Also edited old French keyboard music.

**Gruenberg, Louis** (1884–1964), American composer, pianist, b. Russia. Pupil of Busoni in Berlin and Vienna. Works, influenced by Negro spirituals and jazz, incl. opera *Emperor Jones* (based on O'Neill's play, 1933), 5 symphonies, chamber music, songs and piano pieces, *eg* 'Jazzberries'.

**Grumiaux, Arthur** (1921– ), Belgian violinist. One of finest living exponents of classical repertory from Bach to Bartók.

**gruppetto** (It.), diminutive of *gruppo*.

**gruppo** or **gruppetto** (It.), lit. 'group'. Generic term for various ornaments consisting of one or more decorative notes with melody note, in particular:

(1) shake or TRILL employing both upper and lower accessory notes;
(2) TURN (represented by diminutive *gruppetto*).

**Guadagni, Gaetano** (*c* 1725–92), Italian castrato contralto (and later soprano). Sang in Italy, Ireland, France, Portugal, Austria, Germany and England, where sang solos in Handel's *Messiah* and *Samson*.

**Guadagnini,** family of Italian violin-makers, active throughout 18th cent.

**Guarneri** or **Guarnerius,** family of Italian violin-makers in Cremona. First was Andrea (d. 1698), pupil (like Stradivari) of Nicola Amati. Most celebrated was Giuseppe (1687–1744), known as Giuseppe del Gesù.

**Guédron, Pierre** (*c* 1565–1621), French composer. In service of Henri IV and Louis XIII. Wrote ballets incl. *Ballet de la délivrance de Renaud* (1617), and published collections of *airs de cour*.

**Guerre des Bouffons, La** (Fr., The War of the Comedians), name given to violent controversy that arose in Paris as a result of performances by Italian company (the comedians) in 1752–4. Subject was familiar one of rival merits of French and Italian music, but pursued with unusual intensity.

**Guerrero, Francisco** (1527/8–1599), Spanish composer. Became *maestro de capilla* at Seville Cathedral (1574). One of outstanding composers of church music in 16th cent. Non-liturgical works incl. *Canciones y villanescas espirituales* (1589).

He was first taught by elder brother, **Pedro Guerrero,** some of whose works are preserved in printed lute-tablatures and also in Ms part-books.

**Guglielmi, Pietro** (1728–1804), Italian composer. Pupil of Durante. Became *maestro di cappella* at St Peter's, Rome (1793). Works incl. *c* 100 operas, *eg Il ratto della sposa* (1765), 9 oratorios, motets, and chamber music.

**Gui, Vittorio** (1885–1975), Italian conductor, composer. Conducted opera *eg* at La Scala and Glyndebourne. In 1928 founded orchestra in Florence that became closely involved in creation of Florence Maggio Musicale. Compositions incl. opera *La fata malerba* (1927).

**Guido d'Arezzo** or **Guido Aretinus** (end of 10th cent–*c* 1050), French theorist, teacher. For some time in charge of choir school at Arezzo, Italy. Simplified teaching of choirboys by associating each note of HEXACHORD with particular syllables – *ut, re, mi, fa, sol, la.* This system, called SOLMIZATION, created names of notes still used in France and Italy, and was basis of TONIC SOL-FA in 19th cent. Also extended principle of using horizontal lines to indicate pitch of notes, giving rise to STAFF.

**Guilielmus Monachus** (*fl* 15th cent.), theorist, prob. Italian. His treatise *De praeceptis artis musicae et practicae* contains useful information about the practice of FAUXBOURDON.

**Guillaume de Machaut** or **Machault** (1300–77), French composer, poet, priest. In service of Charles V of France. Became canon of

Rheims. Dominant French composer of 14th cent. Composed first known Ordinary of Mass by single composer. Nearly all his 23 motets are isorhythmic. Secular compositions form first great repertory of polyphonic chansons, comprising *ballades, rondeaux* and *virelais*. Also wrote monophonic *lais* and *virelais*.

**Guillaume Tell,** *see* WILLIAM TELL.

**Guilmant, Félix Alexandre** (1837–1911), French organist, composer. Co-founder of Schola Cantorum. Toured widely as organist. Compositions incl. 2 symphonies for organ and orchestra, sonatas and other works for organ.

**Guiraud, Ernest** (1837–92), French composer, b. US. Works incl. several operas (*eg Piccolino,* 1876). Composed recitatives for Vienna production of Bizet's *Carmen* (1875) - condemned by purists. Also arranged 2nd suite from Bizet's *L'Arlésienne* and revised Offenbach's *The Tales of Hoffmann* (left unfinished by composer).

**guiro,** scraper consisting of notched gourd, played by scraping stick over notches.

**guitar** (Fr., *guitare*; Ger., *Gitarre*; It., *chitarra*; Sp., *guitarra*), plucked string instrument, orig. brought to Spain by Moors in Middle Ages. Differs from lute in having flat back. Modern instrument has 6 strings, tuned: E below bass clef (lowest), A, D, G, B, E (highest). Earliest known compositions date from 16th cent. Related instruments incl. BALALAIKA, BANDURRIA, CITTERN and GITTERN.

**guitare d'amour,** alternative name for ARPEGGIONE.

**Guntram,** opera by Richard Strauss, libretto by composer. First perf. Weimar, 1894. Strauss's first opera, now overshadowed by his later works.

**Gurlitt, Cornelius** (1820-1901), German organist, composer, teacher. Best known for educational piano music.

His grand-nephew, **Wilibald Gurlitt** (1889–1963), was a musicologist. Played important part in revival of old instruments for performance of old music. Edited one vol. of complete edition of works of Praetorius, and wrote valuable study of Bach.

**Gurlitt, Manfred** (1890–1972), German composer, conductor. Pupil of Humperdinck. Works incl. opera *Wozzeck* (1926), setting of Büchner's play (previously set by Berg, 1922).

**Gurney, Ivor Bertie** (1890–1937), English composer, poet. Studied under Vaughan Williams and Stanford. Wounded in WWI; detained in mental hospital from 1922. Composed songs (some to own poetry), 3 song-cycles incl. *Ludlow and Teme* for tenor and string quartet (words by A.E. Housman), piano pieces, and 2 works for violin and piano.

**Gurrelieder** (Ger., *Songs of Gurra*), large scale vocal work by Schoenberg (1911). Scored for soloists, 3 male choruses, mixed choruses, narrator and lavish orchestra. Based on German translation of Danish poems by J.P. Jacobsen.

**Guttoveggio, Joseph,** *see* CRESTON.

**Gwendoline,** opera by Chabrier, libretto by C. Mendès. First perf.

Brussels, 1886. Story concerns Viking king Harald, who falls in love with Gwendoline, daughter of his enemy, Armel the Saxon.

**gymel** (from Lat. *cantus gemellus,* 'twin song'), term first occurring in 15th cent. to denote characteristically English style of singing in 2 parts with same range. Practice goes back to 13th cent., earlier examples making liberal use of parallel thirds.

**Gyrowetz, Adalbert** (Cz. name: Jirovec) (1763–1850), Bohemian composer. Visited London (1789–92), and later lived in Vienna. Several of his symphonies were performed in Paris under Haydn's name. Works incl. *c* 30 operas, melodramas, 40 ballets, 60 symphonies, other orchestral music, much choral, chamber and piano music, and songs.

# H

**H** (Ger.), B natural.

**Haas, Joseph** (1879–1960), German composer. Pupil and disciple of Max Reger. Works incl. operas, oratorios, orchestral, chamber and piano music, and songs.

**Haas, Robert Maria** (1886–1960), Austrian historian, composer, conductor. Edited 7 vols. of *Denkmäler der Tonkunst in Österreich.* Initiated publication of original versions of works of Bruckner (1929), and wrote biography of that composer, and books on 17th and 18th-cent. music.

**Hába, Alois** (1893–1973), Czech composer. Pioneered use of quarter and sixth-tones, which he used in operas *The Mother* (1931) and *Thy Kingdom Come* (1934), piano music, string quartets, and works for violin and cello.

**habanera** (Sp.), Cuban dance adopted in Spain in 19th cent. Usually written in 2/4 time with characteristic syncopated rhythm. Name thought to derive from Habana (Havana).

**Habeneck, François Antoine** (1781–1849), French conductor, violinist, composer. Founded Société des Concerts du Conservatoire in Paris (1828), and introduced many of works of Beethoven into France.

**Haberl, Franz Xaver** (1840–1910), German priest, organist, historian of church music of 15th, 16th and early 17th cents. Edited works of Palestrina, and laid foundation for later research on Dufay.

**Hacomplaynt** or **Hacomblene, Robert** (d. 1528), English composer. His 5-part 'Salve regina' is in *Eton Choirbook.*

**Hadley, Henry Kemball** (1871–1937), American composer, conductor. Works incl. operas, orchestral, choral and chamber music, and songs.

**Hadley, Patrick Arthur Sheldon** (1899–1973), English composer, teacher. Professor at Cambridge (1946–63). Works, mostly for voices and instruments, incl. *The Trees so High* (1931), *La Belle Dame Sans Merci* (1935), and *The Cenci* (1951).

**Hadow, William Henry** (1859–1937), English historian, composer, writer on musical criticism, educationalist. Wrote *Studies in Modern Music* (2 vols. 1894–5) and edited *Oxford History of Music* (of which he wrote vol. 5, *The Viennese Period,* 1904). Chairman of committee that produced Hadow Report, *The Education of the Adolescent* (1927), which emphasized importance of music in education. Knighted 1918.

**'Haffner' Serenade,** serenade in D, K250 (1776), by Mozart, composed with March (K249) for marriage of Elizabeth Haffner.

**'Haffner' Symphony,** symphony in D, K385 (1782), by Mozart, composed for Haffner family and based on serenade (though not K250).

**Hahn, Reynaldo** (1875–1947), French composer, conductor, b. Venezuela. Pupil of Massenet. Works incl. operas (*eg The Merchant of Venice,* 1935), operettas, ballets, incidental, chamber and piano music, and songs to poems by Verlaine and Leconte de Lisle.

**Haieff, Alexei** (1914– ), American composer, b. Russia. Pupil of Nadia Boulanger. Works incl. orchestral and chamber music, and ballet *Beauty and the Beast.*

**Haitink, Bernard** (1929– ), Dutch conductor. Chief conductor of Concertgebouw Orchestra, Amsterdam, from 1964. Has also conducted London Philharmonic Orchestra (1967–77) and at Glyndebourne from 1977. Noted esp. for interpretations of Bruckner and Mahler.

**halb, halbe** (Ger.), half. *Halbe, Halbe Note,* or *Halbetaknote,* minim. *Halbe Pause,* minim rest. *Halbschluss,* half cadence. *Halbsopran,* mezzo-soprano. *Halbtenor*, baritone. *Halbton,* semitone.

**Hale,** *see* ADAM DE LA HALE.

**Halévy, Jacques François,** orig. Fromental Elias Lévy (1799–1862), French composer. Pupil of Cherubini. Works incl. over 30 operas (*eg La Juive,* 1835) and several ballets (one after Prévost's *Manon Lescaut*). Pupils incl. Gounod and Bizet, who married his daughter.

**half cadence** or **half close,** imperfect CADENCE.

**Halffter [Escriche], Ernesto** (1905– ), Spanish composer, conductor, of partly German descent. Settled in Portugal after Spanish Civil War. Works incl. opera *The Death of Carmen,* and orchestral and chamber music.

His brother, **Rodolfo Halffter** (1900– ), is composer and writer on music. Settled in Mexico after Spanish Civil War. Works incl. ballets, violin concerto, and piano pieces.

Their nephew, **Christobal Halffter** (1930– ), is also a composer. Professor of composition at Madrid Conservatory. Works incl. sinfonia, concertino for strings, *Cinco microformas* for orchestra, *Dos movimientos* for timpani and strings, *Espejos* for 4 percussionists and tape, *Antifona pascual* for soloists, chorus and orchestra, *Cantata in Expectione Resurrectionis Domini,* and *Trespiezas* for solo flute.

**half note** (US), minim.

**half step** (US), semitone.

**Hälfte, die** (Ger.), lit. 'the half' – direction indicating that passage is to be performed by only half the usual number of instruments or voices.

**half tone** (US), semitone.

**Hallé Orchestra,** English Manchester-based symphony orchestra, founded 1857 by German-born pianist and conductor Sir Charles Hallé (orig. Carl Hallé, 1819–95). Its conductors have incl. Hans Richter, Sir Hamilton Harty, Sir John Barbirolli, and James Loughran.

**hallelujah,** basically, Biblical word for joyous praise of God. In chant it is spelt *Alleluia.* In 17th, 18th cents., choral compositions often incorporated substantial *Hallelujah* choruses in fugal style. Handel's, in *Messiah*, is most famous example.

**Hallén, Johan Andreas** (1846–1925), Swedish composer, conductor, critic. Works incl. operas, orchestral, choral and theatre music, piano quartet, and songs.

**halling,** popular Norwegian dance, moderately fast in tempo and generally in 2/4 time. Performed by men with much dramatic action incl. leaps in air. Properly accompanied by HARDANGER FIDDLE.

**Hallström, Ivar** (1826–1901), Swedish composer, pianist. Composed operas (one with Prince Gustav, 1847), operettas, ballets, cantatas, piano pieces and songs. Operas, whose use of folk material made them popular in their time, incl. *The Enchanted Cat* (1869), and *The Bewitched One* (1874).

**Halvorsen, Johan** (1864–1935), Norwegian violinist, composer, conductor. Works incl. 2 symphonies, violin concerto and other orchestral works, coronation cantata for King Haakon, incidental, choral and chamber music, and songs. Married niece of Grieg.

**Hamboys,** *see* HANBOYS.

**Hambraeus, Bengt** (1928– ), Swedish composer, organist, musicologist. One of Sweden's most progressive composers. Pioneer of electronic music. Works incl. *Rota* for 3 orchestras, percussion and tape, and *Constellation,* series of pieces for varying instrumental and electronic forces.

**Hamerik, Asger,** orig. Hammerich (1843–1923), Danish composer. Pupil of Gade and Berlioz. Works incl. 7 symphonies, choral, instrumental and chamber music.

His son, **Ebbe Hamerik** (1898–1951), was also composer. Works incl. several operas (*eg The Travelling Companion,* after Hans Andersen), 5 symphonies, *Variations on an Old Danish Folk Tune* for orchestra, chamber and piano music, and songs.

Asger's brother, **Angul Hammerich** (1848–1931), was a critic and historian. Wrote on history of Danish music.

**Hamilton, Iain** (1922– ), Scottish composer, teacher. Has taught in US since 1962. Adoption of 12-note rather than nationalistic idiom caused controversy early in career. Now internationally renowned. Works incl. operas *The Cataline Conspiracy, The Royal Hunt of the Sun* (based on Peter Shaffer's play) and *Anna Karenina*, 2 violin concertos, piano concerto, 2 symphonies and other orchestral works, choral works *The Bermudas* (based on Marvell) and *The Descent of the Celestial City*, chamber and piano music, *Threnos: In Time of War* for organ, inspired by events in Vietnam, and song-cycle *The Spirit of Delight* (to poems by Shelley, 1979).

**Hammerich,** *see* HAMERIK.

**Hammerklavier** (Ger.), lit. 'hammer keyboard' – obsolete German name for piano. Habit of referring to Beethoven's piano sonata op 106 in B flat as 'the "Hammerklavier" sonata' is pointless as Beethoven also used word in titles of other piano sonatas.

**Hammerschmidt, Andreas** (1611/12–75), Bohemian organist,

composer. Important in history of Lutheran music. In his *Dialogues between God and a Faithful Soul* (1645) he applied method of dramatic dialogue to settings of Biblical words for 2, 3, or 4 voices, sometimes with introductory instrumental *sinfonia*. His *Musical Devotions* (1638–53) contains *c* 150 pieces for 1 to 12 voices with figured bass, with or without instruments. Also wrote chamber music and secular songs.

**Hammond organ,** brand of electronic organ.

**Hampel, Anton Joseph** (d. 1771), Czech horn player. Member of Dresden orchestra from 1737. Said to have invented practice of using hand to produce stopped notes on horn. Also wrote horn tutor.

**Hampton, John** (*fl* 15th–16th cents.), English composer. His 5-part setting of 'Salve regina' is in *Eton Choirbook*.

**Hanboys** or **Hamboys, John** (*fl* 15th cent.), theorist. Wrote treatise *Summa super musicam continuam et discretam*.

**Handel, George Frideric,** orig. Georg Friedrich Händel (1685–1759), German-born, English-naturalized composer. Born in Halle. Father was barber-surgeon. Studied music with local organist against wishes of father, who sent him to study law at Halle University. Left after year to become violinist in Hamburg opera house, where first operas, *Almira* and *Nero,* were produced in 1705. Visited Italy (1706–9), where gained knowledge of Italian musical styles, and had success with opera *Agrippina* (1709). Appointed *Kapellmeister* to Elector of Hanover (1710), and produced successful opera *Rinaldo* for London (1711). Returned to London (1712) on leave of absence from Hanover post, which he never resumed, and produced series of operas *eg Il Pastor fido*. Received life pension from Queen Anne, and when former master George I came to throne he soon came back into favour with increased pension.

Became musical director to Duke of Chandos, for whom he wrote *Chandos Anthems* and *Acis and Galatea* (1720). Between 1720 and 1733, produced 20 new operas for Royal Academy of Music (King's Theatre, Haymarket), and wrote much chamber and harpsichord music. Difficulties of maintaining Italian opera and success of first English oratorio *Esther* (1732) led Handel to turn to oratorio, culminating in *Messiah* (1742). During this period produced 15 more operas, but did not achieve real acceptance till last 11 years of life, though these were clouded by blindness from 1753.

Though often perfunctory and sometimes shallow in expression, Handel's writing at its greatest is a brilliant and infallibly effective combination of Italian traditions of solo and instrumental style, English choral tradition, and German contrapuntal style. These qualities are clear in well-known works, but his remarkable versatility and quickness of response to dramatic situations produced many little masterpieces in course of larger compositions. Some of neglected oratorios maintain this high level of inspiration almost throughout. Likewise, instrumental compositions are, at their best, delightful for surety of writing and felicity of expression.

Principal compositions:

(1) Operas: *Almira* (1705), *Rodrigo* (1707), *Agrippina* (1709), *Rinaldo* (1711), *Il Pastor fido* (1712), *Teseo* (1712), *Silla* (1714), *Amadigi* (1715), *Radamisto* (1720), *Muzio Scevola* (1721), *Floridante* (1721), *Ottone* (1723), *Flavio* (1723), *Giulio Cesare* (1724), *Tamerlano* (1724), *Rodelinda* (1725), *Scipione* (1726), *Alessandro* (1726), *Admeto* (1727), *Riccardo Primo* (1727), *Siroe* (1728), *Tolomeo* (1728), *Lotario* (1729), *Partenope* (1730), *Poro* (1731), *Ezio* (1732), *Sosarme* (1732), *Orlando* (1733), *Arianna* (1734), *Ariodante* (1735), *Alcina* (1735), *Atalanta* (1736), *Arminio* (1737), *Giustino* (1737), *Berenice* (1737), *Faramondo* (1738), *Serse* (1738), *Imeneo* (1740), *Deidamia* (1741);

(2) Passions: *St John Passion* (1704), *Der für die Sünden der Welt gemarterte und sterbende Jesus* (1716);

(3) Oratorios: *La Resurrezione* (1708), *Esther* (1720, 1732), *Deborah* (1733), *Athaliah* (1733), *Saul* (1739), *Israel in Egypt* (1739), *Messiah* (1742), *Samson* (1743), *Semele* (1743), *Joseph and his Brethren* (1743), *Belshazzar* (1744), *Hercules* (1744), *Occasional Oratorio* (1746), *Judas Maccabaeus* (1746), *Alexander Balus* (1747), *Joshua* (1747), *Solomon* (1748), *Susanna* (1748), *Theodora* (1749), *Jeptha* (1751), *The Triumph of Time and Truth* (1757);

(4) Secular choral works: *Acis and Galatea* (1720), *Alexander's Feast* (1736), *Ode for St Cecilia's Day* (1739), *L'Allegro, il Penseroso ed il Moderato* (1740);

(5) Church music: Utrecht *Te Deum* (1713), Chandos *Te Deum* (*c* 1718), 11 Chandos anthems (1716–19), 3 coronation anthems (1727), funeral anthem for the death of Queen Caroline (1737), Dettingen *Te Deum* (1743);

(6) Orchestra: *Water Music* (1715–17), 6 concertos ('Oboe Concertos', 1729), 12 organ concertos (1738–40), 12 *concerti grossi* (1739), *Fireworks Music* (1749);

(7) Chamber music: sonatas for flute, recorder, 1 and 2 violins, 2 oboes, with keyboard accompaniment;

(8) Harpsichord: 17 suites (1720, 1733);

(9) Songs: numerous Italian cantatas for 1 and 2 voices.

**Handel's Largo,** *see* OMBRA MA FUI.

**Handel Variations,** set of 20 variations and fugue for piano by Brahms, op 24 (1861). Work is based on Air from Handel's harpsichord suite in B flat.

**hand horn,** 'natural' horn, *ie* one without valves. Some notes other than those of harmonic series could be produced by placing hand in bell.

**Handl, Jakob,** known in Latin as Jacobus Gallus (1550–1591), Austrian or Slovenian composer. Works incl. 19 Masses and numerous motets, ranging from short 4-part pieces to settings in Venetian polychoral style, of which he was one of great masters.

**Handlo, Robert de** (*fl* 14th cent.), English theorist. Wrote on rules of MENSURAL NOTATION.

**Handregistrierung** (Ger.), manual piston on organ.

**Handschin, Jacques** (1886–1955), Swiss musicologist. Wrote extensively on medieval music.

**Handtrommel** (Ger.), tambourine.

**Hans Heiling,** opera by Marschner, libretto by E. Devrient. First perf. Berlin, 1833. Milestone in development of German romantic opera between Weber and Wagner.

**Hansel and Gretel** (Ger., *Hänsel und Gretel*), opera by Humperdinck, libretto by Adelheid Wette (composer's sister), from tale of Brothers Grimm. First perf. Weimar, 1893.

**Hanslick, Eduard** (1825–1904), Austrian critic, musical aesthetician. Very influential. In treatise *The Beautiful in Music* (1854), maintained autonomy of music. In articles, opposed 'New Music' of Liszt and Wagner (though recognized importance of latter's music) and praised Schumann and Brahms. Pilloried by Wagner as Beckmesser in *The Mastersingers.*

**Hanson, Howard** (1896–1981), American composer of Swedish parentage. Works incl. opera *Merry-Mount* (1934), 6 symphonies, symphonic poems, works for chorus and orchestra, piano and chamber music, and songs.

**Hanuš, Jan** (1915– ), Czechoslovak composer. Works incl. several operas *eg The Servant of Two Masters* (after Goldoni) and *The Torch of Prometheus,* 4 symphonies, and chamber music.

**Hardanger fiddle,** Norwegian folk violin, with 4 sympathetic strings in addition to normal 4.

**hardi** (Fr.), bold; *hardiment,* boldly.

**Harfe** (Ger.), harp.

**Harfenquartett,** *see* HARP QUARTET.

**harmonica,** (1) (musical glasses, glass harmonica; Ger., *Glasharmonika*), instrument of 18th-cent. origin in which sounds are produced by application of moist fingers to drinking glasses or glass bowls;

(2) (Ger., *Mundharmonika*), mouth organ.

**harmonic analysis,** study of chords or harmonies of piece of music, both individually and in succession. *See* CHORD, HARMONY.

**harmonic flute** (Fr., *flûte harmonique*), organ stop. Hole is bored mid-way in open cylindrical metal pipe, making predominant pitch the first harmonic, or octave (4ft pitch).

**harmonic minor scale,** *see* SCALE.

**harmonic piccolo,** organ stop similar to harmonic flute, but sounding octave higher (2ft pitch).

**harmonics** (Fr., *sons harmoniques*; Ger., *Flageolett-Töne*; It., *flautato, flautando*), sounds produced on string instrument or harp by touching string lightly at one of its nodes, *ie* exact fractional points. They correspond to upper partials (overtones) of string, and have soft, flute-like quality. On bowed instruments harmonics played on open string are called natural, those played on stopped string (*ie* with one finger stopping string and another touching it lightly) are called artificial. Natural harmonics played on G string of violin, for example, are:

Black notes indicate at what point string is touched.

Harmonics are indicated by writing either small circle over sound to be produced or diamond-shaped note corresponding to point to be touched.

**harmonic series,** composite series of notes produced by vibrating substance or air column. If principal note (or 'fundamental') is C below bass clef, first 16 notes of series will be:

Of these nos 7, 11, 13 and 14 are not in tune with our normal scale. Nos 12–16 (and upwards) are called 'overtones' or 'upper partials'. Actual sound of overtones is faint. Their effect in practice is to enrich sound of principal note. Individual tone-quality of instruments results from presence or absence of particular overtones, and from their relative intensity. Thus clarinet (cylindrical tube, stopped at one end) produces only alternate overtones – 3, 5, 7, *etc.* Individual overtones can be isolated from the principal note: this is done on string instruments by touching string lightly at sectional points (*see* HARMONICS), and on wind instruments (esp. brass) by overblowing. Thus brass instrument without VALVES is able to produce complete series of notes; addition of valves makes available several such series, so providing complete chromatic compass. Same result is achieved on TROMBONE by slide. *See* HORN, TRUMPET.

**harmonie** (Fr.), *Harmonie* (Ger.), ensemble of wind instruments.

**Harmonie der Welt, Die** (Ger., *The Harmony of the World*), opera by Hindemith, libretto by composer (based on life of Kepler). First perf. Munich, 1957.

**Harmoniemesse** (Ger., *Wind Band Mass*), name given to Haydn's Mass in B flat (1802). Has prominent parts for wind instruments.

**Harmonious Blacksmith, The,** nickname given to air and variations in E in 5th suite of Handel's 1st book of harpsichord suites (1720), from erroneous story that he composed it after listening to blacksmith at work.

**harmonium,** small, portable kind of REED-ORGAN. Pedals work bellows which forces air through reeds. Used as substitute for organ.

**harmony,** (1) until 17th cent. term was used in general sense of the sound of music. Chords were viewed as resulting from addition of intervals to original part;

(2) in modern sense harmony means structure, function and relationships of chords. Rameau founded modern theory of harmony in 1722.

Unit of harmony is CHORD. Smallest element of harmonic 'progression', or movement, consists of 2 chords. Pair of chords which marks off period or phrase is called CADENCE. Perfect, imperfect and plagal cadences show in simplest form relation of dominant and subdominant chords of KEY to each other and to tonic chord. Harmonic relationships between chords of key are true for every key, since all keys are transpositions of same 2 MODES, major or minor. Modern theory of harmony is based on chords of major scale. Those of minor scale, though different in quality, are treated as having same functions in relation to each other and to tonic.

TONIC chord, centre of harmony of key, is clearly defined as tonic when it is preceded by DOMINANT chord, as in perfect cadence. Chord which most strongly reinforces that definition by preceding and following perfect cadence is SUBDOMINANT chord. These 3 chords are primary chords of key, and since they contain between them all notes of scale, they may suffice to harmonize any melody which remains in key.

Two of most important parts of Rameau's theory of harmony are (a) theory of inversion (*see* CHORD), in which all chords which do not consist of superimposed thirds (*ie* are not in ROOT position) are held to be inverted positions of, and to derive their harmonic function from, chords which do; and (b) theory of FUNDAMENTAL BASS, in which successive roots of series of chords, represented as notes on staff or by Roman numerals, are held, as consequence of theory of inversion, to give clearest picture of harmonic functions of chords.

Of chords within key, tonic is point of rest, dominant and subdominant play most important parts in harmonic movement, and other chords, except LEADING-NOTE CHORD, have subsidiary functions. Leading-note chord acquires from its bass-note the tendency to 'lead' to tonic. In addition, it has 2 notes in common with dominant, so that it may precede tonic in cadence in same way as dominant, though with less finality. Sense of finality arising from chord relations within key is most important property of harmony. Since key-relations arise from chord-relations, sense of movement is carried over with enhanced quality into modulation. In larger context it becomes sense of movement arising from key-design of forms as wholes.

Harmonic relations between different keys, and possibility and functioning of MODULATION, depend on fact that chord may exist in several keys and can assume function appropriate to it in each of those keys. For example G–B–D is dominant in C and tonic in G, and A–C–E is submediant in C and supertonic in G.

In context of forms as whole, harmonic relationships of keys are basis of harmonic design of all 18th and 19th-cent. forms, however extended the scope of keys involved, and however numerous the incidental modulations. Key-design of SONATA FORM, which may be represented: Tonic — Dominant // Free modulations — Tonic // is same, in enlarged form, as that of earlier BINARY FORM.

Another important property of harmony, which is primarily a property of single chords, is sense of movement caused by use of discords. Movement from (comparative) discord to (comparative) concord is movement from tension to relaxation. Principles and effect of such movement are same whether general level of dissonance is relatively low, as in 18th cent., or high, as in 20th. Richness of colour in 19th-cent. harmony, with its increasing complexity of detail, resulted from extension of function of chromatic chords (*eg* Neapolitan sixth and augmented sixth chord) within key to their relations to other keys, from growing chromaticism of melody, which suggested and necessitated new forms of harmonic relations, and from more continuous use of dissonance to achieve dramatic tension.

**Harold in Italy,** symphony with viola *obbligato* by Berlioz, op 16 (1834). Connection with Byron's *Childe Harold's Pilgrimage* is somewhat remote. Work was commissioned by Paganini, but solo viola part was so unostentatious that he declined to perform it.

**harp** (Fr., *harpe*; Ger., *Harfe*; It., *arpa*), instrument with strings stretched across frame. Played by plucking strings, each string producing single note. Has long recorded history from ancient Sumeria and Babylonia to present day. In West, harp was played in Ireland in early Middle Ages, and was widely known in Europe in centuries before Renaissance. First pedal mechanism was devised *c* 1720, enabling harp to be played in sharp keys as well as diatonically. Modern double action harp with 7 pedals dates from 1820, and is due to Sébastien Érard. Normal key is C flat and each pedal raises its strings a semitone when pressed half-way down, and whole tone when pressed down fully. Compass is from octave below C flat below bass clef to 2 octaves above G sharp above treble clef. Since then harp has been used both as solo instrument and as occasional member of symphony orchestra.

*Chromatic harp,* with string for every semitone, was introduced by Pleyel of Paris in 1897, but has failed to displace pedal harp.

**Harper, Heather** (1930– ), Northern Irish soprano. Has sung at Covent Garden, Glyndebourne and Bayreuth. Sang in first perf. of Britten's *War Requiem.*

**harp-guitar, harp-lute-guitar, harp-lute,** instrument made by E. Light of London, *c* 1800.

**'Harp' Quartet,** nickname commonly given to Beethoven's string quartet in E, op 74 (1809), from *pizzicato* arpeggio in 1st movt.

**harpsichord** (Fr., *clavecin*; Ger., *Flügel, Kielflügel, Klavicimbal*; It., *arpicordo, clavicembalo, gravicembalo, cembalo*), keyboard instrument of horizontal harp or trapezoid shape in which strings are plucked by quill or leather tongue attached to jack, upright piece of wood set in motion by inner end of key. First recorded in 14th cent. In 16th cent., made occasionally in upright form, but more often in 'grand' or 'square' (virginal or spinet) form. In developed form, had 1 or 2 (exceptionally 3) keyboards (2nd being used either for ease of transposing or contrast of tone), and up to 4 stops, for 8ft and 4ft pitch and for producing special effects *eg* lute.

In baroque period, harpsichord was used as solo instrument, in all forms of chamber and ensemble music (except 17th-cent. English viol music), and to accompany voice in opera, cantata and oratorio. As accompanying instrument, main function was to realize harmonies indicated by FIGURED BASS. During later 18th cent. was dropped from orchestra and place in solo and chamber music was taken by piano. In 20th cent. use of harpsichord has been revived for performance of baroque music, and some modern composers (*eg* Poulenc, Falla) have written concertos for it.

**Harris, Renatus** (1652–1724), most famous of family of English organ-builders. Built several cathedral organs, and rebuilt organ in Magdalen College, Oxford, orig. built by his grandfather.

**Harris, Roy** (1898–1979), American composer. Studied with Nadia Boulanger. One of the most prolific of contemporary US composers. Work is distinguished by use of US folk song, assymetrical rhythm, angular melody, and modal and polytonal harmony. Works incl. 16 symphonies, works for chorus and orchestra and for unaccompanied chorus, and chamber and piano music.

**Harrison, Lou** (1917– ), American composer. Pupil of Cowell and Schoenberg. Has worked in many musical forms, and experimented with new sonorities. Some pieces inspired by oriental and Elizabethan music. Works incl. opera *Rapunzel,* several ballets, harpsichord sonatas, works for percussion orchestra, and *Four Strict Songs* for 8 baritones and orchestra in pure intonation. Has also edited several works of Ives, and written orchestral tribute to him.

**Harsányi, Tibor** (1898–1954), Hungarian composer. Resident in Paris from 1923. Works incl. operas, ballets, orchestral works. *Divertimento* no 1 for 2 violins and chamber orchestra, *Divertimento* no 2 for string orchestra and trumpet, and chamber and piano music.

**Hart, Fritz Dennicke** (1874–1949), English-born composer, conductor. Settled in Melbourne (1912) where became director of Conservatory and conductor of Symphony Orchestra. Conductor of Honolulu University (1937–46). Composed *c* 20 operas, choral, orchestral and piano music, and songs.

**Hartmann, Karl Amadeus** (1905–63), German composer. Studied with Webern. In 1945 in Munich founded Music Viva, organization promoting performances of new music. Compositions, reflecting admiration for Berg, incl. 8 symphonies, 2 string quartets, and chamber opera *Simplicius Simplicissimus.*

**Harty, Herbert Hamilton** (1879–1941), Irish conductor, composer. Became conductor of Hallé Orchestra in 1920. Compositions incl. symphony, violin concerto, and works for voices and orchestra, though better known for arrangements of Handel's *Water Music* and *Fireworks Music.* Knighted 1925.

**Harvey, Jonathan** (1939– ), English composer. Works incl. symphony and other orchestral works, music for various instruments and tape, and several cantatas.

**Harwood, Basil** (1859–1949), English organist, composer. Wrote church music, organ works, and cantatas.

**Háry János,** ballad opera by Kodály, founded on Hungarian melodies, libretto by B. Paulini and Z. Harsányi. First perf. Budapest, 1926. Story concerns exploits of Hungarian folk hero. Composer later made suite for orchestra from music.

**Hasse,** married name of Faustina BORDONI.

**Hasse, Johann Adolph** (1699–1783), German composer. Studied under Porpora and A. Scarlatti in Italy. In his day became most popular composer of Italian opera in Neapolitan style. Also wrote church music, oratorios and instrumental music.

**Hassler, Hans Leo** (1564–1612), 1612), German composer, organist. Pupil of A. Gabrieli in Venice. Accomplished master of polyphony and Venetian polychoral style, also wrote secular choral music and works for organ. Wrote tune later used by Bach in *St Matthew Passion* ('O Sacred Head').

**Hatton, John Liptrott** (1809–1886), English composer. Works incl. operas, cantatas, church and incidental music, and songs *eg* 'To Anthea' and 'Simon the Cellarer'.

**Haubiel, Charles** (1892– ), American composer, piano teacher. Founded The Composers Press (1935) for publication of contemporary US music. Composed a musical satire, and incidental, choral, orchestral and chamber music.

**Hauer, Josef Matthias** (1883–1959), Austrian composer, theorist. Developed technique (uninfluenced by Schoenberg) of atonal composition based on groups of notes ('tropes') chosen from 12 notes of chromatic scale. In this system he composed oratorio, orchestral, chamber and piano music, and songs.

**Haugtussa** (Norw., *Troll Maiden*), cycle of 8 songs by Grieg, op 67 (1896–8), with words from poems by Arne Garborg. *Haugtussa* is name of a girl who has gift of seeing and hearing trolls.

**Hauk, Minnie** (1852–1929), American operatic soprano. Performed in US and Europe. Introduced Carmen (her most famous role) to New York and London.

**haupt** (Ger.), principal, chief. *Hauptstimme,* principal part. *Hauptsatz,* main section (or theme). *Haupttonart,* principal key. *Hauptwerk,* great organ.

**Hauptmann, Moritz** (1792–1868), German theorist, composer, violinist. Taught counterpoint at Leipzig Conservatory from 1842, where his pupils incl. von Bülow, Joachim and Sullivan. Chief theoretical work was *The Nature of Harmony and Metre* (Eng. translation 1888). Composed opera *Mathilde,* and chamber and choral music.

**Hausegger, Siegmund von** (1872–1948), Austrian composer, conductor. Conducted in various Austrian and German cities, and in Edinburgh and Glasgow. Composed 2 operas, symphonic poems, programme symphonies, choral works and songs.

**Hausmusik** (Ger.), lit. 'house music', *ie* music for domestic rather than public performance.

**Haussmann** or **Hausman, Valentin** (*fl* late 16th cent.), German composer, organist. Wrote secular songs and instrumental dances, and published works of Marenzio, Vecchi, Gastoldi and Morley with German texts.

**hautbois** (Fr.), OBOE. From Elizabethan period to 18th cent., English equivalent was 'hautboy' (also 'hoeboy', 'hoboy', *etc*).

**haut-dessus** (Fr.), soprano.

**haute-contre** (Fr.), alto.

**havanaise** (Fr.), HABANERA.

**Hawaiian guitar,** style of guitar playing in which steel bar is used to stop strings instead of fingers. In this way, pitch is made to slide between notes.

**Hawkins, Coleman** (1904–69), American tenor saxophonist, one of most important in history of jazz. Famous for his juicy, full-bodied tone. An exceptionally romantic player, he was associated in 1920s and 1930s with Fletcher Henderson, and was later sympathetic to the bop revolution.

**Hawkins, John** (1719–89), English lawyer, historian of music, writer, editor. Wrote *General History of the Science and Practice of Music* (5 vols., 1776). Also edited works of, and wrote lives of, Dr. Johnson and Izaak Walton.

**Haydn, Franz Joseph** (1732–1809), Austrian composer. Born in Rohrau. Father was wheelwright. Became cathedral choirboy in Vienna, then assistant to Porpora. In 1761 began long period of service in Esterházy family, spending much of each year at palace of Esterház. Friendship with Mozart began in 1781. In 1786 wrote 6 symphonies (nos 82–87) for Concert Spirituel in Paris. On death of Prince Nicolaus Esterházy in 1790, family's musical establishment was disbanded, but Haydn retained title and salary, without duties. In 1791 went to London with contract from J. P. Salomon to write opera, 6 symphonies (nos 93–98) and 20 other pieces, and stayed in England for more than a year. Warmly received there, receiving honorary D. Mus. from Oxford. For second visit (1794–5), wrote further set of 6 'Salomon' symphonies (nos 99–104). In 1795 Prince Nicolaus II reconstituted household music, but Haydn's duties were light and consisted principally of composition of Mass each year – the 6 great Masses (1796–1802). During this period he completed 2 big choral works, *The Creation* (1798) and *The Seasons* (1801). During last few years lived quietly in Vienna, composing little.

Haydn's originality and mastery of technical means are apparent in symphonies, quartets and stage works of years 1761–80, after decade in which work was modelled on that of Viennese composers Reutter, Monn and Wagenseil, and C.P.E. Bach. In decade 1781–90, partly under influence of Mozart, music achieved maturity of expression and balance between harmonic and contrapuntal elements in design and texture which are marks of classical style, while retaining individual traits of energy, warmth and humour. His unflagging vitality and fertility of imagination enabled him to write in final period of life his 12 best-known symphonies and his great oratorios and Masses.

Haydn's operas are somewhat provincial and on lower plane than Mozart's; they include *Il Mondo della Luna* (1777) and *Armide* (1784). Concertos tend to lack consistent interest, perhaps because he was not distinguished public soloist. However, importance of keyboard sonatas and piano trios has begun to be recognized, and symphonies and string quartets, remarkable for their richness, tightness of construction, and harmonic and rhythmic verve, form foundation of classical style.

Principal compositions:

(1) Orchestra: 104 symphonies, *c* 13 keyboard concertos, 3 violin concertos, 2 cello concertos, 2 horn concertos, trumpet concerto, 5 concertos for 2 LIRE ORGANIZZATE, *Sinfonia concertante* for violin, cello, oboe and bassoon with orchestra;

(2) Stage works: *c* 18 operas (5 lost), 4 marionette operas;

(3) Oratorios and church music: 8 oratorios and cantatas, 2 solo cantatas, 12 Masses, 2 settings of *Te Deum,* 3 of *Salve Regina,* 1 of *Stabat Mater*;

(4) Chamber music: 84 string quartets (last unfinished), 31 piano trios, 125 *divertimenti* for baryton, viola and cello, *c* 56 string trios, *divertimenti, cassations,* and *notturni* for various instruments;

(5) Keyboard music: 52 sonatas (5 with violin part), 5 sets of variations, fantasia;

(6) Songs: 47 songs, 377 arrangements of Scottish and Welsh airs.

**Haydn, Johann Michael** (1737–1806), Austrian composer, brother of Joseph. In service of Archbishop of Salzburg from 1762. Pupils incl. Weber. Works incl. 24 Masses, 2 Requiem Masses, 4 German Masses and other church music, operas, oratorios and cantatas, 52 symphonies, serenades, divertimenti, 5 concertos, quintets, and other orchestral music.

**'Haydn' Quartets,** name given to Mozart's string quartets nos 14–19, so called because dedicated to Haydn.

**Haydon, Glen** (1896– ), American musicologist. Wrote *The Evolution of the Six-four Chord* (1933) and *Introduction to Musicology* (1941).

**Hayes, William** (1705–77), English organist, composer. Professor of music at Oxford. Composed church music, odes and glees.

His son, **Philip Hayes** (1738–97), was also an organist and composer. Succeeded father as professor at Oxford. Composed anthems, oratorio, masque, and ode.

**Haym, Nicola Francesco** (*c* 1679–1729), Italian musician, of German extraction. Went to England in 1704, where was involved in Italian opera as cellist and arranger in collaboration with Clayton and Dieupart. From 1713 acted as librettist for Handel, Ariosti and Bononcini. Wrote trio sonatas, serenata, and church music.

**Haydn Variations,** *see* 'ST ANTHONY' VARIATIONS.

**head voice,** upper register of voice, as distinct from lower register ('chest voice').

**Heart of Oak,** song in David Garrick's play *Harlequin's Invasion* (1759), set to music by William Boyce. It commemorates British victories of that year.

**Heather** or **Heyther, William** (*c* 1563–1627), English musician. Gentleman of Chapel Royal and lay-vicar of Westminster Abbey. Founded chair of music at Oxford which still bears his name.

**Hebenstreit,** *see* PANTALEON.

**Hebrides, The,** overture by Mendelssohn, op 26 (1832), also known as *Fingal's Cave*. Inspired by visit to Scotland in 1829. Original version (1830) was entitled *The Lonely Island*.

**Heckelclarina** (Ger.), wooden instrument of saxophone type in B flat. Has single reed. Compass is same as soprano saxophone.

**Heckelphone,** double reed instrument corresponding to French baritone oboe, with range octave below oboe. Used for first time by Strauss in *Salome* (1905).

**Heckelphone-clarinet,** wooden instrument of saxophone type designed for use in military bands. Has single reed. Compass is same as alto saxophone.

**heel,** end of bow of string instrument held by hand.

**heftig** (Ger.), violent.

**Heger, Robert** (1886–1978), German conductor, composer, b. Strasbourg. Works incl. operas, 2 symphonies, violin concerto and other instrumental works.

**Heifitz, Jascha** (1901– ), American violinist, b. Russia. Toured as soloist from 1912 with remarkable success. Became US citizen in 1925. Works written for him incl. concertos by Walton and Gruenberg.

**Heiller, Anton** (1923– ), Austrian composer, organist. Works incl. *Symphonie Nordique, Psalm Cantata, Te Deum* and other choral pieces, and much organ music.

**Heimkehr aus der Fremde, Die,** *see* SON AND STRANGER.

**Heinichen, Johann David** (1683–1729), German composer, theorist. Wrote operas, church music, and treatise on figured bass.

**Heintz, Wolff** (*c* 1490–*c*1555), German organist. Two 4-part settings of chorales by him were published in Georg Rhau's collection (1544).

**Heinze, Bernard Thomas** (1894– ), Australian conductor. Pupil of d'Indy. After conducting in various European cities, returned to Australia (1923), where conducted Melbourne Symphony Orchestra (1933–49), and became director of New South Wales Conservatorium in 1956. Knighted 1949.

**Heise, Peter Arnold** (1830–79), Danish composer. Pupil of Gade. Works incl. opera *Drot og Marsk* (King and Marshal, 1878), incidental and choral music, and songs.

**heiter** (Ger.), cheerful.

**Heldenleben, Ein** (Ger., *A Hero's Life*), autobiographical symphonic poem by Richard Strauss (1898).

**Heldentenor** (Ger.; It., *tenor robusto*), lit. 'heroic tenor', *ie* tenor with voice 'heroic' enough to sustain heavier operatic roles esp. those in Wagner.

**helicon,** name given to tuba when made in circular form used in brass bands.

**Hellendaall, Pieter** (1721–99), Dutch violinist, composer, organist. Studied violin with Tartini in Padua. Lived in England from 1752, becoming organist at Pembroke College, Cambridge (1762) and St Peter's College (1777). Published instrumental works, glees and psalms.

**Heller, Stephen** (1813–88), Hungarian pianist, composer. Toured Europe extensively. Composed *c* 150 pieces for piano.

**Hellinck, Lupus** (*c* 1495–1541), Netherlands composer. Works incl. Masses and chorales. For some time confused with Johannes Lupi.

**Helmholtz, Hermann Ludwig Ferdinand von** (1821–94), German physiologist, physicist. In 1862 published *On the Sensations of Tone as a Physiological Basis for the Theory of Music* (Eng. translation 1875), which forms basis of modern theories of consonance, tone-quality, and resultant tones.

**Helmore, Thomas** (1811–90), English writer on church music. Master of the choristers, Chapel Royal, from 1846. Edited several collections of plainsong melodies, hymns and carols, incl. *A Manual of Plainsong.*

**Hely-Hutchinson, Victor** (1901–47), South African-born pianist, composer, conductor. Director of music at B.B.C. (1944–7). Composed *Carol Symphony,* symphony for small orchestra, chamber and choral music, and songs.

**hemidemisemiquaver** (Fr., *quadruplecroche*; Ger., *Vierundsechzigstel*; It., *semibiscroma*; US, sixty-fourth note), quarter of a semiquaver, or 1/64 of semibreve. Single hemidemisemiquaver is written:

group of four

hemidemisemiquaver rest

**hemiola** (Gr.; Fr., *hémiole*; Ger., *Hemiole*; It., *emiolia*; Lat., *sesquialtera*), in medieval and Renaissance theory, proportion of 3/2 in two senses:

(1) interval of perfect fifth, which has vibration ratio 3:2;
(2) rhythmic relation of 3 notes in time of 2.

**Hempel, Frieda** (1885–1955), German soprano. Had uncommonly wide opera repertory, and later in career gave Jenny Lind recitals in costume.

**Hen, The** (Fr., *La Poule*), nickname given to Haydn's symphony no 83 in G minor (1786), one of 'Paris' symphonies. Name usually thought to refer to 'clucking' notes of oboe in 1st movt., though there is slight resemblance in slow movt. to Rameau's harpsichord piece. *La Poule*.

**Henderson, William James** (1855–1937), American critic, writer. Music critic of *New York Times* and *New York Sun*. Books incl. *Some Forerunners of Italian Opera* (1907) and *The Early History of Singing* (1921).

**Henkemans, Hans** (1913– ), Dutch composer, pianist. Authority on Debussy. Compositions incl. 2 piano concertos, concertos for flute, violin, viola and harp, 3 string quartets, and piano music.

**Henry IV** (1367–1413), king of England (1399–1413). *Gloria* and *Sanctus* in OLD HALL MANUSCRIPT, ascribed to 'Roy Henry', may be by either Henry IV or V.

**Henry V** (1387–1422), king of England (1413–22). 'Alleluya' by him survives, and he may be composer of *Gloria* and *Sanctus* in OLD HALL MANUSCRIPT (*see* HENRY IV).

**Henry VIII** (1491–1547), king of England (1509–47). Said to have played well on recorder, lute and virginals; also composer (of no great distinction). Wrote antiphon setting 'Quam pulchra es', 3 and 4-part secular songs, and instrumental pieces.

**Henry, Pierre** (1927– ), French composer. A noted exponent of electronic music, he carried out experimental work for music section of French Radio with Henri Barraud and Pierre Schaeffer in years after WWII.

**Henschel, George,** orig. Isidor Georg (1850–1934), German-born baritone, composer, conductor. First conductor of Boston Symphony Orchestra (1881–4). Settled in Britain. In charge of Scottish Orchestra (1893–5). Compositions incl. 2 operas, choral and instrumental music, and songs. Knighted 1914.

**Hensel, Fanny Cäcilie,** see MENDELSSOHN.

**Henselt, Adolf von** (1814–89), German pianist, composer. Studied piano with Hummel, and became one of greatest players of the age. From 1838 lived in St Petersburg as court pianist. Compositions incl. piano concerto, concert studies, and other piano works.

**Henze, Hans Werner** (1926– ), German composer. Pupil of Fortner and Leibowitz. Established himself as leading German operatic composer with *Boulevard Solitude* (1952), modern version of *Manon Lescaut*. Early works influenced by Stravinsky and Schoenberg, but during years spent in Italy his style softened and gained feeling of Mediterranean romance. Opera *King Stag* (1952–55) contains some of his most ravishing music, some of which he reworked in 5th of 6 symphonies. Next operas were *The Prince of Homburg* (1960) and *Elegy for Young Lovers* (1961), latter with libretto by Auden and Kallman. Was feted on return to Germany; his response was *The Young Lord* (1965), brilliant satire on bourgeois conventions in small German town. Grand opera *The Bassarids* (1966) is based on Euripides, again with libretto by Auden and

Kallman. Second piano concerto is one of few successful big-scale piano concertos since time of Brahms. At this time, Henze declared his commitment to left-wing politics, which have played a dominant part in his music since then, *eg* in powerful, large-scale music drama, *The Raft of The Medusa,* dedicated to Che Guevara. 'Cuban' period resulted in *El Cimarron* (*The Runaway Slave,* 1967), recital for baritone and percussionist, supported by flute and guitar. In next piece of music theatre, *The Long and Weary Journey to the Flat of Natasha Ungeheur* (1970), element of questioning seemed to have entered Henze's politics. However, he has continued political output with works such as song-cycle *Voices*, to texts by Brecht, Ho Chi Minh and others.

**heptachord** (Gr., seven string), scale of 7 notes, *eg* modern major or minor scale.

**Herbert, Victor** (1859–1924), Irish-born composer, conductor, cellist. Settled in US (1886). Composed highly successful operettas, *eg Naughty Marietta* and *Babes in Toyland.* Also wrote cello concerto, symphonic poem *Hero and Leander,* and other orchestral music.

**Herbst, Johann Andreas** (1588–1666), German composer, theorist. Choral works incl. *Theatrum Amoris* (1613) and *Meletemata sacra Davidis* (1619). In *Musica poetica* (1643), was prob. first theorist to disapprove explicitly of 'hidden' fifths and octaves. Other theoretical works are *Musica practica* (1641) and *Arte prattica e poetica* (1653).

**Hercules,** oratorio by Handel, libretto by T. Broughton (after Ovid's *Metamorphoses* ix and Sophocles's *Trachiniae*). First perf. London, 1745.

**Heredia, Pedro** (d. 1648), Spanish composer. *Maestro di cappella* at St Peter's, Rome (1630–48). Works incl. Masses and motets.

**Heredia, Sebastian Aguilera de,** *see* AGUILERA.

**Héretier, Jean L',** *see* L'HÉRETIER.

**Hermannus Contractus** (1013–54), Swiss (or poss. German) composer, theorist. Became monk at Reichenau. Composed antiphon 'Alma redemptoris mater', but not 'Salve regina' long attrib. to him. Theoretical treatises incl. *Musica.*

**hermeneutics,** term usually meaning interpretation of Scriptures, applied by Hermann Kretzschmar (1848–1924) to his method of interpreting musical motifs as expression of human feeling. Method places greater emphasis than 18th-cent. AFFEKTENLEHRE on scientific approach to intervals, rhythms, *etc.*

**Hero's Life, A,** *see* HELDENLEBEN.

**Hérodiade,** opera by Massenet, libretto by P. Milliet and H. Grémont (pseud. of G. Hartmann), founded on story by Flaubert. First perf. Brussels, 1881.

**heroic tenor,** *see* HELDENTENOR.

**Hérold, Louis Joseph Ferdinand** (1791–1833), French composer. Wrote operas and ballets. Best remembered for operas *Zampa* (1831) and *Le Pré aux clercs* (1832).

**Herrmann, Bernard** (1911–75), American composer, conductor.

Works incl. opera *Wuthering Heights* (1965), dramatic cantata *Moby Dick,* film scores *eg* for *Citizen Kane,* and radio music.

**Herrmann, Hugo** (1896–1967), German composer, organist. Wrote operas, works for chorus and orchestra, and instrumental music.

**Hervé,** pseud. of Florimond Ronger (1825–92), French composer. Wrote *c* 100 works for stage esp. operettas, incl. *L'Oeil crevé* (1867), *Childéric* (1868) and *Le Petit Faust* (1869).

**Hervelois,** *see* CAIX D'HERVELOIS.

**hervorgehoben** (Ger.), emphasized.

**Heseltine, Philip,** *see* WARLOCK.

**Hess, Myra** (1890–1965), English pianist. Notable exponent of Beethoven. Toured extensively. Gave daily lunchtime concerts in London National Gallery during WWII. D.B.E., 1941.

**heterophony** (Gr.), lit. 'difference of sounds', *ie* simultaneous playing by 2 or more performers of differently treated forms of same melody. Principle may have been used in Greek music, and is basis of ensemble playing in China, Japan, Java and Bali.

**Heugel,** firm of music-publishers in Paris, founded 1812 by Jean-Antoine Meissonnier (1783–1857). In 1839 Jacques Léopold Heugel (1815–83) became partner of Meissonnier.

**Heure Espagnole, L'** (Fr., The Spanish Hour), opera by Ravel, based on comedy by 'Franc-Nohain' (M. Legrand). First perf. Paris, 1911.

**Heward, Leslie Hays** (1897–1943), English conductor, composer. After conducting with British National Opera Company, went to South Africa in 1924 as director of music of Broadcasting Corporation and conductor of Cape Town Orchestra. On return to Britain, conducted Birmingham Orchestra (1930–43). Compositions incl. unfinished opera, orchestral works, string quartet, and songs.

**Heyborne, Ferdinando,** *see* RICHARDSON.

**Heyden, Sebald** (1499–1561), German theorist, composer. Theoretical treatises incl. *Ars canendi* (1537) and *De arte canendi* (1540). Also composed church music.

**Heyther, William,** *see* HEATHER.

**hexachord** (Gr., six string), scale of 6 notes, adopted by Guido d'Arezzo and incorporated in medieval musical theory.

There were 3 hexachords:

(1)*Hexachordum durum* (hard hexachord: G, A, B, C, D, E;

(2) *Hexachordum naturale* (natural hexachord): C, D, E, F, G, A;

(3) *Hexachordum molle* (soft hexachord): F, G, A, B flat, C, D.

Each hexachord had same succession of intervals: 2 tones, semitone and 2 tones. Range of notes in ordinary use was divided into 7 overlapping hexachords (from G at bottom of bass clef to E at top of treble clef). Application of syllables to notes of hexachords was called SOLMIZATION. In 16th, 17th cents. many compositions used hexachord as *cantus firmus*. Idea was applied to Mass, madrigal and esp. instrumental music.

**Hexenmenuett** (Ger., *Witch Minuet*), nickname given to minuet in Haydn's *Quintenquartett* because of its eerie character.

**Hiawatha,** cantata in 3 sections by Coleridge-Taylor, op 30, with words from Longfellow. Sections are *Hiawatha's Wedding Feast, The Death of Minnehaha* and *Hiawatha's Departure.* First perf. complete, London 1900.

**Hidalgo, Juan** (d. 1685), Spanish composer. Wrote earliest Spanish opera to have partly survived, *Celos aun del ayre matan* ('Jealousy, even of air, is fatal'), libretto by Calderón (1660).

**hidden fifths** and **octaves,** *see* SIMILAR MOTION.

**hi-hat cymbal** or **choke cymbal,** pair of cymbals mounted face to face on stand. Lower one is fixed but upper can be moved by foot pedal and made to strike lower one. Essential part of drum kit.

**Hill, Edward Burlinghame** (1872–1960), American composer, teacher. Pupil of Widor in Paris. Works incl. ballets, orchestral, choral, chamber and piano music, and songs.

**Hiller, Ferdinand** (1811–85), German pianist, composer, conductor. Studied with Hummel. Founded Cologne Conservatorium (1850). Compositions incl. 6 operas, 3 piano concertos, 3 symphonies, and much else.

**Hiller, Johann Adam** (1728–1804), German composer, conductor. Founded and conducted Leipzig Gewandhaus Concerts (1781–5). One of originators of *Singspiel.* First work in form was *Der Teufel ist los* (1766). In these works followed French and Italian models in adopting and developing native *Lied* for stage purposes.

**Hilton, John** (d. 1608), English organist, composer. Wrote anthems and madrigal for *The Triumphes of Oriana.*

**Hilton, John** (1599–1657), English organist, composer. Poss. son of preceding. Composed church music, fancies for viols, and songs. Editor and part-composer of *Catch that catch can* (1652), collection of catches, rounds and canons which initiated long period of popularity of catch in Britain.

**Himmel, Friedrich Heinrich** (1765–1814), German composer. Works incl. LIEDERSPIEL *Frohsinn und Schwärmerei* (1801) and opera *Fanchon, das Leiermädchen* (1804).

**Hindemith, Paul** (1895–1963), German composer. Studied at Hoch Conservatorium, Frankfurt, paying fees by playing in café bands. Leader of Frankfurt Opera Orchestra (1915–25), then became member of Amar-Hindemith Quartet. One of leading figures in Donaueschlingen Festivals of contemporary music (1921–6) and taught at Berlin Hochschule (1927–35). Music was banned by Nazis, who considered it degenerate (though he was not Jewish). Went to Turkey, then to US (1939), became professor of theory at Yale (1942). In 1946 returned to Europe as professor of composition at Zürich University.

One of the most versatile musicians of his day, Hindemith achieved eminence as composer, theoretician, performer, teacher and conductor. Early operas on bizarre subjects, *Murder, Hope of Women* (1921), *Sancta Susanna* (1921), *Cardillac* (1926) and *News of the Day* (1929), reflect expressionist movement. These and instrumental works (mostly chamber music) of 1920s show free and highly resourceful treatment of traditional form and tonality. After 1927, became associated with *Gebrauchsmusik* (utility music), *ie* music with social or political function, often intended for amateur performance.

From *c* 1931 style entered new phase, marked by increased clarity of tonality and form and greater expressiveness of melody, which came to maturity in such works as opera *Mathis der Maler* (1935) and ballet *Nobilissima Visione* (1938). New and more comprehensive theory of tonality of this period was expounded in *The Craft of Musical Composition* (1941–2), and further exemplified in set of preludes and fugues for piano, *Ludus Tonalis* (1942). Other theoretical works incl. text-book on harmony.

Principal compositions since 1931:

(1) Orchestra: Concert Music for strings and brass (1930), *Philharmonic Concerto* (variations, 1932), symphony from opera *Mathis der Maler* (1934), ballet *Nobilissima Visione* (1938), *Symphonic Dances* (1937), symphony in E flat (1940), overture *Cupid and Psyche* (1943), *Symphonic Metamorphoses* on themes by Weber (1943), *Sinfonia serena* (1946), *Hérodiade* (after Mallarmé, 1944) for chamber orchestra, symphony from opera *Die Harmonie der Welt* (1951);

(2) Solo instruments and orchestra: *Der Schwanendreher* for viola and small orchestra (1935), *Trauermusik* for viola and strings (1936), violin concerto (1939), cello concerto (1940), piano concerto (1945), clarinet concerto (1947), horn concerto (1949), *The Four Temperaments* for piano and strings (1940), concerto for trumpet, bassoon and orchestra (1949), concerto for wood-wind, harp and orchestra (1949);

(3) Choral works: oratorio *Das Unaufhörliche* (1931), *Plöner Musiktag* (1932), 'When lilacs last in the dooryard bloom'd' (Whitman, 1946), *Apparebit repentina dies* for chorus and brass (1947), *In Praise of Music* (revision of *Frau Musica,* 1928);

(4) Operas: *Cardillac* (1926, rev. 1952), *Neues vom Tage* (*News of the Day,* 1929, rev. 1953), *Mathis der Maler* (1935), *Die Harmonie der Welt* (1957);

(5) Chamber music: 3 pieces for clarinet, trumpet, violin, double bass and piano, 2 string trios, quartet for clarinet, violin, cello and piano, 6 string quartets, septet for wind instruments, sonatas for piano duet and 2 pianos, sonatas with piano for violin (4), viola, cello, double bass, flute, oboe, cor anglais, clarinet, bassoon, horn, trumpet, trombone;

(6) Solo instruments: 3 sonatas and *Ludus Tonalis* for piano, 3 organ sonatas, harp sonata;

(7) Unaccompanied chorus: *Six chansons, Five Songs on Old Texts;*

(8) Songs: *Das Marienleben* (15 songs, 1922–3, rev. 1948), *Nine English Songs, La Belle Dame sans Merci.*

**Hine, William** (1687–1730), English organist, composer. Works incl. anthems and organ voluntary.

**Hines, Earl** (1905– ), American jazz pianist. Regarded as founder of modern piano style and almost every other from early 1920s, when he was associated *eg* with Louis Armstrong.

**Hingston** or **Hingeston, John** (d. 1683), English organist, composer. Pupil of Orlando Gibbons. In service of Charles I, Cromwell and Charles II. Works incl. fancies with organ accompaniment.

**Hipkins, Alfred James** (1826–1903), English pianist, writer on musical instruments. Developed interest in harpsichord and clavichord, and in problems of tuning and pitch. Wrote *Musical Instruments, Historic, Rare, and Unique* (1888) and *The Standard of Musical Pitch* (1896).

**Hippolyte et Aricie,** opera by Rameau, libretto by S.J. de Pellegrin. First perf. Paris, 1733.

**His** (Ger.), B sharp.

**history of music,** some chief works in English:

GENERAL: C. BURNEY, *General History of Music* (4 vols. 1776–89; modern edition by F. Mercer, 2 vols., 1935). J. HAWKINS, *A General History of Music* (5 vols., 1776; reprinted 1853, 1875). C.H.H. PARRY, *The Evolution of the Art of Music* (1897). *The Oxford History of Music* (7 vols., 1929–34). C.V. STANFORD and C. FORSYTH, *A History of Music* (1916). P. LANDORMY, *A History of Music* (1923). P.A. SCHOLES, *Listener's History of Music* (3 vols., 1923–29). W.H. HADOW, *Music* (1924). C. GRAY, *The History of Music* (1928). G. DYSON, *The Progress of Music* (1932). K. NEF, *An Outline of the History of Music* (1935). D.N. FERGUSON, *A History of Musical Thought* (1935). T.M. FINNEY, *A History of Music* (1935). A. EINSTEIN, *A Short History of Music* (1938; illustrated edition, 1953). H. LEICHTENTRITT, *Music, History, and Ideas* (1938). P. LANG, *Music in Western Civilisation* (1941). C. SACHS, *Our Musical Heritage* (1948; published in the UK as *A Short History of World Music,* 1950). *The New Oxford History of Music* (11 vols., 1954 onwards). D.J. GROUT, *A History of Western Music* (1960). D. STEVENS (editor), *A History of Song* (1960). A. ROBERTSON and D. STEVENS (editors), *The Pelican History of Music* (2 vols., 1960, 1963). A. WARMAN and W. MELLERS, *Man and his Music* (1962). P.H. LANG and N. BRODER, *Contemporary Music in Europe* (1965). W. STERNFIELD, *A History of Western Music* (5 vols.). A. KALLIN and N. NABOKOV: *Twentieth-century Composers* (5 vols.) H. SCHONBERG, *Lives of the Great Composers* (1971).

PERIODS: C. SACHS, *The Rise of Music in the Ancient World* (1943). E. WELLESZ, *A History of Byzantine Music and Hymnography* (1949). H.G. FARMER, *A History of Arabian Music to the 13th Century* (1929). G. REESE, *Music in the Middle Ages* (1940); *Music in the Renaissance* (1954). M. BUKOFZER, *Studies in Mediaeval and Renaissance Music* (1950); *Music in the Baroque Era* (1947). G. ABRAHAM, *A Hundred Years of Music* (1938; new edition 1949). A. EINSTEIN, *Music in the Romantic Era* (1947). G. DYSON, *The New Music* (1924). C. GRAY, *Contemporary Music* (1924). A. SALAZAR, *Music in Our Time* (1948). H.J. FOSS (editor), *The*

*Heritage of Music* (studies of particular composers, 1550–1950) (3vols., 1927, 1934, 1951). N. SLONIMSKY, *Music Since 1900* (1949).

COUNTRIES:

Britain: H. DAVEY, *History of English Music* (1921). P.A. SCHOLES, *The Puritans and Music* (1934); *The Mirror of Music, 1844–1944* (2 vols., 1947). R. NETTEL, *Music in the Five Towns, 1840–1914* (1944). H.G. FARMER, *History of Scottish Music*. E. WALKER, *A History of Music in England*, revised and enlarged by J.A. WESTRUP (1952). PERCY M. YOUNG, *A History of British Music* (1967).

China: J.H. LEWIS, *Foundations of Chinese Musical Art* (1936).

Czechoslovakia: R. NEWMARCH, *The Music of Czechoslovakia* (1942).

France: G. JEAN-AUBRY, *French Music of Today* (1919). E.B. HILL, *Modern French Music* (1924). M. COOPER, *French Music from the Death of Berlioz to the Death of Fauré* (1951).

Hungary: G. CALDY, *A History of Hungarian Music* (1903).

India: A.H. FOX STRANGWAYS, *Music of Hindostan* (1914). A.B. FYZEE-RAHAMIN, *The Music of India* (1925).

Ireland: W.H. GRATTAN FLOOD, *A History of Irish Music* (1905).

Japan: F.T. PIGGOTT, *The Music of the Japanese* (1909).

Java: J. KUNST, *The Music of Java* (2 vols., 1949).

Jews: A.Z. IDELSOHN, *Jewish Music in its Historical Development* (1929).

Latin America: C. SEEGER, *Music in Latin America* (1942). N.SLONIMSKY, *Music of Latin America* (1945).

Mexico: R. STEVENSON, *Music in Mexico* (1952).

Norway: B. QVAMME, *Norwegian Music and Composers* (1949).

Russia: M. MONTAGUE-NATHAN, *A History of Russian Music* (1914). L. SABANEIEV, *Modern Russian Composers* (1927). G. ABRAHAM, *Studies in Russian Music* (1935); *On Russian Music* (1939); *Eight Soviet Composers* (1943).

Spain and Portugal: G. CHASE, *The Music of Spain* (1941). J.B. TREND, *The Music of Spanish History to 1600* (1926).

The United States: F.R. BURTON, *American Primitive Music* (1909). J.T. HOWARD, *Our American Music* (1931). A. COPLAND, *Our New Music* (1941). W. MELLERS, *Music in a New Found Land* (1964).

DICTIONARIES: S. Sadie (ed.), *Grove's Dictionary of Music and Musicians* (20 vols., 1981). W. APEL, *Harvard Dictionary of Music* (1969). A.E. HULL, *Dictionary of Modern Music and Musicians* (1924). P.A. SCHOLES, *The Oxford Companion to Music* (10th edition, 1970). E. BLOM, *Everyman's Dictionary of Music* (5th edition, 1971, edited by Sir Jack Westrup). O. THOMPSON and N. SLONIMSKY (editors), *The International Cyclopedia of Music and Musicians* (1946). H. ROSENTHAL and J. WARRACK, *Concise Oxford Dictionary of Opera* (1964). K. THOMPSON, *A Dictionary of Twentieth-century Composers* (1973).

PERIODICALS (wholly or partly in English): *Acta Musicologica*

(1931 foll.). *Journal of the American Musicological Society* (1948 foll.). *Journal of the Galpin Society* (for the history of musical instruments) (1948 foll.). *Journal of Renaissance and Baroque Music* (1946–7). *Modern Music* (1924–40). *Monthly Musical Record* (1873 foll.). *Musica Disciplina* (1948 foll.). *Musical Antiquary* (1909–13). *Musical Quarterly* (1915 foll.). *Musical Times* (1844 foll.). *Music and Letters* (1920 foll.). *Music Review* (1940 foll.). *Notes of The Music Library Association* (1944 foll.). *Proceedings of the Royal Musical Association* (1874 foll.).

ANTHOLOGIES: (a) Music: A. SCHERING, *History of Music in Examples* (1931; reprinted, 1950). A.T. DAVISON and W. APEL, *Historical Anthology of Music* (vol. 1, to 1600, 1946; vol. 2 to *c* 1780, 1950). J. WOLF, *Music of Earlier Times* (1930; reprinted New York *c* 1948). C. PARRISH and J.F. OHL, *Masterpieces of Music before 1750* (1952).

(b) Writings: O. STRUNK, *Source Readings in Music History* (1950).

(c) Pictures: G. KINSKY, *History of Music in Pictures* (1930).

BIBLIOGRAPHY: W.D. ALLEN, *Philosophies of Music History* (1939; contains a list of histories of music from 1600–1930). E. KROHN, *The History of Music; An Index to a Selected Group of Publications* (1952: an index of the contents of periodicals).

**Hlzbl** (Ger.), abbrev. of HOLZBLÄSER.

**H.M.S. Pinafore,** operetta by Gilbert and Sullivan. First perf. London, 1878.

**Hoboe** (Ger.), oboe.

**Hobrecht,** *see* OBRECHT.

**Hochzeit des Camacho, Die** (Ger., *Camacho's Wedding*), opera by Mendelssohn, libretto by C.A. von Lichtenstein (based on episode from Cervantes's *Don Quixote*). First perf. Berlin, 1827.

**hocket** (Fr., *hocquet, hoquet*; It., *ochetto*; Lat., *hoquetus, ochetus*), breaking of melody into single notes or very short phrases by means of rests, esp. as used in 13th, 14th cents. Most often used in 2 parts at a time, so that one sings while other has rest. In some cases may be based on single melody which is shared by 2 voices. Also used in instrumental music.

**Hoddinott, Alun** (1929– ), Welsh composer. Professor at Cardiff from 1968. Works incl. operas *The Beach of Falesá* (1974), *The Magician* (1976; shown on TV as *Murder the Magician*) and *The Rajah's Diamond* (1978–79), 5 symphonies, 4 sinfoniettas, concertos for piano and other instruments, oratorio *Job*, chamber and instrumental music, and songs.

**Hofer, Josepha,** *see* WEBER, JOSEPHA.

**Høffding, Finn** (1899– ), Danish composer, teacher. Works incl. opera *The Emperor's New Clothes* (after Hans Andersen), orchestral and chamber music, piano pieces and songs.

**Hoffmann, Eduard,** *see* REMENYI.

**Hoffmann, Ernst Theodor Amadeus** (1776–1822), German author, composer. Worked as conductor and civil servant. Composed

11 operas *eg Undine* (1816), symphony, piano sonatas and other works. Style of essays on music was influential in romantic period, and his stories were used as basis of several operas, *eg* Offenbach's *Tales of Hoffmann* (1881).

**Hofhaimer, Paul** (1459–1537), Austrian organist, composer. One of leading organists of his day; founded important school of players and composers. Compositions incl. 3 and 4-part songs.

**Hofmann, Josef Casimir,** orig. Józef Kazimierz Hofmann (1876–1957), Polish-born pianist, composer. Studied with Anton Rubinstein. Toured extensively. Compositions incl. works for piano, symphony, and 'symphonic narrative' for orchestra.

**Hogarth, George** (1783–1870), Scottish writer on music. Settled in London, and became critic of *Morning Chronicle* in 1830. Later became critic of *Daily News,* of which his son-in-law, Charles Dickens, was editor. Books incl. *Musical History, Biography, and Criticism* (1835) and *Memoirs of the Opera.*

**Hohane,** anonymous keyboard piece called *The Irish Hohane* (Gaelic *ochone,* alas) in the *Fitzwilliam Virginal Book.*

**Holborne, Antony** (d. 1602), English composer. Works incl. music for lute, pandora and cittern.

**Holbrooke, Joseph** (1878–1958), English composer, conductor, pianist. Works incl. symphonic poems *The Raven* (1900) and *Byron* (1906), operatic trilogy *The Cauldron of Annwen* (1912–29), orchestral variations on well-known tunes *eg* 'Three Blind Mice'.

**Holiday, Billie** (1915–59), American jazz singer. Her rough-edged voice was equalled in eloquence only by Bessie Smith. Used pop music rather than blues as her inspiration. Numbers incl. 'If dreams come true', 'Am I blue?', 'Gloomy Sunday' and 'Strange Fruit'.

**Holliger, Heinz** (1939– ), Swiss oboist, composer. Repertory incl. oboe music of all periods. Has done much to extend technique of instrument, inspiring composers *eg* Berio, Henze, Křenek, Penderecki, and Stockhausen. Compositions, often experimental, incl. *Siebengesang,* kind of concerto for electronically modified oboe, with vocal postlude.

**Holloway, Robin** (1943– ), English composer. Works incl. opera *Clarissa* (1975), *Homage to Weill* and other orchestral works, choral and chamber music, and songs.

**Holmboe, Vagn** (1909– ), Danish composer. One of most important after Nielsen. Works incl. 10 symphonies, 13 chamber concertos, 10 string quartets, and other chamber music.

**Holmes, John** (*fl* 16th–17th cents.), English composer, organist. His 5-part madrigal 'Thus Bonny-Boots the birthday celebrated' is in *The Triumphes of Oriana* (1601).

**Holmès, Augusta Mary Anne,** orig. Holmes (1847–1903), Irish composer, pianist, b. Paris and later took French nationality. Pupil of Franck. Wrote 4 operas incl. *La Montagne noire* (1895), and series of symphonic poems or dramatic symphonies incl. *Irlande* (1882), *Pologne* (1883) and *Au Pays bleu* (1891).

**Holst, Gustav Theodore,** orig. von Holst (1874–1934), English composer of Swedish descent. Studied composition under Stanford. In 1907 became director of music at Morley College. Teacher of composition at Royal College of Music (1919–24). Also music master at St Paul's Girl's School from 1905 till his death. Integrity of ideals and singleness of purpose enabled him to assimilate diverse elements into style which fuses vitality, clarity and austere mysticism. Early interests were in folk song (*Somerset Rhapsody,* 1907), and in Sanskrit literature and Hindu scales (*Savitri,* 1908, *Hymns from the Rig-Veda,* 1911). Use of 5 and 7-beat bars in this period is continued into next, and is allied with greater harmonic tension and larger choral and orchestral resources, (*The Planets,* 1916, *The Hymn of Jesus,* 1917). In later music Holst pursued experiments in harmony (*Choral Symphony,* 1925, *Egdon Heath,* 1927, *Choral Fantasia,* 1930) and showed leanings towards neo-Baroque forms (*Fugal Concerto,* 1923) and parody (*The Perfect Fool,* 1923).

Principal compositions:

(1) Operas: *Savitri, The Perfect Fool, At The Boar's Head*;

(2) Orchestra: *Somerset Rhapsody, St Paul's Suite* for strings, *The Planets, Fugal Overture, Egdon Heath, Hammersmith*;

(3) Choral works: *Hymns from the Rig-Veda, The Cloud Messenger, The Hymn of Jesus, Ode to Death, Choral Symphony, Choral Fantasia*;

(4) Songs: 9 hymns from the *Rig-Veda,* 12 songs to words by Humbert Wolfe.

**Holst, Imogen** (1907– ), English composer, conductor, writer, teacher. Daughter of Gustav Holst, on whom has written 2 important books. Closely associated with Aldeburgh Festival. Compositions incl. orchestral overture, piano pieces and folk song arrangements.

**Holzbauer, Ignaz** (1711–93), Austrian composer. In 1753 moved to Mannheim and conducted orchestra in period of its greatest fame. Wrote 65 symphonies in style of Stamitz, 11 Italian operas, and one in German, *Günther von Schwartzburg* (1777).

**Holzbläser** (Ger.), woodwind players.

**Holzblasinstrumente** (Ger.), woodwind.

**Home, Sweet Home,** song in opera *Clari, or the Maid of Milan* (London, 1823), words by J.H. Payne (1791–1852), music by Sir Henry Bishop. Its popularity led Bishop to write another opera with title *Home, Sweet Home* (1829).

**Homme armé, L',** title of 15th-cent. *chanson,* used as *cantus firmus* from 15th to 17th cent. for more than 30 Masses, *eg* by Dufay, Ockeghem, Tinctoris, Obrecht, Josquin, Morales, Palestrina and Carissimi.

**homophony,** term applied to music in which one part takes melody and other parts accompany it. Opposite to polyphony, in which all parts play more or less equal part in overall effect. Term also used to describe HOMORHYTHMIC style.

**homorhythmic,** term applied to polyphonic music in which all parts move in same rhythm.

**Honegger, Arthur** (1892–1955), Swiss composer, b. France, and mainly resident there. Pupil of d'Indy and Widor. With Satie, Milhaud and Jean Cocteau formed group *Les Nouveaux Jeunes* which later became *Les Six*. Prolific in many forms. Works incl. portrait of railway engine, *Pacific 231*, for orchestra (1923), oratorio *Le Roi David* (1921), setting of Claudel's *Jeanne d'Arc au Bûcher* (1935), operas *Antigone* (after Sophocles) and *The Eaglet* (with Ibert), 5 symphonies, *Rugby* and *Pastorale d'été* for orchestra, film, chamber and instrumental music, and songs.

**hongroise,** *see* ALL'ONGARESE.

**Hook, James** (1746–1827), English composer, organist. Wrote music for stage, concertos, sonatas, choral works and *c* 2000 songs, incl. 'The Lass of Richmond Hill'.

**Hooper, Edmund** (*c* 1553–1621), English organist, composer. Gentleman of Chapel Royal, and organist at Westminster Abbey. Works incl. anthems and keyboard pieces.

**hopak,** *see* GOPACK.

**Hopkinson, Francis** (1737–91), American statesman, poet, composer. Composed songs, *eg* 'My days have been so wondrous free' (1st published composition by US-born composer).

**hoquet, hoquetus,** *see* HOCKET.

**Horenstein, Jascha** (1898–1973), Russian-born conductor. Pupil of Adolf Busch and Schrecker. Worked internationally as guest conductor. Noted for interpretations of Bruckner, Mahler and Schoenberg.

**horn** (Fr., *cor*; Ger., *Horn*; It., *corno*), brass instrument with conical tube wound into spiral, ending in bell, and funnel-shaped mouthpiece. Known in England since 18th cent. as French horn, as it was perfected in France. In modern form, built in F (*see* TRANSPOSING INSTRUMENTS) and equipped with 3 valves which progressively lower pitch of instrument's natural harmonic series and so make available complete chromatic compass from B below bass clef to F at top of treble clef (written fifth higher in score).

Popular version of instrument has switch which turns it into horn in B flat alto. This facilitates playing of high notes. Stopped notes are played by bringing hand into bell (indicated by + over note in score): sound produced is semitone higher than open note, and tone is muffled. Similar effect is obtained by inserting pear-shaped MUTE into bell, though pitch remains the same. 'Brassy' notes, whether stopped or open, are indicated by terms *cuivré* (brassed) or *schmetternd* (blaring) and are played with increased lip pressure.

Valve horn described above (Fr., *cor à pistons*; Ger., *Ventilhorn*; It., *cornoventile*) came into use in mid 19th cent. Its predecessor was natural horn without valves (Fr., *cor de chasse*; Ger., *Waldhorn*; It., *corno da caccia*); first came into use at end of 17th cent. as improved form of earlier hunting horn *(Jagdhorn)*. In order to play in more than one key players used series of 'crooks' – additional pieces of tubing of varying lengths – to change pitch of instrument. Only means of playing notes other than those of harmonic series was by 'stopping' with hand, which altered pitch of open notes, but also changed tone-quality.

In classical symphony of later 18th cent., 2 horns were used as subsidiary instruments, often sustaining notes of harmony but occasionally coming into foreground. Practice of using 3 horns was introduced by Beethoven in *Eroica* symphony (1804). Concertos for horn have been written by Haydn, Mozart, Strauss and Hindemith.

Name 'horn' is also used misleadingly for 2 woodwind instruments: BASSET HORN (alto clarinet), and English horn or *cor anglais* (alto OBOE).

**horn, basset,** *see* BASSET HORN.

**Horn, Charles Edward** (1786–1849), English composer, singer. Son of Karl Friedrich Horn. Sang in, produced and composed operas in London, Dublin and US. Remembered for song 'Cherry Ripe'.

**horn, English,** *see* OBOE.

**Horn, Karl Friedrich** (1762–1830), German composer, and pianist. Went to London (1782) and entered royal service. Composed some instrumental music and edited, with Samuel Wesley, Bach's *Well-tempered Clavier*.

**hornpipe,** (1) wind instrument with single reed and horn attached to each end, played in Celtic countries. Called pibgorn in Wales, where was in use until 19th cent.;

(2) by beginning of 16th cent. applied to dance in triple time. About mid 18th cent., rhythm changed to 4/4, and it acquired association with sailors.

**Horn Signal, Symphony with the,** *see* AUF DEM ANSTRAND.

**Horowitz, Vladimir** (1904– ), Russian-born pianist. Rapidly acquired international reputation. Settled in US (1928) where married Toscanini's daughter, Wanda. Career interrupted by illness, but returned to platform in 1960s. Noted exponent of Chopin and Scarlatti.

**'Horseman' Quartet,** nickname for Haydn's string quartet in G minor, op 74, no 3 (1793), so called from 'riding' rhythms in 1st movt. and finale. Also called 'Rider' Quartet.

**Horsley, William** (1774–1858), English organist. Organist at several London churches, and one of founders of Philharmonic Society. Composed glees, hymn tunes and piano music, and wrote *An Explanation of Major and Minor Scales* (1825).

**Horwood, William** (d. 1484), English composer. Magnificat and 3 antiphons by him are in *Eton Choirbook*.

**Hothby, John** (d. 1487), English theorist, composer. Travelled in Europe, settling in Florence *c* 1440, and later in Lucca. Returned to England in 1486. Wrote 3 theoretical treatises.

**Hotter, Hans** (1909– ), German baritone, Austrian by naturalization. One of most renowned Wagner exponents of century. Also recitalist and opera producer.

**Hotteterre(-le-Romain), Jacques** (d. *c* 1760), French flautist, author, composer. Member of numerous family of wind instrument makers and players, many in service of Louis XIV. Wrote *Principes* *de la Flûte traversière* (1707). Composed flute pieces, sonatas and suites for 2 flutes and continuo, and a tutor and pieces for the musette.

**Hovhaness, Alan** (1911– ), American composer, of Armenian-Scottish descent. Works influenced by Middle and Far Eastern music, incl. *Lousadzak* (incorporating Chinese and Balinese instruments), many symphonies, operas, choral and chamber music, and *And God Created Great Whales* for taped whale solo and orchestra.

**'How do you do?' Quartet,** nickname given to Haydn's quartet in G, op 33, no 5. Words fit opening theme of work.

**Howells, Herbert** (1892– ), English composer. Studied under Stanford. Compositions incl. works for orchestra, concerto and suite for strings, piano concerto, Requiem, *Hymnus Paradisi, Missa Sabrinensis* for soloists, chorus and orchestra, organ, piano and chamber music, and songs.

**Howes, Frank Stewart** (1891–1974), English critic, author. Chief music critic of *The Times* from 1943. Writings incl. books on Byrd, Beethoven's orchestral works, Walton, and Vaughan Williams.

**Hubay, Jenö,** orig. Eugen Huber (1858–1937), Hungarian violinist, composer. Pupil of Joachim. Composed operas, orchestral works, and concertos and other pieces for violin.

**Huber, Hans** (1852–1921), Swiss composer. Wrote 9 symphonies, 5 operas, and chamber, choral and piano music.

**Huberman, Bronislaw** (1882–1947), Polish violinist. Pupil of Joachim. Made début in Vienna at age of 10, and at age of 14 performed Brahms's violin concerto in composer's presence. Founder of Israel Philharmonic Orchestra.

**Hucbald** (*c* 840–930), theorist and monk of St Amand. Author of *De institutione harmonica.*

**Hudson, George** (*fl* 17th cent.), English violinist, composer. In service of Charles II. Composed music (with Colman, Cooke, Lawes and Locke) for Davenant's *Siege of Rhodes* (1656), first English opera.

**Huë, Georges Adolphe** (1858–1948), French composer. Won *Prix de Rome* in 1879. Works incl. operas, ballets, pantomime, romance for violin and orchestra, symphonic poems, orchestral, incidental and choral music, and songs.

**Hufnagelschrift** (Ger.), lit. 'hobnail script', *ie* type of plainsong notation used in medieval Germany, so-called from shape of notes.

**Hugh the Drover,** ballad opera by Vaughan Williams, libretto by H. Child. First perf. London, 1924. Set in Cotswold village at time of Napoleonic wars.

**Hugo von Reutlingen** or **Hugo Spechtshart** (1285–1359/60), German theorist. Wrote treatise *Flores musicae omnis cantus Gregoriani* (1322, published 1488). His *Chronikon* contains words and melodies of songs of flagellants (*Geisslerlieder*) sung during plague of 1349.

**Huguenots, Les,** opera by Meyerbeer, libretto by A.E. Scribe. First perf. Paris, 1836. Story reaches climax in St Bartholomew Massacre of 1572.

**Hullah, John Pyke** (1812–84), English composer, teacher. Wrote on system of teaching singing in classes. Composed 3 operas incl. *The Village Coquettes* (libretto by Charles Dickens) and many other vocal works.

**Hume, Tobias** (d. 1645), English composer, player on *viola da gamba*. Published *The First Part of Ayres* (1605) which contains some pieces for lyra viol, and *Captain Hume's Poeticall Musicke* (1607).

**Humfrey, Pelham** (1647–74), English composer. In service of Charles II. Wrote anthems, odes and songs.

**Hummel, Johann Nepomuk** (1778–1837), Austrian composer, pianist. Studied under Mozart, Clementi, Albrechtsberger and Salieri. *Kapellmeister* to Prince Esterházy (1804–11). Most important of his many works are 7 concertos and other compositions for piano. Also wrote 9 operas, and chamber and choral music.

**humoresque** (Fr.), **Humoreske** (Ger.), occasionally used as title of capricious piece of music, *eg* by Schumann and Dvořák.

**Humperdinck, Engelbert** (1854–1921), German composer. Assisted Wagner at Bayreuth (1880–1). Later taught in Barcelona, Frankfurt and Berlin. *Hansel and Gretel* is most famous of 6 operas, which show Wagner's influence. Also wrote incidental music, pantomime *The Miracle,* choral works, and songs.

**Huneker, James Gibbons** (1860–1921), American critic, writer. Books incl. studies of Chopin and Liszt.

**Hungarian Dances,** collection of 21 dances by Brahms, orig. written for piano (4 hands). Published in 4 vols. (1852–69). Brahms wrote orchestral arrangements of nos 1, 3 and 10.

**Hungarian Rhapsody,** 19 piano pieces by Liszt in Hungarian gypsy style. Several later published in orchestral arrangements.

**Hungarian String Quartet,** ensemble formed 1935 with Zoltán Székely, Sándor Végh, Dénes Koromzay and Vilmos Palotai.

**Hunnenschlacht** (Ger., *Battle of the Huns*), symphonic poem by Liszt (after painting by Wilhelm von Kaulbach, representing defeat of Huns under Attila in 451). First perf. Weimar, 1857.

**Hunt, The,** *see* CHASSE, LA.

**Hunter, Rita** (1933– ), English soprano. Has sung with English National Opera and at Sadler's Wells and New York Metropolitan. Esp. known for her interpretation of Brünnhilde.

**'Hunt' Quartet,** nickname for Mozart's string quartet in B flat, K 458, so called because opening theme resembles sound of hunting horns.

**Hupfauf** (Ger.), lit. 'hopping up' – one of the names given to NACHTANZ.

**hurdy-gurdy,** medieval stringed instrument in which tone was produced by friction of wooden wheel and pitch was determined by stopping string with rods actuated by keys. Known from 10th cent., when called *organistrum.* Still made in 18th cent., esp. in France.

*Lira organizzata* for which Haydn wrote was 18th-cent. form of instrument. As street instrument it was replaced by street organ, to which name was transferred.

**Huré, Jean** (1877–1930), French organist, composer. Composed 3 symphonies, Masses, motets, and instrumental music.

**Hurlebusch, Konrad** (1696–1765), German organist, composer. Lived in Hamburg, Vienna, Munich, Stockholm and Amsterdam. Composed operas, cantatas, overtures, and works for harpsichord.

**Hurlstone, William Yeates** (1876–1906), English composer, pianist. Studied with Stanford. Works incl. *Fantasie-Variations on a Swedish Air* for orchestra, chamber and piano music, songs and partsongs.

**Husa, Karel** (1921– ), Czech composer. Pupil of Honegger and Nadia Boulanger. Now resident in US. Has written orchestral and chamber music.

**Hutchings, Arthur** (1906– ), English musicologist, teacher. Books incl. studies of Mozart's piano concertos, the baroque concerto, Schubert, and Delius.

**hydraulis,** ancient organ, used in Roman circus. Wind pressure was maintained by water compressor.

**Hygons, Richard** (*c* 1450–*c* 1508), English composer. His 5-part 'Salve regina' is in *Eton Choirbook*.

**hymn,** Christian hymn is poem sung in praise of God. Modern hymn-book is collection of hymns drawn from various times and places. Amongst most important groups are:

(1) early Eastern hymns: *eg* 'Hail, gladdening light'. Greatest hymn writer of Syrian church was St Ephraim (*c* 307–373);

(2) Latin hymns: foundation of Western hymn-writing was laid by St Ambrose (d. 397). Iambic metre used by him was adopted for many hymns sung to plainsong tunes. In later Middle Ages most important development was rise of SEQUENCE. Polyphonic settings of hymns and sequences, either free or based on plainsong tunes, were written from 13th to 16th cents.;

(3) Lutheran CHORALES;

(4) English hymns: hymns sung in English church in 16th, 17th cents. were metrical translations of psalms (*see* PSALTER). Modern hymn began with *Hymns and Spiritual Songs* (1707) of Isaac Watts, whose *Psalms and Hymns* were adopted by Congregationalists, and with John Wesley's Methodist *Collection of Psalms and Hymns* (1737).

**Hymn of Praise** (Ger., *Lobgesang*), Symphony-Cantata by Mendelssohn (1840). Setting of text for chorus and soloists preceded by 3 symphonic movts.

**Hypoaeolian, Hypodorian, etc,** *see* MODE.

# I

**Iberia,** (1) 4 sets of piano pieces (12 in all) by Albéniz, characterized by use of idioms of Spanish popular music. First perf. complete in 1909. 5 pieces later orchestrated by Arbos;

(2) *see* IMAGES.

**Ibert, Jacques François Antoine** (1890–1962), French composer. Pupil of Fauré. Director of Académie de France in Rome from 1937. His witty *divertissement* for chamber orchestra (from incidental music to *The Italian Straw Hat*) is often performed. Also wrote several operas, ballets, symphonic poem after Wilde's *The Ballad of Reading Jail,* orchestral suite *Escales (Ports of Call), concertino da camera* for saxophone and 11 other instruments, film and radio music, and some melodious piano pieces incl. *Le petit âne blanc.*

**idée fixe** (Fr., fixed idea), term used by Berlioz for motto theme, *ie* recurring theme in a piece of music. Most famous example is in Berlioz's *Symphonie Fantastique.*

**idiophone,** any instrument in which solid mass of material (often whole instrument) vibrates to make sound. There are 4 classes: (1) struck idiophones (*eg* bells, xylophone), (2) shaken idiophones (*eg* rattles), (3) plucked idiophones (*eg* jew's harp), (4) rubbed idiophones (*eg* glass harmonica).

**Idomeneo, Rè di Creta** (It., *Idomeneus, King of Crete*), opera by Mozart, libretto by G.B. Varesco. First perf. Munich, 1781. Story concerns Idomeneo, who on way back from Trojan wars vows that if he is delivered home safely will sacrifice to Poseidon first living creature he meets – which turns out to be his own son.

**Illuminations, Les,** cycle of 9 songs by Britten for high voice and strings, op 18 (1939), based on poems by Rimbaud.

**Images,** (1) collective title of 3 symphonic poems by Debussy, 1909: (a) *Gigues,* (b) *Iberia,* (c) *Rondes de Printemps*;

(2) title of 2 sets of piano pieces by Debussy (1905, 1907).

**imitation,** contrapuntal device whereby motif or phrase is presented successively by different voices. If imitation is exact or governed by stated rule (canon), *eg* of AUGMENTATION or DIMINUTION, it is called CANON. Imitation, as term is generally used, is less strict and may extend over less than complete phrase. First came into wide use in church style of 16th cent. and thence became basis of *canzona, ricercar* and English fancy (fantasia). FUGUE results from systematic organization of imitation with regard to key relationship. In classical and romantic periods imitation was occasional device, used with some freedom (*see also* INVERSION, RETROGRADE MOTION).

**imperfect consonance,** intervals of third and sixth.

**'Imperial' Mass,** alternative name for 'NELSON' MASS.

**'Imperial' Symphony,** nickname for Haydn's symphony no 53 in D (*c* 1780). Origin of name unknown.

**Impresario, L',** *see* SCHAUSPIELDIREKTOR.

**impressionism,** term used by analogy with impressionist painting for 'atmospheric' musical style of Debussy, Delius, Ravel and some of their contemporaries. Though impressionist painters' concern with effects of light rather than with shapes is echoed by composers' interest in tones and textures, with latter there is always a coherent underlying structure. This musical style might be more aptly called 'symbolist', as Debussy, with whom it originated, developed his aesthetic ideas in circle of Mallarmé, who regarded music as symbolist art *par excellence*, and Debussy's music shows more evidence of suggestions from symbolist poetry than from impressionist painting. Debussy's first important essay in style was *Prélude à l'après-midi d'un faune* (1892), which evokes imagery of Mallarmé's poem.

**impromptu,** title applied by early romantic composers *eg* Schubert and Chopin, to short piece for piano with something of character of extemporization, or air of delicacy or casualness.

**Improperia** (Lat.), 'reproaches'. Part of RC Liturgy for Good Friday; sung in plainchant, and from 16th cent. set also in homophonic style.

**improvisation,** art of spontaneous composition, variation or ornamentation. Chief forms are improvisation of one or more counterpoints on given theme or CANTUS FIRMUS, of variations on given theme or harmonic framework, of ornamentation which embellishes given melody, and of part of movement, *eg* CADENZA, or of complete movement or set of movements on original or given themes. *See also* DIVISION, FIGURED BASS, JAZZ.

**incidental music,** strictly speaking music for performance during action of play. Commonly used to include overtures and interludes.

**Incoronazione di Poppea, L'** (It., *The Coronation of Poppaea*), opera by Monteverdi, libretto by G.F. Busenello. First perf. Venice, 1642. Monteverdi's last and greatest dramatic work concerns ambition of Poppaea to become Nero's empress.

**Incognita,** opera by Wellesz, libretto by Elizabeth Mackenzie (after Congreve's prose romance). First perf. Oxford, 1951.

**Indes Galantes, Les,** opera-ballet by Rameau, to text by L. Fuzelier. First perf. Paris, 1735. Rameau's most successful opera is exotic story of love in 4 different parts of world.

**indeterminacy,** mode of composition, quite widely used since 1945, which either employs elements of chance (ALEATORY MUSIC) or leaves decisions to performers.

**Indy, Paul Marie Theodore Vincent d'** (1851–1931), French composer. Pupil of Franck. Franck, Liszt and Wagner were most important influences on his musical style, which also sometimes shows his interest in folk song and plainsong. Cofounder of Schola Cantorum in Paris (1894) where he taught composition till his death. Wrote text-book on composition and biographies of Beethoven and Franck. Compositions incl. operas *Fervaal* (1897), *L'Etranger*

(1903) and *La Légende de St Christophe* (1920), symphonies, *Symphonie sur un chant montagnard français* for orchestra and piano (1886), tone-poems *eg Wallenstein* (1882), *Istar* (1896) and *Jour d'été à la montagne* (1905), chamber and piano music, and songs.

**Inextinguishable, The,** title of Carl Nielsen's symphony no 4 (1916).

**inflection,** inflected note is note with ACCIDENTAL placed before it.

**Ingegneri, Marc' Antonio** (*c* 1547–92), Italian composer. Taught Monteverdi. Wrote Masses and other church music, and madrigals.

**Inghelbrecht, Désiré-Emile** (1880–1965), French conductor, composer. Wrote operas, operettas, symphonic poems and other orchestral works, ballets (*eg El Greco*), and chamber and piano music.

**Inglot, William** (1554–1621), English composer. *Fitzwilliam Virginal Book* contains 2 pieces by him.

**innig** (Ger.), 'heartfelt', suggesting quietly intense manner of performance.

**inno** (It.), hymn.

**In Nomine** (Lat.), 'in the name of the Lord'. Title used by English composers of 16th, 17th cents. for instrumental compositions based on part of Benedictus of Taverner's Mass *Gloria tibi Trinitas* set to words 'in nomine Domini'.

**instrumentation,** *see* ORCHESTRATION.

**instruments,** instruments used in Western music may for general purposes be divided into 5 types:

(1) *Woodwind*: recorder, transverse flute, and instruments using single or double reed, even if sometimes made of metal, *eg* oboe, clarinet, bassoon, saxophone; (2) *Brass*: trumpet, cornet, bugle, French horn, trombone, and other lip-reed instruments; (3) *Percussion*: drum, cymbal, triangle *etc*; (4) *Keyboard*: harpsichord, virginal, clavichord, pianoforte, organ, celesta; (5) *String*: viol and violin families, harp, lute, guitar.

Alternative classification on acoustical principles divides instruments into 5 main categories: (1) *Idiophones*: instruments made of naturally sonorous material; (2) *Membranophones*: instruments using stretched membrane; (3) *Aerophones*: woodwind, brass, and those instruments using free reed; (4) *Chordophones*: instruments using strings; (5) *Electrophones*: *eg* etherophone and electronic organ. *See also* ELECTRONIC INSTRUMENTS, MECHANICAL MUSICAL INSTRUMENTS.

**interlude,** term occasionally used as title of part of complete composition. Applied to instrumental phrase between lines or verse of song, hymn or chorale. In more general sense, applied to piece of incidental music for performance during play.

**intermezzo** (Fr., *intermède*; Lat., *intermedium*), play with music, performed between acts of drama or opera. Examples in 16th cent.; custom became general in 17th cent. In early 18th cent. began to be performed separately. Famous example is Pergolesi's *La serva* *padrona*, which gave impulse to cultivation of *opera buffa* and indirectly of French *opéra-comique*. Later the term came to stand for instrumental interlude in course of opera or drama.

**Internationale,** international Communist anthem. National anthem of USSR until 1944. Words by E. Pottier (1871), music by P. Degeyter (1888).

**interpretation,** activity of performer in communicating intentions of composer, esp. those not given explicitly by notation.

**interrupted cadence,** *see* CADENCE.

**interval,** distance in pitch between 2 notes, expressed in terms of number of notes of diatonic scale which they comprise (*eg* third, fifth, ninth), along with qualifying word (perfect, imperfect, major, minor, augmented or diminished). Number is determined by position of notes on staff, qualifying word by number of tones and semitones in interval. Thus

is always third, while

is major third, being distance of 2 tones, and

is minor third, being distance of 1½ tones. Intervals of octave or less are called simple intervals, those of more than octave, compound intervals. For purposes of theory of harmony, compound intervals are equivalent of corresponding simple intervals (*eg* tenth as equivalent of third) except in cases of chord of ninth, and dominant eleventh and dominant thirteenth chords.

The following is a list of names of intervals together with number of tones which they comprise:

unison, 0;
augmented unison, minor second, ½;
major second, diminished third, 1;
augmented second, minor third, 1½;
major third, diminished fourth, 2;
perfect fourth, 2½;
augmented fourth, diminished fifth, 3;
perfect fifth, 3½;
augmented fifth, minor sixth, 4;
major sixth, diminished seventh, 4½;
augmented sixth, minor seventh, 5;
major seventh, 5½;
octave, 6.

In theory of harmony, octaves, fifths, thirds and sixths, when perfect, major or minor, are counted as consonances; seconds, sevenths and all diminished and augmented intervals are counted as dissonances. For inverted intervals, *see* INVERSIONS.

**In The South,** concert overture by Elgar, op 50 (1904), also called *Alassio* after town where he composed it.

**In The Steppes of Central Asia,** 'orchestral picture' by Borodin (1880) describing gradual approach and passing of caravan. Composed as accompaniment to *tableau vivant.*

**Intolleranza 1960,** opera by Luigi Nono, libretta by composer. First perf. Venice, 1961. Work attacks variety of modern social evils. Incorporates serial and electronic techniques.

**intonation,** (1) judgement of pitch by performer;
(2) opening song of plainsong melody.

**intrada** (It.; Fr., *entrée*), term regularly used by 17th-cent. German composers for opening movt. of suite; occasionally used later.

**introduction,** section (usually in slow time) often found at start of symphony, string quartet, sonata or overture; usually written for both structural and dramatic reasons.

**Introit,** first part of Proper of Mass. Orig. antiphon and psalm, now consists of antiphon, verse of psalm, *Gloria Patri* and repeat of antiphon.

**invention,** title used by Bonporti for violin partitas (1712) and by Bach for 2-part pieces in contrapuntal style for clavier; Bach called 3-part pieces *sinfonie*, though now also called 'inventions'.

**inversion,** (1) of interval: interval is inverted when lower note is sounded above upper note, *eg*:

inversion:

Number of interval when inverted is found by subtracting it from nine *eg* inversion of fifth is fourth. Qualifying term of perfect interval is unchanged by inversion, *eg* inversion of perfect fifth is perfect fourth. Major interval when inverted becomes minor, diminished becomes augmented, and vice versa;
(2) of melody: melody is inverted when intervals through which it proceeds are replaced by their inversions (also called contrary motion, and *per arsin et thesin*). Where statement overlaps inversion, result is imitation by contrary motion, also called canon by inversion or 'mirror' canon;
(3) of chord: *see* CHORD;
(4) of counterpoint: *see* invertible COUNTERPOINT.

**inverted mordent,** *see* MORDENT.

**inverted turn,** *see* TURN.

**Invitation to the Dance** (not 'to the Waltz') (Ger., *Aufforderung zum Tanz*), piano piece by Weber, op 65 (1819). Consists of slow introduction, extended dance and reminiscent coda. Orchestrations have been made by Berlioz and Weingartner.

**Iolanthe, or The Peer and the Peri,** comic opera by Gilbert and Sullivan. First perf. London and New York, 1882.

**Ionian mode,** mode which, on piano, uses white notes from C to C.

**Iphigénie en Aulide** (Fr., *Iphigenia in Aulis*), opera by Gluck, libretto by F.L.L. du Roullet (inspired by Racine and Euripides). First perf. Paris, 1774. Story has inspired *c* 30 other works, incl. Cherubini's *Ifigenia in Aulide* (1788).

**Iphigénie en Tauride** (Fr., *Iphigenia in Tauris*), opera by Gluck, libretto by N.F. Guillard. First perf. Paris, 1779. Sequel to *Iphigénie en Aulide*. Piccinni's opera on same subject was produced in Paris 2 years later; supporters of respective composers clashed over performances.

**Ippolitov-Ivanov, Mikhail** (1859–1935), Russian composer. Pupil of Rimsky-Korsakov. Director of Moscow Conservatory (1906–22). Works incl. several operas (also completed Mussorgsky's *The Marriage*), picturesque orchestral pieces *eg Caucasian Sketches*, choral music, and songs. Made study of Russian folk music, reflected in many of his works.

**Ireland, John** (1897–1962), English composer. Pupil of Stanford. Destroyed all his music up to 1908. Thereafter output incl. several picturesque orchestral works *eg The Forgotten Rite* (1913), *Mai-Dun* (1921), *A London Overture* and *Satyricon*, piano concerto (1930), choral *These Things Shall Be* (1937), piano pieces and songs.

**Irmelin,** opera by Delius, libretto by composer. Composed 1892, first perf. Oxford, 1953. Story concerns princess loved by prince disguised as swineherd. So-called 'Prelude' to *Irmelin* was written 39 years after the opera.

**Isaac, Heinrich or Isaak, Hendryk** (*c* 1450–1517), composer, prob. Netherlandish, though Italians called him 'Arrigo tedesco' (Harry the German). In service of Lorenzo de Medici then of Emperor Maximilian, working in Italy and Austria. Composed secular works to French, Italian and Latin texts, and Masses and motets. Greatest work is *Choralis Constantinus*, containing polyphonic settings of parts of Proper of Mass for whole liturgical year. Also made 4-part setting of tune 'Innsbruck', prob. not by him.

**isometric,** same as HOMORHYTHMIC.

**isorhythm,** principle of construction, used *c* 1300–1450 in which same rhythmic pattern is applied to successive divisions or to successive repetitions of melody. Principle is generally applied to tenor, which is usually plainsong melody. Tenor is normally repeated several times in diminishing note values, governed by systems of proportions, to serve as basis for complete composition. Parts written above tenor may also be treated isorhythmically, with more or less strictness. For purpose of analysis term *talea* is used for rhythmic pattern, *color* for melody.

**Isouard, Nicolò** (1775–1818), French composer. Lived in France, Italy and Malta. Wrote many operas and other vocal music, incl. *L'avviso ai maritat* (1794), some in collaboration with other composers, *eg* Méhul, Cherubini, Boïeldieu.

**Israel in Egypt,** oratorio by Handel, with words from Book of Exodus. First perf. London, 1739.

**Israel Philharmonic Orchestra,** Israel's leading orchestra, founded by Bronislaw Huberman. Toscanini conducted inaugural concerts, though orchestra does not have permanent musical director, being run as cooperative. Based in Tel Aviv, though performs regularly in Jerusalem and Haifa.

**Israel Symphony,** work by Bloch for 5 solo voices and orchestra, inspired by Jewish religious festivals. First perf. New York, 1916.

**Istar,** symphonic variations by d'Indy, op 42 (1897). Work concerns Babylonian legend of Istar's descent into limbo, depicted by 7 variations of diminishing complexity; only at end is theme itself performed, in its simplest form.

**istesso tempo, l'** (It.), 'in the same time'. Indication that beat is to remain same even though time-signature changes.

**Istomin, Eugene** (1925– ), American pianist. Apart from appearing as soloist, plays in piano trios with Isaac Stern and Leonard Rose.

**Italiana in Algeri, L'** (It., *The Italian Girl in Algiers*), comic opera by Rossini, libretto by A. Anelli. First perf. Venice, 1813. Story concerns search of Isabella for her lover, Lindoro, a slave of the Mustapha, Bey of Algiers. Rossini's first major comic opera, written in *c* 3 weeks.

**Italian Concerto,** work for harpsichord by Bach, published in 2nd part of Clavierübung (1735). Imitates style of contemporary Italian concerto, reproducing contrast between soloist and *tutti*.

**Italian overture,** type of overture which evolved during 17th, 18th cents. Characterized by 3-movt. layout: quick/slow/quick. Precursor of classical symphony.

**Italian Serenade,** single movt. by Hugo Wolf, orig. for string quartet (1887), later arranged for small orchestra (1892) and intended as first movt. of longer work.

**Italian sixth,** *see* AUGMENTED SIXTH.

**Italian Songbook** (Ger., *Italienisches Liederbuch*), settings by Hugo Wolf (1890–6) of 46 Italian poems in German translation by Heyse.

**Italian Symphony,** Mendelssohn's symphony no 4, op 90 (1831–3), in A major and minor. Inspired by visit to Italy.

**Ivanhoe,** opera by Sullivan, libretto by J. Sturgis (after Scott's novel). First perf. London, 1891. Sullivan's only 'serious' opera, it has failed to hold its place in the repertory.

**Ivan Sussanin,** orig. title of opera by Glinka, libretto by Baron G.F. Rosen. First perf. St Petersburg, 1836. Alternative title is *A Life for the Tsar* (opera was dedicated to Nicholas I). Work was foundation-stone of Russian nationalist school of opera.

**Ivan the Terrible,** (1) name given by Diaghilev to Rimsky-Korsakov's opera *The Maid of Pskov*;

(2) opera by Bizet, libretto by Leroy and Trianon (1865). Thought lost till 1944.

**Ives, Charles Edward** (1874–1954), American composer. Born at Danbury, Connecticut. Received basic musical training from father, who first interested him in polytonality and use of quarter-tones. Although (after studying at Yale) Ives went into business, he became most advanced and adventurous US composer of his day, often anticipating ideas which others did not hit upon for years.

Ives experimented successfully with polytonality, polyrhythms, quarter-tones, chord clusters, musical autobiography and spatial presentation of music. His CONCORD SONATA for piano (1908–15) is dedicated to New England transcendentalists. Second string quartet (1907–13) incorporates linear and rhythmic independence between instruments. Also pioneered use of multiple orchestra to try to recreate sights and sounds of hometown, esp. bands which played different music simultaneously in all 4 corners of square at carnival time. These memories of changing perspectives and traditional US tunes played simultaneously (sometimes in different keys) fill Ives's music, *eg Putnam's Camp* (no 2 of *Three Places in New England,* 1903–14), and *Washington's Birthday* (1913) and esp. in great 4th symphony, which may need up to 4 conductors. However, conflicting bands are only one of the bases of his style. Perhaps essence of Ives is to be found in short philosophical orchestral piece, *The Unanswered Question* (1908), in which 2 orchestral groups represent the Real and the Transcendental, and in which degree of improvisation is required of performers.

During his lifetime, Ives's music was largely neglected and misunderstood, but today he is recognized both as first great US composer and one of pioneers of modern music. Apart from orchestral works, incl. 5 symphonies and *Central Park in the Dark,* he wrote 2 string quartets, 5 sonatas for violin and piano, choral music, and *c* 200 songs.

**Ives, Simon** (1600–62), English composer. Collaborated with William Lawes in composing music for Shirley's masque *The Triumph of Peace* (1633). Other works incl. elegy on death of William Lawes, catches and rounds, and fancies and an *In nomine* for viols.

# J

**Jachet of Mantua** (d. 1559), French composer. Masses, motets, and other church music by him appeared in various Italian publications between 1539 and 1567.

**jack,** *see* HARPSICHORD.

**Jackson, William** (1730–1803), English composer. Wrote church music, odes and canzonets.

**Jacob, Gordon Percival Septimus** (1895– ), English composer. Pupil of Stanford. Authority on orchestration. Compositions incl. music for ballets and films, numerous orchestral works, traditional in style but of expert craftsmanship *eg Passacaglia on a Well-known Theme* ('Oranges and Lemons'), symphonies, suites, concertos for piano, violin, oboe, bassoon and horn, 3-handed piano concerto, and chamber music.

**Jacobi, Frederick** (1891–1952), American composer, conductor. Pupil of Bloch. Studied music of Pueblo Indians, and used it in some of his works, which incl. opera *The Prodigal Son,* orchestral music *eg Indian Dances,* Jewish liturgical works, and chamber music.

**Jacobus de Bononia,** *see* JACOPO DA BOLOGNA.

**Jacobus de Leodio** or **Jacques de Liège** (*c* 1260–*c* 1330), Walloon writer on music. His treatise *Speculum musicae* (*c* 1330) shows strong preference for music of 13th cent. over innovations of *Ars nova* (*see* ARS ANTIQUA) of early 14th cent. Treatise was long attrib. to Johannes de Muris, who took opposite view.

**Jacopo da Bologna** or **Jacobus de Bononia** (*fl* mid-14th cent.), Italian composer, harpist. Wrote secular songs, mainly madrigals.

**Jacotin** or **Jacques Godebrie** or **Jacobus Godefridus** (d. 1529), Flemish composer. Works incl. *chansons.*

**Jacotin** or **Jacobus Picardus** (*fl* late 15th cent.), Italian musician. Prob. composer of motets under this name in Petrucci's *Motetti della corona* (1519).

**Jacques de Liège,** *see* JACOBUS DE LEODIO.

**Jacquet, Elisabeth-Claude** (*c* 1659–1729), French composer, clavecinist. Protégée of Mme. de Montespan. Compositions incl. opera *Céphale et Procris* and other stage music, cantatas, chamber sonatas, and church and harpsichord music.

**Jadassohn, Salomon** (1831–1902), German therorist, composer. Pupil of Liszt. Wrote many theoretical works. Compositions incl. 4 symphonies, and chamber and choral music.

**Jagd** (Ger.), hunt. *Jagdhorn,* hunting horn. *Jagdquartett,* 'Hunt' Quartet – Mozart.

**Jahn, Otto** (1813–69), German archaeologist, philologist, writer on music and art. Wrote important biography of Mozart (1856–59), subsequently remodelled and rewritten by Abert, and prepared material on lives of Haydn and Mozart which he passed on to C.F. Pohl and A.W. Theyer respectively.

**Jahreszeiten, Die,** *see* SEASONS.

**James, Philip** (1890–1975), American composer, conductor. Music, containing element of satire incl. *Station WGZBX* for orchestra, 2 symphonies, *Missa Imaginum* and other choral-music, and chamber and instrumental works.

**Janáček, Leoš** (1854–1928), Czech composer. Son of poor Moravian schoolmaster. Studied at Prague Organ School. After period as conductor of Brno Philharmonic Society and as student at Leipzig and Vienna, founded own organ school in Brno (1881) and directed it till taken over by state (1920); then appointed professor at Prague Conservatory. Janáček was always fascinated by rhythms and intonations of folk song and speech, which helped to give his operas their special character. Wrote many of his greatest works in old age. International reputation rests mainly on his operas, which reveal his lyrical genius; they incl. *Jenůfa* (1894–1903), *The Excursions of Mr Brouček* (1920), *Kátya Kabanová* (1921), *The Cunning Little Vixen* (1924), *The Makropoulos Case* (1926) and *From the House of the Dead* (after Dostoyevsky; uncompleted). His *Sinfonietta* (1926) is also work of great personality, as are his 2 autobiographical string quartets, which are about his love for Kamila Stosslova, married woman nearly 40 years younger than himself. Other works incl. *Glagolitic Mass,* symphonic poem *Taras Bulba,* wind sextet *Mladi* (Youth), chamber and piano music, and *The Diary of One Who Vanished* for voice and piano.

**Janequin, Clement** (*c* 1474–*c* 1560), French composer. His *chansons,* mostly for 4 voices, incl. long 'pictorial' *chansons eg Le Chant des Oiseaux.* Also wrote 2 Masses, motets, and other church music.

**Janissary music,** in 18th cent., European MILITARY BANDS adopted some instruments used by the Janissary (Turkish imperial guards) *eg* triangle, cymbals, and bass drum. Music was imitated by *eg* Mozart in *Die Entführung.*

**Janowitz, Gundula** (1937– ), German soprano. Member of Berlin and Vienna opera companies, and has appeared at world's leading opera houses.

**Jaques-Dalcroze, Emile** (1865–1950), Swiss composer, teacher. In 1915 founded institute in Geneva, where taught and developed principles of training through rhythm known as 'eurhythmics'. Composed 5 operas, 2 violin concertos, choral, orchestral, chamber and piano music, and songs.

**Jarnach, Philipp** (1892– ), Spanish composer, b. France. Pupil of Busoni, whose unfinished opera *Doktor Faust* he completed. Works incl. *Sinfonia Brevis* and other orchestral music, string quartet and other chamber music, instrumental pieces, and songs.

**Järnefelt, Armas** (1869–1958), Finnish composer, conductor. Took Swedish nationality in 1910. Works incl. *Praeludium* and *Berceuse* for orchestra, choral and piano music and songs.

**jazz,** style of music marked by variable degrees of improvisation, intensely rhythmic playing and by individual approach to instrumental tone and rhythmic articulation. Most groups consist of rhythm section of drums, double bass or bass guitar, and piano or guitar (usually amplified) to produce rhythmic springboard for other instruments: usually called horns, these are mostly wind instruments, esp. trumpet, trombone and saxophone.

Jazz orginated in street bands of poor quarters of New Orleans at turn of century, arising from unique fusion of Black and European cultures. Light syncopation of RAGTIME gave way to driving beat and characteristic melodic lines incorporating flattened notes of BLUES. Form and harmony were simple, often being derived from march tunes, but players improvised round them in freewheeling counterpoint. This traditional jazz spread rapidly north, taking with it Louis Armstrong who developed solo style in contrast to collective playing of New Orleans bands, and who improvised solos on harmonic sequence of tunes rather than melodies themselves.

As popularity of jazz spread, bands grew bigger, and SWING style dominated 1930s. Benny Goodman created style, in which routine character of arrangements was often only compensated for by excitement which they generated. However some fine soloists emerged, and one great composer – Duke Ellington.

Mid 1940s saw reaction against routines of swing in return to improvisation. New music, called bebop, rebop or BOP, was marked by introspective and often frenetic virtuosity, complex harmonies, convoluted and totally original melodic lines, and involved rhythms. Chief exponent was Charlie 'Bird' Parker; other important figures incl. Dizzy Gillespie, Art Tatum and Miles Davis.

In 1950s cool style of US west coast and hard bop of New York vied in popularity. From 1960 real break was made by trumpeter Miles Davis, who began to base improvisations on modes rather than harmonies. Harmonic basis was simplified, leading to greater freedom in structure of improvisation. Divergent schools then emerged though both emphasize collective improvisation: one, led by Ornette Colman, continued along path to total freedom (even eschewing regular pulse); other led by Miles Davis, took up propulsive rhythms and electric sounds of rock music.

**Jean de Garlande,** *see* GARLANDE.

**Jeffreys** or **Jeffries, George** (d. 1685), English composer. His many works incl. anthems, services, motets, incidental music, and fancies for strings.

**Jemnitz, Alexander,** orig. Sándor (1890–1963), Hungarian composer, critic. Pupil of Reger and Schoenberg. Works consist mainly of chamber and keyboard music and songs. Concentrated on sonatas for unaccompanied solo instruments. Also wrote ballet *Divertimento*, and 7 *Miniatures* for orchestra.

**Jenkins, John** (1592–1678), English composer. Prolific writer of instrumental music, incl. fancies and dances for viols with organ, airs and fantasia-suites for one or more violins with bass and organ, lyra-viol pieces. Also wrote songs and anthems.

**Jensen, Adolf** (1837–79), German composer. Pupil of Liszt. Numerous songs show influence of Schumann. Also wrote opera, cantatas, part-songs and piano pieces.

**Jenůfa,** opera by Janáček, libretto by composer (based on story by G. Preissová). First perf. Brno, 1904. Orig. title was *Její Pastorkyna* (*Her Foster-daughter*). Work is human drama of Bohemian village life; Jenůfa's illegitimate child is drowned by her foster-mother.

**Jephtha,** (1) Latin oratorio (one of earliest) by Carissimi (1650); (2) oratorio by Handel, libretto by T. Morell. First perf. London, 1752.

**Jeppesen, Knud** (1892– ), Danish musicologist, composer. Pupil of Carl Nielsen. Director of Royal Conservatory at Copenhagen from 1934. Books incl. *The Style of Palestrina and the Dissonance* (1927) and *Counterpoint* (1939). Compositions incl. opera *Rosaura* (after Goldoni), symphony, horn concerto, choral music and songs.

**jeu** (Fr.), organ stop. *Jeux de fonds,* foundation stops. *Jeux d'anches,* reed stops.

**jeu de clochettes, jeu de timbres** (Fr.), glockenspiel.

**Jeune, Claude le,** *see* LE JEUNE.

**Jeune France, La** (Fr.), lit. 'Young France'. Group of French composers – Baudrier, Jolivet, Lesur and Messiaen – who united in 1936 with aim of championing 'sincerity, generosity and artistic good faith'. Claimed music should carry 'personal message', aim not then generally in vogue.

**Jewess, The,** *see* JUIVE.

**Jew's harp,** simple instrument consisting of metal frame to which strip of metal is fixed. Frame is placed loosely between teeth and strip is twanged. Produces several harmonics, which can be made to resonate individually in mouth cavity. Originated in Asia; popular in Europe till 19th cent., when supplanted by mouth organ. Name is corruption of Dutch *jeugdtromp* (child's trumpet).

**jig,** *see* GIGUE.

**'Jig' Fugue,** *see* 'GIGUE' FUGUE.

**jingling johnny,** *see* PAVILLON CHINOIS.

**Joachim, Amalie,** née Schneeweiss (1839–98), Austrian contralto. Sang under name of Amalie Weiss until marriage to Joseph Joachim (1863), from whom she separated in 1884. Made stage debut in 1853 and in 1860s was at Hanover Opera; later devoted herself to concert work, excelling in interpretation of Schumann's songs.

**Joachim, Joseph** (1831–1907), Hungarian violinist, composer. Pupil of Mendelssohn and Schumann. Leader under Liszt of Ducal Orchestra at Weimar (1849–53); director of new Hochschule für Musik in Berlin from 1869. Founded famous quartet (1869). As soloist, most admired for performances of Bach, Beethoven, Mendelssohn and Brahms (who dedicated violin concerto to him). Own compositions incl. works for violin and orchestra, overtures, songs and cadenzas for violin concertos by Mozart, Beethoven and Brahms. Also orchestrated Schubert's *Grand Duo*.

**Jodel,** *see* YODEL.

**Johannes Affligemensis,** *see* COTTON.

**Johannes de Florentia,** *see* GIOVANNI DA CASCIA.

**Johannes de Garlandia,** *see* GARLANDE.

**Johannes de Grocheo,** *see* GROCHEO.

**Johannes de Limburgia** or **John of Limburg** (*fl* early 15th cent.), Netherlands composer, prob. resident in Italy. Wrote church music.

**Johannes de Muris,** *see* MURIS.

**John IV of Portugal** (1604–56), king of Portugal (1640–56). Composed Magnificat and several motets, and wrote *Defensa de la musica moderna* (1649).

**Johnny Strikes Up,** *see* JONNY SPIELT AUF.

**Johnson, John** (d. ?1595), English lutenist, composer. In service of Elizabeth I from 1581. Wrote works for lute.

His son, **Robert Johnson** (*c* 1583–1633), was also composer. Lutenist to James I and Charles I. Wrote music for stage *eg* 2 songs from *The Tempest,* music for instrumental ensemble, and lute music.

**Johnson, Edward** (*fl* 16th–17th cents.), English composer. Contributed 6-part madrigal 'Come, blessed byrd' to *The Triumphes of Oriana* (1601); also wrote instrumental ensemble music.

**Johnson, Robert** (*c* 1485–*c* 1560), Scottish priest and composer. Wrote church music and secular songs.

**Jolie Fille de Perth, La,** *see* FAIR MAID OF PERTH.

**Jolivet, André** (1905–74), French composer. Pupil of Varèse. Associated with JEUNE FRANCE group. Musical director of Comédie-Française from 1945. Works incl. comic opera *Dolores,* ballets, oratorio *La Verité de Jeanne,* concertos (*eg* for Ondes Martenot), orchestral, chamber and piano music, and songs.

**Jomelli, Niccolò** (1714–74), Italian composer. Trained in Neapolitan operatic tradition. Wrote *c* 70 operas. Later worked in Stuttgart, where wrote operas *Vologeso* (1766) and *Fetonte* (1768), in which he paid greater attention than earlier Neapolitan composers to dramatic expression and instrumentation, and increased amount of accompanied recitative. Anticipated Gluck in his dislike of *da capo* aria, and Rossini in his affection for orchestral crescendo. Also wrote church music.

**Jones, Daniel** (1912– ), Welsh composer, conductor. Works incl. operas *The Knife* and *Orestes*, 9 symphonies, violin concerto, incidental music for *Under Milk Wood*, orchestral tribute to Dylan Thomas, and choral and chamber music.

**Jones, Gwyneth** (1936– ), Welsh soprano. Has international reputation, esp. in roles of Leonore, Oktavian and Brünnhilde.

**Jones, Robert** (b. *c* 1577), English composer, lutenist. Wrote madrigals and lute songs – latter among most attractive of period.

**Jongen, Joseph** (1873–1953), Belgian composer, teacher, organist, pianist. Director of Brussels Conservatoire (1925–39). Works incl.

ballet, symphony and other orchestral works, concertos, chamber, choral and keyboard music and songs.

**jongleur,** medieval minstrel and entertainer. Term carried pejorative connotation.

**Jongleur de Notre Dame, Le** (Fr., *Our Lady's Juggler*), opera by Massenet, libretto by M. Léna (after story by Anatole France, in turn based on medieval miracle play). First perf. Monte Carlo, 1902.

**Jonny spielt auf** (Ger., *Johnny Strikes Up*), opera by Křenek, libretto by composer. First perf. Leipzig, 1927. Innovatory use of jazz idioms caused sensation.

**Joplin, Scott** (1868–1917), black American ragtime composer, pianist. Numerous piano rags incl. *Maple Leaf Rag*, *The Entertainer*. Wrote 2 ragtime operas, which were not successful.

**Joseph,** opera by Méhul, libretto by A. Duval. First perf. Paris, 1807. Work is based on Bible story. Title role is scored for contralto. Weber composed set of piano variations, op 28, on theme from opera.

**Joseph and his Brethren,** oratorio by Handel, libretto by T. Morell. First perf. London, 1744.

**Josephs, Wilfred** (1927– ), English composer. Works incl. *The Appointment* (TV opera), *The Nottingham Captain* (music theatre), 9 symphonies, concertos, *Requiem* and other choral works, and chamber music.

**Joshua,** oratorio by Handel, libretto by T. Morell. First perf. London, 1748.

**Josquin des Prés** or **Deprez** (Lat., Jodocus Pratensis) (*c* 1440–1521), Flemish composer, most celebrated of his day. Worked in Milan (1459–79), Papal Chapel (till 1494), and Cambrai (1495–9). From *c* 1500 in Paris in service of Louis XII, then worked in Ferrara from 1503. Towards end of life became Provost of Condé. Composed *c* 30 Masses, *c* 50 motets and *c* 70 *chansons*. In his style he developed some of features which distinguish music of Renaissance from that of later Middle Ages: use of imitation, momentary division of choir into contrasting groups, and more expressive treatment of words. Music combines consummate use of artifice with widest range of expression and feeling.

**Josten, Werner** (1885–1963), American composer, conductor, b. Germany. Settled in US (1921). Works incl. ballets, 2 *concerti sacri*, symphony, and other orchestral works, and vocal and chamber music.

**jota,** Spanish dance from Aragon in moderately fast 3/4 time accompanied by castanets.

**Jour d'Eté à la Montagne** (Fr., *Summer Day on the Mountain*), suite of 3 orchestral pieces by d'Indy, op 61 (1905).

**Judas Maccabaeus,** oratorio by Handel, libretto by T. Morell. First perf. London, 1747.

**Juive, La** (Fr., *The Jewess*), opera by Halévy, libretto by A.E. Scribe. First perf. Paris, 1835. Story Concerns 'Jewess' who, as she is immersed in a vat of boiling water on the orders of the 15th-cent.

Cardinal Brogni, reveals that she is in fact the cardinal's own daughter.

**Julius Caesar [in Egypt]** (It., *Giulio Cesare in Egitto*), opera by Handel, libretto by N. F. Haym. First perf. London, 1724.

**Jullien, Gilles** (*c* 1650–1703), French organist, composer. Published *Livre d'orgue* (1690).

**Junge Lord, Der,** *see* YOUNG LORD.

**Jungfernquartette,** *see* RUSSIAN QUARTETS.

**Juon, Paul** (1872–1940), Russian composer. Pupil of Taneyev and Arensky. Later settled in Germany. Works incl. 2 symphonies, 3 violin concertos, and chamber music.

**Jupiter Symphony,** name given to Mozart's symphony no 41 in C, K551 (1788).

**just intonation,** system of tuning to pure 'natural' scale (*see* TEMPERAMENT), theoretically possible in singing and on bowed string instruments, but not on instruments with fixed pitches which use EQUAL TEMPERAMENT.

# K

**K,** with number following refers to (1) catalogue of Mozart's works compiled by Ludwig von Köchel; (2) catalogue of Domenico Scarlatti's works compiled by Ralph Kirkpatrick.

**Kabalevsky, Dmitri Borisovich** (1904– ), Russian composer. Pupil of Miaskovsky and Scriabin. Works, mainly in diatonic idiom, incl. 4 symphonies, 3 piano concertos, ballets, operas *eg Colas Breugnon* (1938), *Invincible* (1948) and *The Sisters* (1967), piano music and songs.

**Kade, Otto** (1819–1900), German writer on music. Most important publications were vol. of musical examples (supplement to Ambros's *Geschichte der Musik*), and *Die altere Passionskomposition bis zum Jahre 1631* (1892).

**Kadenz** (Ger.), (1) cadence; (2) cadenza.

**Kadosa, Pál** (1903– ), Hungarian pianist, composer. Pupil of Kodály. By his piano recitals and work as composer has done much to further cause of contemporary music. Compositions incl. orchestral, choral and piano music.

**Kagel, Mauricio** (1932– ), Argentinian composer, conductor, director. Resident in West Germany from 1957. Much of his music uses electronic instruments, tapes, aleatory techniques, and latterly has involved highly visual and theatrical style, using *eg* gymnasts and dancers.

**Kaiserlied** (Ger.), *see* EMPEROR'S HYMN.

**Kaiserquartett** (Ger.), *see* EMPEROR QUARTET.

**Kajanus, Robert** (1856–1933), Finnish conductor, composer. Close friend of Sibelius. Founded Philharmonic Society Orchestra, Helsinki (1882). Pioneered appreciation of Finnish music abroad. Compositions incl. several orchestral and choral works.

**Kalbeck, Max** (1850–1921), German music critic, poet. Best known for biography of Brahms (4 vols., 1904–14).

**Kalevala,** *see* LEGENDS.

**Kalinnikov, Vassily Sergeyevich** (1866–1901), Russian composer. Best known for symphony no 1 in G minor.

**Kalischer, Alfred Christlieb Salomo Ludwig** (1842–1909), German poet, critic, teacher. Devoted much of life to study of Beethoven, publishing complete edition of Beethoven's letters.

**Kalkbrenner, Friedrich Wilhelm Michael** (1785–1849), German pianist, composer. Lived in Paris and London. Had great reputation as pianist. As composer, now remembered only for *Etudes*.

**Kalliwoda, Johan Václav** (1801–66). Czech violinist, composer. Compositions incl. 7 symphonies.

**Kamieński, Lucjan** (1885– ), Polish composer, critic, resident in Canada after 1957. Compositions, written under pseud. of Dolega-

Kamienski, incl. comic opera *Damy i Huzary* (Ladies and Hussars, 1932), *Symphonia paschalis* for chorus and orchestra, and many songs, to German and Polish words.

**Kamieński, Maciej** (1734–1821), the first Polish opera composer. His *Nedza Uszczesliwiona* (Misery Contended, 1778) was followed by 7 others. Also wrote church music and cantata for unveiling of monument to Sobieski.

**Kaminski, Heinrich** (1866–1946), German composer. Works, serious in character and polyphonic in style, incl. operas and choral, chamber and organ music.

**Kammenyi Gost,** *see* STONE GUEST.

**Kammer** (Ger.), chamber, room. *Kammermusik*, chamber music. *Kammersymphonie*, chamber symphony.

**Kammerton** (Ger.), 'chamber pitch':

(1) PITCH of orchestral instruments in 17th, 18th cents. in Germany, substantially lower than CHORTON, to which older organs were tuned;

(2) in modern Germany = standard pitch (Fr., *diapason normal*), according to which A in middle of treble clef is established at 440 cycles per second.

**Kapellmeister** (Ger.; Fr., *maître de chapelle*; It., *maestro di cappella*; Sp., *Maestro de capilla*), lit. 'master of the chapel', *ie* director of music to monarch, prince, bishop or nobleman. Term *Kapellmeistermusik* is used contemptuously by German writers to describe music which is correct but lacking in invention.

**Karajan, Herbert von** (1908– ), Austrian conductor. International career began in 1950s, when worked with Philharmonia Orchestra in London; in 1955 became conductor of Berlin Philharmonic. Also musical director of Vienna State Opera (1957–64), founder of Salzburg Easter Festival. Outstanding exponent of Beethoven, Brahms, Schumann, Wagner, Verdi, Bruckner and Richard Strauss.

**Karel, Rudolf** (1880–1945), Czech composer. Pupil of Dvořák. Works incl. operas, and orchestral, chamber and piano music. Died in Nazi concentration camp.

**Karelia,** overture, op 10, and orchestral suite, op 11, by Sibelius (1893).

**Karg-Elert, Sigfrid,** orig. Sigfrid Karg (1877–1933), German composer, organist, pianist. Works incl. many songs and chamber and piano music, but best known for organ works, often extremely elaborate and characterized by over-lush chromaticism.

**Kassation** (Ger.), CASSATION.

**Kastagnetten** (Ger.), castanets.

**Kastner, Jean Georges** (1810–67), Alsatian composer, writer on music. Compositions incl. 9 operas and much popular music. Published books on instrumentation, harmony, counterpoint, military music, and tutors for various instruments.

**Kastner, Macario Santiago** (1908– ), Portuguese pianist, harpsichordist, musicologist, b. England. Has travelled widely as recitalist, and published editions of old Spanish and Portuguese keyboard music. Has also written on history of Spanish and Portuguese music.

**Katchen, Julius** (1926–69), American pianist, b. Russia. Esp. associated with music of Brahms.

**Katerina Ismailova,** opera by Shostakovich, orig. entitled *Lady MacBeth of Mzensk*, libretto by A. Preiss and composer (after novel by Leskov). First perf. Moscow, 1934. Condemned at time by authorities as 'leftist mess', but has now won acceptance.

**Katya Kabanová,** opera by Janáček, libretto by V. Cervinka (based on play by Ostrovsky). First perf. Brno, 1921. Story is domestic tragedy.

**Kaun, Hugo** (1863–1932), German composer. Conducted male-voice choirs in Milwaukee, US (1884–1901). Works incl. pieces for male-voice choir, 3 symphonies, piano concerto, 4 string quartets, piano quintet, 2 piano trios and 4 operas.

**kazoo,** *see* MIRLITON.

**Kegelstatt-Trio** (Ger., 'Skittle-ground Trio'), trio for clarinet, viola and piano by Mozart, K498 (1786). So named because Mozart composed it while playing skittles.

**Keilberth, Joseph** (1908–68), German conductor. Conducted at Karlsruhe, Dresden and Bayreuth, eventually becoming musical director of Bavarian State Opera, Munich, where became famous for performances of Richard Strauss.

**Keiser, Reinhard** (1674–1739), German composer. Long involved with Hamburg opera; later in service of King of Denmark. Wrote *c* 120 operas, much church music and other vocal and instrumental works. Music, melodious and expressive, was extremely popular.

**Keller, Hermann** (1885– ), German organist, editor, teacher. Pupil of Reger. Published books on organ music and organ-playing, and edited several of Bach's keyboard works, Buxtehude's organ works, Frescobaldi's *Fiori musicali, etc.*

**Kelley, Edgar Stillman** (1857–1944), American composer, critic. Works incl. comic opera *Puritania* (1892), 2 symphonies (*Gulliver* and *New England*), incidental and chamber music, and songs.

**Kellner, Johann Peter** (1705–72), German organist, composer. Admirer of Bach and Handel, whom he knew personally. Compositions incl. keyboard works, church cantatas, and an oratorio.

**Kelly, Bryan** (1934– ), English composer. Works incl. children's operas *Herod, do your worst* (1968) and *The Spider Monkey Uncle King* (1971), *The Tempest Suite* and other orchestral works, *Latin Magnificat* and other choral works, and piano and organ music.

**Kelly, Michael** (1762–1826), Irish tenor, composer. Friend of Mozart; sang in first perf. of *Figaro* (1786). Wrote music for many stage productions.

**Kelway, Joseph** (*c* 1702–82), English organist, harpsichordist. Pupil of Geminiani. Gave harpsichord lessons to Queen Charlotte. His elder brother, **Thomas Kelway** (*c* 1695–1744), was organist and composer. Wrote anthems and services.

**Kempe, Rudolf** (1910–76), German conductor. Musical director of

Dresden State Opera (1949–52), then of Bavarian State Opera (1952–4). Had flair esp. for music of Richard Strauss. Also conducted Munich Philharmonic, Royal Philharmonic in Britain, and B.B.C. Symphony Orchestra.

**Kempff, Wilhelm** (1895– ), German pianist. Internationally renowned, esp. for sensitive interpretations of Beethoven, Schubert and Schumann. Has also composed 2 operas, ballets, symphonies and concertos for piano and violin.

**Kennedy-Fraser, Marjorie** (1857–1930), Scottish singer, collector of Hebridean songs. Publications incl. *Songs of the Hebrides* (3 vols., 1909–21). Also wrote libretto for Bantock's opera *The Seal Woman* (1924), which introduces Hebridean melodies.

**Kent bugle,** *see* KEY BUGLE.

**Kentner, Louis** (1905– ), British pianist, b. Hungary. Settled in Britain in 1935. Distinguished exponent of Liszt. Soloist in first perf. of Bartók's 2nd piano concerto (1933).

**Kerle, Jacob van** (1532–91), Flemish organist, composer. Cathedral organist at Augsburg (1568–75). Also worked in Italy, Flanders and Prague. Compositions consist of polyphonic church music, incl. setting of special prayers for Council of Trent (1562).

**Kerll, Johann Caspar** (1627–93), German organist, composer. Works incl. several operas, and church and keyboard music. Handel adapted one of his organ canzonas for *Israel in Egypt*.

**Kertész, István** (1929–73), Hungarian conductor. Worked with London Symphony Orchestra and Cologne Opera. Gifted exponent of Bartók, Kodály and Dvořák.

**kettledrum,** *see* TIMPANI.

**key,** (1) on piano, harpsichord, organ *etc*, one of series of balanced levers operated by fingers which control mechanism for producing sound (Fr., *touche*; Ger., *Taste*; It., *tasto*); *see* KEYBOARD;

(2) on woodwind instruments, metal lever operated by finger which opens or closes one or more soundholes (Fr., *clef*; Ger., *Klappe*; It., *chiave*);

(3) term used to indicate precise tonality of music which uses as its basic material one of major scales and accepts certain relationships between notes of scale and chords built on them (Fr., *ton, tonalité*; Ger., *Tonart*; It., *tonalita*). These relationships have not remained constant, but acceptance of tonic chord (triad on first note of scale) as base or centre is fundamental to conception of key. Keys are of 2 kinds – *major* and *minor* – according to whether they are based on notes of major or minor scale. In all major keys, relationships between notes of scale and chords built on them are exactly the same; the only difference is one of pitch. The same applies to minor keys.

In spite of this identity keys appear to have associations for composers, who frequently use same key to express similar mood. Reasons for this have never been satisfactorily established. Contributing factor in orchestral music is undoubtedly fact that some keys appear brighter than others because they employ open notes of string instruments, thus increasing resonance.

Key of piece of music is partly indicated by KEY SIGNATURE, unless qualified by ACCIDENTALS. For listener, however, key has to be established by harmony. In most 18th-cent. works this is done unequivocally by clear statement of tonic chord (or note) and chords (or notes) associated with it (esp. dominant). Later composers often used deliberately ambiguous openings.

Structural unity makes it desirable that piece or movement should end in key in which it began. Common exceptions to this principle are: (i) piece which began in minor key may end in major key with same tonic (*eg* C major instead of C minor), or even vice versa; (ii) movement which is going to lead directly to another movement may end in key other than tonic in order to provide satisfactory transition.

Relationship between keys varies. Examples of close relationship are:

(i) major and minor keys having same tonic, *eg* C major and C minor. Relationship is strengthened by fact that both keys may have same dominant chord, through sharpening of seventh of scale. C major is said to be *tonic major* of C minor; C minor is *tonic minor* of C major;

(ii) major and minor keys using same series of notes (thus having same key signature) but with different tonic, *eg* C major and A minor, in which tonic in former is C, and in latter A. C major is said to be *relative major* of A minor; A minor is *relative minor* of C major;

(iii) keys whose tonic chords have close association, *eg* in key of C major, chords of F major (subdominant) and G major (dominant) are closely related to tonic chord; and in F major, chord of C major is dominant chord, and in G major it is subdominant.

Relationships between keys facilitate MODULATION from one key to another. Such modulation is normal in any but simplest and shortest pieces. It is quite normal to have one or more sections in piece which are wholly in keys different from principal key. Establishment of different key centres for sake of contrast is basic principle of what is known as SONATA FORM. In all such divergences, principal key of piece is thought of as home base to which music must return at end. Key contrast is also used between several movements of suite, sonata or symphony.

**keyboard** (Fr., *clavier*; Ger., *Klaviatur*; It., *tastatura*), horizontal series of keys which enable performer, by means of intervening mechanism, to produce sound on piano, organ, harpsichord, clavichord *etc*. Basis of system, orig. used on organ, prob. dates from 13th cent. Earliest keyboards were diatonic (*ie* corresponding to white notes on modern keyboard), but chromatic notes had been introduced by early 14th cent. In 14th cent., keyboard was adopted for instruments with vibrating strings, whether plucked or pressed, resulting in HARPSICHORD and CLAVICHORD. On organ, keyboard played by fingers is known as manual. For sake of greater variety and contrast of tone colour organs came to be equipped with 2 manuals, as did harpsichords; some organs now have 4 but few have more. Pedal keyboard, played by feet, was in use for organ in the

15th cent., and was later adopted for harpsichord and sometimes clavichord. Practice of tuning to EQUAL TEMPERAMENT was introduced in 18th cent. On many old instruments white notes of modern keyboard were black and vice versa.

**keyboard music,** generic term for all music written for keyboard instruments, esp. music up to and including time of Bach and Handel, much of which was not designed specifically for any particular keyboard instrument.

**key bugle** (Fr., *bugle à clefs*; Ger., *Klappenhorn*; It., *cornetta a chiavi*), bugle with holes pierced in tube and controlled by keys, patented by Joseph Halliday, 1810. Also called Kent bugle. In course of 19th cent., superseded by brass instruments with valves – flugelhorn and cornet.

**key note,** same as TONIC.

**key signature,** sharps or flats placed at beginning of composition to indicate key. Thus key of A major employs following scale: A–B–C sharp–D–E–F sharp–G sharp–A; since F sharp, G sharp and C sharp are normal notes in key, key signature for A major is:

Same key signature is used for relative minor of A major – F sharp minor.

Modulation and temporary employment of another key do not necessarily involve change of key signature – alterations can be indicated by ACCIDENTALS. However, extended passage in new key is best given new key signature. Key signature of piece is repeated at beginning of each stave and remains in force until new key signature is indicated (usually preceded by double bar). Keys with sharps in signature are called *sharp keys*, and those with flats, *flat keys* (though in 17th, 18th cents., these terms meant major and minor keys respectively). *See* tables on p. 259.

**Khachaturian, Aram Ilich** (1903–78), Russian composer, b. Armenia. Music, influenced by Armenian folk music, is written in direct and comprehensible style favoured by Soviet authorities. Works incl. symphonies, concertos for piano, violin and cello, ballets *Gayaneh* and *Spartacus*, *Song of Stalin* for chorus and orchestra, and chamber, piano and stage music.

**Khovanshchina** (Russ., *The Khovansky Affair*), opera by Mussorgsky, libretto by composer and V.V. Stassov. Completed and orchestrated by Rimsky-Korsakov. First perf. St Petersburg, 1886. Stylistically more authentic completion was made by Shostakovich.

**Khrennikov, Tikhon Nikolayevich** (1913– ), Russian composer. Works incl. 3 operas, 2 symphonies, 2 piano concertos, piano music, and songs (some to words by Robert Burns). As secretary general of Soviet Composers, in 1948 denounced Prokofiev and others for 'formalism'.

**Kidson, Frank** (1855–1926), English antiquarian. Collected and published large number of English folk songs and dances.

**Kielflügel** (Ger.), harpsichord.

**Kiene, Marie,** *see* BIGOT DE MOROGUES.

**Kienzl, Wilhelm** (1857–1941), Austrian composer. Strong admirer of Wagner. Works incl. 9 operas *eg Der Evangelimann* (The Preacher), chamber and piano music, and many songs.

**Kiesewetter, Raphael Georg** (1773–1850), German music historian. Publications incl. works on Greek and Arab music, Guido d'Arezzo and Palestrina.

**Kilpinen, Yrjö** (1892–1959), Finnish composer. Wrote orchestral and chamber works, but best known for *c* 500 imaginative songs in romantic idiom.

**Kindermann, Johann Erasmus** (1616–55), German organist, composer. Works incl. sacred and secular songs for one or more voices with instrumental accompaniment, suites for wind instruments, *canzoni* for strings, and preludes, fugues and Magnificats for organ.

**Kinderscenen** (Ger., *Scenes of Childhood*), suite of 13 easy pieces for piano by Schumann, op 15 (1838). Each piece has descriptive title.

**Kindersymphonie,** *see* TOY SYMPHONY.

**Kindertotenlieder** (Ger., Songs on the death of children), cycle of 5 songs with orchestral accompaniment by Mahler, words by F. Rückert.

**King Arthur,** 'dramatick opera' by Purcell, libretto by Dryden. First perf. London, 1691.

**King Christian II,** incidental music by Sibelius (1898) for A. Paul's play about 16th-cent. Danish King.

**King Stephen** (Ger., *König Stephan*), incidental music by Beethoven, op 117 (1811), for A. von Kotzebue's play about Stephen I of Hungary.

**Kingdom, The,** oratorio by Elgar, op 51, text from Bible. First perf. Birmingham, 1906. Second part of uncompleted trilogy of which *The Apostles* was first.

**Kinkeldey, Otto** (1878–1966), American musicologist. Most important publication is *Orgel und Klavier in der Musik des XVI Jahrhunderts* (1910).

**Kinsky, Georg Ludwig** (1882–1951), German musicologist. Best known for *History of Music in Pictures* (English edition, 1930).

**Kipnis, Alexander** (1896–1978), Russian-born bass-baritone, resident in US. Noted interpreter of Hugo Wolf and Russian songs.

**Kirbye, George** (*c* 1565–1634), English composer. Published volume of madrigals (1597) which show sensitive imagination, esp. in treatment of dissonance.

**Kirchen-** (Ger.), church. *Kirchenkantate*, church CANTATA. *Kirchenschluss*, plagal CADENCE. *Kirchensonate*, church sonata *(sonata da chiesa)*. *Kirchenton*, church (ecclesiastical) MODE.

**Kircher, Athanasius** (1602–80), Jesuit professor of natural science at Würzburg University. Left Germany in 1633; settled in Rome in

**Key signatures of major keys**

**Key signatures of minor keys**

1637. Principal work on music is *Musurgia universalis sive ars magna consoni et dissoni* (2 vols., 1650), which is often interesting but thoroughly unreliable.

**Kirchgessner, Marianne** (1770–1809), blind German musician, who made reputation as player on glass harmonica. Mozart wrote quintet (K617) and solo Adagio (K356) for her.

**Kirchner, Theodor** (1823–1903), German composer, pianist, organist, conductor. Mainly composed works for piano solo or piano duet.

**Kirkman,** firm of harpsichord and piano-manufacturers, founded in London by Jacob Kirkman (orig. Kirchmann), a German who settled there before 1739. Began to make pianos *c* 1775. Amalgamated with Collard in 1896.

**Kirkpatrick, Ralph** (1911– ), American harpsichordist, musicologist. Catalogued works of Domenico Scarlatti – now referred to by Kirkpatrick (or 'K') numbers.

**Kirnberger, Johann Philipp** (1721–83), German composer, violinist, teacher. Pupil of Bach. Composed large number of vocal and instrumental works, and published several technical works.

**Kirshbaum, Ralph** (1946– ), American cellist, conductor. Plays in piano trio with Peter Frankl and György Pauk.

**Kistler, Cyrill** (1848–1907), German opera composer. Pupil of Rheinberger. Operas incl. *Kunhild* (1884), strongly influenced by Wagner, and comic *Eulenspiegel* (1889).

**Kistner,** Leipzig firm of music-publishers, orig. founded by Heinrich Albert Probst in 1823 and taken over by Karl Friedrich Kistner (1797–1844) in 1831. Business was bought by Carl and Richard Linnemann in 1919, and amalgamated with firm of Siegel in 1923, under title Fr. Kistner and C.F.W. Siegel.

**kit** (Fr., *pochette*; Ger., *Taschengeige*), miniature violin, formerly used by dancing-masters. Made either in ordinary shape of violin (from late 17th cent.) or long and narrow like REBEC (earlier form). Known from early 16th cent., and may be much older.

**Kitezh,** opera by Rimsky-Korsakov, libretto by V.I. Bielsky. First perf. St Petersburg, 1907.

**kithara,** LYRE of ancient Greece, later adopted by Romans. Had square box resonator and up to 11 gut strings. Used as accompaniment to voice and as solo instrument.

**Kitson, Charles Herbert** (1874–1944), English organist, teacher, theorist. Wrote books on counterpoint, harmony, fugue, *etc.*

**Kittel, Bruno** (1870–1948), German conductor. Held various posts in Berlin, and founded (1902) and conducted Bruno Kittel Choir.

**Kittel, Johann Christian** (1732–1809), German organist, composer. Pupil of Bach. Had considerable reputation as performer and teacher. Works incl. preludes for organ, piano sonatas, instruction book for organ (3 vols., 1801–8), and *Neues Choralbuch* for Schleswig-Holstein (1803).

**Kittl, Emmy,** *see* DESTINN.

**Kittl, Johann Friedrich** (1806–68), Czech composer. Most

successful of 3 operas was *Bianca und Giuseppe oder die Franzosen vor Nizza* (1848) with libretto by Wagner.

**Kjellstrom, Sven** (1875–1951), Swedish violinist. Founded Kjellstrom Quartet in 1911. Director of Stockholm Conservatoire (1929–40). Toured widely as soloist, often with daughter Ingrid, noted pianist and harpsichordist.

**Kjerulf, Halfdan** (1815–68), Norwegian composer. Works incl. songs, part-songs, and piano pieces.

**Klafsky, Katharina** (1855–96), Hungarian operatic soprano. Began to make name as soloist in Leipzig from 1876, and soon established herself as outstanding Wagnerian singer. Principal soprano at Hamburg Opera (1886–95); also appeared in St Petersburg, London and US.

**Klang** (Ger.), sound, sonority.

**Klangfarbenmelodie** (Ger.), term coined by Schoenberg in *Harmonielehre* (1911) to describe form of composition in which varying tone colours are applied to single level or pitch, or to different pitches, thus establishing timbre as important structural element.

**Klappenhorn** (Ger.), KEY BUGLE.

**Klarinette** (Ger.), clarinet.

**Klaviatur** (Ger.), keyboard.

**Klavier** (Ger., also *Clavier*),
(1) keyboard;
(2) keyboard instruments with strings, *ie* clavichord, harpsichord or piano (*see* CLAVIER, HAMMERKLAVIER);
(3) specifically, in modern German, piano.

**Klavierauszug** (Ger.), piano reduction, piano arrangement.

**Klebe, Giselher** (1925– ), German composer. Pupil of Blacher. Works, sometimes using serialism, incl. several operas *eg Die Räuber* and *Figaro lässt sich scheiden*, and orchestral and chamber music.

**Kleber, Leonhard** (*c* 1490–1556), German organist. Compiled Ms collection of organ music in tablature.

**Kleiber, Erich** (1890–1956), Austrian conductor. As director of Berlin State Opera, gave world première of Berg's *Wozzeck* (1925). Expelled from Germany by Nazis, and became Argentinian citizen. After WWII worked in Germany, Austria and London. Fine, unmannered exponent of classics, and outstanding exponent of operas of Mozart and Strauss.

His son, **Carlos Kleiber** (1930– ), is also conductor. Became Austrian citizen in 1980. Has held various posts with leading opera companies in Austria, Germany and Switzerland. Has also conducted at Bayreuth, Covent Garden and La Scala.

**Kleine Nachtmusik, Eine** (Ger., A Little Serenade), work for string orchestra or string quintet by Mozart, K525 (1787).

**Kleine Orgelmesse** (Ger., Little Organ Mass), name given to Haydn's *Missa brevis Sti. Joannis de Deo* in B (*c* 1775). So called because of part for organ *obbligato*. *See* GROSSE ORGELMESSE.

**Kleine Trommel** (Ger.), side drum.

**Kleinmichel, Richard** (1846–1901), German pianist, composer. Chiefly remembered for simplified piano scores of Wagner's operas. Composed 2 operas, 2 symphonies, and chamber and piano music.

**Klemperer, Otto** (1885–1973), German conductor, composer. Musical director of Kroll Opera, Berlin (1927–31), where presented many important modern works. Joined Berlin State Opera (1931), but expelled from Germany by Nazis (1933). Went to US where conducted Los Angeles Philharmonic until 1939. Returned to Europe after WWII, devoting himself to classics. Became permanent conductor of Philharmonic (later New Philharmonic) Orchestra, London. Esp. noted as interpreter of Beethoven and Brahms, and for magisterial sense of structure.

**Klenau, Paul von** (1883–1946), Danish composer, conductor. Long resident in Germany. Works incl. 7 operas *eg Gudrun auf Island* (1924), ballet, 6 symphonies, orchestral, vocal, chamber and piano music, and songs.

**Klengel, August Alexander** (1783–1852), German composer. Pupil of Clementi. Best known for *Canons et Fugues dans tous les tons majeurs et mineurs*. Other works incl. 2 piano concertos and other works for piano.

**Klengel, Julius** (1859–1933), German cellist, composer. Principal cello of Gewandhaus Orchestra, Leipzig (1881–1924); also taught at Leipzig Conservatorium. Compositions incl. 3 cello concertos and double concerto for violin and cello.

His brother, **Paul Klengel** (1854–1935), was conductor and composer. Held conducting posts at Leipzig, Stuttgart, New York and other cities. Compositions incl. chamber music and songs.

**Klindworth, Karl** (1830–1916), German pianist, conductor. Worked in London, Moscow and Berlin, where founded music school. Made piano scores of Wagner's *Ring* and edited complete works of Chopin. His adopted daughter Winifred married Siegfried Wagner.

**Klose, Friedrich** (1862–1942), German composer. Pupil of Bruckner. Works, influenced by Bruckner, incl. Mass in D minor, 'dramatic symphony' *Ilsebill*, choral and chamber music, and songs.

**Klose, Hyacinthe Eleonore** (1808–80), French clarinettist, b. Corfu. Taught at Paris Conservatoire (1839–68), and successfully adapted to clarinet the Boehm system orig. designed for flute. Composed number of works for his instrument, and instruction books for clarinet and saxophone.

**Klotz,** family of violin-makers active in Mittenwald, Bavaria, in 17th, 18th cents.

**Klughardt, August Friedrich Martin** (1847–1902), German conductor, composer. Works incl. 4 operas, 3 oratorios and other choral works, 4 symphonies, 6 overtures, concertos for oboe, violin and cello, and chamber music.

**Knab, Armin** (1881–1951), German composer. Compositions incl. unaccompanied choral works, expressing enthusiasm for Nazism, and solo songs, combining simplicity of structure with extreme sensibility.

**Knaben Wunderhorn, Des** (Ger., Youth's Magic Horn), collection of German folk poems, several of which were set by Mahler as solo songs, 9 with piano and 13 with orchestra. Settings also appear in Mahler's 2nd, 3rd and 4th symphonies.

**Knarre** (Ger.), rattle.

**Knecht, Justin Heinrich** (1752–1817), German composer, organist. Numerous compositions incl. symphony entitled *Le Portrait musical de la nature,* with similar programme to Beethoven's Pastoral Symphony, which it predates.

**Kneifend** (Ger.), plucking, *ie pizzicato.*

**Kniegeige** (Ger.), viola da gamba.

**Knipper, Lev Konstantinovich** (1898–1974), Russian composer. Works incl. 3 operas *eg Candide*, several symphonies, orchestral suites on folk melodies, chamber music and songs.

**Knorr, Iwan** (1853–1916), German composer, teacher. Pupils incl. Cyril Scott, Balfour Gardiner and Roger Quilter. Works incl. songs and piano pieces.

**Koanga,** opera by Delius, libretto by C.F. Keary (after George Washington Cable's novel *The Grandissimes*). First perf. (in German) Elberfeld, 1904. Story concerns African chief, transported as slave to America. Orchestral interlude, *La Calinda*, is sometimes performed separately.

**Köchel, Ludwig Alois Friedrich, Ritter von** (1800–77), Austrian musical biographer. Made catalogue of Mozart's works (1862, revised by Alfred Einstein, 1937). Numbering (still used) is preceded by letter K, or KV – *Köchel-Verzeichnis* (Köchel Index).

**Kodály, Zoltán** (1882–1967), Hungarian composer. Along with Bartók and Ligeti, one of 3 major Hungarian composers of this century. Studied at Budapest Conservatory, where taught composition from 1907; deputy director from 1919. In 1930 became lecturer at Budapest University. Like Bartók, active in collecting and publishing Hungarian folk songs, which had decided influence on his work. Made no striking break with tradition in his music, which is marked by passionate sincerity and willingness to incorporate elements from folksong.

Principal compositions:

(1) Ballad operas: *Háry János* (1926), *Székely Fonó* (The Spinning Room of the Szekelys, 1932), *Czinka Panna* (1948);

(2) Choral works: *Psalmus Hungaricus* (1923), *Budavari Te Deum* (1936), *Missa brevis* (1945), miscellaneous works for mixed voices, male voices and children's choirs;

(3) Orchestra: Suite from *Háry János*, *Dances of Marosszék* (1930), *Dances of Galánta* (1933), *Peacock Variations* (1939), concertos for orchestra (1943), viola (1947) and string quartet (1947);

(4) Chamber music: 2 string quartets (1908, 1917), cello sonata (1910), duo for violin and cello (1914), sonata for cello solo (1917).

Also wrote piano pieces, songs, arrangements of folk songs, and music for children.

**Koechlin, Charles** (1867–1950), French composer. Pupil of Fauré and Massenet. Works, often very original, incl. 3 string quartets, piano quintet, sonatas for various instruments, many piano pieces and songs, ballets, and small group of orchestral works, some inspired by Kipling's *Jungle Book*. Influence of refined, austere and disciplined style on pupils, *eg* Poulenc, was very marked. Also wrote textbooks.

**Köhler, Christian Louis Heinrich** (1820–86), German composer, conductor, teacher. Composed 3 operas and ballet, but best known for numerous piano works, incl. studies and other educational music.

**Kolisch, Rudolf** (1896– ), Austrian violinist. Pupil of Schreker and Schoenberg. Founded Kolisch Quartet (1922–39), which rapidly gained international reputation for performances (without music) of many modern works. In 1942 became leader of Pro Arte Quartet.

**Koloratur** (Ger.), *see* COLORATURA.

**Königen von Saba, Die,** *see* QUEEN OF SHEBA.

**Königskinder** (Ger., *Children of the King*), opera by Humperdinck, libretto by E. Rosmer (pseud. of E.B. Porges). First perf. New York, 1910. Was orig. play with musical accompaniment; first perf. Munich, 1897.

**Kontakte,** 'dramatic structure' by Stockhausen for electronic sounds, piano and percussion. First perf. at London Proms, 1968.

**Kontrabass** (Ger.), double bass. Also used as prefix to denote instruments octave lower than normal bass members of family, *eg Kontrabassposaune*, double bass trombone.

**Kontrafagott** (Ger.), double bassoon.

**Kontretanz** (Ger.), country dance. *See* CONTREDANSE.

**Konzert** (Ger.), (1) concert; (2) concerto.

**Konzertmeister** (Ger.), principal 1st violin in orchestra.

**Konzertstück,** *see* CONCERTINO (2).

**Koppel, Herman** (1908– ), Danish composer. Estab. reputation with *The Psalms of David* (1949), one of series of choral works written in wake of WWII. Other works, in vigorous, traditional idiom, incl. opera *Macbeth,* 5 symphonies, 4 piano concertos and other orchestral works, and chamber and instrumental music.

**Kornett** (Ger.), modern cornet.

**Korngold, Erich Wolfgang** (1897–1957), Austrian composer, b. Moravia. Showed enormous precocity as child. Prolific composer of chamber and orchestral music incl. violin concerto and symphony in F sharp; also wrote operas *eg The Dead City* (1920). Went to US in 1938, and wrote much film music for Hollywood.

**Köselitz, Johann Heinrich,** *see* GAST.

**Kosleck, Julius** (1835–1905), German trumpeter. In 1884 introduced trumpet in A, with 2 valves, on which he performed with considerable success. In 1894 this trumpet was superseded by trumpet in high D, produced by Belgian firm of Mahillon.

**Kotter, Hans** (1485–1541), Alsatian organist. Worked in Freiburg,

Switzerland (1514–30). His collection of organ pieces in tablature is important source.

**Kotzeluch, Leopold Anton,** *see* KOZELUCH.

**Koussevitsky, Serge,** orig. Sergey Alexandrovich Kussevitsky (1874–1951), Russian conductor. Appointed conductor of Boston Symphony Orchestra (1924) and settled in US. Held post till 1949, bringing orchestra to peak of perfection and presenting many first performances of important works. Encouraged many younger composers, and estab. Koussevitsky Music Foundation as means of sponsorship.

**Koven, Henry Louis Reginald de** (1859–1920), American composer. Successful composer of operettas esp. *Robin Hood* (1890), but less so with serious operas *eg The Canterbury Pilgrims* (1917).

**Kox, Hans** (1926– ), Dutch composer. Pupil of Henk Badings. Works incl. *Concertante Music* for horn, trumpet, trombone and orchestra (1956), concertos for violin, 2 violins and piano, and song cycle *Chansons cruels.*

**Kozeluch, Leopold Anton,** orig. Koželuh (1752–1818), Czech composer. In Vienna from 1778. Works incl. operas, oratorio, symphonies, concertos for piano, 2 pianos, cello, clarinet and basset horn, and chamber and piano music.

**Kraft, Anton** (1752–1820), Austrian composer, cellist, b. Bohemia. Member of Esterházy Orchestra under Haydn (1778–90). Wrote mostly for cello; theory that he composed Haydn's cello concerto in D is now discredited.

**kräftig** (Ger.), vigorously.

**Krakowiak** (Fr., *cracovienne*), Polish dance (named after city of Cracow) in lively 2/4 time with syncopated accents.

**Kramer, Arthur Walter** (1890–1969), American composer, critic. Editor of *Musical America* (1929–36), and managing director of Galaxy Music Corporation. Compositions, for wide variety of vocal and instrumental resources, are numerous.

**Kraus, Joseph Martin** (1756–92), German composer, conductor. Spent much of life in Sweden. Works incl. 4 symphonies, overtures, chamber music, and sacred and secular vocal works.

**Kraus, Lili** (1908– ), Hungarian pianist. Pupil of Bartók and Schnabel. Interned by Japanese in WWII. Took British citizenship during tour of New Zealand. Noted for performances of Mozart, Schubert and modern music. Worked in duo with violinist Szymon Goldberg.

**Krauss, Clemens** (1893–1954), Austrian conductor. Closely associated with music of friend Richard Strauss.

**Krauss, Marie Gabrielle** (1842–1906), Austrian operatic soprano. Appeared in Vienna, Paris, Naples, Milan and St Petersburg. Great-aunt of Clemens Krauss.

**Krebs, Johann Ludwig** (1713–80), German composer, organist. Pupil of Bach. Works incl. *Klavierübungen* for organ, trio sonatas for flute, violin and continuo, flute sonatas, and concerto and preludes for harpsichord.

**Krebs, Karl August** (1804–80), German composer, conductor. Wrote several operas, incl. *Agnes Bernauer* (1833).

**Krebsgang** (Ger.), term for composition that sounds the same when played forwards or backwards.

**Krebskanon** (Ger.), crab CANON.

**Krehbiel, Henry Edward** (1854–1923), American music critic. Worked for *Cincinnati Gazette* and *New York Times*. Books incl. revised edition of Thayer's *Life of Beethoven* (1921), *Studies in Wagnerian Drama* (1891), *How to Listen to Music* (1897), *Music and Manners in the Classical Period* (1898), *Chapters of Opera* (3 vols., 1908–19), and *Afro-American Folksongs* (1914).

**Kreisler, Fritz** (1875–1962), Austrian violinist, composer. Acquired world-wide reputation by brilliance and sophistication of his playing. Gave first perf. of Elgar's violin concerto (1910). Later settled in US. Composed operettas, string quartet, and series of pastiche pieces which (until 1935) he passed off as works of various 17th, 18th-cent. composers *eg* Pugnani.

**Kreisleriana** (Ger.), suite of 8 piano pieces by Schumann, op 16 (1838, rev. 1850). Dedicated to Chopin. Name derives from pseud. used by E. T. A. Hoffmann.

**Krejčí, Iša** (1904–68), Czech composer. Works, in style similar to that of Martinů, incl. comic opera *The Revolt at Ephesus* (1943, after Shakespeare's *Comedy of Errors*), 3 symphonies and other orchestral works, and 3 string quartets.

**Křenek, Ernst** (1900– ), Austrian composer, conductor, pianist of Czech origin. Studied with Schreker. First wife was Mahler's daughter Anna. Emigrated to US (1938). Compositions show various styles. In 1920s became interested in jazz idioms, used successfully in opera *Jonny spielt auf* (Johnny strikes up, 1927). In 1930s adopted 12-note method, and wrote book defending it. Opera *Karl V* (1938) incorporates cinema effects, speech and pantomime within atonal framework. Probably a romantic at heart, as song-cycle *Reisebuch aus den österreichischen Alpen* (Travel Book from the Austrian Alps) would suggest. Latterly has made use of electronic music and aleatory ideas.

Principal compositions:

(1) Operas: *Zwingburg* (1924), *Der Sprung über den Schatten* (1924), *Orpheus und Eurydike* (1926), *Jonny spielt auf* (1927), *Schwergewicht* (*Die Ehre der Nation*, 1928), *Der Diktator* (1928), *Das geheime Königreich* (1928), *Leben des Orest* (1930), *Karl V* (1938), *Tarquin* (1950), *Dark Waters* (1954);

(2) Choral works: *Die Jahreszeiten* (4 unaccompanied choruses), 4 choruses to words by Keller, *Kantate von der Vergänglichkeit des Irdischen*, *Lamentatio Jeremiae*, *Cantata for Wartime;*

(3) Ballets: *Mammon*, *Der vertauschte Cupido*, *Eight Column Line;*

(4) Orchestra: 5 symphonies, 2 *concerti grossi*, *Kleine Symphonie*, 4 piano concertos, violin concerto, *concertino* for flute, violin, harpsi-

chord and strings, *Pot-pourri*, *Theme and thirteen variations*, *Brazilian Sinfonietta* for strings, *Exercises for a Late Hour;*

(5) Chamber music: *Symphonic Music* (9 solo instruments), 7 string quartets, 2 violin sonatas, viola sonata, unaccompanied sonatas for violin (2) and viola, unaccompanied suite for cello;

(6) Piano: 6 sonatas, 5 sonatinas, 2 suites;

(7) Song cycles: *Reisebuch aus den österreichischen Alpen*, *Fiedellieder*, *Durch die Nacht*, *Gesänge des späten Jahres*.

**Kretzschmar, Hermann,** *see* HERMENEUTICS.

**Kreutzer, Konradin** (1780–1849), German composer, conductor. Pupil of Albrechtsberger. Works incl. 30 operas *eg Das Nachtlager von Granada* (1834), oratorio, 3 piano concertos, chamber music, songs, and male-voice choruses.

**Kreutzer, Rodolphe** (1766–1831), French violinist, composer. Toured successfully as soloist, meeting Beethoven. Compositions incl. 40 operas, 19 violin concertos and much chamber music. His 40 *Etudes ou caprices* for solo violin has remained standard work.

**Kreutzer Sonata,** nickname for Beethoven's sonata for violin and piano in A, op 47 (1802–3). Dedicated to French violinist Rodolphe Kreutzer.

**Kreuz** (Ger.), sharp (lit. 'cross' – earlier form of sign).

**Kreuzflöte** (Ger.), transverse FLUTE.

**Křička, Jaroslav** (1882–1969), Czech composer. Works incl. operas *Hypolita* (1917) and *The Gentleman in White* (after Wilde's *The Canterville Ghost*).

**Krieger, Adam** (1634–66), German organist, composer. Pupil of Scheidt. Published collections of songs for up to 5 voices, and *ritornelli* for strings and continuo.

**Krieger, Johann Phillipp** (1649–1725), German composer. Wrote many operas, chamber, organ and church music, and sacred songs.

His brother **Johann Krieger** (1651–1735) was also composer. Works incl. church, organ and harpsichord music.

**Krips, Josef** (1902–74), Austrian conductor. Pupil of Weingartner. Conductor with Vienna State Opera (1933–8, 1945–50), London Symphony Orchestra (1950–4). Also worked in US. Admired exponent of Mozart, Beethoven, Bruckner and Richard Strauss.

**Krohn, Ilmari Henrik Reinhold** (1867–1960), Finnish musicologist, composer. Published collection of *c* 7000 Finnish folk songs, and theoretical works. Compositions incl. opera *Tuhotulva* (Deluge, 1928), church music and songs.

**Krönungskonzert,** *see* CORONATION CONCERTO.

**Krönungsmesse,** *see* CORONATION MASS.

**Kroyer, Theodor** (1873–1945), German musicologist. Pupil of Rheinberger. Founded series *Publikationen älterer Musik* (1926–41), wrote books on Italian madrigal and Rheinberger, and edited music by Ockeghem, Marenzio and others.

**Krumhorn** or **Krummhorn** (Ger.; Fr., *cromorne*, *tournebout*; It., *storto*, *cornamuto torto*), double reed instrument, current in Middle Ages and Renaissance. Tube was curved at end, and reed was enclosed in capsule through which player directed breath without having direct contact with reed. Made in several sizes.

**Kubelík, Jan** (1880–1940), Czech violinist, composer. Toured widely. Became naturalized Hungarian (1903). Works incl. 3 violin concertos.

His son **[Jeronym] Rafael Kubelík** (1914– ) is conductor and composer. Conductor of Czech Philharmonic (1942–8), then emigrated to Britain, and in 1950 went to US as conductor of Chicago Symphony Orchestra. Musical director of Covent Garden Opera (1955–8); conductor of Bavarian State Orchestra from 1961. In 1972 became musical director of New York Metropolitan but resigned almost immediately. Esp. associated with music of Dvořák, Janáček, Smetana and Mahler.

**Kuhlau, Daniel Friedrich** (1786–1832), German composer, flautist. Settled in Copenhagen (1810) and became court composer. Works incl. operas, instrumental music, and many songs.

**Kuhnau, Johann** (1660–1722), German organist, composer. Bach's immediate predecessor at Leipzig. Works incl. church cantatas and keyboard music. Latter is important historically, esp. his *Biblische Historien*, early examples of programme music.

**Kühnel, August** (1645–*c* 1700), German *viola da gamba* player. Active as soloist in Germany and France. Wrote sonatas and partitas for his instrument.

**Kuhreigen,** *see* RANZ DES VACHES.

**Kulenkampff, George** (1898–1948), German violinist. Well known as soloist. Lived in Switzerland from 1943.

**Kullervo,** symphonic poem for soprano, baritone, male chorus and orchestra by Sibelius, op 7. Kullervo is hero from *Kalevala,* Finnish national epic.

**Kunst der Fugue, Die,** *see* ART OF FUGUE.

**Kurth, Ernst** (1886–1946), Austrian musicologist. Resident in Switzerland from 1912. Publications incl. books on Gluck, Bruckner, and harmonic theory.

**Kusser** or **Cousser, Johann Siegmund** (1660–1727), Austrian or Hungarian composer. Lived in Paris (1674–82) where became friend of Lully; subsequently worked in Germany, and finally settled in Dublin. Compositions incl. orchestral suites modelled on French style, several operas *eg Erindo* (1693), and serenades for Queen Anne and George I (1724).

**Kussevitsky,** *see* KOUSSEVITSKY.

**Kutchka** (Russ.), lit. 'handful' – alternative name for The FIVE.

**kylisma,** *see* QUILISMA.

**Kyrie,** short for 'Kyrie eleison' (Gr.), 'Lord, have mercy'. First part of Ordinary of Mass. Only part of Mass in Greek.

# L

**l,** abbrev. of LAH.

**L,** abbrev. for 'Longo'. Letter given before number in identifying works of Domenico Scarlatti, after Alessandro Longo (1864-1945), who catalogued Scarlatti's works. Now superseded by Kirkpatrick's catalogue.

**la,** (Fr., It.), the note A; also 6th note of Guidonian hexachord. *See* SOLMIZATION.

**Labarre, Théodore** (1805–70), French harpist, composer. Wrote operas, ballets, and *Méthode* for harp.

**L'Abbé,** *see* ABBÉ.

**Labey, Marcel** (1875–1968), French composer, conductor, teacher. Pupil of d'Indy, whose style influenced his compositions. Works incl. opera and orchestral and chamber music.

**labial pipes** (Ger., *Labialpfeifen*) same as FLUE PIPES.

**Lablache, Luigi** (1794–1858), Italian-born bass singer, of French and Irish parentage. Made debut in Naples in 1812, and thereafter sang with great success all over Europe. In 1836–7 was Queen Victoria's singing-master.

**Lachner, Franz** (1803–90), German composer, conductor. Worked in Vienna (where became friend of Schubert), Mannheim and Munich. Numerous compositions in many forms, incl. 8 orchestral suites, are now forgotten.

**Lacombe, Louis Trouillon** (1818–84), French pianist, composer. Pupil of Czerny. Composed operas, dramatic symphonies, and chamber and piano music. Wrote *Philosophie et Musique* (published 1895).

**Lacrimosa** ('Ah what weeping'), traditional movt. of Latin Requiem Mass.

**lacrimoso** (It.), sad, mournful.

**Lady Macbeth of Mzensk,** *see* KATERINA ISMAILOVA.

**L'Africaine,** *see* AFRICAINE.

**Lage** (Ger.), (1) position, *eg* on stringed instrument, or of chord; (2) range of instruments or voices.

**lah,** Eng. form of It. *la* (A). In TONIC SOL-FA, 6th note (or submediant) of major scale.

**La Hale [Halle], Adam de,** *see* ADAM.

**lai** (Fr.), type of *trouvère* song closely related in form to SEQUENCE, consisting of sections of irregular length, each with melodic repetition. Single stanza could comprise one or more sections. Became more regular by 14th cent. Complete regularity was observed in *Leich*, German version of *lai*, adopted by *Minnesinger* in 14th cent.

**laissez vibrer** (Fr.), 'let it vibrate'. Direction, given to players of plucked or struck instrument, indicating that sound should not be damped but allowed to die away slowly. Opposite is *étouffez*.

**Lakmé,** opera by Delibes, libretto by E. Gondinet and P. Gille. First perf. Paris, 1883. Story concerns ill-fated love of daughter of Brahmin priest for British army officer.

**Lalande, Michel Richard de** (1657–1726), most significant French composer of church music of his time. In charge of music of Louis XIV's chapel. Wrote 42 motets for chorus and instruments, cantatas, ballets, chamber music, and pieces for solo voice.

**L'Allegro,** *see* ALLEGRO, IL PENSEROSO.

**Lalo, Victor Antoine Edouard** (1823–92), French composer of Spanish origin. Most successful work is *Symphonie espagnole* for violin and orchestra (first perf. 1875). Other works incl. 3 operas *eg Le Roi d'Ys* (1888), ballet *Namouna*, concertos, chamber music, and songs.

**Lambe, Walter** (1451–*c* 1500), English composer, one of most accomplished of his generation. Surviving compositions consist of 6 antiphons, Magnificat, and fragments.

**lambeg drum,** large double-headed bass drum. Found in Northern Ireland, where it is associated with functions of Orange Lodges.

**Lambert, Constant** (1905–51), English composer, conductor, critic. Commissioned by Diaghilev to write music for ballet *Romeo and Juliet* (first perf. 1926). Great success of setting for chorus, solo piano and orchestra without woodwind of Sacheverell Sitwell's *Rio Grande* (1929), which makes use of jazz idioms, was not repeated by later works, which do not achieve consistent style. They incl. *Music for Orchestra* (1931), masque *Summer's Last Will and Testament* (1936), ballet *Horoscope* (1938), piano concerto, piano sonata, and songs. Conducted Sadler's Wells ballet from 1937.

**lament** (Lat., *planctus*), piece of elegiac music. Early European examples may date from 7th cent. In Irish and Scottish folk music, lament is type of song or piece for bagpipes.

**Lamentations,** at Matins *(Tenebrae)* in Holy Week, first 3 lessons, from Lamentations of Jeremiah, are sung to chant.

**'Lamentation' Symphony,** nickname for Haydn's symphony no 26 in D minor, so called because contains thematic resemblances to plainsong melodies used in LAMENTATIONS. Also known as *Weihnachtssymphonie* (Ger., Christmas Symphony).

**L'Amico Fritz,** *see* AMICO FRITZ.

**Lamond, Frederic** (1868–1948), Scottish pianist. Pupil of von Bülow and Liszt, with whose style he was one of last and most famous links. Known internationally esp. for fine playing of Beethoven. Composed symphony and some chamber and piano music.

**L'Amore dei Tre Re,** *see* AMORE DEI TRE RE.

**L'Amour des Trois Oranges,** *see* LOVE OF THREE ORANGES.

**Lamoureux, Charles** (1834–99), French violinist, conductor. Founded Concerts Lamoureux in Paris (1881).

**Lampe, John Frederick** (1703–51), German composer. Went to

Dublin in 1748, and settled in Edinburgh in 1750. Composed music for plays and burlesque operas, incl. *Pyramus and Thisbe*.

**Lampugnani, Giovanni Battista** (1706–81), Italian composer, conductor. Lived in London from 1743. Works incl. operas *eg Semiramide* (1741), and trio sonatas.

**Landi, Stefano** (*c* 1590–*c* 1655), Italian composer. Wrote madrigals, monodies, church music and instrumental canzonas. His *Sant' Alessio* (1632) is important in history of opera.

**Landini** or **Landino, Francesco** (*c* 1335–97), Italian composer, organist. Most famous musician of his age. Blind from childhood. All but 13 of his 154 surviving compositions are in form of BALLATA.

**Landini Cadence, Landini Sixth,** cadential formula, named after composer Francesco Landini in which cadence note is preceded by notes a second and third below it, *ie* by seventh and sixth degrees of its scale. Appears in 14th-cent. music; widely used in 15th cent. by French and English composers.

**Ländler,** Austrian dance in slow waltz-time (though precursor of waltz). Popular in late 18th, early 19th cents. Sometimes used in works of classical period.

**Land of Hope and Glory,** *see* POMP AND CIRCUMSTANCE.

**Landon, H.C. Robbins** (1926– ), American musicologist, resident in Europe from 1947. Leading authority on Haydn, whose works he has edited. Has written books on Haydn and on Viennese classical style. His wife, **Christa Landon-Fuhrmann,** is harpsichordist and musicologist.

**Landowska, Wanda** (1877–1959), Polish-born harpsichordist, pianist. Worked near Paris from 1919, then in New York from 1940. Played important part in revival of harpsichord and its music. Falla and Poulenc wrote harpsichord concertos for her.

**Landré, Guillaume** (1905–68), Dutch composer of French descent. Works incl. opera *Jean Levecq* (after Maupassant's *The Return*), symphonies, violin concerto, and chamber music.

**Lang, Paul Henry** (1901– ), American musicologist, b. Hungary. Became editor of *Music Quarterly* in 1945. Books incl. *Music in Western Civilization* (1941, rev. 1963) and *Handel* (1966).

**Langdon, Michael** (1920– ), English bass-baritone. Principal bass at Covent Garden since 1957. Known esp. for interpretation of Baron Ochs in *Rosenkavalier*.

**Lange, Aloysia,** *see* WEBER, JOSEPHA.

**Lange, Gregor** (*c* 1540–87), German composer. Wrote Latin and German motets for 4 to 8 voices (incl. 'Vae misero mihi', remarkable for its chromaticism), and German songs.

**Langlais, Jean** (1907– ), blind French-born organist, composer. Pupil of Dupré and Dukas. In 1953 became organist at St Clotilde, Paris.

**langsam** (Ger.), slow.

**Lanier or Laniere, Nicholas** (1588–1666), English composer. Most famous of 16th, 17th-cent. family of musicians of French descent. May have been first to write recitative in England when wrote music for Jonson's masque *Lovers made Men*. Wrote music for other masques, and also cantata, songs and dialogues. Master of King's Musick from 1625.

**Lanner, Joseph Franz Karl** (1801–43), Austrian composer. First to produce Viennese dance music on large scale (200 waltzes, polkas *etc*). Founded famous dance orchestra. Partner, then rival, of Johann Strauss the Elder.

**Lantins, Arnold de** (*fl* 15th cent.), Flemish composer. Became singer in Papal chapel in 1431. Wrote sacred compositions incl. Mass, and 3-part *chansons*.

**Lantins, Hugh de** (*fl* early 15th cent.), Flemish composer. Compositions, which show that he spent some time in Italy, incl. liturgical works, Italian *canzoni*, and French *chansons*. Latter make, for their time, remarkably constant use of imitation.

**L'Apprenti Sorcier,** *see* SORCERER'S APPRENTICE.

**L'après-midi d'un faune,** *see* PRÉLUDE À L'APRÈS-MIDI D'UN FAUNE.

**largamente** (It.), broadly.

**largando,** *see* ALLARGANDO.

**large** (Lat., *maxima*), largest note in medieval MENSURAL NOTATION.

**larghetto** (It.), slow and broad, but less so than *largo*.

**largo** (It.), slow and broad.

**Largo, Handel's,** *see* OMBRA MA FUI.

**larigot** (Fr.), organ stop with open cylindrical metal pipes which sound at 19th, *ie* 2 octaves and fifth above normal (8ft) pitch.

**Lark Ascending, The,** 'romance' for violin and orchestra by Vaughan Williams (1914), inspired by poem of Meredith.

**'Lark' Quartet,** nickname of Haydn's string quartet in D, op 64, no 5 (1789). So called because of 1st violin's high, birdlike notes at start of 1st movt.

**L'Arlésienne,** *see* ARLÉSIENNE.

**Larsson, Lars-Erik** (1908– ), Swedish composer, conductor. Pupil of Berg, but uninfluenced by atonalism. Works incl. symphonies and other orchestral music, popular serenade for strings, chamber, choral and film music, and songs.

**La Rue, Pierre de** (*c* 1460–1518), Flemish composer. Disciple of Ockeghem. Wrote 31 Masses, 23 motets, and *c* 30 *chansons*.

**lasciare vibrare** (It.), *see* LAISSEZ VIBRER.

**lassú,** *see* CSÁRDÁS.

**Lassus, Roland de,** also known as Orlando di Lasso (1532–94), Netherlands composer. Most famous contemporary of Palestrina, remarkable for wide range of his forms and versatility of his expression. Choirboy at Mons (his birthplace). Taken to Italy at early age. Choirmaster at St John Lateran, Rome (1553–4). In service of Duke of Bavaria in Munich from 1556, directing his chapel from 1560. Numerous compositions incl. Masses, motets, Magnificats, Passions, psalms, Italian madrigals and *villanelles*, French *chansons*, and German choral *Lieder* and chorale-motets. Style encompasses every resource of 16th-cent. choral technique.

**Last Rose of Summer, The,** Irish air, orig. called 'The Groves of Blarney' (1790), but with new words written by Thomas Moore in 1813. Beethoven and Mendelssohn both made arrangements of the air (latter's taking form of piano fantasia), and Flotow used it in opera *Martha*.

**Last Savage, The,** comic opera by Menotti, libretto by composer. First perf. Paris, 1963. Satirizes pretensions of modern life.

**Laszlò, Magda** (1912– ), Hungarian soprano, resident in Italy from 1946. Created roles of Mother in Dallapiccola's *Il Prigioniero* and Cressida in Walton's *Troilus and Cressida.*

**La Tombelle, Fernand de** (1854–1928), French organist, composer. Pupil of Saint-Saëns. Composed orchestral, choral, organ, harmonium and chamber music, music for the theatre, and songs.

**L'Attaque du moulin,** *see* ATTAQUE DU MOULIN.

**Lattuada, Felice** (1882–1926), Italian opera composer. Works incl. latter-day *Don Giovanni.*

**lauda** (It.), Italian song of popular devotion, prob. dating from time of St Francis (1182–1226). Sung by local fraternities of *Laudisti*, 14th–18th cents. Provided one of points of departure for oratorio.

**'Laudon' Symphony,** nickname for Haydn's symphony no 69 in C (1778), composed in honour of Austrian field marshal Ernst von Laudon.

**Laute** (Ger.), lute.

**Lautenclavicymbel** (Ger.), lute-harpsichord, *ie* harpsichord with gut rather than metal strings. Used 16th–18th cents.

**Lavallée, Calixa** (1842–91), French-Canadian pianist, composer. Best known as composer of Canadian national anthem *O Canada.*

**Lawes, Henry** (1596–1662), English composer. Member of Chapel Royal; wrote coronation anthem for Charles II. Praised in poems by Milton and Herrick. Works incl. songs, music for masques *eg* Milton's *Comus*, part of music for *The Siege of Rhodes*, psalm tunes, and anthems.

His brother **William Lawes** (1602–45) was also composer. Member of Chapel Royal. Joined Royalist army, and was killed in Civil War. Wrote consort suites, anthems, psalms, songs, catches, and masque music.

**Lazarus, or the Feast of the Resurrection,** unfinished cantata by Schubert, based on sacred drama by A. Niemeyer. Work is really half oratorio, half opera. Performance of unfinished score was given after Schubert's death, though was not published until 1892.

**leader,** (1) in Britain, name for principal 1st violin of orchestra (US, concertmaster; Fr., *chef d'attaque*; Ger., *Konzertmeister*):
(2) 1st violin of string quartet or other ensemble;
(3) in US, alternative term for conductor.

**leading motif,** *see* LEITMOTIV.

**leading note** (Fr., *note sensible*; Ger., *Leitton*), seventh degree of scale, so called because of tendency to rise to ('lead to') tonic. It is semitone below tonic in major and both forms of minor scale.

**leading note chord,** chord on leading note contains diminished fifth, and is therefore discord, which is usually resolved on tonic chord. Much more often used in first inversion than in root position. Second inversion normally only occurs in 3-part writing. *See* CHORD, HARMONY.

**Le Bègue, Nicolas Antoine** (1631–1702), French organist, composer. Organist to Louis XIV in 1678. Composed works for organ and wrote *Méthode* for instrument.

**Lebewohl, Das** (Ger.), title of Beethoven's piano sonata in E, op 81a, familiarly (but wrongly) known as *Les Adieux*. Dedicated to Archduke Rudolph on his departure in 1809 from Vienna during French occupation. Titles of 3 movts. are 'Das Lebewohl', 'Die Abwesenheit' and 'Das Wiedersehen' ('Farewell', 'Absence' and 'Return').

**lebhaft** (Ger.), lively.

**Lechner, Leonhard** (*c* 1553–1606), Austrian composer. Choirboy under Lassus in Munich, and thereafter worked in Germany. One of most important and capable German composers of his time. Wrote Masses, motets, Magnificats, St John Passion, and sacred and secular songs. Edited works of Lassus.

**Leclair, Jean Marie** (1697–1764), French composer, violinist. First to adopt French instrumental style to concerto form of Vivaldi. In chamber music he shows both progressive technique and mature command of expression in writing for violin. Also composed operas and ballets. Murdered near home in Paris.

**Lecocq, Alexandre C.** (1832–1918), French composer. Pupil of Halévy. Wrote successful operettas *eg Fleur de Thé*, *La Fille de Madame Angot* and *Giroflé-Girofla*.

**ledger lines,** *see* LEGER LINES.

**Lees, Benjamin** (1924– ), American composer. Pupil of Antheil. Works incl. operas *The Oracle* (1955) and *The Guilded Cage* (1971), 3 symphonies, concertos, and works for voices and instruments.

**Leeuw, Ton de** (1926– ), Dutch composer, pianist, critic. Pupil of Messiaen and Badings. Works incl. opera *The Dream*, oratorio *Job*, and orchestral and chamber music.

**LeFanu, Nicola** (1947– ), English composer. Daughter of Elizabeth Maconchy. Pupil of Wellesz and Petrassi. Works incl. chamber opera *Dawnpath* (1977), ballet *The Last Laugh* (1972), and orchestral, choral, chamber and instrumental music.

**Lefébure-Wély, Louis J.A.** (1817–69), French organist, composer. Gained reputation as lively and inventive player and composer. Works incl. music for organ and harmonium, church and chamber music, symphonies, and opera.

**Lefebvre, Charles Edouard** (1843–1917), French composer. Won *Prix de Rome* in 1870. Composed operas, symphony and other orchestral music, and church and chamber music.

**legatissimo** (It.), as smooth as possible.

**legato** (It.), smooth. In legato bowing (Fr., *louré*), notes, though played in one bow, are each distinct and emphasized. Indicated thus:

**legatura** (It.), **légature** (Fr.), slur.

**Legend of St Elizabeth, The,** oratorio by Liszt, text by O. Roquette. First perf. Budapest (in Hungarian), 1865. Produced as opera in Weimar, 1881.

**Legend of the Czar Saltan, The** (Russ., *Skazka o Tsare Saltane*), opera by Rimsky-Korsakov, libretto by V.I. Belsky (after tale by Pushkin). First perf. Moscow, 1900.

**Legend of the Invisible City of Kitezh, The,** full title of KITEZH.

**Legends,** title of 4 symphonic poems by Sibelius, op 22 (1893–5, rev. 1900), based on Finnish national epic *Kalevala*: (1) *Lemminkäinen and the Maidens*, (2) *Lemminkäinen in Tuonela*, (3) *The Swan of Tuonela*, (4) *Lemminkäinen's Homecoming*.

**leger lines,** short lines above or below staff, used to indicate pitch of notes which lie outside it, *eg*:

**légèrement** (Fr.), lightly.

**leggero, leggiero** (It.), light.

**legno** (It.), wood. In some scores term indicates wood block. *Bacchetta di legno* is direction to percussionist to use wood-headed stick. *Col legno*, *see* BOWING.

**Legrenzi, Giovanni** (1626–90), Italian composer. Important historically. In arias of operas makes some use of short *da capo* form. Early practitioner of trio sonata. Also wrote oratorios, cantatas, ensemble sonatas and church music.

**Lehár, Franz** (orig. Ferencz) (1870–1948), Hungarian-born composer. Studied at Prague Conservatoire then conducted military bands in various cities. Settled in Vienna (1902), and became famous as composer of operettas, of which earliest and most successful was *The Merry Widow* (1905). Later works incl. *The Count of Luxembourg* (1909) and *The Land of Smiles* (1923).

**Lehmann, Lilli** (1848–1929), German soprano. Sang at Berlin Opera from 1870, and at New York Metropolitan (1885–89); associated with Mozart Festivals in Salzburg from 1905. Appeared in first perf. of Wagner's *Ring* at Bayreuth in 1876. Esp. noted for performances of Wagner and Mozart.

**Lehmann, Liza** (1862–1918), English-born soprano, composer, of English/German parentage. Works incl. operas *The Vicar of Wakefield* and *Everyman*, but best remembered for such pieces as *In a Persian Garden* (words from *Omar Khayyam*).

**Lehmann, Lotte** (1888–1976), German-born soprano. Sang both in opera house and concert hall. Particularly associated with operas of Richard Strauss, who wrote *Arabella* for her. Settled in US during Nazi era.

**Lehrstück** (Ger.), lit. 'educational play', a kind of musical drama. Written in Germany in 1920s and early 1930s to reach working-class audiences. Eisler, Hindemith and Weill were chief composers in movement, with Brecht as leading writer. Used documentary material and ideological argument. Typical works are Hindemith's *We build a town* and Weill's *The Yes-Sayer*. Used to counter Nazis till 1933. *See* UTILITY MUSIC.

**Leibowitz, René** (1913–72), Franco-Polish composer. Pupil of Ravel, Schoenberg and Webern. Champion of 12-note music. Wrote orchestral, chamber, choral and piano music, but more distinguished as theoretician.

**Leich,** see LAI.

**leicht** (Ger.), lightly.

**Leichtentritt, Hugo** (1874–1951), German-born musicologist, composer. Wrote history of motet (1908), *Musical Form* (1911), *Music History and Ideas* (1938) and *Serge Koussevitzky* (1946).

**Leidenschaft** (Ger.), passion. *Leidenschaftlich,* passionately.

**Leider, Frida** (1888–1975), German operatic soprano. Excelled in performance of Wagner. Sang in Berlin, Covent Garden, Vienna, and other European opera houses.

**Leier** (Ger.), hurdy-gurdy.

**Leigh, Walter** (1905–42), English composer. Pupil of Hindemith. Works incl. 2 comic operas, and concertino for harpsichord and strings. Killed in action in Libya.

**Leighton, Kenneth** (1929– ), English composer, pianist. Pupil of Petrassi. Works incl. symphonies, concertos for violin, viola, cello, and piano, and chamber and piano music.

**Leighton, William** (d. 1616), English composer, publisher, poet. In 1613 published *Tears or Lamentations of a Sorrowful Soul*, large collection of metrical psalms and hymns written by himself. In 1614 published, under same title, musical settings of 55 of these poems: 8 were set by himself, and the remainder by contemporary composers incl. Byrd, Bull, Dowland, Gibbons, Peerson, Weelkes, and Wilbye. 18 of the pieces are for 3 or 4 vocal parts with instrumental accompaniment; remainder are for 4 or 5 unaccompanied voices.

**Leinsdorf, Erich** (1912– ), American conductor, b. Austria. Held appointments with New York Metropolitan and Boston Symphony Orchestra (1962–9).

**leise** (Ger.), soft, gentle. *Leiser*, softer.

**Leitmotiv** (Ger.), 'leading theme'. Term first used (1887) by H. von Wolzogen in discussion of Wagner's *Götterdämmerung* for numerous recurring themes symbolizing characters, objects, ideas and emotions used in *The Ring*. Recurring themes had been used in earlier years *eg* by Mozart, and device was developed in orchestral music by Berlioz (who used term *idée fixe*), Schumann, and Liszt (who called it 'metamorphosis of themes'). Principle was adopted by others, notably Richard Strauss.

**Leitton** (Ger.), leading note.

**Le Jeune, Claude** (1528–1600), French composer. Involved in composition of MUSIQUE MESURÉE À L'ANTIQUE from 1570. Works incl. *Dix Pseaumes de David* (1564), *chansons* published in *Livre de mélange* (1585), vol. of *Airs* (1594), *Cinquante Pseaumes de David* (1602, 1608), and *Missa ad placitum* (1607).

**Lekeu, Guillaume** (1870–94), Belgian composer. Pupil of Franck and d'Indy. Composed orchestral works *eg* symphonic study after *Hamlet*, *Chant Lyrique* for chorus and orchestra, piano quartet and other chamber music. Showed great promise, but died of typhoid; some works completed by d'Indy.

**Lélio, ou le retour à la vie** (Fr., Lélio, or the return to life), monodrama by Berlioz for narrator, solo voices, chorus, piano and orchestra, op 14b. Composed as sequel to *Symphonie Fantastique*, with which it was first perf. in Paris, 1832.

**Le Maistre or Le Maître, Mattheus** (d. 1577), Dutch composer. Composed Magnificats (1577), 5-part motets (1570), Latin and German sacred music (1563, 1574), German secular songs, and quodlibets.

**Lemminkäinen,** *see* LEGENDS.

**'Leningrad' Symphony,** nickname of Shostakovich's symphony no 7, which portrays siege of Leningrad by Germans in WWII.

**lent** (Fr.), slow. *Lentement*, slowly.

**lento** (It.), slow.

**Lenya, Lotte** (1898–1981), Austrian-born singer, actress. Married to Kurt Weill. She became famous in Brecht-Weill collaborations such as *Mahagonny* and *The Threepenny Opera*. Went to US with Weill in 1933.

**Lenz, Wilhelm von** (1809–83), musical historian. Russian councillor at St Petersburg. Published book on contemporary piano-playing (1872), and collection of essays on Liszt, Chopin and others. In first of 2 books on Beethoven (1852, 1855–60), analysed Beethoven's development in terms of three periods now generally accepted.

**Leo, Leonardo** (1694–1744), Italian composer. Pupils incl. Pergolesi, Piccinni and Jommelli. Works incl. many operas *eg* serious *Demofoonte* (1733) and comic *Amor vuol sofferenza* (1739), church music, concertos, and organ and harpsichord music.

**Leoncavallo, Ruggiero** (1858–1919), Italian composer. Worked as café pianist and travelled widely. Returned to Italy and most successful opera *I Pagliacci* – classic example of Italian *verismo* style – was produced in Milan (1892). Composed operas with own librettos, *eg La Bohème*. Also wrote ballet, and symphonic poem *Serafita*.

**Leonel,** *see* POWER.

**Leoni** or **Leone** (*c* 1560–1627), Italian composer. Works incl. Masses, motets, Magnificats, psalms, *Sacrae cantiones* (1608), madrigals, and concertos in style of G. Gabrieli for 4 voices and 6 instruments.

**Leoni, Franco** (1865–1938), Italian composer. Lived in London for 22 years. Works incl. operas *Ib and Little Christina* (1901) and *L'Oracolo* (1905), 3 oratorios, and songs.

**Leoninus** or **Léonin** (*fl* late 12th cent.), French composer. Worked at Notre Dame, Paris. Notable composer of *organa*.

**Leonore,** (1) title of 3 overtures by Beethoven for opera *Fidelio*. Name is that of heroine. *No 1*, never used; *no 2*, played at first perf., 1805; *no 3*, replaced *no 2* for revised version of opera (1806). For third and final version of opera (1814), Beethoven wrote fourth overture, *Fidelio*;

(2) title of opera by Gaveaux (1798) with plot anticipating *Fidelio*;

(3) Rolf Liebermann's *Leonore 40/45* (1952) sets story during WWII.

**Leopold I** (1640–1705), Holy Roman emperor (1658–1705), composer. Wrote music for opera *Apollo deluso* (1669) by Sances and for many operas by court musician Antonio Draghi. Also wrote Masses, offices and ballet suites.

**L'Epine, Françoise Marguerite de** (d. 1746), French soprano, resident in England from early 18th cent. Appeared in association with composer Jakob Grebor, hence her contemptuous nickname 'Grebor's Peg'. Sang in opera and other dramatic representations (1703–1716). Married J.C. Pepusch.

**Leppard, Raymond** (1927– ), English conductor, musicologist, harpsichordist. Active in reviving neglected 17th-cent. Italian masterpieces. Musical director of English Chamber Orchestra from 1960, conductor of BBC Northern Symphony Orchestra (1973–80).

**Leroux, Xavier Henri Napoléon** (1863–1919), Italian composer. Settled in Paris. Pupil of Massenet. Composed operas *eg Le Chemineau* (1907), incidental music, overture, cantatas, Mass with orchestra, motets, and songs.

**Le Roy, Adrien** (*fl* 16th cent.), French lutenist, composer, music printer. From 1551 to 1571 published over 20 vols. containing original compositions and arrangements of *chansons*, psalms and dances for lute, cittern and guitar, with or without voice; these incl. collection of *airs de cour* for lute (1571). Also wrote instruction books for guitar, cittern and lute.

**Les Adieux,** *see* LEBEWOHL.

**Leschetizky, Theodor** (1830–1915), Polish-born teacher, pianist, composer. Pupil of Czerny. Toured widely as pianist. Settled in Vienna where founded famous school of piano playing and own 'method'. Pupils incl. Paderewski and Schnabel. Composed many piano pieces, and opera.

**Lescurel, Jehan de** (d. *c* 1304), French composer. In his 34 songs (all but one monophonic) was one of first composers to use FORMES FIXES in patterns which remained established throughout 14th and most of 15th cents.

**Les Six,** *see* SIX.

**lesson,** term used in England in 17th, 18th cents.; initially applied to ensemble music, but later to pieces for harpsichord or other solo instrument which would now be called suites or studies.

**Lesueur, Jean François** (1760–1837), French composer. Introduced full orchestra in Mass, causing controversy. Pupils incl. Berlioz and Gounod. In service of Napoleon and Louis XVIII. Wrote operas, oratorios, cantatas, *Te Deum* and Mass for Napoleon's coronation, *c* 30 Masses, psalms, motets, and other church music.

**Lesur, Daniel** (1908– ), French composer, organist. Co-founder of *La Jeune France* with Messiaen, Jolivet and Baudrier. Works incl. ballet *The Child and the Monster* (with Jolivet), orchestral suite, Passacaille for piano and orchestra, chamber, piano and organ music, and songs.

**Let's Make an Opera,** entertainment for children by Britten, text by Eric Crozier. First perf. Aldeburgh, 1949. Work, involving audience participation, shows preparation and performance of children's opera *The Little Sweep.*

**Leveridge, Richard** (*c* 1670–1758), English composer, bass singer. Wrote music for stage and songs *eg* 'The Roast Beef of Old England'.

**Levi, Hermann** (1839–1900), German conductor, composer. Worked in Munich (1872–96), and was esp. famous for conducting of Wagner at Bayreuth and elsewhere; in 1882 conducted première of Wagner's *Parsifal* at Bayreuth. Compositions incl. piano concerto and songs.

**Lévy,** *see* ROLAND-MANUEL.

**Lewis, Anthony** (1915– ), English musicologist, conductor, composer. Principal of Royal Academy of Music, London, from 1968. Founder and general editor of *Musica Britannica.* As conductor, has revived several neglected operas *eg* by Handel. Knighted 1972.

**Lewis, Richard** (1914– ), English tenor. Notable in opera house and concert hall. Originated role of Troilus in Walton's *Troilus and Cressida* and many other roles.

**Ley, Henry George** (1887–1962), English organist, composer. Director of music at Eton College (1926–45). Works incl. church, chamber and organ music, and songs.

**l.h.,** left hand.

**L'Héritier, Jean** (*fl* early 16th cent.), French composer. Pupil of Josquin. From 1521 worked in Rome, and later in Avignon. Works incl. motets, Magnificat and Mass.

**L'Heure Espagnole,** *see* HEURE ESPAGNOLE.

**L'Homme armé,** *see* HOMME ARMÉ.

**Liadov, Anatol Konstantinovich** (1855–1914), Russian composer, teacher, conductor. Pupil of Rimsky-Korsakov. Studied and collected Russian folk songs. Most famous works are symphonic poems *Baba Yaga* (1904), *The Enchanted Lake* (1909) and *Kikimora* (1910). Also wrote 2 orchestral scherzos, choral and piano music, and songs.

**liaison** (Fr.), lit. 'binding', *ie* (1) slur indicating smooth performance, (2) tie or bind.

**Liapunov, Sergey M.** (1859–1924), Russian composer. Pupil of Chaikovsky and Taneyev. Studied and collected Russian folk songs. Works incl. 2 symphonies, 2 concertos and *Rhapsody* for piano and orchestra, folk song settings, and piano music.

**libretto** (It.), lit. 'booklet'. Text of opera or oratorio.

**Libuše,** opera by Smetana, libretto by J. Wenzig (Czech translation by E. Špindler). Written for inauguration of Czech National Theatre, Prague (1881). Story concerns 2 brothers who are rivals in love; they are brought to trial before Libuše, Queen of Bohemia, and are ultimately reconciled.

**licenza** (It.), licence, freedom. *Con alcuna licenza,* with some freedom (in manner of performance).

**Lichfield or Lichfild, Henry** (*fl* 16th–17th cents.), English composer. Published book of 5-part madrigals in 1613.

**lié** (Fr.), lit. 'bound', *ie* (1) slurred, (2) tied.

**Liebe der Danae, Die** (Ger., The Love of Danae), opera by Richard Strauss, libretto by H. von Hoffmannsthal and J. Gregor. Completed 1940; first perf. Salzburg, 1952.

**Liebermann, Rolf** (1910– ), Swiss composer, opera administrator. Works, in style ranging from 12-note technique to jazz, incl. operas *eg Leonore 40/45, Penelope* and *The School for Wives,* and concerto for jazz band and symphony orchestra. Administrator of Hamburg State Opera (1959–72), then of Paris Opéra.

**Liebesflöte** (Ger.), flute built minor third below normal size, now obsolete.

**Liebesgeige** (Ger.), viola d'amore.

**Liebeslieder** (Ger., Songs of Love), set of 18 waltzes for vocal quartet and piano duet by Brahms, op 52 (also published for piano duet as op 52a), to words by G.F. Daumer. Second set, *Neue Liebeslieder,* issued as op 65. Some also arranged for voices and small orchestra.

**Liebesoboe** (Ger.), OBOE d'amore.

**Liebestod** (Ger., love-death), title commonly used for Isolde's death scene at end of *Tristan and Isolde.* Wagner himself, however, applied title, significantly, to love duet in Act 2.

**Liebestraum** (Ger., dream of love), title of Liszt's piano arrangements of 3 of his songs. No 3 is most famous.

**Liebesverbot, Das** (Ger., *The Love Ban*), opera by Wagner, libretto by composer (based on Shakespeare's *Measure for Measure*). First perf. Magdeburg, 1836.

**lieblich** (Ger.), 'sweet'. Applied to family of sweet-toned stops on organ which have stopped pipes, *eg Lieblichflöte.*

**Lied** (Ger., plural *Lieder*), song. Term has come to be applied esp. to German romantic songs of Schubert, Schumann, Brahms, Wolf, Strauss and others, notable for attention paid to mood of words and importance of piano part.

**Liederbuch** (Ger.), songbook.

**Lieder eines fahrenden Gesellen,** *see* SONGS OF A WAYFARER.

**Liederkranz** or **Liederkreis** (Ger.), song cycle.

**Lieder ohne Worte** (Ger.), *see* SONGS WITHOUT WORDS.

**Liederspiel** (Ger.), lit. 'song play': (1) German equivalent of ballad opera; first example, 1800;
(2) also applied to song cycle of which text involves some element of action.

**Liedertafel** (Ger.), lit. 'song table', name given to male-voice choral societies in parts of Germany and German communities in US *etc.*

**Lied von der Erde,** *see* SONG OF THE EARTH.

**Lieutenant Kizhe,** Russian film with music by Prokofiev (1933). Composer later arranged concert suite, op 60, from film music.

**Life for the Tsar, A,** *see* IVAN SUSSANIN.

**ligature,** (1) form used for writing group of notes in plainsong notation from *c* 1150;
(2) slur indicating that syllable is to be sung over group of notes;
(3) tie or bind;
(4) metal band that fixes reed to mouthpiece on clarinet, saxophone *etc.*

**Ligeti, György** (1923– ), Hungarian composer. Left Hungary in 1956 and settled in Austria and Germany. Most important Hungarian composer since Bartók. Makes imaginative use of sliding string textures and strands of wind tone. Such works as *Atmospheres, Lontano* and *Ramifications* reveal fastidious ear for detail, and though idiom is 'advanced' they are not hard to listen to. Other works incl. opera *Le Grande Macabre*, concerto for flute and oboe, chamber music, and Requiem.

**light,** adj. applied (loosely) to music and opera which is easy to listen to.

**Lilliburlero,** words of topical satire on Irish RCs and on appointment of General Talbot as Lord Lieutenant of Ireland in 1687 were set to tune called 'Quick Step' in *The Delightful Companion* (2nd edition 1686), and became most popular political ballad of the day. Set for keyboard by Purcell in *Musick's Hand-Maid* (1689), who also used it as bass of Jig in *The Gordian Knot unty'd* (1691).

**Lily of Killarney, The,** opera by Benedict, libretto by J. Oxenford and D. Boucicault (after latter's *Colleen Bawn*). First perf. London, 1862.

**Limburgia, Johannes de,** *see* JOHANNES DE LIMBURGIA.

**limma,** *see* DIESIS (1).

**Lincoln Portrait, A,** work for narrator and orchestra by Copland, based on Lincoln's letters and speeches. First perf. 1942.

**Lind, Jenny** (1820–87), Swedish soprano. Exceptional range, purity and flexibility of voice earned her nickname 'The Swedish Nightingale'. Settled in London (1847), from where she toured extensively. Confined herself to concert platform after 1849.

**Linda di Chamounix** (It., *Linda of Chamonix*), opera by Donizetti, libretto by G. Rossi. First perf. Vienna, 1842.

**Liniensystem** (Ger.), staff, stave. Usually abbrev. to *System*.

**lining out,** practice in which lines of hymn or psalm are read or sung by minister or preacher before being sung by congregation. Also called 'deaconing'.

**Linley, Thomas** (1733–95), English composer, singing teacher. Works incl. opera, incidental music (with son) for Sheridan's *The Duenna* and for many other stage works, cantatas, part songs, and ballads. Son **Thomas** (1756–78) was violinist, composer and friend of Mozart. Daughter **Elizabeth Ann** (1754–92) was famous soprano and wife of Sheridan.

**'Linz' Symphony,** nickname for Mozart's symphony no 36 in C, K425 (1783), composed and performed at Linz.

**lion's roar,** type of friction drum. Drum head is vibrated by piece of rosined string attached to it.

**Lipatti, Dinu** (1917–50), Romanian pianist, composer. Pupil of Cortot and Nadia Boulanger. One of most gifted pianists of century, with special flair for Mozart, Chopin and Schumann. Compositions, of considerable pianistic interest, incl. concertino for piano and orchestra, *symphonie concertante* for 2 pianos and strings, and sonatina for left hand. Died in Switzerland of leukaemia.

**lira** (It.), stringed instrument played with bow. In use *c* 1580–1650. Made in 2 sizes: smaller *(lira da braccio)* being played on arm, and larger *(lira da gamba)* between knees. *See* LYRA.

**lira organizzata,** *see* VIELLE ORGANISÉE.

**Lisley, John** (*fl* 16th–17th cents.), English composer. Contributed 6-part madrigal to *The Triumphes of Oriana* (1601). Nothing else is known of him.

**Listenius, Magister Nikolaus** (b. *c* 1500), German theorist. His elementary treatise *Rudimenta musicae* was published in 1533, revised under title *Musica* (1537), and appeared in many editions until 1583.

**l'istesso tempo** (It.), the same tempo.

**Liszt, Ferencz** or **Franz** (1811–86), Hungarian composer, pianist. Received piano lessons from father, steward on Esterházy estate. In 1823 went to Vienna, becoming pupil of Czerny and Salieri, and gave recital that impressed Beethoven. Lived in Paris (1823–35), absorbing many artistic influences of city, incl. music of Chopin, Berlioz and Paganini, and writing much piano music. In 1835 eloped to Switzerland with Countess d'Agoult (later known as novelist Daniel Stern); their daughter Cosima (b. 1837) was to marry Wagner. Gave concerts all over Europe (1836–47); acknowledged and adulated as greatest virtuoso of his day. In 1847 met and fell in love with Princess Sayn-Wittgenstein, wife of rich Prussian landowner, for whose sake he settled in Weimar. There was appointed court conductor and musical director, encouraging work of progressive fellow-composers *eg* Wagner. Liszt's own music flourished during this period *eg* in symphonic poems and Hungarian Rhapsodies. Lived in Rome after 1861, composing 2 oratorios, and took minor orders (giving him title Abbé). From 1869 till his death, divided time between Rome, Budapest and Weimar. In later years, received many pupils *eg* Busoni and Weingartner. Died visiting daughter Cosima in Bayreuth.

One of most stimulating musical personalities of 19th cent., Liszt was first of great piano recitalists, unmatched in sheer virtuosity. His symphonies, symphonic poems (a title he invented), concertos and piano music, though sometimes weakened by over-rhetorical style, have great importance in history of PROGRAMME MUSIC, and for their adoption and development of ideas of *idée fixe* and thematic metamorphosis. Some of later piano pieces were to prove far-reaching in their harmonic innovations.

Principal compositions:

(1) Orchestra: *Faust* Symphony (1853–61), *Dante* Symphony (1856), 12 symphonic poems, piano concertos in E flat (1857) and A (1863);

(2) Piano: *Années de Pèlerinage: Suisse* (1852), *Italie* (1848), *Troisième année* (collected 1890), 12 *Études d'Exécution Transcendante* (final form, 1854), 3 *Études de Concert* (1849), *Deux Études de Concert: Waldesrauchen, Gnomenreigen* (1849–63), *Deux Légendes* (1866), 20 Hungarian Rhapsodies (1851–86);

(3) Choral works: oratorios *The Legend of St Elizabeth* (1862) and *Christus* (1866), *Psalm XIII* (1863), Hungarian Coronation Mass (1867).

Also songs and numerous transcriptions of orchestral works, operas, songs, *etc.*

**litany,** series of invocations to God, Blessed Virgin and Saints sung by priest and responded to by people with *Kyrie eleison* or similar response, both to simple plainsong formula.

**lithophones,** ancient group of instruments on which tuned sounds are produced by striking stone surfaces. May be regarded as forerunners of xylophone.

**Litolff, Henry Charles** (1818–91), French composer. Remembered for scherzo from 4th 'symphonic concerto'.

**'Little Russian' Symphony,** nickname for Chaikovsky's symphony no 2 in C minor, op 17 (1873). Name derives from use of Little Russian, *ie* Ukrainian, folk tunes.

**Little Sweep, The,** *see* LET'S MAKE AN OPERA.

**'Little' Symphony,** nickname for Schubert's symphony no 6 in C (1817–18), distinguishing it from Great C Major Symphony (1828).

**liturgical drama,** *see* TROPE.

**liturgy,** term applied to written and official form of service of Christian churches.

**lituus** (Lat.), ancient type of trumpet used in Roman army. Similar in shape to krummhorn.

**liuto** (It.), lute.

**Liuzzi, Fernando** (1884–1940), Italian musicologist, composer. Pupil of Reger and Mottl. In 1939 moved to US. Composed chamber opera for puppets, 3 oratorios, orchestral work, 5 sets of songs, and organ, piano and violin music.

**lizard,** *see* LYZARDEN.

**Lloyd, John** (d. 1523), English composer. Gentleman of Chapel Royal. His 5-part Mass *O quam suavis* is remarkable for 'canons' or riddles used for notation of tenor.

**Lloyd Webber, Andrew** (1948– ), English composer. Best known for successful rock musicals *Joseph and the Amazing Technicolor Dreamcoat* (1968), *Jesus Christ Superstar* (1970) and *Evita* (1976), all with words by Tim Rice.

His brother, **Julian Lloyd Webber** (1951– ), is cellist with growing solo reputation.

**Lobgesang,** *see* HYMN OF PRAISE.

**Locatelli, Pietro** (1695–1764), Italian violinist, composer. Pupil of Corelli. Toured extensively and settled in Amsterdam. Great innovatory violinist. Works incl. 12 *concerti grossi,* flute sonatas, 12 violin concertos, and trio and solo sonatas.

**Locke, Matthew** (?1622–77), English composer. In service of Charles II from 1660. Works incl. music for Shirley's masque *Cupid and Death* (with Christopher Gibbons, 1653), contributions to earliest English operas, Davenant's *Siege of Rhodes* (1653) and Shadwell's *Psyche* (1673), incidental music for plays *eg The Tempest,* consort and church music, and songs.

**Lockwood, Normand** (1906– ), American composer. Won US *Prix de Rome* (1929). Pupil of Boulanger and Respighi. Works incl. choral compositions (some with orchestra), chamber opera *The Scarecrow,* string quartets and other chamber music, and piano pieces.

**loco** (It.), place, *ie* in normal place: (1) used to contradict *8va* or *all'ottava* by indicating that music is to be played at normal pitch, not octave higher or lower;

(2) used in string music to indicate passage is to be played in normal position, after previous contrary indication.

**Locrian mode,** (1) in ancient Greek music, equivalent of white notes on piano from A to A;

(2) in modern usage, applied to equivalent of white notes on piano from B to B. Since interval between 1st and 5th notes is not perfect fifth but diminished fifth, it had virtually only theoretical existence.

**Loder, Edward James** (1813–65), English composer, conductor. His operas *eg Nourjahad* (1834) and *The Night Dancers* (1846) were very popular in his day. Also wrote stage works, cantata, string quartets, and sacred and secular songs.

**Loeffler, Charles Martin** (1861–1935), Alsatian-born composer, violinist. Pupil of Joachim. Settled in US from 1881. Works, in delicate and evocative style somewhat resembling that of Debussy, incl. orchestral *La Mort de Tintagiles* (with viola d'amore, 1905), *A Pagan Poem* (after Virgil, 1905–6), *The Canticle of the Sun* (with solo voice, 1925), *Five Irish Fantasies* (with voice, 1922), choral and chamber music, and songs.

**Loeillet, Jean-Baptiste** (1680–1730), Belgian composer, flautist, oboist. In London from 1705. Composed sonatas for flute, oboe and violin, and harpsichord music. Helped popularize flute in London.

**Loewe, Frederick** (1904– ), American composer, b. Austria. Wrote musicals *eg My Fair Lady* and *Camelot*, to librettos by Alan Jay Lerner.

**Loewe or Loew, Johann Jakob** (1629–1703), German composer, organist. Pupil of Schütz. Composed 2 operas, ballets, instrumental suites (with introductory movements called *Synfonia*), and songs for solo voice.

**Loewe, Johann Karl Gottfried** (1796–1869), German composer, conductor, pianist, singer. Works incl. operas, oratorios, cantata, orchestral, chamber and piano music, songs and part-songs. Most notable as composer and popularizer of dramatic type of *Lied* called 'ballad', *eg* 'Der Erlkönig' and 'Edward'.

**Loewenberg, Alfred** (1902–49), German musicologist. Left Germany in 1934 and settled in London. His *Annals of Opera* (1943, rev. 1955) is valuable chronological tabulation of first and subsequent performances of *c* 4000 operas from 1597 to 1940.

**log drum,** wood drum, usually cylindrical; hollow and sealed off at ends, though with slit that runs almost entire length. Made in various sizes which produce notes of precise pitch.

**Logier, Johann Bernhard** (1777–1846), German-born inventor, flautist, piano teacher, bandmaster, organist. Settled in Dublin (1809). Patented Chiroplast (1814), mechanism to train hands for piano-playing. Wrote *Thoroughbass* and books on his piano-teaching system. Composed piano concerto, trios, ode on 50th year of George III's reign, and piano sonatas.

**Logroscino** or **Lo Groscino, Nicola** (1698–1765), Italian composer. Wrote *c* 25 operas, some in collaboration with Piccinni, but few survive.

**Lohengrin,** opera by Wagner, libretto by composer. First perf. Weimar, 1850 (conducted by Liszt). Story concerns chivalry of Lohengrin, son of Parsifal and knight of Holy Grail.

**Lombardi alla prima corciata, I** (It., *The Lombards at the First Crusade*), opera by Verdi, libretto by T. Solera. First perf. Milan, 1843. Second version, entitled *Jérusalem*, with French libretto by Royer and Vaëz, was first perf. Paris, 1847. Story concerns rival brothers, eventually reconciled during First Crusade, though not before considerable bloodshed.

**Lombardic rhythm,** *see* SCOTCH SNAP.

**Londonderry Air,** Irish folk tune, first printed 1855. Arranged by many composers incl. Percy Grainger. Sung to various words *eg* 'Danny Boy'.

**London Philharmonic Orchestra,** founded in 1932 by Sir Thomas Beecham. Since 1945, conductors have incl. Eduard van Beinum, Sir Adrian Boult, John Pritchard, Bernard Haitink and Sir Georg Solti.

**London Symphony,** (1) nickname for Haydn's last symphony, no 104 in D. First perf. 1795 during Haydn's 2nd visit to London. All of Haydn's last 12 ('Salomon') symphonies were written for London; (2) Vaughan Williams' 2nd symphony (1914, rev. 1920), which incorporates various London sounds *eg* street cries and chimes of Big Ben.

**London Symphony Orchestra,** founded in 1904. Recent conductors have incl. Pierre Monteux, István Kertesz, André Previn and Claudio Abbado.

**long** (Lat., *longa*), in modal and mensural notation, note with value of 2 or 3 breves. Perfect large (Lat., *maxima*) contained 2 or 3 longs.

**Long, Marguérite** (1874–1966), French pianist. Lifelong champion of French music. Ravel dedicated G major piano concerto to her.

**lontano** (It.), distant.

**Loosemore, Henry** (d. 1670), English composer, organist. Composed service, anthems, 2 Latin litanies, and fantasia for 3 viols and organ.
His son, **George Loosemore** (1660–82), was also organist, and composed anthems.

**Lopatnikov, Nicolai Lvovich** (1903–76), Russian composer, pianist. Left Russia (1917), spending time in Finland (where encouraged by Sibelius), and Germany. Settled in US (1939). Works incl. opera *Danton*, 2 symphonies, 2 piano concertos, violin concerto, and chamber and piano music.

**Lorenzani, Paolo** (1640–1713), Italian composer. *Maître de musique* to French queen (1679–83), and choirmaster at St Peter's, Rome, from 1694. Composed operas, Magnificats, cantatas, motets, Italian and French airs, and serenades. His *Nicandro e Fileno* (1681) was only Italian opera given in France between 1662 and 1729.

**Loriod, Yvonne** (1924– ), French pianist. Wife of Messiaen and leading exponent of his keyboard works, and those of other modern composers.

**Loriti, Heinrich,** *see* GLAREANUS.

**Lortzing, Gustav Albert** (1801–51), German composer, singer, conductor, librettist. Composed romantic and comic operas to own libretti, *eg Zar und Zimmermann* (Tsar and Carpenter, 1837).

**Lossius, Lucas** (1508–82), German theorist. Published treatise *Erotemata musicae practicae* (1563) and *Psalmodia sacra veteris ecclesiae* (1553), collection of Latin texts with plainsong melodies for use in Lutheran liturgy.

**Lotti, Antonio** (1667–1740), Italian composer. First organist at St Mark's, Venice, from 1704. Wrote operas, church music, cantatas and madrigals.

**loud pedal,** name often wrongly used to describe sustaining pedal on piano.

**Loughran, James** (1931– ), Scottish conductor. Conducting posts incl. B.B.C. Scottish Symphony Orchestra (1965–71), Hallé Orchestra from 1971, and Bamberg Symphony Orchestra from 1978.

**Louise,** opera by Charpentier, libretto by composer. First perf. Paris, 1900. Story, following Italian *versimo* style, concerns love of dressmaker for artist.

**Louis Ferdinand of Prussia, Prince** (1772–1806), nephew of Frederick the Great, amateur composer and pianist. Friend of

Beethoven, who dedicated C minor piano concerto to him. Wrote 2 rondos for piano and orchestra, and chamber and piano music.

**loure,** type of bagpipe once used in Normandy. Term came to be applied to rustic dance accompanied by this, which was adopted into ballet and orchestral music.

**louré** (Fr.), LEGATO bowing.

**Lourié, Arthur Vincent** (1892–1966), Russian composer. Left Russia (1922), lived in France (where met Stravinsky), and settled in US (1941). Works incl. *Symphonie dialectique* (1930), orchestral, church, choral, chamber and piano music, and song-cycles.

**Love of Three Oranges, The** (Fr., *L'Amour des Trois Oranges*), comic opera by Prokofiev, libretto by composer (in Russian, after Gozzi). First perf. (in French) Chicago, 1921. Music also used for orchestral suite.

**Love of the Three Kings, The,** *see* AMORE DEI TRE RE.

**Love, the Magician** (Sp., *El Amor Brujo*), ballet (with singing) by Falla. First perf. Madrid, 1915.

**Lowe, Edward** (*c* 1610–82), English organist, composer. Organist of Chapel Royal from 1660, and professor of music at Oxford from 1662. Published *A Short Direction for the Performance of Cathedrall Service* (1661) and composed anthems.

**Lualdi, Adriano** (1887–1971), Italian composer, critic. Works incl. operas, *eg The Moon of the Caribbees* (after Eugene O'Neill), symphonic poems, and chamber music.

**Lübeck, Vincent** (1654–1740), German organist, composer. Pupil of Buxtehude. Composed cantatas, chorale preludes and other organ works.

**Lucas, Charles** (1808–69), English conductor, composer, cellist, organist. Principal of Royal Academy of Music (1859–66). Active as music-publisher (1856–65).

**Lucas, Leighton** (1903– ), English composer, conductor. Also worked as ballet-dancer. Works incl. orchestral, choral and film music, ballets, masques, string quartet, and songs.

**Lucia di Lammermoor** (It., *Lucy of Lammermoor*), opera by Donizetti, libretto by S. Cammarano (after Scott's *The Bride of Lammermoor*). First perf. Naples, 1835. Contains most famous operatic mad scene.

**Lucio Silla** (It., *Lucius Sulla*), opera by Mozart, libretto by G. de Gamera (altered by Metastasio). First perf. Milan, 1772. Other operas on same subject were composed by Anfossi and J.C. Bach.

**Lucrezia Borgia,** opera by Donizetti, libretto by F. Romani (after Hugo). First perf. Milan, 1833. In course of poisoning her adversaries, Lucrezia finds she has killed her own son.

**Ludford, Nicholas** (*c* 1485–*c* 1557), English composer. Composed Masses, Magnificat, and antiphons.

**Ludus Tonalis** (Lat., play of tones), work for piano by Hindemith (1942) consisting of 12 fugues and 11 interludes, with prelude and postlude. Intended as 'studies in counterpoint, tonal organization and piano technique' – kind of modern equivalent of Bach's *Well-Tempered Clavier.*

**Ludwig, Christa** (1928– ), German mezzo-soprano. Esp. associated with operas of Beethoven, Mozart and Richard Strauss.

**Luening, Otto** (1900– ), American composer, flautist. Pupil of Busoni. Works incl. opera, symphony, symphonic poems, choral, chamber, piano and organ music, and songs.

**Luftpause** (Ger.), breathing rest.

**Luisa Miller,** opera by Verdi, libretto by S. Cammarano (based on Schiller's drama *Kabale und Liebe*). First perf. Naples, 1849.

**lujon,** percussion instrument. Metal plates, mounted above resonators, are usually beaten by soft-headed sticks, producing sounds of indefinite pitch.

**Lully, Jean-Baptiste,** orig. Giambattista Lulli (1632–87), French composer of Italian origin. Taken to Paris as boy and entered service of Louis XIV's cousin, then of king himself (1652), working as dancer, violinist and composer. From 1664 composed music for comedy-ballets of Molière, incl. *Le Mariage forcé* (1664), *L'Amour médecin* (1665), *Le Sicilien* (1667), *Monsieur de Pourceaugnac* (1669), *Les Amants magnifiques* (1667) and *Le Bourgeois Gentilhomme* (1670), in which he appeared (as he often did) as actor and dancer. By 1673 gained patent to establish opera in Paris, and with poet Quinault, founded French opera, then called *tragédie lyrique.* As king's favourite, amassed privileges and wealth. Died of blood-poisoning, having struck foot with baton while conducting.

Chief characteristics of French opera which he established were: (1) overture in form of slow section in dotted rhythm followed by quick fugal section; (2) extensive use of ballet; (3) important place given to choruses; (4) development of rhetorical style of recitative closely related to rhythms of language. Arias are mostly only of minor importance.

Lully also wrote music for court ballets and *divertissements,* some church music, and 2 orchestral suites.

Operas: *Cadmus et Hermione* (1673), *Alceste* (1674), *Thésée* (1675), *Atys* (1676), *Isis* (1677), *Psyché* (1678), *Bellérophon* (1679), *Proserpine* (1680), *Persée* (1682), *Phaëton* (1683), *Amadis de Gaule* (1684), *Roland* (1685), *Armide et Renaud* (1686), *Acis et Galatée* (1686), *Achille et Polyxène* (with Colasse, 1687).

**Lulu,** unfinished opera by Berg, libretto by composer (after Wedekind's *Earth Spirit* and *Pandora's Box*). First perf. (posthumously) Zürich, 1937. Story concerns sexual *femme fatale* who destroys all her lovers, and is eventually murdered by Jack the Ripper. One of few real operatic masterpieces of 20th cent. Orchestration of 3rd act completed by Friedrich Cerha; first perf. Paris, 1979.

**Lumbye, Hans Christian** (1810–74), Danish conductor, composer. Wrote ballet music, galops and other dances.

**Lumsdaine, David** (1931– ), Australian composer, now resident in

UK. Works incl. *Episodes* and *Hagoromo* for orchestra, and vocal, chamber and piano music.

**lunga pausa** (It.), long pause, long rest.

**Lupo,** name of family of musicians of Italian origin active at English court (1540–1640). They incl. Ambros (d. 1594), Thomas I (d. 1628), Thomas II (d. before 1660) and Theophilus (d. before 1660). Compositions under name Thomas Lupo incl. pieces in Leighton's *Teares or Lamentacions* of 1614 (one by 'Timolphus Thopul', poss. Thomas or Theophilus or both), numerous fantasies in 3 to 6 parts, and *Miserere* for strings in 5 parts.

**Lupu, Radu** (1945– ), Romanian pianist, now resident in UK. Has international reputation as soloist.

**Lupus Hellinck,** *see* HELLINCK.

**lur,** primitive Scandinavian bronze horn.

**Luscinius,** Latin name of Ottomar or Othmar Nacht(i)gall (1487–1537), Alsatian organist, theorist, theologian, composer. Active in Strasbourg, Augsburg, Basle and Freiburg-im-Breisgau. Published 2 treatises, *Musicae Institutiones* (1515) and *Musurgia seu praxis musicae* (1536), and composed organ pieces.

**lusingando** (It.), lit. 'flattering' *ie* in tender manner.

**Lusitano, Vicente** (d. after 1553), Portuguese composer, theorist. Settled in Rome *c* 1550. Published treatise *Introductione facilissima et novissima di canto fermo* (1553), and book of motets (1551).

**lustig** (Ger.), merry, cheerful.

**lustige Witwe, Die,** see MERRY WIDOW.

**Lustigen Weiber von Windsor, Die,** *see* MERRY WIVES OF WINDSOR.

**lute** (Fr., *luth*; Ger., *Laute*; It., *liuto*), plucked string instrument with body shaped like half-pear, fretted finger-board, and peg-box bent back. One of most popular instruments for solo-playing and song accompaniment in 16th, early 17th cents., although history goes back to 2000 BC in Mesopotamia.

In 16th, early 17th cents. lutes had 11 strings in 6 courses, *ie* 5 pairs in double courses at octave and single string, tuned: G (at bottom of bass clef)–C–F–A–D–G. In mid 17th cent. new tuning was generally adopted: A (at bottom of bass clef)–D–F–A–D–F.

Lute music was generally written in TABLATURE. Music for lute solo consisted of dances, variations, preludes, ricercars, and arrangements of choral music and of folk and popular songs. Chief varieties of lute were ARCHLUTE, THEORBO, CHITARRONE, MANDOLA, MANDOLINE, and VIHUELA DA MANO.

**lute-harpsichord,** *see* LAUTENCLAVICYMBEL.

**luth,** *see* LUTE.

**Luther, Martin** (1483–1546), German Protestant reformer. Considered music to be of highest importance after theology, and music was taught thoroughly in Lutheran schools. Composed motet, and may have written music of *Sanctus* in his German Mass and of chorales 'Ein' feste Burg' and 'Mit Fried und Freud'. Wrote words to many hymns still widely sung.

**Lutoslawski, Witold** (1913– ), Polish composer. His *Concerto for Orchestra* (1954) brought him international fame, and *Funeral Music* in memory of Bartók (1958) and *Venetian Games* (1961) helped to consolidate his position as Poland's most important modern composer. Other works incl. symphonies, cello concerto, *Livre pour orchestre, Trois Poèmes d' Henri Michaux* for chorus and orchestra, and *Paroles Tissées* (written for Peter Pears). Music is remarkable for technical and emotional content and for wide range of styles encompassed.

**Lutyens, Elisabeth** (1906– ), English composer. Daughter of architect Sir Edward Lutyens. Works incl. operas *eg Infidelio,* horn concerto, viola concerto, series of chamber concertos, *Rondel* and *Tides* for orchestra, and vocal, chamber and film music. Dedicated exponent of 12-note music.

**Luxon, Benjamin** (1937– ), English baritone. Well known both in concert-hall and opera house. Created title role in Britten's *Owen Wingrave.*

**Luython, Karel** (*c* 1557–1620), Netherlands composer. Court organist in Prague to Emperors Maximilian II and Rudolf II from *c* 1576. Published vols. of madrigals (1582), motets (1603), Lamentations (1604), and Masses (1609). Also wrote organ music, and built harpsichord with separate keys for C and D, D and E, *etc,* to overcome inadequacy of mean-tone system to provide practical tuning for these notes.

**Luzzaschi, Luzzasco** (1545–1607), Italian composer, organist, harpsichordist. Organ pupils incl. Frescobaldi. Published 7 books of madrigals (1575–1604); style of later madrigals resembles that of Gesualdo in its texture, though not in the extent of its chromaticism. Also wrote organ pieces.

**Lvov, Alexis Feodorovich** (1798–1870), Russian composer, violinist. Musical director of Chapel of Nicholas I. Led distinguished string quartet and was high-ranking army officer. Wrote operas and church music, but best remembered for pre-Revolutionary Russian National Anthem.

**Lydian mode,** (1) in ancient Greek music, equivalent of white notes on piano from C to C;

(2) from Middle Ages onwards, equivalent of white notes on piano from F to F. Often found with flattened B, which makes it identical with modern major scale.

**Lympany, Moura** (1916– ), English pianist. Made debut in 1928, since when has acquired international reputation.

**lyra,** alternative name for medieval REBEC, which was continued in Italian LIRA of 17th, 18th cents.

**Lyraflügel** (Ger.), type of upright piano, in form of Greek lyre, made in Germany *c* 1825–50.

**Lyra-glockenspiel,** glockenspiel suitable for marching bands. Also called bell-lyra.

**lyra viol,** bowed instrument used in Britain in 17th cent. Falls in size between bass and tenor viol, and therefore was called *viola bastarda.*

**lyre** (Gr., *lyra*), instrument of ancient Greeks, Assyrians, Hebrews *etc.* Simpler form of kithara, with body of tortoiseshell or wood, 2 horns or wooden arms joined by cross bar, and from 3 to 12 strings.

**Lyric Suite,** string quartet in 6 movts. by Berg (1926). Part of work later arranged for string orchestra.

**lyzarden, lyzardyne, lysard** or **lizard,** medieval English name for largest member of CORNETT family. Forerunner of serpent.

# M

**m,** in TONIC SOL-FA = *me,* third note (or mediant) of major scale.

**M,** as abbrev. M. = *medius,* middle voice (in polyphonic music). M.M. = Maelzel's METRONOME. M.-S. = mezzo-soprano. *m.d.* = *mano destra* or *main droite,* right hand. *mf* = *mezzo forte,* moderately loud. *m.g.* = *main gauche,* left hand. *mp* = *mezzo piano,* moderately soft. *m.s.* = *mano sinistra,* left hand. *m.v.* = *mezza voce,* with moderate volume of tone.

**ma** (It.), but. *Allegro ma non troppo,* quickly but not too quickly.

**Maazel, Lorin** (1930– ), American conductor, violinist. Conducting posts incl. Deutsche Oper (1965–71), Berlin Radio Symphony Orchestra (1965–71), Cleveland Orchestra from 1972. Director of Vienna Opera from 1982.

**Macbeth,** (1) opera by Verdi, libretto by F.M. Piave (after Shakespeare). First perf. Florence, 1847. 'Paris' version (1865) contains some extra music;

(2) symphonic poem by Richard Strauss, op 23. First perf. Weimar, 1890;

(3) opera by Bloch, libretto by E. Fleg. First perf. Paris, 1910;

(4) opera by Lawrence Collingwood. First perf. London, 1934.

**McCabe, John** (1939– ), English composer, pianist. Works incl. operas *The Lion, The Witch, and the Wardrobe* (1968), *The Play of Mother Courage* (1974), ballets, 3 symphonies, concertos, and vocal, chamber, piano and organ music.

**McCormack, John** (1884–1945), Irish-born tenor. Studied in Italy and made debut at Covent Garden in 1907. Sang in US from 1910, and became US citizen in 1917. Excelled in Mozart and Verdi, and also as concert singer. In Britain, best known for interpretations of popular ballads and drawing-room songs.

**MacCunn, Hamish** (1868–1916), Scottish composer, conductor. Pupil of Parry. Best remembered for concert overture *The Land of the Mountain and the Flood* (written at age of 19). Also wrote more ambitious works *eg* opera *Jeannie Deans* (after Scott's *The Heart of Midlothian*).

**MacDowell, Edward Alexander** (1861–1908), American composer. Studied and composed in Europe (with encouragement of Liszt). Returned to US permanently in 1888. Became mentally ill in 1905. Most characteristic works are those for piano. Also wrote symphonic poems, 2 orchestral suites, 2 piano concertos, and songs.

**Mace, Thomas** (*c* 1613–*c* 1709), English writer, instrumentalist. Chiefly known for *Musick's Monument....* (1676), which deals with lute, viol and musical affairs in general. It also contains pieces for various instruments.

**McEwen, John Blackwood** (1868–1948), Scottish composer,

teacher. Principal of Royal Academy of Music, London (1924–36). Wrote 5 symphonies, 3 'Border Ballades' and other orchestral works, 17 string quartets (no 6, *Biscay*), concertos, cantatas, and piano music. Knighted 1931.

**Macfarren, George Alexander** (1813–87), English composer, teacher. Principal of Royal Academy of Music, London from 1876; also professor at Cambridge. Works incl. operas (one on Robin Hood), oratorios, cantatas, orchestral and chamber music, and songs. Knighted 1883.

His brother, **Walter Cecil Macfarren** (1826–1905), was composer and conductor. Works incl. symphony and Shakespearian overtures for orchestra, church and piano music, songs and part-songs.

**Machaut, Guillaume de,** *see* GUILLAUME DE MACHAUT.

**machicotage** (Fr.), ornamentation of solo parts of plainsong.

**machine drums,** TIMPANI fitted with mechanism, such as foot-pedal, capable of making rapid and accurate changes of pitch.

**Mackenzie, Alexander Campbell** (1847–1935), Scottish composer, teacher. Principal of Royal Academy of Music, London from 1888. Works incl. operas, incidental music after Scott and Barrie, cantata on *The Cotter's Saturday Night* (Burns), Scottish rhapsodies, Scottish piano concerto (premièred by Paderewski), and *Pibroch* suite for violin and orchestra. Knighted 1895.

**Mackerras, Charles** (1925– ), Australian conductor, b. US. Settled in Britain (1947). Musical director of English National Opera (1974–8). Esp. associated with Czech music, Handel and Mozart. Made adaptation of music by Sullivan for ballet *Pineapple Poll*.

**MacIntyre, Donald** (1934– ), New Zealand baritone. Member of Sadler's Wells (1960–67) and of Covent Garden from 1967. Internationally admired, esp. in role of Wotan.

**Maconchy, Elizabeth** (1907– ), English composer of Irish parentage. Pupil of Vaughan Williams. Works, in which she developed individual treatment of contemporary idioms within traditional forms, incl. operas, orchestral and ballet music, concertos for piano, viola and clarinet, 9 string quartets and other chamber music.

**Macpherson, Stewart** (1865–1941), English teacher, writer, composer. Wrote textbooks on harmony, counterpoint, form and musical history. Composed symphony and other orchestral works, Mass, piano pieces and songs.

**Macque, Giovanni de** or **Jean de** (*c* 1551–1614), Flemish composer. Pupil of Philippe de Monte. Worked in Rome (1576–82) and Naples (1586–after 1610). Composed some motets and published several books of madrigals. One of his madrigals appeared in Yonge's *Musica Transalpina* (1588) and another in Morley's collection of Italian madrigals (1598).

**Madam Butterfly** (It., *Madama Butterfly*), opera by Puccini, libretto by G. Giacosa and L. Illica (after David Belasco's play based on novel by J.L. Long). First perf. Milan, 1904, was failure; revised version, conducted by Toscanini in same year, was great success.

Story concerns love of Japanese girl, Cio-Cio-San, for Lieutenant Pinkerton, US naval officer.

**Maderna, Bruno** (1920–73), Italian composer, conductor. One of most interesting and musically sensitive of modern Italian composers. Works incl. concertos for piano, 2 pianos, flute and oboe, *Musica du due Dimensioni* for flute, percussion and electronic tape, studies on Kafka's *The Trial* for speaker, soprano and chamber orchestra and other chamber pieces, and electronic music. As conductor, had natural flair for modern music.

**madrigal,** musical setting of poem in several parts. First appeared in 14th-cent. Italy in 2 or 3 parts, with strict form; composers incl. Landini. By 16th cent., madrigal poem was free form, and musical style was derived from *frottola.* This style was followed by that of Willaert and Cipriano de Rore who widened scope of madrigal in expression of words and use of technical resources. 'Classic' Italian madrigal of later 16th cent. was written in imitative polyphony, mostly in 5 parts, and made moderate use of word-painting and word-symbolism (A. Gabrieli, Palestrina, Lassus, Philippe de Monte). Mannered style of late madrigal (Marenzio, Gesualdo, Monteverdi) used less restrained forms of word-painting, chromaticism, and dramatic effects of melodic line and choral texture. Transition from imitative madrigal to madrigal for solo, duet or trio accompanied by continuo, which resulted from pursuit of dramatic expression, can be traced in 7 books of Monteverdi (1587–1619).

Italian madrigals began to appear in England in late 16th cent. English madrigal tradition quickly assumed its own characteristics in hands of Morley, Weelkes, Wilbye and others, partially due to influence of native tradition of secular song as exemplified by Byrd and Gibbons. Notable feature of English madrigal school, when compared with Italian, is lack of suitable literary tradition and presence of greater feeling for tonality and purely musical organization.

**Maelzel, Johann Nepomuk** (1772–1838), German-born inventor. Made various mechanical instruments. Patented the METRONOME (1816), though idea was filched from D.N. Winkel. Later lived in US.

**maestoso** (It.), majestic, dignified.

**maestro al cembalo** (It.), in 18th cent., musician who directed performances of concertos *etc* while seated at harpsichord.

**maestro di cappella,** *see* KAPELLMEISTER.

**Maggini, Giovanni Paolo** (1580–after 1630), Italian violin-maker. Apprentice of Salò in 1602, and later improved on Salò's designs and methods in several respects.

**maggiore** (It.), major mode.

**Magic Flute, The** (Ger., *Die Zauberflöte*), *Singspiel* (opera with dialogue) by Mozart, libretto by E. Schikaneder. First perf. Vienna, 1791. Work is mixture of allegory, fantasy and pantomime which conceals several references to freemasonry and political situation in Austria at time. Story concerns quest of Tamino for Pamina, accompanied by the bird-catcher Papageno.

**Magnard, Albéric** (1865–1914), French composer. Pupil of Massenet and d'Indy. Works, notable for originality, incl. 3 operas *eg Bérénice,* 4 symphonies, and chamber music. Killed (or committed suicide) defending home against invading Germans.

**Magnificat,** canticle of the Virgin sung at RC Vespers and Anglican Evensong. In plainsong, sung antiphonally to one of 8 tones.

**Mahillon, Charles Victor** (1841–1924), Belgian writer. In 1876 became curator of museum of Brussels Conservatoire. Published catalogue of museum and *Les Eléments d'acoustique musicale et instrumentale* (1874).

**Mahler, Gustav** (1860–1911), Austrian composer, conductor, b. Bohemia. Son of Jewish publican, who, though coarse and brutal, recognized and encouraged son's talents. Sent to Vienna Conservatory at age of 15. Also attended Bruckner's lectures at university and came to admire Bruckner's music deeply. Served apprenticeship as opera conductor in various provincial houses, and moved on to Cassel, Prague, Leipzig, Budapest and Hamburg before winning directorship of Vienna State Opera (1897). Period with that company was one of most brilliant and tempestuous in its history. Dismissed in 1907, same year in which his daughter died and his own incurable heart disease was diagnosed. Death of daughter was commemorated in *Das Lied von der Erde,* whose last movt. *(Abschied)* is addressed to life's sweetness and transitoriness – pervading theme of his music. Moved to US where conducted New York Metropolitan Opera and New York Philharmonic Symphony Orchestra. In 1911, failing health precipitated return to Europe. Died in Vienna sanitorium.

His importance as conductor was soon recognized, but importance as composer took longer to establish itself widely. Bruno Walter and Willem Mengelberg were early champions, and by 1960s were joined by many more. Mahler is main musical link between 19th and 20th cents. Schoenberg called him 'classical' composer, but also hailed him as pioneer. Though his music may seem neurotic and self-pitying to some, it can also evoke Austrian landscape with unsurpassed beauty. What once seemed eclectic in his style is now seen as absolutely personal form of expression. Mahler developed and expanded concept of vocal symphony begun by Beethoven. His use of human voice and of orchestra is individual, exceptionally lucid, and instantly recognizable.

Principal compositions (many were later revised):

(1) Symphonies:

No 1 in D major (1884–8)

No 2 in C minor ('Resurrection') for soprano, contralto, mixed chorus and orchestra (1884–94)

No 3 in D minor, for contralto, women's chorus, boys' chorus and orchestra (1895–6)

No 4 in G major, for soprano and orchestra (1899–1900)

No 5 in C sharp minor (1901–2)

No 6 in A minor (1903–5)

No 7 in B minor (1904–5)

No 8 in E flat major ('Symphony of a Thousand') for 8 soloists, mixed chorus, boys' chorus and orchestra

No 9 in D major (1909–10)

No 10 in F sharp major (unfinished) (1910); completed by Deryck Cooke (first perf. 1964);

(2) Songs and other works: *Lieder eines fahrenden Gesellen* for voice and orchestra (1884), *Des Knaben Wunderhorn* for voice and orchestra (1888–9), *Kindertotenlieder* for voice and orchestra (1901–4), 5 Rückert songs for voice and orchestra (1901–2), *Das Lied von der Erde* for alto (or baritone), tenor and orchestra (1907–9), cantata *Das klagende Lied* for 4 soloists, chorus and orchestra (1880).

**Maiden Quartets,** alternative name for Haydn's RUSSIAN QUARTETS.

**Maid of Pskov, The** (Russ., *Pskovitianka*), opera by Rimsky-Korsakov, libretto by composer. First perf. St Petersburg, 1873. Also called *Ivan the Terrible* (after one of principal characters).

**main** (Fr.), hand. *Main droite,* right hand. *Main gauche,* left hand. *Deux mains,* two hands. *Quatre mains,* four hands. Terms mainly applied to piano music.

**Maiskaya Noch,** *see* MAY NIGHT.

**Maistre, Mattheus Le,** *see* LE MAISTRE.

**maître de chapelle,** *see* KAPELLMEISTER.

**maîtrise** (Fr.), choir school of French church, or simply 'church choir'.

**majeur** (Fr.), major.

**major, minor,** 2 predominant scales of western tonal system. Major key is based on major scale, minor key on minor. *See* CHORD, INTERVAL, KEY, SCALE.

**Majorano, Gaetano,** *see* CAFFARELLI.

**malagueña,** Andalusian folk dance originating in Malaga, S Spain. Often sung, but can also be instrumental piece.

**Malcolm, George** (1917– ), English harpsichordist, pianist. Widely know for his recitals.

**Maldeghem, Robert Jullien van** (1810–93), Flemish organist. Edited *Trésor musical* (1865–93), pioneer collection of *chansons* and motets of early 16th cent.

**Malherbe, Charles Théodore** (1853–1911), French writer, composer. Published books on Wagner, Auber, and opéra-comique.

**Malibran, Maria Felicita** (1808–36), Spanish operatic singer, who combined natural contralto with soprano range. Taught by her father Manuel Garcia and by Hérold in Paris. Sang with great success in London, Paris, New York and Italy. Marriage with Malibran was annulled in 1836 and she married Belgian violinist Charles de Bériot. Triumphant career was cut short by fall from horse in 1836, and she died later that year. Robert Russell Bennett wrote opera *Maria Malibran* (1935).

**malinconia** (It.), melancholy (noun). Adj. is *malinconico.*

**Malipiero, Gian Francesco** (1882–1973), Italian composer. Edited works of Monteverdi, Frescobaldi and Stradella. As composer, representative of neo-baroque in modern Italian music. Operas incl. 2 imposing trilogies, *L'Orfeide* (1925) and *Il Mistero di Venezia* (1932), and 2 works after Shakespeare, *Julius Caesar* (1936) and *Anthony and Cleopatra* (1938). Other works incl. series of descriptive symphonies, oratorios, chamber and piano music, and songs.

**Ma mère l'oye,** *see* MOTHER GOOSE.

**Manchester School,** name of group (now dispersed) of young English composers, all of whom studied at Royal Manchester College of Music in 1950s and shared progressive musical ideas. Major figures were Harrison Birtwistle, Peter Maxwell Davies, Alexander Goehr and John Ogdon.

**Manchicourt, Pierre de** (*c* 1510–64), Flemish composer. Became *maestro de capilla* in royal chapel, Madrid, in 1560. Works incl. *chansons* and motets.

**Mancinelli, Luigi** (1848–1921), Italian conductor, composer. Conducted in Italy, London, New York and Buenos Aires. Wrote several operas incl. *A Midsummer Night's Dream*.

**Mancinus,** *see* MENCKEN.

**mandola, mandora** or **mandore** (It.), tenor mandolin.

**mandolin,** member of lute family. Has 8 wire strings tuned as 4 pairs (G–D–A–E), played with plectrum. Stringing makes possible rapid alternations of same note, which is instrument's most characteristic feature.

**mandora, mandore,** *see* MANDOLA.

**Mandyczewski, Eusebius** (1857–1929), Austrian historian, editor. Co-edited complete works of Schubert and Brahms, and began unfinished edition of works of Haydn.

**Manfred,** (1) incidental music to Byron's poem by Schumann, op 115 (1848–9), written for stage performance;

(2) (unnumbered) symphony by Chaikovsky, op 58 (1885), inspired by same poem.

**manico** (It.), finger-board.

**manicorde** (Fr.), 16th-cent. term for clavichord.

**Manieren** (Ger.), 18th-cent. term for ornaments or grace notes.

**Mannheim,** town in western Germany, famous in mid 18th cent. for orchestra. Number of composers wrote symphonies for orchestra, incl. Stamitz, F.X. Richter and Cannabich, and have become known as 'Mannheim School'; played important part in development of symphony.

**Manns, August Friedrich** (1825–1907), German conductor. Became conductor of Crystal Palace band in London in 1855, and was in charge of Crystal Palace Saturday Concerts until 1901. Also conducted Handel Festival there (1883–1900). Knighted 1903.

**mano** (It.), hand. *Mani,* hands.

**Manon,** opera by Massenet, libretto by H. Meilhac and P. Gille (based on Abbé Prévost's novel). First perf. Paris, 1884.

**Manon Lescaut,** opera by Puccini, libretto by M. Praga, D. Oliva and L. Illica (based on Abbé Prévost's novel). First perf. Turin, 1893. Puccini's first major success.

Other operas on subject have been written by Auber (1856), Balfe (*The Maid of Artois,* 1836) and Henze (*Boulevard Solitude,* modernized version of story, 1952).

**manual** (Lat. *manus,* hand), keyboard, esp. on organ or harpsichord. On organ, each manual controls own set of pipes. Number of manuals on instruments varies. Those normally found on English organs are: Solo, Swell, Great, Choir: 3-manual organ will have Swell, Great and Choir; 2-manual organ, Swell and Great. By using COUPLER it is poss. to play on pipes of 2 manuals simultaneously. *See* CHOIR ORGAN, GREAT ORGAN, ORGAN, SOLO ORGAN, SWELL ORGAN.

**Manuel, Roland,** *see* ROLAND-MANUEL.

**Manzoni Requiem,** title sometimes given to Verdi's Requiem, written in memory of Italian novelist and poet Alessandro Manzoni.

**Maometto II** (It., Mahomet II), opera by Rossini, libretto by C. della Valle. First perf. Naples, 1820. Later adapted for France as *Le Siège de Corinth.*

**maraca,** Latin American instrument, essential in rumba bands. Consists of gourd containing dried seeds and handle to shake it. Made in various sizes, and always in pairs.

**Marais, Marin** (1656–1728), French composer, viol player. Pupil of Lully. Solo violist to Louis XIV (1685–1727). Wrote music for viol and other chamber music, operas and some church music.

**Marazzoli, Marco** (? 1619–62), Italian singer, composer. *See* MAZZOCCHI.

**Marbeck** or **Merbecke, John** (*c* 1510–85), English singer, organist, composer, theologian. Arrested as Protestant heretic (1543) and narrowly escaped burning. In 1550 issued well-known *Booke of Common Praier noted,* first musical setting of English liturgy. Also wrote Mass, 2 motets and carol.

**marcato** (It.), marked, emphatic.

**Marcello, Benedetto** (1686–1739), Italian composer, librettist, writer on music, lawyer. Composed settings of 50 paraphrases of psalms by G.A. Giustiniani, cantatas, oratorios, concertos and sonatas.

His elder brother **Alessandro Marcello** (*c* 1684–*c* 1750) was also composer of cantatas, solo sonatas and concertos – some falsely ascribed to brother.

**march** (Fr., *marche*; Ger., *Marsch*; It., *marcia*), basically, piece for marching. Music for procession or parade must necessarily be in duple time (2/4 or 6/8 for quick march) or in quadruple time – common time for regular march and slow common time for funeral march. In form, often consists of main section alternating with one or more trios.

**Marchal, André** (1894– ), French organist. Blind from birth. Master of improvisation, has toured widely as recitalist.

**Marchand, Louis** (1669–1732), French organist, composer. In royal service, but exiled in 1717 and went to Dresden. At concert there, he and Bach improvised variations on same theme; according to legend, Marchand returned to Paris to avoid further contest. Wrote opera, and organ and harpsichord music.

**marche** (Fr.), march.

**Marchesi (de Castrone),** Italian family of singers, most famous of whom were **Salvatore Marchesi** (1822–1908) and his wife **Mathilde Marchesi,** née Graumann (1821–1913). Salvatore fled to US during 1848 revolutions in Europe, but soon returned to Europe, and married Mathilde in 1852.

Mathilde was mezzo-soprano who taught singing in various European cities. Her pupils incl. Emma Calvé, Mary Garden and Nelly Melba. Their daughter **Blanche Marchesi** (1863–1940) was also noted singer and teacher.

**Marchetto or Marchettus de Padua** (*fl* early 14th cent.), Italian theorist. Expounded use of imperfect as well as perfect time and the Italian method of notation of various divisions of breve and semibreve. Wrote 2 treatises on notation, *Ludicarium in arte musicae planae* and *Pomerium in arte musicae mensuratae* (1318) which aroused much opposition.

**marcia** (It.), march. *Tempo di marcia,* march time.

**Marenzio, Luca** (1553–99), Italian composer. Worked briefly at Polish court, but mostly in Rome. One of greatest composers of madrigals, and perhaps most resourceful in expression and technical command. Style had strong influence on madrigal composition in England. Published 16 books of madrigals and one book of *Madrigali spirituali,* besides other volumes of sacred and secular music.

**mariachi** (Sp.), Mexican folk group of varying size, but usually incl. 2 violins, guitar (*jarana*), harp (*arpón*), and large guitar (*guitarron*). Word can also apply to solo folk singer.

**Maria Theresia,** nickname for Haydn's symphony no 48 in C, supposedly performed on occasion of visit of Empress Maria Theresa (Theresia is misspelling) to Esterházy Castle (1773); however, symphony she actually heard was prob. no 50 (also in C).

**Mariazell Mass** (Ger., *Mariazellermesse*), title of Mass in C by Haydn (1782). Named after shrine in Styrian Alps at Mariazell, where A.L. von Kreutzner (who commissioned work) wished to make votive offering on his ennoblement. Also called *Missa Cellensis.*

**Marienleben, Das** (Ger., *The Life of Mary*), cycle of 15 songs for soprano and piano by Hindemith, to words by Rilke. Composed 1922, rev. 1948.

**marimba,** Latin American instrument, of African origin, similar to XYLOPHONE in construction but with larger resonators and usually made of metal. Pitched octave lower than xylophone, and more mellow in tone. Usual compass is 4 octaves starting from octave below middle C. There is also bass version.

**marine trumpet,** *see* TROMBA MARINA.

**Marini, Biago** (*c* 1597–1665), Italian composer, violinist. With Farina, was earliest composer of sonatas for solo violin and continuo. Also wrote music for wide range of instrumental and vocal combinations.

**Mario, Giovanni Matteo** (1810–83), Italian tenor. Sang regularly in opera in Paris and London, and also visited St Petersburg. With wife Giula Grisi, appeared in première of Donizetti's *Don Pasquale* (1843).

**Maritana,** opera by Vincent Wallace, libretto by E. Fitzball (after play by d'Ennery and Dumanoir). First perf. London, 1845. Story concerns Spanish gypsy girl.

**Markevitch, Igor** (1912– ), Russian-born conductor, composer, teacher. Went to Paris (1926) to study under Nadia Boulanger. Works incl. ballets *Rebus,* and *L'Envoi d'Icare,* cantata on Milton's *Paradise Lost,* concerto grosso, sinfonietta, and chamber music. Conductor of Lamoureux Orchestra, Paris (1957–61); director of Monte Carlo Opera from 1968.

**markiert** (Ger.), marked, emphatic.

**Marpurg, Friedrich Wilhelm** (1718–95), German writer on music, composer. His *Handbuch dem Generalbasse* (1755–62) is based on Rameau's theory of harmony. Also wrote treatises on keyboard playing, fugue, and musical history, and preface to 2nd edition of Bach's *Art of Fugue.* Composed sonatas and other keyboard pieces, organ works and songs.

**marqué** (Fr.), marked, emphatic.

**Marriage of Figaro, The** (It., *Le Nozze di Figaro*), opera by Mozart, libretto by L. da Ponte (based on comedy by Beaumarchais). First perf. Vienna, 1786. Figaro, valet to Count Almaviva is going to marry Susanna, Countess's maid. Plot is concerned with his successful frustration of Count's designs on his bride. Opera explores love in all its aspects, and is also social critique.

**Marriner, Neville** (1924– ), English conductor, violinist. Founded (1956) ACADEMY OF ST MARTIN-IN-THE-FIELDS, directing it until 1978.

**Marsch** (Ger.), march.

**Marschner, Heinrich August** (1795–1861), German composer, conductor. Most successful composer of German romantic opera between Weber and Wagner. Operas incl. *The Vampire* (1828), *The Templar and the Jewess* (1829, based on Scott's *Ivanhoe*), and *Hans Heiling* (1833). Also wrote songs and choral music.

**Marseillaise, La** (Fr.), French national anthem. Words and music written by Rouget de Lisle (1792). Acquired name because was sung by troops from Marseille on entering Paris in same year.

**Marson, George** (*c* 1573–1632), English composer. His 5-part madrigal 'The nymphs and shepherds danced lavoltas' is in *The Triumphes of Oriana* (1601). Also wrote church music.

**Marteau sans maître, Le** (Fr., *The Hammer without a Master*), work for contralto and chamber ensemble by Boulez (1955, rev.

1957). Work is based on René Char's surrealist poems of same title (1934).

**martelé,** *see* MARTELLATO.

**martellato** (It.; Fr., *martelé*), lit. 'hammered'. Term used in string-playing, indicating heavy, detached up-and-down strokes, played with point of bow, without taking bow from string. In piano-playing, indicates forceful, detached touch. *Martelé au talon* indicates use of heel of bow.

**Martenot** (Fr.), *see* ONDES MARTENOT.

**Martha,** opera by Flotow, libretto by W. Friedrich (pseud. of F.W. Riese). First perf. Vienna, 1847. Uses Irish song 'The Last Rose of Summer'.

**Martin, Frank** (1890–1974), Swiss composer. Later settled in Holland. His power and originality has been widely recognized. Works, which incorporate very personal use of 12-note technique, incl. operas *The Tempest* and *Monsieur Pourceaugnac*, incidental music for *Oedipus Rex, Oedipus at Colonus* and *Romeo and Juliet,* oratorios *In Terra Pax* and *Golgotha* and other choral music, *Le Vin herbé* for 12 voices, strings and piano (on story of Tristan and Isolde), and orchestral music *eg Petite Symphonie Concertante* for harp, harpsichord, piano and strings.

**Martinelli, Giovanni** (1885–1969), Italian tenor. Sang in European première of Puccini's *La Fanciulla del West* (1911). In 1920s was regarded as Caruso's natural successor at New York Metropolitan. Retired in 1945. Esp. renowned for portrayals of Otello and Radamès (in *Aida*).

**Martini, Giovanni Battista** or **Giambattista,** known as 'Padre Martini' (1706–84), Italian priest, theorist, historian and composer. Most renowned musical *savant* of his day. Corresponded with wide circle of musicians, and gave advice on technical points to many composers, incl. Mozart and J.C. Bach. Wrote unfinished history of music and treatise on counterpoint. Compositions incl. church music, oratorios, and keyboard sonatas.

**Martini il Tedesco** (It., Martini the German), nickname of Johann Paul Aegidius Schwartzendorf (1741–1816), German composer, organist. Settled in France and called himself Giovanni Paolo Martini. Known mainly for song 'Plaisir d'Amour', but also wrote operas, church music *etc.*

**Martinon, Jean** (1909–76), French conductor, composer. Pupil of Roussel. Conducted Chicago Symphony Orchestra and various French orchestras. Works incl. opera *Hecuba* (after Euripides), symphonies, concertos, and choral and chamber music.

**Martinů, Bohuslav** (1890–1959), Czech composer. Pupil of Suk and Roussel. Lived in Paris, then US, and also in Switzerland. Prolific and somewhat eclectic, his works incl. 13 operas *eg Julietta, Comedy on a Bridge, The Marriage* (after Gogol) and *The Greek Passion* (after Kazantzakis's novel *Christ Recrucified*), ballets, 6 symphonies, numerous concertos and other orchestral works, choral music, 7 string quartets, sonatas, and other chamber and instrumental music.

**Martín y Soler, Vicente** (1754–1806), Spanish composer. Produced operas for Florence, Vienna, St Petersburg and London. Melody from most successful opera *Una cosa rara* was used by Mozart in *Don Giovanni*.

**Martucci, Giuseppe** (1856–1909), Italian pianist, conductor, composer. Devoted Wagnerian. Works incl. oratorio *Samuele*, 2 symphonies, piano concerto, chamber and instrumental music, and arrangements of old Italian music.

**Martyre de Saint Sébastien, Le** (Fr., *The Martyrdom of St Sebastian*), mystery play by d'Annunzio with incidental music by Debussy for solo voices, chorus and orchestra (1911).

**Marx, Adolph Bernhard** (1795–1866), German theorist, writer on music., composer. Founded *Berliner allgemeine musikalische Zeitung* (1824), and wrote treatise on composition and books on Handel, Gluck and Beethoven. Compositions incl. operas and oratorios.

**Marx, Joseph** (1882–1964), Austrian composer. Works, in late romantic style, incl. symphonic poems, choral works with orchestra, chamber music, and many songs.

**Marxsen, Eduard** (1806–87), German composer, pianist. His pupils incl. Brahms.

**marziale** (It.), martial, warlike.

**Masaniello,** Italian title for opera by Auber, libretto by A.E. Scribe and G. Delavigne, also known (more correctly) as *La Muette de Portici* (The Dumb Girl of Portici). First perf. Paris, 1828. Story concerns Italian revolutionary hero.

**Mascagni, Pietro** (1863–1945), Italian composer. At age of 26 made name with VERISMO opera *Cavalleria Rusticana*, which won 1st prize in competition, took Europe by storm, and won him fortune. None of his other operas equalled this success. They incl. *L'Amico Fritz* (1891), *Iris* (1898), *Le Maschere* (1901), *Isabeau* (1911) and *Il Piccolo Marat* (1921). As convinced fascist, tried to curry favour with Mussolini with *Nerone* (Nero, 1935).

**Maskarade** (Dan., Masquerade), comic opera by Carl Nielsen, libretto by V. Anderson (after comedy by Holberg). First perf. Copenhagen, 1906.

**mask, maske,** *see* MASQUE.

**Masked Ball, A** (It., *Un Ballo in Maschera*), opera by Verdi, libretto by A. Somma. First perf. Rome, 1859. Story orig. concerned assassination of Swedish King Gustav III, but action was transferred for political reasons (recent attempt on life of Napoleon III) to New England.

**Mason, Lowell** (1792–1872), American organist, teacher. Compiled collection of psalm tunes (1822). Pioneer of musical education in New England schools.

His grandson, **Daniel Gregory Mason** (1873–1953), was composer and writer on music. Pupil of d'Indy. Works incl. 3 symphonies (no 3, *A Lincoln Symphony*) and other orchestral music, choral, chamber and piano music, and songs.

**masque, mask** or **maske,** elaborate court entertainment combining poetry and dancing with vocal and instrumental music, and with scenery, machinery and costume. In England, at height of popularity in early 17th cent. Writers incl. Jonson, Beaumont, Campion, Dekker and Shirley. Composers incl. Campion, Robert Johnson, younger Ferrabosco, Laniere, and brothers Lawes. Inigo Jones designed scenery and machinery for some of Jonson's masques. Masque came closer to opera with increasing use of recitative instead of spoken dialogue, as in 5th entry of Shirley's *Cupid and Death* (1653), with music by Matthew Locke and Christopher Gibbons. After Restoration, masque was still popular, but artistic importance was much less, with exception of Blow's *Venus and Adonis* (actually miniature opera) and masque in Purcell's incidental music for *Dioclesian*. Masques of Arne and others in 18th cent. were light and elegant entertainments.

**Mass,** in musical sense, setting of Ordinary, or invariable parts (KYRIE, GLORIA, CREDO, SANCTUS with BENEDICTUS, AGNUS DEI) of Mass. During 11th–13th cents. original plainsong melodies were used as basis for polyphonic settings of some parts of Ordinary. Settings of Ordinary as musical whole did not become usual till after *c* 1430. Frequent method of establishing musical unity was use of CANTUS FIRMUS; another device was use of common opening for each movt. In 16th cent., settings in imitative polyphony more commonly derived material from motet or *chanson* (*see* PARODY MASS) or were independent compositions *(sine nomine)*. From 15th–17th cents., Mass was often performed in plainsong alternating with organ (*see* ORGAN MASS). Lutheran composers in 17th cent. wrote Masses for combination of voices and instruments: final stage of tradition is seen in Bach's B minor Mass. Masses of subsequent periods reflect dominant style of those periods in other forms. Many of these settings ignore practical requirements of liturgical performance for sake of overall musical conception.

**Massenet, Jules Emile Frédéric** (1842–1912), French composer. Taught composition at Paris Conservatoire (1878–96). Lyrical beauty of his music, and his smooth voluptuous style, helped to establish him as one of favourite composers of period. Though some have dismissed him as feminine Wagner, he still holds place in repertory. Works incl. 27 operas *eg Le Roi de Lahore* (1877), *Hérodiade* (1881), *Manon* (1884), *Werther* (1892) and *Thaïs* (1894), *Le Jongleur de Notre Dame* (1902), *Don Quichotte* (1910), ballets, choral and orchestral music, piano concerto, cantatas *(eg David Rizzio)*, cello fantasy, and *c* 200 songs.

**mässig** (Ger.), moderate.

**Mass of Life, A,** Delius's setting of passages from Nietzsche's *Thus Spake Zarathustra* for soloists, chorus and orchestra (1905).

**Masson, Paul Marie** (1882–1954), French musical historian, pupil of Rolland, d'Indy and Koechlin. Books incl. studies of Florentine carnival songs, Rameau's operas and Berlioz.

**mastersingers,** *see* MEISTERSINGER.

**Mastersingers of Nuremberg, The** (Ger., *Die Meistersinger von Nürnberg*), opera by Wagner, libretto by composer. First perf. Munich, 1868. Story concerns love of knight Walther von Stolzing for Eva, whose father has promised her hand to winner of singing competition. Beckmesser, Walther's rival (caricature of critic Hanslick), attempts to thwart him, but Walther wins competition with assistance of cobbler Hans Sachs.

**Mathias, William** (1934– ), Welsh composer, pianist. Pupil of Berkeley. Works incl. symphony, sinfonietta, *Celtic Dances* for orchestra, 3 piano concertos, and church, choral, chamber and organ music.

**Mathis der Maler** (Ger., *Mathis the Painter*), (1) opera by Hindemith, libretto by composer. First perf. Zürich, 1938. Story is based on life of 16th-cent. painter Matthias Grünewald and deals with conflict of artist's duty to himself and to society;

(2) symphony by Hindemith, based on music from opera. First perf. 1934.

**Matin, Le Midi, Le Soir et La Tempête, Le** (Fr., *Morning, Midday, Evening and Storm*), titles of 3 symphonies by Haydn (no 6 in D, no 7 in C, no 8 in G), composed 1761. Trilogy was clearly meant to be programmatic, but no authentic description of programme survives.

**Matrimonio Segreto,** *see* SECRET MARRIAGE.

**Matteis, Nicola** (*fl* 17th cent.), Italian violinist, composer. Came to London in 1672, and his playing is praised in Evelyn's *Diary*. Published 3 books of 'ayres' for violin, book entitled *The False Consonances of Musick*, and collection of songs in 2 books. Also composed *Ode on St Cecilia's Day*.

**Matthay, Tobias** (1858–1945), English pianist, teacher, composer. Founded own piano school (1900), evolved own method (Matthay System) and became one of leading teachers of Europe. Pupils incl. Myra Hess.

**Mattheson, Johann** (1681–1764), German composer, theorist, organist, opera singer. Took active part in development of church cantata. Works incl. 8 operas, 24 oratorios and cantatas, Passion, and 12 sonatas for flute and violin. Also wrote books on music.

**Matthews, Colin** (1946– ), English composer. Worked with Deryck Cooke on 'performing version' of Mahler's 10th Symphony. Own works incl. *Fourth Sonata* and *Night Music* for orchestra, *5 Sonnets to Orpheus* for voice and harp, and instrumental and piano music.

**Matthews, Denis** (1919– ), English pianist, teacher. Noted exponent of Mozart and Beethoven. Professor of music at Newcastle University from 1971.

**mattinata** (It.), morning song.

**Matton, Roger** (1929– ), French-Canadian composer. Pupil of Nadia Boulanger. Orchestral works incl. series of *Mouvements Symphoniques*.

**Mauduit, Jacques** (1557–1627), French composer. Associated in composition of MUSIQUE MESURÉE À L'ANTIQUE, *eg* 4-part settings of *chansonettes* by de Baïf (1586).

**Maurel, Victor** (1848–1923), French baritone. Was first Iago in Verdi's *Otello* (1887), and first Falstaff (1893). Also sang in Paris, London and New York, where he settled in 1909.

**Má Vlast** (Cz., *My Country*), cycle of 6 symphonic poems by Smetana (1874–9), inspired by Czech countryside and history: (1) *Vyšehrad* (citadel of Prague); (2) *Vltava* (Moldau River); (3) *Šárka* (leader of Bohemian Amazons); (4) *Z Ceskych Luhův a Hájův* (from Bohemia's fields and groves); (5) *Tábor* (stronghold of blind leader of Hussites); (6) *Blaník* (mountain in southern Bohemia).

**Mavra,** comic opera by Stravinsky, libretto by B. Kochno. First perf. Paris, 1922. Work is based on Pushkin's story *The Little House of Kolomna,* and is scored for 4 solo singers and orchestra.

**Maw, Nicholas** (1935– ), English composer. Pupil of Lennox Berkeley and Nadia Boulanger. Lyrical, post-Straussian style is heard at best in vocal music, incl. operas *One Man Show* and *The Rising of the Moon*, and *Scenes and Arias* for 3 female voices and orchestra (on old French texts). Has also written *Nocturne* for mezzo-soprano and orchestra, and *Chamber Music* for piano and wind instruments.

**maxima,** *see* LONG.

**Maxwell Davies,** *see* DAVIES, PETER MAXWELL.

**Maynard, John** (*fl* 16th–17th cents.), English lutenist, composer. In 1611 published *The XII wonders of the world...,* which contains 12 songs describing character-types, and 12 pavans and galliards for lute.

**May Night, A** (Russ., *Maiskaya Noch*), opera by Rimsky-Korsakov, libretto by composer. First perf. St Petersburg, 1880. Based on story by Gogol, story tells how water nymph helps young man to win the girl he loves.

**Mayr, Johann Simon** or **Giovanni Simone** (1763–1845), German-Italian composer, b. Bavaria. Pupils incl. Donizetti. Wrote *c* 70 operas, incl. *Medea in Corinto* (1813), which contains some striking foretastes of Verdi.

**Mayuzumi, Toshiro** (1929– ), Japanese composer. Works incl. orchestral *Bacchanal*, divertimento for chamber ensemble, *Tonepleromas 55* for wind, percussion and musical saw, and electronic music.

**Mazeppa,** (1) opera by Chaikovsky, libretto by V.P. Burenin (pseud. of A. Zhasminov) after Pushkin. First perf. Moscow, 1884. Story concerns Mazeppa's revolt against Peter the Great. Story has also inspired other operas;

(2) symphonic poem by Liszt (1851), based on piano study in *Etudes d'exécution transcendente* and inspired by Hugo's poem.

**mazurka,** Polish folk dance in moderate to fast triple time with 2nd or 3rd beat often strongly accented. First adapted as stylized piece by Chopin, who wrote *c* 50.

**Mazzocchi, Virgilio** (1597–1646), Italian composer. *Maestro di* *cappella* at St Peter's, Rome, from 1629. With Marazzoli, wrote earliest comic opera, *Chi soffre, speri* (1637).

His brother, **Domenico Mazzochi** (1592–1665), was also composer. His book of madrigals of 1638 contains works in both old and new (continuo) styles, and uses signs for *crescendo* and *diminuendo* for first time. Other works incl. opera *La Catena d'Adone* (1626), motets, and monodic *laude*.

**me,** anglicized version of It. *mi* (E). In TONIC SOL-FA, third note (or mediant) of major scale.

**meane** or **mene,** term used in England in 15th, early 16th cents. for voice between treble and tenor (Lat., *medius*); also applied to middle part in 3-part keyboard music.

**mean-tone tuning,** *see* TEMPERAMENT.

**measure** (US), bar. Also applied, more widely, to rhythm or time.

**mechanical musical instruments,** principle of revolving cylinder with protruding pins was applied in 15th, 16th cents. to carillon and keyboard instruments. Addition of clockwork mechanism made it possible to apply to number of contrivances *eg* musical clocks, mechanical organs and orchestras, and musical boxes, which were very popular in 18th cent. *See also* BARREL ORGAN, PIANOLA, STREET PIANO.

**medesimo tempo** (It.), in the same tempo.

**mediant,** third degree of diatonic scale, *eg* E in scale of C.

**Medium, The,** opera by Menotti, libretto by composer. First perf. New York, 1946.

**medley,** mixture, miscellany, potpourri. Operatic medley is therefore selection of excerpts performed non-stop. Term has long musical history, and was used in 16th-cent. keyboard music.

**Medtner, Nikolai Karlovich,** orig. Nikolay Karlovich (1880–1951), Russian composer, pianist, of German descent. Pupil of Arensky and Taneyev. From 1921 lived in Berlin, France and England. Most important compositions, in traditional style, are for piano, and incl. concertos, sonata-trilogy, and series of *Fairy Tales*.

**Mefistofele** (It., *Mephistopheles*), opera by Boito, libretto by composer (based on Goethe's *Faust*). First perf. Milan, 1868.

**Megli, Melio or Melli, Domenico** (*fl* 16th–17th cents.), Italian composer. One of earliest composers of monodic solos and dialogues (published 1602–9).

**mehr** (Ger.), more.

**Mehrstimmigkeit** (Ger.), polyphony.

**Mehta, Zubin** (1936– ), Indian conductor. Has conducted Los Angeles Philharmonic Orchestra (1961–76), New York Philharmonic Orchestra from 1977; musical adviser to Israel Philharmonic Orchestra from 1968; and guest conductor of Vienna Philharmonic Orchestra.

**Méhul, Etienne Henri Nicolas** (1763–1817), French composer. Encouraged by Gluck, wrote several operas. Later operas developed style of Grétry, and he became one of most prominent composers of

Revolution period. Most mature works are *Uthal* (1806) and *Joseph* (1807).

**Meibom or Meibomius, Marcus** (1626–1711), German or Danish philologist. In 1652 printed texts, with Latin translations and commentary, of treatises on music by Aristoxenus, Aristeides, Quintilianus, Nichomachus, Cleonides, Gaudentius, Alypius and Baccheius the Elder.

**Meissen, Heinrich von,** *see* FRAUENLOB.

**Meistersinger** (Ger.), mastersinger, member of literary and musical guilds which were founded in certain German cities in 15th, 16th cents. Composed of traders and craftsmen; succeeded aristocratic MINNESINGER. Hans Sachs was most famous *Meistersinger* of 16th cent.

**Meistersinger von Nürnberg, Die,** *see* MASTERSINGERS OF NUREMBERG.

**Mel, Rinaldo del** (?1554–*c* 1600), Flemish composer. Worked in service of King of Portugal, and in Rome, Bavaria and Bologna. Published 6 books of motets and 15 books of madrigals.

**Melba, Dame Nellie,** orig. Helen Mitchell (1859–1931), Australian operatic soprano. Came to Europe (1886). One of greatest singers of her day in lyric and coloratura roles.

**Melchior, Lauritz** (1890–1973), Danish-born tenor. Sang at Bayreuth (1924–31) and at New York Metropolitan (1926–50). Known for Wagner roles.

**melisma** (Gr., song; pl., *melismata*), unit of melody sung to one syllable, esp. in plainsong. Also applied, more widely, to any florid vocal passage.

**Mellers, Wilfred Howard** (1914– ), English musical historian, composer. Professor of music at York University from 1964. Compositions incl. opera about Christopher Marlowe, cantata *Yggdrasil*, and orchestral, chamber and instrumental music, but is better known for books *eg* on Couperin and The Beatles.

**mellophone,** instrument resembling horn in appearance, and to some extent in tone quality. Easier to play than horn, though inferior. Invented primarily for use in jazz and dance bands; suitable as doubling instrument for trumpet players.

**melodic minor scale,** *see* SCALE.

**mélodie** (Fr.), (1) melody;

(2) song with piano accompaniment, French equivalent of German *Lied*.

**melodrama,** spoken words with musical accompaniment, either as complete work (also called monodrama or duodrama) or as part of opera. Modern use of term, to denote violent or sensational play, is development of original meaning.

**melody,** succession of sounds which achieve distinctive musical shape. Factors which determine character and effect of melody are its MODE, RHYTHM and design in relation to pitch ('contour'). Melody is not necessarily a 'tune' which can be instantly remembered; it may contain very wide leaps, esp. in modern music – however, familiarity breeds understanding, and 'unmelodic' music often turns out to be melodic. *See also* METRE, SEQUENCE.

**membranophone,** generic name for all percussion instruments (*eg* drums) producing sounds by means of vibrating skin or similar substance.

**Mencken** or **Mancinus, Thomas** (1550–1611/12), German composer. Composed setting of Passion (1608), motets and madrigals.

**Mendelssohn Bartholdy, [Jakob Ludwig] Felix** (1809–47), German composer. Born in Hamburg. Son of successful banker, and grandson of Jewish philosopher Moses Mendelssohn. Received first piano lessons from mother; his sister Fanny Cäcilie Hensel (1805–47) was also to develop as pianist and composer, and proved a valuable confidante for him. His remarkable gifts as composer, conductor and pianist were encouraged by his teachers incl. Moscheles. In 1821 visited Goethe in Weimar. By age of 9 was performing in public, by 12 had written piano quartet (op 1), by 14 had own private orchestra, by 16 had produced first masterpiece (octet for strings), and by 17 his second (overture to *A Midsummer Night's Dream*). Led Bach revival, conducting first perf. of St Matthew Passion since Bach's death. In 1829 made first of 10 visits to England, where conducted Philharmonic Society. Also visited Scotland, which inspired Hebrides overture and 'Scottish' Symphony (no 3). These he wrote in Italy (1830–1), where met Berlioz and started 'Italian' Symphony (no 4). Went to Paris (1831–2), where met Liszt and Chopin. Returned to Germany (1833) where he became conductor of Leipzig Gewandhaus Orchestra (initiating its great reputation). Married Cécile Jeanrenaud (1837). With Schumann and others, founded Leipzig Conservatorium. Conducted his oratorio *Elijah* at 1846 Birmingham Festival, one of his greatest triumphs. By now health was weakening, and death of his sister hastened his own.

Mendelssohn's earliest 'mature' works, *A Midsummer Night's Dream* (1826) and *The Hebrides* (1830–2), show superb craftsmanship and individual melodic style, and marked important stage in history of programmatic concert overture. Later compositions show little development in technique or expression. Polish, beauty and harmonic harmlessness of much of his music set canons of mid-Victorian musical taste; but he could be adventurous too, as unusual structure and Wagnerian foretastes of 'Reformation' symphony (no 5) demonstrate.

Principal compositions:

(1) Orchestra: 5 symphonies: no 2, *Hymn of Praise,* symphony-cantata, 1840; no 3, *Scottish,* 1842; no 4, *Italian,* 1833; no 5, *Reformation,* 1830; overtures: *A Midsummer Night's Dream* (1826), *The Hebrides* (1830–2, also called *Fingal's Cave*), *Calm Sea and Prosperous Voyage* (1828), *The Legend of the Fair Melusina* (1833), *Ruy Blas* (1839); piano concertos in G minor (1831) and D minor (1837), violin concerto (1844);

(2) Choral works: oratorios: *St Paul* (1834–6), *Elijah* (1846), *Christus* (unfinished, 1847); symphony-cantata *Hymn of Praise* (1840, also known as symphony no 2), 9 psalms, 9 motets;

(3) Stage music: operas: *Camacho's Wedding* (1825), *Son and Stranger* (1829), *Lorelei* (unfinished, 1847); incidental music: *Antigone* (1841), *The First Witches' Sabbath* (1831, 1842), *Oedipus at Colonus* (1845);

(4) Chamber music: 6 string quartets, 3 piano quartets (1822–5), 2 string quintets (1831, 1845), sextet (1824), string octet (1825), 2 trios (1839, 1845), violin sonata, 2 cello sonatas (1838, 1843);

(5) Piano: *capriccio* (1825), *Rondo capriccioso,* 6 preludes and fugues (1832–7), 8 books of *Songs without Words;*

(6) Organ: 3 preludes and fugues (1833–7), 6 sonatas (1839–44);

(7) Songs and part-songs: 10 sets of songs with piano, 11 sets of part-songs.

**mene,** *see* MEANE.

**Mengelberg, Willem** (1871–1951), Dutch conductor. Conductor of Concertgebouw Orchestra, Amsterdam (1895-1941); developed it into one of finest in Europe, esp. in performance of Mahler, Richard Strauss and French composers. Sympathized with Nazis during WWII and thereafter career declined. Died in Switzerland.

**Mennin, Peter** (1923– ), American composer, conductor. Pupil of Hanson and Koussevitsky. President of Juilliard School of Music, New York, from 1962. Works incl. 8 symphonies, concertos for violin, cello, and piano, 'concertato' (after Melville's *Moby Dick*) and *Canto* for orchestra, *Christmas Cantata*, and chamber and instrumental music.

**meno** or **meno mosso** (It.), with less movement, *ie* less quickly.

**Menotti, Gian Carlo** (1911– ), Italian-born composer. Resident in US from 1928. Operas, incl. *Amelia goes to the Ball, The Island God, The Old Maid and the Thief, The Medium, The Telephone, The Consul, Amahl and the Night Visitors, The Saint of Bleecker Street, The Last Savage* and *Help, help, the Globolinks!* Most of these, esp. *The Consul,* show strong sense of theatre but are musically marred by watery post-Puccini idiom. Piano concerto, despite its fluency, is similarly flawed.

**mensural music** (Lat., *musica mensurata*), medieval term for music with definite relative note-values, as distinct from plainsong *(musica plana)*.

**mensural notation,** system of notation formulated by Franco of Cologne in *Ars cantus mensurabilis* (*c* 1260) and used until gradual adoption of metrical rhythm with bar-lines during 17th cent. In course of 15th cent. black notes began to be written as white and red as black. In white notation, notes and corresponding rests were:

Their relations were governed by time-signature at beginning of part, and by signs of PROPORTION and use of black (imperfect, *ie* duple subdivision) notes instead of white (perfect, *ie* triple subdivision) in course of part. Relation of long to breve was called mode (or 'mood') and was normally imperfect; of breve to semibreve, time; of semibreve to mimim, prolation.

**menuet** (Fr.; Ger., *Menuett*), minuet. Form *menuetto,* often used by German composers, is corruption of It. *minuetto.*

**Menuhin, Yehudi** (1916– ), American-born violinist, conductor. Made debut at age of 7, and soon became internationally famous. Became pupil of Enesco and Adolph Busch. In 1944 commissioned Bartók's solo violin sonata. Also closely associated with Elgar's violin concerto (in which composer coached him). Today he remains world's best-loved violinist, though has also become known as conductor, esp. of chamber music. As player, notable now for warmth of interpretations rather than for technical precision, which is too often erratic. In 1963 founded school in England for exceptionally musical children. Now lives in London, where received K.B.E. (1965). His sisters Hephzibah and Yaltah are both pianists, as is his son Jeremy, who also conducts.

**Mephisto Waltzes,** pieces by Liszt: no 1 (well-known one) and no 2 were written for orchestra and transcribed for piano and for piano duet; nos 3 and 4 are for piano.

**Mer, La** (Fr., The Sea), 3 symphonic sketches by Debussy (1905): (1) *From dawn to midday on the sea*; (2) *Play of the waves*; (3) *Dialogue of the wind and the sea.*

**Merbecke,** *see* MARBECK.

**Mercadente, Giuseppe Saverio Raffaele** (1795–1870), Italian composer. Pupil of Zingarelli. Director of Naples Conservatorio from 1840. Blind from 1862. Works incl. *c* 60 operas *eg Elisa e Claudio* (1821) and *Il Giuramento* (1827), 21 Masses, 4 funeral symphonies, instrumental pieces, and songs.

**Mercure, Pierre** (1927–66), French-Canadian composer. Taught by Nadia Boulanger, Dallapiccola, Pousseur, Nono, and Berio. Works incl. orchestral *Triptique* (1959), *Lignes et Points* (1965), in which electronic sound effects are achieved by purely orchestral means, electronic music, and *musique concrète.* Killed in car accident.

**'Mercury' Symphony,** nickname for Haydn's symphony no 43 in E (*c* 1771). Reason for name is unknown.

**Merlo, Alessandro** or **Alessandro Romano** or **Alessandro della Viola** (b. *c* 1530), Italian singer, violinist, singer, composer. He was bass-tenor with range of 3 octaves. In 1594 became singer in Papal Chapel. Works incl. *canzoni,* madrigals, book of *villanelle,* and book of motets.

**Merlotti,** *see* MERULO.

**Merry Mount,** opera by Howard Hanson, libretto by R. Stokes. First perf. New York, 1934. Work is based on Hawthorne's story *The Maypole of Merry Mount.*

**Merry Widow, The** (Ger., *Die Lustige Witwe*), operetta by Lehár, libretto by V. Léon and L. Stein. First perf. Vienna, 1905. Story is lighthearted piece of amorous and diplomatic intrigue.

**Merry Wives of Windsor, The** (Ger., *Die lustigen Weiber von Windsor*), opera by Nicolai, libretto by S.H. Mosenthal (after Shakespeare). First perf. Berlin, 1849.

**Mersenne** or **Mersennus, Marin** (1588–1648), French theorist. Made acquaintance of Descartes and elder Pascal in Paris. Joined Franciscan order in 1613. Works incl. *De la nature des sons* (1635) and *Harmonie universelle* (1636); latter is comprehensive and scientific study of music theory, which incl. esp. informative sections on musical instruments.

**Merula, Tarquinio** (*c* 1590–1665), Italian composer. Works incl. canzonas, madrigals, motets, sonatas for solo violin and continuo, and keyboard music.

**Merulo, Claudio** or **Claudio da Correggio,** orig. Merlotti (1533–1604), Italian organist, composer. Organist at St Mark's, Venice. Works incl. madrigals, opera *La Tragedia* in madrigal style, 2 books of *Sacrae Cantiones,* 4 Masses, and organ pieces. His organ toccatas are most developed works in form in 16th cent.

**messa di voce** (It.), 'placing of the voice'. Term is used to indicate *crescendo* or *diminuendo* on long note in singing.

**Messager, André Charles Prosper** (1853–1929), French composer, conductor. Pupil of Saint-Saëns. Conducted première of Debussy's *Pelléas et Melisande* (which was dedicated to him). Though wrote serious operas, reputation rests on operettas *eg Véronique* and *Monsieur Beaucaire,* and ballet music *eg Les Deux Pigeons.*

**Messa per i Defunti** (It.), **Messe des Morts** (Fr.), Requiem Mass.

**Messiaen, Olivier Eugène Prosper Charles** (1908– ), French composer, organist. Son of poetess and professor of literature. Pupil of Dukas (composition) and Dupré (organ) at Paris Conservatoire, then taught at École Normale de Musique and Schola Cantorum. Organist at La Trinité, Paris, since 1931. In 1936 with Baudrier, Lesur and Jolivet formed group *La Jeune France.* In 1940 imprisoned by Nazis (*Quartet for the End of Time* was written and performed in concentration camp) but then repatriated, and in 1942 became teacher of harmony at Conservatoire. Though musical roots seem to lie in Franck and Berlioz, Messiaen is one of most original, and influential, of modern composers. Musical language makes use of diverse but (in his case) surprisingly compatible sound sources – bird-song, Indian music (*eg* in *Turangalîla* symphony, 1949), plainsong, timbres of oriental percussion (*eg* in *Chronochromie,* 1960), Franckian harmony, Bartókian night-music – which he employs to immensely spacious and powerful effect. As life-long Catholic, uses nature as symbols of divinity *eg* in *Oiseaux exotiques* (1956) for piano and wind instruments, vast *Catalogue d'oiseaux* (1956–8) for piano, and *Et expecto resurrectionem mortuorum* (1964) for woodwind, brass and percussion (designed to be performed on mountain slopes). *Vingt Regards sur l'Enfant Jésus* (1944) for solo piano shows his religious ecstasy at its most grandly extended, and more recent *Transfiguration de Notre Seigneur Jésus Christ* (1969) for 7 instrumental soloists, chorus and orchestra, in 14 movts., shows no slackening of intensity. Among organ works, *La Nativité du Seigneur* (1935), set of 9 meditations, has established itself as one of few 20th-cent. masterpieces for instrument.

**Messiah** (not *The Messiah*), oratorio by Handel, to text selected from Bible by composer and C. Jennens. Composed in less than month. First perf. Dublin, 1742.

**Messinginstrumente** (Ger.), brass instruments.

**mesto** (It.), sad.

**mesure** (Fr.), (1) bar; (2) time. *Battre de mesure*, to beat time.

**metal block,** instrument similar to wood block or small anvil; produces sound of indefinite pitch. Of recent origin.

**metallophone,** instrument of xylophone family, but made of bronze.

**Metamorphosen** (Ger., *Metamorphoses*), work for 23 solo strings by Richard Strauss (1945), believed to express composer's sense of loss after destruction of Munich. Inscribed 'In Memoriam'. Quotes funeral march from Beethoven's *Eroica* symphony.

**metamorphosis of themes,** *see* LEITMOTIV.

**Metastasio,** orig. Pietro Trapassi (1698–1782), Italian poet, librettist. Stabilized form of opera libretto as alternation of recitatives with arias, which remained basis of form of classical opera until questioned by Calzabigi and Gluck. Some of his libretti were set up to 70 times.

**metre,** scheme of regularly recurring accents, indicated by TIME SIGNATURE, which underlies particular rhythm of melody or harmonic progression. Music in which rhythm was directly related to metre of poetry was written in 16th cent. Bar-lines to show metrical schemes came into general use in 17th cent. Since then rhythmic design of melodies and harmonies has been contained in and related to underlying metrical scheme of each composition, which is indicated by TIME SIGNATURE, *eg* 3/4 time means that basic values are quarter notes (crotchets) and that every third quarter note is accented.

**metrical psalter,** *see* PSALTER.

**metronome,** device which produces regular beats. Model in general use was patented by MAELZEL in 1816 and adopted in following year by Beethoven to indicate tempo of his compositions *eg*

♩ = M.M. 60

indicates 60 crotchet beats per minute (M.M. is abbrev. of Maelzel Metronome)

**Metropolitan Opera House, New York,** most prestigious opera house in US. Opened 1883. Re-housed in 1966.

**Meyerbeer, Giacomo,** orig. Jakob Liebmann Beer (1791–1864),

German-born composer. Pupil of Clementi. Went to Italy (1816) and wrote operas in style of Rossini. After 1830 became dominant composer in most brilliant period of French grand opera in Paris under dramatist Scribe, who wrote his libretti. In this elaborate and spectacular style he found his métier, *eg* in *Robert le Diable* (1831), *Les Huguenots* (1836), *Le Prophète* (1849) and *L'Africaine* (1865). Influenced style of Wagner's *Rienzi* (1842).

**mezzo** (It.), half. *Mezzo forte*, moderately loud (abbrev. *mf*). *Mezzo piano*, moderately soft (abbrev. *mp*). *Mezzo-soprano*, voice between soprano and contralto in range. *Mezza voce*, with moderate volume of tone.

**mi** (Fr., It.), note E. Also third note of Guidonian hexachord (*see* SOLMIZATION).

**Miaskovsky, Nikolai Yakovlevich** (1881–1950), Russian composer. Trained for military career, but studied music with Glière, Rimsky-Korsakov and Liadov. In 1948 denounced with Prokofiev, Shostakovich and others for inharmonious music by Central Committee of Communist Party. Works incl. 27 symphonies, oratorio *Kirov is with us*, 9 string quartets, piano music, and songs, few of which can be deemed inharmonious.

**Michael, Rogier** (*c* 1554–*c* 1619), Flemish singer, composer. Worked in Dresden from 1575. Works incl. introits in motet style, 4-part chorales, and other church music.

His son, **Tobias Michael** (1592–1657), was also a composer. Works incl. collection of sacred concertos entitled *Musikalischer Seelenlust* (1634–7), and other church music.

**Michelangeli, Arturo Benedetti** (1920– ), Italian pianist. One of foremost pianists of the age. Brings exceptional clarity of timbres and textures to everything he plays.

**Micheli, Romano** (*c* 1575–*c* 1659), Italian composer. Works incl. psalms, motets, canons and madrigals.

**microtones,** intervals which are fractions of semitone. Such intervals have always been part of theory and practice of tuning (*see* TEMPERAMENT), but only in modern times have they been introduced into compositions, *eg* by Hába and Ligeti.

**middle C,** note C at (approximately) middle of piano keyboard.

**middle fiddle,** viola (term coined by Percy Grainger).

**Midi, Le,** *see* MATIN.

**Midsummer Marriage, The,** opera by Tippett, libretto by composer. First perf. London, 1955. Work is 'quest opera', consciously modelled as modern equivalent of Mozart's *The Magic Flute*. *Ritual Dances* from opera are sometimes performed in concert hall.

**Midsummer Night's Dream, A,** (1) overture to Shakespeare's play by Mendelssohn, op 21 (1826);

(2) incidental music by Mendelssohn, op 61 (1842);

(3) incidental music by Carl Orff;

(4) opera by Britten (using abbrev. of Shakespeare's text). First perf. Aldeburgh, 1960.

**Mighty Handful, The,** alternative name for The FIVE.

**Mignon,** opera by Ambroise Thomas, libretto by J. Barbier and M. Carré (after Goethe's *Wilhelm Meister*). First perf. Paris, 1866.

**Migot, Georges Elbert** (1891–1976), French composer, painter, aesthetician. Pupil of Widor. Compositions incl. operas, ballets, large-scale choral works, symphonies, and other orchestral music, mainly in personal, polyphonic idiom. Independence from any fashionable school of composition won him nickname of 'Group of One'.

**Mihalovici, Marcel** (1898– ), Romanian composer. Pupil of d'Indy in Paris where he settled. Works incl. opera *L'Intransigeant Pluton*, several ballets, fantasia for orchestra, *Symphonie du temps present* (1943), and chamber music.

**Mikado, The,** operetta by Gilbert and Sullivan. First perf. London, 1885. With its Japanese setting, remains most popular of its creators' works.

**Mikrokosmos** (Gr., microcosm), collection of 153 short piano pieces in 6 progressively graded volumes, by Bartók (1926–37), intended as complete course of instruction in technique and also illustrating rich variety of invention.

**Milán, Luis de** (*c* 1500–after 1561), Spanish composer, *vihuela* (Spanish lute) player. Published book (1536) containing earliest collection of accompanied solo songs of Renaissance period, together with fantasias and pavanes for *vihuela*.

**Milanov, Zinka** (1906– ), Yugoslav soprano. One of leading Verdi sopranos of her generation.

**Milford, Robin Humphrey** (1903–59), English composer. Pupil of Holst and Vaughan Williams. Works incl. 2 oratorios, orchestral works, violin concerto, and songs.

**Milhaud, Darius** (1892–1974), French composer, of Jewish ancestry. Pupil of Widor, d'Indy and Dukas. Diplomat in Brazil (1917–19). On returning to France became member of Les SIX. In 1940 emigrated to California, but returned to France (1947) to teach at Paris Conservatoire. Prolific output reflects varied career. Under spell of Les Six (1919–23) produced jazz-inspired *The Creation of the World*, ballet *The Ox on the Roof* with scenario by Jean Cocteau, and works with texts drawn from agricultural and horticultural catalogues. Collaboration with Paul Claudel resulted in one of most important works, opera *Christophe Colomb* (1930), which uses film effects and Greek chorus. Provençal boyhood is reflected in orchestral *Suite Provençale*, *Carnaval d'Aix* for piano and orchestra (1927), and wind quartet *King René's Chimney* (named after street in Aix). Latin-American period is commemorated by orchestral *Saudades do Brasil* and piano music of same title. Other works incl. opera *David* (1954), numerous symphonies, 18 string quartets, and French version of *The Beggar's Opera*.

**Militärtrommel** (Ger.), side drum.

**military band,** orig. applied only to regimental band, term has, in Britain, come to mean same as 'concert' or 'symphonic' band in US. Inclusion of woodwind distinguishes military from brass band. Instrumentation varies widely, but typical British band might well incl. following parts: piccolo, 2 flutes, 2 oboes, 2 clarinets in E flat, 4 clarinets in B flat, alto saxophone, tenor saxophone, 2 bassoons, 4 horns in F or E flat, 2 cornets in B flat, 2 trumpets in B flat, 2 tenor trombones, bass trombone, euphonium, tubas in E flat and B flat, timpani, side drum, bass drum, and other percussion instruments. Number of players to part varies.

**'Military' Symphony,** Haydn's symphony no 100 in G (1794), 8th of 'Salomon' symphonies written for London. So called from trumpet call in 2nd movt., which also uses triangle, bass drum and cymbals (not normal members of 18th-cent. orchestra).

**Millöcker, Karl** (1842–99), Austrian composer. Wrote numerous operettas, best known being *The Beggar Student* and *Gasparone*.

**Milner, Anthony** (1925– ), English composer. Best known for vocal works incl. Mass and several cantatas. Has also written orchestral and chamber music.

**Milstein, Nathan** (1904– ), Russian-born violinist. Later settled in US. Pupil of Auer and Ysaÿe. Has established international reputation.

**Milton, John** (*c* 1563–1647), English composer, father of the poet. Works incl. madrigal in *The Triumphes of Oriana*, psalms, and 5 fancies for viols.

**minaccevole, minacciando** (It.), in a menacing fashion.

**Mines of Sulphur, The,** opera by Richard Rodney Bennett, libretto by B. Cross. First perf. London, 1965. Work is ghost story.

**mineur** (Fr.), minor.

**miniature score,** score containing all voice and/or instrumental parts of a piece of music, but in smaller type and page-size than full score. Also known as pocket score or study score.

**minim** (US, half-note; Fr., *blanche*; Ger., *Halbe*; It., *minima*), time-value of ½ semibreve (whole-note), represented by sign

𝅗𝅥

Minim rest is

𝄼

**Minnesinger** (Ger., *Minne* = chivalrous love), German poet and musician of period of chivalry, corresponding to TROUBADOUR and TROUVÈRE of Provence and France. Period of aristocratic *Minnesinger* lasted *c* 1150–1450, when traditions were taken over by merchant guilds of MEISTERSINGER. Most famous of *Minnesinger* were Walther von der Vogelweide (*c* 1170–*c* 1230) and Wolfram von Eschenbach (*fl* early 13th cent.).

**Minnesinger fiddle,** forerunner of violin, first appeared in 13th cent.

**minor,** *see* MAJOR.

**minore** (It.), minor mode.

**minstrel,** professional entertainer, esp. performing musician, of Middle Ages, whether attached to household or court, or self-employed. During 16th cent. term 'minstrel' became debased and was applied to wandering ballad singers, and was eventually incorporated into vagrancy laws. 'Respectable' performers now called themselves 'musicians'. *See* JONGLEUR.

**Minton, Yvonne** (1938– ), Australian mezzo-soprano. Has appeared internationally in concert-hall and opera. Created role of Thea in Tippett's *The Knot Garden*.

**minuet** (Fr., *menuet*; Ger., *Menuett*; It., *minuetto*), French dance, of popular origin, in 3/4 time at moderate pace. First introduced as stylized form by Lully *c* 1650, and appeared throughout baroque period. Became one of regular movements in classical sonata and symphony, always in ternary form (minuet-trio-minuet). In music of Beethoven, became transformed into SCHERZO.

**'Minute' Waltz,** nickname for Chopin's waltz in D flat, op 64, no 1 (1847). Played with proper sensitivity, music should last longer than minute. Also called *'Dog' Waltz*, as it is supposed to represent George Sand's dog chasing its tail.

**Miracle, The,** name popularly given to Haydn's symphony no 96 in D (1791). At first performance chandelier supposedly fell and missed audience by miracle. In fact this incident occurred at first performance of Haydn's symphony no 102 in B flat (1794).

**Miraculous Mandarin, The,** mime-play with music by Bartók (1919), scenario by M. Lengyel. First perf. Cologne, 1926. Music also made into concert suite.

**Mireille,** opera by Gounod, libretto by M. Carré (inspired by poem of Mistral). First perf. Paris, 1864. Gounod supplied both tragic and happy ending.

**mirliton** (Fr.), wind instrument consisting of pipe with one end closed by thin parchment or skin and hole in side into which performer sings. Produces tone similar to bleating of sheep. Known as *flûte-eunuque* (eunuch flute) in 17th cent. Now called 'kazoo', and regarded as toy.

**mirror composition,** term applied to composition using either RETROGRADE MOTION or contrary motion – *see* INVERSION (2).

**Miserere** (Lat.), in full *Miserere mei Deus* ('Have mercy upon me, O God'), 51st Psalm (50th in RC Church), sung in Holy Week in RC Church.

**Missa** (Lat.), Mass. *Missa brevis*, short Mass. *Missa Cellensis*, *see* MARIAZELL MASS. *Missa in angustiis*, *see* NELSON MASS. *Missa in tempore belli*, *see* PAUKENMESSE. *Missa pro defunctis*, *see* REQUIEM MASS. *Missa sine nomine*, Mass not founded on any pre-existing melody (or *cantus firmus*) and hence without title *('sine nomine')*. *Missa solemnis* or *Missa solennis*, *see* next entry. *Missa supra voces musicales*, Mass which uses notes of HEXACHORD as *cantus firmus*.

Other titles fall into following categories:

(1) those which indicate plainsong on which Mass is built, or motet from which it borrows material;

(2) those which indicate particular saint's day or festival for which Mass is intended;

(3) those which indicate mode in which Mass is written, *eg Missa quarti toni*, Mass in 4th (Hypophrygian) mode.

**Missa solemnis** (or **solennis**) (Lat.), solemn Mass. Title is usually reserved for Mass of particularly exalted character, esp. Beethoven's in D (op 123).

**misterioso** (It.), mysteriously.

**misura** (It.), measure, term which can be used in English sense of 'bar', but is more usually applied to regularity. Thus *alla misura*, in strict time; *senza misura*, not in strict time (*ie* bar-lines are usually omitted); *misurato*, measured.

**mit** (Ger.), with.

**Mit dem Hornsignal**, *see* AUF DEM ANSTAND.

**Mitridate, Re di Ponte** (It., *Mithridates, King of Pontus*), opera seria, K87, by Mozart, libretto by V.A. Cigna-Santi. First perf. Milan, 1770, when composer was 14. Work is based on tragedy by Racine.

**Mitropoulos, Dimitri** (1896–1960), Greek-born conductor, pianist, composer. Pupil of Busoni. Conductor of Minneapolis Symphony Orchestra from 1937, and of New York Symphony Orchestra from 1950. Noted for conducting of 20th-cent. music. Compositions incl. opera, *concerto grosso*, chamber and instrumental music, and songs.

**mixed voices,** chorus comprising male and female voices.

**Mixolydian mode,** (1) in ancient Greek music, equivalent of white notes on piano from B to B;

(2) from Middle Ages onwards applied to equivalent of white notes on piano from G to G. Sharpening of seventh note makes it identical with modern major scale.

**mixture,** organ stop which produces 3 or 4 sounds higher than pitch corresponding to key which is depressed: 3-rank mixture sounds fifteenth, nineteenth and twenty-second, which are fourth, sixth and eighth notes of harmonic series, above foundation note.

**mock trumpet,** early English name for *chalumeau* or early clarinet.

**mode** (Fr., *ton*; Ger., *Tonart*; It., *tuono*), set of notes which form material of melodic idioms used in composition. Medieval (also called church or ecclesiastical) modes may be represented by scales of white notes on piano. They bear names derived from Greek musical system, though neither this concept of mode nor application of names corresponds to Greek theory:

I Dorian, compass D–D, final D, dominant A
II Hypodorian, compass A–A, final D, dominant F
III Phrygian, compass E–E, final E, dominant C
IV Hypophrygian, compass B–B, final E, dominant A
V Lydian, compass F–F, final F, dominant C
VI Hypolydian, compass C–C, final F, dominant A
VII Mixolydian, compass G–G, final G, dominant D
VIII Hypomixolydian, compass D–D, final G, dominant C
Following modes were added in 16th cent.:
IX Aeolian, compass A–A, final A, dominant E
X Hypoaeolian, compass E–E, final A, dominant C
XI Ionian, compass C–C, final C, dominant G
XII Hypoionian, compass G–G, final C, dominant E

*Final* of mode is note on which its melodies end; *dominant* is reciting note *(tenor)*. Those modes prefixed 'Hypo-' are called *plagal*, the others are called *authentic*; distinction lies in range of melody.

Until end of 16th cent., medieval modal and interval theories were bases of polyphonic composition. By end of 17th cent., exclusive use of 2 modern modes, major and minor (*see* SCALE) was established. Major scale was, melodically, of great antiquity, though not officially recognized by medieval theorists. Occurs frequently in plainsong melodies and secular songs of Middle Ages in form of F mode with flattened B. Intervals are thus identical with those of Ionian mode. Practice of sharpening seventh in Mixolydian mode resulted in similar identity. Minor mode was conflation of Dorian and Aeolian modes, with seventh sharpened as required.

Modal idioms, generally derived from folksong, reappeared in 19th cent., and became element of some importance in style of Debussy, Ravel, Sibelius, Vaughan Williams, and others.

**mode, rhythmic,** *see* RHYTHMIC MODE.

**moderato** (It.), **modéré** (Fr.), moderate (with reference to speed).

**modulation,** basically, change of key, process being achieved by logical harmonic progressions. At its simplest, establishment of new key is effected by perfect CADENCE in that key.

Modulation is often effected by passing through 'pivot' chord, *ie* chord with 2 or more notes belonging to both keys concerned, on way to dominant of new key, *eg* from C to E minor, pivot chord (A–E–A–C) is sub-mediant chord in C, and sub-dominant chord in E minor. Such pivot chords exist, and may be similarly used for modulation, between every major key and key of its supertonic minor, mediant minor, sub-dominant, dominant, relative minor, and leading-note minor, *eg* between C and D minor, E minor, F, G, A minor, and B minor.

Chords of which root and fifth are common to 2 keys concerned are equally effective as pivot chords. Such chords exist between every 2 major keys, except those of which key-notes are tritone apart. Modulation which takes its departure from minor key may be effected along similar lines.

Modulation may also be effected by using as intermediate:

(1) chords which, since they divide octave into equal parts, are inherently capable of assuming as many key-contexts as they have notes (*eg* augmented triad and diminished seventh chord);

(2) chromatic chords which have by historical usage established themselves within key (*eg* Neapolitan sixth and augmented sixth chords). In mediant chord of minor mode with sharpened fifth, which is augmented triad, any one of 3 notes may be used as dominant.

If modulation is repeated from new key as starting point, *ie* transposed into that key, result is modulating or 'real' sequence.

Such formulae as are given above may be basis of modulations which are momentary (sometimes called 'transitions') and are soon followed by return to original key, or are modulations (or 'transitions') on way to further modulation, or are part of large tonal design. Technique and art of modulation is fundamental to artistic use of effects of tonality, to control of tonal design, and thus to art of composition. *See also* HARMONY.

**modus lascivus** (Lat., wanton mode), key of C major, avoided in church music in Middle Ages. Officially recognized as Ionian mode in 16th cent.

**Moeran, Ernest John** (1894–1950), English composer of Irish descent. Pupil of John Ireland. Works, some showing influence of Vaughan Williams and Delius, incl. symphony in G minor (1937), violin concerto (1942), cello concerto (1945) and other orchestral music, choral, church and chamber music, and songs.

**Moeschinger, Albert** (1897– ), Swiss composer, teacher. Works incl. 3 symphonies, 3 piano concertos, orchestral variations and fugue on theme of Purcell, choral, chamber, piano and organ music, and songs.

**Moiseiwitsch, Benno** (1890–1963), Russian-born pianist. Took British nationality (1937). Famed esp. for performances of Rakhmaninov.

**moll** (Ger.), minor, as opposed to major *(dur)*.

**molto** (It.), very. *Allegro molto* (or *Allegro di molto*), very fast.

**Moments Musicaux** (sing. *Moment Musical*), set of 6 short piano pieces by Schubert, op 94 (1828). Title also used by other composers for short piano pieces.

**Mompou, Federico** (1893– ), Spanish (Catalan) composer, pianist. Resident in Paris from early 1920s. Developed individual style of composition called *primitivista*, which has no bar-divisions, key-signatures or cadences. Works are chiefly piano music (*eg Songs and Dances*, based on popular airs) and songs.

**monacordo** (It.), 16th-cent. term for clavichord.

**Mondo della Luna, Il** (It., *The World of the Moon*), comic opera by Haydn, libretto by Goldoni. First perf. Esterházy, 1777.

**Mondonville, Jean Joseph Cassanéa De** (1711–72), French violinist, composer. Became director of Royal Chapel in Paris (1744), and of Concert Spirituel in 1755. Composed operas, incl. *Titon et l'Aurore* (1753), 3 oratorios, motets, and violin sonatas *Les sons harmoniques* (*c* 1738), which make first extended use of harmonics. He was active on French side during *La Guerre des Bouffons*.

**Moniuszko, Stanislaw** (1819–72), Polish composer, organist, conductor. Leading Polish composer of 19th cent. after Chopin. His opera *Halka* (1847) was first Polish opera on national theme. Other works incl. many operas *eg The Haunted Manor* and *The Raftsman*, symphonic poem *Bajka (Fairy Tale)*, choral, incidental and church music, and songs.

**Monn, Georg Matthias** (1717–50), Austrian organist, composer. Works incl. symphonies, quartets, and trio sonatas. His symphony in D of 1740 is earliest known with 4 movts., with minuet as 3rd.

**monochord,** instrument consisting of single string stretched over wooden resonator, with movable bridge. Used, esp. in Middle Ages, to demonstrate relation between musical intervals and division of string.

**monodrama,** (1) dramatic work involving only one character;

(2) in particular, work for speaking voice with instrumental accompaniment. *See* MELODRAMA.

**monody,** solo song with accompaniment. Solo songs with lute were common in 16th cent. Term is particularly applied to Italian monody (for solo voice and continuo) in new style of early 17th cent., which exploited dramatic and expressive possibilities of solo singer. This style appeared in solo monodies and in opera.

**monophony** (Gr., single sound), music which consists of melody only, without independent or supporting accompaniment.

**monothematic,** *see* DEVELOPMENT.

**monotone,** recitation of words on single note.

**Monsigny, Pierre Alexandre** (1729–1817), French composer. Wrote comic operas incl. *Rose et Colas* (1764), *Le Déserteur* (1769), and *La belle Arsène* (1773). Stopped composing in 1777.

**Monte, Philippe de** (1521–1603), Flemish composer. Spent early years in Italy. In service of Philip II of Spain, then became *Kapellmeister* to Emperors Maximilian II and Rudolf II. With Palestrina, Lassus and Victoria, one of great masters of 16th-cent. polyphony, and one of most prolific. Published 36 books of secular madrigals and 5 of *madrigali spirituali*. Also composed French *chansons*, Masses and enormous number of motets.

**Montéclair, Michel Pinolet de** (1667–1737), French composer, violin teacher. Composed operas, cantatas, and church and chamber music, and published textbooks.

**Montemezzi, Italo** (1875–1952), Italian composer. Works incl. operas *eg L'Amore dei Tre Re* (1913), symphonic poem, and elegy for cello and piano.

**monter** (Fr.), to tune (instrument) up in pitch.

**Monteux, Pierre** (1875–1964), French conductor. Conductor of Diaghilev's Ballets Russes from 1912, giving premières of works by Stravinsky, Debussy and Ravel. Conductor of Metropolitan Opera House, New York (1917–19), Boston Symphony Orchestra (1919–24), Orchestre Symphonique de Paris (1929–38), San Francisco Symphony Orchestra (1936–54), and London Symphony Orchestra (1961–4).

**Monteverdi** or **Monteverde, Claudio Giovanni Antonio** (1567–1643), Italian composer. Born in Cremona. Son of doctor. Pupil of Ingegneri. First publication was collection of *Cantiunculae sacrae* (1582). In service of Duke of Mantua as violist (*c* 1590) then as *maestro di cappella* (*c* 1602). Dismissed (1612) but became *maestro di cappella* at St Mark's, Venice (1613). Ordained as priest (1632). Church music incl. 3 Masses, Vespers, Magnificats and numerous motets. Secular vocal music incl. 9 books of madrigals, book of *canzonette* and 2 books of *Scherzi musicali*. For stage wrote at least 12 operas (only 3 survive complete) and ballets.

Monteverdi's madrigals show increasing tendency to break away from tradition by use of new forms of dissonance for sake of pathetic expression, and by writing of melodic lines akin to declamatory style of recitative. Church music may be divided into 2 contrasted groups: one accepts traditional polyphonic style, while other adopts new baroque methods of brilliant and expressive writing for solo voices and chorus, together with effective use of instrumental resources.

Earliest of 3 surviving operas, *Orfeo* (1607), is to some extent modelled on Peri's *Euridice* and also incorporates much choral writing in style of madrigal and motet; but it is also landmark in history of opera on account of remarkable understanding of contribution that music can make to dramatic representation. *Il ritorno d'Ulisse in patria* (1641) and *L'incoronazione di Poppea* (1642) are no less expressive in their declamation but also incorporate rich variety of symmetrical songs and duets.

**Montezuma,** opera by Roger Sessions, libretta by G.A. Borgese. First perf. Berlin, 1964. US première, 1969. Story concerns Spanish invasion of Mexico in 16th cent.

**montre** (Fr.), one of names for 8ft open diapason stop on organ.

**mood,** English term of 16th, 17th cents. for note relationships (mode, time, prolation) of MENSURAL NOTATION.

**moog synthesizer,** type of SYNTHESIZER developed by Robert Moog in 1960s.

**'Moonlight' Sonata,** name given (not by composer) to Beethoven's *Sonata quasi una fantasia* in C minor for piano, op 27, no 2 (1801).

**Moór, Emanuel** (1863–1931), Hungarian composer, pianist, conductor. Invented Duplex-Coupler piano, with 2 manuals which can be coupled to simplify playing of octaves. Compositions incl. operas, symphonies, piano, cello and violin concertos, violin and cello sonatas, many piano pieces and songs.

**Moore, Douglas Stuart** (1893–1969), American composer, teacher. Pupil of Bloch and d'Indy. Professor at Columbia University. Works incl. operas *The Devil and Daniel Webster* (1938, text by Stephen Vincent Benét) and *The Ballad of Baby Doe*, operetta *The Headless Horseman* (1937, text by Benét), and orchestral, choral and chamber music.

**Moore, Gerald** (1899– ), English pianist. Regarded as greatest song accompanist of his day. Worked with *eg* Elizabeth Schwarzkopf, Victoria de los Angeles and Dietrich Fischer-Dieskau. Retired 1967.

**Moore, Thomas** (1779–1852), Irish poet, musician. His songs, incl. 'The Last Rose of Summer', became very popular.

**moqueur** (Fr.), mocking.

**Morales, Cristóbal de** (*c* 1500–53), Spanish composer. Studied under Seville Cathedral choirmaster. Became *maestro de capilla* at Avila (1526). Later went to Rome, where was ordained as priest, and in 1535 became singer in Papal Chapel. He was *maestro de capilla* at Toledo (1545–7), was in service of Duke of Arcos at Marchena in 1550, and was *maestro de capilla* at Málaga in 1551. He was first important Spanish composer of polyphonic church music, publishing 2 books of Masses, Magnificats and motets. Other works incl.

Lamentations, motet for conference at Nice (1538) and some madrigals.

**morasco,** alternative spelling of MORESCA.

**morbido** (It.), soft, delicate, gentle; *morbidezza,* softness, delicacy, gentleness.

**morceau** (Fr., pl. *morceaux*), piece. Satie used term wittily for his *Morceaux en forme de poire* (pieces in the shape of a pear).

**mordent, lower** (Fr., *pincé*; It., *mordente*), ornament played by alternating written note rapidly once or twice with note below it. Speed and number of alternations depend on length of written note, having regard to tempo in which it occurs. It is indicated thus:

and performed thus:

**mordent, upper** or **inverted,** English term for ornament introduced *c* 1750 by C.P.E. Bach and called *Schneller* until *c* 1800, and *Pralltriller* thereafter. Generally occurs on upper of 2 notes in descending second, and is indicated thus:

and played thus:

**Moreau, Jean-Baptiste** (1656–1733), French church musician and composer. Wrote incidental music for Racine's *Esther* (1688) and *Athalie* (1691) and for other plays. Set many poems by Laînez to music. Also taught singing and composition.

**morendo** (It.), 'dying', *ie* decreasing in volume (and poss. also speed) at end of phrase or composition.

**moresca** (It.), dance of 15th, 16th cents., most often sword dance representing fight between Moors and Christians. Related to English morris dance. Appeared as dance in Venetian and Viennese operas of 17th cent. Orig. in triple time, but more often in march rhythm in ballets of opera.

**Morhange,** *see* ALKAN.

**Morin, Jean Baptiste** (1677–1745), French composer. One of first French composers of cantatas; also wrote motets and songs.

**Morlacchi, Francesco** (1784–1841), Italian composer, conductor. Pupil of Zingarelli. Commissioned in 1805 to write cantata for coronation of Napoleon as King of Italy. Conductor of Dresden Opera (where Weber became his rival) from 1810, being succeeded there by Wagner. Works incl. operas *eg Il ritratto* (1807), 10 Masses, oratorios and cantatas.

**Morley, Thomas** (1557–*c* 1602), English composer, theorist. Pupil of Byrd. Organist at St Paul's, London in 1591, gentleman of Chapel Royal in 1592. Granted monopoly of music printing (1598) which he assigned to T. East (1600). Published canzonets, madrigals, ballets (which he introduced into England), consort lessons for 6 instruments, and ayres. Edited *The Triumphes of Oriana* (1601). His *Plaine and Easie Introduction to Practicall Musicke* (1597) was first comprehensive treatise on composition printed in England.

**Morning Heroes,** symphony by Bliss (1930) for orator, chorus and orchestra, with words from Homer, Li-Tai-Po, Whitman, Robert Nichols and Wilfred Owen. Written in memory of composer's brother and others killed in WWI.

**Mornington, Garrett Colley Wellesley, Earl of** (1735–81), Irish-born violinist, organist, composer. In 1757 founded Academy of Music in Dublin, and in 1764 was elected first professor of music at Dublin University. Complete collection of his glees and madrigals was published in 1846. Father of Duke of Wellington.

**morris dance,** traditional English folk dance, believed to originate *c* 15th cent. and to derive name and certain elements (*eg* jingles on dancers' legs) from MORESCA. Music, using wide variety of tunes, was usually played on pipe and tabor.

**Morris, R[eginald] O[wen]** (1886–1948), English teacher, composer, theorist. Taught counterpoint and composition at Royal College of Music, London, and published books on theory. Compositions incl. symphony, violin concerto, chamber music, and songs.

**Mortaro, Antonio** (*fl* 16th–17th cents.), Italian composer, organist. Compositions are written in elaborate polychoral style.

**Moscaglia, Giovanni Battista** (*fl* late 16th cent.), Italian composer. Associate of Marenzio. Published books of madrigals and vol. of villanellas *alla Napolitana*.

**Moscheles, Ignaz** (1794–1870), Bohemian pianist, teacher, composer. Pupil of Albrechtsberger and Salieri. Arranged piano score of opera *Fidelio* under Beethoven's supervision (1814). Toured Europe for 10 years. Gave piano lessons to Mendelssohn. Settled in London (1826–46), then became piano teacher at new Leipzig Conservatorium founded by Mendelssohn. Compositions incl. 8 piano concertos, many piano sonatas and studies, and chamber music.

**Mosè in Egitto** (It., *Moses in Egypt*), opera by Rossini, libretto by A.L. Tottola. First perf. Naples, 1818. Enlarged French version by G.L. Balochi and V.J.E. de Jouy perf. Paris, 1827.

**Moser, Hans Joachim** (1889–1967), German historian, composer, teacher. Numerous books incl. 3-vol. history of German music, and studies of Bach, Schütz, Handel, Gluck and Weber – whose works he edited.

**Moses and Aaron** (Ger., *Moses und Aron*), unfinished opera by Schoenberg, libretto by composer. First perf. (in radio version) Germany, 1954; first staged, Zurich, 1957. Schoenberg completed first 2 acts in 1932, but did not begin last act till 1951. Work is penetrating study of relationship between God and humanity.

**Mosonyi, Mihály,** orig. Michael Brand (1815–70), Austrian-born composer, double-bass player, critic. Beginning in German tradition, became more and more aware of Hungarian folk music, changed his name to a Hungarian one after settling in Budapest, and was honoured after his death as pioneer in development of national style. Works incl. operas, symphonies, string quartets, church and piano music, and songs.

**mosso** (It.), lit. 'moved', *ie* lively. *Piu mosso*, faster. *Meno mosso*, slower. Also used as warning against dragging, *eg Andante mosso*, not too slow.

**Mossolov, Alexander Vassilievich** (1900–73), Russian pianist, composer. Pupil of Glière and Prokofiev. Several of his compositions are influenced by his studies of folk music of Turkmenia and other central Asian republics. Works incl. 3 operas, symphonies and concertos.

**Mosto, Giovanni Battista** (d. *c* 1596), Italian composer. Pupil of Merulo. Published 2 anthologies, and books of madrigals.

**Moszkowski, Moritz** (1854–1925), German-born pianist, composer, of Polish origin. Reputation rests mainly on lighter pieces, esp. *Spanish Dances* for piano duet.

**motet,** term first arose in early 13th cent. by addition of words to hitherto vocalized upper part of 2-part *clausula*. Motet became independent composition, and flourished throughout 13th cent. Most frequently in 3 parts. Lowest part (tenor) was basis; normally taken from plainsong, and disposed in regularly recurring rhythmic pattern. Other parts (*duplum* and *triplum*) had different words, sacred or secular. In latter case, sometimes quoted words and music of well known REFRAIN.

Isorhythmic motet of 1300–1450 (Machaut, Dunstable, Dufay) represented expansion of 13th-cent. motet. Tenor was still basis, and was disposed in 2 or more sections, each with same rhythm in successively diminished note values. Motets of this time could be secular, sacred, or written to mark notable occasion.

From *c* 1450 to 1600 term motet denoted setting for unaccompanied voices of sacred Latin text, all parts having same words. Use of tenor taken from plainsong continued in some cases until after 1500, but after *c* 1530 imitative style with original themes was generally adopted.

In following cents., motet was setting of sacred text in current style of period, for solo voices or choir or both, with or without instrumental accompaniment. Bach's motets are for unaccompanied double chorus, for 5-part chorus, and for 4-part chorus with organ continuo.

**Mother Goose** (Fr., *Ma mère l'oye*), suite of 5 children's pieces for piano duet by Ravel (1908) based on fairy tales of Perrault. Scored for orchestra (1912) and produced as ballet, with added linking passages.

**motif, motive,** *see* PHRASE. Also sometimes implies LEITMOTIV.

**motion,** term describing upward or downward movements of melodic lines. For conjunct and disjunct motion *see* CONJUNCT, for contrary motion *see* INVERSION (2); *see also* OBLIQUE MOTION, PARALLEL MOTION, RETROGRADE MOTION, SIMILAR MOTION.

**moto** (It.), motion. *Con moto*, with motion, *ie* quickly.

**moto perpetuo** (It.), *see* PERPETUUM MOBILE.

**Mottl, Felix** (1856–1911), Austrian conductor, composer. Pupil of Bruckner. Best known for arrangements of Gluck, Wagner and others. Also wrote 3 operas, string quartet, and songs.

**motto** or **motto theme,** recurring theme, used to special dramatic purpose in course of composition. Sometimes theme will have pictorial or symbolic significance, sometimes it will be metamorphosed on each of its appearances, sometimes it will have effect of self-quotation. *See also* LEITMOTIV.

**Motu Proprio** (Lat.), kind of decree issued by Pope, in particular that on sacred music issued by Pope Pius X (1903), in which Gregorian plainsong was affirmed to be supreme model, and which required classical polyphony of Roman school, esp. Palestrina, to be used in ecclesiastical functions.

**Mount of Olives,** *see* CHRIST ON THE MOUNT OF OLIVES.

**'Mourning' Symphony** (Ger., *Trauersinfonie*), nickname for Haydn's symphony no 44 in E minor (*c* 1771). Title is thought to come from Haydn's desire to have slow movt. played at own funeral.

**mouth music** (Gaelic, *port á beul*), type of singing, wordless but articulated, used in Scottish Highlands to accompany dances. Known as 'diddling' in Scottish Lowlands, and 'lilting' in Ireland.

**mouth organ,** small wind instrument, also called harmonica. Blown from side, one of pair of metal reeds for each note being operated by blowing, other by sucking. Chromatic notes are produced by slide.

**Mouton, Jean** (*c* 1459–1522), French composer. Pupil of Josquin des Prés, teacher of Willaert and musician to French court. Works incl. Masses, motets, psalms and *chansons*.

**mouvement** (Fr.), (1) time, speed. *Au mouvement*, in time. *Premier* (or *1er*) *mouvement*, at original speed;
(2) movement (of sonata, symphony *etc*).

**movement** (Fr., *mouvement*; Ger., *Satz*; It., *movimento, tempo*), section, self-contained but not necessarily wholly independent, of extended instrumental composition such as symphony, sonata *etc*. *See* SONATA, SONATA FORM, SYMPHONY.

**movimento** (It.), (1) speed. *Lo stesso movimento*, at same speed;
(2) movement (of sonata, symphony *etc*).

**Mozart, Wolfgang Amadeus** (1756–91), Austrian composer. Born in Salzburg. His father, **Leopold Mozart** (1719–87), was violinist and composer, and author of important violin tutor. Leopold encouraged Wolfgang, who gave recitals at age of 6. In 1763 Wolfgang began long tour with father and sister Maria Anna ('Nannerl'), who as player was also prodigy. Visited Germany, Belgium, Paris, London (1764–5) and Holland. By time of return to Salzburg (1766), had composed first symphonies and *c* 30 other works, and had arranged several piano concertos from sonatas of J.C. Bach (most important of his early influences). In 1768, at age of 12, composed first operas, *La finta semplice* and *Bastien und Bastienne.* Visited Italy with father (1769–71) where took lessons from Martini, and his opera *Mitridate* was acclaimed in Milan.

Despite tremendous international success as child prodigy, Mozart found it singularly difficult to achieve patronage his genius deserved. Entered household of Archbishop of Salzburg, but contempt for employer led to dismissal (1781). Went to Vienna and became first composer ever to attempt to follow independent freelance career, though he always hoped for major musical appointment. This he never achieved, and so suffered from great financial difficulties. Vienna remained his home, and there he taught piano, gave concerts (for which he wrote some of his greatest piano concertos), and married Constanze Weber. Minor appointment as chamber musician to Viennese court (1787) merely involved him in composition of quantities of dances. In 1790 failed to get post of *Kapellmeister* to new Emperor Leopold II. Towards end of life became interested in Freemasonry, which inspired *The Magic Flute* and some other works. Not long before his death, Mozart was greatly perturbed by appearance of mysterious stranger who wanted him to ghost-write *Requiem* – he accepted commission, but died before its completion. Theory that he was poisoned, possibly by rival Salieri, has never been proved, though last illness was never satisfactorily diagnosed.

Music flowed from Mozart unceasingly. He was in habit of composing complete movements in his mind in all their detail before writing them down. Innate liveliness of imagination went with ability to seize essence of another composer's style and to possess it as part of his own – his main influences were J.C. Bach, C.P.E. Bach, Handel, Haydn, Stamitz and Gluck. His surety of technique, infallible command of design, and keen dramatic sense made him the supreme master of the classical style in all the forms of the period. His 6 greatest operas – *Idomeneo, Die Entführung aus dem Serail, The Marriage of Figaro, Don Giovanni, Così fan tutte* and *The Magic Flute* – explore, in music of unsurpassed beauty, aptness and wit, the full range of human emotion. His piano concertos are regarded as greatest ever written.

Mozart's works were catalogued by Ludwig Köchel (1862, rev. Einstein, 1937) and are referred to by 'K' numbers.

Principal compositions:

(1) Operas: *Bastien und Bastienne* (K50, 1788), *Mitridate* (K87, 1770), *Lucio Silla* (K135, 1772), *Il Re pastore* (K208, 1775), *Idomeneo* (K366, 1781), *Die Entfuhrüng aus dem Serail* (K384, 1782), *Der Schauspieldirektor* (K486, 1786), *The Marriage of Figaro* (K492, 1786), *Don Giovanni* (K527, 1787), *Così fan tutte* (K588,

1790), *The Magic Flute* (K620, 1791), *La Clemenza di Tito* (K621, 1791);

(2) Orchestra: 41 symphonies that have acquired numbers, incl. *Paris* (no 31, K297, 1778), *Haffner* (no 35, K385, 1782), *Linz* (no 36, K425, 1783), *Prague* (no 38, K504, 1786), E (no 39, K543, 1788), G minor (no 40, K550, 1788), *Jupiter* (no 41, K551, 1788), and *c* 8 other symphonies. Numerous *divertimenti*, serenades, marches *etc* incl. *Eine kleine Nachtmusik* for strings (K525, 1787);

(3) Concertos: 27 for piano (first 4 are arrangements of pieces by other composers), 1 for 2 pianos, 1 for 3 pianos, 5 for violin, 2 for flute, 1 for clarinet, 4 for horn, 1 for flute and harp, *Sinfonia concertante* for violin and viola (K364, 1779), *Sinfonia concertante* for oboe, clarinet, horn and bassoon (K App. 9, 1778), 14 sonatas for organ and strings, 3 sonatas for organ and orchestra;

(4) Chamber music: 6 string quintets, 23 string quartets, *Adagio and Fugue* in C minor (K546, 1788) for string quartet, 2 piano quartets, 7 piano trios, trio for clarinet, viola and piano (K498, 1786), clarinet quintet, horn quintet, quintet for piano and wind, 2 flute quartets, oboe quartet, 37 violin sonatas (2 unfinished);

(5) Piano: 17 sonatas, 2 Fantasias, 15 sets of variations, sonata for 2 pianos (K488, 1781), 6 sonatas for piano duet, *Adagio* and *Allegro* in F minor (K594, 1790) and *Fantasia* in F minor (K608, 1791) for piano duet (both orig. for mechanical organ);

(6) Church music: 18 Masses, 4 litanies, Requiem (K626, 1791, completed by pupil Sussmayr).

**Mozart and Salieri,** opera by Rimsky-Korsakov, based on Pushkin's dramatic poem about (conjectural) poisoning of Mozart by rival Salieri. First perf. Moscow, 1898.

**Mozartiana,** title of Chaikovsky's 4th orchestral suite, op 61 (1887), comprising orchestrations of 3 keyboard works and motet by Mozart.

**Mudd, Thomas** (b. *c* 1560), English composer. Fellow of Pembroke College, Cambridge. His anthems are confused with those of John Mudd (d. 1639) who was organist of Peterborough Cathedral (1583–1630), and poss. with younger Thomas Mudd (d. 1667), who was organist at Peterborough from 1631. Set of 9 dances in Ms at British Library are by younger Thomas. There was also a Henry Mudd (d. *c* 1588), whose works incl. an *In nomine*.

**Muette de Portici,** *see* MASANIELLO.

**Muffat, Georg** (1653–1704), German composer, organist. Pupil of Lully. Works incl. organ and instrumental music, and orchestral suites *(ouvertures)* in style of Lully.

His son, **Gottlieb** or **Theophil Muffat** (1690–1770), was also composer. Pupil of Fux. From 1717 was court organist in Vienna. Works incl. organ and harpsichord music.

**muffled drum,** drum with piece of cloth or similar material placed on vibrating surfaces. Resulting tone quality is sombre. Often associated with funeral music.

**Muldowney, Dominic** (1952– ), English composer, conductor. Pupil of Birtwistle. Musical director of National Theatre from 1976.

Works incl. theatre music, ballet *Macbeth,* and orchestral, chamber and choral music.

**Mulliner, Thomas** (*fl* 16th cent.), English organist. Compiled, prob. in 1560s, Ms of keyboard compositions and arrangements of period. Important source.

**Munch, Charles** (1891–1968), French (Alsatian) conductor. Conducted Boston Symphony Orchestra (1948–62). Notable for performances of Berlioz and other French composers.

**Münchinger, Karl** (1915– ), German conductor. Founded Stuttgart Chamber Orchestra (1945), which he has conducted ever since.

**Mundharmonica** (Ger.), mouth harmonica or MOUTH ORGAN.

**Mundy, John** (d. 1630), English organist, composer. Educated by father. Gentleman of Chapel Royal. Wrote madrigals, airs and keyboard music.

His father, **William Mundy** (d. *c* 1591), was also composer. Gentleman of Chapel Royal. Works incl. services, anthems, motets, and Latin antiphons and psalms.

**Munrow, David** (1942–76), English musician. Played many early instruments. Founded (1967) and directed Early Music Consort.

**Muris, Johannes de** or **Jean de** (before 1300–*c* 1351), theorist, mathematician and philosopher, of uncertain nationality (poss. Welsh, English, French or Swiss). Supported style and principles of notation of *ars nova.* Treatises incl. *Notitia artis musicae, Compendium musicae practicae,* and *Ars novae musicae.*

**Murrill, Herbert Henry John** (1909–52), English composer. Head of Music at B.B.C. from 1950. Works incl. 2 cello concertos, jazz opera *Man in Cage* (1929), and incidental music for films, ballets and plays.

**musette** (Fr.), type of bagpipe popular among French aristocracy during 17th, 18th cents. Name also given to dance movements incorporating drone bass notes suggestive of instrument, and to 8ft reed stop on organ.

**Musgrave, Thea** (1928– ), Scottish composer. Pupil of Nadia Boulanger. Though early works reveal fastidious musical mind, it was not till 1960s that her full potential began to be revealed in series of orchestral and instrumental works, in which she sought to find vivid dramatic form for abstract instrumental music. Soloist in clarinet concerto and orchestral horns in horn concerto move around concert platform, and in 2nd of 3 chamber concertos there is comic part for viola player in opposition to rest of ensemble. Other works incl. operas *eg The Decision* (1967), *The Voice of Ariadne* (1974), *Mary, Queen of Scots* (1977) and *A Christmas Carol* (after Dickens, 1979), ballet *Beauty and the Beast* and dramatic choral work *The Five Ages of Man*.

**Musica Britannica,** collection of British music published by Royal Musical Association with support of Arts Council of Great Britain. Series was begun in 1951.

**musica colorata** (It.), *see* MUSICA FIGURATA (2).

**musica da camera** (It.), chamber music.

**Musica Enchiriadis,** treatise of disputed authorship (formerly attrib. to Hucbald), written *c* 900. With contemporary treatise, *Scholia enchiriadis,* gives some of earliest examples of ORGANUM.

**musica falsa, musica ficta** (Lat.), former term was used by theorists in early Middle Ages in discussing use of accidentals which lay outside Guidonian hexachord system. Later medieval theorists applied latter term to transpositions of hexachord whereby (in addition to B flat), E flat, A flat and D flat became necessary. This term is also now used in referring to accidentals which, it is presumed, singers in 15th, early 16th cents. supplied to provide B flat in mode on F and leading notes for modes on D, G and A.

**musica figurata** (It.), (1) polyphonic music that is not homorhythmic, *ie* parts have rhythmic independence;
(2) plainsong with decorated melody, also called *musica colorata.*

**musical box,** *see* MECHANICAL MUSICAL INSTRUMENTS.

**musical comedy,** US (and to some extent British) equivalent of operetta, popular during late 19th, early 20th cents., and using music interspersed with spoken dialogue. Later examples came to be known as 'musical play' or simply 'musical'.

**musical glasses,** *see* HARMONICA.

**Musical Joke, A** (Ger., *Ein Musikalischer Spass*), miniature symphony in F by Mozart, K522 (1787), for 2 horns and strings. Work is caricature of work of any third-rate composer of period, remorselessly imitating all threadbare conventions.

**Musical Offering** (Ger., *Musikalisches Opfer*), set of pieces by Bach (1747), incl. 2 *ricercari* (fugues), several canons and sonata, for flute, violin and harpsichord, on theme by Frederick the Great (to whom work was dedicated).

**musical play,** *see* MUSICAL COMEDY.

**musical saw,** *see* SAW.

**musica mensurata,** *see* MENSURAL MUSIC.

**musica plana** (Lat.), medieval term for PLAINSONG.

**musica reservata** (Lat.), term used in latter part of 16th cent., supposedly to indicate music suitable for connoisseurs and private occasions, and more particularly music which gave vivid and faithful expression to spirit of words.

**Musica Transalpina,** title of first printed collection of Italian madrigals with English words, published by Nicholas Yonge (1588). Also contained 2 madrigals by Byrd. Same title was given to 2nd collection (1597).

**music drama,** term used by Wagner to describe his operas.

**Music for strings, percussion and celesta,** work by Bartók, commissioned for 10th anniversary of Basel Chamber Orchestra (1947).

**Music Makers, The,** ode for contralto, chorus and orchestra by Elgar, op 69, to words by A. O'Shaughnessy. First perf. Birmingham, 1912. Music incl. quotations from several earlier works of composer.

**Music of the Future,** term used in 19th cent. to describe music of Liszt, Wagner and other musical 'progressives'.

**musicology** (Fr., *musicologie*; Ger., *Musikwissenschaft*), systematic study of musical composition and its history.

**music theatre,** name for musical-dramatic works, produced (usually) more economically than operas, and employing smaller forces. Such pieces, increasingly composed from 1960s, are suitable for production in concert halls and theatres as well as opera houses, and their composers have not only discarded name 'opera' but also many of its conventions.

**Musikalisches Opfer,** *see* MUSICAL OFFERING.

**Musikalischer Spass,** *see* MUSICAL JOKE.

**Musikwissenschaft** (Ger.), musicology.

**musique concrète** (Fr., concrete music), type of music in which sounds required by composer are recorded on tape and may then be manipulated, combined or distorted by him. Term was coined by Pierre Schaeffer (1910– ), who was prob. first to experiment with this process (at Paris radio station, 1948). Term has now been largely superseded by ELECTRONIC MUSIC.

**musique de chambre** (Fr.), chamber music.

**musique de table,** *see* TABLE (3).

**musique mesurée à l'antique** (Fr.), music in which rhythm was rigidly governed by metre of poetry which it set, practised by composers and poets of *Académie de Poésie et de Musique* (founded Paris, 1570).

**Mussorgsky** or **Musorgsky, Modest Petrovich** (1839–81), Russian composer. Though born well-to-do, spent much of his life in poverty. Intended for military career, but resigned his commission after he met Balakirev and Dargomizhsky in 1858. Though studied under Balakirev, he was too unsystematic to make full-time career of music. Took minor post in civil service, but soon sank into drunkenness and degradation, and died of alcoholic epilepsy in St Petersburg.

Much of Mussorgsky's music was left unfinished and in disorder, but it is surprising he wrote as much as he did. Though a member of the Russian nationalist school 'The FIVE', in many ways he was Russia's most individual and human genius. As vivid and moving portrait of Russian people, his opera *Boris Godunov* (1870) has never been surpassed. His *Pictures at an Exhibition* (1874) was first real masterpiece for solo piano by a Russian. In both these works Mussorgsky's harmonic and rhythmic audacity was mistaken by pedants for ineptitude. Thus Rimsky-Korsakov, in revising *Boris Godunov*, 'corrected' Mussorgsky's errors and turned it into a much more conventional work; however, he helped to popularize *Boris* and was largely responsible for tidying up and completing Mussorgsky's unfinished music. Similarly, Ravel's orchestration of *Pictures at an Exhibition*, though altering character of original, has helped introduce work to wide public. After *Boris,* Mussorgsky's most viable stage works are Gogol-inspired comedy *Sorochintsi Fair* (1874–80, completed by Cherepnin), and *Khovanshchina* (1872–80, completed by Rimsky-Korsakov). Also embarked on operas on Flaubert's *Salammbô* (1863–6, unfinished) and Gogol's *The Marriage* (unfinished). With Rimsky-Korsakov, Borodin and Cui, produced communal ballet-opera *Mlada* (1872), to which he contributed *Night on the Bare Mountain* (well known as orchestral tone poem, adapted by Rimsky-Korsakov) and other material. His feeling for Russian people and their language is heard to powerful effect in *c* 60 songs, incl. 3 great cycles, *The Nursery* (1868–72), *Songs and Dances of Death* (1875–7), and *Sunless* (1874).

**Mustel Organ,** development of HARMONIUM, by Victor Mustel (1815–90) of Paris.

**muta** (It.), imperative of *mutare*, to change. Direction to wind player to change instrument or crook, or to timpani player to change tuning. *Mutano* is used where more than one instrument is concerned.

**mutano,** *see* MUTA.

**mutation,** change from syllables of one HEXACHORD to those of another in SOLMIZATION, *ie* kind of modulation.

**mutation stops,** organ stops which produce sound other than pitch corresponding to key which is depressed or to its octaves. Quint stops sound twelfth (third note of HARMONIC SERIES) and Tierce stops sound seventeenth above foundation note or one of its octaves. *See* MIXTURE, ORGAN.

**mute** (Fr., *sourdine*; Ger., *Dämpfer*; It., *sordino*), any device used to soften or alter normal tone colour of instrument. On bowed instruments it is small fork-shaped clamp that fits onto bridge, thereby reducing vibrations; on brass instruments, it is often made of wood or metal and is pear-shaped, though wide variety are available for trumpets and trombones, each producing distinctive tone colour. Drums, esp. timpani, were formerly muted by placing cloth over drum head; now sponge-headed drumsticks are used. In all these cases, usual indication to play with mutes is *con sordino*, abbrev. *con sord* or *sord*. On piano, muting is effected by depressing soft pedal, and indication is *una corda*.

**Muti, Riccardo** (1941– ), Italian conductor. Chief conductor of Philharmonia Orchestra from 1973, guest conductor of Philadelphia Orchestra from 1977. Artistic director of Florence Festival from 1977.

**My Country,** *see* MÁ VLAST.

**mystic chord,** term for chord invented by Skryabin. Consists of series of ascending fourths, C–F sharp–B flat–E–A–D, and forms basis of *Prometheus*, op 60 (1910) and 7th piano sonata, op 64. Similar chords are found in other Skryabin works.

# N

**Nabokov, Nicholas** (1903–78) Russian-born composer, author, administrator. Worked with Diaghilev's ballet in 1920s, and later settled in US. Works incl. operas *The Death of Rasputin* and *Love's Labours Lost,* ballets, *Sinfonia Biblica,* and other music for concert hall.

**Nabucco** or **Nabucodonosor** (It., Nebuchadnezzar), opera by Verdi, libretto by T. Solera. First perf. La Scala, Milan, 1842. Verdi's first success. Story concerns Babylonian captivity of Jews, and became symbolic of Italy's desire for independence.

**nacchera** (It.), kettledrum. Pl. *nacchera* usually refers to drums designed for military use, esp. by cavalry, as opposed to timpani used in orchestra. *See* NAKER.

**naccherone** (It.), large kettledrum.

**nach** (Ger.), in the manner of, after, towards. Thus '*nach* E' would be instruction to player to tune instrument to E.

**Nachdruck** (Ger.), emphasis.

**nachgehend** (Ger.), following.

**nachlassend** (Ger.), lit. 'leaving behind', *ie* relaxing.

**Nachschlag** (Ger.; Eng., springer, acute; Fr., *accent, aspiration, plainte*), ornament in German music of 17th, 18th cents. In most usual form it was played as short passing note between 2 notes a third apart (French called this *couler les tierces*). In another form, *Nachschlag* is equivalent to English SPRINGER.

In later music, term denotes 2 notes which end trill: notation

played

**Nachtanz** (Ger.), 'following dance'. Dance in quick triple time following dance in duple time, in German instrumental music of 16th, 17th cents. Also called *Proportz, Hupfauf* (hopping up), and *tripla.* Dances most often paired in this way were PAVANE and GALLIARD in 16th cent. and ALLEMANDE and COURANTE in 17th cent. Latter sequence was incorporated into SUITE. Second dance of pair was commonly rhythmically altered form of first.

**Nachtmusik** (Ger.), lit. 'night music', *ie* music of serenade-like character, often in several movts., as in Mozart's *Eine Kleine Nachtmusik,* K525.

**Nachtstück** (Ger.), night piece. Title used by Schumann for set of 4 piano pieces, op 23.

**Nagel, Willibald** (1863–1929), German musical historian. Taught in Zurich, and lived in London (1893–6). Wrote history of English music (2 vols., 1891, 1897), and also wrote on piano sonatas of Beethoven.

**Nagelclavier, Nagelgeige,** *see* NAIL VIOLIN.

**Nageli, Hans Georg** (1773–1836), Swiss musician, publisher. Acquainted with contemporary composers incl. Beethoven. Produced first authentic edition of Bach's 48 preludes and fugues. Also published first editions of some of Beethoven's works, and was active supporter of educational music.

**nail violin** (also nail fiddle and nail harmonica; Ger., *Nagelgeige*), instrument devised by Johann Wilde in St Petersburg in 1740. Consisted of semicircular resonator of wood into which were driven U-shaped nails of graduated lengths. Sound was produced by bow. In 1791 Träger of Bernburg extended idea to nail piano *(Nagelclavier)* in which sound was produced by friction of wheel.

**naker** (Arabic, *naqqara*; It., *nacchera*; Fr., *nacaire*), early English name for small, high-pitched kettledrum of Arabic origin, introduced into Europe in 13th cent. Used in pairs. Tuning could not be altered.

**Namensfeier** (Ger., *Name Day*), overture by Beethoven, op 115, perf. 1815 in honour of name day festivities of Emperor Francis II.

**naqqara,** *see* NAKER.

**Nardini, Pietro** (1722–93), Italian violinist, composer. Pupil of Tartini. Worked in Stuttgart and Florence. Works incl. 6 violin concertos, sonatas, string quartets, and keyboard sonatas.

**Nares, James** (1715–83), English organist, composer. Works incl. church music, harpsichord lessons, glees, and catches.

**Narváez, Luis de** (*fl* 16th cent.), Spanish composer, *vihuela* player. His book of *vihuela* music (*Los seys libros del Delphin de música,* 1538) contains some of earliest examples of variation form.

**Nash, Heddle** (1896–1961), English tenor. Made debut in Milan in 1924. Noted for lyricism and sensitivity of his singing, was at his best in Mozart roles, esp. Ottavio in *Don Giovanni.* Sang for all leading British opera companies.

**national anthem,** song or hymn chosen by country to represent it on official occasions, either at home or abroad.

**nationalism,** in music, nationalist movement first arose in romantic period, with object of accentuating individual musical characteristics of particular country: folk music and folk stories were obvious means of doing so. Composers involved in movement incl. Glinka and The FIVE in Russia, Smetana and Dvořák in Czechoslovakia, Liszt, Kodály and Bartók in Hungary, Grieg in Norway, Sibelius in Finland, Albéniz, Granados and Falla in Spain, and Vaughan Williams in Britain.

**natural,** note which is neither sharp nor flat. Sign

♮

is used to indicate it where this has been made necessary by presence of sharp or flat in key signature or of accidental earlier in same bar.

**natural horn, natural trumpet,** horn or trumpet not furnished with valves or other means of altering length of tubing in use. Except where handstopping can be used, such instruments are limited to notes of harmonic series. *See* HORN, TRUMPET.

**Naumann, Johann Gottlieb** (1741–1801), German composer. Studied in Italy with Tartini and Martini. Worked in Italy and Dresden. Works incl. *c* 26 operas, oratorios, church and chamber music, and songs.

**Naylor, Edward Woodall** (1867–1934), English composer, writer on music. Compositions incl. opera *The Angelus* (1909), church music, songs, and part songs.

His son, **Bernard Naylor** (1907– ), is also composer. Pupil of Vaughan Williams, Holst and Ireland. Works incl. setting of Elizabeth Barrett Browning's *Sonnets from the Portuguese* for voice and string quartet.

**Neapolitan sixth,** name given to 6/3 chord on fourth degree of scale with minor sixth and minor third, *eg* in key of A minor, D–F–B flat. Name seems to be due to use made of it, for pathetic effect, by opera-composers at Naples in 17th cent.

**neben** (Ger.), secondary. *Nebenthema*, second theme (of symphony or sonata).

**neck,** part of stringed instrument that supports finger-board.

**Neefe, Christian Gottlob** (1748–98), German conductor, composer. Pupils incl. 11-year-old Beethoven. Wrote 8 *Singspiele,* and his *Adelheit von Veltheim* (1780) was one of first German operas on Turkish theme.

**Neel, Louis Boyd** (1905–1981), English composer. In 1932 founded Boyd Neel Orchestra, renamed Philomusica of London in 1957, after Neel had become Dean of Royal Conservatory of Music, Toronto.

**Negro spiritual,** *see* SPIRITUAL.

**nei** (Rom.), panpipes, pandean pipes or syrinx. Ancient instrument, commonly associated with Greece, though use today is confined almost entirely to Romania. Consists of number of pipes of whistle type made of wood or reeds, graduated in size, and bound together in row.

**'Nelson' Mass** (Ger., *Nelsonmesse*), nickname of Haydn's Mass in D minor (1798). Dramatic entry of trumpets and timpani in *Benedictus* is said to commemorate Nelson's victory at Battle of the Nile. Haydn's own title for work was *Missa in angustiis* (Mass in time of need). Sometimes known as *Imperial Mass* in Britain.

**Nenna, Pomponio** (*c* 1555–1617), Italian composer. Published 9 books of madrigals; some of his settings closely resemble madrigals by Gesualdo, who may have been his pupil. Also wrote set of Holy Week responses (1607).

**neo-Bechstein piano,** electronic piano invented by Vierling in Berlin 1928–33, and later further developed. Played, and strings struck, in normal way, but sound is modified electronically.

**neo-classicism,** term for 20th-cent. musical movement which (esp. in 1920s) revolted against lush, emotional, chromatic romanticism of late 19th, early 20th-cent. music. Aspects of neo-classical music were emphasis on clarity of texture, lightness of orchestration, coolness of approach, and back-to-18th-cent. (esp. back-to-Bach) respect for counterpoint and close-knit musical forms. Most famous exponent was Stravinsky, whose neo-classical period produced neo-Bachian piano concerto, neo-Pergolesian suite *Pulcinella*, and neo-Mozartian opera *The Rake's Progress*. Other composers attracted to neo-classicism incl. Hindemith, Auric, Poulenc, Casella and Malipiero.

**neo-modalism,** use by some 20th-cent. composers of harmony based on old modes rather than on major and minor scales. Used productively by *eg* Vaughan Williams.

**neo-romanticism,** term for reaction by some 20th-cent. composers against wave of neo-classicism which sprang up during 1920s. Term, however, is not very specific.

**Neri, Massimiliano** (*fl* 17th cent.), Italian organist, composer. Organist at St Mark's, Venice, and later to Elector of Cologne. Works incl. book of motets (1664), *Sonate e canzone in chiesa et in camera* (1644), and sonatas for 3 to 12 instruments. Continued tradition of ensemble *canzona* of Giovanni Gabrieli, and was also practitioner of new style of sonata.

**Nerone** (It., *Nero*), opera by Boito, libretto by composer. Though unfinished when Boito died, music was completed by Tommasini and Toscanini. First perf. Milan, 1924, under Toscanini. Other operas on same subject incl. *Nerone* by Mascagni (1935).

**Netherlands Chamber Orchestra,** ensemble founded 1955 with Szymon Goldberg as its musical director. Orchestra has wide and interesting repertory, and is esp. noted for performances of Bach.

**Neue Liebeslieder,** *see* LIEBESLIEDER.

**Neues vom Tage,** *see* NEWS OF THE DAY.

**Neukomm, Sigismund, Chevalier von** (1778–1858), Austrian composer. Pupil of Michael and Joseph Haydn. Settled in Paris in 1809, where made acquaintance of Grétry, Cherubini and Cuvier. Worked in Rio de Janeiro (1816–21), and subsequently lived alternately in London and Paris. Works incl. operas, oratorios, Masses, Requiem for Louis XVI (1815), choral, chamber, piano and organ music, and *c* 200 songs.

**neuma** or **pneuma,** phrase of melody used by medieval theorists to illustrate characteristics and range of MODE. Occasionally used as tenor in 13th-cent. motets.

**neume** (from Gr. for sign), individual sign in notation used for Eastern chant and Western plainsong.

**Neusiedler, Hans** (*c* 1509–63), German lutenist, composer. Published collections of lute music in German tablature. His *Jew's*

*Dance* has achieved fame as curious example of bitonality, but this is due to wrong transcription of tablature.

**Newman, Ernest** (1868–1959), English music critic. Successively critic of *Manchester Guardian* (1905), *Birmingham Post* (1906), *Observer* (1919) and *Sunday Times* (1920–58). His exhaustive study of Wagner resulted in several books *Wagner as Man and Artist* (1924), *The Life of Richard Wagner* (4 vols., 1933–47), and *Wagner Nights* (1949). Other works incl. books on Gluck and Wolf, *Opera Nights* (1943) and *More Opera Nights* (1955).

**Newmarch, Rosa Harriet** (1857–1940), English writer on music. Helped introduce much important Russian and Czech music to Britain, and wrote books and articles on those subjects.

**new music,** term used of (1) style developed in early 17th cent. by CACCINI and others (*Le Nuove Musiche*); (2) music of Liszt, Wagner and other musical 'progressives' of second half of 19th cent.

**New Philharmonia Orchestra,** *see* PHILHARMONIA ORCHESTRA.

**News of the Day** (Ger., *Neues vom Tage*), opera by Hindemith, libretto by M. Schiffer. First perf. Berlin 1929 (rev. 1953). Music adopts humorous idiom to describe marital conflicts of young couple, and score features parts for 2 typewriters, the bath tub aria, and a hymn to hot water.

**New World Symphony,** *see* FROM THE NEW WORLD.

**New York Philharmonic-Symphony Orchestra,** founded by V. C. Hill in 1842 as Philharmonic Society of New York. Oldest symphony orchestra in US. New York Symphony Society (founded 1878) was absorbed by New York Philharmonic in 1928. Conductors have incl. Mahler (1909–11), Mengelberg (1921–30), Toscanini (1930–6), Barbirolli (1937–40), Rodzinsky (1943–7), Bruno Walter (1947–9), Bernstein (1958–71), and Boulez (1971–7).

**Nibelung's Ring, The,** *see* RING.

**Nichelmann, Christophe** (1717–62), German composer. Pupil of J.S. Bach and Quantz. Worked with C.P.E. Bach for Frederick the Great. Works incl. treatise on melody, and harpsichord concertos and sonatas.

**Nicholson, Richard** (*c* 1570–1639), English organist, composer. Became first professor of music at Oxford (1627). Works incl. anthems, motet, madrigal in *The Triumphes of Oriana,* consort songs, and music for instrumental ensemble.

**Nicholson, Sydney Hugo** (1875–1947), English organist, teacher. Organist at Westminster Abbey (1918–27). Founded (1945) and directed School of English Church Music.

**nicht** (Ger.), not.

**Nicolai, Carl Otto Ehrenfried** (1810–49), German composer, conductor. Founded Vienna Philharmonic concerts (1842) and became director of court opera in Berlin (1847). Most famous work is lively comic opera *The Merry Wives of Windsor* (1849). Also wrote other operas, 2 symphonies, and chamber and church music.

**Nicolai, Philipp** (1556–1608), German poet, musician, Lutheran pastor. His *Freudenspiegel des ewigen Lebens* (1599) contains melodies of 2 chorales frequently used by Lutheran composers down to Bach, namely 'Sleepers, awake' and 'How brightly shines the morning star'.

**Nicolò,** *see* ISOUARD.

**Niecks, Friedrich** (1845–1924), German-born violinist, musical historian. Made debut as violinist in Dusseldorf at age of 13. In 1868 joined A.C. Mackenzie's string quartet in Edinburgh. Appointed Reid Professor of Music at Edinburgh University in 1891. Books incl. *Frederick Chopin* (1888), *A History of Programme Music* (1907), and biography of Schumann.

**Niedt, Fredrich Erhard** (1674–*c* 1717), notary-public of Jena. Published *Musicalische Handleitung,* of which first part gives rules for playing from figured bass. Bach borrowed from it in compiling rules and examples for use in teaching.

**Nielsen, Carl August** (1865–1931), Danish composer. Studied at Copenhagen Conservatory under Gade. Joined Royal Orchestra as violinist (1891), and later conducted it (1908–14). Director of Conservatory and conductor of Musical Society (1915–27). Though soon established himself as Denmark's leading composer, it was not until 1950s that his qualities, esp. as symphonist, began to win international recognition. First symphony (1892) made history by beginning in one key and ending in another – not through eccentricity or clumsiness but through convincing tonal and structural principles which subsequently came to be called 'progressive tonality'. These ideas were cogently worked out in many of his later works.

Each of his 6 symphonies is work of character, strongly felt and powerfully argued, reflecting musical personality that can be both bitter and humorous, thoughtful and breezy, and filled with inimitable dramatic strokes – as when side drum marches starkly into 5th symphony, disrupting its pastoral spirit. This is Nielsen at his fiercest but optimism is usually allowed to break through – as in 4th symphony *(The Inextinguishable)*. Other works incl. concertos for flute, clarinet and violin, operas *Saul and David* (1902) and *Maskarade* (1906), wind quintet and other chamber music, and songs.

**Nielsen, Riccardo** (1908– ), Italian composer. Works incl. opera *The Incubus, Sinfonia concertante* for piano and orchestra, psalms for male voices and orchestra, chamber and piano music, and songs.

**niente** (It.), nothing. *Quasi niente,* indication that tone of voice or instrument is to be refined almost to whisper.

**Nightingale, The,** opera by Stravinsky, libretto by composer and S. Mitusov (after fairy tale by Hans Andersen). First perf. Paris, 1914, under Monteux. Stravinsky later wrote symphonic poem, *The Song of the Nightingale,* based on material from opera, which was used as music for ballet choreographed by Massine (1920).

**Night in May, A,** *see* MAY NIGHT.

**Night on the Bare Mountain,** orchestral work by Mussorgsky, who orig. planned it as incidental music, then turned it into symphonic fantasia (1886–7), used it in opera *Mlada* (1872), and left it as part of unfinished opera *Sorochintsi Fair* (1875). More accurate title is *St*

*John's Night on the Bare Mountain.* Rimsky-Korsakov later re-orchestrated it. Music describes Black Mass.

**Nights in the Gardens of Spain** (Sp., *Noches en los Jardines de España*), 3 symphonic impressions for piano and orchestra by Falla (1909–15).

**Nikisch, Artur** (1855–1922), Hungarian-German conductor. Conducted Leipzig Gewandhaus and Berlin Philharmonic Orchestras. One of greatest and most influential conductors of his time, notably of Bruckner and Chaikovsky.

**Nilsson, Birgit** (1918– ), Swedish soprano. Notable esp. as Brünnhilde in Wagner's *Ring,* and also in title-roles in Strauss's *Salome* and *Elektra* and Puccini's *Turandot.*

**Nilsson, Bo** (1937– ), Swedish composer. Sometimes referred to as *enfant terrible* of modern Scandinavian music. Works incl. *Quantitaten* (1958) for solo piano, *Madchentotenlieder* (1959), for soprano and chamber ensemble, and *Reaktionen* (1960) for 4 percussionists.

**Nin [y Castellanos], Joaquín** (1879–1949), Spanish-Cuban pianist, composer. Pupil of d'Indy. Edited collections of Spanish music and composed piano pieces, works for violin and piano, ballet, and songs for voice and orchestra.

His son, **Joaquín Maria Nin-Culmell** (1908– ), is also composer. Born in Berlin and resident in US. Pupil of Dukas and Falla. Works incl. sonata and concerto for piano, quintet for piano and strings, and songs.

**ninth,** interval of octave and second, totalling 9 steps. For 'chord of the ninth' *see* CHORD.

**Nivers, Guillaume Gabriel** (1632–1714), French composer, theorist. Organist to Louis XIV and music-master to Queen. His 3 books of organ music (1665–75) had considerable influence on French style in later 17th cent. Also published motets, editions of Gregorian chant, and various treatises.

**Nobilissima Visione** (Lat., noblest vision), orchestral suite by Hindemith. First perf. Venice, 1938. Based on ballet of same title (on St Francis of Assisi) which Hindemith produced earlier that year.

**nobilmente** (It.), nobly.

**Noble, Dennis** (1899–1966), English baritone. Sang at Covent Garden, and in Italy and US. Also notable as soloist in choral works.

**Noces, Les,** *see* WEDDING.

**noch** (Ger.), still, yet. *Noch lebhaft,* still lively. *Noch lebhafter*, even livelier.

**Noches en los Jardines de España,** *see* NIGHTS IN THE GARDENS OF SPAIN.

**nocturne,** night-piece. Name introduced by John Field – from whom Chopin adopted it – for piano pieces with *cantabile* melody, often elaborately ornamented, over arpeggiated or chordal accompaniment. *See also* NOTTURNO.

**Nocturnes,** apart from numerous pieces of Field and Chopin, title of

3 orchestral pieces by Debussy (1893–9): *Nuages, Fêtes* and *Sirènes* (last using wordless female chorus).

**node,** *see* HARMONICS.

**noël** (Fr.), Christmas Carol or song.

**noire** (Fr.), crotchet.

**Nola, Giovanni Domenico del Giovane da** (*c* 1510–92), Italian composer. Works incl. motets, madrigals, and villanellas *alla Napolitana,* of which he was one of earliest composers.

**non** (It.), not.

**nonet,** combination of 9 instruments or piece for such a combination.

**non-harmonic note** (US, non-harmonic tone), note which is not part of chord with which it sounds, *ie* passing note or appoggiatura.

**Nonnengeige** (Ger.), lit. 'nun's fiddle', *ie* TROMBA MARINA.

**Nono, Luigi** (1924– ), Italian composer. Pupil of Maderna and Scherchen. Began as follower of Webern and won attention abroad with orchestral variations on note series by Schoenberg (1950). Reputation as one of Italy's major progressive composers was confirmed by opera *Intolleranza 1960,* which used live and recorded performances and mixed actors and film sequences. Other works incl. opera *Al gran sole carico d'amore* (1974–7), *Epitaph for Federico Garcia Lorca* for speaker, singers and orchestra, *Incontri* (Encounters) for chamber ensemble, and *On the Bridge of Hiroshima* for soprano, tenor and orchestra. Uses music as vehicle for left-wing political views.

**Non più andrai,** Figaro's aria at end of Act 1 of Mozart's *The Marriage of Figaro,* in which he tells Cherubino what life will be like in the army.

**Norcombe** or **Norcome, Daniel** (*c* 1576–before 1626), English composer, violinist. Contributed madrigal to *The Triumphes of Oriana.* Pieces for viol in *The Division Violist* (1659) are prob. by relation with same name.

**Nordheim, Arne** (1931– ), Norwegian composer. Works, mostly incorporating electronic elements, incl. ballet *The Tempest* (1979), *Epitaffio* for orchestra and tape, and musical TV play *Favola.*

**Nørgård, Per** (1932– ), Danish composer. Pupil of Holmboe and Nadia Boulanger. Works incl. *Fragment VI* for 6 orchestra groups, opera *The Labyrinth,* ballet *Le jeune homme à marier* (after Ionesco), oratorio *Babel,* and numerous orchestral pieces, chamber music, and songs.

**Norma,** opera by Bellini, libretto by F. Romani. First perf. Milan, 1831. One of most famous and musically perfect of *bel canto* operas. Story concerns Druidic priestess torn between love and duty.

**North, Roger** (1653–1734), English lawyer, amateur musician, attorney-general to James II. His *Memoires of Musick* and *The Musicall Gramarian* contain interesting accounts of music of period. His brother **Francis North, Lord Guildford** (1637–85), published *A Philosophical Essay on Musick* (1677).

**Nose, The,** opera by Shostakovich, based on satirical story by Gogol.

First perf. Leningrad, 1930. Shostakovich's first opera, its progressiveness of outlook alarmed Soviet authorities.

**nota cambiata,** *see* CAMBIATA.

**notation,** the writing down of music so as to indicate its pitch and rhythm. By mid 18th cent., most modern conventions had been more or less universally established. *See* MENSURAL NOTATION, TABLATURE, FIGURED BASS, CHORD SYMBOL, STAFF, CLEF, KEY SIGNATURE, ACCIDENTAL, TIME SIGNATURE, BAR, TEMPO, EXPRESSION MARKS. *See also* appendix of Signs and Symbols.

**note,** (1) tone of definite pitch;
(2) symbol for tone, indicating pitch and duration;
(3) key of piano or other keyboard instrument.

**note cluster** (US, tone cluster), term coined by Henry Cowell for dissonant group of notes, lying close together and usually played on piano. Cowell pioneered effect, which can be obtained by applying fist, forearm or piece of wood to keyboard. Also used notably by Ives in his *Concord Sonata* (1915).

**note de passage** (Fr.), PASSING NOTE.

**note echappée,** *see* ECHAPPÉE.

**note row,** order of notes chosen by composer as basis, or gravitational force, of a composition. In 12-note music, note row would consist of 12 chromatic notes, from which rest of work derives through development and mutation of those notes. Note row need not, however, consist of 12 notes only; nor, except in strictest form of 12-note music, need repetition of note be forbidden until other 11 have been sounded. US expression '12-tone row' is misleading, as octave contains 12 semitones, not 12 tones. *See* TWELVE-NOTE SYSTEM.

**note sensible,** *see* LEADING NOTE.

**notes égales, notes inégales,** *see* DOT (2.iv).

**note value,** the length of time a particular note is to be played in relation to other notes. *See* appendix of Signs and Symbols for values and notations.

**Notker,** known as Balbulus (*ie* the stammerer) (*c* 840–912), most famous member of Music School of St Gall. Wrote poems to melodies of Alleluia of Mass to form SEQUENCES. Also wrote poems, and prob. music, of new sequences.

**Notre Dame** (Fr., Our Lady), cathedral church of Paris. During late 12th, early 13th cents. it was important centre for church music, esp. for development of ORGANUM. Leading composers associated with Notre Dame were Leoninus and Perotinus. Term 'Notre Dame School' is generally applied to all polyphonic music of this period of French or Anglo-French origin.

**Nottebohm, Martin Gustav** (1817–82), German musical historian. Friend of Mendelssohn and Schumann. Lived in Vienna from 1845. Edited Beethoven's sketch-books, and compiled thematic catalogues of Beethoven's and Schubert's works.

**notturno** (It.), night-piece: (1) title given by 18th-cent. composers to music for evening entertainment;
(2) in 19th cent., Italian equivalent of NOCTURNE.

**novachord,** domestic electronic 6-octave keyboard instrument, akin to small organ. Has stops for varying tone colour and pedals for controlling and sustaining volume.

**Novák, Vítezslav** (1870–1949), Czech composer, teacher. Pupil of Dvořák, and encouraged by Brahms. Professor at Prague Conservatory for many years. Music at first influenced by German romantics, but later developed distinctly Czech style. Works incl. operas, cantata *The Spectre's Bride,* symphonic poems, string quartets, piano pieces, and songs.

**Noveletten** (Ger.), 'short stories'. Title given to short instrumental pieces, usually of descriptive character. First used by Schumann of his set of 8 piano pieces, op 21 (1838).

**Novello, Vincent** (1781–1861), London publisher, editor, organist, composer. Founded music-publishing firm of Novello in 1811. Edited many collections of music incl. anthems by Boyce, Croft, and Greene, Masses by Mozart, Haydn and Beethoven, and Purcell's church music.

His son, **Joseph Alfred Novello** (1810–96), succeeded to family business, and instituted cheap editions of standard works. Also produced concerts, and introduced Mendelssohn's music to Britain.

Vincent's daughter **Clara Anastasia Novello** (1818–1908), became one of most famous sopranos of her time, earning praise of Mendelssohn and Schumann.

**Noye's Fludde** (*ie* Noah's Flood), opera by Britten, libretto taken from Chester Miracle Plays. First perf. Aldeburgh, 1958. Work is intended principally for church performance, with audience joining in traditional hymns.

**Nozze di Figaro, Le,** *see* MARRIAGE OF FIGARO.

**Nuits d'Été** (Fr., *Summer Nights*), song cycle, op 7, by Berlioz (1841–56), to poems by Théophile Gautier. First important orchestral song cycle ever written.

**number opera** (Ger., *Nummeroper*), opera consisting of 'numbers', *ie* arias, duets, ensembles *etc*, separated by recitative or spoken dialogue. Prevalent until 18th cent. and even later, until swept aside by Wagner and Verdi, who advocated more continuous form of opera. In 20th cent. some composers have deliberately reverted to number operas, *eg* Stravinsky in *The Rake's Progress.*

**nun's fiddle,** *see* TROMBA MARINA.

**Nuove Musiche, Le** (It.), collection of monodies published in 1602 by Giulio Caccini. In foreword, discusses new style of singing, his own part in developing it, and use of such ornaments as *trillo* and *gruppo.*

**nut,** (1) part of bow held by player of stringed instrument, esp. screw device by which tension of hairs can be adjusted;

(2) strip of ebony at peg-box end of finger-board of stringed instrument which keeps strings slightly raised above level of finger-board and marks off sounding length at that end.

**Nutcracker, The** (Russ., *Shchelkunchik*), ballet by Chaikovsky, choreography by Ivanov (after fairy-tale of E.T.A. Hoffmann). First perf. St Petersburg, 1892. Use of French title *Casse-Noisette* is affectation outside of France.

**Nystroem, Gösta** (1890–1966), Swedish composer. Pupil of d'Indy. Works incl. *Sea Symphony* and other orchestral works, stage music, and songs. Also painter of some distinction.

# O

**obbligato** (It.), lit. 'essential' or 'obligatory'. Term refers to part, usually instrumental, which cannot be dispensed with in performance, as distinct from part which is optional, or *ad libitum*. Obbligato part is therefore usually an important one. In some 19th-cent. music, term was applied in opposite sense to additional, optional part.

**Oberon,** opera by Weber, libretto by J.R. Planché (after poem by Wieland). First perf. Covent Garden, 1826. Action (having nothing to do with Shakespeare's *A Midsummer Night's Dream*) ranges from court of Charlemagne to that of Harun al Rashid.

**obertas or oberek,** Polish round dance in fast triple time.

**Oberto, Conte di San Bonifacio,** opera by Verdi, libretto by Piazza, rev. by Merelli and Solera. Verdi's first opera, first perf. Milan, 1839.

**Oberwerk** (Ger.), swell organ.

**oblique motion,** term describing two melodic lines or parts, one of which moves while other stays on same note.

**oboe,** woodwind instrument with conical bore and double reed. It is non-transposing and has natural scale of D. Although still higher notes are obtainable, generally accepted range is from B flat below middle C to octave above G on top of treble clef.

Oboe-type instruments have long history, stretching back to Sumer and ancient Egypt. Modern oboe is descendant of medieval and Renaissance instruments called SHAWMS. Out of these developed, during 16th, 17th cent., *hautbois* or 'high-wood' instruments, and from them developed hautboys and bassoons of 17th, 18th cents. Early hautboys were harsh and powerful, and could compete with brass. Present day oboes date from time of Mozart and Haydn, although many improvements were made during later 18th, 19th cents.

During late baroque period, oboe was used frequently as solo instrument in chamber music, concertos and cantatas. In classical era, pair of oboes was essential for every symphony orchestra, and later composers sometimes required more.

Oboe family now incl.:

(1) **E flat oboe,** rare instrument pitched minor third above normal oboe;

(2) **oboe d'amore** (It.; Fr., *hautbois d'amour*; Ger., *Liebesoboe*), slightly larger than normal oboe and with pear-shaped bell. Originated in Germany *c* 1720. Tone quality is more tender than oboe's. Pitched minor third lower and treated as transposing instrument. Became obsolete with advent of classical period, but revived by Richard Strauss;

(3) **cor anglais** (Fr.; Ger., *Englisch horn*; It., *corno Inglese*), is neither English nor a horn, but large oboe with bulge-shaped bell. Developed from *oboe da caccia* (see below) and is transposing instrument in F. Sounding range is either E flat or E natural below middle C to A above treble clef. Higher notes are obtainable, but are of better quality on oboe. Came into its own in romantic period: orchestras now have *cor anglais* player who doubles on 3rd or 4th oboe;

(4) **oboe da caccia** (It., lit. 'hunting oboe'; Fr., *taille*; early Eng., tenor hautboy), developed from alto *Pommer* (large shawm). Early form of *cor anglais*; much used by Bach;

(5) **Heckelphone** (Fr., *hautbois baryton*), rarely used instrument pitched octave below oboe.

**Obrecht** or **Hobrecht, Jacob** (1450–1505), Flemish composer. Worked in Berg-op-Zoom (prob. his hometown), Cambrai, Bruges and Antwerp, and twice visited Italy. One of leading composers of his period. Compared with Ockeghem's works in same forms, his 24 Masses and 22 motets show slightly later style in more frequent use of sequence in melodies, of imitation between parts and of definite cadences. Also composed *chansons*.

**Oca del Cairo, L'** (It., *The Goose of Cairo*), unfinished opera by Mozart, libretto by Varesco. Composed 1783; completions by various hands have been made.

**ocarina,** small pear-shaped wind instrument of recorder type and with similar tone quality. With its limited range it is hardly more than a toy.

**O'Carolan, Turlough** (1670–1738), blind Irish harper, composer. Many of his airs were well-known in 18th cent., and some were set to new words by Thomas Moore.

**Occasional Oratorio,** work by Handel, written in celebration of suppression of Jacobite Rebellion (1746). Text was compiled from various sources incl. Milton's psalms.

**Oceanides, The,** symphonic poem, op 73, by Sibelius (1914). Music portrays Aallottaret – Finnish equivalent of sea nymphs of Greek mythology.

**Ocean, thou mighty monster,** aria in Act 2 of Weber's *Oberon* in which heroine, Reiza, hails ocean and boat which she hopes is coming to her rescue. This large-scale aria, one of Weber's grandest conceptions, points way towards Wagnerian music drama.

**ochetto,** *see* HOCKET.

**Ochsenmenuett, Die,** *see* OX MINUET.

**Ockeghem (Okeghem, Ockenheim), Johannes (Jan)** (*c* 1430–*c* 1495), Flemish composer. In service of French king from 1453. Composed *c* 16 Masses, motets, and *chansons*. First in long succession of famous Flemish composers. Style is characterized by continuity of flow, achieved by long overlapping phrases and infrequent use of cadences, and independence of parts (so eschewing imitation).

**Octandre,** work by Varèse (1924) for 7 wind instruments and double bass.

**octave,** (1) INTERVAL between first and eighth notes of diatonic

SCALE. Notes which are octave apart are called by same letter name. Upper note has exactly twice the frequency of vibrations of lower one and two notes have effect of mutual duplication and reinforcement. To play in octaves means that each note is doubled one or more octaves above or below;

(2) 4ft diapason stop on organ, also called principal.

**octave coupler,** mechanical device on organ which automatically doubles at octave above any note which is played. Sub-octave coupler similarly doubles at octave below.

**octave fiddle** (Ger., *Oktargeige*), obsolete, small, 4-stringed instrument, tuned octave below violin.

**octet,** piece for 8 solo instruments or voices, or group that performs such pieces.

**octobass** (Fr., *octo basse*), 3-stringed double bass of vast proportions invented in 1849 by J.B. Vuillaume in Paris. Levers were needed to stop strings because of their thickness. Could descend octave below lowest note of cello (now obtainable on modern 5-stringed double bass). Failed to establish itself.

**ode,** (1) form of strophic poetry;

(2) vocal composition in honour of some person or occasion (though Stravinsky's *Ode* is for orchestra).

**Ode for St Cecilia's Day,** (1) 3 choral works by Purcell (1683, 1692, and ?);

(2) setting by Handel of Dryden's poem (1739).

**Ode to Napoleon,** work by Schoenberg, op 41 (1942), for speaker, strings and piano, to text by Byron, attacking despotism. Spoken part is rhythmically set down, though pitch is left to performer's discretion.

**Odhecaton** (from Gr. for song and hundred), the *Harmonice musices Odhecaton A,* published by Petrucci (1501), was first printed collection of polyphonic music. Contains 96 *chansons* of later 15th cent. by Agricola, Compère, Busnois, Isaac, Josquin, Ockeghem, Obrecht and others. 2 further collections (labelled *B* and *C*) were published in 1502 and 1503.

**Odington, Walter de** or **Walter of Evesham** (before 1278–after 1316), Benedictine monk, musical theorist, astronomer. His treatise *De Speculatione Musicae* (*c* 1300) is one of most informative of period.

**Odo of Cluny** (*c* 879–942), French musical theorist, composer. His *Dialogus de Musica* (*c* 935) contains discussion of MONOCHORD.

**Odysseus** (It., *Ulisse*), opera by Dallapiccola, inspired by Homer. First perf. Berlin, 1968.

**Oedipus at Colonus** (Ger., *Oedipus auf Kolonus*), incidental music, op 93, by Mendelssohn for tragedy of Sophocles. Scored for male chorus and orchestra. First perf. Potsdam, 1845.

**Oedipus Rex,** 'opera-oratorio' by Stravinsky. Libretto is Latin translation by J. Daniélou of play by Cocteau (after Sophocles). First perf. Paris, 1927.

**oeuvre** (Fr.), opus.

**Offenbach, Jacques** (1819–80), German-French composer. Born in Cologne (son of cantor in synagogue) but educated and mostly resident in Paris. In 1849 became conductor at Théâtre Français. Manager of Bouffes Parisiens (1855–61), and of Théâtre de la Gaîté (1873–5). Of his 90 operettas, *Orpheus in the Underworld* (1858), *La Belle Hélène* (1864) and *La Vie Parisienne* (1866) are the most exhilaratingly sparkling and satirical, and achieved very great popularity. Most important work, *The Tales of Hoffmann,* was unfinished at his death, but was completed by Guiraud and produced in 1881.

**offertory** (Lat., *offertorium*; Fr., *offertoire*), part of Proper of Mass, sung after Credo while priest is preparing and offering oblation of bread and wine. Orig. psalm with antiphon, but now consists simply of antiphon.

**Office,** 'Hour Services' of RC Church, also used by Anglican Church for Matins and Evensong. In RC liturgy, Divine Office occurs 8 times daily.

**Offrandes,** work by Varèse (1922) for soprano and chamber orchestra, based on poems by Huidobro and Tablada.

**Ogdon, John** (1937– ), English pianist, composer. Member of 'Manchester School'. Joint winner (with Ashkenazy) of International Chaikovsky Competition in Moscow in 1962. Repertory is unusually large and adventurous, with special emphasis on later 19th cent. and earlier 20th cent. Own compositions, incl. piano concerto, sonata and preludes for piano, reflect tastes as performer.

**ohne** (Ger.), without. *Ohne Dämpfer,* without mute.

**Oistrakh, David** (1908–74), Russian violinist. Did not travel extensively in West till 1950s. Noted for superb qualities as musician and for pure sweetness of tone.

His son **Igor Oistrakh** (1931– ), is also famous violinist.

**Okeghem,** *see* OCKEGHEM.

**Okeover** or **Okar** or **Oker, John** (*fl* 17th cent.), English organist, composer. Composed fancies for viols in 3 and 5 parts, and anthems.

**Oktargeige,** *see* OCTAVE FIDDLE.

**Oktave** (Ger.), octave.

**Old Hall Manuscript,** manuscript collection (made *c* 1410–15) of English polyphonic church music of late 14th, early 15th cents. Long kept at library of St Edmund's College, Old Hall, Herts. Passed to British Library in 1974.

**Old Hundredth,** hymn-tune which first appeared in Genevan Psalter of 1551, set to psalm 134. Adopted in Thomas Sternhold's 'Anglo-Genevan' Psalter of 1561, where it was set to Psalm 100 and also to metrical version of Lord's Prayer. Became known as 'Old Hundredth' after publication of Tate and Brady's new version of Psalter in 1696. In US known as 'Old Hundred'.

**oliphant horn,** small medieval horn or bugle made of elephant's tusk and often elaborately carved.

**Oliver, Joe 'King'** (1885–1938), American jazz cornet player. In 1920s helped to popularize New Orleans style throughout US.

Encouraged young Louis Armstrong and featured him in his Creole Jazz Band, in which they produced some incomparable 2-cornet passages.

**Oliver, Stephen** (1950– ), English composer. Works incl. several operas (*eg Tom Jones*) and pieces of music theatre, symphony, and chamber music.

**Olsen, Ole** (1850–1927), Norwegian composer, critic, conductor. Composed 4 operas, symphonic poems, cantatas, symphony, and oratorio. His suite for Rolfson's children's play *Svein Urd* is still popular in Norway.

**Olympians, The,** opera by Bliss, libretto by J.B. Priestley. First perf. Covent Garden, 1949.

**Ombra ma fui,** correct name for Handel's *Largo,* which is actually marked *larghetto,* and is a song to a tree, being the opening aria of opera *Serse* (Xerxes).

**O mio babbino caro** (It., 'Oh my beloved daddy'), Lauretta's aria in Puccini's *Gianni Schicci* in which she pleads for her father's permission to marry Rinuccio.

**O namenlose Freude,** duet in Act 2 of Beethoven's *Fidelio* in which Leonore and Florestan are reunited.

**ondeggiando,** *see* ONDULÉ.

**Ondes Martenot** or **Ondes Musicales,** electronic instrument patented by Maurice Martenot in 1922. Pitch is infinitely variable, and some variety of tone-colour is possible. Used by such composers as Messiaen, Milhaud and Honegger.

**ondulé** (Fr.; It., *ondeggiando*), 'undulating'. Effect, indicated by sign ~~~ used in violin playing in baroque period either on single note, or on several notes in ARPEGGIO, and produced by undulating motion of bow.

**one-step,** US dance in quick 2/4 time, popular in early 20th cent., but later ousted by slow foxtrot (or two-step).

**Ongarese,** *see* ALL'ONGARESE.

**On Hearing the First Cuckoo in Spring,** orchestral piece by Delius. First perf. Leipzig, 1913. Makes use of Norwegian folk song. Sound of cuckoo is evoked by clarinet.

**Onslow, George [André Georges Louis]** (1784–1853), Franco-British composer. Settled as country squire in France in early middle age. Composed much chamber music, incl. 36 string quartets, works for piano, comic operas, and symphonies.

**On This Island,** cycle of 5 songs by Britten, op 11, to poems by W.H. Auden (1937).

**On Wenlock Edge,** cycle of 6 songs by Vaughan Williams (1909), based on poems from Housman's *A Shropshire Lad.* Scored for tenor, string quartet and piano. Later scored for tenor with orchestra.

**op,** abbrev. of Lat. *opus,* 'work'. Term is traditionally used by composers to indicate numbering of their works in order of composition, *eg* op 95. If opus consists of more than one piece, it may be subdivided, *eg* op 59, no 2. Plural abbrev. is 'opp'. Abbrev. 'op post' or 'op posth' is used to indicate that work received number after composer's death.

**open,** not muted. In brass parts, indicates removal of mute, or discontinuation of hand-stopping (on horns).

**open diapason,** *see* DIAPASON.

**open fifth,** common chord without third is said to have open fifth.

**open notes,** on brass or woodwind instruments, notes produced without use of valves, keys *etc, ie* notes of HARMONIC SERIES.

When used of stringed instruments, term means notes not stopped by finger pressure (also called 'open strings'). Sign ° above note indicates that it is played on open string where poss., or as HARMONIC.

**open strings,** *see* OPEN NOTES.

**opera** (Fr., *opéra*; Ger., *Oper*; It., Sp., *opera*), dramatic work in which whole, or greater part, of text is sung with instrumental accompaniment. Term is abbrev. of *opera in musica* (musical work).

Association of music with ritual and drama is as old as civilization. Music was essential part of liturgical drama of Middle Ages, and it also figured prominently in many dramatic entertainments presented at Italian courts in 16th cent. However, though opera owed much to these entertainments, it was essentially a new form, born when group of artists, musicians and scholars in Florence attempted to revive Greek drama, which they falsely supposed to have been sung throughout.

First product of this movement was Rinuccini's *Dafne* (1597), with music by Peri and Corsi. New type of declamatory song (later called *recitativo*) was found to be suitable musical form, as it gave more room for dramatic expression than complex polyphonic forms. Accompaniment (on lute or keyboard) was treated as subordinate harmonic background. Most important opera on Florentine model was Monteverdi's *Orfeo* (1607), which also included much choral writing.

In 1637 first public opera house was opened in Venice, followed by several others. For economic reasons chorus was neglected in favour of solo singing, and orchestra consisted normally of strings and harpsichord. Tendency to relieve monotony of continuous recitative by incorporating arias (or songs) and duets became well established.

First comic opera was *Chi soffre, speri* by Mazzocchi and Marazzoli (1639). Staple elements of comic opera were rapid recitative, patter songs, and scenes parodying serious opera.

During 17th cent. Italian opera spread abroad. It was introduced into Paris in 1645, but aesthetic and political hostility it aroused led French to produce own operas, which owed much to traditions of spoken drama and to ballet. Success as national form was due to Lully, whose first opera was *Cadmus et Hermione* (1673). Ballet continued to be integral part of French opera right down to 19th cent. In England, where MASQUE was popular in early 17th cent., attempt at establishing opera was made by Davenant, whose *Siege of Rhodes* (1656) had music by several composers, but Restoration society tended to prefer type similar to French *comédie-ballet* (combination of spoken drama with ballet), *eg* Purcell and Dryden's *King Arthur* (1691).

Traditions of Italian opera were continued by Stradella (1644–82) and Alessandro Scarlatti (1660–1725). In work of Scarlatti, aria acquired absolute supremacy: recitative virtually became series of conventional formulas. The standard type of ARIA was in *da capo* form. Overture also developed into standard form – 3 movts. in quick-slow-quick form. French composers preferred slow introduction followed by quick fugal movement.

In Germany Schütz had set translation of Rinuccini's *Dafne* in 1627, but though Italian opera flourished in Germany, German opera did not become fully established till opening of first opera house (Hamburg, 1678), where Handel gained his first operatic experience.

In course of 18th cent. there was growing dissatisfaction with rigidity of operatic conventions. It was felt that vocal virtuosity was exploited at expense of dramatic expression and that overture should be integral part of work, not merely instrumental introduction. Operas of Jommelli and Traetta show awareness of these problems, but it was above all Gluck who demonstrated in his later works, esp. *Alceste* (1767), *Iphigénie en Aulide* (1774) and *Iphigénie en Tauride* (1779), that simple, sincere and direct form of expression could be more truly dramatic than emphasis on fine singing. Rameau had already shown dramatic potential of orchestra: Gluck developed it further.

Comic opera (*opera buffa*) did not become firmly established in Italy till early 18th cent. It aimed above all at being 'natural' in contrast to artificiality of *opera seria*. Hence when Pergolesi's *La serva padrona* was reintroduced to Paris in 1752 it was used by critics of French opera to show up all that was stilted and conventional in French tradition. Violent controversy which ensued was called *La Guerre des Bouffons,* which had important effect of stimulating composition of French *opéras comiques. Opéra comique,* unlike *opera buffa,* employed spoken dialogue in place of recitative. Romantic and pathetic elements came to be introduced into *opera buffa* (*eg* in Mozart's *Don Giovanni,* 1787) and into *opéra comique* – so much so that in 19th cent. *opéra comique* came to mean simply opera with dialogue, as opposed to 'grand opera', which was set to music throughout and produced on lavish scale.

In Britain, comic opera established itself as independent form with Gay's *Beggar's Opera* (1728) in which songs were set to popular themes, either traditional or by composers like Purcell and Handel. This was followed by many similar works, called 'ballad operas'. Ballad opera also had influence in Germany on *Singspiel* (*eg* Mozart's *Die Entführung,* 1782, and *The Magic Flute,* 1791), counterpart to *opéra comique.*

Mozart's principal activity was in field of Italian opera; *Idomeneo* (1781) and *La clemenza di Tito* (1791) are both in *opera seria* form; *The Marriage of Figaro* (1786), *Don Giovanni* (1787) and *Cosi fan tutte* (1789) are outstanding examples of *opera buffa.*

The upheavals of the French Revolution led to composition of *opéras comiques* dealing with dramatic rescues *eg* Cherubini's *Les deux journées* (1800) and Beethoven's *Fidelio* (1805). In Germany, influence of romantic literature is seen in operas of Weber and Marschner.

Contemporary with this movement in Germany was development of grand opera in Paris, which gave scope for historical spectacle on grand scale, *eg* in Rossini's *William Tell* (1829), Meyerbeer's *Les Huguenots* (1836) and Berlioz's *The Trojans* (1856–9).

In Germany, Wagner was familiar with tradition of grand opera and also of romantic German opera. Growing reaction to tradition, however, led him to expound new theory of opera, arguing that form should be union of all the arts, with dignified (*ie* legendary) subject matter, alliterative verse forms, and continuous commentary (explaining action by repetition of significant themes) by orchestra. Theory was put into practice in *The Ring* (1853–74).

In 19th-cent. Italy, traditions were maintained by Rossini, Donizetti and Bellini. Rossini was most original and influential, most notably in *The Barber of Seville* (1816). He assigned greater importance to orchestra, broke with convention of recitative accompanied only by keyboard instrument, and put end to improvised ornamentation by singers. Verdi inherited traditions of predecessors, but he developed new mastery of orchestra and remarkable instinct for dramatic effect, culminating in *Aida* (1871), *Otello* (1887) and *Falstaff* (1893).

Simultaneously, growth of nationalism was having stimulating effects in other countries, esp. Russia and what is now Czechoslovakia. Foundations of Russian opera, hitherto dependent on Italy, were laid by Glinka in 1836. His successors were Mussorgsky (esp. with *Boris Godunov,* 1868), Borodin and Rimsky-Korsakov. Chaikovsky's style leaned more to that of West. In Czechoslovakia, Smetana, though attacked by critics as 'Wagnerian', won popular success with *The Bartered Bride* (1866).

In 20th cent., opera has pursued no consistent path. In Germany, Richard Strauss applied Wagnerian musical tradition to combination of bourgeois sentiment and wild extravagance, *eg* in *Der Rosenkavalier* (1911). In France, Debussy's impressionistic *Pélleas and Mélisande* proved highly influential. In Italy, *verismo* (realism), foreshadowed by Bizet's *Carmen* (1875), was inaugurated by Mascagni's *Cavalleria rusticana* (1890) and Leoncavallo's *I Pagliacci* (1892) and used by Puccini, *eg* in *La Bohème* (1896) and *Madame Butterfly* (1904). Realism, of more subtle kind, is also characteristic of Berg's *Wozzeck* (1925) and *Lulu* (1937).

Since WWII, leading composers of opera have been Britten and Henze. Forms and directions have multiplied. Symbolism has emerged as reaction to realism, and CHAMBER OPERA and return to 18th-cent. conventions (as in Stravinsky's *The Rake's Progress*) have both evolved as reactions to Wagnerian style. One of most recent significant developments is MUSIC THEATRE, which abandons both name and conventions of opera.

**Opera Ball, The** (Ger., *Der Opernball*), operetta by Heuberger, after farce *Les Dominos Roses* by Delacour and Hennequin. First perf. Vienna, 1898.

**opéra-ballet,** type of stage work which flourished in France in 17th, 18th cents., in which song and dance were given more or less equal importance. Important exponents incl. Lully and Rameau.

**opéra-bouffe** (Fr.), species of French comic opera.

**opera buffa** (It.), comic opera. Developed in Italy in 18th cent. Used light subject matter and drew characters from normal life, as opposed to mythological or regal subjects of *opera seria,* and its music was generally simpler and less long-winded.

**opéra-comique** (Fr.), lit. 'comic opera', though applied in 19th cent. to any French opera with spoken dialogue.

**opera-oratorio,** hybrid stage work, involving elements of opera and oratorio.

**opera semiseria** (It.), serious opera containing comic elements.

**opera seria** (It.), 'serious' opera. Most prevalent operatic form of 17th, earlier 18th cents., characterized by noble subjects, serious, elaborate arias, and general air of formality. Libretto was in Italian, and important roles were often given to castrato singers.

**operetta,** orig. diminutive of 'opera'. Term came to be used in 19th cent. for type of opera with dialogue which employed music of popular character, and used for subject matter judicious mixture of romantic sentiment, comedy, and parody of serious opera. Also called 'light opera'. Outstanding 19th-cent. composers of genre were Offenbach, Johann Strauss and Sullivan. *See also* MUSICAL COMEDY.

**ophicleide,** bass of key bugle family. Regular member of orchestra for period during 19th cent. Range is just over 3 octaves, and usual function was to apply bass to other brass instruments, esp. trombones. Was also important member of military bands, but tone is somewhat coarse and it was eventually ousted by smoother toned tuba. Made in various sizes from alto to double bass, but C and B flat versions were most common.

**opp, opus,** *see* OP.

**Opieński, Henryk** (1870–1942), Polish composer, conductor. Pupil of Paderewski, d'Indy and Nikisch. Composed operas, choral works, symphonic poems and songs, and published books on Polish music and edition of Chopin's letters.

**oratorio,** setting of text on sacred or epic theme for chorus, soloists and orchestra, for performance in church or concert hall. Name arose from Oratory of church in Vallicella where St Philip Neri instituted, in later 16th cent., performance of sacred plays with music. Carissimi was first important composer of oratorios, which adopted forms of opera with more extensive use of chorus – subsequently a common characteristic of oratorio. Later Italian composers of oratorio incl. Draghi, A. Scarlatti and Caldara. In Germany and Austria, most important composers have been Schütz, J.S. Bach, C.P.E. Bach, Haydn and Mendelssohn; in England, Handel, Arne, Parry, Elgar, Vaughan Williams and Walton; in France, M.A. Charpentier,

Berlioz, Franck, Saint-Saëns and d'Indy. Successful modern examples of form have been written by *eg* Honegger and Kodály.

**Orchésographie** (Fr.), treatise on dance, in form of dialogue, by Thoinot Arbeau (anagram of his real name, Jehan Tabourot), published 1589. Earliest surviving book on dance which prints tunes.

**orchestra,** as a definite group of instruments, the orchestra emerged in 17th-cent. opera houses. Groups (consorts) of instruments, *eg* strings or recorders, had earlier played together and occasionally several groups had been joined. First orchestras were temporary and very variable. Regular orchestra of baroque period consisted of strings, usually with oboes and bassoons, and other instruments were added for solo parts. Standardization took place in classical period, with division of orchestra into 4 groups: strings, woodwind (1 or 2 flutes, 2 oboes, 2 bassoons, and later, clarinets), brass (2 horns, 2 trumpets), and 2 kettledrums. In 19th cent., orchestra was expanded on this basis to incl. triple or quadruple woodwind, complete brass section, harp, and auxiliary percussion. Typical composition of late romantic orchestra might be:

*Woodwind:*
piccolo
3 flutes
3 oboes
cor anglais (also playing 4th oboe)
E flat clarinet
2 B flat clarinets
bass clarinet
3 bassoons
double bassoon
*Brass:*
8 horns
5 trumpets
3 trombones
B flat tenor tuba
bass tuba
*Percussion:*
kettledrums (mechanical)
bass drum
cymbals
small side-drum
tenor drum
*Strings:*
16 first violins
16 second violins
12 violas
12 cellos
8 double basses
2 harps

Reaction to large scale of orchestra (in which economics played part) arose after WWI, and many later composers have been content with more modest forces.

**orchestration,** art of writing for orchestra, concerned with tone colour, technical capacity, and effective range of instruments, with textures arising in combinations of instruments, and with setting out of orchestral score.

**orchestre** (Fr.), orchestra.

**orchestrion,** mechanical instrument able to imitate sounds of various orchestral instruments.

**Ordinary,** parts of Mass with invariable texts, *ie Kyrie, Gloria, Credo, Sanctus* and *Agnus Dei,* as distinct from PROPER.

**ordre** (Fr.), name given to various harpsichord suites by François Couperin.

**Orfeo, L'** (It., *The Story of Orpheus*), opera by Monteverdi, libretto by A. Striggio. First perf. Mantua, 1607.

**Orfeo ed Euridice** (It., *Orpheus and Eurydice*), opera by Gluck, libretto by R. de' Calzabigi. First perf. Vienna, 1762. Revised version, *Orphée* (translated by P.L. Moline), first perf. Paris, 1774.

**Orff, Carl** (1895–1982), German composer, teacher, educationalist. In 1930s wrote *Schulwerk*, quantity of short pieces for various instruments, suitable for schoolchildren. Other compositions consist mainly of stage works. 'Scenic cantatas', involving optional action and dance, incl. *Carmina Burana* (1937) and *Carmina Catulli* (1943). Operas incl. *The Moon* (1939), *The Clever Girl* (1943), *Antigone* (1949), *Oedipus the Tyrant* (1959), and *Prometheus* (1968). Music is strongly rhythmic, often percussive, and non-contrapuntal, and is effective for both drama and comedy.

**Orff-Schulwerk,** collection of percussion instruments of simple construction designed by Carl Orff for educational purposes.

**organ** (Fr., *orgue*; Ger., *Orgel*; It., *organo*), keyboard instrument, played with hands and feet, in which wind under pressure sounds notes through series of pipes. Mechanism of organ comprises:

(1) supply of wind under constant pressure, by hand pump or electric blower;

(2) one or more MANUALS (keyboards) and PEDAL BOARD, connected with pipes by trackers, electro-pneumatic devices, or electric contacts and wires;

(3) pipes, of flute type, and usually also reed type;

(4) stops, to admit wind to each register or set of pipes;

(5) couplers, to join actions of manuals to each other, and to that of pedal.

Flue pipes are of whistle (*ie* recorder) type, and may be open or stopped; stopping lowers pitch by octave. Reed pipes have beating reed and cylindrical or conical resonator. They consist of chorus reeds and solo reeds. Range of pitch within which stop sounds is indicated by reference to length, which is *c* 8ft, of unstopped pipe which sounds C below bass clef. Since this is lowest note of keyboard, it is taken as convenient standard of measurement: 8ft stop sounds at pitch corresponding to key which is depressed, 4ft stop an octave higher, 2ft stop 2 octaves higher, and 16ft and 32ft stops an octave and 2 octaves lower. MIXTURE STOP has 3 or 4 sets (ranks) of pipes which sound octave, fifteenth, double octave *etc* above normal pitch of key; MUTATION STOPS sound at twelfth or seventeenth, or their octaves.

Total design of each of 3 manuals, GREAT, CHOIR and SWELL, is complete in itself: Great incl. most powerful stops, Swell the softest. In large organs, pedal stops will also have own tonal design, and Solo manual will have stops of more individual character. Large organs may also have ECHO ORGAN. Following stops are basic: diapasons of 16, 8, 4 and 2ft and mutation stop on Great and Swell; one or more flute stops on each manual; flue stop of string quality (gamba) on Choir, Swell and Solo; chorus reeds (*eg* trumpet, clarion) on Great and Solo; solo reeds (*eg* clarinet, oboe) on Choir, Swell and Solo; diapasons and flute stops of 16, 8 and 4ft (and on large organs reed of 16ft), and diapason of 32ft on Pedal Organ.

Swell is always enclosed in box, as usually are Choir and Solo; this enables *crescendo*, controlled by pedal, to be made by opening one side of box.

Organ is one of most ancient instruments still in use. Known to Greeks and Romans as *hydraulis*. Used in churches all through Middle Ages. Smaller medieval organs were called, according to size, POSITIVE and PORTATIVE. Greatest period of organ music began with Merulo and ended with Bach. In 19th cent. action was completely changed by use of electricity, and organs increased steadily in size, some having as many as 7 manuals.

**organ, electronic,** instrument, of which Hammond organ and Compton Electrone are examples, with manuals and pedals in which tone is produced and amplified electronically. Some variety of tone colour can be obtained by controls which select and regulate intensity of certain number of overtones. *See* ACOUSTICS, ELECTRONIC INSTRUMENTS.

**organetto** (It.), small medieval PORTATIVE ORGAN.

**organistrum** (Lat.), hurdy-gurdy.

**Organ Mass,** Mass in which music of Ordinary is performed by singers and organ in alternating phrases. Singers sang plainsong and organist played polyphonic elaboration of it. Custom dates from 15th cent. *See also* GROSSE ORGELMESSE, KLEINE ORGELMESSE.

**organo** (It.), organ.

**organo di choro** (It.), choir organ.

**organo di legno** (It.), lit. 'wooden organ'. Term used in 16th, 17th cents. for small organ with flue pipes, as opposed to REGAL, which was reed organ.

**organo pieno** (It.; Lat., *organo pleno*), full organ.

**organ point,** same as PEDAL POINT.

**organum** (Lat.), (1) organ;

(2) term for method of composition used in several stages of medieval polyphony. In first stage (expounded *c* 900), added part follows plainsong in parallel fifths or fourths, also using thirds and

unison. In next stage (11th, 12th cents.) added part moves in perfect intervals (octaves, fifths and fourths) above plainsong. This is earliest form of true polyphony. By mid 12th cent., added part had become much more florid, and plainsong must have been sung quite slowly. Form gave rise to MOTET. *See also* CLAUSULA.

**orgatron,** electronic organ invented (1934) by Everett of Michigan.

**Orgel** (Ger.), organ.

**Orgelbüchlein** (Ger.), 'little organ book'. Collection of 46 short chorale preludes by Bach (1708–17), intended for beginner on instrument.

**Orgelmesse,** *see* GROSSE ORGELMESSE, KLEINE ORGELMESSE.

**Orgelpunkt** (Ger.), PEDAL POINT.

**Orgelwalze** (Ger.), mechanical organ.

**orgue** or **orgues** (Fr.), organ.

**orgue expressif** (Fr.), harmonium.

**Orlando,** opera by Handel, libretto by G. Bracciotti (after Ariosto's *Orlando Furioso*). First perf. London, 1733.

**Ormandy, Eugene** (1899– ), Hungarian-born conductor. Started as child prodigy on violin. Settled in US (1921). Conductor of Minneapolis Symphony Orchestra (1931–6) then of Philadelphia Orchestra.

**ornaments** (Fr., *agréments*; Ger., *Manieren*; It., *abellimenti*), in some periods, ornaments (graces or embellishments) have been important feature of melodic style, whether added extemporaneously by performer or indicated by composer in form of signs, or incorporated in notation. In 17th, 18th cents., principal types for which signs were used were: TRILL, MORDENT, APPOGGIATURA, ARPEGGIO, TURN, SPRINGER or NACHSCHLAG. In later periods most ornaments have been written out by composer. *See also* ACCIACCATURA.

**Ornithoparcus, Andreas** (*c* 1485–1535), German theorist. His *Musicae activae micrologus* (1517) was translated into English by John Dowland (1609).

**Ornstein, Leo** (1892– ), American composer, pianist, b. Russia. As pianist, was early champion of Schoenberg. Early works *eg Wild Men's Dance* for piano (1912) were considered very avant-garde. Later works incl. *Lysistrata Suite* for orchestra (1933) and piano music.

**orpharion,** type of CITTERN.

**Orphée** (Fr., *Orpheus*), *see* ORFEO ED EURIDICE.

**Orpheus,** (1) symphonic poem by Liszt (1854);
(2) ballet by Stravinsky, choreography by Ballanchine. First perf. New York, 1948.
*See also* ORFEO.

**Orpheus Britannicus,** collection of songs by Purcell (1659–95), published in 2 vols. (1698, 1702; enlarged edition, 1706, 1711).

**Orpheus in the Underworld** (Fr., *Orphée aux enfers*), operetta by Offenbach, libretto by H. Crémieux and L. Halévy. First perf. Paris, 1858. Satirizes Second Empire in terms of Greek gods, and burlesques legend, esp. Gluck's treatment of it.

**Orr, Robin** (1909– ), Scottish composer. Pupil of Casella and Nadia Boulanger. Professor of music at Glasgow University (1956–65) then at Cambridge. Works incl. operas *Full Circle* and *Weir of Hermiston,* 3 symphonies and other orchestral works, chamber and instrumental music, choral music and songs.

**Ortiz, Diego** (b. *c* 1510), Spanish composer. Court *maestro di cappella* in Naples from 1553. Wrote treatise *Tratado de glosas ... en la música de Violones* (1553) on extemporizing of variations (*glosas, diferencias*) on viola da gamba in style originated by Luis de Narvaez for lute. Also wrote church music.

**Orto, Marbriano de** (d. 1529), Flemish singer, composer. Singer in Papal Chapel, and later at court of Philip of Burgundy. His *Ave Maria* and a *chanson* were printed in Petrucci's *Odhecaton* (1501), and Masses and motets in later publications of Petrucci.

**Ory, 'Kid'** (1889–1973), American jazz trombonist. Heyday was in 1920s, when appeared with King Oliver, Jelly Roll Morton and Louis Armstrong. His lusty style was also notable in his work with his own Kid Ory's Creole Jazz Band.

**Osiander, Lucas** (1534–1604), German musician, theologian. His *Fünfzig geistliche Lieder und Psalmen* (1586) was first collection of chorales in which tune was put in the treble; previously tune was put in tenor.

**O soave fanciulla** (It., lovely maid in the moonlight), love duet for Mimi and Rudolfo in Act 1 of Puccini's *La Bohème.*

**ossia** (It.), or. Used to indicate alternative (usually simplified) to passage in composition.

**ostinato** (It.), persistently repeated musical figure which may occur during section of composition or even throughout whole piece. Ostinato patterns very often occur in bass, so *basso ostinato* = GROUND BASS.

**Otello,** (1) opera by Verdi, libretto by A. Boito (after Shakespeare). First perf. Milan, 1887;

(2) opera by Rossini, libretto by F.B. di Salsa (after Shakespeare). First perf. Naples, 1816.

**ôtez** (Fr.), remove (*eg* mutes).

**Othmayr, Caspar** (1515–53), German composer. Wrote settings of German songs, motets, and settings of Lutheran hymns. His *Symbola* (1547) is collection of 5-part pieces each in honour of notable person of his time.

**ottava** (It.), octave. Abbrev. *8va. All'ottava* or *8va,* octave higher or lower (generally former); *ottava alta* or *ottava sopra,* octave higher; *ottava bassa* or *ottava sotto,* octave lower; *coll' ottava* or *con ottava,* doubled at octave above or below. Indications are written above notes when they refer to higher octave, below when they refer to lower. Dotted line indicates how long indication is valid. When term *8va* (or equivalents) ceases to be valid, it is often contradicted by *loco* '[in the normal] place'.

**ottavino** (It.), piccolo.

**Ottobi, Giovanni,** *see* HOTHBY.

**ottone** (It.), brass, *Strumenti d'ottone* (or *ottoni* alone), brass instruments.

**Ottone, Re di Germania** (It., *Otho, King of Germany*), opera by Handel, libretto by N.F. Haym. First perf. London, 1723.

**Our Hunting Fathers,** symphonic song cycle by Britten, op 8, to text devised by W.H. Auden (1936).

**Ours, L',** *see* BEAR.

**Our Town,** music by Copland for film of Thornton Wilder's drama. Written in 1940, Copland later transformed it into orchestral suite.

**Ousely, Frederick Arthur Gore** (1825–89), English composer, musical historian. At age of 6 played piano duet with Mendelssohn. Professor at Oxford from 1855. Edited sacred music of Orlando Gibbons.

**Out of Doors,** set of 5 piano pieces by Bartók (1926).

**ouvert** (Fr.; Lat., *apertum*; It., *verto*), open. *See* CLOS.

**ouverture** (Fr.), overture.

**overblowing,** means whereby HARMONICS are produced on woodwind instruments instead of fundamental notes. Normally there is special key opening small hole near mouth piece to assist overblowing, and when it is brought into use, player merely duplicates fingering in lower register to produce same note transposed. Most woodwind instruments produce first harmonic when overblown (octave above fundamental), but clarinets overblow at second harmonic (twelfth above fundamental). Other harmonics are brought into use for higher notes.

**overstrung,** method for positioning strings in pianos so that they are on 2 levels and cross each other diagonally. This allows strings of greater length to be used in small instruments than would otherwise be possible.

**overtones,** *see* HARMONIC SERIES.

**overture,** introductory music to opera, oratorio, ballet, play, or other large-scale work. CONCERT OVERTURE, however, is written as independent concert piece.

First established form was French overture of Lully, which consisted of slow section in pompous dotted rhythm followed by fast section in imitative style. In some cases Allegro ended with short section in similar style to opening. Instrumental 'overtures' of German composers such as Telemann and Bach are French overtures followed by dance movements and are now called SUITES.

Italian opera overture *(sinfonia avanti l'opera)* in 3 movts., Allegro-Adagio-Allegro, was established by A. Scarlatti after 1680, and its later history merged with that of symphony. Opera overture of classical period was single movt., usually in sonata form. Gluck's idea that it should prepare audience for nature of action by using musical themes from main work was adopted in many later overtures.

Following Wagner's *Lohengrin* (1847), operas and incidental music frequently opened with PRELUDE – often (though not necessarily) shorter than overture and leading straight into 1st act. Sometimes later acts of opera have preludes.

**Owen Wingrave,** TV opera by Britten, libretto by M. Piper (based on ghost story by Henry James). First screened in Britain, 1971. Later revised for stage.

**Oxford Symphony,** name given to Haydn's symphony no 92 in G after it was performed at Oxford (July 1791) during his visit there to receive hon. D. Mus. Work was actually written 3 years earlier without this occasion in mind.

**Ox Minuet, The** (Ger., *Ochsenmenuett*), title of *Singspiel* by Seyfried. First perf. Vienna, 1823. Music is arranged from works by Haydn. Title is often misattrib. to one of Haydn's minuets.

**Ozawa, Seiji** (1935– ), Japanese conductor. Pupil of Karajan. Conducting posts incl. Toronto (1965–69), San Francisco (1970–76) and Boston (1974– ) Symphony Orchestras.

# P

**p,** abbrev. (1) for *piano* (It., soft); *pf, poco forte,* moderately loud; *pp, pianissimo,* very soft; *mp, mezzo piano,* moderately soft;

(2) in French organ music, for *pédales, ie* pedals, or for *positif.*

**Pachelbel, Johann** (1653–1706), German organist, composer. As composer of suites for harpsichord and of chorale preludes in fughetta style for organ he was important precursor of Bach. Also wrote several motets, arias, concertos, and cantatas, though many are now lost.

His son, **Wilhelm Hieronymous Pachelbel** (1685–1764), was also a composer. Works incl. organ music.

**Pachmann, Vladimir de** (1848–1933), Russian pianist. Excelled in performance of Chopin, whose works he played with remarkable delicacy.

**Pacific 231,** 'symphonic movement' for orchestra by Honegger (1923) evoking US railway engine in terms of 'visual impression and physical enjoyment'.

**Pacini, Giovanni** (1796–1867), Italian composer. Works incl. *c* 70 stage works, Masses, oratorios and cantatas.

**Pacius, Fredrik** (1809–91), German composer, violinist, resident in Finland from 1834. His *Kung Carls Jakt* is generally regarded as first Finnish opera; first perf. (in Swedish) Helsinki, 1852; revived in Finnish translation, 1905.

**Paderewski, Ignacy Jan** (1860–1941), Polish pianist, composer, statesman. Pupil of Leschetizky. Became one of most renowned pianists of his day, esp. in performances of Chopin. From 1915 worked for Polish independence, and became prime minister in 1919. Resumed concert tours in 1922. Composed many works incl. piano concerto, opera *Manru,* symphony, and songs.

**padiglione,** *see* PAVILLON.

**padiglione cinese,** *see* PAVILLON CHINOIS.

**Padilla, Juan de** (1605–73), Spanish composer. Works incl. motets and *villancicos.*

**Padilla, Juan Gutiérrez de** (*c* 1595–1664), Spanish-Mexican composer. Worked at Puebla, Mexico, from *c* 1620. Composed much church music, incl. 5 Masses; several of his works are for double choir.

**Padmâvatî,** opera-ballet by Roussel, libretto by L. Lalois. First perf. Paris, 1923. Story is based on violent episode in 13th-cent. Indian history.

**Paer, Ferdinando** (1771–1839), Italian-born composer. Settled in France (where known as Paër) and became musical director to Napoleon. Wrote *c* 40 operas incl. sequel to Mozart's *Marriage of Figaro* called *The New Figaro* (1797), and *Leonora,* which has same plot as Beethoven's *Fidelio* (pre-dating it by a year). Also wrote 2 oratorios, cantatas, church music and some instrumental music.

**Paesiello,** *see* PAISIELLO.

**Paganini, Niccolò** (1782–1840), Italian violinist, composer. One of most famous performers in musical history. Made first concert tour at 13. Music director to Princess of Lucca (1805–13). In 1828 began tour that took in Vienna, Germany, Paris and British Isles. Also played guitar and viola, and commissioned work for latter from Berlioz. Result was *Harold in Italy* (1834), but Paganini never played it – reputedly because solo part was insufficiently brilliant.

Paganini performed his greatest feats as exponent of his own works. Verve and demonic intensity with which he played led many to believe him to be inspired by the Devil. Extraordinary range of his technical mastery can be found in his 24 caprices, op 1, for solo violin. Some of new technical developments in these pieces were adapted to piano in studies of Liszt and Schumann, and used for piano variations by Brahms and Rakhmaninov. Also wrote at least 5 violin concertos, *The Carnival of Venice* and other pieces for violin, and chamber music for guitar and strings.

**Pagliacci, I** (It., The Clowns), opera by Leoncavallo, libretto by composer. First perf. Milan, 1892 (under Toscanini). One of finest examples of Italian *verismo* style. Story concerns jealous actor who murders his wife and her lover during performance of comedy. Traditionally staged with Mascagni's *Cavalleria Rusticana.*

**Paine, John Knowles** (1839–1906), American composer. Built up music faculty at Harvard University. Works incl. 2 symphonies, symphonic poems, and choral, chamber, piano, organ and incidental music.

**Paisiello** or **Paesiello, Giovanni** (1740–1816), Italian composer. Pupil of Durante. Began as composer of church music, but from 1863 found his true *mėtier* in *opera buffa.* Worked in St Petersburg (for Catherine the Great), Paris (for Napoleon) and Naples. His *Barber of Seville* (1792) was most famous setting of text before Rossini's. Works incl. *c* 100 operas, church music, symphonies, concertos, and chamber music.

**Paladilhe, Émile** (1844–1926), French composer. Pupil of Halévy. Won *Prix de Rome* (1860). Composed operas, symphony, 2 Masses, and songs.

**Palestrina, Giovanni Pierluigi da** (*c* 1525–94), Italian composer. Took name from birthplace, Palestrina, near Rome. Choirmaster of Julian Chapel, member of Papal Choir, successor of Lassus as director of St John Lateran, director of Julian Chapel, and holder of other important posts. On death of wife in 1580 almost entered priesthood, but remarried instead.

Palestrina's style has been regarded by RC Church as purest model of devotional polyphony, and by musical historians as exemplar of greatest age of counterpoint. However, though his style is noteworthy for its serenity of expression, artistic discipline and thorough consistency, it is by no means representative of 16th-cent. contrapuntal style as a whole.

Palestrina's most typical style is a diatonic and modal imitative polyphony, beautifully balanced in rhythm, melody, and use of dissonance. In compositions of 6 or more parts it leans more often towards the originally Venetian and more homophonic style of antiphonal writing for divided choir, as in *Stabat Mater*. Many of his Masses, for 4 to 8 voices, are PARODY MASSES; some are based on plainsong *cantus firmus* or on secular song. Other works incl. motets in 4 to 8 and in 12 parts, Lamentations, Magnificats, Litanies, Psalms, and sacred and secular madrigals.

**Palestrina,** opera by Pfitzner, libretto by composer, based on (unfounded) legend that Palestrina wrote his *Missa Papae Marcelli* through angelic inspiration, thereby persuading Council of Trent not to ban polyphonic music. First perf. Munich, 1917.

**palindrome,** in music, phrase or piece which reads same forwards as backwards, *ie* in which second half is first half in RETROGRADE MOTION.

**Pallavicini** or **Pallavicino, Carlo** (*c* 1630–88), Italian composer. Lived in Venice and Dresden. Contributed greatly to development of aria in Venetian opera. Most mature of his 21 operas is *Gerusalemme liberata* (1687).

**Palmer, Felicity** (1944– ), English soprano. Sings in both opera and concert-hall. Known esp. for interpretations of French songs.

**Palmer, Robert** (1915– ), American composer. Pupil of Hanson, Harris and Copland. Works incl. 2 symphonies, piano concerto, *Abraham Lincoln Walks at Midnight* (1948) and other choral works, and chamber music.

**Palmgren, Selim** (1878–1951), Finnish composer, pianist, conductor. Taught in US (1923–30). Works incl. piano concertos, choral and orchestral music, operas, songs, and piano pieces.

**Pammelia,** title of Thomas Ravenscroft's collection (1609) of anonymous canons, rounds and catches. Continuation, *Deuteromelia,* was published in same year.

**pancake drum** (Fr., *tarole*), side drum of normal diameter but only *c* 8cm deep. Tone is crisp and high pitched.

**pandean pipes,** *see* NEI.

**pandora,** also called pandore, bandora or bandore, plucked string instrument of CITTERN family, developed in England in mid 16th cent.

**pandorina,** small lute.

**pandoura,** instrument of lute type with long neck. Still played in Balkans and Middle East.

**pandura,** name applied by Greeks to 3-stringed lute, for which vernacular term was *trichordon.*

**Panharmonicon,** mechanical orchestra invented by Maelzel. Beethoven wrote *The Battle of Vittoria* for it.

**panpipes,** *see* NEI.

**pantaleon,** type of DULCIMER invented during 18th cent. by Pantaleon Hebenstreit, and named after him by Louis XIV.

**pantomime,** traditionally, play in dumb-show. In England in 18th cent. name was used to refer to stage entertainment with music similar to Italian *commedia dell'arte.* This led in turn to still popular Christmas show, in which fairy-tale or traditional story is enacted in spoken words interspersed with music.

**pantonality,** term referring to music not written in definite key. Schoenberg preferred this term to 'atonality'.

**Panufnik, Andrzej** (1914– ), Polish composer, conductor. Pupil of Weingartner. During WWII composed patriotic songs under pseudonym. Dislike of political situation led him to move to Britain (1954) where he conducted Birmingham Symphony Orchestra (1957–9). Compositions, mainly for orchestra, incl. *Sinfonia rustica* (1948), *Sinfonia sacra* (1963), *Sinfonia Mistica* (1977), and ballets *eg Miss Julie* (1970).

**Papillons** (Fr., *Butterflies*), 12 short piano pieces by Schumann, op 2 (1832). Music contains thematic and atmospheric links with *Carnaval,* op 9.

**paradiddle,** method of executing repeated pattern of notes (usually 4) on side drum so that successive principal beats are not played by same hand.

**Paradies** or **Paradisi, Pietro Domenico** (1707–91), Italian composer. Taught in London from 1747. Works incl. harpsichord sonatas and operas.

**Paradise and the Peri,** (1) (Ger., *Das Paradies und die Peri*), work for soloists, chorus and orchestra by Schumann, op 50 (1843), with words from German translation of poem in Thomas Moore's *Lalla Rookh;*

(2) fantasia-overture by Sterndale Bennett, op 42 (1862), based on same poem.

**Paradisi,** *see* PARADIES.

**parallel intervals,** *see* CONSECUTIVE INTERVALS.

**parallel motion,** movement of 2 or more parts of same INTERVAL. *See* CONSECUTIVE INTERVALS.

**Paray, Paul M.A. Charles** (1886–1979), French conductor, composer. Won *Prix de Rome* (1911). Conductor of Colonne Orchestra, Paris, for many years. Conducted Detroit Symphony Orchestra (1952–64).

**pardessus de viole** (Fr.), descant viol made in 18th cent. Tuned fourth higher than treble viol *(dessus de viole)*.

**Paride e Elena** (It., Paris and Helen), opera by Gluck, libretto by R. de' Calzabigi. First perf. Vienna, 1770.

**Parikian, Manoug** (1920– ), Turkish-born violinist, now UK citizen. Has given first perfs. of many modern British works. Musical director of Manchester Camerata from 1980.

**Paris Symphonies,** set of 6 symphonies by Haydn commissioned by the Concert de la Loge Olympique in Paris:

no 82 in C, The Bear, 1786;
no 83 in G minor, The Hen, 1785;
no 84 in E flat, 1786;

no 85 in B flat, The Queen of France, *c* 1786;
no 86 in D, 1786;
no 87 in A, 1785.

**Paris Symphony,** title given to Mozart's symphony no 31 in D, K 297 (1778), which he composed for Concert Spirituel during visit to Paris. Work contains some witty references to symphonic style in fashion in Paris.

**Parker, Charlie 'Bird'** (1920–55), black American jazz musician. Brilliant alto saxophonist. Principal figure of 1945 jazz revolution, when swing was replaced by BOP. His complex, wriggling, often astoundingly fast improvisations inspired the direction modern jazz was to take after his early death.

**Parker, Horatio William** (1863–1919), American organist, composer. Pupil of Rheinberger. Composed oratorios incl. *Hora Novissima,* and orchestral and keyboard music.

**parlando** (It.), lit. 'speaking', *ie* style of singing, found esp. in opera, in which tone approximates that of speech.

**parody Mass** (lat., *missa parodia*), term used, since 19th cent., for polyphonic Mass composed by using existing music, in more or less complete sections, of motet or *chanson,* a procedure adopted by many composers from Ockeghem to Palestrina.

**Parry [Charles] Hubert [Hastings]** (1848–1918), English composer, musical historian. Series of choral works, incl. *Ode on St Cecilia's Day* (1889), *L'Allegro ed il Penseroso* (1890), *Job* (1892), *The Lotus-Eaters* (1892), *Ode to Music* (1901), *The Pied Piper of Hamelin* (1905) and *Songs of Farewell* (1916–18), and his work as director of the Royal College of Music from 1894, established him as leader, with Stanford, of 'English Musical Renaissance'. Now remembered for setting of Milton's *Blest Pair of Sirens* (1887), and song *Jerusalem*. Knighted, 1898; baronetcy, 1903. Professor of music at Oxford (1900–8).

**Parry, Joseph** (1841–1903), Welsh composer. Works incl. operas, oratorios, cantatas and hymn tunes *eg* 'Aberystwyth'.

**Parsifal,** opera by Wagner, libretto by composer. First perf. Bayreuth, 1882. Described by Wagner as *Bühnenweihfestspiel* (sacred festival drama), and was his last stage work. Story is based on medieval legend related to that of Lohengrin, and concerns Parsifal, guileless forest lad who becomes knight and uncovers Holy Grail.

**Parsley, Osbert** (*c* 1511–85), English composer, singer. Works incl. church music.

**Parsons, Robert** (d. 1570), English composer. Gentleman of Chapel Royal from 1563. Composed services, anthems, motets, consort songs, and pieces for viols. His music had important influence on early works of Byrd.

**part,** any voice or instrument in ensemble, or music for it.

**part-book,** when large CHOIRBOOKS began to go out of use in early 16th cent. it became usual to write and print parts in separate part-books. Since *c* 1600 SCORE form has been adopted, while various parts have been published separately for performance.

**parte** (It.), voice-part.

**Parthenia** (Gr., maidenhood), title of collection of 21 pieces for virginals by Byrd, Bull and Gibbons (1612/13). Sister volume, *Parthenia Inviolata* (*c* 1625), contained 20 anonymous arrangements for virginals and bass and viol.

**partials,** tones of HARMONIC SERIES: lowest is known as first partial, and others are upper partials, or overtones.

**partial signature,** term used to denote situation common in music of *c* 1350–*c* 1520 in which key signatures of some parts, usually higher parts, have fewer flats than those of others, usually lower parts. Theoretical implications have not been fully explained. From it arose frequent occurrences of FALSE RELATION, which was persistent idiom in English music until Purcell.

**partita,** division. In 17th cent., term meant variation. It is not clear why German composers in late 17th cent. began to use it in sense of SUITE, as Bach did. Term is still sometimes used by composers today.

**partition** (Fr.), score. *Partition d'orchestre,* full score. *Partition chant et piano,* vocal score.

**Partitur** (Ger.), score.

**partitura** (It.), score.

**partiturophon,** one of group of electronic instruments using oscillating frequencies. Difference between 2 electrical frequencies produces sound which is then amplified.

**Partridge, Ian** (1938– ), English tenor. Known for recitals of *Lieder* and English songs.

**part song,** term used, esp. in 19th, 20th cents., for short unaccompanied piece for choir in HOMOPHONIC style.

**part writing** (Ger., *Stimmführung*; US, voice leading), writing of parts of polyphonic composition so as to produce good melodic line in each part.

**pasodoble** or **paso doble** (Sp.), 'double step', modern Spanish dance in quick 2/4 time.

**paspy,** 17th-cent. Eng. equivalent of *passepied.*

**Pasquini, Bernardo** (1637–1710), Italian composer, organist, harpsichordist. Pupil of Cesti. Pupils incl. Durante, Muffat, Gasparini and D. Scarlatti. Composed keyboard music, operas, oratorios and cantatas.

**passacaglia** (It.; Fr., *passecaille*), slow and stately dance introduced into keyboard music in early 17th cent.; later term came to mean piece in which theme is continually repeated. Composers made no effective distinction between passacaglia and CHACONNE; both were normally in triple time, composed in regular phrases of 2, 4 or 8 bars, and had perfect CADENCE at end of each phrase. French composers wrote passacaglia in RONDO form (*passecaille en rondeau*). German composers usually wrote passacaglia in variation form, over regular GROUND BASS.

**passage,** section of piece of music. Term may be used to imply section of little value or interest apart from opportunity it gives for virtuoso display.

**passamezzo** (It.), 'half step', dance in duple time with fairly quick tempo, popular in later 16th cent. Terms 'passinge mesures' and 'passa measures' appeared in English virginal books of period. Also called *passemezzo.*

**passecaille** (Fr.), passacaglia.

**passemezzo,** *see* PASSAMEZZO.

**passepied** (Fr.), French dance in quick triple time, poss. Breton in origin, introduced into French ballet *c* 1650 and thence into SUITE. Called 'paspy' in England.

**passing note** (Fr., *note de passage*; Ger., *Durchgangsnote*), note (or notes) taken scalewise between 2 notes consonant with prevailing harmony, which may itself be dissonant with that harmony. Called unaccented or accented according to whether it falls on weak or strong beat.

**passing shake,** same as upper MORDENT.

**Passion,** from *c* 12th cent., plainsong to which gospel accounts of Passion were recited during Holy Week was divided between 3 singers who recited parts of Christ (*bassa voce,* in low range), Evangelist (*media voce,* in middle range), and crowd or *turba* (*alto voce,* in high range). In 15th cent. part singing began to be used for words of *turba,* other parts still being sung in plainsong. Method of setting whole text in polyphony, sometimes using plainsong as CANTUS FIRMUS in tenor, arose at *c* beginning of 16th cent. In next 150 years Passions were written in either of these ways by *eg* Lassus, Victoria, Byrd and Schütz. New features in settings of Passion by Lutheran composers after 1640 were use of recitative, and introduction of contemplative poems in form of chorales and arias. Bach's *St John* (1723) and *St Matthew* (1729) Passions are final flowering of this development.

**Passione, La** (It., The Passion), name given to Haydn's symphony no 49 in F minor (1768). Poss. intended for performance in Holy Week, but title may simply refer to sombre intensity of music.

**pasticcio** (It.), lit. 'pie', *ie* work that has been put together by taking items from works of various composers, as was often done in 18th-cent. operas.

**pastiche** (Fr.), piece in which composer deliberately apes style of another (usually well-known) composer. *See also* PASTICCIO.

**pastoral,** as noun (1) alternative name for madrigal;
(2) any work representing country life.

**pastorale** (It.), (1) instrumental movement, usually in 6/8 or 12/8 time, with long bass notes, giving drone effect similar to that of MUSETTE;
(2) stage entertainment based on legendary or rustic subject, orig. with little or no music, but during 18th cent. more operatic in style, *eg* Handel's *Acis and Galatea.*

**'Pastoral' Sonata,** name given to Beethoven's piano sonata in D, op 28 (1801), prob. because finale has elements of rustic dance.

**Pastoral Symphony,** (1) Beethoven's symphony no 6 in F, op 68

(1808), entitled *Sinfonia pastorale,* and described by composer as 'an expression of emotion rather than tone-painting'. Five movts. are:

1. *Awakening of happy feelings on arriving in the country;*
2. *Scene by the Brook,* incl. calls of nightingale (flute), quail (oboe) and cuckoo (clarinet);
3. *Merry gathering of peasants,* interrupted by
4. *Thunderstorm,* leading to
5. *Shepherd's song. Cheerful and thankful feelings after the storm;*

(2) Vaughan Williams' 3rd symphony (first perf. 1922, rev. 1955); incorporates wordless soprano voice;

(3) name given to instrumental piece in *siciliano* rhythm in Handel's *Messiah* (1742). Called 'Pifa' by composer;

(4) also applied to instrumental piece in same rhythm in Bach's *Christmas Oratorio* (1734).

**Pastor fido, Il** (It., *The Faithful Shepherd*), opera by Handel, libretto by G. Rossi (from Guarini's pastoral play). First perf. London, 1712.

**'Pathetic' Sonata,** *see* SONATA PATHÉTIQUE.

**'Pathetic' Symphony,** *see* SYMPHONIE PATHÉTIQUE.

**Patience,** comic opera by Gilbert and Sullivan. Satirizes 'aestheticism'. First perf. London, 1881.

**Patrick, Nathaniel** (d. 1595), English organist, composer. Composed services and consort songs.

**Patterson, Paul** (1947– ), English composer. Works incl. *Strange Meeting* and other orchestral works, concertos for trumpet and horn, and choral, chamber, brass band and organ music.

**patter song,** kind of song, popular in comic opera, involving rapid, tongue-twisting enunciation of syllables.

**Patti, Adelina** or **Adela Juana Maria** (1843–1919), Spanish-born soprano, of Italian parentage. Made opera debut in 1859 in New York. Sang in Britain, Europe, and North and South America, and made last public appearance in 1914. Most famous soprano of her time, excelling in both opera and oratorio.

**Patzak, Julius** (1898–1974), Austrian tenor. Sang at Munich and Vienna Operas, and was famed exponent of Florestan in *Fidelio* and of Palestrina in Pfitzner's opera.

**Pauk, György** (1936– ), Hungarian-born violinist, now resident in UK. Plays as soloist and in piano trio with Peter Frankl and Ralph Kirshbaum.

**Pauken** (Ger.), timpani.

**Paukenmesse** (Ger., *Drum Mass*), nickname given to Haydn's Mass in C (1796) because of prominent part for timpani. Haydn called work *Missa in tempore belli* (Mass in time of war).

**Paukenschlag, Symphonie mit dem,** *see* SURPRISE SYMPHONY.

**Paukenwirbel, Symphonie mit dem,** *see* DRUM ROLL SYMPHONY.

**Paulus,** *see* ST PAUL.

**Paumann, Conrad** (*c* 1410–1473), blind German organist, composer. His *Fundamentum organisandi* (foundations of composition) of 1452 is one of earliest Mss of keyboard tablature. It contains exercises in composing in organ style and arrangements of German songs.

**Paumgartner, Bernhard** (1887–1971), Austrian musicologist, conductor, composer. Director of Salzburg Mozarteum 1917–38, and again after 1945. Published biography of Mozart, and edited (with O.E. Deutsch) Leopold Mozart's letters to his daughter. Compositions incl. operas, ballets, and incidental music for Goethe's *Faust*.

**Paur, Emil** (1855–1932), Austrian conductor. After holding posts in Germany, became conductor of Boston Symphony Orchestra (1893), New York Philharmonic Orchestra (1898), Pittsburgh Orchestra (1903), and Berlin Royal Opera (1912).

**pausa** (It.), rest.

**pause,** (1) (Eng.), wait of indefinite length on note or rest, indicated by sign

𝄐

(Fr., *point d'orgue*; Ger., *Fermate*; It., *fermata*);
(2) (Fr.), rest (esp. semibreve rest).
*See also* GENERALPAUSE.

**pavane** (also called pavan, pavana, paven, pavin), dance, normally in slow duple time, introduced into instrumental music in early 16th cent. After *c* 1550 usually followed by GALLIARD, often using same theme.

**Pavane for a dead Infanta** (Fr., *Pavane pour une Infante défunte*), piano piece by Ravel (1899). More famous orchestral version dates from 1912.

**Pavarotti, Luciano** (1935– ), Italian tenor. Made debut in 1961. Has sung in world's leading opera houses.

**pavillon** (Fr.; It., *padiglione*), lit. 'pavilion', 'tent', hence (by shape) bell of brass instrument. *Pavillons en l'air* is instruction to brass (esp. horn) players to raise bells of instruments in order to increase volume.

**pavillon chinois** (Fr.; It., *padiglione cinese*), percussion instrument shaped like pavilion or tent with little bells hanging from it. Also called Turkish crescent or jingling johnny.

**Payne, Anthony** (1936– ), English composer, critic, writer on music. Works incl. *Phoenix Mass* and other choral music, *Fire on Whaleness* for brass band and percussion, and chamber and piano music.

**Pearl-Fishers, The** (Fr., *Les Pêcheurs de perles*), opera by Bizet, libretto by E. Cormon and M. Carré. First perf. Paris, 1863. Set in Ceylon.

**Pears, Peter** (1910– ), English tenor. Closely associated with music of Britten, much of which was written with Pears's voice in mind. Also distinguished singer of Bach and *Lieder* (latter with Britten as accompanist). Knighted 1978.

**Peasant Cantata,** orig. *Mer hahn en neue Oberkeet* (Eng., We have a new magistracy), secular cantata no 10 (cantata no 212) by Bach

(1742) for solo voices, chorus and orchestra, with words in Saxon dialect.

**pedal,** (1) part of mechanism of instrument, controlled by feet. *See* HARP, ORGAN, PEDAL BOARD, PIANOFORTE;
(2) *see* PEDAL POINT;
(3) FUNDAMENTAL on brass instrument.

**pedal board,** pedals were added to organ in Netherlands and Germany in 14th cent., and were used in Italy from 15th cent., and in England from *c* 1720, though many English organs did not have pedals till mid 19th cent. Modern organ has concave and radiating pedal board with compass from C below bass clef to G on treble clef. *See also* PEDAL HARPSICHORD, PEDAL PIANO.

**pedal clarinet,** alternative name, now little used, for CONTRABASS CLARINET.

**pedalcoppel** (Ger.), pedal coupler (on organ).

**pedale** (It.), (1) pedal (of organ, piano *etc*);
(2) PEDAL POINT.

**Pedalflügel** (Ger.), pedal piano.

**pedal harp,** name sometimes used to distinguish ordinary harp from chromatic harp.

**pedal harpsichord,** harpsichord with pedal board for practising organ music.

**pédalier** (Fr.), pedaliera (It.), pedal board.

**pedal notes,** *see* PEDAL (3).

**Pedalpauken** (Ger.), *see* TIMPANI.

**pedal piano** (Fr., *pédalier pianoforte*; Ger., *Pedalflügel*), piano with pedal board. Made sporadic appearances in 19th cent.

**pedal point** (Fr., *point d'orgue*; Ger., *Orgelpunkt*; It., *pedale*), note, most commonly in bass, which is held while harmonic progressions, with which it may be discordant, continue above it. Generally known simply as 'pedal'. Pedal on tonic frequently comes at end of piece, and dominant pedal often precedes re-establishment of tonic, after series of modulations, as at end of DEVELOPMENT in sonata form. Drones, which occur in folk music and in some branches of Eastern chant, are form of pedal point.

**Pedrell, Felipe** (1841–1922), Spanish composer, musicologist. Pupils incl. Albéniz, Granados, Falla and Gerhard – hence known as 'midwife' of 20th-cent. Spanish nationalist school of composition. Edited complete works of Victoria. Composed operas, symphonic poems and other orchestral music, chamber music, cantatas, and songs. Extensively researched older Spanish music.

**Peer Gynt,** (1) incidental music by Grieg for original production of Ibsen's drama (1876). Later arranged in 2 suites;
(2) incidental music to Ibsen's play by Saeverud (1947);
(3) opera by Egk, libretto by composer (after Ibsen). First perf. Berlin, 1938.

**Peerson, Martin** (*c* 1572–1650), English composer, organist. Master of choristers at St Paul's, London. Wrote church and other vocal music, music for viols, and keyboard works.

**Peeters, Flor** (1903– ), Belgian organist, composer, writer. Works incl. organ, church and piano music, and important organ treatise.

**Peitsche** (Ger.), whip. *See* SLAPSTICK.

**Pélleas et Mélisande** (Fr.), (1) opera by Debussy, set to play by Maeterlinck. First perf. Paris, 1902. Story concerns ill-fated lovers and jealous husband;

(2) incidental music to Maeterlinck's play by Fauré, op 80 (1898), and Sibelius, op 46 (1905);

(3) symphonic poem by Schoenberg, op 5 (1903).

**Pellegrini, Vincenzo** (d. *c* 1631), Italian composer. Composed Masses, canzonets for organ, secular canzonets for voices, and 3 and 4-part instrumental pieces.

**Penderecki, Krzysztof** (1933– ), Polish composer. One of most important and progressive figures to have emerged in Poland since WWII. Though has all modern techniques at his fingertips – note clusters, indeterminate pitch, sound of instruments or voices at extremes of their registers, use of orchestra as reservoir from which to extract variety of colours – he is not a difficult composer, and his *St Luke Passion* (1965) and its successor *Utrenja* (Morning Service, 1971) have enjoyed wide popularity. Other works incl. operas *The Devils of Loudon* (1969) and *Paradise Lost* (after Milton, 1979), *Threnody for the Victims of Hiroshima* (1960) for 52 strings, *Dies Irae* (dedicated to victims of Auschwitz), violin concerto (for Isaac Stern), cello concerto, capriccio for violin and orchestra, symphony, *Partita* for harpsichord, 5 solo instruments and orchestra, and choral Magnificat.

**Pénélope,** opera by Fauré, libretto by R. Fauchois. First perf. Monte Carlo, 1913. Story is based on episode in *The Odyssey*. Other operas on same subject have been composed by Cimarosa, Galuppi, and by Rolf Liebermann (1954, set in WWII).

**Penitential Psalms,** psalms of penitential character, *ie* nos 6, 32 (31), 38 (37), 51 (50), 102 (101), 130 (129), and 143 (142). Numbers in brackets are those of RC Bible. Set complete by Lassus (1565).

**Penna, Lorenzo** (1613–93), Italian composer. Wrote Masses, psalms and other church music, and 'French Correntes' in 4 parts. 3rd part of his *Li Primi Albori Musicali* (1672) is one of the important 17th–cent. treatments of rules for playing organ from figured bass, with examples of use of trill.

**penny whistle,** *see* TIN WHISTLE.

**penorcon,** type of CITTERN used in 17th cent.

**pentatonic scale,** scale which has 5 notes in octave, *eg* C–D–F–G–A. Can also be played by striking black notes of piano. Used in traditional music of China, Japan and Far East, and in Africa. Also used in some Scottish and Irish folk songs, in US Negro spirituals, and by some 20th-cent. composers, *eg* Debussy and Ravel, to achieve oriental effect.

**Pepping, Ernst** (1901– ), German composer. Works incl. much Protestant church music, symphonies, chamber, piano and organ music, and songs.

**Pepusch, Johann Christoph** (1667–1752), German-born composer, theorist. Settled in London (1700). Co-founder of Academy of Ancient Music (1710); music director of Lincoln's Inn Fields Theatre from 1713. Composed music for masques, odes, cantatas, motets, and selected and arranged tunes for *Beggar's Opera* (1728). Published *A Treatise on Harmony* (1730).

**Perahia, Murray** (1947– ), American pianist, conductor. Has acquired international reputation. Known esp. for interpretations of Mozart concertos, which he conducts from piano.

**percussion band,** normally confined to schools, this ensemble usually consists of more manageable percussion instruments of indefinite pitch, along with piano. Should not be confused with percussion ensemble.

**percussion instruments,** instruments which produce sound when struck or shaken. Can be divided into those with definite and those with indefinite pitch. Latter usually serve purely rhythmic or colouristic function. General characteristic is inability to sustain sounds (thus piano is often classified as percussion rather than string instrument, though main reason for being so classified is that it is struck), although in some cases rapid repetition can have this effect. Percussion instruments incl. timpani and other drums, castanets, tambourine, *pavillon chinois,* triangle, gong, cymbals, Glockenspiel, xylophone, marimba, and chimes. Also incl. non-percussive instruments *eg* wind machine and whistle.

**perdendosi** (It.), 'losing itself', *ie* gradually dying away.

**perfect cadence,** *see* CADENCE.

**perfect consonances,** INTERVALS of octave, fifth and fourth.

**perfect pitch,** sense of pitch so acute that it can identify any note by name, without reference to tuning fork or musical instrument.

**perfect time,** triple time in medieval music.

**Perfect Fool, The,** comic opera by Holst, libretto by composer. First perf. London, 1923. Work is parody of operatic conventions. Now known by orchestral suite of same title.

**Pergolesi, Giovanni Battista** (1710–36), Italian composer. Pupil of Durante in Naples. His comic intermezzo *La serva padrona* (for serious opera *Il prigionier superbo,* 1733) became prototype of later form of *opera buffa.* When produced in Paris (1752) became centre of GUERRE DES BOUFFONS. Also wrote much church music, incl. *Stabat mater.* His trio sonatas cultivate melodious style of allegro movt. later adopted by Bach; also made some contribution to development of sonata form. His fame was such that many works ascribed to him were not in fact by him.

**Peri, Jacopo** (1561–1633), Italian composer, singer. As member of *camerata* (Florentine artistic set), composed music (not extant) of first opera, *La Dafne* (text by Rinuccini), first perf. Florence, 1597. His *Euridice* (text by Rinuccini, 1600) is first opera with music still extant.

**Péri, La** (Fr., *The Peri*), dance-poem by Dukas, produced as ballet (Paris, 1912).

**Perlman, Itzhak** (1945– ), Israeli violinist. Soloist with leading orchestras. Plays in chamber music with *eg* Barenboim.

**Perosi, Lorenzo** (1872–1956), Italian composer, church musician, priest. *Maestro di cappella* at Sistine Chapel from 1898. Works incl. oratorios, Masses, cantatas, motets, and orchestral, organ and chamber music.

**Perotinus Magnus** or **Pérotin** (*fl* 1180–1210), French composer. Prob. worked at Notre Dame, Paris. Wrote liturgical music incl. *organa,* notable for structural organization.

**perpetual canon,** *see* CANON.

**perpetuum mobile** (Lat.), 'perpetually in motion', *ie* rapid piece of music in which repetitive note-pattern is maintained from start to finish. Paganini's *Moto Perpetuo,* op 11, is classic example.

**per recte et retro,** *see* RETROGRADE MOTION.

**Persée** (Fr., Perseus), opera by Lully, libretto by P. Quinault. First perf. Paris, 1682.

**Persephone,** MELODRAMA by Stravinsky for orchestra, chorus, tenor and speaking voice. Based on poem by André Gide (after Greek myth). First perf. Paris, 1934.

**Pert, Morris** (1947– ), Scottish composer. Worked with Stomu Yamash'ta, then formed experimental group Suntreader. Works incl. orchestral *Xumbu-Ata,* 2 symphonies, ballets, chamber and vocal music, and works for piano and tape.

**pes** (Lat.), foot. Name used in English music of 13th, 14th cents. for tenor of motet, and esp. for lower parts of *Sumer is icumen in.*

**pesante** (It.), heavy, ponderous, solid.

**Pescetti, Giovanni Battista** (1704–66), Italian composer. Pupil of Lotti. Became director of Covent Garden (1739), and of King's Theatre, London (1740). On returning to Venice, became organist at St Mark's (1762). Composed operas, oratorio, church music, and harpsichord sonatas.

**Peter and the Wolf,** 'musical tale for children' by Prokofiev, op 67. First perf. Moscow, 1936. Scored for storyteller and orchestra. Each character is represented by different instrument or group of instruments.

**Peter Grimes,** opera by Britten, libretto by M. Slater (after Crabbe's poem *The Borough*). First perf. London, 1945. Anti-hero, fisherman Grimes, is outcast from society.

**Peters,** firm of music-publishers founded in Leipzig in 1814 by C.F. Peters, who bought business of Kühnel and Hoffmeister. Dr H. Hinrichsen became head of firm in 1900, and publishing is now carried on under original name in London and New York by Hinrichsen family.

**Peterson-Berger, Olof Wilhelm** (1867–1942), Swedish composer, music critic, poet. Director of Royal Opera, Stockholm (1908–11). Works incl. operas, 5 symphonies, festival cantatas, violin sonatas, piano pieces, and songs.

**petite flûte** (Fr.), piccolo.

**Petits Riens, Les** (Fr., *The Little Nothings*), ballet with music by

Mozart, K App. 10, and choreography by J. Noverre. First perf. Paris, 1778.

**Petrassi, Goffredo** (1904– ), Italian composer. Though sometimes called 'elder statesman' of Italian music, remains remarkably progressive composer, youthful and adventurous in outlook. Works incl. 2 short operas, comic *The Tapestry* and tragic *Death in the Air*, concertos for orchestra, *Portrait of Don Quixote* for orchestra, Magnificat and other choral works, settings of Edward Lear's nonsense poems, and chamber and piano music.

**Petri, Egon** (1881–1962), German-born pianist, son of Dutch violinist Henri Petri (1856–1914), who settled in Germany in 1877. Egon initially studied violin, playing in father's quartet (1899–1901). Having decided to become pianist, studied with Busoni, with whom he edited Bach's keyboard music. Became renowned as distinguished concert pianist, and taught successively in Manchester, Basle, Berlin and Poland. Emigrated to US in 1939.

**Pétrouchka,** *see* PETRUSHKA.

**Petrucci, Ottaviano dei** (1466–1539), Italian music printer. Published first printed collection of polyphonic music, *Harmonice Musices Odhecaton A*, in 1501 (*see* ODHECATON), and published further 61 vols. of music between 1501 and 1520.

**Petrushka,** ballet with music by Stravinsky, choreography by Fokine. First perf. Paris, 1911, by Diaghilev's Ballets Russes. Tells of fate of Russian puppet who comes to life. Made into concert suite (1914, rev. 1947).

**Peuerl, Peurl, Bäurl, Beurlin** or **Bäwerl, Paul** (*c* 1570–after 1625), Austrian composer. His *Newe Padouan, Intrada, Däntz, und Galliarda* (1611) contains earliest known examples of variation suite. Also published *Weltspiegel* (1613), containing secular part-songs, and *Gantz Neue Padouanen* (1625).

**pezzo** (It.), piece.

**Pfeife** (Ger.), pipe.

**Pfitzner, Hans** (1869–1949), German composer, teacher, conductor, b. Moscow. As romantic in tradition of Schumann and Brahms, fought what he considered to be corrupting influences in modern music. Best known work is opera *Palestrina* (1917), but reputation outside Germany has been tenuous. Also wrote other operas, symphonies, concertos, choral and chamber music, and 100 songs.

**Phaéton,** opera by Lully, libretto by P. Quinault. First perf. Versailles, 1683.

**phagotus,** extraordinary instrument, long obsolete, developed from bagpipe in 16th cent. Had 2 pipes with holes for fingering, but wind was supplied by hand bellows. Unrelated to bassoon (It., *fagotto*).

**Phantasie** (Ger.), fantasy.

**phantasy,** title used for several chamber compositions written 1906–30 for competitions instituted by W.W. Cobbett, incl. works by Bridge, Ireland, Vaughan Williams and Britten.

**Philadelphia Orchestra,** one of most famous US symphony orchestras, founded 1900 by Fritz Scheel, who conducted it till 1907.

Later conductors have been Karl Pohlig (1907–12), Leopold Stokowski (1912–38), and Eugene Ormandy (1938– ).

**Philémon et Baucis,** opera by Gounod, libretto by J. Barbier and M. Carré (after Ovid). First perf. Paris, 1860.

**Philharmonia Orchestra,** London-based symphony orchestra formed in 1964 as New Philharmonia Orchestra after predecessor (Philharmonia Orchestra, founded 1945) had been disbanded. 'New' dropped from name in 1977.

**philharmonic** (Gr.), 'loving harmony'. Adj. used in titles of various orchestras, societies *etc.* Unlike 'symphony orchestra' does not imply kind of orchestra.

**Philidor, François André Danican** (1726–95), French composer, chess player. Composed operas incl. *Tom Jones,* motets, and Requiem for Rameau (1766). His father, André, was also composer, and his half-brother founded *Concert Spirituel* in Paris (1725). Family's orig. name was Danican.

**Philips, Peter** (*c* 1560–1628), English composer, organist. As RC, lived abroad from 1582, in Rome, Antwerp and Brussels. In style closer to Continental than English contemporaries. Works incl. madrigals, keyboard pieces, and music for viols.

**Philosopher, The** (Ger., *Der Philosoph*), nickname of Haydn's symphony no 22 in E flat (1764) – perhaps because of slow, solemn opening movt.

**Phinot** or **Finot, Dominicus** (*fl* 16th cent.), French composer. Wrote 2 books of motets (1547–8), 2 books of *chansons* (1548), book of psalms and Magnificats (1555), and other church music.

**photona,** electronic instrument with 2-manual keyboard. Photo-electric cell is used to produce sound.

**phrase,** unit of melody, of indeterminate length. In classical period, most frequently of 4 bars, and since it usually ends with some form of cadence, it is also unit of harmonic progression. A smaller unit is usually called *motive.* Art of 'phrasing' concerns articulation both of complete phrases and of their details, chiefly indicated by slur and *staccato* dot.

**Phrygian cadence,** Phrygian mode was only mode in which interval between final and note above was semitone. Hence harmonization of cadence in this mode presented problem, as seventh note of scale (D) could not be sharpened because that would create augmented sixth, and to sharpen note above final would have destroyed character of mode. Standard harmonization of cadence (with TIERCE DE PICARDIE, or major third) in final chord therefore came to be:

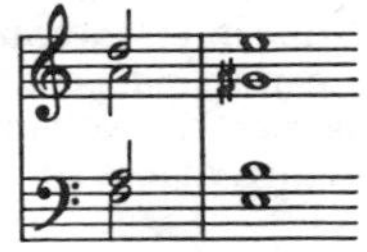

With establishment of major and minor modes in 17th cent., this cadence survived in use, but with changed implication, final chord now suggesting dominant harmony in minor key. Cadence was therefore no longer final and was regularly used in 17th, early 18th cents. as transition between movts. This became so much a convention that new movt. did not necessarily accept concluding chord of previous movt. as dominant but began instead in related key. This practice was esp. common where 1st and 3rd movements of sonata or concerto were in major key and middle movement in minor key.

**Phrygian mode,** (1) in ancient Greek music, equivalent of white notes on piano from D to D;

(2) from Middle Ages onwards applied to equivalent of white notes on piano from E to E. Dominant was orig. B (fifth above tonic, as in other modes) but was changed to C in 11th cent., since B was regarded as ambiguous note: its relation to F was dissonant and it was one note not common to all 3 hexachords. Change, though accepted by theorists, was not always observed in practice.

**physharmonica,** precursor of HARMONIUM, invented 1818.

**piacere** (It.), pleasure. *A piacere,* 'at the performer's pleasure', *ie* strict adherence to tempo and rhythm need not be observed.

**piacevole** (It.), in an agreeable, pleasant manner.

**pianette,** tiny upright piano, even smaller than PIANINO.

**piangendo** (It.), 'crying', *ie* in a plaintive manner.

**pianino,** small upright piano.

**pianissimo** (It.), very soft. Abbrev. *pp.*

**piano,** (1) (It.), soft. Abbrev. *p*;

(2) (Eng., Fr.), standard abbrev. of PIANOFORTE.

**piano accordion,** *see* ACCORDION.

**piano duet,** term normally applied to 2 players at 1 instrument.

**pianoforte, piano,** mechanism of piano consists of keyboard, action, hammers, dampers, strings, and pedals. Keyboard of modern piano has compass of 7 octaves or 7 octaves and minor third. Damper stops vibration of strings when key returns to normal position. Right (or sustaining) pedal suspends action of dampers, allowing strings to vibrate freely; left (or soft) pedal mutes sound by moving hammers either towards strings so that their length of travel is shortened or parallel to strings so that they strike only 1 or 2 of strings which are provided for each note. On some pianos 3rd pedal allows notes to continue sounding which have been played before pedal is depressed, while any other notes remain unaffected.

Piano and its name originated in instruments made in Florence *c* 1710 by Bartolommeo Cristofori, who described them as 'harpsichords which can produce *piano* and *forte* by touch'. Cristofori devised hammer action (still, in essence, used today), hammer being hinged to rail and free to rise independently of key. By principle called escapement, spring-jack raises hammer with help of underlever and then, when hammer strikes string, allows hammer to drop away.

Main developments in 18th cent. were escapement, which allowed hammer to return for repetition of note though key was still down, pedal (Broadwood, 1783), and return to Cristofori's 'grand' shape in addition to square. Main developments in 19th cent. were extension of compass, increase in sonority, double escapement which allowed quicker repetition, and adoption of upright shape (first successful model by J.I. Hawkins, 1800).

In 20th cent., piano's percussive qualities have tended to be emphasized. Composers have demanded that performer pluck, thump or tickle actual strings, or have used PREPARED PIANO. Possibilities of quarter-tone piano have also been explored.

**pianola,** piano played mechanically by means of rolls pierced with holes corresponding to duration and pitch of notes, thus allowing air under pressure to act on device which moves hammers. Widely used from late 19th cent. till rise of gramophone and wireless. Also called 'player-piano'.

**piano organ,** mechanical instrument similar to BARREL ORGAN but without pipes. Notes are produced by hammers striking strings.

**piano quartet,** term usually applied to quartet for piano, violin, viola and cello.

**piano quintet,** combination of piano with (usually) string quartet.

**piano trio,** piece for piano, violin and cello.

**Pianotron,** electronic upright piano. Evolved from NEO-BECHSTEIN PIANO. Produced by Selmer (1938).

**piatti** (It.), cymbals.

**Piatti, Alfredo Carlo** (1822–1901), Italian cellist, composer. Gave concerts in Munich (with Liszt, 1843), Paris, the British Isles, Italy and Russia. Became leading solo cellist of 19th cent. Composed cello concertos, songs with cello accompaniment, and sonatas and other works for his instrument.

**pibgorn,** *see* HORNPIPE.

**pibroch** (Gaelic, *piobaireachd,* 'pipe-tune'), most important category of Scottish bagpipe music. Consists of variations on theme *(urlar)*, played with many grace notes.

**Picardy third,** *see* TIERCE DE PICARDIE.

**Picchi, Giovanni** (*fl* 17th cent.), Italian organist, composer. Wrote book of harpsichord music, canzonas and sonatas for instruments, and church music. Toccata by him is in *Fitzwilliam Virginal Book.*

**Piccinni, Niccolò** (1728–1800), Italian composer. Pupil of Leo and Durante in Naples. From 1755 produced operas in Naples and Rome, then in Paris from 1776. Management of Opéra took advantage of feud between his supporters and those of Gluck by commissioning setting of *Iphigénie en Tauride* from both composers. Piccinni's version (1781) was not unsuccessful, though posterity has deemed Gluck's the greater. Wrote *c* 120 operas, incl. *La buona figliola* (*The Good Girl,* 1760) with libretto by Goldoni (after Richardson's *Pamela*).

**piccolo** (Fr., *petite flûte*; Ger., *kleine Flöte, Pickeflöte*; It., *flauto piccolo, ottavino*), abbrev. of *flauto piccolo,* little flute. Small flute, with natural scale of D and range written from D below treble clef to octave above C above treble clef, and sounding octave higher. Not regular member of orchestra till mid 19th cent. *See* FLUTE.

**piccolo timpano** (It.), very small kettledrum capable of producing middle C.

**picco pipe,** instrument of recorder type.

**Pickelflöte,** *see* PICCOLO.

**Pictures at an Exhibition,** set of piano pieces by Mussorgsky (1874), composed in memory of painter and architect V.A. Hartmann and containing musical pictures of some of his works. Orchestral arrangements have been made by Ravel, Henry Wood, Walter Goehr and Tushmalov.

**pieno** (It.), full. *Organo pieno,* full organ. *A voce piena,* with full voice.

**Pierné, [Henri Constant] Gabriel** (1863–1937), French composer, organist, conductor. Pupil of Franck and Massenet. Wrote operas, ballets, pantomimes, oratorios, orchestral, chamber, incidental and piano music, and songs. Now remembered for *Entry of the Little Fauns* from ballet *Cydalise and the Satyr*.

**Pierrot Lunaire** (Fr., *Moonstruck Pierrot*), melodrama by Schoenberg, op 21, first perf. 1912. Consists of 21 settings of poems by Albert Giraud in German translation by O.E. Hartleben, scored for voice (using SPRECHGESANG technique) and instrumental ensemble.

**Pierson, Heinrich Hugo,** orig. Henry Hugh Pearson (1815–73), English composer, mostly resident in Germany. Wrote operas, oratorios, overtures, music to 2nd part of Goethe's *Faust* (1854), church music, and songs, incl. 'Ye Mariners of England'.

**pietoso** (It.), compassionate, sympathetic.

**Pifa,** Handel's name for 'Pastoral Symphony' in *Messiah,* indicating that it is intended to represent sound of shepherds' *pifferi.*

**piffero** (It.), small flute or shepherd's pipe, of 18th cent.

**Pijper, Willem** (1894–1947), Dutch composer, pianist, writer on music. Director of Rotterdam Conservatory from 1930. Father of modern Dutch music. Wrote 3 symphonies, 6 Symphonic Epigrams, string quartets and other chamber works, concertos for piano, cello and violin, opera *Halewijn,* choral, incidental and piano music, songs, and essays on music and musicians.

**Pikovaya Dama,** *see* QUEEN OF SPADES.

**Pilgrims from Mecca, The,** *see* RENCONTRE IMPRÉVUE.

**Pilgrim's Progress, The,** opera by Vaughan Williams, libretto by composer (after Bunyan). First perf. London, 1951. Incorporates most of earlier one-act opera *The Shepherds of the Delectable Mountains* (1922).

**pincé** (Fr.), mordent.

**Pincherle, Marc** (1888– ), Algerian-born musicologist. Studied and taught in Paris. Published books on history of violin, on Corelli (1934), and on Vivaldi (2 vols., 1948; contains thematic catalogue of Vivaldi's works).

**Pines of Rome, The** (It., *Pini di Roma*), symphonic poem by Respighi, in 4 linked movts. depicting pine trees in 4 areas of city.

First perf. Rome, 1924. Incorporates gramophone record of nightingale's song. Intended as companion to *The Fountains of Rome.*

**pipe,** hollow cylinder in which vibrating air produces either single note, as in organ pipe, or series of notes when effective length can be altered by opening and closing holes with fingers.

**pipe and tabor,** combination of 2 primitive instruments. Player holds small pipe in one hand while beats time with other on tabor (small drum), which either hangs from shoulder or is strapped to waist.

**Pique-Dame,** *see* QUEEN OF SPADES.

**Pirata, Il** (It., *The Pirate*), opera by Bellini, libretto by F. Romani. First perf. Milan, 1827. Successfully revived in present century by Maria Callas. Heroine, Imogene, loses her reason after her (unloved) husband is murdered by her pirate-lover.

**Pirates of Penzance, The,** comic opera by Gilbert and Sullivan. First perf. Paignton, 1879.

**Pirro, André** (1869–1943), French musicologist. Studied organ under Franck and Widor. Became director of Schola Cantorum at its foundation in 1896. Succeeded Romain Rolland as Professor of musical history at Sorbonne (1912), and became leading French musicologist of his time. Works incl. books on Bach, Buxtehude and Schütz, and history of music in 15th and 16th cents.

**Pisendel, Johann Georg** (1687–1755), German violinist, composer. Pupil of Vivaldi. Travelled widely in Europe, and was leader of Dresden court orchestra from 1730. Composed symphony, 2 *concerti grossi,* 8 violin concertos and other works for violin.

**Pistocchi, Francesco Antonio Mamiliano** (1659–1726), Sicilian-born composer, conductor, singer. Published *Cappricci puerili* for keyboard and other instruments at age of 8. First appeared as opera singer in 1675, and became *Kapellmeister* to Margrave of Ansbach in 1696. Later founded important school of singing in Bologna. Composed operas, oratorios, cantatas and other church music, vocal duets, trios and arias.

**piston,** (1) (Fr.), short for *cornet à pistons,* modern cornet;
(2) valve on brass instrument.

**Piston, Walter** (1894–1976), American composer. Pupil of Nadia Boulanger. Taught composition at Harvard from 1932; professor there from 1944. Compositions, in direct and vigorously traditional style, incl. 8 symphonies and other orchestral works, violin concerto, 5 string quartets, sonatas and other chamber music, and ballet *The Incredible Flautist.* Also wrote several important textbooks.

**pistone** (It.), cornet pitched fourth above normal instrument.

**pitch,** relative height or depth of sound, determined by rate of vibration (frequency) of medium. Up to 19th cent. standard pitch varied for different kinds of music, until international standard ('Concert Pitch') was adopted in 1889. In 1939 this was amended, so that A in treble clef was fixed at frequency of 440 cycles per second. *See* CHORTON, KAMMERTON.

**pitch pipe,** small pipe with graduated stopper by which any note of scale can be produced. Used for giving pitch to choir about to sing without accompaniment.

**più** (It.), more. *Più allegro, più mosso,* faster. *Più forte,* louder. *Più andante* is ambiguous: if *andante* is taken literally as 'moving' it means 'a little faster'; if it is taken as 'moderately slow' it means 'slower'. *Più* by itself = *più mosso. Il più* = the most; *il più piano possibile,* as soft as possible.

**piuttosto** (It.), rather. *Andante piuttosto allegro,* rather fast than slow, *ie* not too much on the slow side. *See also* TOSTO.

**piva** (It.), bagpipe.

**pizz.,** *see* PIZZICATO.

**Pizzetti, Ildebrando** (1880–1968), Italian composer, writer on music. Held important academic appointments in Florence, Milan and Rome. Operas, for which he mostly wrote own librettos, are on tragic or religious subjects, and incl. *Debora e Jaele* (1922), *Vanna Lupa* (1949), and *Murder in The Cathedral* (after T.S. Eliot, 1958). Choral style is polyphonic, and songs are mostly in serious vein. Also composed orchestral music, concertos for cello and piano, and chamber and piano music.

**pizzicato** (It.), plucked. Abbrev. *pizz.* Used to indicate plucking of string by finger on bowed instrument. Paganini introduced *pizzicato* for left hand, with or without another note being bowed. 'Bartók *pizzicato*' allows string to rebound off finger-board with snap. *Pizzicato tremolando,* term used by Elgar in violin concerto as indication to orchestral string players to produce rapid thrumming sound with fingers across strings.

**Pk.,** abbrev. of *Pauken* (Ger.), timpani.

**plagal cadence,** *see* CADENCE.

**plagal mode,** *see* MODE.

**plainsong** (Lat., *cantus planus*), term most commonly used of GREGORIAN CHANT. Liturgical melodies of other Western and Eastern rites (*eg* Ambrosian, Byzantine *etc*) are usually referred to simply as 'chant'.

**Plainsong and Mediaeval Music Society,** society formed in 1888 with object of cataloguing and publishing sources for plainsong and medieval music in England and promoting performances of it.

**plainte** (Fr.), ornament used in 17th, 18th-cent. French music, equivalent to German NACHSCHLAG.

**Planets, The,** suite for orchestra, organ and (in last movt.) female chorus by Holst, op 32 (1915), in 7 movts. entitled: (1) *Mars, the Bringer of War,* (2) *Venus, the Bringer of Peace,* (3) *Mercury, the Winged Messenger*, (4) *Jupiter, the Bringer of Jollity,* (5) *Saturn, the Bringer of Old Age,* (6) *Uranus, the Magician,* (7) *Neptune, the Mystic.*

**player-piano,** *see* PIANOLA.

**Playford, John** (1623–86), first regular music-publisher in England, and most active in 17th cent. Publications incl. *The English Dancing Master* (1651), *A Musicall Banquet* (1651), *Introduction to the Skill of Musick* (written by himself, 1654), *The Whole Book of Psalms*

(1677) and *Choice Ayres* (5 books, 1676–84). His son, Henry Playford, continued his business.

**plectrum,** small piece of horn, ivory, wood *etc* used to pluck strings of mandolin, guitar, zither *etc.*

**plein jeu** (Fr.), full organ.

**pleno** (It.), full; hence full organ.

**Pleyel, Ignaz Joseph** (1757–1831), Austrian pianist, violinist, composer. Pupil of Haydn. Founded famous piano-making firm in Paris (1807). Numerous compositions (some much admired by Haydn and Mozart) incl. 29 symphonies, concertos for piano and violin, string quintets and quartets, piano sonatas, and songs.

**plica** (medieval Lat.), lit. 'plait'. Ornament is early medieval notation; passing note sung with effect resembling TREMOLO.

**Plunket Greene, Harry,** *see* GREENE.

**pneuma,** *see* NEUMA.

**pochette,** *see* KIT.

**pochettino** (It.), very little, very slightly.

**poco** (It.), little, *ie* slightly, rather. *Poco più lento,* rather slower. *Poco diminuendo,* getting slightly softer. *Poco a poco,* little by little, gradually.

**podium,** dais on which conductor stands to direct orchestra. Term widely used in US. Term 'rostrum' is preferred in Britain.

**Poem of Ecstasy,** symphonic poem by Skryabin, op 54 (1908). Depicts artist's joy in creative activity.

**poème symphonique** (Fr.), symphonic poem.

**Poglietti, Alessandro** (d. 1683), Italian composer. Organist at court chapel in Vienna from 1661 until killed during Turkish siege. Composed *ricercari* for organ, suites for harpsichord, and church music. One of his suites depicts Hungarian rebellion of 1671, and another, written for birthday of 3rd wife of Emperor Leopold I, contains German air with 22 variations, some of which illustrate style of regional dances, *eg* Bohemian, Dutch and Bavarian.

**Pohjola's Daughter,** symphonic fantasia by Sibelius, op 49, based on Finnish epic *Kalevala.* First perf. St Petersburg (conducted by composer), 1906.

**Pohl, Carl Ferdinand** (1819–87), Austrian musicologist, organist. Lived in London (1863–66), researching Haydn and Mozart. Wrote *Mozart and Haydn in London* (1867) and *Joseph Haydn* (1875–82, completed by Hugo Botstiber, 1927).

**Pohl, Richard** (1826–96), German music critic. Friend of Liszt. Wrote 3-vol. work on Wagner, and studies of Liszt and Berlioz.

**poi** (It.), then. Word usually used when section of music is to follow another in way not made clear by notation, *eg scherzo da capo, poi la coda,* 'repeat the scherzo, then [play] the coda'.

**point,** (1) end of bow opposite heel. *See* PUNTA D'ARCO;

(2) 16th-cent. English term for theme used in passage in imitative counterpoint.

**point d'orgue** (Fr.), 'organ point' *ie*: (1) pedal point; (2) pause; (3) cadenza.

**pointé** (Fr.), *see* DOT (2, iv).

**pointe d'archet** (Fr.), point of the bow.

**pointillism,** term for spare, pointed style, often using pizzicato effects, adopted by some 20th-cent. composers (*eg* Webern) in some of their works. Has been likened to pointillist school of painting, characterized by use of dots of colour to convey painter's visual impression.

**pointing,** *see* ANGLICAN CHANT.

**Poisoned Kiss, The,** comic opera by Vaughan Williams, libretto by E. Sharp. First perf. Cambridge, 1936. Based on story by Richard Garnet, *The Poison Maid,* opera concerns sorcerer's daughter who has power to bestow kisses of death; but when she falls sincerely in love, magic spell is broken.

**polacca** (It.), polonaise.

**polka,** dance in moderately quick 2/4 time, said to have originated in Bohemia *c* 1830. After 1835 spread through Europe and US and achieved great popularity.

**Pollini, Maurizio** (1942– ), Italian pianist. Pupil of Michelangeli. One of greatest pianists of his generation, known for performances of new music as well as classics.

**Polly,** ballad opera with text by John Gay and musical arrangements by Pepusch. Sequel to *The Beggar's Opera.* Published 1729, but banned as subversive till performed with alterations in 1777. Modern musical arrangement made by F. Austin (1922).

**polo,** Andalusian folk dance in moderately fast 3/4 time, frequently syncopated, and with periodic ornamental phrases on syllable such as 'Ay!'.

**polonaise** (Fr.; It., *polacca*), Polish dance in moderately fast 3/4 time. Chief characteristics are stately rhythm in persistent pattern, and use of feminine ending. Examples are found in works of Bach, though most famous are Chopin's great series.

**Polovtsian Dances,** *see* PRINCE IGOR.

**polychoral style,** style of composition using several choirs performing both separately and jointly. Notably employed by Venetian polyphonic composers of 16th cent., *eg* Willaert and G. Gabrieli.

**polymetry** (adj., polymetrical), simultaneous combination of different metres, *eg* 2/4 against 3/4 or 6/8.

**polyphony** (Gr., multiplication of sounds; Ger., *Mehrstimmigkeit*), style of music in which composer pays particular attention to melodic value of each part (*see* COUNTERPOINT), as distinct from HOMOPHONY, style consisting of melody with chordal accompaniment. Most important polyphonic forms are MOTET, polyphonic MASS, CANON and round, polyphonic CHANSON, CANZONA, RICERCAR, and FUGUE. True polyphony was first written in 2nd stage (11th–12th cent.) of ORGANUM. Medieval polyphony was written by method of successive composition, *ie* by addition of complete part(s) to first complete part (*see* MOTET, CANTUS FIRMUS). Imitative polyphony of 16th-cent. choral music and *canzona* and *ricercar* was composed by disposing same theme in each of parts successively. Tonal or harmonic polyphony of 18th-cent. fugue was composed in similar fashion, but normally used single theme (subject) throughout, and was organized according to principles of tonality (*see* KEY). In modern compositions employment of polyphony may follow principles of chromatic tonality or of antonality.

**polyrhythm,** simultaneous use of several markedly different rhythms sounding in different parts.

**polytonality,** use of 2 or more keys simultaneously, generally by superimposing chords, arpeggios or melodies each of which unequivocally defines different key (tonality). Composers who have used it incl. Stravinsky, Bartók, Milhaud and Holst. *See also* BITONALITY.

**pommer,** name of double-reed instruments from which OBOE family eventually derived. *See also* SHAWM.

**Pomo d'Oro, Il** (It., *The Golden Apple*), opera by Cesti, libretto by F. Sbarra. First perf. Vienna, 1667.

**Pomone,** opera by Cambert, libretto by P. Perrin. First perf. Paris, 1671.

**Pomp and Circumstance,** set of 5 military marches for orchestra by Elgar, op 39 (nos 1–4, 1901–7, no 5, 1930). Elgar used part of no 1 for *Coronation Ode* (1902) with words 'Land of hope and glory'.

**pomposo** (It.), in a pompous manner.

**Ponce, Manuel** (1882–1948), Mexican composer. Studied in Germany and Italy, and later (at age of 40) under Dukas in Paris. Wrote orchestral works, concertos *eg* for guitar (for Segovia), chamber and piano music, and songs (incl. popular 'Estrellita'). Also collected and arranged Mexican folk songs.

**Ponchielli, Amilcare** (1834–86), Italian composer. Of his 9 operas only *La Gioconda* (1876) – containing famous *Dance of the Hours* – is still regularly performed. Also wrote ballets and cantatas (one in memory of Garibaldi).

**Ponte, Lorenzo Da** (1749–1838), Italian-born poet, librettist, of Jewish parentage. Became priest in 1773, but his life was irregular. Banished from Venice as result of scandal in 1779. Became poet to court opera in Vienna (1784), where met Mozart and wrote librettos for *The Marriage of Figaro, Don Giovanni* and *Così fan tutte*. Later lived in London, Holland and New York.

**ponticello** (It.), bridge of stringed instrument. *Sul ponticello, see* BOWING.

**Poot, Marcel** (1901– ), Belgian composer. Pupil of Dukas. Became director of Brussels Conservatoire (1949). Works incl. operas, ballets, oratorios, symphonies, and symphonic poem *Charlot* (inspired by Charlie Chaplin).

**Popov, Gavryil Nikolaievich** (1904– ), Russian composer. Wrote operas, symphony, suites for orchestra, and film, chamber and piano music.

**Popper, David** (1843–1913), Czech-born cellist. Composed concertos and many other works for cello.

**Porgy and Bess,** opera by Gershwin, libretto by D. Hayward and Ira Gershwin (composer's brother). First perf. (by all black cast) Boston,

1935. Though music uses certain Negro idioms, songs are genuine Gershwin, and incl. famous 'Summertime'.

**Porpora, Niccolò Antonio** (1686–1767), Italian composer, singing teacher (one of most famous ever). Worked in Italy, Germany, London (where became rival conductor to Handel) and Austria (where Haydn became his pupil and accompanist). Wrote 53 operas, and church, chamber and harpsichord music.

**Porta, Costanzo** (*c* 1530–1601), Italian composer, Franciscan monk. Wrote Masses, motets, hymns and other church music, and madrigals.

**portamento** (It.; Fr., *port de voix*), lit. 'carrying'. Effect used in singing or on bowed instruments, obtained by carrying sound in continuous glide from one note to next.

**portative** or **portative organ** (It., *organetto*), small portable organ, developed in Middle Ages.

**portato** (It.), *mezzo staccato* (*see* STACCATO).

**port de voix** (Fr.), (1) 17th, 18th-cent. term for APPOGGIATURA;
(2) PORTAMENTO.

**portée** (Fr.), staff, stave.

**Porter, Cole** (1893–1964), American composer. Pupil of d'Indy. One of principal and most evergreen composers in field of popular song and American musical. Subtle melodist, with keen ear for syncopation, he also wrote equally subtle and witty words to his songs, *eg* 'You're the top'. Most famous musicals are *Anything Goes* and *Kiss Me Kate* (modern spoof on *The Taming of the Shrew*).

**Porter, Quincy** (1897–1966), American composer. Pupil of d'Indy and Bloch. Professor at Yale from 1946. Works incl. 2 symphonies, symphonic suite *New England Episodes,* concertos for viola and 2 pianos, 10 string quartets, and incidental music.

**Porter, Walter** (*c* 1587/95–1659), English composer. Pupil of Monteverdi. Works incl. madrigals (with instrumental interpolations) and motets.

**Portsmouth Point,** concert overture by Walton, after drawing by Rowlandson depicting bustling quayside scene. First perf. Zürich, 1926.

**Posaune** (Ger.), trombone.

**Posch, Isaak** (d. before 1623), Austrian or German composer. Organist at Ljubljana. Published books of instrumental dances, incl. *Musicalische Tafelfreudt,* which contains several Paduana-Gagliarda pairs, each pair being thematically related, followed by several Intrada-Couranta -pairs, similarly related. Other works incl. *Harmonia concertans* (1623), set of sacred concertos for 1 to 4 voices with continuo.

**positif** (Fr.), choir organ.

**position,** (1) on stringed instrument, placing of left hand on string in relation to open note of string. Thus in first position on G string first finger plays A, in second position it plays B, and so on. Thumb is used in higher positions on cello;
(2) placing of slide of TROMBONE;

(3) disposition of CHORD in relation to its ROOT; root position and inversions of chord are all said to be positions of that chord.

**Positive,** choir organ.

**positive organ,** orig., small chamber organ which, unlike PORTATIVE, was fixed in position. Later, name was given to part of large organ controlled by CHOIR ORGAN manual.

**Possenti, Pellegrino** (*fl* early 17th cent.), Italian composer. Published 2 books of madrigals (1623, 1625), and was one of earliest composers of sonatas for 2, 3, and 4 instruments with continuo (*Concentus armonici,* 1628).

**posthorn,** simple brass instrument akin to bugle but usually straight and so much longer. Used by postillions in 18th, 19th cents. Had no valves; could only produce notes of HARMONIC SERIES.

**postlude,** generally, final piece or closing section of composition. May also apply to organ piece played at end of service.

**Poston, Elizabeth** (1905– ), English composer, writer on music. Compositions incl. vocal and piano pieces, but is best known for arrangements of British folk songs.

**Pothier, Dom Joseph** (1835–1923), Benedictine authority on plainsong. Entered Abbey of Solesmes (1859), and in 1898 became abbot of St Wandrille monastery, which was later moved to Belgium. Published many works on plainsong, and initiated series *Paleographie musicale* for publishing Mss of 9th–16th cent. Chaired committee responsible for preparation and publication of Vatican edition of liturgical chant.

**pot-pourri** (Fr.), succession of familiar tunes fashioned, with links, into continuous composition.

**Potter, [Philip] Cipriani [Hambly]** (1792–1871), English pianist, composer, conductor. Advised by Beethoven in Vienna. Principal of Royal Academy of Music, London (1832–59). Works incl. 9 symphonies, 4 overtures, piano concertos, cantata, and chamber and piano music.

**Pougin, François Auguste Arthur** (1834–1921), French writer on music. Edited *Le Ménestrel* from 1885, and wrote many biographies of composers.

**Poule, La,** *see* HEN.

**Poulenc, Francis** (1899–1963), French composer, pianist. Pupil of Koechlin. Became member of Les SIX. Influenced by Satie. Composed *opéra burlesque (Les Mamelles de Tirésias)*, ballets (*eg Les Biches*), concerto for 2 pianos and many piano pieces, concerto for harpsichord, chamber and choral works (incl. cantata), and numerous songs. Style combines classical clarity with irrepressible talent for satire and caricature, though after WWII his music gained new vein of seriousness, esp. in opera *Les Dialogues des Carmélites* (*The Carmelites,* 1957) and concerto for strings and timpani. As pianist appeared frequently with baritone Pierre Bernac.

**Pouplinière, Alexandre Jean Joseph le Riche de la** (1693–1762), French amateur musician, patron of music. Pupil of Rameau, who lived in his house for some years and conducted his private orchestra.

Patron of concerts conducted by Johann Stamitz in Paris (1754–5), and on advice of Stamitz added clarinets, horns, and harp to his orchestra for first time in France.

**poussé** (Fr.), lit. 'pushed', *ie* up-bow, as opposed to *tiré* ('pulled'), down-bow.

**Pousseur, Henri** (1929– ), Belgian composer. Started writing electronic music in 1950s. Other works incl. operas *Votre Faust* and *Die Erprobung des Petrus Hebraïcus, Les Ephemerides d'Icare II, L'Effacement de Prince Igor* and other orchestral works, and chamber, piano and vocal music.

**poussez** (Fr.), lit. 'push ahead', *ie* quicken tempo.

**Power, Leonel** (d. 1445), English composer. Most important contemporary of Dunstable. Music, with that of Dunstable and other English composers, had considerable influence on Continent. His *Alma redemptoris* Mass is earliest complete Mass on *cantus firmus*. Many of his works are in OLD HALL MANUSCRIPT.

**pp,** abbrev. for *pianissimo,* very soft.

**praeludium** (Lat.), prelude.

**Pré aux clercs, Le** (Fr., *The Scholars' Meadow*), opera by Hérold, libretto by F.A.E. de Planard. First perf. Paris, 1832. Work is based on Mérimée's *Chronique de Régne de Charles IX*.

**Praetorius, Hieronymous** (1560–1629), German organist, composer. Works incl. Masses, Magnificats, and motets.

**Praetorius, Michael** (1571–1621), German composer, theorist. One of most versatile and prolific musicians of his time, and one of foremost German composers to practise Venetian polychoral style. Works for church incl. settings of both Latin and German words, *eg* Magnificat, Kyries, Glorias *etc,* and many settings of Lutheran chorales ranging from simple harmonizations to elaborate contrapuntal treatment. Some choral works have independent instrumental accompaniment. Also wrote dances for instrumental ensemble, and organ settings. His book *Syntagma Musicum* (3 vols., 1614–20) contains valuable information about 17th-cent. music and performance.

**'Prague' Symphony,** nickname given to Mozart's symphony no 38 in D, K504 (1786); first perf. Prague, 1787.

**Pralltriller** (Ger.), ornament used in 18th-cent. instrumental music. C.P.E. Bach gives this example:

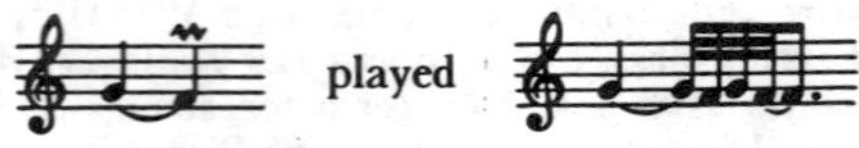


He points out that it occurs only on lower of 2 notes in descending second played legato, and that it must be played very fast and with 'snap'. When it is marked over pause note preceded by appoggiatura, latter is held, and *Pralltriller* is played immediately before end of note:

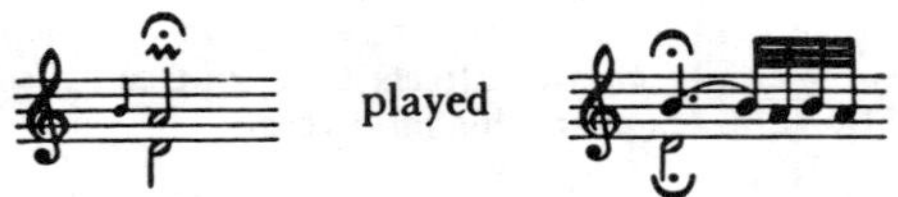


Since *c* 1800 name has been applied to ornament formerly called *Schneller*, now commonly called inverted MORDENT. *See also* TRILL.

**Präludium** (Ger.), prelude.

**precentor,** (1) official in charge of music of cathedral, college chapel or monastery;

(2) official of Presbyterian Churches of Scotland and of 17th, 18th-cent. Puritan churches of New England who gave out and led psalms and hymns.

**Preciosa,** play by P.A. Wolff (based on Cervantes' *La Gilanella*) for which Weber wrote overture and other music. First perf. Berlin, 1821.

**precipitato, precipitoso** (It.), 'precipitately', *ie* impetuously.

**preciso** (It.), precise (as regards time).

**preclassical,** term for music written before time of Haydn and Mozart (or, more loosely, before Bach).

**prelude** (Lat., *praeludium*; Fr., *Prélude*; Ger., *Präludium*), introductory movement; also, in Chopin and later composers, short self-contained piano piece in one movement. Preludes for organ, lute and virginals in 15th, 16th cents. were free pieces in extemporary style (It., *tastar*; Sp., *tañer*). Some of SUITE preludes of baroque period continued this style; in others more regular and extended form was adopted. Chopin's 24 preludes, while romantic in style, use, like preludes of Bach's *Forty-eight,* single theme and complete cycle of keys. Later sets, though not always using complete key sequence, have followed same plan, *eg* those by Rakhmaninov and Debussy.

Since *c* 1840 many composers have written short orchestral piece as prelude to, and usually taking its music from, an opera, as in Wagner's *Lohengrin* and *Tristan and Isolde* and Verdi's *La Traviata,* rather than full-length OVERTURE.

*See also* CHORALE PRELUDE.

**Prélude à l'après-midi d'un faune** (Fr., *Prelude to the afternoon of a faun*), orchestral piece by Debussy (1894), designed to illustrate poem by Mallarmé. Orig. intended to be first of set of 3 pieces. Nijinsky later based ballet on music.

**Préludes, Les,** symphonic poem by Liszt, inspired by poem of Lamartine. First perf. 1854. Orig. intended as overture to *Les quatre éléments,* choral setting of 4 poems by J. Autran. Lamartine only came in when Liszt rewrote work as symphonic poem. Definitive version is prefaced by words suggesting life is merely series of preludes to hereafter.

**preparation,** harmonic device whereby impact of discord is softened by first sounding note of chord which makes chord dissonant in preceding chord in which it is consonant.

**prepared piano,** piano that has been 'prepared' by having various objects, *eg* pieces of rubber and screws, placed between selected strings. This not only greatly affects tone, but can also alter pitch. Much used by John Cage and his followers.

**Prés, Josquin des,** *see* JOSQUIN.

**près de la table** (Fr.), *see* TABLE (2).

**prestant,** 4ft open diapason stop on organ.

**presto** (It.), orig. 'lively', 'brisk', but came to be used to indicate fastest speed in normal use. Superlative *prestissimo* can only mean fastest speed of which performer is capable.

**Previn, André** (1929– ), German-born conductor, pianist, composer. Moved to US at start of WWII. Joined music department of MGM (at age of 16) and later won 4 Oscars for film scores. Studied conducting with Monteux and composition with Castelnuovo-Tedesco. After period as outstanding jazz pianist became conductor of Houston Symphony Orchestra (1967), then of London Symphony Orchestra (1968) and of Pittsburgh Symphony Orchestra (from 1976). Compositions incl. concertos for cello and guitar, 2 wind quintets, suite of piano preludes, and music for Tom Stoppard's play *Every Good Boy Deserves Favour*.

**prick song,** term derived from 'pricking', in sense of writing musical notes, used in England in earlier 16th cent. to distinguish written polyphonic music from plainsong, and later extended to incl. all music except plainsong, whether written down or not.

**prima** (It.), 'first of all', 'formerly'. *Come prima,* as at first, *ie* resume original tempo of piece or movt.

**prima donna** (It.), 'first lady'. Singer of most important female part in an opera. Corresponding term in 18th cent. for singer of most important castrato or tenor role was *primo uomo*.

**prima prattica, seconda prattica** (It.), first and second practice. Terms used by Monteverdi to distinguish between old contrapuntal style of 16th cent. and new style of 17th cent. in which solo instruments or voices were exploited, with figured-bass accompaniment. *See also* STILE.

**Primavera, Giovanni Leonardo** (*c* 1540–after 1585), Italian composer. Wrote madrigals and *canzone napolitane* for 3 voices. Palestrina composed PARODY MASS on his madrigal 'Nasce la gioia mia'.

**prima volta,** *see* VOLTA (1).

**prime,** interval 'zero' or unison.

**primo** (It.), 'first': (1) upper part of piano duet, lower part being termed *secondo* (second);

(2) first of 2 or more players or singers, or of 2 or more groups of performers. *Violino primo,* first violin in string quartet, or whole body of first violins in orchestra. *Flauto (oboe, clarinetto etc) primo,* first flute (oboe, clarinet *etc*). In orchestral score parts for 2 wind instruments of same kind are generally printed on same stave. Hence

when only 1 is playing, *primo* (abbrev. *Imo* or *I*) indicates that first player is intended. So also *violino secondo*, second violin(s), and so on;

(3) *tempo primo* (abbrev. *tempo Imo* or *tempo I*), 'original speed'. Indication that speed of opening of movt. or piece is to be resumed after section(s) in different tempo.

**primo uomo,** *see* PRIMA DONNA.

**Primrose, William** (1904–82), Scottish-born viola player. Resident in US since 1937. Most famous viola player of his day; had numerous works written for him incl. Bartók's viola concerto.

**Prince Igor** (Russ., *Kniaz Igor*), unfinished opera by Borodin, to own libretto. Completed after his death by Rimsky-Korsakov and Glazunov. First perf. St Petersburg, 1890. Concerns capture of 12th-cent. Russian hero by Polovtsians, whose leader, Khan Konchak, treats him with respect and entertains him with display of Polovtsian dances (often performed separately).

**Prince of the Pagodas, The,** ballet with music by Britten, choreography and scenario by J. Cranko. First perf. London, 1957.

**Princess Ida,** or **Castle Adamant,** comic opera by Gilbert and Sullivan. First perf. London, 1884.

**principal,** (1) in orchestra, first player of particular group of instruments (*eg* 'principal violin');

(2) in opera company, singer who takes leading parts, but not chief ones;

(3) organ stop: in Britain, 4ft diapason; in Germany (*Prinzipal*) and Italy *(principale)*, 8ft diapason.

**principale,** term used for trumpet parts till *c* 1750.

**Printz, Wolfgang Kaspar** (1641–1717), German composer. His *Historische Beschreibung der edlen Sing- und Klingkunst...* (1690) was first history of music written in German.

**Prinzipal,** *see* PRINCIPAL (3).

**Prise de Troie, La,** *see* TROJANS.

**Pritchard, John** (1921– ), English conductor. Principally associated with Glyndebourne Festival Opera, starting as répétiteur (1947) and becoming musical director (1969–77). Esp. associated with operas of Mozart and Richard Strauss. Has also been musical director of Royal Liverpool Philharmonic and London Philharmonic Orchestras, and conductor of Stuttgart Opera (from 1978).

**Prix de Rome** (Fr.), prize given by French Government for excellence in each of following fields: painting, sculpture, engraving, architecture and music. Winners reside for 3 years in Rome, submitting work for inspection. First awarded 1803. Winners incl. Hérold (1812), Halévy (1819), Berlioz (1830), Gounod (1839), Bizet (1857), Massenet (1863), Debussy (1884), Charpentier (1887), Caplet (1901), L. Boulanger (1913), Ibert (1919). Prize has not always been gauge of musical inspiration – Ravel failed to win it.

**Prodaná Nevësta,** *see* BARTERED BRIDE.

**Prodigal Son, The,** church parable by Britten, libretto by W. Plomer. Third of Britten's church parables (really short operas for church performance), others being *Curlew River* and *The Burning Fiery Furnace.* First perf. Aldeburgh Festival, 1968.

**programme music,** music in which sound is used to depict concrete elements of, and whose form is governed by, story or image, as distinct from ABSOLUTE MUSIC. Some pictorial passages may be found in music before 19th cent., but only in rare instances are both form and themes directly related to programme. Beethoven affirmed that his *Pastoral Symphony* was 'expression of emotion rather than tone-painting', but 4th movt. (storm scene) is programme music. Berlioz, on other hand, wrote out programme for his *Symphonie Fantastique,* and regarded it as instrumental drama 'deprived of the resource of words'. Mendelssohn kept pictorial elements in his concert overtures well within limits of traditional form, but Liszt's SYMPHONIC POEMS were in form and expression so closely related to their subject that he provided programme 'to guard the listener against a wrong poetical interpretation'. Liszt regarded composer of programme music as 'tone-poet' whose music expressed 'adventures of his soul', as compared to 'mere musician' who played games according to certain established rules. Idea that all music is by its nature an expression of some programme was vigorously attacked by critic Hanslick. Richard Strauss's symphonic poems brought pictorial possibilities of orchestral music with accompanying programme to their final point. General view in 20th cent. has tended to be that judgement of value of programme music rests on its purely musical qualities.

**progressive tonality,** *see* NIELSEN, CARL.

**Prokofiev, Sergey Sergeyevich** (1891–1953), Russian composer. Born at Sontsovka, in Ekaterinoslav region. Mother was pianist and ensured his precocious gifts as composer and pianist were speedily encouraged. Became pupil of Glière, then, at St Petersburg Conservatory, of Rimsky-Korsakov, Liadov and Cherepnin. Won Rubenstein prize for 1st piano concerto. His *Scythian Suite* (1916), with its bludgeoning rhythms, established him as one of Russia's most progressive composers, and his *Classical Symphony* (1917) revealed his talent for pastiche. Left Russia during Revolution and travelled widely, living in London, Japan, US, and (from 1922) Paris, where he wrote music for Diaghilev's Ballets Russes. Returned to Russia in 1934 and adopted Soviet citizenship. There his previously astringent musical style gradually mellowed, though his outlook was still sufficiently uncompromising to provoke criticism from Soviet authorities, who required readily comprehensible music. However, he continued to compose more or less as he liked. Awarded Stalin Prize in 1951.

Prokofiev composed important works in most musical forms. Of his operas, *War and Peace, The Fiery Angel, The Gambler* and *The Love of Three Oranges* hold their place in 20th-cent. repertory. His ballet *Romeo and Juliet* still seems greatest work of its kind since Chaikovsky's *Sleeping Beauty.* Of his symphonies, 5th is most glamorous, though darker, more disturbing 6th is preferred by connoisseurs. Piano and violin concertos continue to be popular. Cantata *Alexander Nevsky* is one of greatest and most picturesque of modern choral works (also superlative piece of film music in its original form). Piano music is notable for wit, pugnacity and lyricism.

Principal compositions:

(1) Stage works: operas: *Magdalen* (1913), *The Gambler* (1915–16), *Love for Three Oranges* (1919), *The Fiery Angel* (1919–26), *Semyon Kotko* (1939), *Betrothal in a Monastery* (1940), *War and Peace* (1941–52), *The Story of a Real Man* (1947–8); 6 ballets, incl. *Romeo and Juliet* (1936) and *Cinderella* (1946);

(2) Orchestra: 7 symphonies, sinfonietta, overtures, symphonic suites, film music for *Lieutenant Kizhe, The Queen of Spades, Ivan the Terrible etc,* 5 piano concertos, 2 violin concertos, cello concerto;

(3) Chamber works: quintet for wind and strings, string quintet, 2 string quartets;

(4) Piano: 9 sonatas, 2 sonatinas, suites, studies.

Also choral cantatas, and *Peter and the Wolf* (1936) for speaker and orchestra.

**prolation,** *see* MENSURAL NOTATION.

**Promenade Concerts,** first of such concerts in London were given in 1838. Present London 'Proms' were instituted in 1895 by Robert Newman, and conducted till 1944 by Sir Henry Wood. His most popular successor was Sir Malcolm Sargent. Organization of concerts was taken over by B.B.C. in 1927. Name is misnomer: though there is standing room, people do not walk about.

**Prometheus,** (1) *Die Geschöpfe des Prometheus* (Ger., *The Creatures of Prometheus*), ballet with music by Beethoven, op 43 (1800);

(2) symphonic poem by Liszt (1850);

(3) *Prometheus: the Poem of Fire,* tone poem for orchestra by Skryabin, op 60 (1819). Score calls for *tastiera per luce,* keyboard instrument which projects colours on screen;

(4) song settings of Goethe's poem by Schubert, Wolf and others.

**Proper,** parts of MASS with texts and music proper to day or season, as distinct from ORDINARY (parts with invariable text): Introit, Gradual, Alleluia (Tract in penitential seasons), Offertory, and Communion.

**Prophète, Le** (Fr., *The Prophet*), opera by Meyerbeer, libretto by A.E. Scribe. First perf. Paris, 1849. Plot concerns Anabaptist rising in Holland in 16th cent.

**proportion,** rhythmic system of all part-music is based on proportion. Our present TIME-SIGNATURES are derived from signs of proportion used in mensural notation to show relation between new note-value and immediately preceding one. Relation could be one of AUGMENTATION or, more frequently, of DIMINUTION, and was shown by fraction or ratio.

**Proportz,** *see* NACHTANZ.

**propriety** (Lat., *proprietas*), in combination (ligature) of 2 notes in MENSURAL NOTATION, normal ('proper' and 'perfect') sequence was considered to be that which had shorter note (*brevis*) followed by longer (*longa*). Term propriety referred to first note, so that ligature of 2 or more notes beginning with breve was defined as ligature 'with propriety' (*cum propriete*), and ligature beginning with a long was 'without propriety' (*sine propriete*). Ligature beginning with 2 semibreves, shown by upward stem, was defined as ligature 'with opposite propriety' (*cum opposita propriete*).

**prosa,** *see* SEQUENCE (2).

**Proske, Karl** (1794–1861), Silesian editor of church music. Visited Italy, and collected and published church music of 16th and 17th cents. in *Musica divina* (4 vols., 1853–62) and *Selectus novus missarum* (1855–59), which contributed greatly to revival of music of Palestrina and his contemporaries.

**Prout, Ebenezer** (1835–1909), English composer, organist, theorist. Wrote widely used textbooks.

**Provençal tambourin,** *see* TAMBOURIN.

**Provenzale, Francesco** (*c* 1627–1704), Italian composer. Wrote operas, cantatas, oratorios, motets and other church music, and was first of line of Neapolitan composers who assumed leadership in development of opera in late baroque period.

**Prunières, Henry** (1886–1942), French musicologist. Pupil of Romain Rolland. Founded (1920) and edited *La Revue Musicale*, and edited works of Lully. Wrote books on opera in 17th cent., and on Lully, Monteverdi, and Cavalli.

**Prussian Quartets,** nickname of set of 3 string quartets by Mozart, composed (1789–90) for King Frederick William of Prussia, who was amateur cellist: no 1 in D, K575; no 2 in B flat, K589; no 3 in F, K590. All have prominent parts for cello.

**Psalmody,** oldest part of Christian liturgical music. Verses of complete psalm are normally sung in alternation by 2 sides of choir to ANGLICAN CHANT, or to 1 of 8 psalm-tones of plainsong – *see* TONE (4). Orig. ANTIPHON was sung after each verse, later only before and after psalm. Psalm-tone is chosen to agree with MODE of antiphon. Verse of psalm is sung in more elaborate plainsong as part of RESPOND. *See also* TONUS PEREGRINUS, TRACT.

**psalm-tone,** *see* TONE (4), PSALMODY.

**Psalmus Hungaricus** (Lat., Hungarian Psalm), setting for tenor, chorus and orchestra by Kodály, op 13, of Psalm 55 in translation by 16th-cent. poet Michael Vég. Commissioned by Hungarian government in 1923 for 50th anniversary of union of cities of Buda and Pest.

**psalter, metrical,** in 16th cent., Reformed Churches of Netherlands, England, Scotland and Switzerland decided to replace singing of psalms to plainsong by singing of metrical translations of psalms to tunes suitable for congregational use. Tunes were set in imitative style, or more frequently in homophonic style with tune in tenor or treble.

**psalterion,** *see* PSALTERY.

**psaltery** (Fr., *psalterion*; It., *salterio*), medieval instrument of zither type with plucked strings, of similar shape to DULCIMER, strings of which were struck. Usually had trapezoid shape; half-psaltery had wing shape, which was kept when it was developed into harpsichord by addition of keyboard.

**Pskovitianka,** *see* MAID OF PSKOV.

**Puccini, Giacomo Antonio Domenico Michele Secondo Maria** (1858–1924), Italian opera composer. From musical family, studied in Lucca and at Milan Conservatorio, where was pupil of Ponchielli. First success was *Manon Lescaut* (1893), followed by *La Bohème* (1896), *Tosca* (1900), and *Madame Butterfly* (1904, initially a failure). Success of these was not equalled by *La Fanciulla del West* (*The Girl of the Golden West,* 1910), nor by *Il Trittico,* triptych of one-act operas *(Il Tabarro, Suor Angelica, Gianni Schicchi)* on which he worked during WWI, although latter contains some of his best music. Final duet of *Turandot,* left unfinished at his death, was completed by Alfano. Puccini was gifted with vivid stage sense and natural melodic talent, and developed impressive resource in harmony and orchestration which have made his operas among most successful of past century, even though he was more superficial and limited than his predecessor, Verdi.

**Pugnani, Gaetano** (1731–98), Italian violinist, teacher. Pupil of Tartini. Toured as violinist (1754–70), spending some time in London. Also composed operas, ballets, cantatas, violin concertos, and chamber music, but not 'Praeludium and Allegro' once ascribed to him, which was in fact pastiche by Kreisler.

**Pujol, Juan Pablo** (1573–1626), Spanish composer, priest. Composed Masses and other church music, and secular songs.

**Pulcinella,** ballet with music (incorporating songs) by Stravinsky (after Pergolesi), choreography by Massine and décor by Picasso. First perf. Paris, 1920. Music later arranged as orchestral suite.

**Pult** (Ger.), DESK.

**Punch and Judy,** opera by Harrison Birtwhistle, libretto by S. Pruslin. First perf. Aldeburgh Festival, 1968. Work uses familiar fairground puppet-play as basis of what librettist describes as 'a source opera after the events'.

**punctum** or **punctus** (Lat.), 'point'. (1) a note, as in *contrapunctus,* counterpoint;

(2) in mensural notation, point after note (*punctus additionis*) adds one half of its value; point placed between 2 notes or beside stem of note (*punctus divisionis*) marks off group of 3 notes in PERFECT TIME or perfect prolation (*see* MENSURAL NOTATION);

(3) each of repeated sections in ESTAMPIE;

(4) theorist Anonymous IV uses *punctum* as alternative for CLAUSULA (*clausulae sive puncta*) in discussing composition of Perotin.

**punta d'arco** (It.), point of the bow, at opposite end to heel. *A punta d'arco,* direction to use only last few inches of bow on strings.

**Purcell, Henry** (1659–95), English composer, organist. Son of Gentleman of Chapel Royal. Chorister of Chapel Royal (*c*

1668–73). Became composer for violins (1677). Organist at Westminster Abbey from 1674, and at Chapel Royal from 1682. Appointed keeper of king's instruments (1683).

Purcell was most original and gifted English composer of his time. Active in every field of music. Early work shows certain attachment to past combined with awareness of newer harmonic resources. As he developed he came to accept conventions of baroque music – clearcut outlines, brilliance, and inclination to pathetic expression – without ever sacrificing his own personality. Theatre music incl. 6 operas, only one of which *(Dido and Aeneas)* is set to continuous music – others contain much spoken dialogue. Church music incl. both full anthems in traditional style and up-to-date verse anthems with solos for counter-tenor, tenor and bass. Odes are rich in contrasts between solo voices, chorus and orchestra. As writer of solo songs he has never been surpassed. Most remarkable of his instrumental works are fantasias for viols (*c* 1680), which handle traditional form in curiously individual way. His trio sonatas are most striking evidence of his capacity for mastering Italian style, for which he professed admiration.

Principal compositions:

(1) Stage music: *Dido and Aeneas* (1689), *Dioclesian* (1690), *King Arthur* (1691), *The Fairy Queen* (1692), *The Indian Queen* (1695), *The Tempest* (1695), and music for *c* 40 plays;

(2) Odes: 17 for king and other members of royal family, 4 for St Cecilia's day, 3 for other occasions;

(3) Songs and cantatas: 9 cantatas for 2 or more voices with instruments, 41 secular duets, *c* 100 secular songs, sacred songs, duets, trios, quartets, numerous catches;

(4) Church music: 12 complete full anthems, *c* 40 verse anthems, 3 services;

(5) Chamber music: Fantasias in 3, 4 and 5 parts, 2 In Nomines, 12 *Sonatas of III Parts* (1683), 10 *Sonatas of IV Parts* (1697);

(6) Keyboard works: various pieces printed in *Musick's Hand-Maid,* ii (1689) and *A Choice Collection of Lessons* (1696), and others in MS.

His brother **Daniel Purcell** (*c* 1663–1717) was also composer and organist. Wrote music for theatre, incl. setting of Congreve's *The Judgement of Paris,* and completion of brother's *The Indian Queen.* Also wrote odes, anthems, sacred and secular songs, 6 solo cantatas, flute and violin sonatas, and psalm settings for organ or harpsichord.

**Puritani, I** (It., *The Puritans*), opera by Bellini, libretto by C. Pepoli (after Scott's *Old Mortality*). First perf. Paris, 1835.

# Q

**Q,** as abbrev., = *quintus, quinto* or *quinto pars,* 5th part in 16th-cent. composition for 5 or more voices or instruments.

**quadrille,** French dance fashionable in early 19th cent., introduced into Britain in 1815 and Germany in 1821. Danced by 2 or 4 couples. Had 5 parts in 6/8 and 2/4 alternately. Operatic music was often arranged as quadrille.

**quadruple counterpoint,** *see* COUNTERPOINT.

**quadruple croche** (Fr.), hemidemisemiquaver.

**quadruple fugue,** fugue with 4 different subjects.

**quadruple stop,** chord of 4 notes played on bowed string instrument. Term applies even if some of notes are open strings.

**quadruplet,** group of 4 notes to be played in time of 3, written:

**quadruple time,** same as COMMON TIME.

**quadruplum** (Lat.), 4th part above tenor (tenor being 1st part) of ORGANUM and CLAUSULA of period *c* 1200. Hence term also applied to whole composition, *eg* by Perotin.

**Quagliati, Paolo** (*c* 1555–1628), Italian composer. Music stands between old and new styles of early 17th cent. Works incl. pageant *Il carro di fedeltà d'amore* (1606), which contains both monodic and polyphonic music, 4-part madrigals (1608), sung either as monodies or as madrigals with continuo, *Sfera armoniosa* (1623), containing duets with obbligato instrumental solos, and keyboard music.

**quail,** toy instrument that imitates sound of quail.

**Quantz, Johann Joachim** (1697–1773), German composer, flautist. Studied counterpoint under Fux. In service of Frederick the Great. Composed *c* 300 flute concertos, sonatas, and *c* 200 other works for flute. His treatise on flute-playing also gives important information on performance of 18th-cent. music.

**quarter note** (US), crotchet.

**quarter tone,** half a semitone, which is smallest interval traditionally used in Western music. Had place in ENHARMONIC tetrachord of Greek music. Used by some modern composers as occasional effect or as complete system (*eg* by Bloch, Hába, Boulez, Stockhausen and Ligeti). Notes are indicated by modified forms of usual signs for accidentals. *See also* MICROTONES.

**quartet** (Fr., *quatuor*; Ger., *Quartett*; It., *quartetto*), composition for 4 performers. Since mid 18th cent., most common forms have been

STRING QUARTET, PIANO QUARTET, quartet for mixed instruments, and vocal quartets.

**Quartet for the End of Time** (Fr., *Quatuor pour la fin du temps*), work in 8 movts. for violin, clarinet, cello and piano by Messiaen. Written while composer was prisoner of war in Silesia; unusual scoring was dictated by instruments played by fellow prisoners.

**Quartettsatz** (Ger., quartet movement), single allegro movt. in C minor for string quartet by Schubert (1820). Intended as 1st movt. of complete quartet.

**Quartfagott** (Ger.), large bassoon pitched fourth below normal instrument. Used in Germany up to early 19th cent.

**Quartgeige,** *see* VIOLINO PICCOLO.

**Quartposaune** (Ger.), TROMBONE pitched fourth below tenor trombone in B flat, *ie* bass trombone in F.

**quasi** (It.), 'as if', 'nearly', as in tempo mark *Andante quasi allegretto,* or in *quasi niente,* 'almost nothing', *ie* as softly as possible.

**Quatorze Juillet, Le** (Fr., The Fourteenth of July), incidental music to play by Romain Rolland, composed in combination by Auric, Honegger, Ibert, Koechlin, Lazarus, Milhaud and Roussel. First perf. Paris, 1936.

**quatreble,** term used in 15th, early 16th cents. (equivalent of Lat. *quadruplex*) for highest voice in choir, being 4th above tenor (tenor being 1st part); parts between were meane and treble. Quatreble SIGHT was twelfth above tenor.

**Quattro Rusteghi, I** (Eng., *School for Fathers*), comic opera by Wolf-Ferrari, libretto by G. Pizzolato (after Goldoni). First perf. (in German) Munich, 1906.

**quatuor** (Fr.), quartet.

**quaver** (US, eighth note; Fr., *croche*; Ger., *Achtel*; It., *croma*), note which is half length of crotchet, and eighth of semibreve (whole note). Written

♪ grouped ♫

Quaver rest is written 𝄾

**Queen of France, The** (Fr., *La Reine*), nickname given to Haydn's symphony no 85 in B flat (1785), one of 6 'Paris' Symphonies. Reputed to be favourite of Marie Antoinette.

**Queen of Sheba, The** (Ger., *Die Königen von Saba*), opera by Goldmark, libretto by S.H. Mosenthal. First perf. Vienna, 1875. Story concerns wooing of Queen of Sheba by Assad, King Solomon's favourite courtier, who ends by being banished.

**Queen of Spades, The** (Russ., *Pikovaya Dama*; Fr., *Pique-Dame*), opera by Chaikovsky, libretto by Modest Chaikovsky, composer's brother (after Pushkin). First perf. St Petersburg, 1890.

**Quercu, Simon de** or **Simon van Eycken** (*fl* 15th–16th cents.), Flemish theorist. Worked in Milan and Vienna. Published treatise on elementary theory, *Opusculum musices* (1509), and vol. of motets (1513).

**Querflöte** (Ger.), *see* FLUTE.

**Querstand** (Ger.), FALSE RELATION.

**Questa o quella** (It., the one or the other), flirtatious aria sung by Duke of Mantua in Act 1 of *Rigoletto* in which he proclaims that all women please him equally.

**quest opera,** opera in which principal character(s) undergoes various hardships, tests, or difficult journeys before reaching his goal. Famous example is *The Magic Flute.*

**queue** (Fr.), 'tail'. *Piano à queue,* grand piano.

**quickstep,** march in quick steps; also, modern ballroom dance notable for quick beat.

**Quiet City,** work by Copland for trumpet, cor anglais and strings. First perf. 1941. Based on incidental music for play of same title.

**Quiet Flows the Don,** opera by Dzerjinsky, libretto by composer (after novel by Sholokhov). First perf. Leningrad, 1935. Work was dedicated to Shostakovich, and was proclaimed in Russia as outstanding example of Soviet opera. Story concerns Cossack who leads peasant revolt.

**quilisma,** NEUME used in notation of plainsong. Usually came between 2 notes a third apart, and was prob. sung with trill or tremolo in same way as later PLICA. Occurs in Byzantine chant as *kylisma,* where it indicated 'rolling and rotating of the voice'.

**Quilter, Roger** (1877–1953), English composer. Composed song settings of Shakespeare, Herrick *etc,* small orchestral works (incl. *A Children's Overture*), incidental music, and pieces for piano and violin.

**Quinet, Fernand** (1898– ), Belgian composer, cellist. Member of Pro Arte String Quartet. Became director of Conservatoires at Charleroi and Liège. Composed chamber music and songs.

**quint,** 5-stringed tenor VIOL.

**Quintadena,** *see* QUINTATÖN.

**Quintatön** (Ger.), organ stop of stopped flue type in which twelfth, *ie* 3rd note of HARMONIC SERIES, is present as well as fundamental. Smaller size is called *Quintadena.*

**quinte** (Fr.), term used in France in 17th, early 18th cents. for 5th part (Lat., *quinta pars*) in 5-part instrumental piece; applied specifically to viola.

**Quintenquartett** (Ger., 'Fifths Quartet'), nickname given to Haydn's string quartet in D minor, op 76, no 2 (1797–8). Principal theme begins with 2 falling fifths.

**quintet** (Fr., *quintette, quintuor*; Ger., *Quintett*; It., *quintetto*), composition for 5 performers. String quintet is usually for 2 violins, 2 violas and cello, as in those of Mozart, Beethoven, Mendelssohn and Brahms. Boccherini wrote quintets for 2 violins, viola and 2 cellos, combination also used in Schubert's great C major quintet. Combination for piano with string quartet is called piano quintet; similarly with clarinet quintet *etc.*

**quinto** (It.), specific kind of trumpet, prescribed by Monteverdi in *Orfeo*.

**quinton,** violin with 5 strings used in France in 18th cent.

**Quintposaune** (Ger.), TROMBONE pitched fifth below tenor trombone in B flat; *ie* bass trombone in E flat.

**Quintsaite** (Ger.), misleading name for E or 1st string of violin.

**Quint stops,** *see* MUTATION STOPS.

**quintuor** (Fr.), quintet.

**quintuple time,** 5 beats, usually crotchets, in bar, *ie* 5/4 time. In practice usually resolves into alternation, regular or irregular, of 3/4 and 2/4, or occasionally into 4/4 plus 1/4. Quite uncommon before 20th cent.

**quintuplet,** group of 5 notes to be performed in time of 4, written:

**quintus, quinto, quinta pars,** *see* Q.

**quodlibet** (Lat.), 'what you will': (1) composition, extemporized or written down, in which 2 or more well-known tunes are sung or played simultaneously. Practised in 17th, 18th cents., esp. by German composers;

(2) succession of pieces or songs spontaneously strung together.

# R

**r,** abbrev. of RAY.

**R,** abbrev. of Respond.

**Rabaud, Henri Benjamin** (1873–1949), French composer. Pupil of Massenet. Worked as conductor then as director of Paris Conservatoire (1920–40). Wrote operas incl. successful *Marouf, savetier de Caire* (1914) and one on Synge's *Riders to the Sea,* 2 symphonies and other orchestral music (incl. orchestration of Fauré's *Dolly* suite), chamber music, oratorio, and songs.

**rabbia** (It.), 'rage'.

**Rachmaninoff, Rachmaninov,** *see* RAKHMANINOV.

**racket, rackett** or **ranket,** double reed woodwind instrument used late 16th–early 18th cents. Consisted of solid body pierced by number of parallel vertical channels, connected alternately at top and bottom so as to form continuous tube. Holes pierced in side made limited scale available. Because of shape, called *Cervelas* (saveloy) in France and *Wurstfagott* (sausage bassoon) in Germany.

**Radamisto** (It., Rhadamistus), opera by Handel, libretto by N.F. Haym. First perf. London, 1720.

**raddoppiamento** (It.), 'doubling', usually to indicate doubling of bass at octave below.

**Radetzky March,** march by Johann Strauss the elder (1848). Named after Austrian field-marshal, music has come to be regarded as symbol of Hapsburg monarchy.

**radio-synthetic organ,** electronic organ in which electrical waves are converted to sound. Invented by Abbé Puget in 1934.

**Radziwill, Prince Antoni Henryk** (1775–1833), German cellist, singer, composer. Governor of Posen. Friend of Beethoven and Chopin. Composed incidental music to Goethe's *Faust,* vocal duets, part songs, and songs with guitar and cello. Beethoven dedicated to him his *Namensfeier* overture, op 115.

**Raff, Joseph Joachim** (1822–82), Swiss composer, teacher, music critic. Friend of Liszt and Mendelssohn. Director of Frankfurt Hoch Conservatorium from 1877. Works incl. 11 symphonies, concertos, overtures, incidental and piano music, and songs.

**Raft of the Medusa** (Ger., *Das Floss der Medusa*), oratorio for speaker, solo voices, chorus and orchestra by Henze, text by E. Schnabel, written for Hamburg Radio in 1968. First perf. was broken up by police after noisy demonstrations. Work is dedicated to Che Guevara and was inspired by Géricault's famous painting (1819).

**raga,** basically, Indian scale, but term refers more widely to piece of music which has raga as its basis, and whose mood and atmosphere is determined by constant use of certain notes of raga. Each piece has its own fixed scale material, used without modulation throughout performance.

**ragtime,** style of dance music popular from late 19th cent. till early years of jazz age. Used various kinds of syncopation against regular rhythmic background in 2/4 or 4/4 time. Piano rags of Scott Joplin are esp. famous. Stravinsky wrote *Ragtime* for 11 instruments in 1918, and *Piano Rag-Music* in 1920.

**Raimondi, Pietro** (1786–1853), Italian composer, conductor. Director of Royal Theatre, Naples, from 1824; *maestro di cappella* at St Peter's, Rome, from 1852. Composed 62 operas, 21 ballets, 8 oratorios, Masses, Requiems, psalms and other church music. Famed as deviser of multiple counterpoint; wrote 3 opera-oratorios that could be performed simultaneously.

**'Raindrop' Prelude,** nickname for Chopin's piano prelude in D flat, op 28, no 15 (1839). Repeated note A flat (G sharp) was thought to resemble raindrops dripping from roof of composer's (temporary) residence in Majorca.

**Rainier, Priaulx** (1903– ), South African composer, now resident in Britain. Pupil of Nadia Boulanger. Works incl. cello concerto, *Sinfonia da camera* for strings, string quartet, viola sonata, and songs.

**Raison, André** (*fl* 17th–18th cents.), French organist, composer. Wrote 2 books of organ works; Bach used theme of passacaglia in G minor as first 4 bars of his passacaglia in C minor for organ.

**Rake's Progress, The,** opera by Stravinsky, libretto by W. H. Auden and C. Kallman. First perf. Venice, 1951. Inspired by Hogarth's series of 18th-cent. pictures.

**Rakhmaninov, Sergey Vassilievich** (1873–1943), Russian composer, pianist. Studied in St Petersburg and at Moscow Conservatory under Arensky. Early compositions were influenced by warm admiration of Chaikovsky. Lived in Dresden for several years, gave concerts in US (1909–10), then returned to Moscow, where conducted Philharmonic concerts (1911–13). Left Russia in 1917, and later settled in US. Composed 3 operas, 3 symphonies, tone poem *The Isle of the Dead* (1907) and other works for orchestra, 4 piano concertos, *Rhapsody on a Theme by Paganini* (same as that used in Brahms's Variations) for piano and orchestra, piano music (incl. series of preludes and *études-tableaux*), choral works, chamber music, and songs.

It used to be said that Rakhmaninov was a romantic born out of his period, that many of his large-scale works were flawed by 'structural weaknesses', and that his inspiration dwindled as he grew older. However, the 2nd symphony, his largest orchestral work, is probably also his best: it has great emotional power and melodic intensity, and is structurally sound. His romanticism was an asset rather than a liability, and anyway was irrelevant to finely integrated works like the 3rd piano concerto and *Rhapsody on a Theme of Paganini.* As for loss of inspiration, one of his most progressive and compelling works, *Symphonic Dances,* dates from the very end of his career.

**Rákóczi March,** Hungarian national tune, named after leader of revolt against Austria, 1703–11. Used by Berlioz (Hungarian March in *Damnation of Faust*), Liszt (Hungarian Rhapsody for piano, and *Rákóczi March* for orchestra), Johann Strauss *(The Gipsy Baron)*, and others.

**rallentando** (It.), becoming gradually slower. Abbrev. *rall.*

**Rameau, Jean Philippe** (1683–1764), French composer, theorist. First part of life was spent as organist in Clermont-Ferrand (1702–6), Paris, Lyons, and from 1722 again at Clermont. In 1706 published 1st book of *Pièces de clavecin,* modelled on those of Couperin. Laid foundation of modern musical theory in various treatises, setting forth principles of key-centre, fundamental bass, and roots and inversions of chords. Settled in Paris (1732) and met Voltaire, who was several times his librettist. With *Hippolyte et Aricie* (1733) began, at age of 50, new and distinguished career as most important composer of French opera since Lully. Chief stage works were operas *Castor et Pollux* (1737) and *Dardanus* (1739), opera-ballets *Les Indes galantes* (1735) and *Les Fêtes d'Hébé* (1739), and ballet-bouffon *Platée* (1745). Revival of *Platée* in 1754 sealed fate of Italian *intermezzo* in Paris, Rameau leading French faction against Pergolesi's champions in 'La Guerre des Bouffons'. Also wrote trio sonatas and church music.

**Ramis** or **Ramos de Pareja, Bartolomé** (*c* 1440–1521?), Spanish theorist, composer. In his *Musica practica* (1482) set forth simpler method of dividing string than Pythagorean tuning given by Boethius and taught throughout Middle Ages. This system was disputed by Gafori and developed by Zarlino.

**Rands, Bernard** (1935– ), English composer. Pupil of Dallapiccola, Boulez, Maderna and Berio. Works incl. *Serena* (music theatre), *Ology* for jazz orchestra, *Ballad 3* for soprano and tape, and chamber and instrumental music.

**Ranelagh Gardens,** gardens on bank of Thames in London in which Rotunda was built for concerts (1742). Arne and other English composers wrote music and arranged concerts for Ranelagh, and Mozart played there at age of 8. Gardens closed in 1803.

**Rangström, Anders Johan Türe** (1884–1947), Swedish composer, conductor. Pupil of Pfitzner. Works incl. numerous songs, operas, symphonic poems and symphonies (1st in memory of Strindberg), suites, cantatas, choral works with orchestra, and incidental, chamber and piano music.

**rank,** set of pipes belonging to one stop on organ. Word is most often used in connection with MUTATION STOPS; thus mixture is referred to as 3-rank or 4-rank according to number of pipes which sound for each note.

**ranket,** *see* RACKET.

**Rankl, Karl** (1898–1968), Austrian-born conductor, composer. Pupil of Schoenberg and Webern. Musical director at Covent Garden (1946–51). Conductor of Scottish National Orchestra (1952–7), then directed Elizabethan Trust Opera in Australia (1957–60). Compositions incl. opera *Deirdre of the Sorrows* (after Synge), 8 symphonies, chamber music, and songs.

**ranks,** 2 strings tuned to same note on instruments of LUTE family.

**rant,** term used of various English dances of 17th cent.

**Ranz des Vaches** (Fr.; Ger., *Kuhreigen*), melody sung or played on Alpine horn by Swiss cowherds to call their cattle. Exists in various forms. Used in Rossini's William Tell overture, Beethoven's *Pastoral Symphony,* Berlioz's *Symphonie Fantastique,* and Walton's *Façade.*

**Rape of Lucretia, The,** chamber opera by Britten, libretto by R. Duncan (after A. Obey's play). First perf. Glyndebourne, 1946.

**rappresentativo,** *see* STILE (3).

**Rappresentazione di anima e di corpo** (It., Representation of soul and body), morality play set to music by Emilio de' Cavalieri. First perf. Rome, 1600. Often described as first oratorio, though now normally performed as opera.

**Rapsodie espagnole** (Fr., *Spanish Rhapsody*), orchestral work by Ravel (1907).

**rasch** (Ger.), quick.

**Raselius** or **Rasel, Andreas** (*c* 1563–1602), German composer. Wrote numerous motets, in both German and Latin, and theoretical treatise *Hexachordum seu quaestiones musicae practicae* (1589).

**Rasiermesserquartett,** *see* RAZOR QUARTET.

**Rasumovsky Quartets,** 3 quartets, op 59 (1806) by Beethoven, dedicated to Count Rasumovsky, Russian ambassador in Vienna, who played violin in own string quartet. Quartets contain some Russian folk music elements.

**rataplan,** term for solos or ensembles in opera which have character of military march.

**Rathaus, Karol** (1895–1954), Polish-born composer. Pupil of Schreker in Vienna and Berlin, where he later taught. Subsequently lived in Paris, London and US. Composed symphonies, opera, ballets, string quartets and other chamber music, choral, incidental, piano and organ music, and songs.

**Ratsche** (Ger.), rattle.

**rattle** (Fr., *crécelle*; Ger., *Knarre, Ratsche*), occasionally used percussion instrument in which sound is produced by piece of hard but flexible wood striking against ratchet-toothed cogwheel.

**Rattle, Simon** (1955– ), English conductor. Has worked with many orchestras in Britain, Europe and US. Principal conductor of City of Birmingham Symphony Orchestra from 1980.

**Rauzzini, Venanzio** (1746–1810), Italian castrato singer, composer. Settled in England in 1774. Of his operas, *Piramo e Tisbe* (1775) was most successful.

**Ravanello, Oreste** (1871–1938), Italian organist, composer. Wrote Masses and other church music, method for organ, and treatise on rhythm of Gregorian chant.

**Ravel, Maurice** (1875–1937), French composer, of Swiss and Basque descent. Pupil of Fauré and Gédalge at Paris Conservatoire. Progressive outlook resulted in his losing Prix de Rome 3 times, and being forbidden to make 4th attempt. Served as ambulance driver at front during WWI. Refused Légion d'Honneur (1920), but accepted honorary doctorate from Oxford (1928).

First mature works showed virtuosity of means and compact clarity of form which were characteristic of his style. Like Debussy, was strongly influenced by Chabrier and Satie, but interest in French harpsichord music, in orchestration of Rimsky-Korsakov, and in piano writing of Liszt led his development away from impressionism to precise and often wittily ironic style based on traditional harmonies and forms. Source of his inspiration, however, was more often poetic than abstract, and most of his orchestral works were originally written for theatre or as piano pieces. His orchestration was masterfully lucid. Later works tended towards greater economy of means without losing in deftness of expression and versatility of technique.

Principal compositions:

(1) Ballets: *Daphnis et Chloé* (1912), *Ma mère l'oye* (from suite for piano duet (1915);

(2) Operas: *L'Heure espagnole* (1907), *L'Enfant et les sortilèges* (1925);

(3) Orchestra: *Rapsodie espagnole* (1907), *La Valse* (1920), *Bolero* (1928), concerto for piano (left hand only) and orchestra (1931), concerto for piano and orchestra(1931);

(4) Chamber music: string quartet (1903), *Introduction and Allegro* for harp, string quartet, flute, clarinet (1906), piano trio (1915), cello sonata (1922), violin sonata (1927);

(5) Piano: *Jeux d'eau* (1901), *Miroirs* (1905), *Sonatine* (1905), *Gaspard de la Nuit* (1908), *Ma mère l'oye* (piano duet, 1908), *Valses nobles et sentimentales* (1911), *Le Tombeau de Couperin* (1917);

(6) Songs: *Shéhérazade* (1903; accompaniment was later orchestrated), *Histoires naturelles* (1906), *Deux mélodies hébraïques* (1914), *Ronsard à son âme* (1924), *Chansons madécasses* (for voice, flute, cello, piano, 1926), *Don Quichotte à Dulcinée* (baritone and chamber orchestra, 1932).

**Ravenscroft, Thomas** (*c* 1590–*c* 1633), English composer, editor. Published collections of rounds, catches and arrangements of popular songs, entitled *Pammelia* (1609), *Deuteromelia* (1609) and *Melismata* (1611). Compositions incl. anthems and instrumental works.

**Rawsthorne, Alan** (1905–71), English composer. Initially studied dentistry. Compositions, usually written in vigorously contrapuntal style, incl. *Symphonic Studies* (1938), 3 symphonies, *Street Corner* overture, 2 piano concertos, 2 violin concertos, clarinet concerto and other orchestral works, 3 string quartets and other chamber music, piano pieces, and songs.

**ray,** anglicized form of Italian *re* (D). In TONIC SOL-FA, second note (or supertonic) of major scale.

**Raymond,** opera by Ambroise Thomas, libretto by A. de Leuven and J.B. Rosier (after Dumas's *The Man in the Iron Mask*). First perf. Paris, 1851.

**Razor Quartet** (Ger., *Rasiermesserquartett*), name given to Haydn's string quartet in F minor and major, op 55, no 2 (published 1789). When Haydn was visited by John Bland (London music publisher), he said he would give his 'best quartet for a good razor'; Bland presented him with own set of razors and Haydn later produced promised quartet.

**re,** (1) second note of hexachord (*see* SOLMIZATION);
(2) (It., Fr.), the note D.

**Read, Gardner** (1913– ), American composer. Compositions incl. symphonies and other orchestral works, and chamber, vocal and keyboard music.

**Reading, John** (d. 1692), English organist. Organist of Winchester Cathedral from 1675, and of Winchester College from 1681, for which he composed Latin Graces and Winchester school song, *Dulce domum*.

**Reading, John** (1677–1774), English organist, prob. son or otherwise related to above. Held various posts, and published book of *New Songs (after the Italian manner)* and book of anthems.

**Reading rota,** *see* SUMER IS ICUMEN IN.

**real answer,** *see* ANSWER.

**realization,** act of completing harmony of 17th or 18th-cent. work by providing keyboard accompaniment based on indications by FIGURED BASS.

**rebec** or **rebeck** (It., *ribeca*), also rebab, rebibe, ribibe, ribible, rubible, rubybe and rybibe: small bowed instrument of elongated pear-shape, adapted from Arabian *rebâb,* used in Europe from 16th cent. Treble size had 3 strings tuned as lower 3 strings of violin. It was one of instruments from which violin developed in course of 16th cent. In form with 4 strings, survived into 18th cent. as KIT used by dancing masters.

**Rebikov, Vladimir** (1866–1920), Russian composer. Composed operas, ballets, suites and other orchestral works, and church, vocal and piano music. Considered advanced in his time because of his occasional use of whole-tone scale and parallel fifths.

**rebop,** *see* BOP.

**rebute,** French form of JEW'S HARP.

**recapitulation,** *see* SONATA FORM.

**récit** (Fr.), (1) recitative;
(2) swell organ.

**recital,** public programme of music for 1 or 2 performers – where more performers are involved, term is usually 'concert'.

**recitative** (Fr., *récit, récitatif*; Ger., *Rezitativ, Sprechgesang*; It., *recitativo*), style of singing which is more closely related in pitch and rhythm to dramatic speech than to song. Originated *c* 1590 in works of Florentine composers, *eg* Peri, and was adopted in operas, oratorios, cantatas and some forms of church music during first half of 17th cent. Generally accompanied by harpsichord, organ, or other CONTINUO instrument, with or without string bass. Earliest operas are largely recitative, but technique was soon used mainly for narrative and less lyrical sections of operas and oratorios.

In 18th cent., accepted style of recitative was that of Italian opera, called *recitativo secco.* This was sung in quick free rhythm of stage dialogue, composer's notation merely indicating approximate note-values. Recitative in more expressive style accompanied by orchestra, as used by Bach, was called *recitativo stromentato* or *accompagnato.* Style of recitative was sometimes transferred to instrumental music.

In Wagner's later operas distinction between aria and recitative became blurred: both were absorbed into vocal line and used as freely as dramatic situation required. Opera since Wagner has tended to use recitative to the exclusion of all but shortest passages in aria style. At same time, orchestral part, as in Wagner, has assumed function of providing thematic continuity and development.

**recitativo** (It.), *see* RECITATIVE.

**reciting note** (Lat., *repercussio, tuba*), note on which intermediate words of each verse of psalm are sung in plainsong. It is dominant of MODE in which psalm-tone is written. *See* PSALMODY.

**recorder** (Fr., *flûte douce, flûte à bec*; Ger., *Blockflöte*; It., *flauto dolce*), straight or end-blown flute, as distinct from transverse or side-blown flute. It was used from Middle Ages till 18th cent., and has been revived in modern times. It has sweet and gentle tone. In 16th cent., recorders were made in sets, or consorts: most usual sizes were descant (in Germany, soprano or treble), treble (in Germany, alto), tenor, and bass, whose lowest notes were respectively C on treble clef, F on treble clef, middle C, and F on bass clef. Bach calls recorder simply *flauto,* and transverse flute *traversa.*

**recte et retro, per,** *see* RETROGRADE MOTION.

**recueilli** (Fr.), meditative, collected.

**Redford, John** (d. 1547), English organist, composer, dramatist. Organist and master of choristers at St Paul's from *c* 1530. One of most important English composers of liturgical organ music before Reformation. Other works incl. music for Office and Mass.

**reduction** (Fr., *réduction*), arrangement (*eg* for piano) of piece of music that reduces or simplifies composer's original scoring.

**redundant entry,** *see* FUGUE.

**reed** (Fr., *anche*; Ger., *Zunge*; It., *ancia*), vibrating element in many musical instruments, usually made of cane or metal. Single beating reed, *ie* one which vibrates against material of instrument, is used in reed stops of organ (metal reed) and in clarinet and saxophone. Double beating reeds, *ie* 2 reeds of cane which vibrate against each other, are used in oboe family, *eg* cor anglais and bassoon. Free, as distinct from beating, reeds – *ie* reeds of metal which vibrate freely in slot – are used in harmonium and concertina. Pitch of metal reed, being determined by its length and thickness, is fixed; that of cane reed is variable, being determined by length of pipe to which it is attached.

**Reed, William Henry** (1876–1942), English composer of orchestral and chamber music.

**reed-organ,** name covering many instruments, both old and modern, which have no pipes and use free-beating reeds (one for each note) to produce their notes. *See* ACCORDION, AMERICAN ORGAN, CONCERTINA, HARMONIUM, MOUTH ORGAN, REGAL.

**reed pipe,** *see* ORGAN, REED.

**reed stops,** organ stops controlling reed pipes.

**reel,** dance, prob. of Celtic origin, practised in northern countries of Europe, in which dancers stand face to face and perform figures of eight. Music is usually in quick 4/4 time and in regular 4-bar phrases. Scottish strathspey is related to reel, but is danced in slower tempo, and is characterized by constant use of rhythms

𝅘𝅥𝅮. 𝅘𝅥𝅯 and 𝅘𝅥𝅯 𝅘𝅥𝅮.

**Reese, Gustave** (1899–   ), American musicologist. Associate editor (1933) then editor (1944–5) of *The Music Quarterly,* and one of founders of American Musicological Society (1934). His *Music in the Middle Ages* (1940) and *Music in the Renaissance* (1954) are standard works.

**'Reformation' Symphony** (Ger., *Reformationssinfonie*), title given by Mendelssohn to his symphony no 5 in D, op 107 (1830), which was composed for tercentenary of Augsburg Conference but (because of RC opposition) not performed there. Uses 'Dresden Amen' in 1st movt. and chorale 'Ein' feste Burg' in finale – so balancing RC and Protestant musical quotation.

**refrain,** lines in song that recur at end of each verse, usually set to same music.

**regal,** portable reed organ used in 16th, 17th cents. Had beating reeds, and unlike portable organ with flue pipes, was capable of *crescendo* and *diminuendo.*

**Reger, Max** (1873–1916), German composer, pianist, organist, conductor, teacher. Musically conservative, though claimed to be progressive, so made enemies in both camps. Attachment to Bach and Brahms is seen in his mastery of counterpoint and of complete resources of late romantic harmony. Avoided any kind of programme in his instrumental music, building up large structures on basis of classical and pre-classical forms to degree of harmonic complexity that at its best is splendidly massive but too often tends to become turgid and cumbersome. Greater discipline began to appear in his later works, but did not live to develop it. Organ music, incl. chorale preludes, preludes and fugues, passacaglias, and many shorter pieces, has important place in literature of instrument, esp. in Germany. Other works incl. concertos, orchestral, chamber choral and piano music, and songs. Orchestral *Variations on a theme of Mozart* is still occasionally performed.

**reggae,** type of West Indian popular music having 4 beats to the bar, upbeat being strongly accented. Words often involve social and political comment. Bob Marley (1945–81) was one of greatest exponents.

**Regino (of Prüm)** (d. 915), Benedictine monk, musical theorist. Abbot of monastery of Prüm (near Trier), and was later at St Maximin in Trier. Works incl. *De harmonica institutione* and *Tonarius,* latter being one of earliest examples of classification of plainsong melodies according to mode.

**Regis, Johannes** (*c* 1430–*c* 1485), Flemish composer. Became secretary to Dufay. Surviving works consist of Masses, motets and *chansons.*

**régisseur** (Fr.), term used in France and Germany for person in charge of artistic and technical parts of production of opera.

**register,** (1) set of pipes, which may consist of one or more RANKS, controlled by single stop on organ;

(2) division in compass of singer's voice, *eg* head register, chest register. Also applied to instrument's compass, *eg* Chalumeau register of clarinet.

**registration,** art of choosing and combining stops in organ playing. Indications given by composer may incl. changes of manual, particular type of solo stop, or relative weight of sound.

**Regnart, François** (*c* 1530–*c* 1600), Flemish composer. Wrote motets and vol. of *chansons* entitled *Poésies de P. Ronsard et autre poètes* (1575).

His brother, **Jacques Regnart** (*c* 1540–99), was singer and composer. Worked in Vienna, Prague and Innsbruck. Works incl. Masses, motets, vol. of 5-part German songs (1580), and 3 vols. of 3-part songs to German words after style of Neapolitan or Italian villanellas (1576–79).

**Regnault, Pierre,** *see* SANDRIN.

**Reichardt, Johann Friedrich** (1752–1814), German composer. Musical director at Prussian court (1776–93). Works incl. operas and incidental music, but best known for songs – he was important forerunner of Schubert. Also wrote several books on music.

**Reid,** orig. **Robertson, John** (1721–1807), Scottish-born army general. Left his fortune to Edinburgh University where he had studied, mainly for foundation of chair of music and annual Reid concert.

**Reimann, Aribert** (1936– ), German composer, pianist. Pupil of Blacher. Works incl. operas *Melusine* (1971) and *Lear* (1978), *Dance of Death* for baritone and orchestra, and chamber and ballet music.

**Reinagle, Alexander** (1756–1809), English pianist, composer, conductor. Settled in US. In 1793 built theatre in Philadelphia with Thomas Wignell, for which he directed music. Composed incidental music, songs, quartets, and concerto for 'Improved Pianoforte with Additional Keys'.

**Reine, La,** *see* QUEEN OF FRANCE.

**Reinecke, Carl Heinrich Carsten** (1824–1910), German pianist, violinist, composer, conductor, writer on music. Composed operas, choral works, symphonies, and songs.

**Reiner, Fritz** (1888–1963), Hungarian-born conductor. Settled in

US. Conducted Pittsburgh Symphony Orchestra (1938–48), and Chicago Symphony Orchestra from 1953.

**Reinken (Reincken), Johann (Jan) Adam** (1623–1722), German organist, composer, poss. of Dutch extraction. Bach made several visits to Hamburg to hear him play. His chorale preludes for organ are in extended fantasia style practised by North German organists of period. Also wrote music for 2 violins, viola da gamba and continuo.

**Reissiger, Karl Gottlieb** (1798–1859), German composer, conductor. Succeeded Marschner as director of Dresden Opera, and directed Dresden Conservatorium (1856–9). Composed operas, church music, symphony, 27 piano trios and other chamber music, many works for piano, and songs.

**Reiterquartett** (Ger.), Haydn's 'HORSEMAN' QUARTET.

**Reizenstein, Franz** (1911–68), German-born composer, pianist. Pupil of Hindemith and Vaughan Williams. Settled in England, 1934. Works, which show influence of both his teachers, incl. radio opera *Anna Kraus,* concertos, cantata *Voices of Night,* and chamber and piano music.

**Rejcha, Antonin** (1770–1836), Bohemian composer, theorist. At age of 18 went to Bonn, where became friend of Beethoven; later lived in Hamburg, Vienna, and Paris, where his pupils incl. Berlioz, Liszt, Gounod and Franck. Composed operas, 2 symphonies and other orchestral works, 24 quintets for woodwind and horn, 20 string quartets, 24 horn trios and other chamber music, duets for flutes and for violins, violin and piano sonatas, and piano pieces. Also wrote treatises on harmony, melody and composition.

**réjouissance** (Fr.), lit. 'enjoyment'. Title of spirited movt. sometimes found in suites of Bach–Handel era.

**Relâché,** surrealist ballet by Satie (1924), with choreography by J. Borlin and film episode directed by René Clair. Title refers to term employed in France to indicate that theatre is closed and that there will be no performance. On 'official' first night, audience found theatre in darkness; actual première took place 3 days later. Ballet score is also performed as concert suite.

**related,** term describing harmonic relationship between keys. Thus D major and A major are closely related, because latter is dominant of former and there is difference of only one sharp between key-signatures. On the other hand, relationship between B major and E flat major is more distant, and thus modulation between them would be harder to achieve.

**relative major, relative minor,** *see* KEY (3).

**Reményi, Eduard** (1830–98), Hungarian violinist, whose real name was Hoffman. Fled to US after taking part in 1848 Revolution. Toured Germany with Brahms (1852–53), introducing him to Hungarian gypsy music. Became friend of Liszt in Weimar, and was appointed violinist to Queen Victoria (1854) and at Austrian court (1860). Gave many concerts and made world tour in 1887. Composed violin concerto and other works for violin.

**Renaissance music,** term flexibly used to refer to music composed from about the middle of the 15th cent. to the end of the 16th cent. The word 'Renaissance' referred particularly to the revival of the ideas of antiquity, but in music this aspect did not become important until towards the end of the period, mainly because of the lack of examples of Greek music.

The beginning of the Renaissance period in music saw Dufay at the height of his career, and Ockeghem and Busnois at the threshold of their creative lives. It was marked by some important changes, for example: the replacement of isolated settings of individual Mass movements by cyclic settings of the 5-section Ordinary of the Mass unified by a single tenor melody, or by common headmotifs, or both; the abandonment of ISORHYTHM and other medieval structures in MOTET composition in favour of free forms which took their inspiration from the text, itself no longer tied to the liturgy; the disappearance of the old FORMES FIXES in song writing, again in the interests of greater freedom and flexibility, and a shift in emphasis from courtly to popular types of song. Associated with these changes was a move away from successive composition (the medieval tendency to work out one voice at a time) to a simultaneous method of composition. The central sonority became a 4-part texture with each part corresponding to one of the 4 principal ranges of the human voice. Mixtures of voices and instruments were eschewed in the writing (though not necessarily the performance) of music in favour of a homogenous texture, which displayed a steadily evolving feeling for harmony.

In the forefront of these developments were the composers of the Flemish School, and their successors, Obrecht, La Rue, and above all Josquin des Prés. Josquin and his generation refined the technique of imitation, which became the established method of polyphonic writing in the first half of the 16th cent., whether on original or derived themes (*see* PARODY MASS), and caused the method of *cantus firmus* treatment to be regarded as old-fashioned.

The chief characteristic of imitative polyphony was the direct relation of the themes to the words, which, in the secular forms, was carried further into details of word-painting and word-symbolism (*see* MADRIGAL). In conformity with the more expressive treatment of words the melodic style of Renaissance music was less florid than that of the 15th cent., the rhythms were simpler and more controlled, and the use of dissonance was more clearly regulated. Other accomplishments of the early 16th cent. were the emergence of instrumental music and writings about instruments (*see* SCHLICK, VIRDUNG), and the displacement of the modes by major and minor.

Attempts to revive the musical practices of antiquity were a feature of the latter part of the Renaissance. Notable were the experiments in relating poetic metres to musical rhythm, as in the odes of Tritonius and in MUSIQUE MESURÉE À L'ANTIQUE, in what was conceived to be the modern equivalent of Greek tragedy; and in the theory and practice of chromatic and enharmonic intervals, as in the writings of Vicentino and Zarlino and in Luython's chromatic harpsichord. More far reaching, however, was the criticism of the polyphonic style by Galilei and others, and the appearance of MONODY, which, though founded on a false Renaissance concept of the nature of Greek music, and allied to the lute-songs of the 16th cent., became one of the chief embodiments of the baroque style. Other late Renaissance styles which were maintained and developed in the early baroque period were the divided-choir style (*see* CORI SPEZZATI), the styles of the keyboard toccata, fantasia and variations, of the homophonic dance-piece, and of the English fantasia for viols.

**Renard,** burlesque by Stravinsky, to text by composer adapted from Russian folk tales about fox, cock, cat and goat (or ram). First perf. by Russian Opéra, Paris, 1922.

**Rencontre imprévue, La** (Fr., *The Unforeseen Encounter*), comic opera by Gluck, libretto by L.H. Dancourt (from earlier French *vaudeville* by Lesage and d'Orneval). First perf. Vienna, 1764. German version entitled *Die Pilger von Mekka* (*The Pilgrims from Mecca*) was first perf. Frankfurt, 1771.

**Re Pastore, Il** (It., *The King as Shepherd*), (1) opera by Gluck, libretto by Metastasio. First perf. Vienna, 1756.

(2) *opera seria* by Mozart, to same libretto. First perf. Salzburg, 1775. Metastasio's story was set to music by at least 12 composers.

**repeat,** exact restatement of section of composition. Passage to be repeated is indicated by sign

||:

at beginning and sign

:||

at end (repeat marks); former is omitted if repeat is from very beginning of composition or movement. Repeat of 1st section after middle section, as in aria and minuet and trio, is marked *Da capo* (from the beginning); repeat from sign

𝄋

in such a case is marked *Dal segno* (from the sign). Repeats of exposition in music in sonata form should be observed, as they are often of structural importance. *See also* CLOS.

**repercussio,** *see* RECITING NOTE.

**répétiteur** (Fr.; Ger., *Repetitor*; It., *repetitore*), coach, generally in opera house, who teaches singers their parts.

**répétition** (Fr.), rehearsal. *Répétition generale,* dress rehearsal.

**replica** (It.), REPEAT.

**reports,** term used in England and Scotland in 17th cent. for entries in IMITATION, esp. in connection with psalm-tunes.

**reprise** (Fr.), (1) REPEAT;

(2) recapitulation (*see* SONATA FORM);

(3) recurrence of 1st section as latter part of 2nd section of BINARY FORM, as commonly in classical minuet.

**Requiem** (Fr., *messe des morts*; Ger., *Totenmesse*; It., *messa per i* *defunti*; Lat., *missa pro defunctis*), Mass for the dead in RC Church, so called from opening words, '*Requiem aeternam dona eis, Domine*' ('Lord, grant them eternal rest'). Normally consists of following sections:

(1) *Introit: 'Requiem aeternam'* (Grant them eternal rest);
(2) *Kyrie* (Lord, have mercy upon us);
(3) *Sequence: 'Dies irae'* (Day of wrath);
(4) *Offertorium: 'Domine Jesu'* (Lord Jesus Christ, King of glory);
(5) *Sanctus* (Holy, holy, holy);
(6) *Benedictus* (Blessed is he that cometh);
(7) *Agnus Dei* (O Lamb of God);
(8) *Communion: 'Lux aeterna'* (Light eternal shine on them).

To these may be added (at end) *Responsorium*: *'Libera me Domine'* (Deliver me, O Lord). *Gloria* and *Credo* of ordinary Mass are not included.

Notable settings have been made for soloists, chorus and orchestra by Mozart, Berlioz, Dvořák, Verdi and Fauré. Delius's Requiem is setting of text compiled from Nietzsche; Britten's *War Requiem* combines Latin text and poems by Wilfred Owen; Brahms's *German Requiem* is setting of passages from German Bible.

**Requiem Canticles,** Stravinsky's pocket requiem, composed for Princeton University in 1966, and scored for contralto, bass, chorus and orchestra. Stravinsky's last major work, it successfully compresses the whole spirit of a vast 19th-cent. Requiem into 15 minutes, using short passages from the Latin Requiem Mass.

**resin,** *see* ROSIN.

**resolution,** term used in harmony for process by which discord progresses to concord. *See also* HARMONY, SUSPENSION.

**resonance,** creation by vibrating body of vibrations in another body. Occurs in form of:

(1) *sympathetic vibrations* in such cases as tuning forks of same pitch;
(2) sung note acting on free strings of piano;
(3) stopped string on violin acting on open string of same pitch;
(4) overtones of vibrating string on piano acting on corresponding higher strings when sustaining pedal is held down.

In wind instrument played with reed, vibrating column of air which determines pitch causes reed to vibrate in its period. Resonance occurs in form of *forced vibrations* in sounding board of piano and belly of violin, which do not naturally vibrate in same period as notes of strings.

**Respighi, Ottorino** (1879–1936), Italian composer. Became leading viola in opera orchestra at St Petersburg, and there studied composition and orchestration with Rimsky-Korsakov. Taught composition in Rome, becoming director of Conservatorio Regio in 1923. As composer, had considerable talent but lacked decided musical personality. Nevertheless, some of his orchestral works are so strikingly written and so colourful that they have remained in repertory. These incl. suites *The Fountains of Rome* and *The Pines of Rome*. His numerous effective arrangements incl. *La Boutique Fantasque* (*The Fantastic Toyshop* – ballet music based on Rossini), *The Birds* (bird pieces by old masters), and *Ancient Airs and Dances for Lute.* Also wrote 9 operas *eg La Fiamma,* tone poems and other orchestral works, concertos, chamber and choral music, and songs.

**respond, responsory,** plainsong chant sung by chorus alternating with one or more solo verses. Used *eg* between lessons at Matins and for Gradual and Alleluia in Mass.

**rest** (Fr., *pause*; Ger., *Pause*; It., *pausa*), a silence. For notation of rests of different lengths, *see* CROTCHET, QUAVER *etc.*

**resultant tone,** *see* COMBINATION TONE.

**'Resurrection' Symphony,** nickname for Mahler's symphony no 2 (1894), which ends with choral setting of Klopstock's poem *Auferstehen* ('Resurrection').

His brother, **Jean** or **Jan Mieczyslaw de Reszke** (1850–1925), was operatic tenor (orig. baritone). Appeared in Venice, London, Paris and Madrid.

**retardation,** SUSPENSION in which dissonant note is resolved upwards rather than downwards.

**retenu** (Fr.), held back (with reference to speed).

**Reti, Rudolph** (1885–1957), Serbo-Austrian critic, composer, pianist, who became US citizen. A champion of modern music, he was a founder of International Society for Contemporary Music in 1922. His theories about thematic unity, expounded in *The Thematic Process in Music* (1950), have come to seem increasingly valuable. Also wrote *Tonality, Atonality and Pantonality* (1958). Compositions incl. opera *Ivan and the Drum* (after Tolstoy), opera-ballet *David and Goliath,* orchestral and choral music, and songs.

**retrograde motion** (It., *al rovescio*; Lat., *cancrizans, per recte et retro*), use of retrograde, *ie* backwards, motion has been applied in composition both to melodies (melody is played backwards), as contrapuntal device, and to entire textures, as formal device. Special kind of retrograde motion, combined with inversion, is produced when music is performed with page turned upside down.

**returning note,** cambiata in which movement is back to original note. *See* CAMBIATA (2).

**Return of Lemminkäinen, The,** *see* LEGENDS.

**Reubke, Julius** (1834–58), German pianist, composer. Pupil of Liszt. Known only for programme-sonata for organ, *The Ninety-fourth Psalm,* published posthumously, as were some piano pieces and songs.

**Reusner, Esajas** (1636–79), German lutenist, composer. Composed 3 books of dance suites for lute, and published several books of lute arrangements.

**Reutlingen, Hugo von,** *see* HUGO VON REUTLINGEN.

**Reutter, Hermann** (1900– ), German composer, pianist. Works incl. operas, ballet, choral, chamber and piano music, and songs.

**Reutter, Johann Adam Karl Georg** (1708–72), Austrian composer. Ennobled in 1740, becoming von Reutter. *Kapellmeister* at St

Stephen's when Haydn was choirboy there, but took little interest in Haydn's efforts at composition and expelled him from choir-school in 1749. Composed symphonies, *c* 40 operas, 80 Masses, 6 Requiems, and 120 motets.

**'Revolutionary' Etude,** nickname for Chopin's étude in C minor, op 10, no 12 (1831). Music is believed to represent Chopin's patriotic feelings on hearing that Russians had invaded Warsaw.

**Revueltas, Silvestre** (1899–1940), Mexican composer, violinist, pianist. Worked for Republicans during Spanish Civil War. Works, strongly Mexican in character, incl. symphonic poems, string quartets, songs, and numerous film scores.

**Reyer, Ernest,** pseud. of Louis Ernest Etienne Rey (1823–1909), French composer, critic. Friend of Gautier, Flaubert and Méry, who provided texts for his compositions. He was staunch Wagnerian. Works incl. operas *eg Sigurd* (1884) and *Salammbô* (1890), ballet-pantomime, choral music, and songs.

**Rezitativ** (Ger.), recitative.

**Rezniček, Emil Nikolaus von** (1860–1945), Austrian composer, conductor. Settled in Germany. Remembered mainly for vivacious overture to opera *Donna Diana*. Numerous other operas incl. *The Maid of Orleans* (after Schiller) and *Till Eulenspiegel*. Also composed 4 symphonies, choral, chamber and keyboard music, and songs.

**rf, rfz,** abbrevs. of RINFORZANDO.

**r.h.,** right hand.

**rhapsody,** title given by 19th, 20th-cent. composers to instrumental works of heroic, national, or rhetorical character.

**Rhapsody in Blue,** work for piano and orchestra by Gershwin. First perf. New York, 1924, with composer as soloist. First important 'concert' work to bridge gap between jazz band and symphony orchestra. Orchestrated by F. Grofé.

**Rhau** or **Rhaw, Georg** (1488–1548), German composer, publisher. Published many of early collections of Lutheran church music. Also wrote handbook of elementary theory, *Enchiridion utriusque musicae practicae*.

**Rheinberger, Joseph Gabriel** (1839–1901), Liechtenstein-born organist, composer. Appointed to post as organist at age of 7. Studied at Munich Royal Conservatorium, where he taught from 1859 almost continually till his death. Composed operas, orchestral, choral and church music, 2 organ concertos, 20 sonatas and other works for organ, piano pieces, and songs.

**Rheingold, Das,** *see* RING DES NIBELUNGEN.

**Rheinische Sinfonie,** *see* RHENISH SYMPHONY.

**Rhené-Baton,** pseud. of René Baton (1879–1940), French conductor, composer. Worked at Opéra-Comique and conducted Concerts Pasdeloup (1918–32). Composed lyric drama, ballet, orchestral and piano music, and songs.

**'Rhenish' Symphony** (Ger., *Rheinische Sinfonie*), name given to Schumann's symphony no 3 in E, op 97 (1850), which incorporated impressions he received on visit to Cologne.

**Rhine Gold, The,** *see* RING DES NIBELUNGEN.

**rhythm,** organization of music in respect to time. Rhythm may be:

(1) free, as in some types of Oriental music;

(2) flexible, as in plainsong, where each note is regarded as having approximately same length;

(3) measured, either in RHYTHMIC MODES as in 11th–12th cents., or in complete system of duple and triple note-values, as in MENSURAL NOTATION of 13th–16th cents.;

(4) metrical, *ie* accentual, as from 16th cent. to present.

Within each of these systems, rhythmic character of phrase, period, section or movement of composition is fundamental element in its style, and also chief criterion of distinctions of style, *eg* between movements, or between themes within movement, in symphony and sonata.

*See* ACCENT, BAR, METRE, SYNCOPATION, TIME SIGNATURE.

**rhythmic modes,** term mode had rhythmic meaning in notation of *c* 1150–*c* 1250, and denoted rhythmic pattern used more or less consistently in each part of polyphonic composition. These patterns were arrangements of long and breve (extended in later MENSURAL NOTATION to incl. semibreves and minims) used in various combinations referred to as Modes I to VI.

**rhythmicon,** electrical instrument incorporating photo-electric cell invented by Léon THÉRÉMIN and Henry Cowell. Although possessing keyboard it is concerned not with pitch but with producing cross-rhythms, esp. complex ones. Has character, therefore, of percussion instrument.

**ribeca, ribibe, ribible,** *see* REBEC.

**ributhe,** Scottish form of JEW'S HARP.

**Riccardo I, Re d'Inghilterra** (It., *Richard I, King of England*), opera by Handel, libretto by P.A. Rolli. First perf. London, 1727.

**Ricci, Luigi** (1805–59), Italian composer. Pupil of Zingarelli. Conducted opera at Trieste and directed music at cathedral. Composed *c* 30 operas, some with brother **Federico Ricci** (1809–77); most successful collaboration was in comic opera *Crispino e la Comare* (1850).

**Riccio, Antonio Teodoro** (*c* 1540–*c* 1603), Italian composer. Held posts in Breccia, Ansbach and Königsberg. Composed Masses, motets, Magnificats, madrigals and *Canzone alla napolitana.*

**ricercar** (It., from *ricercare,* to seek out), term used in general sense of essay or study as title of certain instrumental compositions in 16th, 17th cents. Many are in imitative polyphony. Ricercar is based on one or more themes of rather abstract character, is usually in 4/2 time, and is not clearly distinguishable in style from contrapuntal FANTASIA (term preferred by German composers till late 17th cent.). Later ricercars on one theme are fugues, which is sense in which Bach uses term. Alternative name is *ricercata.*

**Richafort, Jean** (*c* 1480–*c* 1547), Flemish composer. Pupil of Josquin des Prés. Composed Requiem, Masses, motets and *chansons.* Willaert wrote Mass on his motet 'Christus resurgens'.

**Richard Coeur-de-Lion,** opera by Grétry, libretto by J.M. Sedaine. First perf. Paris, 1784. Beethoven composed set of piano variations on song from it.

**Richardson,** orig. **Heyborne, Ferdinando** (*c* 1558–1618), English composer, poet. Pupil of Tallis. Groom of Privy Chamber (1587–1611). Works incl. 2 pavanes and 2 galliards, each with variation, in *Fitzwilliam Virginal Book*.

**Richter, Ernst Friedrich Eduard** (1808–79), German theorist, organist, composer. Books incl. *Harmony, Simple and Double Counterpoint* and *Fugue*. Composed church, chamber and organ music, and songs.

**Richter, Franz Xaver** (1709–89), Moravian composer, violinist, singer. Leading member of group of composers connected with Mannheim orchestra whose work contributed much to early history of symphony. Works incl. 69 symphonies, 6 harpsichord concertos with string orchestra, 12 trio sonatas for 2 violins and continuo and other chamber music, 28 Masses, 2 Requiems, motets, and other church music.

**Richter, Hans** (1843–1916), Austro-Hungarian conductor. Worked with Wagner preparing score of *The Mastersingers* and *The Ring* for publication. Conducted first perf. of latter (Bayreuth, 1876). One of great conductors of his age, did much to improve performing standards and to further knowledge of Wagner's works. Conducted Hallé Orchestra, Manchester (1900–11).

**Richter, Sviatoslav** (1914– ), Russian pianist. One of most outstanding musicians of USSR. Esp. associated with Beethoven and Schubert. Has often appeared in recitals with cellist Rostropovich. Prokofiev's 9th piano sonata was dedicated to him.

**ricochet** (Fr., *jeté*), kind of bowing in which upper part of bow is thrown on strings, producing rapid series of bouncing notes on down-bow.

**riddle canon,** canon in which composer deliberately supplies only one part, leaving it to performer to decide where and at what pitch other parts enter.

**'Rider' Quartet,** *see* 'HORSEMAN' QUARTET.

**Riders to the Sea,** opera by Vaughan Williams, setting (nearly word-for-word) of Synge's play. First perf. London, 1937.

**Riegger, Wallingford** (1885–1961), American composer. Studied and conducted in Germany for some years. Composed numerous works for modern dancers incl. Martha Graham, symphonies and other orchestral works, and chamber music, incl. *Study in Sonority* for 10 violins.

**Riemann, Karl Wilhelm Julius Hugo** (1849–1919), German musicologist, theorist. Wrote many books on musical history and theory, and edited collections of music. Also wrote *Musiklexicon* (1882).

**Rienzi, der Letzte der Tribunen** (Ger., *Rienzi, the Last of the Tribunes*), opera by Wagner, libretto by composer (after Bulwer Lytton's novel about 14th-cent. patriot). First perf. Dresden, 1842.

**Ries, Ferdinand** (1784–1838), German pianist, composer, conductor. Member of family of musicians. Studied under Beethoven. Composed 3 operas, 2 oratorios, 6 symphonies, chamber music, and many works for piano.

**Riesco, Carlos** (1925– ), Chilean composer. Pupil of Copland, Diamond and Nadia Boulanger. Works, in which Latin-American idioms are discernible, incl. ballet *Candelaría,* violin concerto, and other orchestral music.

**Rieti, Vittorio** (1898– ), Italian composer, b. Egypt. Pupil of Respighi. Settled in US, 1939. Works incl. ballets (one on Robinson Crusoe), opera (on Lorca's play *Don Perimplin*), 5 symphonies, concertos, chamber music, and piano pieces.

**Rietz, Julius** (1812–77), German cellist, conductor, composer. Assistant conductor to Mendelssohn at Düsseldorf Opera in 1834, succeeding him in 1835. In Leipzig, was conductor of Opera and director of Gewandhaus Concerts. Worked in Dresden from 1860 as Court conductor and director of Conservatorium.

**rigaudon** (Fr.), **rigadoon** (Eng.), Provençal dance in lively 2/2 time. Adopted into suite and into ballet of French operas in late 17th cent.

**rigo** (It.), staff, stave.

**Rigoletto,** opera by Verdi, libretto by F.M. Piave (after Hugo's *Le Roi s'amuse*). First perf. Venice, 1851. Rigoletto is humpbacked court jester, who has his daughter killed in mistake for her lover, the Duke. Most famous aria is 'La donna è mobile'.

**Riisage, Knutåge** (1897–1974), Danish composer. Pupil of Roussel. Works incl. opera *Susanne,* 4 symphonies and other orchestral works, ballet, choral, chamber and piano music, and songs.

**Riley, Terry** (1935– ), American composer, saxophonist. Performs own works, which incl. *Poppy Nogood and the Phantom Band* for soprano saxophone, tape, time-lag and feedback system (1968). Music consists of constantly reiterated rhythms and phrases built up into large structures.

**Rimbault, Edward Francis** (1816–76), English musical historian, organist. Editor of Motet Society publications, edited many collections of early English music, and wrote books on music history.

**Rimsky-Korsakov, Nikolay Andreyevich** (1844–1908), Russian composer. Joined Navy at age of 12, and 5 years later met Balakirev, Cui and Mussorgsky, and began serious study of music under Balakirev. Appointed professor of composition at St Petersburg Conservatory in 1871, and director of New Free School of Music in 1874. Soon became leader of new group of composers incl. Liadov, Glazunov and Arensky. After performance of Wagner's *Ring* in St Petersburg in 1888, began to write for larger orchestra and to develop ideas on orchestration that were published in *Principles of Orchestration.* In 1902 met Stravinsky, who became his pupil. Showed sympathy with 1905 Revolution and was dismissed from Conservatory, but later reinstated. Element of satire on government in last work, opera based on Pushkin's *The Golden Cockerel* (1907), caused it to be banned till 1910.

Like other members of The FIVE, Rimsky-Korsakov was strongly influenced by national ideas in his early work. His later development acquired solid foundation through concentrated work on technical matters after 1871, work on collection of folk songs, and experience of editing Glinka's operas. After 1887–8, when he wrote his most mature orchestral pieces (*Spanish Capriccio, Sheherazade* and *Russian Easter Festival* overture), he re-orchestrated many earlier works, but concentrated on composition of operas – *Mlada* (1890), *Christmas Eve* (1895), *Sadko* (1896), *Czar Saltan* (1898), *Kitezh* (1904), and *The Golden Cockerel* – which are his greatest achievement. Also edited and arranged (some would now say disarranged) operas by other Russian composers, incl. Mussorgsky's *Boris Godunov* and Borodin's *Prince Igor*. His clear and brilliant orchestrations had marked effect on Stravinsky, and, through Stravinsky, on many contemporary composers.

**Rinaldo,** opera by Handel, libretto by G. Rossi (after Tasso's *Jerusalem Delivered*). First perf. London, 1711.

**Rinck, Johann Christian Heinrich** (1770–1846), German organist, composer. Wrote *Practical Organ School* and other organ works, and church and chamber music.

**rinforzando** (It.), lit. 'reinforcing', sudden strong accent on note or chord. More or less the same as *sforzando*. Abbrev. *rf, rfz,* or *rinf.*

**Ring des Nibelungen, Der** (Ger., *The Ring of the Nibelung*), cycle of 4 operas by Wagner, libretto by composer. Dedicated to Ludwig II of Bavaria. Described by him as 'festival drama for three days and a preliminary evening':

(1) *Das Rheingold* (The Rhine Gold), first perf. Munich, 1869;
(2) *Die Walküre* (The Valkyrie), first perf. Munich, 1870;
(3) *Siegfried,* first perf. Bayreuth, 1876;
(4) *Götterdämmerung* (Twilight of the Gods), first perf. Bayreuth, 1876.

Complete cycle first perf. Bayreuth, 13–17th Aug. 1876. Story is based on Nordic Nibelung saga: ring gives mastery of the world but at cost of renunciation of love. Work is most complete embodiment of Wagner's musical and ethical beliefs.

**Rio Grande, The,** work by Constant Lambert for piano, contralto, chorus and orchestra, to words by Sacheverell Sitwell. First perf. 1929. Work successfully incorporates jazz elements.

**ripieno** (It.), lit. 'full'. Term refers – esp. in baroque *concerto grosso* – to full body of orchestra, as distinct from soloist or group of soloists (*concertino*). *Senza ripieni* indicates that 1st desks only of accompanying orchestra are to play.

**Rippe, Albert de** or **Alberto da Ripa** or **Alberto Mantovano** (*c* 1500–51), Italian lutenist, one of most famous of his time. Spent most of career at court of Francis I of France. Lute compositions consist of *fantasies,* dances, and transcriptions of *chansons* and motets.

**ripresa** (It.), 'repeat': (1) REFRAIN in 14th cent. Italian BALLATTA; (2) in 16th cent., dance movt. for lute in form of variation;

(3) in later music, any REPEAT or recapitulation (*see* SONATA FORM).

**Rise and Fall of the City of Mahagonny, The** (Ger., *Aufstieg und Fall der Stadt Mahagonny*), opera by Kurt Weill, libretto by Bertolt Brecht. First perf. Leipzig, 1930. Work is ferocious political satire on capitalist morality. Earlier, simpler version first perf. Baden-Baden, 1927.

**risoluto** (It.), in a resolute manner.

**rispetto,** Italian improvised folk-poem with inter-rhyming lines, sung to popular tunes.

**risposta** (It.), (1) answer in FUGUE or IMITATION;
(2) COMES in canon.

**risvegliato** (It.), in an animated (or re-animated) manner.

**ritardando** (It.), becoming gradually slower – equivalent of *rallentando*. Abbrev. *rit.*

**ritenuto** (It.), held back in tempo, *ie* slower, though sometimes used as equivalent of *ritardando*.

**Rite of Spring, The** (Fr., *Le Sacre du printemps*), ballet with music by Stravinsky. First perf. Paris, 1913 – when uncompromising ferocity of music's grinding discords and rhythms caused riot.

**ritmo** (It.), rhythm. *Ritmo di tre battute* means that music is to be performed in groups of 3 bars – *ie* tempo is so fast that there is only 1 beat per bar, and each group of 3 bars forms rhythmical unit. Similarly, *ritmo di quattro battute* refers to group of 4 bars.

**ritornello** (It.), 'return': (1) passage for full orchestra in concerto, during which soloist is silent;
(2) last section of 14th-cent. Italian MADRIGAL which is thus conclusion, not return;
(3) instrumental piece in early opera;
(4) orchestral prelude, interludes and postlude in 17th, 18th-cent. aria, and recurrences of *tutti* theme in main movts. of baroque *concerto grosso.* In both cases intermediate *ritornelli* are in closely related keys and final one is in tonic;
(5) interlude for instrumental ensemble played after each verse of 17th-cent. German songs.

**Ritorno d'ulisse in Patria, Il** (It., *The Return of Ulysses to his Fatherland*), opera by Monteverdi, libretto by G. Badoaro. First perf. Venice, 1641. Modern arrangements have been made by Dallapiccola and Raymond Leppard.

**Rittquartett** (Ger.), Haydn's 'HORSEMAN' QUARTET.

**Rivier, Jean** (1896– ), French composer. Prolific in output and accessible in idiom. Works incl. 7 symphonies, concertos, chamber music, and songs.

**Roberday, François** (1624–80), French composer. Attached to courts of Queen Anne of Austria and Queen Marie-Thérèse. Was one of teachers of Lully, and organist at Church of the Petits-pères in Paris. Published *Fugues et caprices* for organ (1660).

**Robert le Diable** (Fr., *Robert the Devil*), opera by Meyerbeer, libretto by A.E. Scribe. First perf. Paris, 1831. Hero is Robert, Duke of Normandy, son of mortal and devil.

**Robeson, Paul** (1898–1976), black American bass, actor. World-renowned for performances of Negro songs and spirituals.

**Rochberg, George** (1918– ), American composer. Works, some using serialism, incl. 4 symphonies, violin concerto, *Imago Mundi* and other orchestral music, and vocal, chamber and piano music.

**rock music,** form of popular music originating in mid-1950s. Derives in part from American rhythm and blues, gospel, and country and western music. Early exponents incl. Bill Haley, Elvis Presley, Chuck Berry (rock-and-roll). Status of rock music as vehicle for artistic expression was enhanced by such performers as the Beatles, Rolling Stones and Bob Dylan in mid-1960s. Modern rock music has absorbed such influences as Eastern music, jazz, electronic and classical music.

**rococo,** *see* STYLE GALANT.

**Rode, Jacques Pierre Joseph** (1774–1830), French violinist, composer. Became court violinist at St Petersburg under Boïeldieu in 1803. Played Beethoven's sonata in G, op 96, for composer in Vienna. Works incl. studies, caprices, concertos and duets for violin, and quartets.

**Rodelinda,** opera by Handel, libretto by A. Salvi (altered by N.F. Haym). First perf. London, 1725.

**Rodeo,** ballet with music by Copland. First perf. New York, 1942. Action takes place in Wild West, and quotes traditional US songs. Later arranged as concert suite.

**Rodgers, Richard** (1902–80), American composer. Wrote successful musicals with Lorenz Hart as librettist, *eg Pal Joey,* then with Oscar Hammerstein II, *eg Oklahoma!* and *South Pacific.*

**Rodrigo, Joaquin** (1902– ), Spanish composer. Blind from age of 3. Pupil of Dukas. Has written number of sensitively written works of Spanish character, *eg Concerto de Aranjuez* for guitar and orchestra, and concertos for flute and cello.

**Rodzinski, Artur** (1892–1958), Polish-Yugoslav conductor. Emigrated to US, where conducted in Los Angeles, Cleveland, New York and Chicago.

**Roger-Ducasse, Jean Jules Amable** (1873–1954), French composer. Pupil of Fauré. Succeeded Dukas as teacher of composition at Paris Conservatoire in 1935. Composed opera *Cantegril,* mime-drama *Orphée,* orchestral, choral, chamber and piano music, and songs.

**Rogers, Bernard** (1893–1968), American composer. Pupil of Bloch, Frank Bridge and Nadia Boulanger. Composed 4 operas, 4 symphonies and other orchestral works, choral and chamber music, and songs.

**Rohrflöte** (Ger.; Fr., *flûte à cheminée*), 'chimney flute'. Organ stop of flute type; pipe is stopped at one end, but stopper is pierced by hole, in which metal tube or chimney is inserted.

**Rohrwerk** (Ger.), reed stops on organ.

**Roi de Lahore, Le** (Fr., *The King of Lahore*), opera by Massenet, libretto by L. Gallet. First perf. Paris, 1877. Story tells how King Alim is murdered by treacherous minister, but is allowed by gods to return to earth as beggar.

**Roi d'Ys, Le** (Fr., *The King of Ys*), opera by Lalo, libretto by E. Blau. First perf. Paris, 1888. Story is based on legend of submerged city off Breton coast – also the subject of Debussy's piano prelude, *La Cathédrale engloutie*.

**Roi l'a dit, Le** (Fr., *The King has said it*), opera by Delibes, libretto by E. Gondinet. First perf. Paris, 1873. Story concerns marquis who recruits peasant boy as his pretended son.

**Roi malgré lui, Le** (Fr., *The King in spite of himself*), opera by Chabrier, libretto by E. de Najac and P. Burani (after comedy by A. Ancelot). First perf. Paris, 1887.

**Roland,** opera by Lully, libretto by P. Quinault. First perf. Versailles, 1685.

**Roland-Manuel,** orig. Roland Alexis Manuel Lévy (1891–1966), French composer, writer on music. Pupil of Roussel and Ravel. Composed operas, ballets, and orchestral, chamber and film music. Wrote 3 books on Ravel.

**roll,** succession of notes on drum or other percussion instrument so rapid that it approximates to continuous sound.

**Rolland, Romain** (1866–1944), French writer, musical historian. Became president of musical division of Ecole des Hautes-Etudes Sociales in 1901, and lectured on musical history at Sorbonne (1903–13), then moved to Switzerland. Returned to France in 1938, and was put in concentration camp by Germans and only released when mortally ill. Books incl. valuable work on 17th-cent. opera, biographies of Handel and Beethoven, and studies of other composers. Subject of his 10-vol. novel *Jean-Christophe* (1904–12) is a musician.

**Rolle, Johann Heinrich** (1718–85), German composer, organist. In service of Frederick the Great (1741–6). Wrote 20 oratorios, set of cantatas, 5 Passions, motets, and organ works.

**Rolltrommel,** *see* TENOR DRUM.

**Roman, Johan Helmich** (1694–1758), Swedish composer. Pupil of Pepusch in London; influenced by Handel. Returned to Stockholm in 1720. Works incl. 21 symphonies, overtures, concertos, and church, vocal and chamber music.

**romance** (Ger., *Romanze*; It., *romanza*), title used occasionally – and somewhat vaguely – for lyrical piece of instrumental or vocal music.

**Roman de Fauvel** (Fr.), poem written 1310–14 by Gervais du Bus, attacking abuses prevalent in Church at the time. One of Mss of poem contains several musical pieces copied by Chaillou de Pesstain in 1316, consisting of motets (many adaptations of pieces written up to a century earlier), monophonic pieces, and plainsong pieces.

**romanesca,** particular harmonic bass line used as basis for variations (mid 16th–early 17th cent.) in same way as was PASSAMEZZO bass, which differs from *romanesca* only in first note.

**Romano, Alessandro,** *see* MERLO, ALESSANDRO.

**romantic music,** romantic era in music may be dated *c* 1820–*c* 1920. Broadly, change from classical age to romantic may be described as change of emphasis from universal to individual, from conservative to liberal, and from abstract to poetic.

In this period, music, because its language and symbols are more remote than those of other arts, was considered ideal of arts. Music and poetry were more closely allied, and union of arts became highest form of art. These ideas are clearly related to chief forms developed in 19th cent.: *Lied,* poetic piano-piece, symphonic poem, and music-drama.

Within broad unifying ideas of romantic music there developed such apparent contradictions as those between musician's growing remoteness from society, in that he regarded himself as essentially different from his fellows, and his closeness to it, expressed in use of folk song and national idioms and in development of virtuosos and public concerts; between 'modernist' and more conservative elements in movement itself, which led to controversy between supporters of 'New Music' of Liszt and Wagner, and supporters of Brahms; between cultivation of smaller and more intimate forms and creation of largest and most spectacular. Attitude of romantic musician to past, which was chiefly rejection of immediate past, sometimes took form of valuing it for its remoteness (*eg* use of exotic or medieval subjects for operas), adopting its methods (*eg* Brahms's use of fugue and variations), and investigating and publishing its productions.

Changes of style which took place in romantic period can be most clearly seen in (1) harmony, which went through very rapid development of chromaticism (valuable to romantic composer because of its ambiguity, sense of remoteness, and tension) to its extreme forms in *Tristan* and in writing of Strauss and Schoenberg between 1900 and 1910; (2) orchestra, which grew rapidly from Berlioz's new conception of its possibilities of dramatic and poetic expression to monster orchestras of 1900–10 used by Strauss, Schoenberg and Mahler; (3) technique of instruments, which from invention of valve mechanism in 1813 kept pace with development of chromatic harmony and growth of orchestra; extension of capacities of piano and organ provided solo players with greatly increased power and range.

Also of importance were changes in (1) melodic style, which tended to become more lyrical in small forms and more rhetorical in large, (2) in rhythmic style, which sometimes tended to become more diffused by use of conflicting metres and rubato, and (3) in form, in which romantic composers aimed at greater continuity of texture, more 'organic' unfolding and development of themes, and closer relation to programme in symphonic poem or to dramatic conflict in music-drama.

**Romanze, romanza,** *see* ROMANCE.

**Romberg, Andreas Jakob** (1767–1821), German violinist, composer. Composed operas, choral works, symphonies, numerous violin concertos, string quartets and other chamber music, part-songs, and pieces for violin.

His cousin **Bernhard Romberg** (1767–1841), was cellist and composer. Performed internationally. Composed operas, 10 cello concertos and other cello works, and incidental and chamber music.

**Romberg, Sigmund** (1887–1951), Hungarian-born composer. Settled in US, 1909. Wrote successful operettas incl. *The Student Prince, The Desert Song* and *New Moon*.

**Romeo and Juliet,** works based on Shakespeare's tragedy incl.:

(1) dramatic symphony for soloists, chorus and orchestra by Berlioz, op 17 (1839) – dedicated to Paganini;

(2) opera by Gounod, libretto by Barbier and Carré. First perf. Paris, 1867;

(3) orchestral piece by Chaikovsky, orig. (1869) described as 'overture'. Revised 1870 and 1880, and finally called 'overture-fantasia';

(4) ballet by Prokofiev. First perf. Moscow, 1935. Also arranged as 2 orchestral suites.

**Rome Prize,** *see* PRIX DE ROME.

**ronde** (Fr.), semibreve.

**rondeau** (Fr.), (1) form of medieval French poetry, written and set to music from 13th to 15th cents. Poems have refrain which occurs 2 or 3 times in single strophe. Music is composed in 2 sections, which serve for refrain and verses;

(2) form of French instrumental music in baroque period, in which opening section recurs after different sections called *couplets*.

**Rondes de Printemps,** *see* IMAGES.

**Rondine, La** (Fr., *The Swallow*), opera by Puccini, libretto by G. Adami (adapted from German of A.M. Willner and H. Reichert). First perf. Monte Carlo, 1917. In this lyric comedy, Puccini attempted to write Italian equivalent of Viennese operetta. Story is reminiscent of *La Traviata* (though heroine does not suffer from consumption).

**rondo,** form of instrumental music with recurring section. May occur as single piece, or more often as last movt. of sonata, symphony or concerto. Chief varieties of form are: (a) simple rondo, in which opening section alternates with number of different sections ('episodes'), in form *ABACADA* . . . , (b) symmetrical rondo, in which 1st episode, initially in dominant, returns at later stage in tonic. In this variety, as in sonata-rondo, there are commonly transitions between sections and coda, and recurring section is varied and shortened, though always in tonic key; (c) sonata-rondo, having 3 sections, corresponding to exposition, development and recapitulation of SONATA FORM, and 2 episodes, of which 1st returns in dominant and 2nd is actually development. Variety of (b) and (c) is short-circuited rondo, in which 3rd appearance of *A* is omitted, so that form is *ABACBA*.

**Ronger, Florimond,** *see* HERVÉ.

**Röntgen, Julius** (1855–1932), German composer of Dutch descent.

In 1885 helped found new Amsterdam Conservatory, which he directed (1918–24). Friend of Brahms and Grieg. Compositions incl. 2 operas, symphony, concertos for piano and violin, chamber music, and arrangements of Dutch folk songs.

**root,** 'fundamental' or 'generating' note of chord. Thus chords C-E-G and E-G-C have same 'root' C; former is said to be in root position, *ie* having root in lowest part, and latter is first inversion. *See* CHORD, HARMONY.

**Rootham, Cyril Bradley** (1875–1938), English organist, composer. Pupil of Stanford. Composed opera *The Two Sisters* (1922), 2 symphonies, choral, chamber and instrumental music, and songs.

**Ropartz, [Joseph] Guy [Marie]** (1864–1955), French composer. Pupil of Massenet and Franck. Works incl. 5 symphonies, 2 operas, chamber, instrumental, choral and incidental music, and songs.

**Rore, Cipriano de** (1516–65), Flemish composer. Studied under Willaert in Italy, where held various church and court posts. Published 5 books of 5-part and 3 books of 4-part madrigals, motets, Masses, St John Passion (1557) and other church music, and volume of 3-part fantasias and *ricercari* (with Willaert, 1549). Greatest madrigal writer of his time: established 5-part madrigal in imitative polyphony as norm, and after 1550 added to his style expressive chromaticism and harmonic experiments which were developed by later composers *eg* Marenzio and Gesualdo.

**Rorem, Ned** (1923– ), American composer, author. Pupil of Copland and Virgil Thompson. Works incl. several operas *eg Miss Julie* (after Strindberg, 1964), song cycles, 3 symphonies and other orchestral music, 3 piano concertos, *Paris Journal* and *Letters from Paris* for chorus and orchestra. Numerous songs have so far been most successful side of his output.

**Rosamunde, Fürstin von Cypern** (Ger., *Rosamund, Princess of Cyprus*), play by H. von Chézy, with incidental music by Schubert. First perf. Vienna, 1823. Overture played then had in fact been written for *Alfonso and Estrella.* Overture now known as *Rosamunde* was orig. overture to *The Magic Harp* (1820), and was published in piano duet arrangement under title *Ouvertüre zum Drama Rosamunde* (*c* 1827). Rest of music consists of 3 entr'actes, 2 ballet movts., and various vocal numbers. Some authorities believe that B minor entr'acte is 'lost' finale of *'Unfinished' Symphony*.

**Rosbaud, Hans** (1895–1962), Austrian conductor. Famous for performances of 20th-cent. music. Gave première (in concert version) of Schoenberg's *Moses and Aaron* at few days' notice (Hamburg, 1954).

**Roseingrave, Daniel** (*c* 1650–1727), English organist, composer. Wrote services, anthems and other church music.

His son, **Ralph Roseingrave** (1695–1747), was also organist and composer. Wrote services and anthems.

Ralph's brother, **Thomas Roseingrave** (1690–1766), was also organist and composer. Travelled to Italy in 1710 and became friend of Domenico Scarlatti. Subsequently lived in London then Dublin.

Composed opera, 6 Italian cantatas, services and other church music, *Fifteen Voluntarys and Fugues* for organ or harpsichord, lessons for harpsichord or spinet, pieces for German flute with continuo, and additional songs for Scarlatti's opera *Narciso,* which he produced in London (1720). Edited collection of sonatas by Scarlatti.

**Rosenberg, Hilding** (1892– ), Swedish composer, conductor. Works incl. series of dramatic oratorios based on Thomas Mann's *Joseph and his Brethren,* 6 symphonies (no 4 is oratorio-symphony entitled *The Revelation of St John*), concertos, 12 string quartets (showing influence of Schoenberg school), instrumental pieces, and witty ballet music *Orpheus in Town.*

**Rosenkavalier, Der** (Ger., *The Knight of the Rose*), opera by Richard Strauss, libretto by Hugo von Hofmannsthal. First perf. Dresden, 1911. Story concerns Marschallin and her lover Octavian, who is chosen by Baron Ochs to present rose (as betrothal token) to Sophie. Octavian falls in love with Sophie, Ochs is ridiculed, and Marschallin blesses match, being resigned to her loss.

**Rosenmüller, Johann** (*c* 1620–84), German composer. One of most important composers of Lutheran church music between Schütz and Buxtehude. Works incl. Masses, Latin and German motets with instruments and continuo, cantatas, psalms, and sonatas and dance suites for instruments.

**Rosenthal, Manuel** (1904– ), French composer, conductor. Pupil of Ravel, from whose style his music derives. Compositions incl. operas and operettas, oratorio *St Francis of Assisi,* symphonic suite *Joan of Arc* and other orchestral music, songs, and piano pieces. Has orchestrated some of Ravel's music.

**rosin,** hard brittle resin, applied to bows of violin family to increase friction (and hence sonority) between hairs of bow and strings.

**Roslavetz, Nikolay Andreivich** (1881–1944), Russian composer. Notable for his forward-looking style, he wrote cantata *Heaven and Earth* (after Byron), symphony, 2 symphonic poems, chamber and piano music, and songs.

**Rosseter, Philip** (1570–1623), English composer. Published *A Book of Ayres* (1601) with Thomas Campion, to which he contributed 21 lute songs. His *Lessons for Consort* (1609) is collection of settings of pieces by various authors.

**Rossi, Luigi** (*c* 1598–1653), Italian composer. Wrote numerous cantatas in monodic style. Also wrote *Orfeo,* first Italian opera commissioned for Paris (1647) though not first to be played there.

**Rossi, Michelangelo** (*fl* early 17th cent.), Italian organist, composer. Pupil of Frescobaldi. Composed operas incl. *Erminia sul Giordano* (1633), and book of *Toccate e Corrente* for organ or harpsichord.

**Rossi, Salomone** (*c* 1570–*c* 1630), Jewish composer. At court of Mantua (1587–1628). Published 5 books of 5-part madrigals (1600–22) – 2nd is earliest book of madrigals with continuo part. Modernist outlook is also seen in his early use of trio sonata in 2 vols. of *Sinfonie e gagliarde* for 3 to 5 instruments. Also wrote vocal music for synagogue.

**Rossini, Gioacchino Antonio** (1792–1868), Italian composer. Son of musical parents. Studied at Liceo Musicale in Bologna. Produced 1st comic opera, *La cambiole di matrimonio* in 1810, and 1st *opera seria, Tancredi*, in 1813, both in Venice. Under title *Almaviva,* his *Il barbiere di Siviglia (The Barber of Seville)* had unfortunate 1st night in Rome (1816), but later became his greatest triumph, and today still represents high watermark of *opera buffa.* Between 1816 and 1824, when he became director of Théâtre Italien in Paris, *Otello, Mosè in Egitto, La Cenerentola* and *Semiramide* were produced in Italy; in Paris were staged *Moïse* (rev. version of *Mosè in Egitto*), *Le Comte Ory* and *Guillaume Tell* (*William Tell,* his greatest work after *The Barber*). After success of *Guillaume Tell* in 1829, wrote no more operas. He had written 36 operas in 19 years, but during rest of life wrote only *Stabat Mater* (1842), *Petite messe solenelle* (1864), and numerous short pieces. Lived in Italy 1830–55, then settled in Paris. Compositions besides opera incl. cantatas, songs, piano pieces (*Péchés de vieillesse,* 1857–68), and 6 instrumental quartets.

**Rostropovich, Mstislav Leopoldovich** (1927– ), Russian cellist, pianist, conductor. One of most renowned performers of 20th cent. Studied and later taught at Moscow Conservatory. First played in West in 1951. Composers who have written works for him incl. Prokofiev, Shostakovich and Britten. Frequently appears as piano accompanist to wife, soprano Galina Vishnevskaya. As conductor has built up distinguished career at Bolshoi Theatre. Co-director of Aldeburgh Festival from 1977.

**rota,** (1) round (*see* CANON);
(2) *see* ROTE.

**Rota, Nino** (1911–79), Italian composer. Pupil of Pizzetti and Casella. Works incl. operas, music for broadcasting, orchestral, instrumental and church music, and songs. Film music incl. *The Legend of the Glass Mountain.*

**rotary valve,** special type of brass instrument valve. In Britain and US use is largely confined to horns, but equally common on trumpets on Continent.

**rote, rotte, rota** or **rotta,** medieval instrument of LYRE type, similar to CRWTH.

**Rouget de Lisle, Claude Joseph** (1760–1836), French royalist soldier, poet, violinist, composer. Wrote words and music of the *Marseillaise* (1792). Imprisoned during Revolution, but later released and re-entered army. Went on to write patriotic hymns, romances with violin obbligato, *Chants français* with piano, and libretti for operas.

**roulade,** ornamental vocal phrase, usually quite extended and traditionally (though not invariably) consisting of descending scale with intermediate notes rising by one degree.

**round,** *see* CANON.

**Rousseau, Jean-Jacques** (1712–78), French philosopher, composer, writer on music. His intermezzo *Le Devin du village* had immediate and lasting success, as did Favart's parody, *Bastien et Bastienne*

(German version set by Mozart). Other compositions incl. volume of songs. Took Italian side in *La Guerre des Bouffons*, though wrote pamphlets supporting Gluck. In 1743 proposed new system of musical notation. His articles on music in Diderot's *Encyclopédie* were severely criticized by Rameau, but his *Dictionnaire de musique* (1767) has valuable information on musical terminology and ideas of period.

**Roussel, Albert** (1869–1937), French composer. Served as marine officer in Indo-China (1887–93) then studied music under d'Indy at Schola Cantorum, Paris, where became teacher of counterpoint in 1902. Visit to Cochin China and India in 1909 inspired orchestral *Évocations* (1911) and opera-ballet *Padmâvati* (1914–18). In WWI, served with Red Cross, seriously damaging his health. Composed operas, ballets (incl. *Bacchus and Ariadne* and *The Spider's Banquet*), 4 symphonies, chamber music, piano pieces, and songs. Taking its departure from late romantic style of Franck and d'Indy, as in 1st symphony *(Le Poème de la forêt)* of 1908, his music developed through period of impressionism to mature and impressive writing of *Eightieth Psalm* for chorus and orchestra (1928) and 3rd symphony (1930).

**rovescio, al** (It.), 'in reverse':
(1) melodic INVERSION;
(2) RETROGRADE MOTION.

**Rowley, Alec** (1892–1958), English composer, pianist, organist, teacher. Works incl. 2 piano concertos, ballet, orchestral, choral, chamber and instrumental pieces, and songs, mostly in traditional British idiom.

**Roxolane, La,** name of Haydn's symphony no 63 in C (*c* 1780). Haydn himself applied name to slow movt., set of variations which owes name to heroine of play that had been recent success.

**Royal Philharmonic Orchestra,** one of London's 5 major orchestras, founded by Sir Thomas Beecham in 1946. In 1961 Rudolf Kempe succeeded Beecham as conductor. Since then conductors have been Antal Dorati and Walter Weller.

**Royal Philharmonic Society,** society for the encouragement of orchestral and instrumental music, founded in London, 1813. Title 'Royal' was granted on its centenary. Among those involved in early concerts were Clementi, Saloman and Spohr. Works commissioned by Society incl. Beethoven's 9th symphony, Mendelssohn's *Italian* symphony, Dvořák's *Husitzka* overture, and Saint-Saëns's symphony in C minor.

**Rozhdestvensky, Gennady** (1931– ), Russian conductor. Posts incl. USSR Radio and TV Orchestra (1960–65, 1970–74), Bolshoi Theatre (1965–70), Stockholm Philharmonic Orchestra from 1975 and B.B.C. Symphony Orchestra from 1978.

**Rózsa, Miklós** (1907– ), Hungarian-born composer. Settled in US, and worked in film industry from 1939. Works incl. *Ballet Hungarica,* symphony and other orchestral pieces, chamber music, and many film scores.

**rubato** (It.), lit. 'robbed'. Controlled flexibility of tempo, by which notes are deprived of part of their length by slight quickening of tempo, or given more than their strict length by slight slowing. Commonly applied to performance of 19th-cent. music.

**Rubbra, [Charles] Edmund** (1901– ), English composer. Pupil of Vaughan Williams and Holst. Lecturer in composition at Oxford (1947–68). As pianist, has directed own piano trio. Interest in 16th-cent. music has resulted in acute awareness of melody and in use of every kind of contrapuntal elaboration. Vocal music has been less successful than instrumental works. Orchestration, at first almost excessively austere, has shown greater interest in colour in later works. Compositions incl. 10 symphonies, concertos for viola and piano, *Festival Overture,* Masses, motets, madrigals, string quartets, piano trio sonatas, and songs.

**rubible,** *see* REBEC.

**Rubinstein, Anton Gregoryevich** (1821–94), Russian composer. Toured Europe as pianist. Settled in St Petersburg in 1858, where founded Conservatory and was its director (1862–7, 1887–90). As composer and teacher, represented traditional Western and anti-national ideas in Russian music. Adopted methods of Liszt in such works as 3 *Musical Portraits* for orchestra, but now known only for some songs and piano pieces *eg* Melody in F.

His brother, **Nicholas Rubinstein** (1835–81), was conductor and composer. Settled in Moscow, where founded Conservatory in 1866. Pupils incl. Taneyev. Introduced early works of Chaikovsky, who dedicated to him piano trio in A minor, op 50.

**Rubinstein, Artur** (1887– ), Polish-born pianist. Pupil of Paderewski. Made debut at age of 12 in concert conducted by Joachim in Berlin. Became US citizen in 1946. One of greatest pianists of his time; performances are notable for intelligence, warmth and exceptional clarity of line. Esp. associated with Chopin, Beethoven, Schubert, Schumann and Brahms.

**rubybe,** *see* REBEC.

**Ruckers,** famous family of harpsichord makers in Antwerp, active *c* 1580–1670.

**Ruddigore, or the Witch's Curse,** comic opera by Gilbert and Sullivan. First perf. London, 1887. Plot is parody of Victorian melodrama.

**Rue,** *see* LA RUE.

**Ruffo, Vincenzo** (*c* 1510–87), Italian composer. Published Masses, motets, Magnificats (1578) and 5-part psalms (1574) written 'in conformity with the decree of the Council of Trent'. His 9 books of madrigals, without reaching great depth of expression, have considerable variety of style, at times approaching later *canzonetta* in lightness of touch. Also published *Capricci in Musica* (1564), vol. of 3-part ensemble music.

**Rugby,** symphonic movt. by Honegger (1928) depicting game of rugby football.

**ruggiero,** internationally known ballad and dance tune of late 16th, early 17th cents. Bass was used as pattern for variations and for new melodies in same way as were PASSAMEZZO and ROMANESCA.

**Ruggles, Carl** (1876–1971), American composer, painter. Associate of Varèse. Developed fiercely dissonant and personal idiom, with leanings towards Schoenberg. With Ives, one of most important questing figures of US music. Works incl. *Angels* for 7 muted trumpets and trombones, *Marching Mountains* for chamber orchestra (1924, rev. 1936), *Portals* for string orchestra (1926), *Suntreader* (1933) and *Organum* (1945) for orchestra, and *Vox Clamans in Deserto,* song-cycle for mezzo-soprano and chamber orchestra.

**Rührtrommel,** *see* TENOR DRUM.

**Ruins of Athens, The** (Ger., *Die Ruinen von Athen*), play by Kotzebue with incidental music by Beethoven, op 113, comprising overture and 8 pieces for chorus and orchestra. First perf. at opening of German Theatre at Pest, Hungary, 1812.

**Rule Britannia,** song with words prob. by James Thomson and music by Arne, first perf. in masque *Alfred* (1740). Generally sung today in garbled version.

**rule of the octave,** simple rule for harmonizing bass rising and descending stepwise through octave, used in teaching harmony in 18th cent.

**rumba,** fast Afro-Cuban dance in syncopated 2/4 time, often divided in 8 beats in pattern 3 + 3 + 2. Introduced into ballroom dancing and jazz in 1930s.

**Russian bassoon** (Fr., *basson russe*; Ger., *Russisches Fagott*), brass instrument with cup mouthpiece, unrelated to bassoon, which paved way for and was then ousted by OPHICLEIDE. Fingering was similar to that of SERPENT. Compass extended from about D below bass clef upwards for 2½ octaves, but many notes lacked quality and accuracy of pitch.

**Russian Easter Festival,** overture by Rimsky-Korsakov (1888); uses melodies associated with Russian Orthodox Church.

**Russian Quartets** (Ger., *Russische Quartette*), title given to set of 6 string quartets by Haydn, op 33 (1781), dedicated to Grand Duke Paul of Russia. Also called *Gli Scherzi* (as Haydn gave name *scherzo* to minuet movts.) or *Jungfernquartette* (*'Maiden Quartets'*). Set comprises no 1 in B minor, no 2 in E (*The Joke*), no 3 in C (*The Bird* or *Birds*), no 4 in B, no 5 in G (*How do you do?*), no 6 in D.

**Russlan and Ludmilla,** opera by Glinka, libretto by V. F. Shirkov and K. A. Bakhturin (after Pushkin's poem). First perf. St Petersburg, 1842.

**Rust, Wilhelm** (1822–92), German pianist, violinist, composer. Wrote vocal and piano music. Edited 18 vols. of *Bach Gesellschaft* and piano sonatas of grandfather, **Friedrich Wilhelm Rust** (1739–96), with additions of his own.

**Rustle of Spring,** piano piece (3rd of set of 6, 1909) by Sinding, his only work now widely played.

**Ruthe** (Ger.), kind of birch occasionally used on bass drum, often while ordinary stick beats on other head.

**Ruy Blas,** play by Hugo for which Mendelssohn composed overture (C minor, op 95) and 2-part song (1839).

**rybibe,** *see* REBEC.

**Rzewski, Frederic Anthony** (1938– ), American composer, pianist. Experimental compositions, often using tape and mixed media, are influenced by Stockhausen and John Cage.

# S

**s.,** abbrev. for (1) *soh,* in TONIC SOL-FA, fifth note (or dominant) of major scale;
(2) *superius,* highest part in 16th-cent. music;
(3) *segno,* as in *d.s., dal segno* (*see* REPEAT);
(4) *sinistra,* as in *m.s.* (in keyboard music), *mano sinistra,* left hand.

**S.,** abbrev. for SCHMIEDER in catalogue of Bach's works.

**Sabaneyev, Leonid Leonidovich** (1881– ), Russian music critic, writer, composer. Pupil of Taneyev. Left Russia in 1924. Works incl. *Modern Russian Composers* (1927), *Music for the Films* (1935), books on Wagner, Medtner and Skryabin, and a history of Russian music. Also composed songs and piano pieces.

**Sabata, Victor de** (1892–1967), Italian conductor, composer. Conducted at La Scala and elsewhere in Europe, and in US. Composed operas, ballet, and orchestral and chamber works.

**Sacchini, Antonio Maria Gasparo** (1730-86), Italian composer. Lived in Germany, London (1772–82) and Paris. Works incl. *c* 60 operas *eg Oedipe à Colone* (1786), 2 symphonies, church and chamber music, and harpsichord and violin sonatas.

**Sacher, Paul** (1906- ), Swiss conductor. Pupil of Weingartner. Founded Basel Chamber Orchestra in 1926, and became conductor of Collegium Musicum in Zurich from 1941. Has given many premières of modern works.

**Sachs, Hans** (1494–1576), German shoemaker, poet, composer. Most famous personality of 16th-cent. MEISTERSINGER. Hero of Wagner's opera *The Mastersingers of Nuremberg.*

**Sachs, Kurt** (1881–1959), German musicologist. Pupil of Fleischer, Kretzschmar and Wolf. After holding various posts in Berlin, became professor of musicology at New York University in 1938. Books incl. *The Rise of Music in the Ancient World* (1943), *History of Musical Instruments* (1943), *The Commonwealth of Art* (1946), and *Our Musical Heritage* (1948; published in Britain as *A Short History of World Music,* 1950).

**sackbut,** though often said to be merely early name for TROMBONE, sackbut was smaller in both bell and bore – so lighter in tone, and suitable for use in chamber music.

**Sackpfeife,** *see* BAGPIPE.

**Sacre du Printemps, Le,** *see* RITE OF SPRING.

**Sadie, Stanley** (1930– ), English critic, editor. Editor of *Musical Times* from 1967. Edited *New Grove Dictionary of Music* (6th ed., 1981).

**Sadko,** opera by Rimsky-Korsakov, libretto by composer and V.I. Belsky. First perf. Moscow, 1898. Also title of symphonic poem by same composer.

**Sadler's Wells,** London theatre dating from 17th cent. Reopened 1931, through efforts of Lilian Baylis, for opera, ballet and drama. Drama soon moved to Old Vic. Home of Sadler's Wells opera company till 1968; company changed name to English National Opera in 1974.

**Saeverud, Harald** (1897– ), Norwegian composer. Works incl. 9 symphonies and incidental music to Ibsen's *Peer Gynt* (1947). Most characteristic works are for piano: *Ballad of Revolt* and other aphoristic pieces have established him as one of leading Scandinavian composers of 20th cent.

**Saga, En** (Fin., *A Tale*), symphonic poem by Sibelius, op 9 (1892, rev. 1901). Composer's earliest work in form; has narrative quality, but no specific programme.

**Sagittarius, Henricus,** *see* SCHÜTZ.

**St Anne,** hymn-tune, prob. by Croft, published 1708. By coincidence, Fugue in E flat in Pt. III of Bach's *Clavierübung* has same theme, and so is known as 'St Anne' Fugue.

**'St Anthony' Variations,** work by Brahms; exists in 2 forms – for orchestra, op 56a, and for 2 pianos, op 56b. Based on theme called 'St Anthony' Chorale from partita for wind instruments by Haydn, who is thought to have borrowed it from someone else. Hence used to be called (incorrectly) 'Variations on a theme of Haydn'. First perf. 1873.

**St Cecilia,** *see* CECILIA, ST.

**Saint-Foix, Georges de** (1874–1954), French musicologist. Wrote famous study of Mozart in 5 vols. (first 2 in collaboration with Théodore de Wyzéwa).

**St John Passion,** accepted name for Bach's *Passion according to St John*. First perf. Leipzig, 1723. Scored for solo voices, chorus and orchestra. Text from Gospel of St John, with interpolations.

**St John's Night on the Bare Mountain,** *see* NIGHT ON THE BARE MOUNTAIN.

**St Martial School,** important school located in vicinity of Abbey of St Martial, Limoges, France, which produced sequences, tropes and *prosulae* in 10th and 11th cents., and polyphonic settings of sacred songs, sequences and Benidicamus *prosulae* in 12th cent. Latter employ style of both melismatic ORGANUM and note-for-note DISCANT, overlapping with repertory of NOTRE DAME School.

**St Matthew Passion,** accepted name for Bach's *Passion according to St Matthew*. First perf. Leipzig, 1729. Scored for solo voices, chorus and orchestra. On much grander scale than St John Passion. Text again incl. interpolations.

**St Nicolas,** cantata by Britten, op 43 (1948), text by Eric Crozier. Scored for tenor solo, mixed voices, string orchestra, piano duet, percussion and organ.

**Saint of Bleecker Street, The,** opera by Menotti, libretto by composer. First perf. New York, 1954. Work is religious melodrama set in New York's Italian quarter.

**St Paul** (Ger., *Paulus*), oratorio by Mendelssohn, op 36 (1836). Text from Bible.

**St Paul's Suite,** work for strings by Holst (1913), written for orchestra of St Paul's Girls School, London, where Holst was teacher of music.

**Saint-Saëns, Charles Camille** (1835–1921), French composer, pianist. Gave concert at age of 10. From 1848 studied composition (under Halévy) and organ at Conservatoire. Became organist at Madeleine in 1857. Influence of Liszt, whom he met in 1852, turned him towards 'cyclic' design in symphonies and concertos – 3rd symphony is based on single theme – and towards symphonic poem (*Le Rouet d'Omphale,* 1871, *Phaëton,* 1873, *Danse macabre,* 1874, *La Jeunesse d'Hercule,* 1877). Operas incl. *Le Timbre d'argent* (1864–5, perf. 1877) and *Samson et Dalila;* latter was refused by Paris Opera till 1892, but has proved his most lasting work. He was extremely prolific composer, but music, though meticulously crafted, suffers from superficiality and lack of adventurousness. His *Carnival of the Animals,* 'zoological fantasy' for 2 pianos and chamber ensemble, retains its wit and charm, and 2nd piano concerto in G minor remains popular with soloists.

**Saite** (Ger.), string. *Saiteninstrumente,* string instruments.

**salicional, salicet, salcional,** soft 8ft metal organ-stop producing tone bearing some resemblance to that of string instruments.

**Salieri, Antonio** (1750–1825), Italian composer, conductor and teacher. Lived in Vienna from 1766. Teacher of Beethoven, Schubert and Liszt. His intrigues against Mozart were inflated into story that he poisoned Mozart, used in dramatic poem by Pushkin (1830) which became libretto of Rimsky-Korsakov's opera *Mozart and Salieri* (1898). Works incl. *c* 40 operas, 4 oratorios, Passion, Masses and other church music, symphony, concertos for organ, 2 pianos and flute and oboe, and vocal pieces.

**Salinas, Francisco de** (1513–90), Spanish musical theorist, organist, blind from age of 10. Worked in Italy (1538–61). In theoretical treatise *De musica libri septem* (1577), expounded theories of Zarlino and quoted several Spanish folk songs.

**salmo** (It.), psalm.

**Salò** (orig. **di Bertolotti**), **Gasparo da** (1540–1609), Italian violin-maker, grandson of lute-maker Santino di Bertolotti. One of first to use form of violin instead of viol.

**Salome,** opera by Richard Strauss, setting of German translation of Oscar Wilde's French drama. First perf. Dresden, 1905. In early days caused scandal almost everywhere it was performed.

**Salomon, Johann Peter** (1745–1815), German-born violinist, composer, concert promoter. Settled in London where played symphonies by Haydn and Mozart in his concerts. Arranged Haydn's visits to England (1791–2, 1794–5); hence 12 symphonies written for those visits are known as 'Salomon' symphonies.

**Salón México, El,** orchestral work by Copland. First perf. Mexico

City, 1937. Music evokes Mexican dance hall, and incorporates folk song material.

**saltando,** *see* BOWING.

**saltarello** or **salterello** (It., from *saltare,* to jump), Italian dance in quick tempo, usually 6/8 with jumping effect in rhythm. In general, somewhat like jerky version of tarantella. Example survives from 14th cent. In 16th, early 17th cents. usually followed passamezzo. Used in finale of Mendelssohn's 'Italian' symphony.

**salterio** (It.), psaltery. *Salterio tedesco,* dulcimer.

**Salve Regina** (Lat.), 'hail, Queen'; antiphon to Virgin sung at end of Compline, last service of day, in Latin liturgy.

**Salzédo, Carlos** (1885–1961), French-born harpist, composer. Settled in US. With Varèse, founded International Composers' Guild (1921). Wrote works for harp solo and for harp with various combinations of instruments.

**Salzman, Eric** (1933– ), American composer, critic. Pupil of Sessions and Babbitt. Many of his works are for voice, instruments and prerecorded tape, incl. *Foxes and Hedgehogs* (1967), piece of music theatre with words by John Ashbery. Other works incl. Series of *Verses* (1967) for voice, guitar and multitrack tape, ballet *The Peloponnesian War* (1968), and *The Nude Paper Sermon* for speaker, Renaissance consort and electronics. Also wrote *Twentieth-Century Music: an Introduction* (1967).

**samba,** dance of Brazilian origin, basically in 2/4 time but with syncopated rhythmic patterns. Traditional form of carnival music in Brazil, where it is danced by groups forming circle. In ballroom, danced by couples at more moderate tempo.

**Saminsky, Lazare** (1882–1959), Russian-born composer, writer on music. Pupil of Rimsky-Korsakov and Glazunov. Settled in US (1920), where was cofounder of American League of Composers (1932). Works incl. 5 symphonies, symphonic poems, Requiem, opera-ballet *Jephtha's Daughter,* chamber, choral and piano music, and songs.

**Sammartini** or **San Martini, Giovanni Battista** (*c* 1698–1775), Italian composer, organist. Taught Gluck (1737–41). Prolific output (said to exceed 2,000 works) incl. operas, serenatas, more than 23 symphonies, overtures, church music, *concerti grossi,* chamber music, violin concertos and other works for violin. Most important Italian composer of symphonies of his day; his instrumental style contains notable foretastes of Haydn and Mozart.

His brother, **Giuseppe Sammartini** (1693–1750) was oboist and composer. Settled in London *c* 1727, and later became musical director of chamber concerts for Prince of Wales. Composed 12 *concerti grossi,* overtures, concertos for violin and for harpsichord, oratorio, trio sonatas and other chamber music, violin sonatas and flute solos and duets.

**Samson,** oratorio by Handel, text by N. Hamilton based on poems by Milton. First perf. London, 1743.

**Samson and Delilah** (Fr., *Samson et Dalila*), opera by Saint-Saëns, by F. Lemaire (after Bible). First perf. Weimar, 1877.

**San Carlo, Naples, Teatro di,** one of Italy's leading opera houses, built in 1737. Destroyed by fire in 1816, but rebuilt. Rossini wrote several operas for this theatre, and Donizetti his *Lucia di Lammermoor* (1835).

**Sances, Giovanni Felice** (*c* 1600–79), Italian composer, singer. Became *Kapellmeister* at Vienna Court Chapel (1669). Composed operas (one with Emperor Leopold I), oratorios, and monodies and duets with continuo.

**Sancta Civitas** (Lat., *The Holy City*), oratorio by Vaughan Williams for solo voices, chorus and orchestra, with text from Bible and other sources. First perf. Oxford, 1926.

**Sanctus** (Lat.), 'holy, holy'. Part of Ordinary of Mass and Communion Service. Text usually consists of *Sanctus, Pleni sunt coeli* and *Benedictus qui venit.*

**Sándor, György** (1912– ), Hungarian-born pianist, resident in US since 1939. Pupil of Kodály and Bartók, and specializes in performance of their piano music, and that of Prokofiev. Gave first perf. of Bartók's 3rd piano concerto (1946).

**Sandrin, Pierre,** orig. **Regnault** (d. after 1561), French composer. Worked in Paris, Ferrara and Sienna. Wrote 50 *chansons* and poss. one Italian madrigal. His 'Douce memoire' became one of most popular *chansons* of 16th cent.

**sanft** (Ger.), soft, gentle.

**San Martini,** *see* SAMMARTINI.

**Sappho** (Fr., *Sapho*), (1) opera by Gounod (revised several times), libretto by E. Augier. First perf. Paris, 1851. Gounod's first opera, written for prima donna Pauline Viardot, concerns the Greek poetess;

(2) opera by Massenet (1897), based on novel by Alphonse Daudet whose hero falls in love with artist's model of Sappho.

**sarabande** (Fr.), dance in slow 3/2 or 3/4 time, one of regular dances of SUITE. Orig. seems to have been introduced from East to Spain.

**Sarasate [y Navascues], Pablo Martín Melitón** (1844–1908), Spanish violinist, composer. Rapidly made reputation as soloist, and toured widely in Europe and US. Composed works for violin and transcriptions of Spanish dances.

**sardana** (Sp.), national dance of Catalonia, often in fast 6/8 time and performed in circle to pipe and drum accompaniment.

**Sargent, [Harold] Malcolm [Watts]** (1895–1967), English conductor, one of most popular of his day. Began career as organist, pianist (trained by Moiseiwitsch), and composer, but turned increasingly towards conducting, in which capacity was esp. associated with British music. Posts incl. conductor of Royal Choral Society (from 1928) and B.B.C. Symphony Orchestra (1951–7). For last 16 years of his life was conductor-in-chief of London Proms, winning enthusiasm of huge young audience. Knighted 1947.

**Sarro** or **Sarri, Domenico** (1678–1744), Italian composer. Works incl. *c* 50 operas, oratorios, cantatas, Masses and other church music, concerto for strings and flute, serenades, and arias. Set Metastasio's first libretto, *Dido abbandonata* (1724).

**sarrusophone,** family of double reed brass instruments with wide conical bore. Invented in later 19th cent. by French bandmaster called Sarrus. Constructed on basis of bassoon and has same fingering. Primarily intended for use in military bands as substitutes for oboes and bassoons.

**Sarti, Guiseppe** (1729–1802), Italian composer, conductor. Pupil of Martini. Worked in Italy, Denmark and Russia. Taught Cherubini. Works incl. *c* 70 operas, church and choral music, 2 concertos, and harpsichord sonatas. Mozart used aria from his opera *Fra due litiganti* (1782) in *Don Giovanni* and wrote piano variations on it, K460.

**Sarum Rite,** liturgy, with its plainsong, of cathedral church of Salisbury. Most widely used rite in England till Reformation.

**sassofone** (It.), SAXOPHONE.

**Satie, Erik Alfred Leslie** (1866–1925), French composer, of partly Scottish descent. Studied at Paris Conservatoire from 1879 and at Schola Cantorum under d'Indy and Roussel (1905–8). Became friend of Debussy in 1890 and had some influence on his style. Worked for period as café pianist, and this affected personality of his music. Wrote 3 ballets (incl. *Parade,* produced with Cocteau, Picasso and Diaghilev in Paris, 1917), operettas, symphonic drama *Socrate, Messe des pauvres* for voice and organ, 4 sets of songs, and many piano pieces. Ironically humorous character of his style, in strong contrast to impressionism of period, is indicated in satirical titles of piano pieces, *eg Pièces en forme de poire, Aperçus désagréables*. Once regarded merely as talented eccentric, but his importance is now recognized. Inspired Les SIX and ECOLE D'ARCUEIL.

**Satz** (Ger.), (1) movement of sonata, symphony, suite *etc, eg erster Satz,* 'first movement'. *See also* QUARTETTSATZ;

(2) composition or musical setting (in full *Tonsatz,* 'musical composition');

(3) style in composition, *eg freier Satz,* free style, *strenger Satz,* strict style;

(4) theme or subject, *eg Hauptsatz,* first subject, *Seitensatz,* second subject.

**saudades,** Portuguese word, usually used in plural, suggesting 'nostalgia' or 'wistful yearning'. Used as title of set of songs by Warlock.

**Saudades do Brasil** (Port., *Nostalgia for Brazil*), 2 vols. of piano pieces by Milhaud (1920–1), written after period spent in Rio de Janeiro. Also title of orchestral suite by Milhaud.

**Sauguet, Henri** (1901– ), French composer, critic. Pupil of Koechlin and disciple of Satie. Music, notable for clarity and wit, incl. several operas *eg Les Caprices de Marianne,* ballets *eg Les Forains,* 3 symphonies and other orchestral works, cantatas, chamber music, and songs.

**Saul,** oratorio by Handel, text by C. Jennens (after Bible). First perf. London, 1739. So-called 'Dead March' has long enjoyed separate popularity.

**Saul and David,** opera by Nielsen, libretto by E. Christiansen (based on Old Testament). First perf. Copenhagen, 1902. First of Nielsen's 2 operas.

**sausage bassoon,** *see* RACKET.

**sautillé,** *see* BOWING.

**Savitri,** chamber opera by Holst, libretto by composer based on episode in *Mahabharata* (Hindu scriptures). Composed 1908; first perf. London, 1916.

**Savoy Operas,** *see* SULLIVAN.

**saw, musical,** hand-saw held between knees and played with bow while left hand alters pitch by bending blade. *See also* FLEXATONE.

**Sax, Adolphe,** orig. Antoine Joseph Sax (1814–94), Belgian inventor of saxhorn and saxophone.

**saxhorn,** family of instruments patented by Adolphe Sax in 1845. Invention resulted from application of valves instead of keys to BUGLE family. Made in at least 7 sizes. Often referred to as FLUGELHORNS, but though similar in most respects they have smaller bore and consequently different tone quality. There is some confusion in nomenclature owing to variety of names given to instruments in different countries.

**saxophone** (Ger., *Saxophon*; It., *sassofone*), family of instruments patented by Adolphe Sax in 1846. Although made of brass, properly belongs to woodwind group. Single reed is set in clarinet-type mouthpiece, though conical shape of bore as well as fingering relate instrument to oboe. Family has 7 members: little used soprano in E flat is straight, like clarinet, while alto in E flat, tenor in B flat, baritone in E flat, bass in B flat and rare contrabass in E flat all have upturned bell like bass clarinet; soprano in B flat is made in both shapes. For practical purposes family can be reduced to 4 instruments, all with written compass from B flat below middle C to octave above F at top of treble clef: soprano sounds tone lower; alto, major sixth lower; tenor, major ninth lower; baritone, major thirteenth lower. Higher notes can be produced by harmonic technique using unorthodox fingerings. Sections of saxophones form essential part of larger jazz and dance bands; usually found singly in symphony orchestra.

**Scacchi, Marco** (*c* 1600–before 1685), Italian composer. Composer at Polish Court in Warsaw (1623–48). Composed opera, oratorio, Masses, motets and madrigals. Published (1643–4) critical examination of style of Psalms of Paul Siefert, and proposed division of styles into those appropriate to church, chamber and theatre.

**Scala, La,** properly Teatro alla Scala, Milan, Italy's leading opera house. Opened 1778.

**Scala di Seta, La,** *see* SILKEN LADDER.

**scale** (Fr., *gamme*; Ger., *Torleiter*; It., *scala*), progression of notes in ascending or descending order, so arranged for theoretical purposes, vocal or instrumental exercise, or as part of composition.

Scale consists of certain number of divisions of a fourth (TETRACHORD) or OCTAVE. Manner of such division is MODE, though scale is commonly used in sense of mode in referring to PENTATONIC SCALE, major or minor scale, CHROMATIC SCALE and WHOLE-TONE SCALE. Medieval HEXACHORD was 6-note scale.

Modern DIATONIC scale has 2 modes: major (TTSTTTS, where T = tone, S = semitone) and minor (TSTTSTT). Latter only has theoretical existence; in practice has 2 forms, both of which involve element of chromaticism in treatment of LEADING NOTE: harmonic minor scale (TSTTS1½TS), and melodic minor scale, in which ascending form (TSTTTTS) differs from descending form (TTSTTST).

In system of EQUAL TEMPERAMENT each of 2 modes may begin on any of 12 notes from C upwards to B by using sharps or flats, usually shown by KEY SIGNATURE, thus giving rise to 12 scales in major mode and 12 scales in minor, on which music has been based since early 18th cent. Notes of scale are designated in both modes and in all positions by name which indicates their function in relation to their KEY, viz: tonic, supertonic, mediant, subdominant, dominant, submediant, leading note. These are *scale degrees,* numbered from I to VII respectively, used in harmonic analysis.

**scale degrees,** *see* SCALE.

**Scandello** or **Scandellus, Antonio** (1517–80), Italian composer, cornett-player. Became assistant *Kapellmeister* to Le Maistre at Dresden Court in 1566, and *Kapellmeister* in 1568. Composed Masses, Passion and other church music, 2 books of *Canzoni napolitane* (1566, 1577), and sacred and secular choral songs to German words. His *St John Passion* (*c* 1560) is intermediate in method between those with plainsong narrative and polyphonic choruses and those set in polyphony throughout.

**Scapino,** comedy overture by Walton (1940, rev. 1950), inspired by Callot's etching (1619) of rascally servant of Commedia dell'arte.

**Scarlatti, Alessandro** (1660–1725), Italian composer. Held various posts in Rome, Florence and in Naples. Pupils incl. Logroscino, Durante and Hasse. Greatest and most prolific of composers of Italian opera in period when its forms were assuming their most lasting characteristics. In his mature works are found fully developed *da capo* aria with instrumental accompaniment and *ritornelli,* rapid style and special cadence formulas of *secco* recitative, and use of accompanied recitative for more intense dramatic effects. In later operas used 3-movt. form which became distinguishing mark of Italian overture. Of his 115 operas few survive in repertory, despite their immense historical importance. Also wrote 150 oratorios, *c* 600 cantatas with continuo and 61 with instrumental accompaniment, Masses, Passion, motets and other church music, concertos, chamber music and pieces for harpsichord.

His son, **[Giuseppe] Domenico Scarlatti** (1685–1757) was composer and harpsichordist. Pupil of father, Gasparini and Pasquini. Held various posts in Rome, Lisbon and Madrid. Greatest Italian writer for harpsichord of his time. Composed *c* 600 single-movt. pieces, now generally called sonatas, though some published in his lifetime were called *Esercizi*. Most are written in BINARY FORM, within which there is inexhaustible variety in character of themes and continuous flexibility in texture and treatment. They contain many original and characteristic technical devices incl. wide skips, crossing of hands, rapidly repeated notes, and repeated dissonant chords which suggest strumming of guitar. Catalogue of Scarlatti's works has been made by Ralph Kirkpatrick, and works are referred to by 'K' numbers.

**scat singing,** jazz term for use of nonsense syllables and other wordless effects in course of vocal number.

**scena** (It.), 'scene': (1) stage (of theatre);

(2) dramatic scene in opera, consisting of extended aria, usually of dramatic character; (3) concert piece for solo voice with accompaniment, similar in character to (2).

**Scenes of Childhood,** *see* KINDERSCENEN.

**Schaeffer, Pierre** (1910– ), French composer. In 1948 began first experiments in MUSIQUE CONCRÈTE (term which he coined). In 1951 established first electronic music studio at RTF radio station, Paris. His compositions, mostly in collaboration with Pierre Henry, incl. *Orphée 53* for violin, harpsichord, 2 voices and tape.

**Schalen, Schallbecken** (Ger.), CYMBALS.

**Schalmei,** *see* SHAWM.

**Scharwenka, Franz Xaver** (1850–1924), German-born pianist, composer, teacher. Founded conservatory in Berlin in 1881 (which joined Klindworth Conservatorium in 1893). With Walter Petzet founded new Master School in 1914. Toured extensively as pianist in Europe and US, where he lived (1891–98) and founded conservatory in New York. Composed opera, symphony, 4 piano concertos, piano trios, church music, songs, sonatas and other piano pieces, edited piano works of Schumann and wrote (with A. Spanuth) *Methodik des Klavierspiels* (1908).

His brother, **Ludwig Philipp Scharwenka** (1847–1917), was also composer and teacher. Held various posts at his brother's conservatory in Berlin. Composed opera, 2 symphonies, symphonic poems and other orchestral works, works for solo voices, chorus and orchestra, violin concerto, piano and chamber music, and songs.

**Schat, Piet** (1935– ), Dutch composer. One of Holland's most progressive composers. Works incl. opera *Labyrinth* (1966), *Signalement* (1962) and *On Escalation* (1968) for percussion and other instruments, and *The Fifth Season* (1973), piece of music theatre about Vietnam War.

**Schauspieldirektor, Der** (Ger., *The Impresario*; It., *L'Impresario*), 'comedy with music' by Mozart. First perf. Vienna, 1786.

**Scheherazade,** Ger. spelling of SHEHERAZADE.

**Scheibe, Johann Adolph** (1708–76), German composer, writer. Held various posts in Germany and Denmark. Published periodical entitled *Der critische Musicus* (1737–40) in which he denounced

Italian operatic conventions and also style of J.S. Bach (though withdrew latter attack in 2nd edition of his paper, 1745). Works incl. opera, choral music, 150 flute concertos, 30 violin concertos, 70 quartet-symphonies, incidental music, trios, flute sonatas, and songs.

**Scheidemann, Heinrich** (*c* 1596–1663), German organist, composer. Pupil of Sweelinck in Amsterdam. His organ music is of some historical importance. Wrote 10 chorale melodies for Rist's 5th book of chorales (1651), and published vol. of sacred dialogues (1658).

**Scheidt, Samuel** (1587–1654), German organist, composer. Wrote music for various combinations of voices and instruments, separately and combined. For organ, wrote harmonized chorales and *Tabulatura nova* (3 vols., 1624), which contains variations on sacred and secular melodies, fantasies, dance movts., and complete set of liturgical organ music for Lutheran Mass and Vespers; work uses staff notation in place of TABLATURE, hence title.

**Schein, Johann Hermann** (1586–1630), German composer. First Lutheran composer to adapt Italian monodic style to treatment of chorale melodies. Also wrote *Cymbalum Sionium* (1615) in Venetian polychoral style, secular vocal pieces, and instrumental suites notable for early use of same theme in different movts. ('variation-suite').

**Schelle, Johann** (1648–1701), German singer, composer. Composed cantatas and motets to German words, Latin motets, Magnificats, and Mass.

**Schellen** (Ger.), jingles, sleigh-bells.

**Schellenbaum** (Ger.), PAVILLON CHINOIS.

**Schellengeläute** (Ger.), sleighbells.

**Schellentrommel** (Ger.), tambourine.

**Schelling, Ernest** (1876–1939), American composer, pianist. Studied in Europe under Bruckner, Leschetizky, Paderewski and Moszkowski. Works incl. symphony, *Symphonic Legend, A Victory Ball* and *Morocco* for orchestra, *Fantastic Impressions from an Artist's Life* for piano and orchestra, chamber and piano music, and songs.

**Schemelli, Georg Christian** (*c* 1676–1762), German musician. Published collection of songs entitled *Musicalisches Gesangbuch* (1736, known as 'Schemelli Hymn-book'), edited and in part composed by Bach.

**Schenk** or **Schenck, Johann** (?1656–after 1712), German composer, *viola da gamba* player. Later lived in Amsterdam. Wrote suites and sonatas for bass viol, chamber sonatas for 2 violins, bass viol and continuo, sonatas for bass viol and continuo, opera, setting of *Song of Solomon* for voice and continuo, and *Scherzi musicali,* book of suites for *viola da gamba* and continuo.

**Schenker, Heinrich** (1868–1935), Austrian theorist, teacher. Pupil of Bruckner. Best known for methods of detailed analysis of form, harmony and tonality in 18th, 19th-cent. music. Known as 'Schenker system', these methods attempt to prove that every composition can be reduced to a few simple patterns or simple tone structure, from which grows its continuity and coherence.

**Scherchen, Hermann** (1891–1966), German-born conductor. Settled in Switzerland (1932). Specialized in modern music, esp. that of 12-note school. Wrote *A Handbook of Conducting*.

**Scherer, Sebastian Anton** (1631–1712), German composer. Published vol. of Masses, psalms and motets (1657), vol. of *Tabulatura in cymbalo et organo* containing intonations in the 8 modes, with 2nd part (*Partitura*) containing toccatas in the 8 modes (1664), and set of 14 trio sonatas (1680).

**scherzando** (It.), playfully, in a light-hearted fashion.

**scherzetto, scherzino** (It.), short SCHERZO.

**Scherzi, Gli,** *see* RUSSIAN QUARTETS.

**scherzo** (It.), lit. 'joke'. Term occasionally used for both vocal and instrumental compositions before 1750. Scherzo (and trio) after 1750 is almost always in quick triple time, and is generally movt. in sonata, symphony *etc* where it takes place of minuet.

**Schicksalslied,** *see* SONG OF DESTINY.

**Schikaneder, [Johann] Emanuel** (1751–1812), German librettist, singer, theatre manager. In 1784 settled in Vienna, where he managed several theatres, incl. Theater auf der Wieden, for which Mozart composed *The Magic Flute* (1791), with Schikaneder as librettist, producer and exponent of role of Papageno. In 1801 opened Theater an der Wien, for which Beethoven wrote *Fidelio*. Also wrote librettos for operas by Süssmayr and Paisiello.

**Schildt, Melchior** (*c* 1593–1667), German organist, composer. Pupil of Sweelinck in Amsterdam, and held various posts in Germany and Denmark. Works incl. 2 sets of harpsichord variations, 2 preludes and 2 chorales for organ.

**Schillinger, Joseph** (1895–1943), Russian-born composer, theorist. Settled in US (1929), where taught mathematical musical method invented by himself. Pupils incl. Gershwin. Works incl. *March of the Orient*, and *First Airphonic Suite* for THÉRÉMIN, orchestra and piano.

**Schillings, Max von** (1868–1933), German conductor, composer. Became music director at Court Opera, Stuttgart (1911), and director of Berlin State Opera (1919–25). His 4 operas, Wagnerian in style, incl. highly successful *Mona Lisa* (1915).

**Schindler, Anton** (1794–1864), Austrian violinist, conductor. Held various posts in Vienna, Münster, Aix-la-Chapelle and Frankfurt. Met Beethoven in 1814, became his secretary in 1816, lived in his house (1822–24) and returned in 1826 to care for him until his death. Wrote famous biography of Beethoven (1840), but its accuracy leaves something to be desired.

**Schiøtz, Aksel** (1906–75), Danish tenor. Appeared in opera at Glyndebourne and in US. Also a notable *Lieder* singer.

**Schipa, Tito** (1890–1965), Italian tenor. Gave recitals internationally, esp. in US.

**Schirmer,** firm of New York music-publishers, founded 1861 by Gustav Schirmer and B. Beer. Schirmer assumed sole control in 1866. In 1915 firm founded periodical *Musical Quarterly*.

**Schlag** (Ger.), beat.
**Schlägel** (Ger.), drumstick.
**Schlaginstrumente** (Ger.), percussion instruments.
**Schlagzither** (Ger.), type of ZITHER in which strings, instead of being plucked, are struck with hammers. In fact more like dulcimer than zither.
**Schlagenrohr** (Ger.), SERPENT.
**Schlegel** (Ger.), drumstick.
**Schleifer** (Ger.), slide or slur, *ie* appoggiatura consisting of 2 grace notes.
**schleppen** (Ger.), 'to drag'. *Nicht schleppen,* do not drag.
**Schlick, Arnolt** (before 1460–after 1517), blind organist, composer, active in Germany and Holland. Wrote book on organs and methods of constructing them, *Spiegel der Orgelmacher und Organisten* (1511). Also wrote *Tabulaturen etlicher Lobgesang und Lidlein* (1512), containing organ settings.
**Schluss** (Ger.), end, conclusion, cadence.
**Schlüssel** (Ger.), clef.
**Schmelzer, Johann Heinrich** (*c* 1623–80), Austrian composer. Works incl. 3 vols. of chamber music, ballets for Viennese court opera, and *Nuptial Mass.*

His son, **Andreas Anton Schmelzer** (1653–1701), also composed music for ballets.

**schmetternd** (Ger.), 'blaring', indication to horn players to use harsh, brassy tone.
**Schmidt, Bernhard** or **Bernard Smith** (*c* 1630–1708), German organ-builder. Settled in England in 1660, where was known as 'Father Smith', and was appointed Organmaker in Ordinary to the King and later court organ-builder to Queen Anne.
**Schmidt, Franz** (1874–1939), Austrian composer, cellist, organist, pianist. Works, in Viennese style of period, incl. 2 operas, oratorio *The Book of the Seven Seals,* 4 symphonies, 2 piano concertos (orig. for left hand only), and chamber and organ music.
**Schmidt-Isserstedt, Hans** (1900–73), German conductor, composer. Became conductor of Hamburg State Opera and Deutsche Oper Berlin. In 1945 founded Hamburg Radio Symphony Orchestra, with which he toured world.
**Schmieder, Wolfgang** (1900–73), German musicologist. His thematic index of Bach's works is basis of present numbering system. Numbers bear prefix BWV, *ie Bach Werke-Verzeichnis* (Index to Bach's Works).
**Schmitt, Florent** (1870–1958), French composer, pianist, writer on music. Pupil of Massenet and Fauré. Works incl. ballets, orchestral, choral, chamber and piano music, and songs. Though style was based on French impressionism, music has distinctive personality, notably in ballet *The Tragedy of Salome* and choral setting of Psalm 47 (1904).
**Schnabel, Artur** (1882–1951), Austrian pianist, teacher, composer. Pupil of Leschetizky. Settled in Berlin, touring extensively, then

lived in New York after Nazis came to power. In later years composed symphony, orchestral rhapsody and other works in advanced atonal idiom. As pianist, renowned for intellectually authoritative performances of Viennese classics, esp. Beethoven.

**Schnabelflöte** (Ger.), 'beaked flute', obsolete name for RECORDER.

**Schnarre** (Ger.), rattle. *Schnarretrommel,* snare drum. *Schnarrsaite,* 'rattle string', *ie* snare. *Schnarrwerk,* reed section of organ.

**schnell** (Ger.), quick. *Schneller,* quicker.

**Schneller,** *see* upper MORDENT.

**Schobert, Johann** (*c* 1720–67), German harpsichordist, composer. Settled in Paris (1760). His keyboard style had some influence on Mozart; 2nd movt. of Mozart's piano concerto K39 (1767) is arrangement of movt. from sonata by Schobert.

**Schoeck, Othmar** (1886–1957), Swiss composer, conductor. Pupil of Reger. Works incl. 6 operas, concertos for violin, cello and horn, choral and chamber music, and *c* 400 songs.

**Schoenberg, Arnold,** orig. Schönberg (1874–1951), Austrian composer. One of major figures of 20th-cent. music. Largely self-taught. Composed *Verklärte Nacht* (*Transfigured Night*) for string sextet in 1899, and began massively scored *Gurrelieder* in 1900, completed in 1911. Between then and 1920s taught in Berlin and Vienna. In 1933, having been condemned by Nazis for musical 'decadence' (he was Jewish), he moved to US, settling in California and changing spelling of his name to Schoenberg. From early works which showed complete command of late romantic style, Schoenberg turned *c* 1907, under self-confessed 'inner compulsion', to period of experimentation in such music as *Three Piano Pieces,* op 11 (1909), 15 songs from Stefan George's *The Book of the Hanging Gardens,* op 15 (1907–9), *Five Pieces for Orchestra,* op 16 (1909), monodrama *Erwartung* (Expectation), op 17 (1909), drama with music *Die glückliche Hand* (*The Lucky Hand*), op 18 (1913), and 21 songs from Albert Giraud's *Pierrot Lunaire* for SPRECHGESANG and instruments, op 21 (1912). Technique towards which these very controversial works had been moving was formulated *c* 1921 in principle of TWELVE-NOTE system, essentially a return to polyphony, which composer regarded as ascent to 'higher and better order'. Working of system is exemplified esp. in works written 1921–33, incl. *Five Pieces,* op 23, and *Suite,* op 25, for piano, *Serenade* for 7 instruments and bass baritone, op 24, quintet for wind instruments, op 26, 3rd string quartet, op 30, and *Variations for Orchestra,* op 31.

In many of works written in US Schoenberg returned to more traditional principles of form and tonality (he always regarded 'atonality' as misnomer), *eg* in string suite in G (1935) and *Theme and Variations for Band,* op 43 (1943), first works to have key-signature since 2nd quartet (1907). Most notable works of this last period were violin concerto, op 36 (1936), 4th string quartet, op 37 (1936), *Ode to Napoleon,* setting of Byron's poem, for piano, strings and narrator, op 41 (1943), piano concerto, op 42 (1943), string trio, op 45 (1946), and *A Survivor from Warsaw* for narrator, male chorus and orchestra, op 46 (1947). Left opera *Moses and Aaron* unfinished at death.

Schoenberg's most distinguished pupils were Berg, Webern and Wellesz. His *Harmonielehre* (1911) is one of most important modern treatises on harmony. He was also active as painter in expressionist style, esp. in period 1907–10.

**schola cantorum,** papal choir and song school, prob. originating long before 8th cent. Schola Cantorum founded by d'Indy (1894) in Paris is full-scale conservatory.

**Scholes, Percy Alfred** (1877–1958), English music critic, author, lexicographer. Founded and edited the *Musical Student* (1908) and *Music and Youth,* and worked for London *Evening Standard, The Observer* and the BBC. Lived for some years in Switzerland. Books incl. *The Listener's History of Music* (1923–8), *The Oxford Companion to Music* (1938, 10th edition, 1970), *The Mirror of Music, 1844–1944* (1947), *The Concise Oxford Dictionary of Music* (1952, 3rd edition, 1980), and *Sir John Hawkins* (1953).

**Schönberg,** *see* SCHOENBERG.

**Schöne Müllerin, Die** (*The Fair Maid of the Mill*), cycle of 20 songs by Schubert (1823), set to poems by W. Muller telling story of initially happy but finally tragic courtship.

**Schöne Melusine, Die** (Ger., *The Fair Melusina*), overture by Mendelssohn, op 32 (1833), composed after performance of opera *Melusina* by Kreutzer, with libretto by Grillparzer.

**School for Fathers,** *see* QUATTRO RUSTEGHI.

**Schoolmaster, The** (Ger., *Der Schulmeister*), nickname given to Haydn's symphony no 55 in E flat (1774), poss. from serious character of slow movt. Has been suggested that dotted figure of main theme represents teacher's wagging forefinger.

**Schop** or **Schopp, Johann** (*c* 1590–1667), German composer, violinist, lutenist, trombonist. Worked in Wolfenbüttel, Copenhagen and Hamburg. Composed sacred concertos (1643–44), sacred songs (1654) and instrumental music, of which little has survived. One of musical editors of Rist's collections of sacred and secular songs.

**Schöpfung, Die,** *see* CREATION.

**Schöpfungsmesse,** *see* 'CREATION' MASS.

**Schottische** (Ger.), lit. 'Scottish', round polka dance, similar to but slower than 19th-cent. polka. Not to be confused with *écossaise.*

**Schott und Söhne,** firm of music-publishers, founded in Mainz in 1773 by Bernhard Schott. Later opened branches in Belgium, Paris and London. Now publishes many modern scores, incl. works by Henze, Tippett and Orff.

**Schrammel quartet,** Viennese ensemble usually consisting of 2 violins, guitar and accordion or clarinet. Owes name to Joseph Schrammel (1850–93) who led such a quartet.

**Schreker, Franz** (1878–1934), German composer, conductor. Founded (1911) and conducted Philharmonic Chorus of Vienna. Director of Berlin Hochschule (1920–32) but was harassed and sacked by Nazis. First major work was opera *Der ferne Klang* (*The*

*Distant Sound*, 1912), which influenced other composers of period *eg* Berg; 8 other operas incl. *Der Schatzgräber* (*The Digger for Treasure*, 1920). Chamber symphony (1916) also helped to establish him as avant-garde leader, but music lacks sustaining power and has recently been neglected.

**schrittmässig, schrittweise** (Ger.), 'step-style', 'stepwise', *ie* at walking speed; equivalent of *andante*.

**Schröder-Devrient, Wilhelmine** (1804–60), German soprano. Made debut in Vienna (1821) and sang Leonore in *Fidelio* in Beethoven's presence (1822). Sang at court opera in Dresden (1823–47), and also appeared in Paris, London and Berlin. Sang Adriano in first perf. of Wagner's *Rienzi*, Senta in *The Flying Dutchman*, and Venus in *Tannhäuser*. Wife of baritone Eduard Devrient.

**Schröter, Corona** (1751–1802), German singer, composer, actress. Invited by Goethe to write music for his play *Die Fischerin*. Also acted in Goethe's plays.

**Schröter, Leonhart** (*c* 1532–*c* 1601), German composer. Published several collections of music for Lutheran service, incl. settings of Latin and German hymns, psalms, 8-part German Te Deum, and Latin Te Deum.

**Schubart, Christian Friedrich Daniel** (1739–91), German musician, poet, editor. In 1774 founded *Deutsche Chronik*. Director of Stuttgart Court Opera. Wrote words for 3 songs by Schubert, autobiography, and book on musical aesthetics. Also composed songs and piano pieces.

**Schubert, Franz** (1808–78), German composer, violinist. His violin solo *L'Abeille* (Fr., *The Bee*) has sometimes been mistaken for work of his great namesake.

**Schubert, Franz Peter** (1797–1828), Austrian composer. Born in Vienna. Son of music-loving schoolmaster. At age of 8 began to learn violin from father and piano from elder brother Ignaz, and soon progressed to organ and study of counterpoint. Admitted as chorister at Imperial Chapel in Vienna (1808), in due course becoming leader, and often conductor, of chapel orchestra. Composed 1st song at age of 14. Took lessons from Salieri after leaving school at age of 16. From this period dated 1st symphony (1813) and first 3 string quartets. 'Maturity' was reached at 17 with song 'Gretchen am Spinnrade' ('Gretchen at the spinning wheel'), followed by 2nd and 3rd symphonies (1815) and several operettas and melodramas. Thereafter Schubert continued to produce rapid stream of masterpieces. Failed to gain any important musical post, and as freelance composer was even less successful than Mozart, though he did not seem to desire fame. Lived on casual earnings and generosity of friends, initially enjoying his Bohemian existence in Vienna. When Graz Musical Society elected him honorary member (1822) he sent them 'Unfinished' Symphony, which was forgotten and not performed till 1865. However, he did finish 'Great' C major symphony, C major string quintet, several string quartets, and 2 of greatest song cycles ever written – *Die schöne Müllerin* (1823) and *Winterreise* (1827). Almost morbid loneliness of latter reflects Schubert's feelings at this time. Though did not lack women friends, remained unmarried; his Bohemian existence had begun to go stale, and he was short of money and increasingly unwell. Towards end of life, considered taking refresher course in counterpoint. Died of typhus at age of 31.

At centre of Schubert's art are his songs, sheer number of which – more than 600 – testifies to his immediate and spontaneous response to early romantic poetry. He could create a masterpiece out of mediocre verse as easily as out of good. His songs are duets for singer and pianist on equal terms, and in range of musical resources they form compendium, as well as foundation, of whole vocabulary of romantic musical speech. Up to 1823 made strenuous but unsuccessful efforts to achieve practicable opera as distinct from *Singspiel.* However, choral works of last years show breadth and consistency of style which might have developed into something very impressive. It was in his great instrumental works – 'Unfinished' Symphony and 'Great' C major symphony (1828), chamber music, esp. A minor (1824), D minor (*Death and the Maiden,* 1824–6) and G major (1826) string quartets, piano trios in B flat (1826) and E flat (1827), *Trout* quintet (1819), C major string quintet (1828), octet for wind and strings (1824), and piano sonatas and duets – that his lyrical melodic style is most perfectly allied to largeness of conception and form and to consummate sense of key-design and harmonic detail.

Deutsch's numbering (prefixed by 'D') of Schubert's works should always be used in preference to opus numbers, which are chronologically inaccurate. Main divisions in Deutsch's catalogue (complete edition, 1884–97) are: I. 8 symphonies; II. 10 overtures and other orchestral works; III. 3 octets; IV. string quintet; V. 15 string quartets; VI. string trio; VII. 3 piano trios, piano quartet, piano quintet; VIII. 8 works for piano and other instrument; IX. 32 works for piano duet; X. 15 piano sonatas; XI. 16 other works for piano; XII. 31 dances for piano; XIII. 7 Masses; XIV. 22 sacred works; XV. 15 stage works; XVI. 46 works for male choir; XVII. 19 works for mixed chorus; XVIII. 6 works for female choir; XIX. 36 vocal trios and duets; XX. 567 songs with piano and 36 other solo vocal pieces; XXI. supplement of 31 instrumental pieces and 13 vocal pieces.

**Schübler Chorales,** set of 6 chorale preludes by Bach, so called because they were published (*c* 1747) by Schübler.

**Schuhplattler** (Ger.), Bavarian dance, usually in 3/4 time, in which performers slap knees and soles of feet with hands.

**Schuller, Gunther** (1925– ), American composer, horn player. Style is interesting compound of jazz and serialism, which he calls 'Third Stream' music. Most substantial work is opera *The Visitation* (1966), but international reputation rests mainly on *Seven Studies on Themes of Paul Klee* for orchestra (1959). Other works incl. concertos, ballet and chamber music.

**Schulmeister, Der,** *see* SCHOOLMASTER.

**Schulwerk, Das** (Ger., *Schoolwork*), educational work by Orff

(1930–33). Consists of numerous short pieces using instruments, incl. recorders and percussion, likely to be found in schools.

**Schulz, Johann Abraham Peter** (1747–1800), German conductor, author, composer. Held posts at Rheinsberg and Copenhagen. His songs with piano in folk song style (3 books, 1782–90) were first of their kind, and some are still well known in Germany. Composed 5 operas to French texts incl. *Le Barbier de Séville* (1786) and *Aline, reine de Golconde* (1787), and 3 operas to Danish texts.

**Schuman, William Howard** (1910– ), American composer. Pupil of Roy Harris. Head of Juilliard School of Music, New York (1945–61). Music, often distinctively US in flavour, incl. 9 symphonies, *American Festival* and *William Billings* overtures, *New England Triptych,* concertos for violin and piano, ballets, opera *The Mighty Casey* (about baseball player), and choral and chamber music.

**Schumann, Clara Josephine,** née Wieck (1819–96), German pianist, composer. Daughter and pupil of Friedrich Wieck (1788–1873). Gave first recital in 1830 in Leipzig, subsequently playing in Germany, Paris and Vienna. After considerable opposition from father, married Robert Schumann in 1840. After husband's death in 1856, played frequently in Britain. One of outstanding interpreters of her time, esp. of husband's music. Also influential as teacher. Compositions incl. piano music and songs.

**Schumann, Elisabeth** (1888–1952), German soprano. Famous both in opera and in *Lieder* recitals for silvery delicacy of her voice. Member of Vienna State Opera (1919–37). Left Austria for US before WWII.

**Schumann, Robert** (1810–56), German composer. Born at Zwickau. Encouraged by father – bookseller, publisher and writer – to develop both musical and literary interests. Developed burning admiration for extravagantly romantic sentiment of writer Jean Paul [Richter]. After father's death, mother insisted he study law at Leipzig, but he neglected legal studies and in 1829 began to study piano and harmony with Friedrich Wieck, his future (unwilling) father-in-law. At end of 1830 gave up law for music, and wrote *Abegg Variations* for piano, op 1. In 1832 right hand became crippled, so ending aspirations to become concert pianist. However, infirmity made him devote more time to composition, and during 1830s he wrote bulk of piano works. In 1833 founded *Neue Zeitschrift für Musik,* journal to champion new romantic style. In 1840, against opposition of her father (his former teacher), he married Clara Wieck, who became most renowned interpreter of his piano music. Up to 1839 wrote only for piano, but in 1840 turned, equally obsessively, to art of song, and in that year wrote 15 sets. In 1841 wrote 1st symphony, which marked start of orchestral phase, and in 1842 began writing chamber music. Appointed teacher of composition at newly founded Leipzig Conservatorium (1843), but moved in 1844 to Dresden, and in 1850 to Düsseldorf as conductor. From 1843 work had been disturbed by periodic crises of mental instability; in 1854 threw himself in Rhine and spent last years in asylum near Bonn, composing fitfully.

Schumann's piano music embodies many traits which became idioms of piano style of romantic period, *eg* impetuous waywardness of rhythm expressed in syncopations and in combinations of different metres, and new effects of tonal distance resulting from sudden changes of harmony and of sonority and fusion from use of pedal. Subjective and literary element in his music takes form of (1) deriving themes from names, *eg* in ABEGG VARIATIONS, and (2) relating musical styles to personalities, *eg* Chopin, Paganini, Clara, Eusebius and Florestan (extrovert and introvert aspects of his own personality) in *Carnaval.* He did not tend to use the kind of dramatic musical narrative employed by Berlioz.

His quick and intuitive insight into romantic poetry shows itself in varied forms and intimate expression of his songs. Apart from 1st symphony (inspired by poem by A. Böttger), 3rd (*Rhenish*) symphony and 3 concert overtures, his orchestral and chamber music is without programmatic titles. D minor symphony (no 4) is remarkable pioneering example of thematic transformation, being based almost entirely on 2 motives. So-called ineptitude which at times mars his orchestral scoring is due to lack of orchestral training and experience, and his inherently 'pianistic' way of thinking; however, weaknesses have been greatly exaggerated. In his writings Schumann deprecated prevalent taste of 1830s and was enthusiastic about Bach and Beethoven, and new music of contemporaries such as Chopin and Brahms.

Principal compositions: (1) Piano solo: 3 sonatas, 3 'sonatas for the Young', *Fantasie,* 12 studies on CAPRICES by Paganini, *Abegg Variations,* Impromptus on theme by Clara Wieck, 12 studies in form of Variations (*Études symphoniques*), 3 Romances, 4 Fugues and 7 'Little Fugues' (*Clavierstücke in Fughettenform*), 4 Marches, sets of pieces with titles *Papillons, Intermezzi, Davidsbündlertänze, Carnaval, Fantasiestücke* (two) *Kinderscenen* (Scenes from Childhood), *Kreisleriana, Novelletten, Nachtstücke* (Nightpieces), *Faschingsschwank aus Wien* (Carnival Jest from Vienna), *Clavierstücke, Album für die Jugend* (Album for the Young), *Waldscenen* (Woodland Scenes), *Bunte Blätter* (Motley Leaves), *Albumblätter, Gesänge der Frühe* (Songs of the Early Morning), Toccata, Allegro in B minor, *Arabeske, Blumenstücke* (Flower Pieces), *Humoreske*;

(2) Piano duet: 8 Polonaises, 6 Impromptus (*Bilder aus Osten*), 12 pieces for 'small and big children', 9 dances (*Ball-Scenen*), 6 Easy Dances (*Kinderball*);

(3) 2 pianos: Andante and Variations, 8 Polonaises;

(4) Pedal-piano: 6 studies and 4 sketches;

(5) Organ or pedal-piano: 6 Fugues on name of Bach;

(6) Orchestra: 4 symphonies, Overture, Scherzo and Finale, overtures to Schiller's *Braut von Messina* (Bride of Messina), Shakespeare's *Julius Caesar,* Goethe's *Hermann und Dorothea,* piano concerto in A minor, Introduction and Allegro Appassionato in G and *Concert Allegro* in D for piano and orchestra, violin concerto,

*Phantasie* for violin and orchestra, cello concerto, *Concertstücke* for 4 horns and orchestra;

(7) Chamber music: 3 quartets, 3 trios, 4 *Fantasiestücke* for trio, piano quartet, piano quintet, *Märchenerzählungen* for piano, clarinet (or violin) and viola, 2 violin sonatas, *Märchenbilder* for viola and piano, 5 pieces 'in folk song style' for cello and piano, 3 Romances for oboe and piano, *Fantasiestücke* for clarinet and piano, Adagio and Allegro for horn and piano;

(8) Vocal works: 33 sets or cycles and 14 single songs with piano, 3 ballads for declamation to piano, 4 sets of vocal duets, 1 of vocal trios and 4 of vocal quartets with piano, 7 sets of part-songs for mixed voices, 4 for male voices and 2 for female voices, 15 choral works with orchestra;

(9) Stage works: opera *Genoveva,* incidental music to Byron's *Manfred.*

**Schumann-Heink, Ernestine** (1861–1936), German-American contralto. Made operatic debut in 1878, appeared regularly at Bayreuth (1896–1906), and played Klytemnestra in première of Strauss's *Elektra* (1909). Later joined New York Metropolitan.

**Schuppanzigh, Ignaz** (1776–1830), Austrian violinist. Friend and teacher of Beethoven. Member of Prince Lichnowsky's quartet (1794–95), conductor of Augarten concerts (1798–99) and founder leader of Rasumovsky Quartet (1808), which toured Germany, Russia and Poland (1815–24) and gave first perfs. of quartets by Beethoven and Schubert. Conducted Vienna Court Opera from 1828.

**Schürmann, Georg Caspar** (*c* 1672–1751), German composer, singer. After Keiser (d. 1739) was most important composer for German stage in baroque period, and wrote *c* 40 operas. Court opera conductor at Wolfenbüttel from 1707.

**Schütz, Heinrich,** also called Henricus Sagittarius (1585–1672), German composer. Pupil of G. Gabrieli in Venice. Worked in Cassel and Copenhagen, but mostly lived in Dresden. Greatest German composer of his century. Earliest published works were Italian madrigals (1611). In series of compositions for Lutheran church (*Psalms of David*, 1619, *Resurrection Story*, 1623, *Cantiones Sacrae*, 1625, *Symphoniae Sacrae*, 1629-50, *Kleine geistliche Konzerte*, 1636–9) he adopted the elaborate polychoral style of Gabrieli, continuo madrigal style and some elements of opera style of Monteverdi, and *concertante* style for voices and instrument of his Italian contemporaries. In *Twelve Sacred Songs* (1657) and *Christmas Oratorio* he achieved perfect balance between Italian style and Lutheran polyphonic tradition, and in 3 Passions (St Matthew, St Luke, St John, 1665–6) he refined style even further by composing words of Evangelist in unaccompanied chant modelled on that of earliest Lutheran Passions. Made much less use of chorale melodies than did Lutheran composers before and after him.

**schwach** (Ger.), weak, soft. *Schwächen*, to weaken.

**Schwanda the Bagpiper,** *see* ŠVANDA THE BAGPIPER.

**Schwanengesang** (Ger., *Swan Song*), set of 14 songs by Schubert

(1828), published posthumously. Title supplied by publisher. Songs do not form narrative unity; 7 are based on poems by Heine.

**Schwarz, Rudolf** (1905– ), Austrian-born conductor. Director of Jewish Cultural Union in Berlin till 1941, when was sent by Nazis to Belsen concentration camp. Having survived this, came to Britain in 1947 as conductor of Bournemouth Municipal Orchestra. Conducted City of Birmingham Orchestra (1951–7), then B.B.C. Symphony Orchestra (1957–62) and Northern Sinfonia Orchestra, Newcastle (1964–73).

**Schwarzkopf, Elisabeth** (1915– ), German soprano. In her prime, outstanding exponent of Mozart and Strauss opera roles. As *Lieder* singer, one of most sensitive and communicative artists of 20th cent., with repertory ranging from Mozart to Wolf and beyond.

**Schweigsame, Frau** (Ger., *The Silent Woman*), comic opera by Richard Strauss, libretto by Stefan Zweig (after Ben Jonson's *Epicne*). First perf. Dresden, 1935, but soon ran into Nazi disapproval (Zweig was a Jew), and was withdrawn. Story is similar to that of Donizetti's *Don Pasquale*.

**Schweitzer, Albert** (1875–1965), French-Alsatian theologian, medical missionary, organist and musical historian. Organist of Strasbourg Bach concerts from 1896 and Paris Bach Society concerts from 1906. Thereafter became missionary in French Congo though made visits to Europe to give lectures and recitals. Author of important book on Bach. Awarded Nobel Peace Prize (1952).

**Schweitzer, Anton** (1735–87), German conductor, composer. Composed several successful *Singspiele,* incl. *Die Dorfgala* (1772). His *Alceste* (1773), to libretto by C.M. Wieland, was major step towards creation of serious German opera. His setting of J.J. Rousseau's *Pygmalion* (1772) was first important melodrama written by German composer.

**Schweller** (Ger.), swell. *Schwellkasten*, swell box. *Schwellwerk*, swell organ.

**schwindend** (Ger.), dying away.

**Schwirrholz,** *see* THUNDER STICK.

**Schwung** (Ger.), swing. *Schwungvol*, spirited.

**sciolto** (It.), free and easy.

**Scipione** (It., *Scipio*), opera by Handel, libretto by P.A. Rolli (based on Zeno's *Scipione nelle Spagne*). First perf. London, 1726.

**scoop,** in singing, to slide tentatively up to note instead of hitting it accurately.

**scordatura** (It.), 'mis-tuning'. Term used for tuning of stringed instrument to abnormal notes, for sake of effect.

**score** (Fr., *partition*; Ger., *Partitur*; It., *partitura*), music written down so that parts for different performers appear vertically above one another. 'Full' orchestral score comprises all parts of orchestral composition, or of opera or work for chorus and orchestra. 'Short' score (piano score, piano reduction) is reduction of essential parts of orchestral or choral work to 2 staves. Vocal score contains separate vocal parts of opera or other composition for voices and orchestra together with reduction of orchestral part to 2 staves for use with piano and organ. 'Miniature' score contains same material as full score, but reduces it in size to make it cheaper and easily transportable.

Modern full score is set down in following vertical order: woodwind, brass, percussion, harp and keyboard instruments, solo instrument(s) (in a concerto), voices, 1st and 2nd violins, violas, cellos and double basses.

**scorrevole** (It.), scurrying, gliding.

**Scotch snap,** name for rhythm consisting of short note on beat, followed by longer note:

Rhythm is one of idioms of Scottish folk music (esp. strathspey), but is not peculiar to Scotland; called 'Lombardic' rhythm on Continent.

**'Scotch'** or **'Scottish' Symphony,** 3rd of Mendelssohn's mature symphonies, op 56, in A minor. Inspired by visit to Scotland in 1829 and completed in 1842. Though contains certain Scottish characteristics, work is no more programmatic than 'Italian' Symphony. Dedicated to Queen Victoria.

**Scott, Cyril Meir** (1879–1970), English composer, poet. Music incl. many works for piano, *eg* sonata (1909), *Five poems* (1912) and concerto (1915). These helped to earn him nickname 'the English Debussy', though his music was more original than that implies. Other compositions incl. orchestral, choral and chamber works, violin concerto, songs, and opera *The Alchemist* (1925). Also wrote on occultism and music.

**Scott, Francis George** (1880–1958), Scottish composer. Pupil of Roger-Ducasse. Sensitive and prolific composer of songs set to Scottish poems from 16th to 20th cents., which recreate in musical terms speech rhythms and inflections of Scottish folk poetry.

**Scottish National Orchestra,** originally founded (1891) as Scottish Orchestra; present name adopted 1950. First conductor was George Henschel; successors have incl. Max Bruch, Barbirolli, Szell, Süsskind, Rankl, and (from 1959) Alexander Gibson.

**Scottish Opera,** one of Britain's leading opera companies, based in Glasgow. Founded in 1962 by Alexander Gibson, who has been its principal conductor ever since. Repertory ranges from Purcell to Henze and contemporary Scottish composers.

**Scriabin,** *see* SKRYABIN.

**Sculthorpe, Peter** (1929– ), Australian composer. Output incl. series of vivid orchestral works each entitled *Sun Music,* 8 string quartets and choral, stage and piano music.

**Scythian Suite,** also called *Ala and Lolli,* work by Prokofiev, orig. intended as ballet, but released as concert suite in 1916. Reminiscent in orchestral ferocity to Stravinsky's *Rite of Spring.*

**Sea, The,** *see* MER, LA.

**Sea Drift,** setting of poem by Walt Whitman for baritone solo, chorus and orchestra by Delius (1903).

**Seaman, Christopher** (1942– ), English conductor. Principal conductor of B.B.C. Scottish Symphony Orchestra (1971–77) and of Northern Sinfonia (1973–79). Also conducts orchestras in Germany and Holland.

**Sea Symphony, A,** title of Vaughan Williams' 1st symphony, which is setting for solo singers, chorus and orchestra of sea poems by Walt Whitman. First perf. 1910.

**Searle, Humphrey** (1915–82), English composer. Pupil of Ireland and Webern. One of first and leading British exponents of 12-note technique. Works incl. operas *The Diary of a Madman* (after Gogol), *The Photo of the Colonel* (after Ionesco) and *Hamlet,* trilogy for speakers and orchestra comprising *Gold Coast Customs* and *The Shadows of Cain* (to texts by Edith Sitwell) and *The Riverrun* (Joyce), 5 symphonies, 2 piano concertos, ballet *Noctambules,* setting of Lear's *The Owl and the Pussy Cat* for speaker and chamber ensemble, piano sonata, and songs.

**Seasons, The,** (1) secular oratorio by Haydn (Ger., *Die Jahreszeiten*), words translated and adapted from Thomson's poem by Baron van Swieten. First perf. Vienna, 1801;
(2) ballet music by Glazunov (1900).
*See also* FOUR SEASONS (Vivaldi).

**Sebastiani, Johann** (1622–83), German composer. His *St Matthew Passion* (1663) incl. chorales for solo voice accompanied by 4 *viole da gamba,* and illustrates one of steps in development of Lutheran Passion between 16th cent. and J.S. Bach. Also published 2 vols. of sacred and secular songs, entitled *Parnassblumen* (1672, 1675).

**sec** (Fr.), dry.

**secco,** *see* RECITATIVE.

**Sechzehntel** (Ger.), semiquaver.

**second,** INTERVAL of semitone (minor second *eg* G–A flat), tone (major second *eg* G–A), or tone and a half (augmented second *eg* G-A sharp) when 2 notes concerned have adjacent letter names.

**seconda prattica,** *see* PRIMA PRATTICA.

**seconda volta,** *see* VOLTA (1).

**secondary dominant** (Ger., *Wechseldominante,* 'exchange dominant'), 'dominant of the dominant', *eg* D in key of C (G being dominant). *See* DOMINANT.

**secondo,** *see* PRIMO.

**Secret, The** (Cz., *Tajemství*), opera by Smetana, libretto by E. Krásnohorská. First perf. Prague, 1878. One of Smetana's most distinguished operas, it deals with separation and eventual reunion of 2 lovers.

**Secret Marriage, The** (It., *Il Matrimonio Segreto*), comic opera by Cimarosa, libretto by G. Bertati (based on *The Clandestine Marriage* by Garrick and Colman). First perf. Vienna, 1792.

**Segal, Uri** (1944– ), Israeli conductor. Worked under Bernstein and Szell, and has subsequently conducted leading European orchestras.

Principal conductor of Bournemouth Symphony Orchestra from 1980.

**segno, dal,** *see* DAL SEGNO.

**Segovia, Andrés** (1893– ), Spanish guitarist, most famous in world. By technique and artistry, extended expressive range of instrument, and inspired numerous composers (*eg* Villa-Lobos and Castelnuovo-Tedesco) to write music for him.

**Segreto di Susanna, Il,** *see* SUSANNA'S SECRET.

**segue** (It.), 'follows'. Used as direction (1) to proceed to following movt. without break;

(2) to continue formula which has been indicated, such as arpeggiating of chords or doubling in octaves.

**Seguidilla,** Spanish dance in 3/8 or 3/4 time in style of, but faster than, bolero, with sung passages called *coplas*. Often accompanied by castanets.

**sehr** (Ger.), very.

**Seiber, Mátyás György** (1905–60), Hungarian-born composer, cellist, conductor. Pupil of Kodály. Resident in Britain from 1935. Interests ranged from 16th-cent. music to jazz and 12-note music. Music incl. several choral works (*eg Ulysses,* after Joyce), clarinet concerto, stage, film, chamber, piano and educational music, and songs.

**Seidl, Anton** (1850–98), Hungarian-born conductor. Became Wagner's assistant at Bayreuth (1872). Conductor of Liepzig opera (1879–82), and toured Germany, Holland and England as conductor of 'Nibelungen' opera company. Appointed conductor of Bremen Opera in 1883, of German opera at New York Metropolitan in 1885, and of New York Philharmonic in 1891. Conducted US premières of *Tristan und Isolde* (1886), complete *Ring* (1889), and Dvořák's *New World* symphony (1893).

**Seiffert, Max** (1868–1948), German musicologist. Numerous publications incl. *Geschichte der Klaviermusik* (1899). Edited complete works of Sweelinck and completed Chrysander's edition of *Messiah.* Also responsible for large number of practical editions of works by Bach, Handel and other 18th-cent. composers, and edited series of old music entitled *Organum.*

**Seikilos song,** one of few surviving examples of Greek music, inscribed on tomb of Seikilos (2nd or 1st cent. BC) at Tralles in Asia Minor.

**Seiten** (Ger.), side. *Seitenthema,* second theme of movement in sonata form, *etc.*

**Selle, Thomas** (1599–1663), German composer. Published several sets of solo songs with continuo, of sacred concertos, and of secular choral pieces, and contributed melodies to Rist's collections of chorale texts. One of first to introduce settings of other words into Passion: his *St John Passion* (1643) contains choruses to words from Isaiah and from Psalm 22.

**Semele,** secular oratorio by Handel, to text adapted from earlier opera libretto by Congreve. First perf. London, 1744. Now often staged as opera.

**semibiscroma** (It.), hemidemisemiquaver.

**semibreve** (US, whole-note; Fr., *ronde*; Ger., *ganze Note*; It., *semibreve*), 'half a breve'. Longest note-value normally used in modern notation, written 𝅝 Semibreve rest is written –
In 13th cent. was shortest note; in 15th cent. became normal beat (tactus), and in 18th cent. became theoretical term of reference for all time-signatures and for all other note-values.

**semicroma** (It.), semiquaver.

**semidemisemiquaver,** same as HEMIDEMISEMIQUAVER.

**semihemidemisemiquaver,** note with half time value of HEMIDEMISEMIQUAVER, and 128th time value of semibreve.

**semiminima** (It.), crotchet.

**semiquaver** (US, sixteenth note; Fr., *double croche*; Ger., *Sechzehntel*; It., *semicroma*), note with half time value of quaver, and sixteenth time value of semibreve. Written:

𝅘𝅥𝅯 grouped ♬

Semiquaver rest is written

𝄿

**Semiramide** (It., *Semiramis*), opera by Rossini, libretto by G. Rossi (based on Voltaire's tragedy). First perf. Venice, 1823. Story of legendary Queen of Babylon who kills husband and falls in love with son has inspired operas by many other composers, incl. Porpora, Vivaldi, Gluck, Paisiello, Salieri, Cimarosa, Meyerbeer and Respighi.

**semiseria** (It.), 'half-serious'; 18th cent. term for *opera seria* with some comic scenes.

**semitone,** half a tone – smallest interval in regular use in western music. Can be regarded either as augmented unison (*eg* interval between G and G sharp) or as minor second (*eg* G and A flat) according to context. In EQUAL TEMPERAMENT there are 12 equal semitones in octave.

**semplice** (It.), in a simple manner.

**sempre** (It.), 'always', 'still', as in *sempre piano,* still softly.

**Semyon Kotko,** first of Prokofiev's Soviet operas, composed 1939–40, after his return to Russia. Story (based on Katayev's novel *I, Son of the Working Class*) concerns Ukrainian soldier returning from fighting for Revolution, but whose fiancée's father is an anti-revolutionary.

**Senaillé, Jean Baptiste** (1687–1730), French violinist, composer. Pupil of Vitali. Introduced Italian violin techniques to France. One of first French composers of solo sonatas for violin.

**Senfl, Senffl, Sänftli** or **Senfel, Ludwig** (*c* 1489–1543), Swiss composer. Worked in Vienna, Augsburg and Munich. Corresponded with Luther, and composed polyphonic choral settings of Lutheran chorales. Other works incl. settings of German secular songs, settings of Latin hymns, Magnificats in 8 tones, motets and Masses.

**sennet** (also synnet, cynet, signet), direction in Elizabethan plays that instrumental music is to be played.

**sensibile, sensibilita** (It.; Fr., *sensible*), sensitive. *Nota sensibile,* leading note.

**senza** (It.), without. *Senza rall.,* without slowing down. *Senza sordino,* without mute.

**septet** (Fr., *septette, septuor*; Ger., *Septett*; It., *settimino*), group of 7 performers, or composition, usually instrumental, written for such a group.

**septuor** (Fr.), septet.

**septuplet,** group of 7 notes to be played in time of 4 or 6.

**sequence,** (1) repetition of same melodic pattern at different pitch. Sequential melody, if based on more than one chord, is usually accompanied by sequential harmony. If such a sequence is in exact transposition, involving modulation, it is called 'real' or modulating sequence; if not, 'tonal' or diatonic;

(2) form of Latin poetry widely used in Middle Ages, esp. in France and England, as accretion to liturgy. Early texts were usually in prose, hence Latin term *prosa.* In form, normally consisted of series of pairs of lines, each pair being sung to same melody. Examples are *Dies irae* and *Stabat mater.*

**Seraglio, Il,** *see* ENTFÜHRUNG.

**serenade,** (1) song of amorous devotion, traditionally sung in evening below beloved's window, often with guitar or mandolin accompaniment;

(2) set of movts. for chamber orchestra or wind instruments similar in style to cassation and divertimento, composed for evening entertainment in 18th cent.

**Serenade to Music,** work by Vaughan Williams for 16 solo voices and orchestra, based on speech in *The Merchant of Venice.* Composed in honour of Sir Henry Wood's jubilee as conductor, 1938.

**serenata** (It.), title used in early 18th cent. for secular cantata or short opera written in homage to patron.

**serialism,** method of composition deriving from Schoenberg's TWELVE-NOTE SYSTEM.

**series,** succession of notes presented in certain order, not necessarily to create melody, but to establish relationship between them. Thus note row of TWELVE-NOTE SYSTEM is 'series', which can be treated in various ways – played backwards, turned upside down, *etc* – once original order has been established.

**serio, seria** (It.), serious (also *serioso, seriosa*).

**Serkin, Rudolf** (1903– ), Austrian-born pianist. Resident in US since 1939. One of most distinguished exponents of the classics, esp. Mozart, Beethoven, Schubert and Brahms.

**Serov, Alexander Nikolayevich** (1820–71), Russian composer, music critic. Champion of Wagner. Operas incl. *Judith* and *The Power of Evil.* Also wrote orchestral and choral works.

**serpent** (Fr.; Ger., *Serpent*; It., *serpentone*), obsolete wind instrument, bass of cornett family. Name was suggested by shape. Made of wood covered with leather. Used from 16th to 19th cents. *See* BASS HORN, RUSSIAN BASSOON.

**serré** (Fr.), equivalent of STRINGENDO.

**Serse,** *see* XERXES.

**Serva Padrona, La** (It., *The Maid as Mistress*), comic opera by Pergolesi, libretto by G.A. Federico. First perf. as 2 *intermezzi* in composer's serious opera *Il prigionier superbo,* Naples, 1733. Soon widely perf. on its own, giving impulse to cultivation of *opera buffa,* and indirectly of French *opéra-comique*.

**service,** musical setting of canticles at Morning and Evening Prayer and of congregational part of Communion service in Anglican liturgy. In Morning Service are *Te Deum* and *Benedictus* (or *Jubilate*); in Evening Service, *Magnificat* (or *Cantate domino*) and *Nunc dimittis* (or *Deus misereatur*); in Communion Service, *Kyrie, Sanctus* and *Gloria in excelsis,* and also, in modern times, *Benedictus* and *Agnus Dei*. Full service contains settings of all these parts, which are sung in English. In 16th cent. 'short' service was set in simple style, and 'great' service in more elaborate polyphonic or antiphonal style.

**sesquialtera** (Lat.), (1) HEMIOLA;

(2) MUTATION STOP on organ, normally with 2 ranks of 2⅔ft and 1⅗ft giving intervals of twelfth and seventeenth above fundamental.

**Sessions, Roger** (1896– ), American composer. Pupil of Bloch. Lived in Europe (1925–33), then at various US universities. Works incl. operas *The Trial of Lucullus* (after Brecht, 1947) and *Montezuma* (1954), 8 symphonies, concertos for violin, violin and cello, and piano, chamber music, and songs. Author of various books on music.

**sestetto,** *see* SEXTET.

**settimino,** *see* SEPTET.

**Seven Last Words of the Saviour on the Cross** (Ger., *Die Sieben Worte des Erlösers am Kreuze*), orchestral work in 7 slow movts. by Haydn (1785) commissioned by Cathedral of Cadiz. Later arranged as string quartet, op 51 (1787) and as choral work (1796). Oratorio on same subject was composed by Schütz (1645) with text from Gospels.

**seventh,** INTERVAL comprising first and last of any series of 7 notes in diatonic scale *eg* F-E. Major seventh is semitone less than octave *eg* C-B. Minor seventh is tone less than octave *eg* C–B flat. Diminished seventh is 1½ tones less than octave *eg* C sharp–B flat. Since seventh is dissonance, chord containing seventh required resolution in traditional harmony. Most important chords containing sevenths are DOMINANT seventh and DIMINISHED SEVENTH chords.

**sextet** (Fr., *sextette, sextuor*; Ger., *Sextett*; It., *sestetto*), group of 6 performers, of composition written for such a group. String sextet usually contains 2 violins, 2 violas and 2 cellos. In vocal music term is usually only applied to operatic ensembles.

**sextolet, sextuplet,** group of 6 notes to be performed in time of 4.

**sextuor,** *see* SEXTET.

**sfogato** (It.), 'evaporated'. Term used by Chopin and others to indicate airy quality of playing.

**sforzando, sforzato** (It.), 'forcing', *ie* giving strong accent on single note or chord. Abbrev. *sfz* or *sf.* Abbrev. *sfp* indicates that *sforzando* is to be followed immediately by softness of tone.

**Sgambati, Giovanni** (1841–1914), Italian pianist, conductor, composer. Pupil of Liszt. Disciple of Liszt and Wagner. Works incl. 2 symphonies, *Requiem*, chamber music, and songs.

**shake,** alternative name for TRILL.

**Shaliapin,** *see* CHALIAPIN.

**Shankar, Ravi** (1920– ), Indian musician. One of greatest exponents of SITAR, has done much to arouse Western interest in Indian music.

**shanty,** work-song sung by sailors in days of sailing ships. Usually have decided rhythm and are in form of solo verses and chorus.

**Shapero, Harold** (1920– ), American composer. Pupil of Hindemith, Křenek, Piston and Nadia Boulanger. Works incl. symphony, *Nine-minute Overture,* and chamber and piano music.

**Shaporin, Yuri Alexandrovich** (1889–1966), Russian composer. Works incl. symphony for orchestra, brass band and chorus (1932), setting for chorus, soloists and orchestra of Blok's poem *On the Field of Kulikovo* (1939), oratorio *The Battle on Russian Soil* (1944), opera *The Decembrists* (1941), incidental and piano music, and songs.

**sharp** (Fr., *dièse*; Ger., *Kreuz*; It., diesis), the sign

♯

which raises by semitone pitch of line or space in stave on which it stands. Thus C sharp is semitone higher than C natural.

**Sharp, Cecil James** (1859–1924), collector of English folk music. In 1911 founded English Folk Dance Society and became director of School of Folksong and Dance, Stratford-on-Avon. His collections laid foundation of English folk song and folk dance revival. Also collected in Appalachian Mountains of US.

**sharp mixture,** organ stop sounding high harmonics in addition to fundamental note, so giving bright tone ('sharp' refers to tone quality, not pitch).

**Shaw, George Bernard** (1856–1950), Irish-born dramatist, critic. His musical writings, though peripheral to his career, offer unsurpassed picture of music in London at end of 19th cent. His witty and penetrating reviews appeared in the *Star* and the *World,* often under pseud. of Corno di Bassetto; their moments of wrong-headedness are a small price to pay for their vitality.

**shawm, shawn,** primitive and coarse sounding instrument that gave rise to OBOE. Sometimes confused with CHALUMEAU, forerunner of clarinet, since this name was often loosely used to describe any member of woodwind family. Made in various sizes: in Germany, small, high ones were called *Schalmei* and large ones *Pommern* (Fr., *bombarde*); latter had tubes curved back from pipe to mouthpiece like bassoon.

**Shchedrin, Rodion** (1932– ), Russian composer. works incl. ballet *The Little Hump-Backed Horse,* symphonies, piano music, and songs.

**Shebalin, Vissarion Yakovlevich** (1902–63), Russian composer. Pupil of Miaskovsky at Moscow Conservatory, of which he later became director. Criticized by authorities in 1948 for 'inharmonious music', but at other times won approval. Works incl. opera *The Embassy Bridegroom,* 5 symphonies (3rd, *Lenin,* with chorus), cantatas, overtures, concertos for violin and cello, chamber and instrumental music, and songs.

**Sheep may safely graze** (Ger., *Schafe können sicher weiden*), aria for soprano with 2 recorders and figured bass from Bach's earliest secular cantata *Was mir behagt* (1716).

**Sheherazade,** symphonic suite by Rimsky-Korsakov, op 35 (1888), based on stories from *Arabian Nights.* Fokine's ballet based on music was first perf. Paris, 1910.

**Shéhérazade** (Fr.), set of 3 songs with orchestra by Ravel (1903), to poems by Tristan Klingsor. Subject matter has no connection with Rimsky-Korsakov's suite.

**Shelomo** (Heb., *Solomon*), rhapsody for cello and orchestra by Bloch (1915). German spelling *Schelomo* is often used.

**Shepherd, Arthur** (1880–1958), American composer, conductor. *Horizons* (1st of 2 symphonies) incl. traditional cowboy music. Also wrote violin concerto, fantasy for piano and orchestra, 3 string quartets, instrumental music, and songs.

**Shepherds of the Delectable Mountain, The,** *see* PILGRIM'S PROGRESS.

**shepherd's pipe,** primitive double reed wind instrument. Resembles bagpipe chanter.

**Shield, William** (1748–1829), English composer. Pupil of Avison. Composer to Covent Garden (1782–91, 1792–7), Master of King's Musick from 1817. 'Composed and selected' music for many stage works *eg* opera *Rosina* (1782). Also wrote songs, string trios, violin duets, and theoretical works.

**shift,** (1) change of POSITION of left hand on stringed instrument; (2) change of position of slide of trombone.

**Shirley, George** (1934– ), American tenor. Has appeared at New York Metropolitan, Covent Garden and other leading opera houses.

**Shirley-Quirk, John** (1931– ), English baritone. Known for *Lieder* recitals and in opera. Created roles in several of Britten's operas.

**shofar, shophar,** ancient Jewish wind instrument still used in synagogue. Made from ram's horn. Notes are produced in same way as on bugle.

**short octave,** lowest notes on keyboard instruments in 16th, 17th cents. were often arranged so as to provide within compass of sixth (short octave) bass notes normally required, leaving out those which did not occur on account of restricted range of keys used.

**short score,** *see* SCORE.

**Shostakovich, Dmitri** (1906–75), Russian composer. Most important Russian composer after death of Prokofiev. Born in St Petersburg, and there studied composition under Steinberg. Wrote Scherzo for orchestra at 13, and 1st symphony was performed in Leningrad in 1926. Works of next few years were either political, as in 2nd symphony (1927, dedicated to October Revolution of 1917), and 3rd (*May the First*, 1930), or else satirical, as in opera *The Nose* (1927–8), and ballet *The Golden Age* (1930). Official disfavour fell on more extreme forms of social caricature in his music, and opera *Lady Macbeth of Mzensk* (*Katerina Ismailova*) was denounced in 1936 as 'bourgeois and formalistic'. 4th symphony was withdrawn (1936) in rehearsal, and 5th (1937), in more serious vein and in traditional form, was described by composer as 'a Soviet artist's practical reply to criticism'. 7th symphony was composed during siege of Leningrad in 1941 and depicts peace, struggle and victory. After renewed official criticism in 1948, Shostakovich undertook to bring his work closer to 'folk art'. Nevertheless he succeeded in producing some of the most internationally impressive music of our time, and proved himself a composer of remarkable staying power. Wrote total of 15 symphonies: no 10 is perhaps finest of all his works; nos 13 (song-symphony based on poems by Yevtushenko), 14 (inspired by poems about death), and 15 reveal vein of pessimism unusual in Soviet music. His string quartets are among finest modern examples of this form. Also wrote violin, cello and piano concertos, piano quintet, piano trio, duo sonatas, and solo piano music (incl. set of preludes and fugues). In most of his works he replenished traditional classical forms with fresh vitality and meaning.

**shoulder-viol** (It., *viola da spalla*), viol midway in size between that of *viola da braccio* (arm viol) and *viola da gamba* (leg viol). It was played held in front of the body, and sometimes fastened to it. This made it suitable for playing while walking, and in Italy it was much used for church processions.

**Shropshire Lad, A,** orchestral rhapsody by Butterworth (1912), inspired by Housman's poems. Butterworth also wrote song-cycle on some of Housman poems.

**Shudi, Burkat** or **Burkhardt Tschudi** (1702–73), Swiss harpsichord-maker. Became apprentice in London in 1718, and founded own business in 1742. His son-in-law John Broadwood succeeded him. Patented Venetian SWELL for harpsichord in 1769.

**si** (Fr., It.), the note B.

**Sibelius, Jean** (1865–1957), Finnish composer, most famous ever to emerge from that country. Studied in Helsinki, Berlin and Vienna. Works of 1890–1900 expressed aspirations of Finland towards national musical culture; incl. tone poems *En Saga* (1892) and *Finlandia* (1899), and 4 *Legends* based on Finnish epic *Kalevala*: *Lemminkaïnen and the Maidens* (1895), *Lemminkaïnen in Tuonela*

(1895), *The Swan of Tuonela* (1893), *The Return of Lemminkaïnen* (1895). These works show individual approach to treatment of orchestra and of thematic material which is further developed in 7 symphonies (1899–1924). In exposition of 1st movt. of 2nd symphony several short motifs are presented, which are built into long phrases in development, and combined and compressed in recapitulation. 4th symphony is concise in form and is mainly based on melodic and harmonic relation of tritone. In 7th symphony, normal scheme is compressed into single movt., final section being partial recapitulation of 1st section. Other notable works incl. symphonic *Ride and Sunrise* (1909), *The Bard* (1913), *The Oceanides* (written after visit to US in 1914), *Tapiola* (1925), incidental music to Shakespeare's *The Tempest* (1926), violin concerto (1903–5), and string quartet *Voces Intimae* (1909). Also wrote many pieces for violin and piano, cello and piano, voice and piano, piano solo, and chorus – but these are of minor importance. In 1897 Finnish govt. granted him annual stipend to enable him to compose without distraction. In 1904 retired to country house at Järvenpäa to compose in seclusion. Ceased to compose in 1926, though output up to then was large enough and imposing enough to establish him (esp. in Britain) as major composer, even though was less influential than was once hoped. His symphonies and symphonic poems, without being revolutionary works, speak with taut, decisive and individual voice.

**siciliano** (It.; Fr., *sicilienne*; Eng., *siciliana*), type of Sicilian dance used in baroque period in instrumental music and arias, written in moderately slow 6/8 or 12/8 time, and often in minor key. In style and in frequent use of rhythm

it is similar to PASTORALE.

**Sicilian Vespers, The** (Fr., *Les Vêpres Siciliennes*; It., *I Vespri Siciliani*), opera by Verdi, libretto by A.E. Scribe and C. Duveyrier. First perf. Paris, 1855. Story concerns 13th-cent. rising of Sicilians against French rulers.

**side drum** (Fr., *tambour, tambour militaire, caisse claire*; Ger., *Kleine Trommel, Militärtrommel*; It., *tamburo militare*), cylindrically shaped drum, also called snare drum; smallest drum normally used in orchestra. Snares made of gut or metal are stretched across lower of 2 parchment heads, giving drum its characteristic rattling sound; snares can be thrown out of action instantly, giving totally different tone.

**Sieben Worte, Die,** *see* SEVEN LAST WORDS.

**Siefert, Paul** (1586–1666), German composer, organist. Pupil of Sweelinck in Amsterdam. Held posts in Warsaw and Danzig. Style of his *Psalmen Davids* (1640) was criticized by Marco Scacchi, provoking extended controversy. Also composed fantasies for organ, and 2nd vol. of Psalms (1651).

**Siege of Corinth, The** (Fr., *Le Siège de Corinthe*), opera by Rossini. First perf. Paris, 1826. Based on earlier opera MAOMETTO II.

**Siegfried,** *see* RING DES NIBELUNGEN.

**Siegfried Idyll,** work for small orchestra by Wagner (1870), celebrating birth of his son Siegfried, and using themes from opera of same name.

**sight,** system used in England in 15th, 16th cents. for teaching choristers to descant, *ie* to extemporize simple part to go with plainsong melody. Singer imagined his notes to be on same staff as plainsong (tenor) but sang them at pitch suitable to compass of his voice. Thus, to treble descanter, who sang octave above his 'sight' pitch, third below plainsong in 'sight' actually sounded sixth above plainsong. *See* DESCANT.

**sight reading,** playing or singing piece of music at first sight.

**signature,** *see* KEY SIGNATURE, TIME SIGNATURE.

**Signor Bruschino, Il,** comic opera by Rossini, libretto by Foppa. First perf. Venice, 1813. Story, a typical 18th-cent. marital tangle, is based on French comedy by de Chazy and Ourry. Overture, often performed separately, requires violinists to tap music stands with bows.

**Sigurd Jorsalfar** (Norw., *Sigurd the Crusader*), incidental music by Grieg for play by Bjørnson, incl. well-known *Homage March*.

**Si j'etais roi** (Fr., If I were King), opera by Adam, libretto by A.P. d'Ennery and J. Brésil. First perf. Paris, 1852.

**Silbermann, Gottfried** (1683–1753), most celebrated member of German family of organ-builders and harpsichord-makers. Built organs in Freiburg, Saxony and Dresden. Also built clavichords and harpsichords, and was first German to make pianos. His nephews Johann Daniel, Johann Andreas and Johann Heinrich carried on the trade.

**Silken Ladder, The** (It., *La Scala di seta*), opera by Rossini, libretto by G. Rossi (after comedy by F.A.E. de Planard). First perf. Venice, 1812. Known for sparkling overture.

**Sills, Beverly,** orig. Belle Silverstein (1929– ), American soprano. Made opera debut in 1953. Known esp. for colaratura roles. Has appeared at La Scala, New York Metropolitan and Covent Garden. Long associated with New York City Opera, becoming director in 1979.

**Siloti, Alexander Ilyich** (1863–1945), Russian pianist. Pupil of Chaikovsky, N. Rubinstein and Liszt. Later settled in US. His edition of Chaikovsky's 2nd piano concerto is still widely performed, though it contains reprehensible cuts.

**silver band,** common name for brass band in days when instruments were silver plated.

**similar motion,** movement of 2 or more parts or melodies in same direction, either up or down. When parts move by same interval, parallel or CONSECUTIVE INTERVALS result. When 2 parts rise to fifth or octave, effect is referred to as 'hidden' fifths or octaves, and is usually avoided between outer parts in contrapuntal writing, unless higher part moves by step to next degree of scale.

**simile** (It.), 'like', 'similar', used as direction to continue formula which has been indicated, *eg* arpeggiating of chords. Abbrev. *sim.*

**Simon Boccanegra,** opera by Verdi, libretto by F.M. Piave (based on Spanish drama by A.G. Gutierrez). First perf. Venice, 1857, was failure. Rev. version (with libretto altered by A. Boito) successfully staged at Milan, 1881. Story concerns 14th-cent. Doge of Genoa.

**simple time,** *see* COMPOUND TIME.

**Simpson, Robert** (1921– ), English composer, writer on music. Pupil of Howells. Works incl. 7 symphonies, 2 concertos, 7 string quartets and other chamber music. Has written important studies of Nielsen and Bruckner.

**sin',** *see* SINO.

**Sinding, Christian** (1856–1941), Norwegian composer, pianist. Studied in Germany. Lived in Oslo and Berlin. Taught in US 1921–2. Works incl. opera, 3 symphonies and violin concerto, but now remembered only for miniatures *eg Rustle of Spring* for piano.

**sine nomine** (Lat.), 'without name'; *see* MASS.

**sinfonia** (It.), symphony – but word has wider meanings than this would suggest. Orig. simply meant instrumental piece, and title was used thus by Bach and others. Then could also mean prelude or overture to opera, cantata or suite (*see* OVERTURE). Now sometimes used as performing name of small orchestra.

**Sinfonia Antartica** (It., *Antarctic Symphony*), Vaughan Williams' 7th symphony, based on music written for film *Scott of the Antarctic* (1949). First perf. 1953.

**sinfonia concertante** (It.), orchestral work, normally in several movts., in which there are parts for solo instruments, generally 2 or more, usually with less emphasis on display than in solo concerto.

**Sinfonia da Requiem,** symphony by Britten, composed (1940) in memory of his parents.

**Sinfonia Domestica,** *see* DOMESTIC SYMPHONY.

**Sinfonia Espansiva,** Nielsen's 3rd symphony, op 27 (1912). Music is 'expansive' both in its picture of Danish landscape and in its attitude to humanity. Slow movt. contains wordless parts for solo soprano and baritone.

**Sinfonie, Symphonie** (Ger.), symphony.

**sinfonietta** (It.), short, small-scale symphony. Sometimes also used as performing name of small orchestra.

**Sinfonische Dichtung** (Ger.), symphonic poem.

**Singakademie** (Ger.), 'singing academy'. Society for concert-giving founded by K.F.C. Fasch in Berlin, 1791. Today name is used by many choirs in German-speaking countries.

**Singspiel** (Ger.), lit. 'sing-play', *ie* German comic opera with spoken dialogue. Earliest examples (mid 18th cent.) were imitations of English ballad operas, but thereafter form developed independently. Mozart's *Die Entführung* (1782) and *The Magic Flute* (1791) are outstanding examples. In early 19th cent. history of form merges with that of German romantic opera. Later term came to be used in Germany as equivalent of musical comedy.

**Sinigaglia, Leone** (1868–1944), Italian composer. Pupil of Dvořák, who prob. aroused his interest in folk music. Works incl. set of Piedmontese dances, *Piedmontese Rhapsody* for violin and orchestra, collection of Piedmontese popular songs for voice and piano, and chamber and instrumental music.

**sinistra** (It.), left hand.

**sink-a-pace,** *see* CINQUE-PACE.

**sino, sin'** (It.), until, *eg sin' al segno,* go on until the sign.

**Sins of My Old Age** (Fr., *Péchés de vieillesse*), title given by Rossini to several sets of songs and instrumental pieces which he wrote after abandoning career as opera composer (with *William Tell,* 1829). Music is characterized by wit and by comic titles.

**sistema** (It.), staff.

**sistrum,** ancient percussion instrument, prob. originated in Egypt. Best known form has wooden discs or metal bars strung onto frame; when instrument is shaken these strike against each other, producing rattling sound. More developed version has sets of tuned bells that can be played with beater. Recently this type has been improved by addition of keyboard.

**Sir John in Love,** opera by Vaughan Williams, to libretto drawn from Shakespeare's *The Merry Wives of Windsor* – the hero being Sir John Falstaff. First perf. London, 1929.

**Siroe, Re di Persia** (It., *Siroes, King of Persia*), opera by Handel, libretto adapted from Metastasio. First perf. London, 1728.

**sitar,** Indian type of long-necked lute with movable frets and from 3 to 7 strings, below which are *c* 12 sympathetic strings. Ravi Shankar is distinguished modern exponent.

**Sitzprobe** (Ger.), term used in opera for a 'sitting rehearsal', *ie* one in which singers play their roles sitting down, with accompaniments played by orchestra.

**Six, Les** (Fr.), 'The Six'. Name given by H. Collet in 1920 to group of 6 young French composers influenced by Satie's emphasis on simplicity and by artistic ideals of Cocteau. Members of group, who soon ceased to be 6, were Milhaud, Honegger, Poulenc, Auric, Durey and Tailleferre.

**six-four chord,** chord containing sixth and fourth from its bass note. It is second inversion of chord based on note which is fourth from its bass, *eg* 6/4 chord G–C–E is second inversion of C–E–G. *See* CHORD.

**sixte ajoutée,** *see* ADDED SIXTH.

**sixteenth-note** (US), semiquaver.

**sixth,** INTERVAL comprising first and last of any 6 notes in diatonic scale *eg* F–D. Sixth may be minor *eg* F–D flat, major *eg* F–D, or augmented *eg* F–D sharp. Sixth, like third, of which it is INVERSION, is imperfect consonance. Term 'sixth chord' is sometimes used in referring to SIX-THREE CHORD. *See* AUGMENTED SIXTH, CHORD.

**sixth, added,** *see* ADDED SIXTH.

**six-three chord,** chord containing sixth and third from its bass note. It is first inversion of chord based on note which is sixth from its bass, *eg* 6/3 chord E–G–C is first inversion of C–E–G. *See* CHORD.

**sixty-fourth note** (US), hemidemisemiquaver.

**Skalkottas, Nikos** (1904–49), Greek composer, violinist. Pupil of Schoenberg and Weill in Berlin. Earlier works show influence of Schoenberg, but later developed own style, in which Greek folk music played part. Works incl. *Greek Dances* for orchestra, concertos, music for strings, and 4 string quartets. Misunderstood till after his death, when began to win international acclaim.

**Skazka o Tsare Saltane,** *see* LEGEND OF THE CZAR SALTAN.

**Skilton, Charles Sanford** (1868–1941), American composer. Works, often incorporating American Indian elements, incl. operas, and orchestral, choral, piano and organ music.

**Skryabin, Alexander Nikolaievich** (1872–1915), Russian composer, pianist. Pupil of Taneyev and Arensky. In 1896 toured Europe, giving concerts of own works. Taught piano at Moscow Conservatory (1898–1908), lived in Switzerland till 1905, and in Brussels (1908–10). Early works (2 symphonies, piano concerto, 3 sonatas, 7 sets of preludes, and other works for piano) had little relation to Russian music of time (1890–1903), but showed influence of Chopin, Liszt and Wagner, coupled with subtle sense of harmony. In succeeding compositions (*The Divine Poem* and *Poem of Ecstasy* for orchestra, 7 further sonatas, 8 further sets of preludes, 6 *Poems, Vers la flamme,* and other piano works) he embarked on experiments with esoteric harmonies connected with his ideas on theosophy. As basis for harmonies he devised so-called MYSTIC CHORD. In last works (*Prometheus* and unfinished *Mystery*) he was moving towards conception of synthesis of arts – score of *Prometheus* incl. 'colour organ' (TASTIERA PER LUCE) invented by Rimington.

**slancio** (It.), impetus.

**slapstick** or **whip** (Fr., *fouet*; Ger., *Peitsche*; It., *frustra*), percussion instrument consisting of 2 strips of hardboard hinged together but with spring that normally keeps them at an angle. Sound of strips striking each other resembles crack of whip.

**slått** (pl., *slåtter*), type of Norwegian folk tune, often in march rhythm, played on fiddle. Inspired several piano pieces by Grieg, and has attracted other Norwegian composers.

**Slavonic Dances,** 2 sets of dances by Dvořák (1878, 1886), orig. for piano duet but later orchestrated. Though tunes are suggestive of folk music, they are in fact original.

**Slavonic Rhapsodies,** 3 orchestral works by Dvořák (1878). Though tunes are suggestive of folk music, they are in fact original.

**Sleepers Awake,** *see* WACHET AUF.

**Sleeping Beauty, The,** ballet by Chaikovsky, choreography by Petipa. First perf. St Petersburg, 1890.

**sleigh-bells** (Fr., *grelots*; Ger., *Schellen, Schellengeläute*; It., *sonagli*), small metal bells containing steel ball. Normally fastened to leather strap, but for orchestral use they are fixed to steel frame connected to wooden handle, allowing for high degree of rhythmic precision when hand taps frame or *vice versa*.

**slentando** (It.), becoming gradually slower.

**slide** (Fr., *coulé, flatté*; Ger., *Schleifer*), (1) ornament used in 17th, early 18th cents., also called 'elevation' or 'wholefall', consisting of 2 grace notes moving up by step to principal note. Indicated in variety of ways:

played

and

Purcell, who calls it 'slur', gives

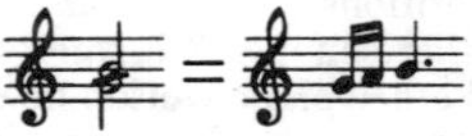

and Chambonnières gives

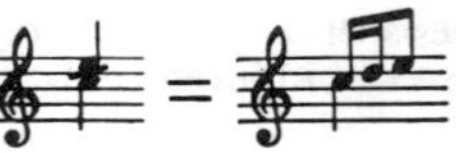

Later composers and editors usually write out grace notes;

(2) movement of left hand on violin which effects quick change of POSITION, at same time producing slight PORTAMENTO. Paganini extended use of slide to rapid playing of chromatic scale passages;

(3) device which alters length of air column in TROMBONE.

**slide trumpet,** *see* TRUMPET.

**Slit drum,** *see* WOOD DRUMS.

**slughorn** or **slughorne,** although mentioned by Browning and Chatterton, no such musical instrument has ever existed.

**slur** (Fr., *légature*; Ger., *Bindungszeichen*; It., *legatura*), (1) curved line over or under group of notes indicating that they are to be played or sung smoothly, or, on stringed instrument, in one bow. If slur is combined with staccato marks, indicates phrase should be performed semi-staccato;

(2) Purcell used term as equivalent of SLIDE.

**Smalley, Roger** (1943– ), English composer, pianist. Pupil of Stockhausen. One of Britain's leading exponents of electronic music.

Works incl. *Beat Music* for orchestra and electronic instruments (1971), and vocal, chamber and piano music.

**Smetana, Bedřich** (1824–84), Czech composer. Son of brewer. Studied composition in Prague, where taught and composed till 1856. Lived as conductor and teacher in Göteborg, Sweden (1857–9, 1860–1). Visited Liszt in Weimar, and during 1858–61 wrote 3 symphonic poems, *Richard III, Wallenstein's Camp* and *Hakon Jarl.* Returned to Prague in 1863. Went on to write most famous opera *The Bartered Bride* (1866), and 3 other operas on national subjects by 1874, when suddenly became completely deaf. Nevertheless in following years composed best instrumental works – *Má Vlast* (*My Country,* set of 6 musical landscapes), and 1st string quartet entitled *From My Life.* Though very seldom used actual folk songs, his Czech operas are thoroughly national in subject and feeling. Also wrote trio, 2nd string quartet, piano pieces, choruses, and songs. His operas are: *The Brandenburgers in Bohemia* (1866), *The Bartered Bride* (1866), *Dalibor* (1868), *Libuše* (written 1871–2, perf. 1881), *The Two Widows* (1874), *The Kiss* (1876), *The Secret* (1878), *The Devil's Wall* (1882), and unfinished *Viola.* Smetana was Czechoslovakia's first great nationalist composer during period of country's rising opposition to Austrian rule, and his patriotism is strongly reflected in his operas – most heroically in *Dalibor.* His comedies are equally characteristic, and just as deeply Czech.

**Smith, Bernard** ('Father Smith'), *see* SCHMIDT, BERNHARD.

**Smith, Bessie** (1895–1937), black American singer. Known as 'Empress of the Blues'. Greatest exponent of 'classic' blues form. Recordings provide vivid evidence of majesty of her style and intensity of her response to songs she sang – many of them about loneliness and wretchedness.

**Smith, John Stafford** (1750–1836), English organist, composer, editor. Pupil of Boyce. Collected and published early English music. Works incl. glees, catches, canons, madrigals, anthems, part-songs, and songs. Tune of his 'Anacreon in Heaven' was adopted for 'The Star-Spangled Banner'.

**Smith Brindle, Reginald** (1917– ), English composer, author. Pupil of Dallapiccola, spending several years in Italy. Works, which show influence of Berio and Nono, incl. opera *Antigone* (1969), symphony, *Apocalypse* and other orchestral works, and choral, chamber, electronic and guitar music. Books incl. *The New Music* (1975).

**smorzando** (It.), dying away.

**Smyth, Ethel Mary** (1858–1944), English composer, author. Studied in Germany. Back in Britain became leader in women's suffrage movement and was jailed in 1911. Created Dame in 1922. Wrote operas *Fantasio* (1898), *The Wood* (1902), *The Wreckers* (first perf. as *Strandrecht,* Leipzig, 1906), *The Boatswain's Mate* (1916), *Fête galante* (1923), and *Entente Cordiale* (1926). Also wrote Mass, *The Prison* (1930), and other choral works.

**snare drum, snares,** *see* SIDE DRUM.

**Snegourochka,** *see* SNOW MAIDEN.

**Snow Maiden, The** (Russ., *Snegourochka*), opera by Rimsky-Korsakov, libretto by composer (after play by A. Ostrovsky). First perf. St Petersburg, 1882.

**soave** (It.), in a smooth and gentle manner.

**Söderström, Elisabeth** (1927– ), Swedish soprano. One of greatest opera singers of her generation, known esp. in Strauss roles.

**soft pedal,** *see* PIANO.

**soggetto** (It.), 'subject', 'theme', (1) subject of fugue or other contrapuntal piece which is short and of abstract or stock type, so distinguished from *andamento* (longer subject of more individual character), and from *attacco* (POINT of imitation);

(2) term *soggetto cavato* ('carved-out' or derived subject) was used by 16th-cent. theorists for theme derived from words by using SOLMIZATION syllables corresponding to vowels of words.

**soh;** anglicized form of Italian *sol* (G). In TONIC SOL-FA, fifth note (or dominant) of major scale.

**Soirées musicales** (Fr., musical evenings), collection of songs and other pieces by Rossini, published 1835. Respighi's ballet *La Boutique Fantasque* and Britten's *Soirées musicales* are both orchestrations of some of Rossini's music.

**Soir et la Tempête, Le,** *see* MATIN.

**sol** (Fr., It.), the note G. Also fifth note of hexachord. *See* SOLMIZATION.

**Soldier's Tale, The** (Fr., *L'Histoire du soldat*), work by Stravinsky based on text by C.F. Ramuz. Tale, inspired by Russian folklore, concerns soldier, violin, Devil, and princess. Scored for narrator, 2 actors, dancer, and instrumental ensemble. First perf. Lausanne, 1918.

**solenne** (It.), solemn.

**Soler, Padre Antonio** (1729–83), Spanish composer, monk. Wrote church music, harpsichord sonatas (influenced by D. Scarlatti), incidental music, 6 quintets for strings and other chamber music, and theoretical treatise.

**Solesmes,** Benedictine monastery near Le Mans. Chief centre of study of plainsong. Since 1904 Solesmes editions of liturgical chant have been official Vatican editions.

**sol-fa,** *see* TONIC SOL-FA.

**solfeggio** (It.; Fr., *solfège*), study of ear-training through singing of exercises to syllables of sol-fa. In more advanced forms, exercises are sung to vowels and are then more properly called *vocalizzi* (Fr., *vocalises*). In France term *solfège* is applied to course of ear-training and general musicianship.

**solmization,** use of syllables to designate notes of hexachord. Those adopted by Guido d'Arezzo were used in medieval theory as system of reference and as means of ear-training: ut, re, mi, fa, sol, la. These developed into modern French and Italian names for notes, and TONIC SOL-FA system.

**solo** (It.), alone. Piece to be performed by one person alone, or with others merely accompanying (as in concerto).

**Solomon,** secular oratorio by Handel, to text, based on Bible, attrib. (without sufficient authority) to T. Morell. First perf. London, 1749.

**solo organ,** manual on ORGAN which incl. stops intended for solo, rather than combined, use. Found on organs of 4 or more manuals and is placed above swell. Its stops are enclosed in swell-box. Normally contains set of loud reeds and *eg* viola da gamba, concert flute, clarinet, orchestral oboe and French horn. More recently MUTATION STOPS have been incl.

**solovox,** electronic instrument usually attached to piano, but with own keyboard. Imitates sounds of various instruments, but can only produce one note at a time.

**soltanto** (It.), solely.

**Solti, Georg** (1912– ), Hungarian-born conductor. Pupil of Dohnányi and Kodály. Resident in Switzerland during WWII. Became director of Munich Opera (1946), Frankfurt Opera (1952), and musical director of Covent Garden (1961–71), where was esp. associated with Wagner and Strauss. Later became conductor of Chicago Symphony Orchestra and London Philharmonic Orchestra. Knighted 1972.

**Sombrero de tres picos, El,** *see* THREE-CORNERED HAT.

**Somervell, Arthur** (1863–1937), English composer. Pupil of Stanford and Parry. Works incl. symphony, choral and chamber music, and songs. Knighted 1929.

**Somis, Giovanni Battista** (1686–1763), Italian violinist, composer. Pupil of Correlli and Vivaldi. Works incl. 2 violin concertos, solo sonatas, and trio sonatas. His pupils incl. Leclair, Giardini and Pugnani.

**Sommernachtstraum** (Ger.), *see* MIDSUMMER NIGHT'S DREAM.

**Son and Stranger** (Ger., *Die Heimkehr aus der Fremde*), operetta by Mendelssohn. First perf. privately, Berlin, 1829. First public perf., Leipzig, 1851.

**sonata,** before 1750, composition for single instrument, or for one or more solo instruments accompanied by continuo. After 1750, term denotes composition in several movts. for solo instrument, or for solo instrument and piano. Orig. term was used as equivalent of CANZONA (*canzon da sonar*), but was soon applied to pieces for 1 or 2 violins and continuo – in later 17th cent. these became 2 chief media for sonata.

Sonata for solo instrument and continuo (*sonata a due*) was called solo sonata, though part was also written for bass. Sonata for 2 instruments (usually violins) and continuo was called trio sonata, and also had bass part (usually cello). Many sonatas for instrumental ensemble were also published in later 17th cent. Term *sonata da camera* ('chamber sonata') was applied to series of dance movts. preceded by prelude (*sinfonia*), and was adopted by Corelli. Corelli also adopted term *sonata da chiesa* ('church sonata') for trio sonatas of 1683 and 1689, which have 4 movts. – slow-fast-slow-fast; though

| | (Introduction) Exposition | |
|---|---|---|
| TONALITY | 1st group<br>(In major mode)<br>Tonic<br><br>(In minor mode)<br>Tonic | 2nd group<br><br>Dominant<br><br><br>Relative major |
| THEMATIC CHARACTER | Leading theme is direct and concise. | Leading theme is *cantabile.* |
| THEMATIC TREATMENT | Complete and successive presentation. | |

number of movts. in sonatas up to 1750 varies considerably, this scheme was used consistently by Bach and Handel. Sonatas for unaccompanied string instrument were comparatively rare, and term was rarely used of keyboard works before D. Scarlatti's 1-movt. pieces (also called *Esercizi*).

Modern convention which restricts use of term sonata to instrumental solos and duets is based on distinction of medium rather than form: 3-movt. form (I. Allegro in SONATA FORM; II. Slow movt.; III. Allegro in sonata or rondo form) of classical and romantic duet-sonata is shared by trio, string quartet, quintet *etc* as well as by concerto and symphony. In sonatas of earlier classical period (early Mozart, Haydn, J.C. Bach) violin plays accompanying role (sometimes optional) to keyboard instrument. True duet style was developed in Mozart's mature violin sonatas. His 3-movt. scheme, Allegro-Adagio-Allegro, was continued by Beethoven (who sometimes included Scherzo), and became standard; 2nd or 3rd movts. were sometimes in form of theme and variations. Classical basis of form has remained relatively stable.

Modern keyboard sonata takes its departure from works of C.P.E. Bach. In piano sonatas of Haydn, Mozart and Clementi, 3 movts. are normal; Beethoven uses 4 in earlier sonatas. Beethoven's sonatas op 90 and 111 have only 2 movts. Liszt's attempt at more fluid form in Sonata in B minor (1854) had little effect on later history of form, though single movt. sonatas have been written by modern composers.

**sonata form,** term for design most often used since *c* 1750 for 1st movt., and sometimes slow movt. and finale, of symphony, sonata, trio, quartet *etc,* and often for overture. Procedures denoted by names of 3 sections – exposition (*ie* presentation), DEVELOPMENT (*ie* discursive treatment), and recapitulation (*ie* return) – were present

| Development | Recapitulation (Coda) | |
|---|---|---|
| | 1st group | 2nd group |
| Varying | Tonic | Tonic |
| Varying | Tonic | Tonic major |
| Varying | As exposition | |
| Discursive, e.g. by dismemberment, transposition, contrapuntal treatment, combination. | Re-presentation | |

in earlier music, and both these and basis of its scheme of tonality were developed from its immediate ancestor, BINARY FORM of later baroque period. Special characteristics are definite distinction between parts that these procedures play in design, and complete co-ordination of thematic character, thematic treatment and tonality in making that design clear, logical and symmetrical. Its basic plan in late 18th cent. is shown in table above. Introduction is usually unrelated to exposition before Beethoven, and is often dispensed with. Leading theme of 1st group and that of 2nd group are commonly called '1st subject' and '2nd subject'; 1st group frequently contains single theme, 2nd group seldom less than 2, and in Beethoven's longer movts. as many as 6. Latter part of 1st group in exposition normally has function of making transition to related key; hence, corresponding part of 1st group in recapitulation differs from it, not having that function. Recapitulation may differ from exposition in details, *eg* in orchestration and in use of new accompaniments to themes. Latter part of development has function of preparing for return of tonic. Coda, which in classical sonata was usually short addendum by way of 'rounding off', was extended by Beethoven in many cases to length of other sections, and treated as 2nd development.

Interest which this design has had for composers for more than 200 years arises from its capacity for expansion and contraction, its scope for inter-relations between sections and for varieties of treatment of development and coda, and its cheerful submission to those departures from its inherent principles, which depend for their effect on strength and clarity of basic scheme. Since calculated plan of tonality is essential to its working, its development in late romantic and modern periods has chiefly been in direction of greater flexibility in proportions and relations of sections. Object in many cases has been to give form, which was originally sectional and symmetrical, effect of continuous and organic growth.

**sonata-rondo form,** combination of SONATA FORM and RONDO form.

**Sonate Pathétique** (Fr., *Pathetic Sonata*), Beethoven's piano sonata in C minor, op 13, published 1799 with composer's title *Grande sonate pathétique* (intended to mean 'with emotion' rather than 'with pathos').

**sonatina,** short sonata, usually elementary in its technical requirements.

**Sondheim, Stephen** (1930– ), American composer, lyric-writer. Musicals incl. *A Little Night Music* and *Company*.

**song,** short composition for voice. Of indeterminate antiquity though earliest recorded examples in Western Europe date from 10th cent. These songs are in Latin, which continued in popular use till end of 13th cent. Melodies show simple symmetrical structure similar to that of folk song. This symmetry is characteristic also of vernacular songs of *troubadours* in Provence (11th–13th cents.), *trouvères* in N France (12th–13th cents.) and *Minnesinger* in Germany and Austria (12th–14th cents.), Spanish CANTIGAS and Italian *laudi spirituali* (*see* LAUDA). Neither in form nor tonality is there any valid distinction between sacred and secular songs. None of these has any written accompaniment.

Though traditions of this kind of song were continued in Germany by MEISTERSINGER in 15th, 16th cents., elsewhere 14th cent. saw considerable change. Songs and duets of highly sophisticated character, with instrumental accompaniment, were composed in France and Italy by *eg* Machaut and Landini. Simple structure of earlier songs had now been largely replaced by greater subtlety of rhythm and form. Elaborate ornamentation was common, esp. in late 14th cent., as was intimate relationship between 2 voices or voice and accompaniment (*eg* imitation, canon). With temporary decline of Italian music in 15th cent., French song (*chanson*) became dominant form of secular vocal music.

Both at this period and in 16th cent. there were no hard and fast conditions for performance. Words were often applied to accompanying instrumental parts, so blurring distinction between solo and part songs. This easy-going attitude is found in Italian *frottole* of early 16th cent., French *airs de cour,* and songs of English lutenists of late 16th, early 17th cents. Many 16th-cent. madrigals and church motets were arranged for solo and lute, by then most favoured accompanying instrument. Old tradition of solo song accompanied by instrumental ensemble survives in English music of late 16th cent. Lute-song, as opposed to transcriptions of madrigals, originated in Spain with publication of Milán's collection (1536).

Significant development in Italy in late 16th cent. was cultivation of new form of declamatory song called RECITATIVE, which proved to be ideal medium for new opera. Both in opera and chamber cantata, ARIA became indispensable element in course of 17th cent.

Domination of opera continued through 18th cent., relieved

however by popular style of songs in English BALLAD OPERA, imitated in German SINGSPIEL. But songs of this kind received little attention from serious composers. Songs with keyboard accompaniment written by Haydn and Mozart form minor (though very attractive) part of their output. Nor did Beethoven, in spite of having written earliest known song cycle (*An die ferne Geliebte,* 1816), contribute enormously to form. It was Schubert who showed how traditional simplicity of German popular song could be combined with romantic awareness of text and how imaginative accompaniment could illuminate words.

Schubert's example had powerful influence on romantic composers of 19th cent., notably Schumann and Brahms. Schumann's songs often seem like piano solo to which voice part has been added. Brahms's accompaniments are generally more traditional, and in many cases vocal melodies show influence of popular song. Songs of Wolf are strongly influenced by Wagner, and accompaniments are often orchestral in character. Influence of Wolf is apparent in Strauss's songs, and that of Brahms in songs of Mahler.

More advanced 20th-cent. composers have tended to ignore tradition that vocal line should be naturally flowing. Some composers, *eg* Schoenberg, have used form of declamation called SPRECHGESANG.

**song cycle** (Ger., *Liederkreis*), set of songs, normally performed complete, to words by single poet, or which have some other form of unity. First use of term was in Beethoven's *An die ferne Geliebte* (1816). Other notable examples incl. those by Schubert and Schumann.

**song form** (Ger., *Liedform*), basic form ABA, also used in many instrumental pieces, *eg* minuet and trio.

**Song of Destiny** (Ger., *Schicksalslied*), work for chorus and orchestra by Brahms, op 54 (1871), with words from poem by Hölderlin.

**Song of the Earth, The** (Ger., *Das Lied von der Erde*), unnumbered song-symphony by Mahler, scored for mezzo-soprano, tenor and orchestra, with words from German translation of 8th-cent. Chinese poems. Completed 1908, first perf. 1911 (after composer's death).

**Song of the Flea, The,** setting by Mussorgsky (1879) of Mephistopheles' song from Goethe's *Faust.*

**Song of the High Hills,** work for chorus and orchestra by Delius (1912). Chorus sings without words.

**Songs and Dances of Death,** 4 songs by Mussorgsky (1875–7), to poems by Golenishchev-Kutuzov.

**Songs of a Wayfarer** (Ger., *Lieder eines Fahrenden Gesellen*), set of 4 songs for voice and orchestra by Mahler (1884), to texts by composer reflecting moods of young man spurned in love. Mahler later re-used some of musical material in 1st symphony.

**Songs of Gurra,** *see* GURRELIEDER.

**Songs without Words** (Ger., *Lieder ohne Worte*), title given by Mendelssohn to 8 books of piano pieces (1830–45).

**Sonnambula, La** (It., *The Sleepwalker*), opera by Bellini, libretto by

F. Romani. First perf. Milan, 1831. Story concerns girl whose somnambulism leads her into potentially compromising situation.

**Sonneck, Oscar George Theodore** (1873–1928), American author, musical historian. First chief music librarian at Library of Congress (1902–17), where produced important musical catalogues. Also worked as editor for Schirmer's.

**Sonnenquartetten,** *see* SUN QUARTETS.

**sonore** (Fr.), **sonoro** (It.), sonorous, with full tone.

**sons bouchés** (Fr), stopped notes on HORN.

**sons étouffés** (Fr.), lit. 'damped sound'. Indication, most frequently found in harp music, meaning that vibrations should be damped by hand immediately after string(s) have been plucked, thereby producing dry sound. Alternative is *sec* (Fr.; It., *secco*), and opposite is *laissez vibrer*.

**sons harmoniques** (Fr.), harmonics.

**sons près de la table,** *see* PRÈS DE LA TABLE.

**sopra** (It.), 'above'. In piano music term used to indicate that one hand has to pass over the other.

**sopranino** (It.), 'little soprano'. Term used of instrument higher in range than soprano of certain families (*eg* flugelhorn, saxophone).

**soprano,** female voice of highest register with range extending approx. from middle C upwards for 2 octaves. Term is also applied to some instruments, *eg* soprano saxophone. Boy trebles can achieve soprano range, as could *castrati*.

**Sor, Fernando** or **Ferdinand,** orig. Ferdinando Sors (1778–1839), Spanish composer, guitarist. Taught in Paris and London. Composed several operas (earliest at age of 19), ballets, and guitar music.

**Sorabji, Kaikhosru Shapurji,** orig. Leon Dudley Sorabji (1892– ), English-born composer, pianist, writer on music, son of Parsee father and Spanish mother. Works incl. 2 symphonies for orchestra with chorus, piano and organ, 5 piano concertos, symphonic variations for piano and orchestra, piano quintets, piano sonatas, elaborate 2-hour work for piano entitled *Opus Clavicembalisticum,* organ symphonies, 5 Michelangelo sonnets for baritone and chamber orchestra, and songs. Much of his music is of exceptional complexity, and all of it has until recently been banned by composer from public performance.

**Sorcerer, The,** comic opera by Gilbert and Sullivan. First perf. London, 1877.

**Sorcerer's Apprentice, The** (Fr., *L'Apprenti sorcier*), symphonic scherzo by Dukas (1897), inspired by Goethe's ballad about apprentice who learns how to cast spell but not how to stop it.

**sordino, sordina** (It.; Fr., *sourdine*; Ger., *Dämpfer*), abbrev. *sord.*, (1) mute (of string or wind instrument). *Con sordino*, with mute. *Senza sordino,* without mute;

(2) damper (in piano). *Senza sordini* indicates that dampers are to be raised, *ie* strings are to be left free to vibrate. This is done by using right-hand (sustaining) pedal – hence alternative indication *Ped.*

**Sordun** (Ger.; It., *sordone*), instrument of bassoon family, current in late 16th, early 17th cents. Sound was muffled. Made in several sizes.

**Sore,** *see* AGRICOLA, MARTIN.

**Soriano, Suriano, Surianus** or **Suriani, Francesco** (1549–1620), Italian singer, composer. Pupil of Palestrina. Held various posts, incl. *maestro di cappella* at St Peter's, Rome (1603). Composed Masses, motets, psalms, 110 canons on *Ave maris stella,* Magnificats, Passion and other church music, madrigals and *villanelle.*

**Sorochintsi Fair** (Russ., *Sorochinskaya Yamarka*), opera by Mussorgsky, libretto by composer (after Gogol). Left incomplete and without orchestration. Performed versions incl. those by Cui (1917), Cherepnin (1923), and Shebalin (1931).

**Sors,** *see* SOR.

**Sosarme, Re di Media** (It., *Sosarmes, King of Media*), opera by Handel, libretto adapted from *Alfonso Primo* by Matteo Noris. First perf. London, 1732.

**sospiro** (It.), lit. 'sigh', *ie* crotchet rest.

**sostenuto** (It.), 'sustained', direction to sustain tone, usually equivalent to slowing tempo.

**sostenuto pedal,** whereas sustaining pedal on piano removes all dampers from strings, sostenuto pedal (only fitted on more expensive instruments) enables player to pre-select specific notes he wishes to be sustained.

**sotto** (It.), under. In piano music term used to indicate that one hand has to pass under the other.

**sotto voce** (It.), in an under tone, quietly.

**soubrette** (Fr.), 'cunning', 'shrewd'. Term used in opera to describe soprano who sings role of cunning servant girl.

**sound board,** resonant wooden part of certain instruments, incl. piano, organ and dulcimer, over which strings are stretched. It vibrates sympathetically and so amplifies notes sounded.

**sound hole,** variously shaped opening in belly of stringed instruments: *f* shape is usual, while earlier instruments, *eg* viols, had *c* shapes, and guitars' and lutes' sound holes are circular. Hole allows belly more flexibility, and freer passage of air vibrations from body of instrument.

**soundpost,** piece of wood, usually pine, that connects 2 surfaces (belly and back) of stringed instruments. Purposes are to strengthen, and to distribute vibrations.

**soupir** (Fr.), lit. 'sigh', *ie* crotchet rest. *Demi-soupir,* quaver rest; *quart de soupir,* semiquaver rest; *huitième de soupir,* demisemiquaver rest; *seizième de soupir,* hemidemisemiquaver rest.

**sourdine,** *see* SORDINO.

**Sousa, John Philip** (1854–1932), American bandmaster, composer. Leader of US Marine Corps Band (1880). In 1892 organized own band which later made European tours and world tour (1910–11). Composed many marches incl. *The Stars and Stripes Forever* and *Washington Post*; also light operas, orchestral suites, and songs.

**sousaphone,** type of TUBA first made in 1899 specially for Sousa's band. Tubing encircles player's body and ends in large bell facing forwards above his head. Much in evidence in early jazz bands and still occasionally used.

**soutenu** (Fr.), equivalent of SOSTENUTO.

**Souterliedekens** (Flem.), *Psalter Songs,* title of Flemish Psalter which contained earliest metrical translations of all the Psalms, with their melodies (which were folk songs), published 1540. Clemens non Papa made 3-part settings of tunes, with melodies in tenor (4 vols., 1556–57).

**Sowerby, Leo** (1895–1968), American composer, pianist, organist. Works incl. symphonies, choral, chamber, organ and piano music, and songs.

**Spanisches Liederbuch,** *see* SPANISH SONGBOOK.

**Spanish Caprice,** orchestral work by Rimsky-Korsakov (1887), using Spanish folk song idioms. Familiar title, *Capriccio Espagnol,* is pointless snobbism, being mixture of Italian and French.

**Spanish Rhapsody,** *see* RAPSODIE ESPAGNOLE.

**Spanish Songbook** (Ger., *Spanisches Liederbuch*), settings by Wolf (completed 1890) of German translations of 44 Spanish poems of 16th, 17th cents.

**spassapensieri** (It.), JEW'S HARP.

**Spataro, Spadaro** or **Spadarius, Giovanni** (*c* 1458–1541), Italian musical theorist, composer. Defended system of tuning monochord advocated by Ramis de Pareja against criticisms of Burzio (*Musices opusculum,* 1487) and Gafori (*Apologia,* 1520). Compositions incl. Masses, motets and secular works.

**speaker-key,** key on reed instrument, *eg* oboe or clarinet, which opens hole at such a point as to facilitate playing of notes which are sounded by overblowing at octave, twelfth or fifteenth.

**Specht, Richard** (1870–1932), Austrian music critic, writer. Esp. associated with music of Mahler, but also with Brahms and Richard Strauss.

**species,** method of teaching strict COUNTERPOINT formulated by Fux in *Gradus ad Parnassum* (1725). Fux listed 5 processes, or species, of counterpoint whereby one voice part (*ie* melody) could be set against another:

(1) added voice part moves at same speed as given one (*ie* note for note);

(2) added voice part moves at 2 or 3 times speed of given one (*ie* with 2 or 3 notes for each given note);

(3) added voice part moves at 4 or 6 times speed of given one (*ie* with 4 or 6 notes for each given note);

(4) notes of added voice part are in syncopated positions;

(5) added voice part contains mixture of above processes (called florid counterpoint).

**Spectre's Bride, The** (Cz., *Svatební košile*), cantata for 3 solo singers, chorus and orchestra by Dvořák based on ballad by K.J. Erben. First perf. (in English) Birmingham, 1885. Later setting of ballad was made by Novák (1913).

**speech-song,** *see* SPRECHGESANG.

**spezzato** (It.), 'divided', as in CORI SPEZZATI.

**spianato** (It.), smooth, even.

**spiccato** (It.), 'clearly articulated'. Term used in string playing for light staccato played with middle of bow and loose wrist.

**Spieltenor** (Ger.), light operatic tenor voice.

**spinet** (Fr., *épinette*; Ger., *Spinett*; It., *spinetta*), term which replaced word 'virginals' in course of 17th cent. in England for small, 1-manual HARPSICHORD. In 16th cent., Italian spinet was made in pentagonal shape; Flemish spinet, like virginals, was rectangular. Octave or 4ft spinet was triangular, with strings at angle of 45° to keyboard, and English makers adopted enlarged version of this shape for 8ft or normal pitch spinet towards end of 17th cent.

**spinto** (It.), 'pushed', urged on.

**Spiral,** work by Stockhausen for soloist and short-wave receiver (1968). Esp. associated with oboist Heinz Holliger. Soloist has to respond to random sounds received from receiver, thus making each performance different.

**spirito** (It.), spirit. *Con spirito,* with spirit, lively.

**spiritoso** (It.), in a spirited manner.

**spiritual,** religious song of North American Negro. Melodic style is simple, with occasional use of modes or of pentatonic scale. Rhythms are frequently syncopated, and harmonies similar to those of hymns of early Baptists and Methodists. Often makes use of call-and-response patterns, and may be partly or wholly extemporized. First attracted attention in 19th cent.

**Spitta, Julius August Philipp** (1841–94), German musicologist. His *Life of Bach* (2 vols., 1873, 1880) was first comprehensive work on life and music of Bach, the Lutheran tradition, and the Italian and other influences on his music. Also edited complete works of Schütz, organ works of Buxtehude, and selection of pieces by Frederick the Great.

**Spitze** (Ger.), point. *An der Spitze,* indication to string players to use point of bow.

**Spohr, Ludwig** or **Louis** (1784–1859), German violinist, composer, conductor, teacher. Held various posts in Germany, and gave concerts in Switzerland, Italy, Holland, Paris and London (where caused sensation by using baton to conduct – he was one of first to do so). His 9 symphonies and 15 violin concertos were highly regarded in their time. Most successful of his 10 operas were *Faust* (1816), *Zemire und Azor* (1819) and *Jessonda* (1823). Chamber music incl. still popular nonet, 36 quartets and 2 double quartets, trios, and duets for 2 violins. Also wrote choral, piano and harp music.

**Spontini, Gasparo Luigi Pacifico** (1774–1851), Italian composer. Pupil of Piccinni. Worked in Palermo, Paris and Berlin, returning to Italy in 1848. Most famous and successful operas, *La Vestale* (1807) and *Fernand Cortez* (1809), were written for Paris, and were first to reflect taste of Napoleonic era for operas with sumptuous production and plots with historical and political significance.

**Sprechgesang** (Ger.), speechsong, *ie* type of voice production midway between song and speech. Most famous example is Schoenberg's *Pierrot Lunaire,* in which approx. pitch of voice is indicated by musical notation.

**Sprechstimme** (Ger.), 'speaking part', *ie* voice part employing SPRECHGESANG.

**springer,** ornament used in 17th-cent. English music. Equivalent to one of forms of German NACHSCHLAG. Notated

played

**Spring Sonata** (Ger., *Frühlingssonate*), title given – though not by composer – to Beethoven's sonata in F for violin and piano, op 24 (1801).

**Spring Symphony,** (1) (Ger., *Frühlingssymphonie*) the title, authorized by composer, of Schumann's symphony no 1 in B flat, op 38 (1841);

(2) song–symphony for 3 solo singers, mixed chorus, boys' chorus and orchestra by Britten, op 44 (1949). Based on poems on spring by various authors.

**Squarcialupi, Antonio** (1416–80), Italian musician, organist. Known chiefly as owner of Ms (Squarcialupi Manuscript), which is largest surviving collection of 14th-cent. Italian music. Contains pieces by 12 composers, incl. Landini.

**square piano,** early form of piano, oblong in shape and strung horizontally.

**Squire, William Barclay** (1855–1927), English music librarian, editor. Became superintendent of printed music at British Museum. Edited catalogues of various collections of music, incl. *Catalogue of Printed Music 1487–1800.* Edited *Fitzwilliam Virginal Book* (with J.A. Fuller-Maitland), Purcell's harpsichord music, works by Byrd and Palestrina, and anthology of madrigals.

**Staatskapelle** (Ger.), state orchestra.

**Staatsoper** (Ger.), state opera house and/or company.

**Stabat Mater** (Lat.), 'the Mother was standing'. Initial words of sequence prob. written by Jacopone da Todi (*c* 1228–1306). Earliest polyphonic settings (*c* 1500) incl. one by Josquin des Prés. Later settings incl. those by Palestrina, Pergolesi, Haydn, Schubert, Rossini, Verdi, Dvořák and Stanford.

**Stabreim** (Ger.), alliteration; term for alliterative verse used by Wagner in his music dramas.

**staccado-pastorole,** type of XYLOPHONE used in 18th cent.

**staccato** (It.), 'detached'. May be indicated either by pointed dash ▼ indicating that note is to be as short as poss., or by DOT, indicating that it is to be short. In *mezzo-staccato,* also called *portato,* indicated by combination of slur and dots, notes are to be slightly detached.

**Stadler, Anton** (1753–1812), Austrian clarinettist. His virtuosity and beauty of tone encouraged Mozart to write several works for him, incl. trio in E for clarinet, viola and piano, K498, clarinet quintet, K581, and clarinet concerto, K622.

**Stadler, Maximilian** (1748–1833), Austrian composer, organist, Benedictine monk. Friend of Mozart and Haydn. Completed Mozart's piano sonata in A, K402, and his trio in D, K442, and wrote 2 pamphlets in defence of his Requiem. Own compositions incl. 2 Requiems and other church music, instrumental works, and songs.

**Städtische Oper** (Ger.), civic opera house and/or company.

**Stadtpfeifer** (Ger.), performer on wind instrument employed by municipality. Equivalent of English WAIT.

**staff** or **stave** (Fr., *portée*; Ger., *Liniensystem, System*; It., *rigo, sistema*), set of horizontal lines, each representing different pitch (as do spaces between them), on which music is written. 5 lines are now used for all music except plainsong, which uses 4. LEGER LINES are used for notes above and below staff, and CLEF indicates pitch of one of lines and hence particular pitch-position of staff.

**Stahlspiel** (Ger.), percussion instrument with steel bars and played with hammers. Virtually a GLOCKENSPIEL designed for military bands. Because manufactured in shape of lyre for British military bands, has acquired misleading name of lyra.

**Stainer, John** (1840–1901), English organist, composer. Professor at Oxford from 1889. Composed numerous choral works incl. *The Crucifixion* (1887). Knighted 1888.

**Stamitz, Karl,** orig. Karel Stamic (1745–1801), German-born violinist, composer, of Czech parentage (son of Johann Stamitz). Member of 'Mannheim School'. Works incl. 70 symphonies (some with 2 *concertante* violin parts), symphony for 2 orchestras, concertos for piano, viola and viola d'amore, string quartets, trio sonatas, and 2 operas.

His father, **Johann Wenzel Anton Stamitz,** orig. Jan Vaclav Stamic (1717–57), was Czech-born composer, violinist. Became chamber music director to court of Mannheim (1745), and is regarded as founder of 'Mannheim School'. Was most important of composers attached to Mannheim orchestra who developed some of chief traits in style of symphony. Works incl. *c* 50 symphonies, 100 orchestral trios, and chamber music.

**stampita,** form of ESTAMPIE.

**Ständchen** (Ger.), serenade.

**Stanford, Charles Villiers** (1852–1924), Irish-born composer. Taught composition at Royal College of Music from 1883, professor at Cambridge from 1887 till his death. One of leaders of English musical renaissance. Pupils incl. Bliss and Vaughan Williams. Little of his own prolific musical output has survived. Some works are coloured by Irish folk song esp. opera *Shamus O'Brien* (1896), *Irish Rhapsodies* and 3rd symphony (*Irish,* 1887), and there are continental influences in opera *The Veiled Prophet of Khorassan* (1881), Requiem (1897), and in chamber music. Also wrote church music. Knighted 1901.

**Stanley, John** (1713–86), English composer, organist. Blind from age of 2. Pupil of Greene. Master of the King's Musick from 1779. Works incl. cantatas and songs for solo voice and instruments, oratorios, 6 concertos for strings, a dramatic pastoral, pieces for flute, violin or harpsichord, and organ voluntaries.

**stantipes,** form of ESTAMPIE.

**stark** (Ger.), strong, loud. *Stark blasend,* strongly blown.

**Starker, János** (1924– ), Hungarian-born cellist. Settled in US (1946). Internationally renowned for performances of Bach.

**Starokadomsky, Mikhail** (1901–54), Russian composer. Pupil of Miaskovsky. Works incl. opera *Sot,* oratorio *Simon Proshakov,* concerto for orchestra, 2 suites for orchestra, organ concerto, violin concerto, and 2 string quartets.

**Star-Spangled Banner, The,** song officially adopted as US national anthem in 1931, though used as such long before then. Tune prob. written by Englishman, John Stafford Smith (*c* 1750–1836), with words supplied by Francis Scott Key (1779–1843) in 1814.

**Stasov, Vladimir** (1824–1906), Russian critic, writer on music. Friend of The FIVE, for whom he coined nickname 'the Mighty Handful'. His writings offer vivid picture of musical life in 19th-cent. Russia.

**stave,** *see* STAFF.

**Steffani, Agostino** (1654–1728), Italian composer, diplomat, priest. Court music director in Hanover (succeeded by Handel), and from 1703 in service of Elector Palatine in Düsseldorf. His 16 operas combine features of Italian, French and German styles in manner afterwards developed by Handel, and his chamber duets also served Handel as models. Also wrote church music.

**Steg** (Ger.), bridge of stringed instrument. *Am Steg, see* BOWING.

**Steibelt, Daniel** (1765–1823), German pianist, composer. Worked in Paris, London and from 1808 in St Petersburg. Wrote operas, ballets, concertos, and instrumental pieces.

**Stein, Erwin** (1886–1958), Austrian music critic, writer, who settled in Britain. Authority on Mahler and succeeding Viennese composers, on whom his book, *Orpheus in New Guises,* provides valuable commentary.

**Steinberg, Maximilian Osseievich** (1883–1946), Russian composer. Pupil of Liadov, Glazunov and Rimsky-Korsakov, whose daughter he married. Director (1934) of Leningrad Conservatory. Pupils incl. Shostakovich and Shaporin. Works incl. 4 symphonies, ballets, choral music, piano concertos and sonatas, string quartets, and songs.

**Steinberg, William,** orig. Hans Wilhelm (1899–1978), German-born conductor. Settled in US. Conductor of Pittsburgh Symphony Orchestra from 1952, London Philharmonic (1958–60), and Boston Symphony Orchestra (1969–72).

**Steinway,** New York firm of piano manufacturers, founded 1853 by Henry Engelhard Steinway (orig. Steinweg), who was previously established in Brunswick. London branch opened 1875.

**Stenhammar, Karl Vilhelm Eugen** (1871–1927), Swedish composer, conductor, pianist. Works incl. operas, 2 symphonies, 2 piano concertos, chamber and piano music, and songs.

**stentando** (It.), 'labouring', *ie* holding back each note; hence equivalent to *molto ritenuto*. Abbrev. *stent.*

**Stern, Isaac** (1920– ), Russian-born violinist. Taken to US as child and made debut in San Francisco at age of 13. One of most distinguished violinists of the age.

**Sterndale Bennett, William,** *see* BENNETT.

**Stevens, Bernard** (1916– ), English composer. Output incl. *Symphony of Liberation* (1945), and other orchestral works, and choral, chamber and instrumental music.

**Stevens, Denis** (1922– ), English musicologist, conductor. In 1964 became professor at Columbia University, US. Has edited many works by Monteverdi, and Mulliner Book. As conductor, associated with Accademia Monteverdiana and Ambrosian Singers. Has also written *A History of Song* and *Tudor Church Music.*

**Stierhorn** (Ger.), cow horn. Has coarse quality and is limited to single note.

**Stiffelio,** opera by Verdi, libretto by F. Piave (after play by Souvestre and Bourgeois). First perf. (unsuccessfully) Trieste, 1850. Revised under title *Aroldo* in 1857. Story concerns matrimonial problems of Stiffelio, 16th-cent. Protestant pastor.

**stile** (It.), style. In particular: (1) *stile antico*: contrapuntal style of 16th cent. as practised by Italian composers and formulated by Italian theorists in 17th, 18th cents. Principles expounded by Fux in *Gradus ad Parnassum* (1725) and thereafter became rules of 'strict' COUNTERPOINT;

(2) *stile rappresentativo*: style of dramatic RECITATIVE practised in earliest operas;

(3) *stile moderno* (*concertato*): 'modern' style of early 17th cent., in which (a) continuo, with or without other instruments with independent parts, was used to accompany voice or voices, as distinct from older practice of doubling or replacing voices by instruments, or in which (b) parts in instrumental composition were written for specific instruments and accompanied by continuo.

*See also* PRIMA PRATTICA.

**Still, William Grant** (1895–1978), American composer. World's 1st black symphonist (Afro-American Symphony, 1931). Music, often with distinctive Negro stamp, incl. 6 operas *eg Troubled Island* (*ie* Haiti, 1938). Other works incl. *Darker America* (1927), *And They Lynched him on a Tree* (1940), and *Highway no 1, USA* (1963).

**Stimme** (Ger.), (1) voice;
(2) separate part, vocal or instrumental. *Stimmbuch,* partbook.

**Stimmen** (Ger.), to tune. *Stimmung,* tuning.

**Stimmflöte, Stimmhorn, Stimmpfeife** (Ger.), pitch pipe.

**Stimmführung** (Ger.), part-writing.

**Stimmgabel** (Ger.), tuning fork.

**Stimmung,** large-scale work for 6 vocalists by Stockhausen (1968). Composer has declared that title has many meanings, incl. 'intonation', 'tuning in' and 'attuning'. Performers sit on floor in circle, and music is mostly very quiet and mesmeric.

**stock and horn, stock in horn,** or **stockhorn,** primitive Scottish instrument, fitted with single reed and played in same way as chanter of bagpipe. Made of either wood or bone and fitted to a cowhorn.

**Stockhausen, Karlheinz** (1928– ), German composer. Pupil of Messiaen and Milhaud. During 1950s became associated with electronic studios of West German Radio at Cologne, and through works such as *Mikrophonie I* and *II* soon established himself as world's leading electronic composer. At same time he was writing for more conventional forces (though often employed in unconventional way). His *Gruppen* (Groups) for 3 orchestras and conductors (1955–7), with its exploration of spatial effects, has proved to be one of milestones of 20th-cent. orchestral music, just as 11 *Klavierstücke* (1952–7) have come to seem modern equivalent of Chopin's preludes and Bach's preludes and fugues. Other works of period incl. *Kontra-Punkte* for 10 instruments (1952–3), *Zeitmesse* ('Tempi') for woodwind quintet (1955–6), *Carré* for 4 orchestras and choruses (1959–60), and *Zyklus* (Cycle) for solo percussionist (1959). Elements of indeterminacy have increasingly featured in his music: in some works performers simply receive advice from composer. He has been strongly inspired by mystical philosophy in his more recent music. Other important works incl. *Stimmung* (Attuning) for 6 voices (1968), *Mantra* for 2 pianists (1970), *Prozession* for mixed instrumental and electronic forces, *Hymnen* (Anthems) for purely electronic forces (1967) and *Licht* (1977–78), Part I for dancers and orchestra, Part II for trumpet and ensemble.

**Stokowski, Leopold Anton Stanislaw** (1882–1977), English-born conductor, son of Polish father and British mother. Pupil of Stanford. Became US citizen, 1915. Conductor of Philadelphia Orchestra (1913–36) and other orchestras. Made orchestral transcriptions of many works of Bach, and appeared in Walt Disney's *Fantasia* and other films.

**Stollen** (Ger.), 1st portion of stanza of Minnesinger or Meistersinger song commonly consisted of 2 *Stollen* (lit. 'props'), music of 1st being repeated for 2nd.

**Stolzer, Thomas** (*c* 1480–1526), German composer. *Kapellmeister* to King Louis of Hungary and Bohemia. Composed Masses, Latin motets, psalms and hymns, and German psalms and secular hymns.

**Stolzel, Gottfried Heinrich** (1690–1749), German composer. Wrote 22 operas, 14 oratorios, Masses, 8 sets of cantatas and motets for church year, chamber cantatas with piano, concertos, trio sonatas, and 2 theoretical treatises. His song 'Bist du bei mir' has often been wrongly attrib. to Bach.

**Stone Flower, The,** ballet by Prokofiev (1948–50). Story, based on folk tales, tells of potter who leaves village and his fiancée to seek legendary stone flower which will enable him to perfect his art.

**Stone Guest, The** (Russ., *Kamennyi Gost*), opera by Dargomizhsky, based (word for word) on Pushkin's play, on same subject as Mozart's *Don Giovanni*. Composer died before completion; finished by Cui and Rimsky-Korsakov. First perf. St Petersburg, 1872.

**stop,** on organ, handle or drawstop which controls admission of wind to particular register, or set of pipes. Term is also applied to register itself. On harpsichord, stops were formerly used to produce variations of tone or pitch; their function is now generally performed by pedals.

**stopped notes,** *see* STOPPING, HORN.

**stopped pipe,** on organ, pipe in which upper end is closed, so lowering pitch by octave.

**stopping,** on stringed instruments, placing of fingers of left hand on strings, thereby shortening effective vibrating length and therefore raising pitch. Playing 2, 3 and 4 notes simultaneously this way is referred to as double, treble and quadruple stopping respectively, even when open strings are used. *See also* HORN.

**Storace, Stephen** (1763–96), English composer. Studied in Naples, met Mozart in Vienna, and returned to England in 1787. Composed operas incl. *No Song, no Supper* (1790), ballet, chamber music, harpsichord sonatas, and songs.

**storto** (It.), Krummhorn.

**Story of a Real Man, The,** opera by Prokofiev, libretto by composer's wife. First perf. Leningrad, 1948. This was Prokofiev's reply to severe criticism of him made by General Committee of Communist Party. Though music was intended to be more readily comprehensible, and hero was legless Russian pilot, opera was condemned for its 'infatuation with modernist trickery'.

**Stradella, Alessandro** (1644–82), Italian composer, violinist, singer. Attempt to murder him following his elopement with mistress of Venetian nobleman is basis of opera by Flotow (1844); later attempt was successful. Composed 6 oratorios incl. *S. Giovanni Battista* (1676) – perhaps his best work – sacred and secular cantatas, operas, serenatas, concertos for strings, and trio sonatas. He is important in history both of vocal forms and of concerto – in latter he separated solo instruments from *concerto grosso.*

**Stradivari** or **Stradivarius, Antonio** (1644–1737), Italian violin-maker. Apprenticed to Nicolo Amati and founded own workshop at Cremona. Made best instruments 1700–1720; unsurpassed in craftsmanship and quality of tone. Assisted by 2 of his sons, Francesco and Omobono, who carried on father's work after his death.

**strambotto** (It.), (1) form of Italian poetry of 15th, 16th cents. Consists of verse of 8 lines with rhyming scheme *abababcc,* or less frequently *abababab*. Musical settings in Petrucci's 4th collection of *frottole* (1505) have music for first pair of lines, to be repeated for other 3 pairs;

(2) Malipiero used term in his *Rispetti e Strambotti* for string quartet, intended to evoke 'character of old Italian poetry'. Work is in form of 20 instrumental 'stanzas' each preceded by recurring 'ritornello'.

**Strandrecht,** *see* WRECKERS.

**Strangeways,** *see* FOX STRANGEWAYS.

**Straniera, La** (It., *The Stranger*), opera by Bellini, libretto by F. Romani. First perf. Milan, 1829. Story of this lakeside romantic drama revolves round various complex problems of identity.

**strascinando** (It.), dragging.

**strathspey,** *see* REEL.

**Straube, Karl** (1873–1950), German organist, conductor. Excelled in performance of Reger's organ works, many written for him. His various collections of organ music are indispensable to organists.

**Straus, Oscar** (1870–1954), Austrian-born composer, conductor. Took French nationality, 1939. Pupil of Bruch. Wrote several Viennese operettas incl. *The Chocolate Soldier* and *A Waltz Dream*.

**Strauss, Christoph** (*c* 1580–1631), Austrian composer. Published collection of 36 motets in 5 to 10 parts (1613), and set of 16 Masses in 8 to 20 parts with continuo (1631).

**Strauss, Johann** (the elder; 1804–49), Austrian conductor, composer. Wrote waltzes and other pieces, incl. famous *Radetzky March*.

His son, **Johann Strauss** (the younger; 1825–99), was violinist, conductor and prolific composer of Viennese light music. Founded own orchestra (1844) and joined it with father's (1849), and subsequently toured widely. Composed 16 operettas incl. *Die Fledermaus* (*The Bat*, 1874) and *Die Zigeunerbaron* (*The Gypsy Baron*, 1885), waltzes, polkas, galops and other dances. Many of his waltzes, often containing exceptionally delicate orchestration, are substantial and picturesque enough to be regarded as Viennese symphonic poems; they incl. *The Blue Danube, Tales from the Vienna Woods* and *The Emperor Waltz*.

Johann the younger's brother, **Joseph Strauss** (1827–70), was also distinguished composer of waltzes – his output running to 283 works, incl. *Music of the Spheres* and *The Village Swallows of Austria*. Another brother, **Eduard Strauss** (1835–1916), added *c* 200 pieces to Strauss family repertory.

**Strauss, Richard** (1864–1949), German composer. Born in Munich. Son of horn player, who gave him thoroughly musical upbringing. Started composing before he reached his teens. In 1885, after abandoning studies at Munich University, became assistant to von Bülow at Meiningen, and within year succeeded him as 1st conductor. As composer, turned from style of Brahms to that of Liszt and Wagner. With *Aus Italien* (1887) began series of daring symphonic poems and illustrative symphonies which helped to bring him fame and fortune and caused much controversy about merits of programme music. Meanwhile his conducting career developed by way of appointments with Munich Opera and Weimar Court Opera. Conducted *Tannhäuser* at Bayreuth (1891), and in 1894, influenced by Wagner, completed 1st opera, *Guntram*. By then he seemed to be Wagner's most successful successor. In 1894 became conductor of Berlin Philharmonic, in 1898 conductor of Berlin Royal Opera, and later conductor of Vienna Opera (1919–24). His home, however, was at Garmisch in Upper Bavaria, where he settled after composing *Salome* (1905) – his first sensational, and very controversial, operatic success. Next opera, *Elektra* (1909), was almost equally sensational; Hugo von Hofmannsthal, poet and dramatist, wrote libretto, and subsequently wrote 5 more for Strauss.

Hofmannsthal is usually credited with having diverted Strauss from morbid excesses of works like *Salome* and *Elektra* to more genial style of his later music, with *Der Rosenkavalier* marking rococo turning point. Opinion remains divided as to whether this was a good thing; however, it is possible to appreciate both early and late works for themselves.

Principal compositions:

(1) Operas: *Guntram* (1894), *Feuersnot* (1901), *Salome* (1905), *Elektra* (1909), *Der Rosenkavalier* (1911), *Ariadne auf Naxos* (1912, rev. 1916), *Die Frau ohne Schatten* (1919), *Intermezzo* (1924), *Die Aegyptische Helena* (1928), *Arabella* (1933), *Die schweigsame Frau* (1935), *Friedenstag* (1938), *Daphne* (1938), *Capriccio* (1942), *Die Liebe der Danae* (1952);

(2) Ballets: *Josephslegende* (1914), *Schlagobers* (1924);

(3) Orchestra: tone poems: *Aus Italien* (1887), *Macbeth* (1887), *Don Juan* (1888), *Death and Transfiguration* (1889), *Till Eulenspiegel* (1895), *Thus spake Zarathustra* (1896), *Don Quixote* (1897), *Ein Heldenleben* (1898), *Symphonia domestica* (1903), *An Alpine Symphony* (1915); symphony in F minor (1884), violin concerto (1883), 2 horn concertos (1884, 1942), oboe concerto (1945), duet-concertino for clarinet and bassoon (1948), *Metamorphosen* for 23 strings (1945), suite for *Le Bourgeois gentilhomme* (1919);

(4) Chamber music: string quartet (1881), cello sonata (1883), piano quartet (1884), violin sonata (1887);

(5) Songs: 4 sets with orchestra (1897–1921), 26 sets with piano (1882–1929), *Four Last Songs* with orchestra (1948);

(6) Piano: sonata in B minor (1881), 2 sets of short pieces (1881, 1883).

**Stravinsky, Igor Feodorovich** (1882–1971), Russian composer. Born near St Petersburg. Son of bass singer at Imperial Opera. Met Rimsky-Korsakov (1903) and became his pupil (1907); 1st symphony performed in 1908. However, individuality did not become apparent till came into contact with Diaghilev and composed 1st major ballet, *The Firebird* (Paris, 1910). Influence of Rimsky-Korsakov can be seen in its orchestral colours, but in other respects it looked forward to *Petrushka* (1911) and *The Rite of Spring* (1913), also written for Diaghilev's company. Première of latter in Paris created famous uproar. In contrast with chromaticism of Wagner, *The Rite* is primarily concerned with rhythm, employed to orgiastic effect – even its harmony, often involving clash of one tonality against another, is predominantly percussive. In its liberation of rhythm, *The Rite* was epoch-making, but was the end of a line for Stravinsky. Only rarely thereafter was he to require such heavy orchestral forces. *The Soldier's Tale* (1918), basically an anti-opera in which no one actually sings, involves acting, dancing and spoken narration and music for 7 instruments, notable for nervy economy of style.

Main outcome of his prolonged stay in Western Europe (lived mainly in Paris after 1914) was his adoption of neoclassicism in such works as ballet *Pulcinella* (after Pergolesi, 1920) and opera *The Rake's Progress* (1951) – basically a classical number opera, energized by Stravinsky's very personal rhythms and harmonies. Stravinsky settled in US in 1939, and there belatedly found inspiration in serialism and, from *Agon* (1957) onwards, produced remarkable series of masterpieces in old age. It has been said that Stravinsky's works provide 'map' of 20th-cent. musical developments – certainly no other composer has ranged more widely.

Principal compositions: (1) Stage works: ballets: *The Firebird* (1910), *Petrushka* (1911), *The Rite of Spring* (1913), *The Wedding* (with chorus, 1923), *The Soldier's Tale* (with speaking voice, 1918), *Pulcinella* (after Pergolesi, 1920), *Apollo* (1928), *The Fairy's Kiss* (1928), *Card Game* (1937), *Orpheus* (1948), *Agon* (1957); operas: *The Nightingale* (1914), *Mavra* (1922), *The Rake's Progress* (1951); opera-oratorio: *Oedipus Rex* (1927); melodrama: *Persephone* (1933); *The Flood* (1961–2);

(2) Orchestra: *Fireworks* (1908), *Symphonies for Wind Instruments* (1920), *Dumbarton Oaks* concerto (1938), symphony in C (1940), *Danses concertantes* (1942), symphony in 3 movements (1945), concerto for string orchestra (1946), concerto for piano and wind (1924), *Capriccio* for piano and orchestra (1929), violin concerto (1931), *Ebony Concerto* for dance band (1945), *Movements* for piano and orchestra (1958–9), *Variations* for orchestra (Aldous Huxley *in memoriam*, 1963–4);

(3) Choral works: *Symphony of Psalms* (1930), *Mass* (1948), cantata (1951–2), *Canticum sacrum* (1956), *Threni* (1957–8), *A Sermon, a narrative, and a Prayer* (1960–1), *Requiem Canticles* (1965–6);

(4) Other works: *Berceuses du chat* (4 songs for female voice and 3 clarinets, 1916), octet for wind (1923), concerto for 2 pianos (1935), sonata for 2 pianos (1944), septet for clarinet, bassoon, horn, violin, viola, cello and piano (1954), *In memoriam Dylan Thomas* (tenor, string quartet and 4 trombones), *Abraham and Isaac* for baritone (or mezzo-soprano) and 3 clarinets (1964).

**straw fiddle** (Ger., *Strohfiedel*), type of XYLOPHONE.

**street piano,** mechanical type of piano with barrel-and-pin action similar to that of musical box. Played in same way as barrel organ by turning handle and is thus sometimes called piano organ. Formerly much favoured by itinerant performers.

**Streich** (Ger.), bow (of bowed instrument). *Streichinstrumente*, bowed instruments. *Streichquartette*, string quartet.

**strepitoso** (It.), noisy.

**stretto** (It.), close, narrow, drawn together: (1) bringing in of overlapping entries of subject in fugue 'closer', *ie* after shorter intervals of time than those at which they originally came (Ger., *Engführung*); (2) quickening of tempo towards end of piece.

**Strich** (Ger.), bow stroke.

**Striggio, Alessandro** (*c* 1535–*c* 1589), Italian composer, *lira da gamba* player, nobleman. One of earliest composers of *intermezzi*, his *Psiche ed Amore* was perf. in 1565. Published 7 books of madrigals and set of programme madrigals. Keyboard transcription of his madrigal 'Chifara fede al cielo' by Peter Philips is in *Fitzwilliam Virginal Book*.

His son, **Alessandro Striggio** (*fl* 16th–17th cents.), was *lira* player and librettist. Wrote libretto of Monteverdi's *Orfeo* (1607).

**string(s)**, lengths of wire or gut on which sounds are produced in many diverse instruments, incl. piano, harp, violin family, guitar, mandolin and lute; also used to mean stringed instruments, but in this case usually refers only to violin family and its predecessors.

**stringed instruments**, *see* INSTRUMENTS.

**stringendo** (It.), 'tightening', *ie* increasing tension and (usually) accelerating tempo.

**string orchestra**, strictly, band consisting of stringed instruments only, as distinct from wind or brass band.

**string quartet**, medium (and music for medium) of 2 violins, viola and cello. In effect it is SONATA in 3 or 4 movts. History began 1750–60 with early quartets of Haydn, prob. written for outdoor performance – hence absence of continuo. From op 3 (*c* 1765) onwards he adopted 4-movt. form, and continued development of medium for rest of his life. Mozart dedicated to Haydn first 6 of his 10 mature quartets. In Beethoven's last quartets, their linear style and treatment of thematic development and tonality places them closer to modern quartets than to those of 19th cent. Between Schubert and Brahms, quartet, an apt medium for lyrical expression but not for rhetoric, has patchy history. With Debussy's quartet of 1893 it entered new phase, which later incl. remarkable series of 6 quartets by Bartók and some of most characteristic compositions of Ravel, Schoenberg, Berg, Webern, Hindemith, Shostakovitch and Walton.

**string quintet**, *see* QUINTET.

**Strogers, Nicholas** (*fl* 1570–90), English composer. Works incl. services, anthems, motets, consort songs, *In Nomines* for strings, and keyboard music. Fantasia by him is in *Fitzwilliam Virginal Book*.

**Strohfiedel**, *see* STRAW FIDDLE.

**Stroh violin, viola, cello, mandolin, guitar**, instruments, invented by Charles Stroh (1901), in which normal body is replaced by amplifying horn. Not to be confused with *Strohfiedel* (*see* STRAW FIDDLE).

**stromentato** (It.), played by instruments. *Recitativo stromentato, see* RECITATIVE.

**stromento,** same as STRUMENTO.

**Strong, George Templeton** (1856–1948), American composer. Disciple of Liszt. Settled in Switzerland (1892). Works incl. 3 symphonies, symphonic poem *Undine,* and choral and chamber music.

**strophic,** term used for song which uses same music for each verse. Opposite is 'through-composed' (Ger., *durchkomponiert*).

**strumento** (It.), instrument. *Strumenti a corde,* string instruments; *strumenti a fiato,* wind instruments; *strumenti a percossa* (or *percussione*), percussion instruments; *strumenti di legno,* woodwind instruments; *strumenti d'ottone,* brass instruments.

**Strungk, Nikolaus Adam** (1640–1700), German composer, violinist, organist. On visit to Italy his violin-playing was praised by Corelli. Works incl. operas *eg Alceste,* and organ works.

**Stück** (Ger.), piece, composition.

**Stuckenschmidt, H.H.** (1901– ), German critic, author, composer. Became friend of Schoenberg in Berlin. Left Berlin in 1937 because of opposition to Nazis, and went to Prague. Returning to Berlin after WWII, became president of German section of International Society for Contemporary Music, and professor of musical history at Berlin Technical University. Books incl. studies of Schoenberg, Busoni and Ravel.

**study** (Fr., *étude*), piece of music designed to give practice in some branch of instrumental technique. Those by *eg* Clementi and Chopin (for piano) also have great artistic merit.

**Stump,** obsolete and now virtually non-existent type of CITTERN. Apparently invented *c* 1600 by one Daniel Farrant.

**Sturgeon, Nicholas** (*c* 1390–1454), English composer. Received annuity from Henry V in 1419. Prob. had part in writing of OLD HALL MANUSCRIPT, which contains 3 *Glorias,* 2 *Credos* (1 incomplete), *Sanctus* with incomplete *Benedictus,* and isorhythmic motet by him.

**Sturm und Drang** (Ger.), 'storm and stress'. Term for wave of powerful romantic expressiveness which swept Austrian and German music in 1760s and 1770s, esp. evident in Haydn's symphonies of that time. Term was coined by C. Kaufmann in connection with play *Wirrwarr* (1776) by F.M. Klinger and is also applied to German literature of period *c* 1770–85.

**Style,** the tracing of the history of musical styles, and of the changes in social, technical and aesthetic ideas which accompany and interact with changes in musical style, is one of the chief objects of the study of musical history. The style of a composition is its manner of treating form, melody, rhythm, counterpoint, harmony and tone-colour; it is closely related to and limited by its medium, but not entirely dependent on it, since features of the style appropriate to one medium may be transferred to another. The analysis of compositions written in a particular period, in a particular genre and by a particular composer provides the material for the history of the style of that period, genre or composer.

Musical historians have adopted from historians of painting and sculpture terms for the main periods in the history of style, the use of which is obviously justified by their convenience (gothic, 1150–1475; renaissance, 1475–1600; baroque, 1600–1750; rococo or galant, 1730–1770; classical, 1750–1820; romantic, 1820–90; impressionist, 1890–1910; expressionist, 1910–30), although their implications in terms of musical styles may not have been fully investigated. The history of the style of a genre (more commonly called 'form' in this context, eg. opera, concerto, etc.) includes changes in its form as well as in its other technical elements.

Among the genres which have been studied in this way are Mass, motet, Italian madrigal, opera, concerto, symphony and suite, and oratorio. The progress of a composer's style assumes a pattern which may be determined by a variety of circumstances, such as his response to outside influences, as in Schütz, his writing in different genres, as in Rameau and Schumann, or an inner development in clearly defined phases, as in Beethoven.

*See also* NATIONALISM, STILE.

**style galant** (Fr.; Ger., *galanter Stil*), term adopted by German writers on music in 18th cent. for homophonic and rather elaborately ornamented style of French and Italian music, *eg* that of F. Couperin and D. Scarlatti, as opposed to contrapuntal style (*gearbeiteter Stil*) of main German tradition. It is thus equivalent of rococo style in painting. This style appears in Bach's music in variable dances in suite (*Galanterien*).

Its adoption by such contemporaries of Bach as Telemann and Mattheson led to its becoming important factor in marked change of style between Bach and his sons C.P.E. Bach and J.C. Bach, from whom it passed into early works of Haydn and Mozart. Period of style may be dated *c* 1730–*c* 1770, overlapping late baroque and early classical styles.

**subdominant,** fourth degree of diatonic scale, *eg* F in scale of C. Subdominant, dominant and tonic triads are 3 'primary' or principal triads in a key. Chord of subdominant followed by tonic chord forms plagal CADENCE. Addition of sixth to subdominant chord forms chord of ADDED SIXTH.

**subito** (It.), suddenly. *Piano subito,* suddenly soft.

**subject,** theme (or group of notes) used as basis of musical form *eg* subject in fugue, and 1st and 2nd subjects (or group of subjects) in movt. in sonata form.

**submediant,** sixth degree of diatonic scale, *eg* A in scale of C major.

**succentor,** official in charge of music, under supervision of precentor, in cathedral, college, chapel or monastery.

**Such Sweet Thunder,** Shakespearian suite by Duke Ellington, combining considerable verve and wit, compiled during 1950s.

**Suggia, Guilhermina** (1888–1950), cellist of mixed Portuguese and Italian origin. Pupil of Casals, to whom she was married for 6 years.

**suite,** before *c* 1750, composition consisting of group of dance movts., all in same key. Prototypes of baroque suite were pairs (*see* NACHTANZ) or groups of dance pieces in keyboard and lute music of 16th cent. In early 17th cent. some German composers published instrumental dances in sets of 4 or more; some or all of dances were related thematically, forming what is known as 'variation suite'.

Later in 17th cent. Froberger's keyboard suites had order allemande–courante–sarabande, with or without gigue after allemande or courante. Ballet-suites varied in number and type of dances according to nature of ballet. When Froberger's suites were published in 1693 they were disposed in order allemande–courante–sarabande–gigue, which was adopted by Bach and Handel. In addition, Bach's suites and partitas contain one or more dances of French type (*Galanterien*), *eg* bourrée, gavotte, minuet, passepied, after sarabande, or occasionally, in partitas, after courante. Bach's English Suites and Partitas also contain prelude, which may be in quite extended form.

Each of François Couperin's suites for harpsichord (which he called *Ordres*) consists of considerable number of movts. which have title of dance or descriptive idea *eg Les Abeilles, L'Enchanteresse.* Another type of French suite, modelled on overture and set of dances which came at beginning of opera and opera-ballet of Lully, was adopted by German composers, *eg* Georg Muffat, Telemann *(Musique de Table)* and Bach, and called *Ouverture.* As in Bach's 4 *Overtures* (now generally called *Orchestral Suites*), dances are French and vary in number and type.

There were dance movts. in *divertimenti* of mid 18th cent. and minuet became one of movts. of sonata, but use of word 'suite' was not resumed until late in 19th cent., when was used with more generalized meaning of composition consisting of any group of instrumental movts., frequently drawn from ballet or incidental music.

**Suite bergamasque,** piano suite by Debussy, published 1905. Incl. famous *Clair de lune.*

**suivez** (Fr.), 'follow': (1) begin next movt. or section without break *(attacca)*;

(2) accompaniment is to follow any modifications of tempo made by soloist (It., *colla parte*).

**Suk, Josef** (1874–1935), Czech composer, violinist, viola player. Pupil and son-in-law of Dvořák. Member of Bohemian String Quartet from 1892. Compositions incl. 2 symphonies, symphonic poems, overtures, Mass, chamber and piano music, and part-songs.

His grandson, **Josef Suk** (1929– ), is also violinist of international reputation.

**sulla tastiera,** *see* BOWING.

**Sullivan, Arthur Seymour** (1842–1900), English composer, organist, conductor. Studied under Sterndale Bennett and at Leipzig. Became principal of National Training School of Music (1876).

Knighted 1883. His light operas, to libretti by W.S. Gilbert, have been highly successful in many parts of the world. Also wrote grand opera *Ivanhoe* (after Scott, 1891), 2 ballets, oratorios, cantatas, symphony, overtures, incidental, church and piano music, and songs. In operettas, often called 'Savoy Operas' because first perf. (by D'Oyly Carte company) at Savoy Theatre, London, Sullivan combined tunefulness with neat craftsmanship and brilliant flair for parody. More important are: *Cox and Box* (1867, libretto by F.C. Burnand, all others except *The Rose of Persia* by W.S. Gilbert), *Thespis* (1871), *Trial by Jury* (1875), *The Sorcerer* (1877), *H.M.S. Pinafore* (1878), *The Pirates of Penzance* (1879), *Patience* (1881), *Iolanthe* (1882), *Princess Ida* (1884), *The Mikado* (1885), *Ruddigore* (1887), *The Yeomen of the Guard* (1888), *The Gondoliers* (1889), *Utopia Limited* (1893), *The Grand Duke* (1896), *The Rose of Persia* (1899, libretto by B. Hood).

**sul ponticello** (It.), *see* BOWING.

**sul tasto,** *see* BOWING.

**Sumer is icumen in,** *rota* (or round) found in Ms written at Reading Abbey *c* 1240. Ms also has Latin words and directions for performance. Melody is sung by 4 voices with 2 voices adding *pes* (ground bass). Earliest extant piece in 6 parts and earliest extant canon.

**summation tone,** *see* COMBINATION TONE.

**Sun Quartets** (Ger., *Sonnenquartetten*), name given to Haydn's 6 string quartets, op 20 (1772). So called from publisher's trade mark on title-page of old editions.

**Suor Angelica,** *see* TRITTICO.

**supertonic,** second degree of diatonic scale, *eg* D in scale of C.

**Suppé, Franz von,** orig. Francesco Ezechiele Ermenegildo Cavaliere Suppé-Demelli (1819–95), Dalmatian-born composer, conductor, of Belgian descent. Conducted at theatres in Vienna, Pressburg and Baden. Works incl. 31 operettas *eg Light Cavalry* and *The Beautiful Galatea,* farces, ballets, incidental music, Mass, Requiem, symphony, quartets, and songs.

**Suriano, Francesco,** *see* SORIANO.

**sur la touche,** *see* BOWING.

**Surprise Symphony** (Ger., *Symphonie mit dem Paukenschlag*), symphony no 94 in G by Haydn (1791), so called from abrupt *fortissimo* chord for full orchestra which interrupts quiet opening of slow movt. *Paukenschlag* = stroke on timpani. Not to be confused with *Drum Roll Symphony,* no 103 (Ger., *Symphonie mit dem Paukenwirbel*).

**Survivor from Warsaw, A,** cantata by Schoenberg, op 46, for speaker, men's chorus and orchestra. First perf. 1948. Text (in English, with German interpolations and Hebrew prayer) describes atrocities against Jews in Nazi concentration camp.

**Susanna,** oratorio by Handel, with anonymous text based on Apocrypha. First perf. London, 1749.

**Susanna's Secret** (It., *Il Segreto di Susanna*), comic opera by Wolf-

Ferrari, libretto by E. Golisciani. First perf. in German version by M. Kalbeck (*Susannens Geheimnis*), Munich, 1909. Susanna's secret is that she smokes.

**Susato, Tylman, Tielmann** or **Thielemann** (end of 15th cent.–before 1564), Flemish music-printer, composer. Published collections of polyphonic *chansons,* madrigals, motets, Masses and instrumental pieces, many containing compositions of his own.

**suspension,** harmonic device whereby note sounded as part of chord is sustained while second chord is sounded. Result is discord, which is then usually resolved by movement of dissonant note one step downwards (suspended leading note resolves upwards). Process consists of (1) preparation by consonance on relatively weak beat, (2) suspension on dissonance on relatively strong beat, (3) resolution of consonance on relatively weak beat. Suspension is delayed movement in part, and so is as much rhythmic as harmonic in effect, hence it is essential that point of dissonance should coincide with metrical accent. *See also* ANTICIPATION, PREPARATION, RETARDATION.

**Süsskind, Walter** (1913–80), Czech-born conductor, pianist. Moved to UK in 1938. Conducting posts incl. Scottish Orchestra (1946–52), and symphony orchestras in Melbourne (1953–55), Toronto (1956–65) and St Louis (1968–75).

**Süssmayr** or **Süssmayer, Franz Xaver** (1766–1803), Austrian composer. Pupil of Salieri and Mozart. Wrote recitatives for Mozart's *La clemenza di Tito* (1791) and helped to complete Mozart's unfinished Requiem. Also wrote operas, 2 ballets, cantatas, clarinet concerto, and church and instrumental music.

**sustaining pedal,** *see* PIANO.

**Sutermeister, Heinrich** (1910– ), Swiss composer. Earlier works show influence of Orff, with whom he studied, in their emphasis on simplicity and clear outlines. Works incl. operas based on *Romeo and Juliet* and Dostoyevsky's *Crime and Punishment,* piano concertos, and choral music.

**Sutherland, Joan** (1926– ), Australian soprano. Internationally renowned for performances of *bel canto* roles.

**Švanda the Bagpiper** (Cz., *Švanda Dudák*), comic opera by Weinberger, libretto by M. Kareš. First perf. Prague, 1927. Spelling 'Schwanda' is pointless outside German-speaking countries.

**Svendsen, Johan Severin** (1842–1911), Norwegian composer, violinist, conductor. Studied in Leipzig. Works incl. 2 symphonies, concertos for violin and cello, and chamber music, but best remembered for occasional pieces *eg Carnival in Paris* for orchestra.

**swanee whistle,** whistle with slide at opposite end to mouthpiece that can be pulled in and out by player, so varying length of tube and hence pitch of note. Small models are no more than a toy, but Ravel used more substantial one, which he called *flûte à coulisse,* in opera *L'Enfant et les sortilèges.*

**Swan Lake,** ballet by Chaikovsky (1876), choreography by Petipa and Ivanov.

**Swan of Tuonela, The,** *see* LEGENDS.

**Swanson, Howard** (1909– ), black American composer. Pupil of Nadia Boulanger in Paris, where he stayed until 1940, when returned to US. Marian Anderson helped to establish him as composer by singing his songs in New York. In 1952 his *Short Symphony* won New York Music Critics' Circle Award. Other works incl. orchestral works, cello suite, and piano music.

**Swan Song,** *see* SCHWANENGESANG.

**Swayne, Giles** (1946– ), English composer. Pupil of Messiaen. Works incl. *Orlando's Music* (1974) and *Pentecost Music* (1977) for orchestra, chamber, instrumental, choral, organ and piano music, and songs.

**Sweelinck, Jan Pieterszoon** (1562–1621), Dutch composer, organist, harpsichordist, teacher. Studied in Venice. Most important compositions are for keyboard, and were much influenced by English virginalists. Developed their style in variations on psalm tunes and secular songs, and in fantasias, which are constructed on single subject, anticipating form of fugue. Toccatas and 'echo' fantasias, however, are in Venetian tradition. Handed on these styles to pupils who incl. Scheidt. Also wrote vocal music.

**swell,** device for producing *crescendo* or *diminuendo* on organ or harpsichord. Most successful form, Venetian swell, incorporates slatted blind, operated by pedal, which can be opened and closed gradually, so allowing continuous change of volume.

**swell box,** box containing several organ pipes and fitted with Venetian SWELL.

**swell organ** (Fr., *récit*; Ger., *Oberwerk*), manual organ in which pipes are enclosed in SWELL BOX. In most modern organs, Choir organ and Solo organ are similarly enclosed.

**Swieten, Gottfried, Baron van** (1734–1803), Dutch-born amateur musician, diplomat. Became director of Royal Library in Vienna, and founded Musikalische Gesellschaft. Patron of Mozart (who wrote accompaniments to Handel oratorios for concerts presented by van Swieten), Haydn (for whom he translated *The Creation* and *The Seasons* into German), C.P.E. Bach (from whom he commissioned 6 string quartets), and Beethoven (who dedicated his 1st symphony to him).

**swing,** (1) basic ingredient of jazz; quality differentiating good jazz performance (which should 'swing', *ie* have rhythmic momentum beyond actual note values) from bad one;

(2) specific era and style in jazz history. Began *c* 1935; characterized by use of big bands and powerful contrasts between brass and reed (*ie* saxophone and clarinet) sections. Most famous exponent was Benny Goodman. Style swept America, but was itself swept aside by BOP revolution of 1945.

**Sylphides, Les** (Fr., *The Sylphs*), ballet adapted from various piano pieces by Chopin, with choreography by Fokine. First perf. Paris, 1909.

**Sylvia,** ballet by Delibes, choreography by Merante. First perf. Paris, 1876.

**sympathetic resonance** or **sympathetic vibrations,** acoustical phenomenon that occurs when resonant body, *eg* piano string, glass or tuning fork, vibrates and sounds note without being touched when same note is played or sung nearby. Certain old stringed instruments, incl. viola d'amore, use effect by having 'free' or sympathetic strings immediately under those played by bow.

**symphonia** (Lat., from Gr. for simultaneous sound), (1) in ancient Greek theory (a) unison, (b) consonant interval;

(2) 14th-cent. name for HURDY-GURDY;

(3) in 16th, 17th cents., apparently alternative name for virginals;

(4) symphony.

**Symphonia Domestica,** *see* DOMESTIC SYMPHONY.

**symphonic poem** (Fr., *poème symphonique*; Ger., *symphonische Dichtung, Tondichtung*), term applied by Liszt to programmatic orchestral piece (*see* PROGRAMME MUSIC). Immediate ancestors were concert overture *eg* Mendelssohn's *Midsummer Night's Dream,* and programmatic symphony *eg* Berlioz's *Symphonie fantastique.* Liszt wrote symphonic poems in single movt., abandoning sonata form for more flexible treatment of thematic material.

After Liszt, symphonic poems (or 'tone pictures' or 'fantasies') were written by various composers incl. Borodin, Smetana, Franck, Dukas, Sibelius (*Tapiola* and several other important works), Delius, and Elgar (*eg* 'symphonic study' *Falstaff*). Most famous are series by Richard Strauss, who used term 'tone poem' (*Tondichtung*) and brought genre to highest point of circumstantial and realistic depiction. 'Fantasy Overtures' of Chaikovsky are dramatic concert overtures rather than symphonic poems. Form was ideal for impressionist style; Debussy's chief orchestral works are 5 symphonic poems in 1 or more movts. More recently form has been much less cultivated.

**symphonic study,** vague term used by Schumann for set of piano variations, and by Elgar for orchestral work *Falstaff,* and variously by other composers.

**symphonie** (Fr.), **Symphonie** (Ger., also *Sinfonie*), symphony.

**Symphonie cévenole,** *see* SYMPHONY ON A FRENCH MOUNTAIN SONG.

**symphonie concertante** (Fr.), SINFONIA CONCERTANTE.

**Symphonie espagnole** (Fr., *Spanish Symphony*), work for violin and orchestra by Lalo. First perf. 1875.

**Symphonie fantastique** (Fr., *Fantastic Symphony*), orchestral work in 5 movts. by Berlioz, op 14 (1830), also entitled *Épisode de la vie d'un artiste* (episode in an artist's life). Berlioz issued detailed programme for work based on own hopeless love for Harriet Smithson: hero attempts to poison himself with opium, dreams he has killed his beloved and is led to execution, then finds himself at witches' sabbath. His beloved is represented by musical *idée fixe* which recurs throughout in various forms.

**Symphonie funèbre et triomphale** (Fr., Funeral and Triumphant Symphony), symphony by Berlioz, op 15 (1840), for military band, string orchestra and chorus, commissioned by French Government and performed on 10th anniversary of 1830 Revolution.

**Symphonie mit dem Paukenschlag,** *see* SURPRISE SYMPHONY.

**Symphonie mit dem Paukenwirbel,** *see* DRUM ROLL SYMPHONY.

**Symphonie pathétique** (Fr., Pathetic Symphony), Chaikovsky's 6th symphony in B minor, op 74 (1893). Title was authorized by composer.

**Symphonie sur un chant montagnard français,** *see* SYMPHONY ON A FRENCH MOUNTAIN SONG.

**Symphonische Dichtung** (Ger.), symphonic poem.

**symphony** (Fr., *symphonie*; Ger., *Sinfonie, Symphonie*; It., *sinfonia*), since *c* 1750, SONATA for orchestra. Previously word was used variously, usually for instrumental music. Applied to instrumental movts. in operas, prelude to cantata or instrumental suite, Italian opera overture (*sinfonia avanti l'opera*), introduction to song, and, exceptionally, by Bach to 3-part Inventions.

Modern symphony emerged as independent piece, modelled on Italian OVERTURE, between 1730 and 1750. Minuet was added to 3 movts. of Italian overture in some of symphonies of Viennese composers Monn and Wagenseil, and in those of members of 'Mannheim School' *eg* F.X. Richter and J. Stamitz. Some of Haydn's first 30 or so symphonies (his first dates from 1759) have 3 movts., either omitting or ending with minuet, and some have resemblances to *concerto grosso* in use of solo instruments.

In 4-movt. form which became normal after *c* 1765 symphony drew elements of its style from overture, *concerto grosso,* suite, and aria and finale of opera. In symphonies written after 1780 (incl. Salomon Symphonies, nos 93–104), Haydn absorbed some of grace and delicacy of Mozart, but kept his characteristic humour and spontaneity. Mozart's symphonies were influenced by those of J.C. Bach, and of Mannheim and Viennese composers, incl. Haydn. In last 3 symphonies (1788) he attained consummate balance of expression and design.

Beethoven's *Eroica* symphony expanded form and deepened expression, but only radical departure from tradition was variation form of last movt. It is the ancestor of all romantic symphonies, and, with 9th (choral) symphony, the largest conception of the form before Mahler. Few works before Mahler followed Beethoven's use of human voice in 9th symphony, exceptions being Mendelssohn's *Hymn of Praise,* Liszt's *Dante* and *Faust* symphonies, and Berlioz's *Symphonie funèbre et triomphale.* Tendency towards narrative 'programme' in Beethoven's 6th symphony was pursued by Berlioz in *Symphonie fantastique* and 'dramatic symphony' *Romeo and Juliette,* and was diverted by Liszt into new form of SYMPHONIC POEM.

Schubert's 8 extant symphonies encompassed classical, lyrical (*Unfinished*) and grand (Great C Major) styles. Main tradition goes through Mendelssohn and Schumann (who had some new and progressive ideas on symphonic form) to 4 symphonies of Brahms (1875–85), 9 of Bruckner (1866–94), 2 of Borodin (1862–76), 6 of

Chaikovsky (1868–93), 9 of Dvořák (1880–93), 10 of Mahler (1888–1909), and 7 of Sibelius (1898–1924). Form was not unaffected by use of thematic transformation, first applied in comprehensive way by Schumann in D minor symphony, and developed in symphonic poem. Device is found in Brahms's 1st and Chaikovsky's 4th symphony, and in symphonies of Franck and Saint-Säens.

Mahler treated traditional number and disposition of movts. quite flexibly, Sibelius less so; Mahler tended towards expansion, Sibelius to contraction and concentration. Mahler used voices in 4 of his symphonies, culminating in no 8 (*Symphony of a Thousand*) scored for massive choral and orchestral forces. Tendency to contraction is noticeable in 4th and 6th symphonies of Sibelius, and 7th is in single movt. Carl Nielsen also brought strong and individual style to his 6 symphonies, using (like Mahler) idea of 'progressive tonality' – *ie* ending work or movt. in different key from that with which it started.

In general, modern composers tend to use flexible number of movts. Notable symphonies written since 1914 incl. those by Vaughan Williams (9), Prokofiev (7), Shostakovich (15), Hindemith (2), Stravinsky (3), Walton (2), Henze (6), Tippett (4), Gerhard and Roy Harris.

**'Symphony of a Thousand',** misleading nickname given to Mahler's symphony no 8 (completed 1906) because of massive forces required: large orchestra, 8 soloists, 2 mixed choirs and children's choir.

**Symphony of Psalms,** 3-movt. symphony for chorus and orchestra by Stravinsky. First perf. 1930. Latin texts are from Psalms.

**Symphony on a French Mountain Song** (Fr., *Symphonie sur un chant montagnard français*), symphony for orchestra and piano by d'Indy, op 25 (1886), also known as *Symphonie cévenole* because it uses theme from region of Cévennes mountains.

**syncopation,** placing of accent(s) on parts of bar not usually accented. Can occur in various ways *eg* by (1) rhythmic anticipation, (2) rhythmic suspension, (3) indicated stress on unaccented beat or on subdivision of beat, (4) by having rest on beat and sound on subdivision of beat. If regularly syncopated rhythm is continued for more than bar it has effect of displaced metre superimposed on basic metre. Rhythms made up of different metres in succession have similar, but not identical, effect, since there is no continuous basic metre. Syncopation is characteristic idiom of Negro spirituals, ragtime and jazz.

**synthesizer,** integrated array of electronic devices for generation and modification of sound. Evolved in 1960s to solve practical difficulties faced by composers of early electronic music who had to use large quantities of inflexible and bulky equipment designed for quite other purposes. Synthesizers can modify 'live' external sounds, imitate specific instruments, or create completely new sounds. Can also be pre-programmed for live performance. Synthesizers come in all shapes and sizes and are used in production of both live and prerecorded music of all kinds.

**syrinx,** *see* NEI.

**Syrinx,** piece for solo flute by Debussy (1912), orig. called *Flûte de Pan* and intended as incidental music to G. Mourey's play *Psyché*.

**System** (Ger.), STAFF (abbrev. of *Liniensystem*).

**Székely, Zoltán** (1903– ), Hungarian violinist, composer. Pupil of Hubay and Kodály. In 1935 founded Hungarian String Quartet, in which he played 1st violin. Closely associated with music of Bartók, whose 2nd violin concerto and 2nd rhapsody for violin and piano were both written for him.

**Szell, George,** orig. Georg (1896–1970), Hungarian-born conductor, pianist, composer. Held various posts in Germany before WWII. Conductor of Cleveland Orchestra in US from 1946 till his death, transforming it into ensemble of unsurpassed excellence.

**Szeryng, Henryk** (1918– ), Polish-born violinist, Mexican citizen since 1946. His playing has met with international acclaim.

**Szigeti, Joseph** (1892–1973), Hungarian-born violinist. Resident in Britain then in US. Toured extensively. Esp. famous for interpretations of Bartók and Prokofiev.

**Szokolay, Sándor** (1931– ), Hungarian composer. Works incl. operas based on Lorca's *Blood Wedding* and *Hamlet,* ballets, oratorios, *Negro Cantata,* settings of Negro folk poetry in Hungarian translation, and instrumental music.

**Szymanowski, Karol** (1882–1937), Polish composer, b. Ukraine. Studied in Warsaw, then lived in Berlin and Russia, returning to Poland after Revolution. Director of Warsaw Conservatory from 1926. Regarded as father of modern Polish music. Though style was initially indebted to Chopin, Skryabin and Debussy, it soon became remarkably forward looking. Works incl. 2 operas *eg King Roger,* ballets, 3 symphonies, works for solo voices, chorus and orchestra, 2 violin concertos, *Symphonie concertante* for piano and orchestra, chamber and piano music, and songs.

# T

**t,** abbrev. for (1) *corde* in *tutte le corde* or *tre corde* (*see* CORDA);
(2) trill (or shake) in 17th-cent. music; modern sign is *tr.*;
(3) *tasto;* t.s. = *tasto solo* (*see* TASTO);
(4) *te,* in TONIC SOL-FA, seventh note (or leading note) of major scale.

**T.,** as abbrev. = tenor, tonic.

**Tabarro, Il,** *see* TRITTICO.

**tabla,** type of oriental drum beaten by hands. Indian and Arabic forms are most familiar. Indian version is single-headed, producing similar sound to *timpano*; has clearly defined pitch and sets of up to 12, providing complete chromatic compass, have been used. Arabic version has much drier tone.

**tablature** (Ger., *Tablatura*; It., *intavolatura*), type of notation used esp. in 16th, 17th cents. for writing music for lute, *vihuela,* organ and other instruments, in which pitch of notes is shown by letters or numbers, indicating position of fingers or notes of scale; time values of notes were usually indicated in normal way. Modern notation for guitar and similar instruments is tablature in form of diagram of strings and frets on which dots indicate positions of fingers.

**table** (Fr.), (1) belly, or upper part of sound box of string instrument;
(2) sounding board of harp, rising diagonally from foot of vertical pillar to upper end of neck. *Près de la table,* play near sounding board, thus producing metallic sound similar to that of banjo;
(3) *musique de table* (Ger., *Tafelmusik*), music for a banquet.

**tabor,** small drum. *See* PIPE AND TABOR, TAMBOURIN.

**Tábor,** *see* MÁ VLAST.

**taboret,** small tabor.

**tabourin** (Fr.), tabor.

**tabrete** (early Eng.), drum.

**tacet** (Lat.), 'is silent'. Indication in part that performer does not play in particular movt. or section.

**tactus** (Lat.), term used for 'beat' by theorists of 15th, 16th cents.

**Tafelklavier** (Ger.), spinet or virginals.

**Tafelmusik,** *see* TABLE (3).

**taille** (Fr.), term used in 17th, 18th cents. for: (1) tenor or middle part of composition;
(2) tenor member of family of instruments, *eg taille de violin,* viola. *Taille* by itself = (a) viola, (b) *oboe da caccia.*

**Tailleferre, Germaine** (1892– ), French composer, pianist. Member of Les SIX. Settled in US in 1942. Works, in characteristically lucid style, incl. piano concerto, Ballade for piano and orchestra, ballet, *Pastorale* for small orchestra, quartet and other chamber music, and songs.

**Takemitsu, Toru** (1930– ), Japanese composer, internationally most famous of the day. Music incorporates both Japanese and European elements. Works incl. *November Steps* (1967) for *biwa* and *shakuhachi* (traditional Japanese instruments) and orchestra, *Water Music* for Noh-dancer and tape, percussion pieces closely associated with the percussionist Stomu Yamash'ta, and piano music.

**Takt** (Ger.), (1) bar, (2) beat, (3) time.

**Taktstrich** (Ger.), bar-line.

**Tal, Joseph** (1910– ), Israeli composer, b. Poland. Compositions incl. opera *Ashmedai* (1973), choreographic poem *Exodus* for baritone and orchestra, and other orchestral works.

**talea,** *see* ISORHYTHM.

**Tale of Two Cities, A,** opera by Arthur Benjamin, libretto by C. Cliffe (after Dickens). Broadcast 1953; first staged London, 1957.

**Tales of Hoffmann, The** (Fr., *Les Contes d'Hoffmann*), opera by Offenbach, libretto by J. Barbier and M. Carré. Left incomplete at composer's death; finished by E. Guiraud. First perf. Paris, 1881. Presents 3 love-affairs in life of E.T.A. Hoffmann (1776–1822), on whose stories libretto is based.

**Tálich, Václav** (1883–1961), Czech conductor. Pupil of Nikisch. Outstanding exponent of Dvořák. Conducted Czech Philharmonic from 1919.

**Tallis, Thomas** (*c* 1505–85), English composer, organist. Gentleman of Chapel Royal from *c* 1545, and organist of Chapel with Byrd. In 1575 he and Byrd were granted sole right to print music in England. Composed 2 Magnificats, 2 Masses, Lamentations for 5 voices, Latin motets, services, psalms, anthems and other church music, 2 *In Nomines* for strings, secular vocal works and keyboard pieces. Such works as 40-part motet and 7-part canon 'Miserere nostri' are both technically skilful and artistically satisfying. Deeper aspects of his style are more evident in Mass *Salve intemerata*, in Lamentations, and in motets of *Cantiones Sacrae* (which also contains motets by Byrd), works which place him among greatest of composers of mid 16th cent. 'Tallis's Canon' is adaptation of one of his tunes (1567).

**talon** (Fr.), nut of bow. *Au talon,* play with nut-end or heel of bow.

**Tamagno, Francesco** (1851–1905), Italian tenor. Made debut in 1873, and was La Scala's leading tenor by early 1880s. Created role of Otello in 1887, and sang the part all over the world.

**tambour** (Fr.), drum. *Tambour militaire,* side drum. *Tambour de basque,* tambourine.

**tamboura,** alternative name for PANDOURA.

**tambourin** (Fr.), (1) long narrow drum, played with 1 stick when used, esp. in Provence (*tambourin de Provence*), with small, 1-handed recorder (*flûtet, galoubet*) to accompany dancing;

(2) *tambourin de Béarn* (It., *altobasso*) was DULCIMER with gut strings sounding only tonic and dominant, and was used similarly with type of flageolet (*galouvet*) to accompany dance (also called *tambourin*).

**tambourine** (Fr., *tambour de Basques*; Ger., *Tamburin, Baskische*

*Trommel, Schellentrommel*; It., *tamburino, tamburo basso*; Sp., *panderete*), small drum with single head fastened to narrow circular wooden frame slotted to accommodate several pairs of tiny, loosely hanging cymbals, called jingles. Normally held in one hand and struck by fingers, knuckles or palm of other. Jingles can be sounded without striking head, either by shaking or by rubbing moistened thumb round head, thereby setting up vibrations. *Tamburello* is Italian type of tambourine without jingles.

**tamburello,** *see* TAMBOURINE.

**Tamburini, Antonio** (1800–76), Italian baritone. Created roles of Dr Malatesta in Donizetti's *Don Pasquale* and Riccardo in Bellini's *I Puritani*. Began career in Italy, but achieved greatest fame in Paris and London.

**tamburino,** *see* TAMBOURINE.

**tamburo** (It.), drum. *Tamburo grande, tamburo grosso,* old terms for bass drum. *Tamburo rullante,* tenor drum. *Tamburo militare,* snare drum.

**tamburo basso,** *see* TAMBOURINE.

**tamburo piccolo** (It.), side drum.

**Tamerlano** (It., *Tamburlaine*), opera by Handel, libretto by A. Pioverne, adapted by N.F. Haym. First perf. London, 1724.

**Taming of the Shrew, The** (Ger., *Der widerspänstigen Zähmung*), opera by Goetz, after Shakespeare's comedy. Several other operas have been based on play, as well as Cole Porter's musical *Kiss Me Kate* (1948).

**tampon** (Fr.), 2-headed drumstick held in middle and used with alternating motion of wrists to produce roll on bass drum.

**tam-tam,** variety of gong.

**Tancredi,** opera by Rossini, libretto by G. Rossi (after Tasso and Voltaire). First perf. Venice, 1813. Overture is well-known in concert hall.

**tañer,** *see* TASTAR.

**Taneyev, Sergey Ivanovich** (1856–1915), Russian composer. Pupil of Chaikovsky and N. Rubinstein. Teacher at Moscow Conservatory (1880–1906), and director (1885–9). Composed symphonies, overture, string quartets and other chamber music, operatic trilogy, choral works, and songs.

**tangent,** *see* CLAVICHORD.

**tango,** dance in moderately slow 2/4 time with syncopated rhythms. Originated in urban Argentina and appeared in Europe and US *c* 1910.

**Tannhäuser,** in full *Tannhäuser, und der Sängerkrieg auf Wartburg* (Ger., *Tannhäuser, and the Tournament of Song at Wartburg*), opera by Wagner, libretto by composer. First perf. Dresden, 1845. Revised for Paris production in 1861. Tannhäuser is minstrel knight torn between love for Venus and for landgrave's pious niece Elizabeth.

**Tansman, Alexandre** (1897– ), Polish-born composer, pianist. Resident in Paris from 1920, spending war years in US. Works incl.

operas, ballets, 7 symphonies, concertos, string quartets, film and piano music, and songs.

**tanto** (It.), 'so much'. Used as equivalent of *troppo, eg allegro non tanto,* not too fast.

**Tans'ur, William,** orig. **Tanzer** (1706–83), English composer, teacher, organist. Published books of metrical psalms containing some composed by himself and some with words by himself. His *A New Musical Grammar* (1746–56, later published as *The Elements of Musick Display'd,* 1772) was widely used and reprinted as late as 1829.

**Tanz** (Ger.), dance.

**tap box,** same as CHINESE BLOCK.

**tape music,** *see* ELECTRONIC MUSIC.

**Tapiola,** symphonic poem by Sibelius op 112 (1925). Tapio is forest god in Finnish mythology.

**Tapissier, Jean** (*fl* early 15th cent.), French composer. Surviving works consist of *Credo* and *Sanctus* in 3 parts, and 4-part motet.

**tarantella,** very fast Italian dance in 6/8 time, usually with alternating major and minor sections. Long regarded as cure for bite of tarantula spider (both named after Taranto in S Italy).

**Taras Bulba,** rhapsody for orchestra by Janáček (1928), based on Gogol's novel about 15th-cent. conflict between Poles and Ukrainian Cossacks.

**tarbouka,** North African drum used by Berlioz in Slave Dance in *The Trojans.*

**tardo** (It.), slow. *Tardando,* becoming slower.

**tárogató,** Hungarian woodwind instrument with oriental origins. Orig. had double reed, now single. Resembles straight soprano saxophone in appearance and tone.

**Tartini, Giuseppe** (1692–1770), Italian violinist, composer, teacher, theorist. Worked in various Italian towns and in Prague (1723–6). In 1728 established school of violin-playing in Padua; pupils incl. Graun, Nardini and Pugnani. Discovered COMBINATION TONES. Wrote many treatises on violin-playing and on acoustical problems. Composed *c* 100 violin concertos, symphonies, numerous sonatas (incl. *The Devil's Trill*), and some church music.

**Tasso,** symphonic poem by Liszt, inspired by poem by Byron. First perf. Weimar, 1849, as overture to Goethe's drama *Torquato Tasso.* In 1850–1 composer revised and extended score.

**tastar** (It.; Sp., *tañer*), 'touching'; 16th-cent. term for lute prelude in extemporary style.

**tastatura** (It.), keyboard.

**Taste** (Ger.), key of keyboard instrument.

**tastiera** (It.), finger-board. *Sulla tastiera, see* BOWING.

**tastiera per luce** (It.), 'keyboard for light', instrument invented by Rimington which projected colours. Had 12 notes 'tuned' to 'scale' of colours based on musical cycle of fifths. Prescribed by Skryabin in *Prometheus.*

**tasto** (It.), (1) key of keyboard instrument. *Tasto solo,* in figured bass, play only bass notes without adding harmonies above;
(2) fret on lute, guitar, viol *etc;*
(3) fingerboard of stringed instrument. *Sul tasto, see* BOWING.

**Tate, Phyllis** (1911– ), British composer. Works incl. operas *The Lodger* (1958) and *Dark Pilgrimage* (1963), saxophone concerto, sonata for clarinet and cello, and *A Secular Requiem* for voices, organ and orchestra.

**tatto** (It.), obs. term for *acciaccatura.*

**Tatum, Art** (1910–56), American jazz pianist. Florid style was immensely influential – though few could match his Lisztian technique. Heard at his best in solo capacity.

**Tauber, Richard,** orig. Ernst Seiffert (1892–1948), Austrian-born tenor. Sang in Dresden, Vienna and Covent Garden. Took British nationality. Famed esp. in Mozart and Lehár. Also composed.

**Tausig, Carl** (1841–71), Polish pianist, composer. Settled in Germany. Pupil of Liszt. One of greatest piano virtuosos of his day. Composed symphonic poems, piano concerto, and studies and transcriptions for piano, incl. some Bach organ works.

**Tavener, John** (1944– ), English composer, pianist, organist. Works incl. operas *Thérèse* and *A Gentle Spirit, A Celtic Requiem,* and dramatic cantatas *The Whale* and *Cain and Abel.*

**Taverner,** opera by Peter Maxwell Davies, libretto by composer. First perf. Covent Garden, 1971. Based on career of John Taverner (see below).

**Taverner, John** (*c* 1490–1545), English composer. Master of choristers at Cardinal College (later Christ Church), Oxford (1526–30), where was briefly imprisoned for heresy. Later settled in Boston, Lincolnshire. There is no firm historical basis for story that he renounced composition in 1530 and worked as agent of Thomas Cromwell in suppression of monasteries.

He was one of the last and greatest of composers to write Masses, Magnificats and antiphons to the Virgin in the elaborate style of early 16th-cent. English composers. He made greater use of imitation than his immediate predecessors. Masses show interesting variety of method: 3 (including *Gloria tibi Trinitas* whose 'In nomine' section was starting point of IN NOMINE) are large works on *cantus firmus* in older style; *The Western Wynde* is set of variations on secular tune; 3 are in 'familiar' (*ie* chordal) style making use of divided choir technique (*see* CORI SPEZZATI) to some extent; and *Mater Christi* is parody Mass.

**Taylor, [Joseph] Deems** (1885–1966), American composer, critic, writer on music. Works incl. operas *The King's Henchman* (1927) and *Peter Ibbetson* (1931), ballet, symphonic poems, suites *eg Through the Looking Glass* (after Lewis Carroll), and choral and incidental music.

**Tchaikovsky,** *see* CHAIKOVSKY.

**Tchaikowsky, André** (1935– ), Polish-born pianist, now resident in UK. Has acquired international reputation, esp. for recitals.

**Tcherepnin,** *see* CHEREPNIN.

**te,** Eng. substitution for It. *si* (B), used in TONIC SOL-FA for seventh note (or leading note) of major scale.

**Teagarden, Jack** (1905–64), American jazz trombonist, most famous of his day. Created style of playing on trombone which was counterpart of Louis Armstrong's on trumpet. Heyday was 1930s, when appeared frequently with Ben Pollack and Paul Whiteman, as well as with own bands. Also worked as singer, often performing in partnership with Louis Armstrong.

**Tebaldi, Renata** (1922– ), Italian soprano. One of most important since WWII. Esp. associated with dramatic roles of Verdi and Puccini.

**tecla** (Sp.), term for key or keyboard, dating from 16th, 17th cents. *Música para tecla,* keyboard music.

**tedesca** (It.), short for *danza tedesca,* 'German dance'. *See* ALLA TEDESCA, ALLEMANDE, DEUTSCHER TANZ.

**Te Deum** (Lat.), opening words of 'Te Deum laudamus' (We praise thee, God), Christian hymn sung at Matins on festivals, on occasions of thanksgiving, and (in Eng. translation) at Morning Prayer in Anglican service. Notable settings have been made by Purcell, Handel, Berlioz, Bruckner, Dvořák, Verdi, Stanford, Parry, Vaughan Williams and Walton.

**Teil** (Ger.), section, part (of work). *Erste Teil,* 'Part One', *etc.*

**Te Kanawa, Kiri** (1944– ), New Zealand soprano. Known esp. for roles in Strauss, Mozart and Verdi operas.

**Telemann, Georg Philipp** (1681–1767), German composer. Studied law at Leipzig University. Musically self-taught, he worked in Sorau, Eisenach (where became friend of Bach), Frankfurt, Bayreuth and Hamburg. One of most prolific composers ever. Wrote 12 cycles of cantatas for church year, 44 Passions, oratorios and much other church music, 40 operas, 600 French overtures (*ie* suites for orchestra), concertos, much chamber music, fantasies for harpsichord, and short fugues for organ.

His grandson, **Georg Michael Telemann** (1748–1831), was composer and writer. Published introduction to figured bass (1773), and composed trio sonatas, solo sonatas, organ preludes and church music. Cantor at Riga *c* 1775.

**Telemusik,** work by Stockhausen (1966), incorporating recorded *objets trouvés* from all over world, esp. Japan.

**Telephone, The,** opera by Menotti, libretto by composer. First perf. New York, 1947. Story concerns young man who has to compete with incessantly ringing telephone for his beloved's attention.

**Telmányi, Emil** (1892– ), Hungarian violinist. Resident in Denmark, where married Nielsen's daughter. Invented 'Bach bow', which enables chords to be played without spreading.

**tema** (It.), theme. *Tema con variazioni,* theme and variations.

**temperament,** system of tuning in which intervals are 'tempered' (*ie* slightly lessened or enlarged) away from 'natural' scale. Devised when gradual introduction of chromatic tones made inadequate systems based on physical laws, where intervals agree with those found by successive fractional division of string.

After *c* 1500, system of mean-tone temperament was generally adopted for keyboard instruments, which was adequate for normal chords of modal harmony and for keys not involving more than 2 sharps or flats. With use in composition of complete cycle of major and minor keys (as in Bach's *The Well-Tempered Clavier*), system of EQUAL TEMPERAMENT began to be adopted, though not universally accepted till *c* 1850. *See* DIESIS.

**Tempest, The,** (1) opera with dialogue by Purcell (1695), text adapted from Shakespeare by Thomas Shadwell;
(2) incidental music for play by Sibelius, op 109 (1926);
(3) symphonic fantasy by Chaikovsky, op 18 (1873), based on play;
(4) operas based on play by several composers, incl. Frank Martin (1956).

**temple block,** also called Chinese or Korean temple block; not to be confused with CHINESE BLOCK. Made of hard wood with slits and shaped like skull. Usually made in sets of 5. Played with sticks and tone varies with hardness of these – but is anyway deeper and mellower than that of Chinese block. They produce recognizable notes, though not of very definite pitch.

**tempo** (It.), (1) time. Pace of composition as determined by speed of beat to which it is performed. Towards end of 17th cent. modern tempo indications, *eg largo, adagio, allegro, presto,* were adopted in Italy and gradually came into general use. Within certain limits interpretation of these is up to performer. *See also* GIUSTO, PRIMO;
(2) movement (of sonata, symphony *etc*). *Il Secondo tempo,* the second movement.

**temps** (Fr.), beat. *Temps fort,* strong beat. *Temps faible,* weak beat.

**Tender Land, The,** opera by Copland, libretto by H. Everett. First perf. New York, 1954. Concerns farmer's daughter who falls in love with harvester on father's Midwest farm.

**Tenebrae,** RC services of Matins and Lauds for Wednesday, Thursday and Friday of Holy Week, during which are sung LAMENTATIONS and *Miserere*. Name derives from practice of gradually extinguishing lights through services.

**tenendo** (It.), sustaining.

**teneramente** (It.), tenderly.

**Tennstedt, Klaus** (1926– ), German conductor, violinist. Has worked with Kiel Opera, Minnesota Orchestra, Hamburg Radio Symphony Orchestra and London Philharmonic Orchestra. Noted exponent of Mahler.

**tenor,** (1) RECITING NOTE in psalmody;
(2) in sacred polyphonic music until *c* 1450, lowest part, often derived from plainsong, on which composition was based. In polyphonic *chanson* of same period, part which formed, with highest part (*cantus*), 2-part framework of composition. It was as melodious as *cantus* part and could be used as tenor of Mass;
(3) in music after *c* 1450, when bass part began to be used, part

above bass in 4-part vocal composition (S.A.T.B.). Term hence applied to adult male voice intermediate between bass and alto;

(4) as prefix to name of instrument, indicates size intermediate between alto (or treble) member of family and bass, *eg* tenor saxophone, tenor trombone;

(5) obs. Eng. term for viola (tenor violin);

(6) tenor clef is C clef on 4th line (*see* CLEF).

**tenor cor,** alternative name for MELLOPHONE.

**tenor drum** (Fr., *caisse roulante*; Ger., *Rolltrommel, Rührtrommel*; It., *tamburo rullante*), snareless drum larger than side drum but considerably smaller than bass drum. Long used in military and drum-and-fife bands, though rarely in orchestra.

**Tenorfagott,** *see* TENOROON.

**Tenorgeige** (Ger.), lit. 'tenor violin', *ie* viola.

**tenor hautboy,** obs. Eng. term for *cor anglais* (*see* OBOE).

**Tenor Horn, Tenorhorn** (Ger.), name sometimes given to tenor SAXHORN and occasionally to corresponding member of FLUGELHORN family.

**tenoroon** (Fr., *basson quinte*; Ger., *Tenorfagott*; It., *fagottino*), tenor bassoon, long obs., pitched fifth higher than normal instrument.

**Tenorposaune** (Ger.), tenor TROMBONE.

**tenth,** interval of octave plus third. Treated as equivalent of third in theory of harmony and in figured bass.

**tento,** *see* TIENTO.

**tenuto** (It.), 'held'. Indication that single note or chord should be held for full value (or even longer) in context in which performer might be inclined to play it *staccato*. Abbrev. *ten.*

**ternary form,** form, represented by formula *ABA,* in which 1st section is restated, with or without modifications or embellishments, after middle section of different content. Where restatement is without change it is often indicated by *da capo al fine* at end of middle section, as in *da capo* aria, and minuet or scherzo with trio; where it is abbreviated, it is indicated by *dal segno al fine*. Most of short piano pieces of romantic period (nocturne, impromptu, intermezzo, rhapsody *etc*) are in ternary form. SONATA FORM, having evolved from earlier BINARY FORM, is special case of ternary form in which middle section is development, recapitulation involves partial change of key, and coda may be as long as each of other sections.

**Terradellas** or **Terradeglias, Domingo Miguel Bernabe (Domenico)** (*c* 1713–51), Spanish composer. Pupil of Durante in Naples. Lived in London, Paris and Rome. Composed operas, incl. *Artaserse* (1744) and *Bellerofonte* (1747); latter made early use of crescendo. Also composed some church music.

**Terry, Charles Stanford** (1864–1936), English historian. Published many books and essays on Bach and his music.

**Terry, Richard Runciman** (1865–1938), English organist, composer, editor. Organist at Westminster Cathedral (1901–24), and gave many performances of early English church music. Edited Tudor motets and *The Westminster Hymnal* (1912). Published several books on church music, and collection of sea shanties. Composed 5 Masses, Requiem, and motets.

**tertian harmony,** harmonic system based on third or triad, *ie* standard western system of harmony.

**Tertis, Lionel** (1876–1975), English viola player, teacher. Toured Europe and US. Retired from concert platform in 1936. Several composers, incl. Bax and Bliss, wrote works for him. Laid down new technical specifications for making of violas.

**Terz** (Ger.), third. *Terzdezime,* thirteenth, or upper sixth.

**terzetto** (It.; Ger., *Terzett*), vocal trio. Also applied (rarely) to piece for 3 instruments.

**terzina** (It.), triplet.

**Teschner, Melchior** (1584–1635), German church musician. Composer of hymn 'Valet will ich dir geben', sung in English as 'All glory, laud and honour'.

**Teseo** (It., *Theseus*), opera by Handel, libretto by N.F. Haym. First perf. London, 1713.

**Tessarini, Carlo** (1690–*c* 1762), Italian violinist, composer. Prob. pupil of Vivaldi. Works incl. violin sonatas, trio sonatas, violin duets, *concertini* and *concerti grossi* for strings. His *Grammatica di musica* (1741) was published in French and English translations.

**Tessier, Charles** (born *c* 1550), French composer, lutenist. Was chamber musician to Henry IV, and visited England. Composed book of *Chansons et airs de cour* for 4 to 5 voices (London, 1597), and *Airs et villanelles* for 3 to 5 voices (Paris, 1604). Also set song from Sidney's *Astrophel and Stella,* printed in R. Dowland's *A Musicall Banquet* (1610).

**tessitura** (It.), 'texture'. Compass to which particular singer's voice naturally inclines, or compass of vocal or instrumental part in particular piece.

**testo** (It.), lit. 'text', *ie* narrator in early oratorio.

**testudo** (Lat.), lit. 'tortoise', 'tortoise-shell', hence (1) in Graeco-Roman world, LYRE;

(2) in 16th, 17th cents., lute.

**tetrachord** (Gr., four string), segment of scale of ancient Greek music, consisting of 4 notes descending through perfect fourth in order tone-tone-semitone *eg* A–G–F–E. This diatonic tetrachord was basis of complete diatonic scale. CHROMATIC tetrachord had 2 steps of semitone above lowest note; ENHARMONIC tetrachord had 2 steps of quarter tone above lowest note.

**Tetrazzini, Luisa** (1871–1940), Italian operatic soprano. Started career in Italy, then joined companies in Argentina (from 1898) and Mexico (from 1905). Sang in various European and American cities, and later returned to Italy.

**Teutsch,** *see* DEUTSCHER TANZ.

**Teyte, Maggie** (1888–1976), British soprano. Achieved success on French opera stage. Also famous as recitalist, esp. in French repertory of late 19th, early 20th cent.

**Thaïs,** opera by Massenet, libretto by L. Gallet (after novel by

Anatole France). First perf. Paris, 1894. Heroine is 4th-cent. courtesan who becomes nun. Orchestral interlude known as 'Meditation from Thaïs' is often performed out of context.

**Thalben-Ball,** *see* BALL.

**Thalberg, Sigismond** (1812–71), Austrian pianist, composer. Pupil of Hummel. Toured Europe, US and Brazil. Rival of Liszt in Paris. Works incl. operas, piano concerto, sonata, studies and much else for piano, transcriptions for piano, and songs.

**Thamos, König in Agypten** (Ger., *King Thamos in Egypt*), incidental music by Mozart K345 (1773) for play by Tobias Philipp, Baron von Gebler. Music consists of choruses and entr'actes.

**Thayer, Alexander Wheelock** (1817–97), American writer on music. Lived in Trieste from 1865 as US consul. His life of Beethoven (3 vols., 1866–79, vol. 4 uncompleted) is standard biographical work on composer; English edition translated and completed by H.E. Krehbiel (1921). Also published chronological index of Beethoven's compositions (1865).

**theme,** musical entity (consisting of group of notes, usually melodic) which is chief idea, or one of chief ideas, in a composition. Used esp. of idea in instrumental work which is used as basis for discussion, development or variation. *See also* SUBJECT.

**Theodora,** oratorio by Handel, text by T. Morell. First perf. London, 1750. On story of Christian martyr.

**Theodorakis, Mikis** (1925– ), Greek composer. His melodious songs did much to revive Greek popular music in 1960s. Has also written symphony, piano concerto and other concert works, and music for film *Zorba the Greek*. Imprisoned for Communist sympathies; music was banned during rule of junta (1967–74).

**theorbo** (Fr., *théorbe*; Ger., *Theorbe*; It., *tiorba*), small bass lute or ARCHLUTE used in 17th cent. as continuo instrument in ensembles, and less frequently to accompany monodies.

**theory of music,** according to period when they were written, works on theory of music may deal with one or more of following aspects of the subject: acoustics, notation, melody, rhythm, harmony, counterpoint, composition, form, and musical aesthetics.

**Thérémin,** electronic instrument (purely melodic) invented by Russian physicist Leon Thérémin (1896– ), first demonstrated in 1920. Notes are produced by variations in frequency of oscillating electric circuit, controlled by movement of player's hand in air towards or away from antenna.

**Theresienmesse** (Ger., *Theresa Mass*), Mass in B flat by Haydn (1799). No satisfactory explanation of name has been advanced.

**thesis,** *see* ARSIS.

**Thibaud, Jacques** (1880–1953), French violinist. Toured widely as soloist, and in piano trio with Cortot and Casals. Killed in air crash.

**Thieving Magpie, The** (It., *La Gazza ladra*), opera by Rossini, libretto by G. Gherardini. First perf. Milan, 1817. Story concerns maidservant who is condemned to death for theft until it is realized that magpie was real thief. Overture is often played out of context.

**third,** interval comprised by first and last notes of any 3 notes in diatonic scale (*ie* 2 notes written on adjacent lines or spaces on staff), *eg* F–A. Major third has 2 whole tones (*eg* F sharp–A sharp), minor third has tone and semitone (*eg* F sharp–A) and diminished third has whole tone (*eg* F sharp–A flat).

**Third Stream,** *see* SCHULLER.

**thirteenth,** interval of octave plus sixth. For 'chord of the thirteenth' *see* CHORD.

**thirty-second note** (US), demisemiquaver.

**Thoinan, Ernest,** pseud. of Antoine Ernest Roquet (1827–94), French musical scholar. Collected works of music, and contributed to *La France musicale, L'Art musical* and other periodicals.

**Thomas, Arthur Goring** (1850–92), English composer. Studied in Paris; later pupil of Sullivan and Bruch. Works incl. operas *eg Esmeralda* and *Nadeshda,* 4 concert-scenes, cantatas and other choral works, orchestral *Suite de Ballet,* and many songs (chiefly to French words).

**Thomas, [Charles Louis] Ambroise** (1811–96), French composer. Won *Prix de Rome* (1832). Became director of Paris Conservatoire (1871). Works incl. operas *eg Mignon* (1866) and *Hamlet* (1868), Fantasia for piano and orchestra, cantatas, church, chamber and piano music, songs and part-songs.

**Thomas, Theodore** (1835–1905), American conductor, violinist, b. Germany. Founded own orchestra (1862), and conducted Brooklyn Philharmonic (1866), New York Philharmonic (1877), and Chicago Symphony Orchestra (1891–1905). Gave many first perfs. in US of modern music.

**Thomé, Francis,** orig. Joseph-François Luc Thomé (1850–1909), French composer, b. Mauritius. Wrote operas, operettas, incidental and choral music, but best remembered for piano piece *Simple Aveu.*

**Thompson, Randall** (1899– ), American composer, teacher, music critic. Works incl. opera *Solomon and Balkis,* 3 symphonies, *Jazz Poem* for piano and orchestra and other orchestral works, choral, incidental, chamber and piano music, and songs.

**Thomson, Virgil** (1896– ), American composer, music critic. Pupil of Nadia Boulanger. Lived in Paris (1925–32), where was influenced by Satie, Les Six, Cocteau and Stravinsky. Works incl. operas *Four Saints in Three Acts* (1934), *The Mother of us all* (1947) – both to texts by Gertrude Stein – and *Lord Byron* (1968), 3 symphonies, cello concerto and other orchestral works, ballet, choral, chamber, incidental, film, organ and piano music, songs (many to French words), and series of *Portraits* for various media.

**thorough bass,** *see* FIGURED BASS.

**Thorne, John** (d. 1573), English composer. His motet 'Stella coeli' was printed in Hawkins' *History of Music.*

**Three Choirs Festival,** annual festival, founded 1724, given by combined choirs of Gloucester, Worcester and Hereford, and held in each cathedral in turn.

**Three-Cornered Hat, The** (Sp., *El sombrero de tres picos*), ballet by

Falla, based on Pedro de Alarcón's story. First perf. with title *The Magistrate and the Miller's Wife* in Madrid. Rev. version with present title first perf. London, 1919, with choreography by Massine and sets and costumes by Picasso.

**Threepenny Opera, The** (Ger., *Die Dreigroschenoper*), opera by Kurt Weill, text by Brecht, (with some lyrics from Kipling and Villon). Work is modern interpretation of *The Beggar's Opera.* First perf. Berlin, 1928.

**Threni,** work for soloists, chorus and orchestra by Stravinsky. First perf. 1958. Latin text based on *Lamentations* in Jeremiah.

**through-composed,** *see* DURCHKOMPONIERT.

**Thuille, Ludwig** (1861–1907), German composer. Pupil of Rheinberger, and friend of Richard Strauss. Works incl. 4 operas (1 unfinished), overture and other orchestral works, music for female and for male choirs, chamber and piano music, and songs.

**thump,** early Eng. word for *pizzicato,* esp. on lyra viol; also applied to piece so performed.

**thunder horn,** early name for 'folded' as opposed to 'straight' trumpet.

**thunder machine,** device consisting of hard balls inside large rotating drum, used to produce thunder effects.

**thunder stick, bull roarer** or **whizzer** (Fr., *planchette ronflante*; Ger., *Schwirrholz*), instrument consisting simply of flat piece of wood fastened to piece of string. When swung rapidly round head produces groaning or roaring sound varying in pitch with speed. Long used by natives of North America, Australia, central Africa *etc.*

**Thus spoke Zarathustra,** *see* ALSO SPRACH ZARATHUSTRA.

**tibia** (Lat., pipe), (1) Greek AULOS;

(2) organ stop, usually with qualification *eg tibia clausa,* flue stop of large scale.

**tie** (Fr., *liaison*; Ger., *Bindung*; It., *legatura*), curved line, also called bind, joining 2 notes of same pitch into continuous sound.

**Tiefland** (Ger., *Lowland*), opera by d'Albert, libretto by R. Lothar (pseud. of R. Spitzer), based on play *Terra baixa* by Catalan writer Angel Guimerá. First perf. Prague, 1903. An example of German *verismo,* work is melodrama of passion, betrayal and death.

**tiento** (Sp.; Port., *tento*), lit. 'touch', 16th-cent. term for *ricercar.*

**tierce de Picardie** (Fr., Picardy third), major third used in final chord of composition in minor mode, replacing expected minor third.

**tierce flute,** 18th-cent. name for flute built minor third higher than normal, also called 'third flute'.

**Tierce stops,** *see* MUTATION STOPS.

**Tiersot, Jean Baptiste Elisée Julien** (1857–1936), French historian, composer. Pupil of Massenet and Franck. Wrote many books on musical history and folk music, edited collections of folk songs, and worked with Saint-Saëns on Pelletan edition of Gluck's works. Composed works for chorus and orchestra, suite and other orchestral works, and incidental music for Corneille's *Andromède.*

**Tietjens, Therese** (1831–77), German soprano. Made debut in

1849. Built up substantial repertory, excelling in 19th-cent. operas, which she sang with great richness.

**Tigrini, Orazio** (*c* 1535–91), Italian composer, theorist. Composed book of madrigals for 4 voices (1573), and 2 books for 6 voices (1582, 1591). Also wrote 4-vol. work on counterpoint (*Compendio della musica,* 1588), from which Morley quoted in his *Plaine and Easie Introduction* (1597).

**Till Eulenspiegel,** in full *Till Eulenspiegels lustige Streiche* (Ger., 'Tyll Eulenspiegel's Merry Pranks'), symphonic poem by Richard Strauss, op 28 (1895), based on 15th-cent. German folk tale about exploits of lovable rogue. Story also inspired opera by Rezniček.

**Tillyard, Henry Julius Wetenhall** (1881–1968), English scholar, authority on Byzantine music. One of editors of *Monumenta Musicae Byzantinae*; also published several studies in Byzantine music and musical notation.

**timbales,** (1) (Fr.), TIMPANI;

(2) *timbales créoles,* single-headed drums of Latin American origin, similar to BONGOS and CONGAS, but played with sticks. Used in sets of 2 or 3.

**timbre** (Fr.), quality of tone, also used in English as alternative to TONE-COLOUR.

**timbrel,** rare term for TAMBOURINE.

**time,** time of piece of music is its division into beats per bar. Since *c* 1700 has been indicated by bar-lines and TIME SIGNATURE. Time in this sense may be duple (2 beats per bar), triple, quadruple, quintuple *etc.* Each of these is called 'simple' when beat is simple note value *ie* semibreve, minim, crotchet *etc, eg* simple triple time (3/4) has 3 crotchet beats per bar. 'Compound' time is one in which beat is ternary note-value, always represented by dotted note, *eg* compound duple time (6/8) has 6 quavers per bar making 2 dotted crotchet beats per bar. *See also* METRE, RHYTHM.

**time signature,** indication at start of piece of music of number and type of note-values in each bar. Consists of figures placed one above the other directly after key signature *eg*

$\substack{3\\4}$ = 3 crotchets in bar,

$\substack{6\\8}$ = 6 quavers in bar.

Lower figure gives value of each unit of measurement in relation to semibreve (or whole-note). Upper figure gives number of these in bar (these are usually equivalent to beats per bar in simple, but not in compound, TIME). Sign C is also used for 4/4 time, and

¢

for 2/2 time, also called ALLA BREVE. *See also* METRE.

**timpan,** string instrument used by Irish in early Middle Ages. Played with nails or plectrum and was thus early type of PSALTERY. In later Middle Ages strings were struck with rod as on DULCIMER.

**timpani** (It.; Fr., *timbales*; Ger., *Pauken*), drums of Arabian origin, most important of all orchestral percussion instruments. Also called kettledrums. Sing. *timpano* is very rare. *Timpani coperti* or *sordi* indicates muffled timpani.

Instrument consists of basin-shaped shell of copper or brass across which is stretched head, formerly of calfskin but now using synthetic substitute. Shell is mounted on legs. Drums are played with 2 sticks, most often of hard felt, although other materials are used for different effects, and drums may be muffled or muted. Head's tension can be adjusted by screws, allowing accurate tuning and alterations of pitch within limited compass.

Screw-tensioning device was added in 17th cent., when timpani were first used in orchestra. Up to Beethoven, only 2 instruments were used, tuned to tonic and dominant of piece being played. Combined range was approx. octave from F below bass clef. Beethoven used only 2 instruments, but introduced other tunings and sometimes brought them to fore for solos. Berlioz increased expressive range further, and called for large numbers. As demands of composers on instruments increased, tuning problems sometimes arose during performance – overcome by methods of tuning mechanically by foot pedal. On pedal drums (pedal timpani, machine drums; Ger., *Pedalpauken*) pitch can be changed instantly, so giving virtually complete chromatic compass and allowing glissandi to be played. Orchestras now have small drum extending range up to middle C, and modern timpanist rarely has less than 4 instruments.

**Tinctoris, Joannes** (*c* 1435–1511), Flemish theorist, composer. Held posts in Louvain, Naples and Nivelles. In his *Liber de arte contrapuncti* (1477) he remarks that no music written more than 40 years before that time was thought worth hearing. In his *Proportionale musices* (before 1476), observes that 'fount and origin' of this new art was considered to be among the English, esp. Dunstable. Published first dictionary of music, *Terminorum musicae diffinitorium* (*c* 1495), and *De inventione et usu musicae* (*c* 1484). Compositions incl. 4 Masses, 2 motets, Lamentations, and 7 *chansons*.

**Tin Pan Alley,** US slang expression (now obsolete) for pop music industry. Term originated in early 20th cent., when popular song publishing was based largely in West 28th Street, New York.

**Tinsley, Pauline** (1928– ), English soprano. Has sung with leading British opera companies. Esp. noted for Verdi roles.

**Tintagel,** symphonic poem by Bax (1917), evoking the cliff-top castle in Cornwall.

**tin whistle** or **penny whistle,** metal instrument with 6 finger holes, modelled on recorder. Its shrill sound is feature of Irish folk music.

**tiorba** (It.), THEORBO.

**Tippett, Michael Kemp** (1905– ), English composer. Pupil of C. Wood and R.O. Morris at Royal College of Music, London. Subsequently became director of music at Morley College. His music, like Britten's, reveals deep compassion for mankind, esp. in oratorio

*A Child of Our Time* (1941) and 3rd symphony. Otherwise music is very different from Britten's, being less fluent, more contrapuntal and 'chiselled'. Style has been influenced by cross-rhythms of 16th-cent. English composers, by American blues, and also in mature years by late Beethoven. Output, though not enormous, is of almost consistently high quality. Works incl. operas *The Midsummer Marriage* (1955), *King Priam* (1962), *The Knot Garden* (1970) and *The Ice Break* (1977), cantata *The Vision of St Augustine* (1966), 4 symphonies, *Concerto for Orchestra* (1963), piano concerto, triple concerto (1980) and other orchestral works, instrumental and chamber music incl. 4 string quartets, and song cycles. Knighted 1966.

**tirade** (Fr.), **tirata** (It.), baroque ornamental scale passage linking 2 notes of melody, or 2 chords.

**tirasse** (Fr.), *see* COUPLER (3).

**tiré** (Fr.), *see* POUSSÉ.

**Titelouze, Jean** (1563–1633), French organist, composer. Wrote organ hymns, Magnificats, and Mass *In ecclesia.*

**toccata,** (1) piece for keyboard instrument. Towards end of 16th cent. 2 types of toccata were written by Italian composers. First, practised by A. and G. Gabrieli, Luzzaschi and later by Frescobaldi, was in free style with much elaborate passage-work. Second, practised by Merulo and later by Frescobaldi, used sections in this style alternating with sections in imitative style.

Sweelinck and German organists (*eg* Scheidt) adopted both Italian types, later cultivated by Froberger, Pachelbel and Buxtehude. One short toccata of Pachelbel in free style is followed by fugue; others were of kind also written by Italian composers of his time (*eg* Pasquini) in which free style became much less diffuse, and each piece tended to pursue one particular form of figuration. Bach's harpsichord toccatas are of alternating type, divided into 3 or more distinct sections; all his organ toccatas are followed by fugue. Toccatas by later composers are usually in fast tempo with continuous rhythm based on one kind of figuration;

(2) word was also applied *c* 1600 to short piece with character of fanfare, for brass with or without other instruments (Eng., *tucket*; Ger., *Tusch*).

**Toch, Ernst** (1887–1964), Austrian-born composer, later resident in US. Works incl. 4 operas *eg The Princess and the Pea,* and orchestral, chamber, film and radio music.

**Tod und das Mädchen, Der,** *see* DEATH AND THE MAIDEN.

**Tod und Verklärung,** *see* DEATH AND TRANSFIGURATION.

**Toeschi, Carlo Giuseppe** (1724–88), Italian-born composer, violinist. Pupil of J. Stamitz. Leader of MANNHEIM Court Orchestra. Composed 63 symphonies, ballet and chamber music *etc.*

**Togni, Camillo** (1922– ), Italian composer, pianist. Pupil of Casella. Has written choral works incl. settings of T.S. Eliot, and chamber and piano music.

**Tolomeo, Re d'Egitto** (It., *Ptolemy, King of Egypt*), opera by Handel, libretto by N.F. Haym. First perf. London, 1728.

**Tolstoy, Count Theophil Matveivich** (1809–81), Russian composer, critic. Began work as music critic (under pseud. Rostislav) in 1850. Works incl. opera and *c* 200 songs.

**Tomašek, Václav Jan,** Germanized form Wenzel Johann Tomaschek (1774–1850), Bohemian composer, pianist. Works incl. 3 operas, symphony, piano concerto, church, chamber and piano music, and songs.

**Tomasi, Henri** (1901–71), French composer, conductor, of Corsican parentage. Works incl. operas *Sampiero Corso* and *The Silence of the Sea,* ballets, and orchestral and radio music.

**Tomasini, Luigi** (1741–1808), Italian-born violinist, composer. Joined Prince Esterházy's orchestra (1757), was appointed leader by Haydn (1761), and later became chamber music director. Haydn wrote many pieces for him, incl. several violin concertos. His son Luigi was also violinist in Esterházy orchestra.

**tombeau** (Fr.), 'tomb', 'tombstone'. Title used by French composers in 17th cent. for lament on death of notable person. Idea revived by Ravel in *Le Tombeau de Couperin.*

**Tombelle, Fernand de la,** *see* LA TOMBELLE.

**Tomkins, Thomas** (1572–1656), English composer, organist. Most famous of family of musicians. Pupil of Byrd. Organist of Worcester Cathedral (1596–1646) and at Chapel Royal from 1621. Composed services, 93 anthems, part-songs, keyboard and consort music. Also wrote coronation music for Charles I (1625).

**Tommasini, Vincenzo** (1878–1950), Italian composer. Pupil of Bruch. Composed 2 operas, ballet (on music by D. Scarlatti), orchestral suites, symphonic poems, choral settings of poems by Dante and others, chamber and piano music, and songs.

**tom-tom,** snareless drum, usually with 2 heads but occasionally with only 1. Rarely found singly, sets of 7 being quite common. Used both as pitchless and tuned instruments. In latter case, sometimes employed as upward extension of timpani. They have clear tone which varies according to type of stick used; also played with fingers. When no specific note is required, 2 heads are tuned differently. When clear pitch is needed, lower head is usually removed.

**ton** (Fr.), (1) key, mode;
(2) pitch;
(3) equivalent of TONE (1);
(4) *demi-ton,* semitone;
(5) *ton de rechange,* crook (of brass instrument).

**Ton** (Ger.), (1) sound, music. *Tondichter,* lit. 'poet in sound', *ie* composer;
(2) note;
(3) *Ganzton* = TONE (1);
(4) *Halbton,* semitone;
(5) quality of sound. *Tonfarbe,* tone colour;
(6) *Kirchenton,* church mode.

**tonada** (Sp.), tune set to poem or dance, usually with contrasts between slow and fast tempi.

**tonadilla** (Sp.), diminutive of TONADA. Term for type of scenic cantata, often with vocal, choral and instrumental movts., used in Spanish stage entertainment. Orig. light intermezzi presented between acts of play or serious opera. Flourished from mid 18th to early 19th cents.

**tonal answer,** *see* ANSWER.

**tonality,** *see* KEY, POLYTONALITY.

**Tonart** (Ger.), key, mode.

**tonary,** medieval catalogue of chants performed in conjunction with psalm verses. Facilitated selection of correct TONE (sense 4).

**Tondichtung** (Ger.), tone poem. *See* SYMPHONIC POEM.

**tone,** (1) interval of major second, *eg* between C and D, or E flat and F, sometimes called whole tone. May be subdivided into 2 semitones. Some 20th-cent. composers have divided it further into quarter tones and smaller microtones. On keyboard instruments interval of tone is always the same (*see* EQUAL TEMPERAMENT). *See* KEY, SCALE, SECOND;

(2) (US), musical note. In Britain used in this sense only in acoustics, *eg* pure tone (note without upper partials or overtones), COMBINATION TONE, *etc*;

(3) quality of sound, *eg* good tone, harsh tone, brittle tone;

(4) in plainsong, melodic formula used for recitation of psalms, canticles and other parts of liturgy (Lat., *tonus*). There are 8 ordinary psalm-tones, corresponding to 8 modes, and most have several alternative endings. *See* PSALMODY, TONUS PEREGRINUS.

(5) in 17th cent., also used in sense of KEY (3).

**tone cluster** (US), NOTE CLUSTER.

**tone colour** (Fr., *timbre*; Ger., *Klangfarbe*), characteristic quality of tone of instrument or voice. Effective combination of tone colours is chief art of ORCHESTRATION. Tone colour of note depends on number, selection and relative strengths of overtones of which it is composed (*see* HARMONIC SERIES); these are different in different kinds of instruments. Tone quality of individual instrument depends on extent to which vibrations of body are in resonance with overtones produced by strings.

**tone poem,** *see* SYMPHONIC POEM.

**tone row** (US), NOTE ROW.

**tongue,** to tongue note on wind instruments is to give impetus to its attack. Tonguing depends on phrasing required. *See* DOUBLE TONGUING, TRIPLE TONGUING, FLATTERZUNGE.

**tonic,** first note of scale (*eg* C in case of C major and C minor) which is its key note and centre of its tonality, and key note of composition written in that tonality.

**tonic sol-fa,** system of ear-training and sight-singing in which notes are sung to syllables and ear is trained to recognize and reproduce, through syllables, intervals between notes of scale, and between each note and tonic. In British system, established and taught by John

Curwen in 1840s, tonic of major scale is always *doh,* whatever the key ('movable *doh*'), whereas in French *solfège* (SOLFEGGIO) syllables are fixed ('fixed *doh*'), C always being *ut.* Tonic of 'natural' minor scale is *lah,* so that same relation holds as in major scale, and *ba* is used for sixth degree of ascending harmonic minor scale. Vowel *e* is used for sharps, and *a* for flats: *eg* in C major – A minor:

In tonic sol-fa notation, syllables are represented by initial letters, time values by barlines and dots. Idea is derived from SOLMIZATION.

**Tonkunst** (Ger.), lit 'art of sound', *ie* music.

**Tonleiter** (Ger.), scale.

**tono** or **tuono** (It.), key, mode, tone. Also means thunder.

**Tonreihe** (Ger.), note row.

**Tonstück** (Ger.), piece of music.

**tonus peregrinus** (Lat.), 'the strange [or alien] tone'. Additional psalm-tone to 8 regular tones – see PSALMODY, TONE (4) – which is irregular in that 2nd half has different dominant (reciting note) from 1st. Sung to Psalm 114 (113 in Vulgate Bible), and adapted as Anglican chant.

**torch song,** sentimental ditty of unrequited love, usually sung by a woman, and with jazz or pop associations. Idea is that singer is 'carrying a torch' for the loved one.

**tordion,** lively French dance, current in 15th, 16th cents., used to form contrast with stately BASSE DANSE.

**Torelli, Gasparo** (d. after 1613), Italian composer. Wrote *I fidi amanti* (1600), pastoral fable in madrigal style for 4 voices, book of madrigals for 5 voices (1598), and 4 books of *canzonette* mainly for 3 voices (1593–1608).

**Tortelier, Paul** (1914– ), French cellist, composer. Famous as soloist and in chamber music. Repertory ranges from Bach's solo suites to 20th-cent. works. Compositions incl. concerto for 2 cellos.

**Tosca,** opera by Puccini, libretto by G. Giacosa and L. Illica (based on play by Sardou). First perf. Rome, 1900. Tosca is famous singer who kills corrupt police chief who has arrested her lover; her lover is executed and she commits suicide.

**Toscanini, Arturo** (1867-1957), Italian conductor, one of greatest in musical history. Conductor at La Scala, Milan (1898–1903, 1921–9), Metropolitan Opera, New York (1908–15), then of New York Philharmonic Orchestra (1926–36), and at festivals at Bayreuth (1930–1) and at Salzburg (1933, 1935–7); conductor of National Broadcasting Company Symphony Orchestra, New York, from 1937. Latterly lived in US, refusing to perform under German or Italian fascism. Gave many important first performances incl. Puccini's *Turandot* (1926). As renowned in German music as in Italian, his interpretations being characterized by exceptional clarity and vigour.

**Tosti, Francesco Paolo** (1846–1916), Italian composer, singing master. Pupil of Mercadente. Settled in London (1880) as singing master to royal family. Compositions consist mostly of songs, *eg* 'Farewell'. Knighted 1908.

**Tost Quartets,** collective name for 12 string quartets by Haydn (1789–90): op 54, nos 1–3, op 55, nos 1–3, op 64, nos 1–6. Dedicated to violinist Johann Tost.

**tosto** (It.), (1) quick, rapid. *Più tosto,* faster;
(2) quickly, soon. *Più tosto* or *piuttosto,* sooner, rather.

**Totenmesse** (Ger.), Requiem Mass.

**Totentanz** (Ger.), 'dance of death'. Title of work by Liszt for piano and orchestra.

**Tote Stadt, Die** (Ger., *The Dead Town*), opera by Korngold, libretto by P. Schott (from G. Rodenbach's play *Bruges-la-Morte*). First perf., simultaneously, in Hamburg and Cologne, 1920.

**touche** (Fr.), (1) key of keyboard instrument;
(2) fret on lute, viol, guitar *etc;*
(3) finger-board on stringed instrument. *Sur la touche, see* BOWING.

**Tournemire, Charles Arnould** (1870–1939), French composer, organist. Pupil of d'Indy. Works incl. 2 operas, 8 symphonies, choral, chamber, organ and piano music, and songs. In organ music was leader of movement towards more liturgical use of organ.

**Tourte bow,** normal type of bow used by string players, invented by François Tourte (1747–1835). Unlike earlier type, stick curves inwards towards hair instead of outwards. *See* BOW.

**Tovey, Donald Francis** (1875–1940), English musical historian, pianist, composer, conductor. Pupil of Parry. Professor of music at Edinburgh University from 1914. Composed opera *The Bride of Dionysus,* symphony, concertos for piano and cello, anthems, chamber and piano music, and songs, but renowned mainly for his writing on music. Also composed conjectural completion of final unfinished fugue in Bach's *The Art of Fugue.*

**toye,** term occasionally used in English instrumental music of 16th, 17th cents. for piece of simple, playful character in dance rhythm.

**Toye, Geoffrey** (1889–1942), English conductor, composer. Conducted Beecham Opera Company, Royal Philharmonic Society Concerts and D'Oyly Carte Opera. Manager of opera at Sadler's Wells (1931–4) and managing director of Royal Opera, Covent

Garden (1934–6). Works incl. opera and radio opera, 2 ballets, masque (with his brother), symphony, and songs.

His brother, **John Francis Toye** (1883–1964) was music critic and author. Books incl. *The Well-Tempered Musician* (1925), *Verdi* (1931), and *Rossini* (1934).

**Toy Symphony** (Ger., *Kindersymphonie*, Children's Symphony), instrumental work with parts for toy instruments (cuckoo, rattle *etc*), added to ordinary score. Earliest example, in 3 movts., is often attrib. to Haydn, though music also exists as part of *divertimento* attrib. to Leopald Mozart. Among later examples best known is by Andreas Romberg.

**tr,** as abbrev. = trill.

**Trabaci, Giovanni Maria** (*c* 1575–1647), Neapolitan composer. Composed motets for 5 to 8 voices (1602), 2 books of madrigals for 5 voices (1606, 1611), Masses (some for double choir), psalms, and 2 books of *ricercare* and other organ pieces (1603, 1615).

**tracker,** flat strip of wood used as part of mechanism which connected key of organ with lid ('pallet') which admitted wind to pipe. Now replaced by some form of electric action.

**tract,** part of Proper of Mass, sung in penitential seasons in place of Alleluia. Tracts are among oldest part of plainsong, and are all in 2nd or 8th mode. Words are from psalms.

**Traetta, Tommaso** (1727–79), Italian composer, teacher. Worked in St Petersburg (1768–74). Prolific output incl. 42 operas, *divertimento* for 4 orchestras, church music, arias and duets.

**tragédie lyrique** (Fr.), 17th-cent. term for opera, esp. those of Lully (also called *tragédie en musique*), all of which were settings of tragedies by Quinault and Corneille.

**Tragic Overture** (Ger., *Tragische Ouvertüre*), concert overture by Brahms, op 81 (1880). Not intended as overture to any particular tragedy.

**'Tragic' Symphony,** Schubert's symphony no 4 in C minor (1816), entitled *Tragische Symphonie* by composer.

**Tragoedia,** work for wind quintet, string quartet and harp by Harrison Birtwhistle (1965), in which composer seeks to capture spirit of Greek tragedy without implying any specific events or plot. Some of material later reappeared in Birtwhistle's opera *Punch and Judy*.

**tranquillo** (It.), calm.

**Trans,** orchestral work by Stockhausen (1971), reflecting his oriental experiences.

**transcription,** same as ARRANGEMENT.

**Transfiguration de Notre Seigneur Jésus Christ, La** (Fr., *The Transfiguration of our Lord Jesus Christ*), large-scale work for chorus, orchestra, and vocal and instrumental soloists by Messiaen (1969). Text, in Latin, is drawn from Bible and other sources.

**Transfigured Night,** *see* VERKLÄRTE NACHT.

**transition,** (1) incidental change of key in course of composition; (2) linking passage which (usually) involves change of key.

**transposing instruments,** instruments which sound different notes than those written for them. One reason for this is to avoid large numbers of leger lines. Consequently music is written in higher or lower key or octave than notes produced. Music for celesta is written in lower octave, that for double bass and guitar in higher, and that for glockenspiel usually 2 octaves below. In case of most transposing woodwind or brass instruments, written notes represent fingering as opposed to pitch, greatly easing problems of switching from one instrument to another of higher or lower pitch, *eg* when clarinetist fingers C on instruments in E flat, D, B flat and A, those notes result. Other instruments similarly affected incl. *oboe d'amore, cor anglais,* piccolo, double bassoon, alto flutes, saxophones, modern trumpets, cornets and horns. Trombones in E, B flat, G and F are non-transposing, as is bass tuba. In brass bands, as opposed to symphony orchestras, all instruments apart from bass tuba (only one to use bass clef) are written for as transposing instruments.

**transposing keyboards,** devices whereby keyboard MANUALS could be moved in order to produce higher or lower keys. Player therefore had no need to transpose when music was required in key other than written one. Fitted to organs in 16th cent.; later applied to piano.

**transposition,** performance or writing down of music at another pitch, and therefore in different key, from that in which it was originally written. *See* TRANSPOSING INSTRUMENTS.

**transverse flute,** *see* FLUTE.

**Trapassi, Pietro,** *see* METASTASIO.

**Trapp, Max** (1887–1971), German composer, pianist. Pupil of Dohnányi. Works incl. 6 symphonies and many other orchestral works, chamber music, and songs.

**traps,** (1) kit used by drummers in dance and jazz bands;
(2) in dance or theatre orchestras, devices used for special effects *eg* whistle, whip crack, cowbell *etc.*

**Trauermarsch** (Ger.), funeral march.

**Trauer-Ode** (Ger., *Funeral Ode*), cantata no 198 by Bach (1727), with text by J.C. Gottsched. Perf. in Leipzig at memorial ceremony of Christiane Eberhardine, Queen-Electress of Poland-Saxony, 1727.

**Trauersinfonie,** *see* MOURNING SYMPHONY.

**Trauerwalzer** (Ger., *Mourning Waltz*), title given by publisher to piano composition by Schubert, op 9, no 2 (1816, published 1821). Also known as *Le Désir,* and was often attrib. to Beethoven, since corrupt version of it was published under his name.

**Träumerei** (Ger.), 'dreaming'. Title of piano piece by Schumann, from his *Scenes of Childhood* (1838).

**träumerisch** (Ger.), dreamy.

**traurig** (Ger.), sad.

**Trautonium,** electronic instrument similar to SOLOVOX, invented in Germany (1930).

**Travers, John** (*c* 1703–58), English organist, composer. Became organist of Chapel Royal (1737). Composed *The Whole Book of*

*Psalms* for 1 to 5 voices with continuo for harpsichord (1750), anthems, services, Te Deum, canzonets for 2 and 3 voices, and voluntaries for organ and harpsichord.

**traversa** (It.), 18th-cent. name for *flauto traverso,* transverse FLUTE.

**Traviata, La** (It., The Woman who was led astray), opera by Verdi, libretto by F.M. Piave (after play *La Dame aux camélias* by Alexandre Dumas the younger). First perf. Venice, 1853. Story concerns courtesan who gives up her respectable lover, is spurned by him, but dies in his arms.

**trayn** or **traynour** (Fr.), term referred to by 14th-cent. Italian theorist Philippus de Caserta (in *Tractatus de diversis figuris*) as applied to combination of different rhythmic groups, *eg* 4 notes against 3, 9 against 2.

**treble,** (1) highest voice in choir, esp. when sung by boys; otherwise 'soprano' is more often used;
(2) treble clef is G clef on 2nd line (*see* CLEF).

**treble flute,** instrument approx, midway in pitch between ordinary flute and piccolo.

**treble recorder, treble trombone etc,** *see* RECORDER, TROMBONE *etc.*

**tre corde,** *see* CORDA.

**Tregian, Francis,** *see* FITZWILLIAM VIRGINAL BOOK.

**tremblement** (Fr.), trill.

**tremolando** (It.), using TREMOLO.

**tremolo,** rapid reiteration of single note or alternation of 2 or more.

**tremulant,** device used on organ to produce effect resembling VIBRATO by alternately increasing and decreasing wind pressure.

**Trent Codices,** 6 Ms vols. of 15th-cent. music, discovered by Haberl in chapter library of Cathedral of Trent; further vol. was discovered in 1920. They form largest extant collection of music of period, comprising over 1500 sacred and secular pieces by *c* 75 French, English, Italian and German composers. Selections have been published in *Denkmäler der Tonkunst in Osterreich.*

**Trepak,** Cossack dance in quick 2/4 time.

**Trésor musical,** *see* MALDEGHEM.

**triad,** chord of 3 notes in which lowest note is accompanied by third and fifth above. *See* CHORD.

**Trial by Jury,** comic opera by Gilbert and Sullivan. First perf. London, 1875.

**triangle** (Fr., *triangle*; Ger., *Triangel*; It., *triangolo*), percussion instrument consisting of thin steel bar bent in shape of triangle but with one corner left open. Normally struck by thin metal beater; for less brilliant sound, wooden stick is sometimes used.

**tricinium** (Lat.), title used in 16th, early 17th cents. for short 3-part piece.

**trill** or **shake** (Fr., *cadence, tremblement, trille*; Ger., *Triller*; It., *gruppo, trillo*), (1) ornament consisting of rapid alternation of note

**with second above. In 17th, 18th cents., trill was begun on upper note, and was indicated by various signs, *eg*:**

played:

It might also begin with upper appoggiatura *eg*:

played:

with lower appoggiatura *eg*:

played:

or with turn *eg*:

played:

and might end with turn *eg*:

played:

Number of notes in trill depended on length of note (could be played as turn if note was very short) and turn was frequently used to end it, whether indicated or not. This is also true of modern trill (abbrev., *tr*), introduced early in 19th cent., which is begun on principal note *eg*:

played:

unless beginning on upper note is indicated by grace note;

(2) in Italian terminology of early 17th cent., trill was called *gruppo* or *tremolo,* and term *trillo* (Eng., 'plain shake') denoted rapid reiteration of note.

*See also* MORDENT, PRALLTRILLER.

**Trillo del Diavolo, Il,** *see* DEVIL'S TRILL.

**Trinklied** (Ger.), drinking song.

**trio,** (1) instrumental or vocal piece for 3 performers. Most frequent instrumental types are piano trio (piano, violin, cello) and string trio (violin, viola, cello). For trio sonata, *see* SONATA;

(2) middle section of minuet or scherzo after which 1st section is repeated. Orig. written in 3 parts; title was retained after this custom was dropped.

**Triole** (Ger.), **triolet** (Fr.), triplet.

**Trionfi,** trilogy of 3 short operas or scenic cantatas by Carl Orff. Works, usually perf. separately, are *Carmina Burana, Catulli Carmina* and *Trionfo d'Afrodite.* First perf. as entity, Milan, 1953, conducted by Karajan.

**Trionfo di Dori, Il** (It., The Triumph of Doris), anthology of 29 Italian madrigals by various composers (1592). Refrain 'Viva la bella Dori' (long live the fair Doris) is common to all the poems. It was model for English anthology THE TRIUMPHES OF ORIANA.

**trio sonata** *see* SONATA.

**tripla,** *see* NACHTANZ.

**triple concerto,** concerto for 3 solo instruments with orchestra, *eg* Beethoven's op 56 for piano, violin, cello and orchestra.

**triple counterpoint,** *see* COUNTERPOINT.

**triple croche** (Fr.), demisemiquaver.

**triple stop,** any chord of 3 notes played on bowed string instrument, whether or not all 3 strings are stopped by fingers.

**triplet** (Fr., *triolet*; Ger., *Triole*; It., *terzina*), group of 3 notes played in time of 2. Written:

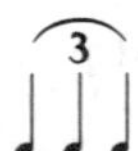

**triple time,** time in which number of beats in bar is 3, *eg* 3/8, 3/4, 3/2. *See* TIME.

**triple tonguing,** method of tonguing on wind instruments in which consonants T-K-T are articulated. Can be done at great speed, and passages of triplets can be played much faster than is poss. using simple tonguing. Difficult to accomplish on reed instruments.

**triplum,** *see* DUPLUM.

**Tristan and Isolde** (Ger., *Tristan und Isolde*), opera by Wagner, libretto by composer. First perf. Munich, 1865. Story concerns the famous lovers who drink love-potion that eventually leads to death of both.

**Tristano, Lennie** (1919– ), American jazz pianist. Founder of experimental school of jazz performers, specializing in free improvisation and in breakdown of certain traditional features of jazz. Pieces incl. *Intuition* and *Digression* (dating from 1940s).

**tritone,** interval comprising 3 whole tones, *ie* augmented fourth. In EQUAL TEMPERAMENT, identical in sound (though not in function) to its inversion, diminished fifth. Normally avoided in plainsong and medieval polyphony (*see* DIABOLUS).

**Trittico, Il** (It., *The Triptych*), group of 3 one-act operas by Puccini: *Il tabarro* (The Cloak, libretto by G. Adami), *Suor Angelica* (Sister Angelica, libretto by G. Forzano), and *Gianni Schicchi* (libretto by G. Forzano). First perf. as entity, New York, 1918.

**Triumphes of Oriana, The,** collection of 25 madrigals, poss. in honour of Queen Elizabeth I, edited by Morley, published 1601. Each madrigal ends 'Long live fair Oriana'.

**Triumphlied** (Ger., *Song of Triumph*), work by Brahms, op 55 (1870–1) for chorus, orchestra and organ *ad lib.*, with words from Revelation of St John. Composed to celebrate German victory in Franco-Prussian War.

**Triumph of Time and Enlightenment** (It., *Il Trionfo del Tempo e del Disinganno*), oratorio by Handel, text by Cardinal Benedetto Pamfili. First perf. Rome, 1708. *See also* TRIUMPH OF TIME AND TRUTH.

**Triumph of Time and Truth, The,** oratorio by Handel (1757). Text translated by T. Morell from Handel's earlier work *Il Trionfo de Tempo e della Verita* (1737), a revision of still earlier *Il Trionfo del Tempo e del Disinganno* (1708). Several of movts. were adapted from *Il Trionfo del Tempo* and other works.

**Troilus and Cressida,** opera by Walton, libretto by C. Hassall (after Chaucer). First perf. Covent Garden, 1954.

**Trojans, The** (Fr., *Les Troyens*), opera in 2 parts by Berlioz, libretto by composer (after Virgil): (1) 'The Capture of Troy' (*La Prise de Troie*) first perf. (in German) Karlsruhe, 1890; (2) 'The Trojans at Carthage' (*Les Troyens à Carthage*), first perf. Paris, 1863.

**tromba** (It.), trumpet. *Tromba cromatica, tromba ventile,* valve trumpet. *Tromba da tirarsi,* slide trumpet.

**tromba da tirarsi** (It.), slide trumpet. *See* TRUMPET.

**tromba marina,** stringed instrument up to 2m (7ft) long and consisting of single string mounted on thin and slightly tapered box. Player used bow and had to stand; only notes he could produce were natural harmonics. Inside box were *c* 20 sympathetic strings. Bridge had one foot fixed and the other, slightly shorter, drummed against sound board. Sound produced was loud and trumpet-like, hence 'tromba', but no explanation of 'marina' has been found. Instrument was frequently played by nuns, hence Ger. '*Nonengeige*' (nun's fiddle).

**tromba ventile** (It.), valve TRUMPET.

**trombone** (Eng., Fr., It.; Ger. *Posaune*), modern trombone is brass instrument with 2 parts: cylindrical bore expanding to bell over lower third of its length, with cup-shaped mouthpiece; and U-shaped slide which moves parallel to other part to vary effective length of tuba.

Apart from extra mechanism added to some (but not all) instruments, trombone has remained basically unchanged for 500 years or more. It is the old SACKBUT with larger bell and bore increased in size to produce weightier tone. Because they have always been fully chromatic, trombones are non-transposing instruments.

By altering length of tubing in use, slide alters pitch in same way as VALVES on trumpets and horns. There are 7 slide positions, which on B flat tenor trombone give series of fundamental (or pedal) notes one octave below following series:

In practice only upper 3 fundamentals are used at all frequently. Except that low E can be 'lipped' down to E flat, there was no means of bridging gap between 2nd harmonic in 7th position (E) and fundamental note in 1st (B flat) until valve-operated mechanism, throwing into play additional length of tubing, was added. This lowers pitch of tenor trombone from B flat to F, E or E flat. Instrument so equipped is often referred to as tenor-bass trombone. Similar mechanism was also applied to bass trombone, normally built in F or G. Compass of members of trombone family is *c* 3½ octaves from 1st pedal note, or 4 from 7th, highest note demanded from tenor being F at top of treble stave.

Of 6 members of family, highest pitched or soprano trombone, often called slide trumpet, is long obsolete; alto in E has recently enjoyed revival. Tenor is by far most frequently encountered now that bass in old form has virtually disappeared. It has been replaced by large-bore tenor, complete with extension mechanism, that is taking over name as well as function of bass trombone. This instrument also substitutes effectively for contrabass trombone (built in C or B flat). Valve trombone is still occasionally used, but not in symphony orchestra. It is tenor with valves instead of slide; its only advantage is that successions of notes requiring extreme and rapid changes of slide position are negotiated more easily.

**trombone à pistons** (Fr.), valve TROMBONE.

**trombone stop,** 16ft reed stop on organ with powerful tone.

**trombonino** (It.), alto TROMBONE.

**Trommelflöte** (Ger.), fife.

**tromp, trompe, trompede Béarn, trompe de Bern, trompe de Laquais,** forms of Jew's harp.

**Trompete** (Ger.), trumpet. *Ventiltrompete,* valve trumpet. *Zugtrompete,* slide trumpet.

**trompette** (Fr.), (1) trumpet. *Trompette à pistons,* valve trumpet; (2) *trompette marine,* tromba marina.

**tronco** (It.), 'truncated', *ie* abruptly cut off note or chord.

**trope** (Lat., *tropus*), additional music and words which preceded, were interpolated with, or followed piece of liturgical plainsong. Many such additions were written between 9th and 11th cents. In later Middle Ages polyphonic settings of liturgy often incorporated additional unofficial sections of text. Such additions were eliminated from RC liturgy by Council of Trent in 16th cent.

**troppo** (It.), too much. *Allegro non troppo,* fast, but not too fast.

**troubadours** (Fr., from Provençal, *trobadors*), poet-musicians of early Middle Ages who lived in S France and wrote in *langue d'or* (Provençal). Many were of aristocratic birth. Cultivation of lyrical song spread to N France in late 12th cent., word *trobador* being translated into Fr. equivalent *trouvère.* Music of troubadours and *trouvères* was monophonic. Many songs show influence of Gregorian chant, while others, by use of modes alien to RC Church, seem to owe their musical style to heritage of secular song now lost. Melodic styles had considerable influence on polyphonic motet of 13th cent. Majority of surviving melodies have no indication of rhythm, no doubt because they were not sung in strict time. In German-speaking countries, art of troubadours and *trouvères* was imitated by MINNESINGER.

**Trouble in Tahiti,** opera by Leonard Bernstein, libretto by composer. First perf. Waltham, Mass., 1952. This comedy depicts day of domestic strife between US suburban couple.

**Trouluffe** or **Truelove, John** (*fl* 15th–16th cent.), English composer. Wrote, apparently with Richard Smert, carols and other sacred pieces.

**Trout Quintet** (Ger., *Forellenquintett*), popular name of Schubert's quintet in A major for violin, viola, cello, double bass and piano, composed 1819, published posthumously (1829) as op 114. 4th movt. consists of variations on Schubert's song *Die Forelle* (The Trout).

**trouvères,** *see* TROUBADOURS.

**Trovatore, Il** (It., *The Troubadour*), opera by Verdi, libretto by S. Cammarano (after Spanish play by A.G. Gutierrez). First perf. Rome, 1853. Story concerns nobleman's son, kidnapped by gypsy as child, who becomes troubadour.

**Troyens, Les,** *see* TROJANS.

**trumpet** (Fr., *trompette*; Ger., *Trompete*; It., *tromba, clarino*), name applied to wide variety of instruments, some of which have little in common apart from being made of metal (usually brass) and having funnel-shaped mouthpiece. Oldest ancestor was animal's horn fitted with mouthpiece, but long before Christian era this was replaced by straight trumpet. During 13th cent. folded trumpet first appeared, shaped like small saxophone. Familiar type of folded trumpet appeared only in 15th cent., and was called claro or clarion, name trumpet being reserved for straight variety. Being restricted to selection of notes from HARMONIC SERIES, trumpets were for long suited only to ceremonial and military occasions, but invention of crooks gave them greater scope, and they joined orchestra in early 17th cent. Crooks were lengths of tubing that could be inserted into instrument, thereby altering pitch. Limitations of harmonic series remained, but instrument could now be crooked in almost any key, and range of notes could be increased by using several trumpets with different crooks. Aided by shallow mouthpieces players developed technique enabling them to exploit fluently upper register, where notes of harmonic series lie close together. Thus, during baroque period, trumpet became melodic instrument. Degree of virtuosity required can be seen in Bach's and Handel's more elaborate trumpet parts. For solo work most usual key was D. This highly specialized technique apparently vanished during mid 18th cent., presumably because composers ceased to demand it. In consequence trumpet now fulfilled humbler role, using relatively few notes and often merely adding weight to sound of full orchestra. These limitations led, in late 18th cent., to experiments being made with keys similar to those on woodwind instruments. Keyed trumpet (Fr., *trompette à clefs*; Ger., *Klappentrompete*; It., *tromba a chiavi*) enjoyed only brief existence, for early in 19th cent. it was replaced by valve trumpet (Fr., *trompette à pistons*; Ger., *Ventiltrompete*; It., *tromba ventile*). Since this possessed complete chromatic compass crooks were no longer needed, and F trumpet became standard instrument. Large F trumpet (not to be confused with small one) remained in general use well into 20th cent. Nowadays parts for it and for earlier valveless trumpets are always played on modern instruments, usually those in C or B flat. These are very different instruments, being *c* half the size of older F trumpet. Trumpet in B flat sounds tone lower than written; its sounding range is from E below treble clef to C above treble clef. Many trumpets in C have extension mechanism that puts them instantly into B flat; similarly B flat trumpets have one that lowers pitch to A. Several higher pitched trumpets in use today all derive from, and use same section of harmonic series as, B flat and C trumpets. Most common are those in D and E flat (sounded tone and minor third above written note). Little F, despite being modern invention, is misleadingly called Bach trumpet, since it was designed for 2nd Brandenburg Concerto and similar parts. Modern bass trumpet corresponds to B flat and C trumpets but sounds octave lower; also made in E flat, but C is usual form. So-called slide trumpet (used in 17th cent.) is really soprano TROMBONE or treble SACKBUT.

**trumpet-cornet,** cross between trumpet and cornet, said by its exponents to combine tone of former with ease of playing of latter.

**trumpet stop,** 8ft reed stop on organ.

**Trumpet Voluntary,** popular name for piece, falsely attrib. to Purcell, which occurs among harpsichord solos of Jeremiah Clarke (*c* 1673–1707) under title 'The Prince of Denmark's March'.

**t.s.,** = *tasto solo* (*see* TASTO).

**Tsar's Bride, The** (Russ., *Tsarskaya Nevesta*), opera by Rimsky-Korsakov, libretto by I.F. Tyumenev (based on play by L.A. Mey). First perf. Moscow, 1899. Tsar is Ivan and his bride is Martha, who is loved by 2 other men. In the end she is poisoned, and while dying goes mad on hearing that only man she loves has been beheaded by tsar.

**Tsarskaya Nevesta,** *see* TSAR'S BRIDE.

**Tschudi, Burkhardt,** *see* SHUDI.

**tuba,** (1) brass instrument of saxhorn type which has conical bore and 3 to 5 valves, and uses cup-shaped mouthpiece. There are 3 sizes: (a) bass-cum-tenor, also called EUPHONIUM (Ger., *Barytonhorn*) in B flat with range from B flat below bass clef upwards for 3 octaves; (b) bass, fourth or fifth lower, in F (used in orchestra) or E flat (used in military and brass bands); former has range from F octave below bass clef upwards for 3 octaves, latter has range tone lower; (c) double bass in B flat, octave below (a). Latter 2 sizes are also called bombardon, or if made in circular shape for marching, helicon. Music for tubas is normally written in bass clef, with actual sounds and key signature (except in brass band music);

(2) 'Wagner tubas' designed for use in *The Ring* are group of 5 instruments consisting of 2 pairs and bass. Upper pair are modified horns, with funnel-shaped mouthpiece, in B flat with range from B flat on bass clef to F at top of treble clef; lower pair are similar, but fourth lower, in F, with range from B flat below bass clef to G on treble clef. Wagner wrote for these as TRANSPOSING INSTRUMENTS; also used in Bruckner's last 3 symphonies. Bass of group is double bass tuba;

(3) organ stop of reed type with loud tone, chiefly used as solo stop. Tuba of 8ft pitch is sometimes called *tuba mirabilis* or *tuba major,* that of 4th pitch, tuba clarion;

(4) (Lat.), (a) trumpet; (b) RECITING NOTE.

**tuba major, tuba mirabilis** or simply **tuba,** 8ft reed stop on organ.

Although of great power, its range is considerably higher than orchestral tuba.

**tubaphone** or **tubophone,** percussion instrument producing bell-like sounds when its metal tubes, laid out like piano keyboard, are struck with hammers.

**tubular bells,** *see* BELL.

**tuck,** early English word for sound of drum, esp. drum-taps.

**tucket,** *see* TOCCATA (2).

**Tuckwell, Barry** (1931– ), Australian horn-player, resident in UK from 1951. In demand as soloist; also plays in own wind quintet.

**Tudor, David** (1926– ), American composer, pianist. Disciple of John Cage, experimenting in ALEATORY MUSIC and in compositions involving visual elements *eg Video/Laser.*

**Tudor Church Music,** edition of church music by English composers of 16th and early 17th cents. published in 10 vols. (1923–29). Contents are: Vol. I, Masses by Taverner; Vol. II, English church music by Byrd; Vol. III, Magnificats and motets by Taverner; Vol. IV, Services and anthems by Orlando Gibbons; Vol. V, Latin and English church music by Robert White; Vol. VI, Latin church music by Tallis; Vol. VII, Byrd's *Gradualia* I and II; Vol. VIII, Responses, psalms and services by Tomkins; Vol. IX, Latin church music by Byrd; Vol. X, works by Aston, Marbeck and Parsley. Appendix, containing supplements from sources discovered later, was published in 1948.

**Tudway, Thomas** (*c* 1650–1726), English organist, composer. Professor at Cambridge from 1705. Edited collection of cathedral music. Composed church music.

**Tunder, Franz** (1614–67), German composer, organist. Preceded son-in-law Buxtehude as organist at Marienkirche in Lübeck. As composer, esp. associated with 'variation-cantata', in which each verse of chorale is based on melody treated in different way; example is his setting of 'Ein feste Burg'.

**tune,** *see* MELODY.

**tuning,** *see* TEMPERAMENT.

**tuning fork** (Fr., *diapason*; Ger., *Stimmgabel*; It., *corsita*), 2-pronged device for accurately giving pitch of single note, invented 1711 by trumpeter John Shore (d. 1752). Sound given is practically pure note, without overtones.

**tuono,** *see* TONO.

**Turandot,** opera by Puccini, completed by Alfano after Puccini's death, libretto by G. Adami and R. Simone (after Gozzi). First perf. Milan, 1926 (under Toscanini). Story concerns Chinese princess who proclaims she will marry any man who can answer 3 riddles, but any who fail will be executed. Other composers inspired to write operas on same subject incl. Busoni (1917).

**Turangalîla Symphony,** large-scale work in 10 movts. by Messiaen. First perf. 1949. Title is Sanskrit, defined by composer as 'love song'. Work is influenced by Indian music, and incl. important parts for piano and ONDES MARTENOT.

**turba,** *see* PASSION.

**turca, alla** (It.), 'in the Turkish style' (*see* JANISSARY MUSIC). Mozart's *Rondo alla turca* is last movt. of piano sonata in A major, K331.

**Turchi, Guido** (1916– ), Italian composer. Works incl. *Concerto Breve* in memory of Bartók and *Five Comments on the Bacchae of Euripides* for orchestra.

**Turco in Italia, Il** (It., *The Turk in Italy*), opera by Rossini, libretto by Romani. First perf. Milan, 1814. Revived for Maria Callas in 1950. Story is conventional comedy of intrigue.

**Tureck, Rosalyn** (1914– ), American pianist, conductor. Known for performances of Bach on piano.

**Turges (Sturges), Edmund** (*c* 1450–after 1502), English composer. Works incl. church music and secular songs.

**Turina, Joaquin** (1882–1949), Spanish composer, pianist, conductor. Pupil of d'Indy and Moszkowski. Works incl. operas, symphonic poems, piano and guitar pieces, and songs.

**Türk, Daniel Gottlob** (1756–1813), German composer, writer on music. Published some useful textbooks, and treatise on figured bass. Compositions incl. piano sonatas, symphonies, songs and church music.

**Turkish crescent,** *see* PAVILLON CHINOIS.

**turn** (Fr., *double, double cadence, brise*; Ger., *Doppelschlag*; It., *grupetto*), ornament which takes turn around note, beginning with note above. In commonest forms it is indicated over note thus:

and played thus:

or between 2 notes thus:

and played thus:

or thus:

played thus:

It may occasionally begin on principal note, indicated by grace note thus:

played:

or be inverted, shown by sign:

played:

In music of second half of 18th cent. it may be more appropriate to play first 2 notes of turn more quickly than others, in which case

would be played:

**Turner, William** (1651–1740), English composer, singer. Gentleman of Chapel Royal. Composed services, anthems, hymns, masque, songs (some for plays), odes and catches.

**Turnhout, Gerard de** (*c* 1520–80), Flemish composer, singer.

Attached to court of Philip II in Madrid from 1572. Wrote Mass, and book of sacred and secular songs for 3 voices (1569). His younger relative, Jean de Turnhout, composed madrigals and motets.

**Turn of the Screw, The,** opera by Britten, libretto by M. Piper (after story by Henry James). First perf. Venice, 1954. Story concerns ghostly possession of 2 children, and their relationship with their governess.

**Tusch,** *see* TOCCATA (2).

**tutte le corde,** *see* CORDA.

**tutti** (It.), 'all' (pl.). Term used, most often in concertos, to indicate entrance of full orchestra, as distinct from passages for soloist.

**Tveitt, Geirr** (1908– ), Norwegian composer, pianist. Collected and arranged Norwegian folk music. Prodigious output incl. 5 operas, 5 piano concertos, *c* 30 piano sonatas, and orchestral arrangements for *c* 100 folk tunes.

**twelfth,** (1) interval of an octave plus a fifth;

(2) organ stop of diapason quality and $2^2{}_3$ft pitch. Sounds produced are twelfth above notes played.

**twelve-note system** (US, twelve-tone system; Ger., *Zwölftonsystem*), method of composition, also known as dodecaphony, formulated by Schoenberg *c* 1921 after period of experimentation in writing music without tonality and without using traditional ways of building chords. In it, basis of both melodies and chords of composition is arrangement of 12 notes of chromatic scale in particular order, called NOTE ROW. This series is always used complete, but may be transposed to any of 11 other possible positions, inverted, reversed (RETROGRADE MOTION), or reversed and inverted. It thus has 48 forms, and in addition any note of series may be used in any of its octaves. Schoenberg used method much less rigidly in his later works than in pieces written in 1920s. It was adopted as working basis by his pupils Webern and Berg, and later by Křenek and others.

**twelve-tone system** (US), twelve-note system.

**Twilight of the Gods,** *see* RING DES NIBELUNGEN.

**Tye, Christopher** (*c* 1500–73), English composer. Wrote 4-part setting of Acts of the Apostles (first 14 chapters) to metrical translation by himself, Masses, motets, anthems, services, and In Nomines for strings.

**tymbal,** early Eng. name for kettledrum (*see* TIMPANI).

**tympanon** (Fr.), DULCIMER.

**typophone** (Fr.), DULCITONE.

**Tyrolienne** (Fr.), country dance, akin to *Ländler,* in slow waltz-time. Though believed to be of Tyrolean origin, prob. had source in various 19th-cent. operas and ballets.

**Tyrwhitt-Wilson,** *see* BERNERS.

**tzigane, tsigane** (Fr.), term for Hungarian gypsies and their music.

# U

**über** (Ger.), 'over', 'above'.
**Übung** (Ger.), 'exercise'. *Clavierübung*, keyboard exercise.
**Ugolini, Vincenzo** (*c* 1570–1638), Italian composer. Wrote Masses, motets, psalms, vespers and other church music, and madrigals.
**Uhr, Die,** German title for Haydn's 'CLOCK' SYMPHONY.
**uillean pipe,** *see* UNION PIPE.
**ukulele, ukelele,** small easily-learnt 4-stringed guitar from Hawaii, though orig. Portuguese. Very popular in 1920s.
**Ulysses** (It., *Ulisse*), opera by Dallapiccola, based on Homer. First perf. West Berlin, 1968. Also title of cantata by Sieber inspired by Joyce's novel.
**Umkehrung** (Ger.), 'turning round', 'reversal', 'inversion'. *Kanon in der Umkehrung,* canon by inversion.
**Umlauf, Ignaz** (1746–96), Austrian composer. Director of German national *Singspiel.* Wrote *Singspiele, eg Bergknappen* (1778), comic opera, and incidental music.

His son, **Michael Umlauf** (1781–1842), was composer and conductor. From 1814 gave beat to orchestra in perfs. of Beethoven's works, while composer (then growing deaf) conducted. Composed 12 ballets, *Singspiel,* opera, church music, and piano sonatas.
**umore** (It.), humour. *Con umore,* with humour.
**una corda,** *see* CORDA.
**Una Cosa Rara** (It., A rare thing), opera by Martín y Soler, libretto by L. da Ponte (based on story by L.V. de Guevara). First perf. Vienna, 1786, stealing success of Mozart's *The Marriage of Figaro.* Mozart quoted from it in Supper Scene of *Don Giovanni.*
**Una furtiva lacrima** (It., A furtive tear), Nemorino's aria in Act 2 of Donizetti's *L'Elisir d'Amore,* in which he detects tears in his beloved Adina's eyes – proof, he hopes, that his love is returned.
**Una voce poco fa,** Rosina's aria in Act 1 of Rossini's *The Barber of Seville,* in which she reads love letter from Lindoro (really Count Almaviva in disguise).
**Un Ballo in Maschera,** *see* MASKED BALL.
**Un bel di vedremo,** aria in Act 2 of Puccini's *Madame Butterfly* in which Cio-Cio-San looks forward to return of Pinkerton. Famous in English as 'One fine day'.
**unda maris** (Lat.), 'wave of the sea'. Organ stop of soft tone, tuned slightly flat, or which has 2 ranks slightly mistuned, so that beat results which has effect similar to vibrato. Also called *voix céleste, vox coelestis* or *vox angelica.*
**Un di felice,** love duet between Alfredo and Violetta in Act 1 of Verdi's *La Traviata.*
**Undine,** opera by Lortzing, libretto by composer (based on story by F.

de la Motte Fouqué). First perf. Magdeburg, 1845. Story, of water-nymph who lured her unfaithful lover to his death, also inspired operas by E.T.A. Hoffmann (1816), Mori (1865) and Sporck (1877), and ballet by Henze.

**'Unfinished' Symphony,** title given to Schubert's symphony no 8 in B minor (1822), of which he completed only 2 movts., though sketches of 3rd movt. have survived. It was sent to Musical Society at Graz in return for his election as honorary member and apparently forgotten, but recovered and first perf. in 1865 in Vienna. Several attempts have been made to complete work *eg* by Gerald Abraham (1971).

**unichord,** same as MONOCHORD.

**Union pipe,** form of BAGPIPE, popular in Ireland since early 18th cent. Blown by bellows and has relatively quiet tone which makes it suitable for indoor use. Also called 'uillean pipe' (Gael. *uillean* = elbow).

**unison,** combined sound of 2 or more notes of same pitch. Term 'singing in unison' is used when song is performed by several voices, all at same pitch (or octave apart with male and female singers).

**unit organ,** small organ constructed to save space and expense, with certain pipes shared by different stops.

**unruhig** (Ger.), 'restless'.

**unter** (Ger.), 'under', 'lower'.

**Unterwerk** (Ger.), choir organ.

**up-beat,** upward movement of conductor's baton or hand, indicating beat before main accent in bar of music.

**up-bow,** bow stroke on stringed instrument from point to heel.

**upper partials,** *see* HARMONIC SERIES.

**Uppman, Theodore** (1920– ), American baritone. Sang title role in Britten's *Billy Budd* at Covent Garden première (1951).

**upright piano,** ordinary domestic piano in which, to save space, strings are laid out vertically instead of horizontally as in grand piano. *See* PIANO.

**Urio, Francesco Antonio** (b. *c* 1660), Italian composer, Franciscan monk. Wrote *Te Deum,* oratorios, motets for voices and instruments, and psalms. Considerable amount of material from *Te Deum* was used by Handel in his *Dettingen Te Deum, Saul, Israel in Egypt* and *L'Allegro,* though some say Handel was composer of *Te Deum* attrib. to Urio.

**Usper, Francesco Spongia** (d. 1641), Italian organist, composer, priest. Wrote church music, madrigals, *ricercari* and other instrumental pieces. Made early use of tremolo on violin.

**Ussachevsky, Vladimir** (1911– ), American composer of Russian parentage, b. Manchuria. His tape-recorder experiments in 1950s made him one of pioneers of US electronic music.

**ut** (Fr.), the note C. Also first note of Guidonian hexachord (*see* SOLMIZATION).

**utility music** (Ger., *Gebrauchsmusik*), term employed by Hindemith, Weill and other German composers of 1920s to describe works intended to have social or political function rather than be music for music's sake. Works tended to deal with everyday subjects in everyday style.

**Utopia Limited** or **The Flowers of Progress,** comic opera by Sullivan, libretto by W.S. Gilbert. First perf. London, 1893. Story concerns Utopia run on lines of British limited liability company.

**Utrecht Te Deum,** choral work by Handel, composed (with Jubilate) for Peace of Utrecht. First perf. St Paul's Cathedral, London, 1713.

**Utrenja,** large-scale choral work by Penderecki in 2 parts – *The Entombment of Christ* and *The Resurrection of Christ.* Title refers to morning service of Eastern Church, work consisting mainly of settings of extracts from 2 such services. Part 1 first perf. Altenburg Cathedral, 1970; Part 2 completed 1971.

# V

**V,** as abbrev., V. = violin, voice. V. = verse (in Gregorian chant). Vc. = cello. Vla. = viola. Vln. = violin. V.S. = *volti subito* (*see* VOLTI).

**Vaccai, Nicola** (1790–1848), Italian opera composer. Pupil of Paisiello. Most successful of his works was *Giulietta e Romeo* (1825), last scene of which came to be substituted for corresponding section of Bellini's *I Capuleti ed i Montecchi* (1830), a setting of same libretto (after Shakespeare's *Romeo and Juliet*). Also wrote popular treatise on singing.

**Vaet, Jakob** (1529–67), Flemish composer. *Kapellmeister* to Emperor Maximilian II in Vienna. Composed church music, some of it published under title *Modulationes quinque vocum (volgo motecta) noncupatae* (1562).

**Vakula the Smith,** opera by Chaikovsky, libretto by Y. Polonsky (after Gogol's story *Christmas Eve*). First perf. St Petersburg, 1876. Revised in 1885 under title *Cherevichki* (Russ., *The Little Shoes*); first perf. Moscow, 1887.

**Valen, Olav Fartein** (1887–1952), Norwegian composer. Spent early years in Madagascar. Pupil of Reger in Berlin. Works, in which he adapted Schoenbergian methods to his own purposes, incl. 5 symphonies, 2 string quartets, violin concerto, choral and piano music, and songs.

**Valkyrie, The,** *see* RING DES NIBELUNGEN.

**Vallas, Léon** (1879–1956), French music critic, teacher. Founded *Revue musicale de Lyon,* 1903 (later *Revue française de musique* and *Nouvelle revue musicale*), and wrote books on Debussy and d'Indy.

**Vallin, Ninon** (1886–1961), French soprano. Began career as concert singer, but in 1912 joined Opéra-Comique in Paris, where became leading exponent of title roles in Charpentier's *Louise* and Massenet's *Manon.*

**valse** (Fr.), waltz.

**Valse, La** (Fr., *The Waltz*), 'choreographic poem' for orchestra by Ravel. First perf. 1920.

**Valses Nobles et Sentimentales** (Fr., *Noble and Sentimental Waltzes*), set of 7 waltzes for piano by Ravel. Title is allusion to Schubert's *Valses nobles* and *Valses sentimentales* for piano. First perf. 1911. Later orchestrated as ballet *Adélaïde, ou Le Langage des fleurs.*

**Valse triste** (Fr., *Sad Waltz*), orchestral piece by Sibelius, part of incidental music (op 44, 1903) to Arvid Järnefelt's play *Kuolema.*

**valve** (Fr., *piston*; Ger., *Ventil*; It., *pistone*), device enabling brass instruments to command complete chromatic compass. Used on horn, cornet, trumpet, flugelhorn, saxhorn, euphonium, tuba, and, less frequently, on trombone, where same result is normally achieved by slide. Valves either open length of extra tubing, so lowering pitch, or cut off length of tubing, so raising pitch: in this way different HARMONIC SERIES can be used, so providing complete chromatic compass.

**valve horn, valve trombone, etc,** *see* HORN, TROMBONE, *etc.*

**vamp,** to improvise accompaniment, usually to song.

**Vampyr, Der** (Ger., *The Vampire*), opera by Marschner, libretto by W.A. Wöhlbruck (based on story by J.W. Polidori). First perf. Leipzig, 1828. Story tells how Lord Ruthven avoids death for 3 years by annually sacrificing a pure maiden. In the end he is exposed as vampire, and is struck down by flash of lightning.

**Van den Borren, Charles,** *see* BORREN.

**Van Dieren,** *see* DIEREN.

**Vanessa,** opera by Samuel Barber (his first), libretto by G.C. Menotti. First perf. New York, 1958. Concerns 3 women, representing 3 generations of a family, living in castle in a northern country in 1905.

**Vanhall,** *see* WANHAL.

**Va, pensiero, sull' ali dorate,** patriotic chorus in Act 3 of Verdi's *Nabucco,* in which Hebrew prisoners by banks of Euphrates sing of their lost homeland.

**Varèse, Edgard** (1885–1965), French-born composer. Pupil of d'Indy, Roussel and Widor. Encouraged by Debussy. Served in French army in WWI, but health failed and he emigrated to US in 1916. Co-founder (1921) of International Composers Guild, and subsequently did much to further cause of modern music in US. As dedicated experimentalist, used sound-quality (what he called 'density') of each instrument as starting-point of his musical ideas. Most famous piece is *Density 21.5* for solo flute (1936). Other works, many making pioneering use of bold instrumental combinations, incl. *Ionization* for 13 percussionists (1933), *Equatorial* for chorus, brass, piano, organ, 2 Ondes Martenots and percussion (1934, rev. 1961), *Etude* and *Espaces* for chorus, 2 pianos and percussion (1947), and *Déserts* for orchestra and 2 tracks of 'organized sounds' on magnetic tape (1950–4).

**variation,** process of modifying theme, figure or passage so that resulting product is recognizably derived from original.

Basic elements to be found in series of variations are: variation of melody; variation of figuration or texture; variation of rhythm; variation of tonality (*eg* minor for major or vice versa); and variation of harmony. Any or all of these may be combined in same variation.

From late 18th cent. variations have frequently figured as complete movt. in sonata, symphony or similar composition. In more general sense, DEVELOPMENT of theme(s) consists in realizing possibilities inherent in material and so is itself a form of variation. *See also* CANTUS FIRMUS, CHACONNE, DIVISION, DOUBLE, GROUND, PASSACAGLIA.

**Variations on a theme of Haydn,** *see* 'ST ANTHONY' VARIATIONS.

**variazione** (It.), variation. *Tema con variazioni*, theme and variations.

**Varnay, Astrid** (1918– ), American soprano, b. Stockholm, of Austro-Hungarian parentage. Outstanding exponent of Wagner and Strauss.

**varsovienne** (Fr.), Warsaw dance. Dance in fairly slow 3/4 time, in mazurka rhythm, popular in Paris during Second Empire.

**Vásáry, Tamás** (1933– ), Hungarian pianist. One of finest exponents of Mozart and Chopin of his generation.

**Vassilenko, Sergei Nikiphorovich** (1872–1956), Russian composer. Began as nationalist composer, later developed more cosmopolitan style, but subsequently reverted, under influence of Oriental melodies which he collected, to characteristically Russian idiom. Works incl. opera *Son of the Sun* (1929), cantata *The Legend of the City of Kitezh* (later rewritten as opera), 4 other operas, 6 ballets, 4 symphonies, symphonic poems *The Garden of Death* (after Oscar Wilde) and *Witches' Flight* (*hircus Nocturnus*) and other orchestral works, violin concerto, incidental and chamber music, and songs.

**vaudeville** (Fr.), popular song, esp. topical song to well-known tune, sung in Paris in early 18th cent. Later meant final song in entertainment in which each character sings verse in turn (as in Mozart's *Die Entführung*, 1782). In 19th cent., term was applied to comedies interspersed with songs. Term is now used of variety entertainment.

**Vaughan, Elizabeth** (1937– ), Welsh soprano. Has sung in many of world's leading opera houses. Noted esp. for roles in Italian opera.

**Vaughan Williams, Ralph** (1872–1958), English composer. Studied at Royal College of Music with Parry and Stanford, in Berlin with Bruch, and in Paris with Ravel. Joined R.C.M. as teacher of composition in 1918, conducted Bach Choir (1920–6), and became president of English Folk Dance and Song Society (1932), and for many years directed Leith Hill Festival, Dorking. Active as collector of English folk song, and discovered affinity between traditional melodies and own aspirations. Folk song began to colour his work more and more, but this was combined with influence of Tudor polyphony and restrained by independence of outlook which gave wholly individual flavour to his mature work. Made occasional use of polytonality *eg* in *Flos campi*. Range of expression of his work is considerable: brutal violence, robust jollity, and almost mystical tranquillity – all find a place, often in the same work. Contrasts between them are not contradictions but related facets of same personality.

Principal compositions:

(1) Orchestra: *A London Symphony* (1914, rev. 1920), *A Pastoral Symphony* (1922), symphony in F minor (no 4, 1935), symphony in D (no 5, 1943), symphony in E minor (no 6, 1948), *Sinfonia Antartica* (1953), symphony in D minor (no 8, 1956), symphony in E minor (no 9, 1958), 3 Norfolk rhapsodies (1906–7), Fantasia on a Theme by Tallis (1910), *The Lark Ascending* for violin and orchestra (1914), *Flos campi* for viola, orchestra and voices (1925),

*Concerto accademico* for violin (1925), piano concerto (1933), suite for viola and orchestra (1934), *Five Variants of 'Dives and Lazarus'* for strings and harp (1939), oboe concerto (1948);

(2) Choral works: *Toward the Unknown Region* (1907), *A Sea Symphony* (1910), *Five Mystical Songs* (1911), Fantasia on Christmas carols (1912), Mass in G minor (1923), *Sancta Civitas* (1926), *Benedicite* (1930), 3 choral hymns (1930), *Magnificat* (1932), *Dona nobis pacem* (1936), *Five Tudor Portraits* (1936), *Te Deum* (1937), *Serenade to Music* (1938), *The Sons of Light* (1950);

(3) Operas: *Hugh the Drover* (1914), *Riders to the Sea* (1927), *The Poisoned Kiss* (1928), *Sir John in Love* (1929), *The Pilgrim's Progress* (1951, incorporating most of 1-act *The Shepherds of the Delectable Mountains,* 1922);

(4) Other stage works: incidental music to *The Wasps* of Aristophanes (1909); ballets *Old King Cole* (1923) and *Job* (1930);

(5) Chamber music: piano quintet, 2 string quartets, fantasy quintet for strings;

(6) Songs: *The House of Life* (6 sonnets by Rossetti), *Songs of Travel* (Stevenson), *On Wenlock Edge* (song cycle; Housman), and many individual songs.

Also works for organ and piano, and film music.

**Vautor, Thomas** (*fl* early 17th cent.), English composer. Published vol. of 5 and 6-part madrigals (1619).

**Vauxhall Gardens,** house and grounds at Lambeth, London, opened to public at Restoration under name 'Spring Garden'. Name 'Vauxhall Gardens' was first used in 1786. Used for concerts in 18th cent., and also for dramatic entertainments in early 19th cent.

**Vc.,** abbrev. for cello.

**Vecchi, Orazio** (1550–1605), Italian composer, priest. Held various church and court posts. Published 6 books of *canzonette,* 2 books of madrigals, Masses, motets, and 4 collections for voices, of which best known is *Amfiparnaso,* in which characters from *commedia dell'arte* are presented in series of madrigalian compositions – work was not, however, intended for stage presentation.

**Vecchi, Orfeo** (*fl* late 16th cent.), Italian composer. Wrote mostly church music, incl. motets, Masses and psalms.

**veloce** (It.), fast.

**Venegas de Henestrosa, Luys** (*c* 1505–after 1557), Spanish musician. Compiled and published in 1557 *Libro de cifra nueva para tecla, harpa, y vihuela* (Book of new tablature for keyboard, harp and *vihuela*), which contains several pieces by Cabezón.

**Venetian swell,** *see* SWELL.

**Venite** (Lat.), first word of Psalm 95, 'Venite, exultemus Domino' ('O come let us sing praise unto the Lord'), sung as canticle before psalms at Matins in Anglican service. Incl. in choral settings of service by pre-Commonwealth composers, but since Restoration has been sung as chant, like psalms.

**Ventil** (Ger.), valve.

**Venus and Adonis,** masque by Blow, librettist unknown. First perf. at court of Charles II, *c* 1682.

**Vêpres Siciliennes, Les,** *see* SICILIAN VESPERS.

**Veränderungen** (Ger.), variations.

**verbunkos,** Hungarian military dance, once used to aid recruitment, esp. in late 18th, early 19th cents. Form of slow introduction (*lassú*) followed by rapid section (*friss*) has been used as basis of various Hungarian rhapsodies (*eg* those of Liszt and Bartók).

**Verdelot** or **Deslouges, Philippe** (*fl* 16th cent.), Flemish composer. Mostly resident in Italy. One of earlier composers of Italian madrigals. Also wrote Masses and motets.

**Verdi, Giuseppe** (1813–1901), Italian composer. Born near Busseto. Son of grocer. Began career playing organ at village church and acting as assistant conductor of Busseto Philharmonic Society. Failed to gain admission to Milan Conservatorio (1832). Studied privately with Lavigna, répétiteur at La Scala. His first opera, *Oberto, Conte di S. Bonifacio,* was successfully produced at La Scala in 1839. La Scala immediately commissioned 3 more operas. First of these, comedy *Un giorno di regno* (1840), was a flop. Moreover, it coincided with death of Verdi's wife and 2 children, and Verdi vowed he would write no more music. Eventually, however, he was inspired by Solera's patriotic libretto for *Nabucco,* and resulting opera was huge success, leading to many commissions from opera houses in Italy and elsewhere. *Rigoletto* (one of several works that ran into censorship trouble because of politically controversial texts) was written for Venice (1851) and *Il Trovatore* for Rome (1853). Latter was said by composer to be 'new sort of opera' in which drama would have precedence. *La Traviata* (1853), though initially a failure, soon established itself as intimate obverse of *Trovatore.* There followed series of operas (*eg Don Carlos*) in which Verdi's Shakespearian qualities come to the fore. After *Aida* (1871) Verdi wrote no operas for 16 years, but then came truly Shakespearian operas *Otello* (1887) and *Falstaff* (1893) which crowned his achievement. In later years also composed some church music incl. Manzoni Requiem (1873), one of great choral requiems of 19th cent., in tribute to Italy's great poet, novelist and patriot.

Brought up in traditions of Italian opera, which exalted singer at expense of orchestra, Verdi began by accepting them wholeheartedly and only gradually developed the form for his own use. Early works show great gift of melody and typical red-bloodedness, but as he matured, he developed steady growth in musicianship, increased sensitivity, and resourceful and imaginative treatment of orchestra, until he reached supreme mastery in operas of his old age.

Principal compositions:

(1) Operas: *Oberto, Conte di San Bonifacio* (1839), *Un giorno di regno* (1840), *Nabucco* (*Nabucodonosor,* 1842), *I Lombardi alla prima crociata* (1843, rev. as *Jérusalem,* 1847), *Ernarni* (1844), *I due Foscari* (1844), *Giovanna d'Arco* (1845), *Alzira* (1845), *Attila* (1846), *Macbeth* (1847, rev. 1865), *I masnadiere* (1847), *Il corsaro*

(1848), *La battaglia di Legnano* (1849), *Luisa Miller* (1849), *Stiffelio* (1850, rev. as *Aroldo*, 1857), *Rigoletto* (1851), *Il Trovatore* (1853), *La Traviata* (1853), *Les Vêpres siciliennes* (1857, rev. 1881), *Un ballo in maschera* (1859), *La forza del destino* (1862), *Don Carlos* (1867), *Aida* (1871), *Otello* (1887), *Falstaff* (1893);

(2) Choral works: *Inno delle nazioni* (1862), *Messa da Requiem* (1874), *Pater Noster, Ave Maria* (1889), *Stabat Mater* (1898), *Te Deum* (1898), *Lauda alla Vergine Maria* (1898);

(3) Chamber music: string quartet (1873);

(4) Songs: part-song and 16 songs.

**Veress, Sándor** (1907– ), Hungarian composer, pianist, critic. Now resident in Switzerland. Pupil of Bartók and Kodály. Music has been influenced by activity as collector of folk songs, by Bartók, and by neo-classical style of Stravinsky. Works incl. opera for children, ballets, 2 symphonies, choral and chamber music, concertos for violin and piano, and *Sinfonia Minneapolitana* (for Minneapolis Symphony Orchestra).

**Veretti, Antonio** (1900–78), Italian composer. Pupil of Alfano. Works, in diversified styles, incl. *Sinfonia Sacra* for chorus and orchestra and opera-ballet *Burlesca.*

**verismo** (It., from *vero,* 'true'), anglicized as 'verism'. Artistic movement originating in late 19th cent. which aimed at vivid and realistic representation of contemporary life. In opera this resulted in melodramatic treatment which tended to exploit individual moments at expense of development or structural unity. Best examples are Mascagni's *Cavalleria rusticana* (1890), Leoncavallo's *I Pagliacci* (1892) and Charpentier's *Louise* (1900); in all these, participants are people of humble birth. Influenced many of Puccini's operas *eg Il tabarro,* set on Paris barge.

**Verklärte Nacht** (Ger., *Transfigured Night*), string sextet by Schoenberg, op 4 (1899), inspired by R. Dehmel's poem about moonlit walk by man and woman. Milestone in development of modern music. Later arranged for string orchestra (1917).

**Vermeulen, Matthijs** (1888–1967), Dutch composer, critic. At one time resident in France. Works incl. 6 symphonies, chamber music, and songs.

**Véronique,** operetta by Messager. First perf. Paris, 1898.

**Verschiebung** (Ger.), soft pedal of piano.

**Verschworenen, Die** (Ger., *The Conspirators*), opera by Schubert, inspired by Aristophanes' *Lysistrata.* First perf. Frankfurt, 1861.

**verse anthem,** anthem in which important sections are assigned to one or more solo voices with independent accompaniment.

**Verset,** organ piece based on plainsong melody and used to replace verse of psalm, Magnificat, or section of item of Mass. Performance would thus alternate between choir and organ. Many examples from 16th–18th cents. survive.

**versicle,** in RC and Anglican church, short text (usually from Bible) which is sung by officiant, with responses from choir or congregation.

**vers mesuré,** *see* MUSIQUE MESURÉE À L'ANTIQUE.

**verto** (It.), *ouvert* (*see* CLOS).

**Vespers,** service preceding Compline in office of RC rite. Incl. series of psalms with their antiphons, hymn and Magnificat. Elaborate settings for voices and orchestra were made by Monteverdi and Mozart (K321 and 339).

**Vestale, La** (Fr., *The Vestal Virgin*), opera by Spontini, libretto by V.J.E. de Jouy. First perf. Paris, 1807.

**Vesti la giubba,** Canio's aria from Act 1 of Leoncavallo's *I Pagliaci*. Familiarly known as 'On with the motley', it bemoans fate of clown who has to act in comedy while his heart is breaking.

**Via Crucis,** work for soloists, chorus and organ by Liszt (1879), depicting Stations of the Cross. Text makes use of Biblical quotations, Latin hymns and German chorales. Neither performed nor published till *c* 40 years after Liszt's death.

**Viadana, Lodovico,** orig. Lodovico Grossi (*c* 1560–1627), Italian composer, monk. Held various church posts. Works incl. canzonets, instrumental ensemble music, and church music. His *Cento concerti ecclesiastici* (1602) is provided with unfigured *basso continuo* and incl. detailed instruction for its performance by organist.

**Viaggio a Reims, Il** (It., *The Journey to Rheims*), opera by Rossini. First perf. Paris, 1825, for coronation of Charles X. Performance was failure, but composer salvaged much of music, which reappeared in *Le Comte Ory* (1828).

**vial, viall,** alternative names for viol.

**Viardot-Garcia, Pauline,** orig. Michelle Ferdinande Pauline (1821–1910), French mezzo-soprano of Spanish parentage. Daughter of singer Manuel Garcia and sister of Maria Malibran. Studied piano with Liszt. Sang with great success in opera in Brussels, London, Paris and Berlin. A close friend of Turgenev, she composed operettas to librettos by him.

**vibraharp** (US), vibraphone.

**vibraphone** or **vibes,** instrument, probably developed from glockenspiel, which first appeared after WWI. In appearance resembles xylophone, but bars are made of metal instead of hardwood. Beneath bars are resonators, in which discs are set spinning by electric or clockwork motor. This action helps to sustain notes and gives them controllable vibrato. Duration of notes is also controlled by damper pedal. Vibraphone is capable of substantial variety of tone colours, determined, apart from motor, by type of beaters used. Most common model has 3-octave compass from F in bass clef. Used extensively in jazz.

**vibrato** (It.), lit. 'shaking'. In music, method of giving expressive quality to note by rapid and minute fluctuations of pitch. This is achieved in following ways:

(1) on string instruments by oscillations of left hand, which is used to stop strings;

(2) on clavichord by repeating pressure of finger on key without releasing it. Generally known as BEBUNG;

(3) on wind instruments by suitably manipulating supply of air.

This is done by lips or EMBOUCHURE, by shaking instrument slightly, or (on trombone) by means of slide;

(4) in singing by method similar to that used on wind instruments; easily abused by those with defective technique.

Note that tremolo, often used as synonym for vibrato, properly means rapid reiteration of same note.

**Vicentino, Nicola** (1511–1576), Italian composer, theorist. Pupil of Willaert. Works incl. 2 books of 5-part madrigals. Wrote unscientific treatise entitled *L'antica musica ridotta alla moderna prattica* (1555), which argues that diatonic, chromatic and enharmonic genera of Greek music should be used as basis of composition. In pursuit of this theory, he invented keyboard instrument called *arcicembalo* (with 6 manuals) and another called *arciorgano*.

**Vickers, Jon** (1926–   ), Canadian tenor. Made debut in 1956, and has since established himself as one of finest Verdi and Wagner singers of the day.

**Victoria, Tomás Luis de,** also known as Vitoria or Vittoria (*c* 1548–1611), Spanish composer, priest. Held various church posts in Rome, then became chaplain to Empress Maria (sister of Philip II of Spain) and returned with her to Spain (*c* 1580), becoming director of music in Madrid convent in 1596. Compositions, exclusively for church, incl. motets, Masses, Magnificats, hymns and psalms – some are elaborate works for 8 to 12 voices with organ. His mastery of subtle and expressive polyphony makes him one of outstanding figures of 16th-cent. church music, and one of most remarkable in history of Spanish music.

**Vida Breve, La** (Sp., *Life is short*), opera by Falla, libretto by C.F. Shaw (in Spanish). First perf. (in French version by P. Milliet) Nice, 1913. Story concerns gypsy girl who curses man she loves when she discovers he is about to marry someone else; then, overcome with remorse, she falls dead at his feet.

**vide** (Fr.), empty. *Corde à vide,* open string.

**vide** (Lat.), lit 'see'. Term indicates optional omission in score (with syllables *Vi-* and *-de* usually at either end of cut).

**vielle, vielle-à-manivelle** (Fr.), hurdy-gurdy.

**vielle organisée** (Fr.; It., *lira organizzata*), 'organ' hurdy-gurdy incorporating set(s) of organ pipes.

**Vienna Philharmonic Orchestra,** self-governing body of players founded 1842 by members of Vienna Court Opera Orchestra. First conductor was Otto Nicolai, whose successors have incl. Hans Richter, Mahler, Felix Weingartner, Furtwängler, Clemens Krauss, Bruno Walter, Karajan, Karl Böhm and Claudio Abbado.

**Vienna State Opera,** orig. Vienna Court Opera, present name adopted 1918. First opera was given in Vienna in 1641, and rapidly became popular as court entertainment. One of world's leading opera companies, it has had a glittering history. Conductors have incl. Gluck, Donizetti, Richter, Mahler, Weingartner, Schalk, Richard Strauss, Clemens Krauss, Walter, Böhm and Karajan.

**Viennese School,** general term for composers active in Vienna in late

18th, early 19th cents., notably Haydn, Mozart, Beethoven and Schubert. So-called Second Viennese School grew up in 20th cent., with Schoenberg, Berg and Webern as its principal members.

**Vie parisienne, La** (Fr., *Life in Paris*), operetta by Offenbach, libretto by Meilhac and Halévy. First perf. Paris, 1866.

**Vier Grobiane, Die** (Eng., The four rustics), German title of I QUATTRO RUSTEGHI.

**Vierhebigkeit** (Ger.), term for musical phrases containing 4 bars or accents, or their multiples.

**Vierne, Louis Victor Jules** (1870–1937), French organist, composer. Blind from birth. Pupil of Franck and Widor. Organist at Notre Dame, where died while performing. Pupils incl. Nadia Boulanger. Works for organ incl. 6 large-scale 'symphonies'. Also wrote orchestral symphony, and choral and chamber music.

**Viertel** (Ger.), 'quarter', *ie* crotchet.

**Vierundsechzigstel** (Ger.), 'sixty-fourth', *ie* hemidemisemiquaver.

**Vieuxtemps, Henri** (1820–81), Belgian violinist, composer. Travelled widely in Europe and US. Compositions for violin incl. concertos.

**vif** (Fr.), lively.

**vihuela, vihuela da mano** (Sp.), Spanish lute. Usually 6-stringed and shaped like guitar. Became obsolete in late 16th cent. Most commonly plucked with fingers, though plectrum sometimes used (*vihuela da pendola*). Earlier, term was applied generically to any form of stringed instrument.

**vihuela de arco** (Sp.), viol.

**vihuela de flandes** (Sp.), ordinary as opposed to Spanish lute (*vihuela*).

**Village Romeo and Juliet, A,** opera by Delius, libretto by composer (after story by G. Keller). First perf. (in German) Berlin, 1907. Contains well-known orchestral interlude *The Walk to the Paradise Garden*.

**Villa-Lobos, Heitor** (1887–1959), Brazilian composer. First South American composer to become internationally famous. Numerous compositions show influence of South American Indian music and Brazilian folk song. Works incl. operas, symphonies, symphonic poems, cello concerto, 13 *choros* (serenades) for various media, chamber, choral and piano music, and songs. Most popular works, series of *Bachianas Brasileiras,* attempt to evoke spirit of Bach in Brazilian terms.

**villancico** (Sp., from *villano,* rustic), (1) type of song in popular but sophisticated style, current in Spain in late 15th, 16th cents. Begins with refrain, repeated after each verse;

(2) in 17th, 18th cents., cantata for soloists and chorus with instrumental accompaniment, frequently on subject of Christmas;

(3) (modern Sp.) Christmas carol.

**villanella** (It.), lit. 'rustic song'. Popular but sophisticated form of part-song in 17th-cent. Italy. Originated in Naples, hence also known as *napolitana* (Eng., Neapolitan). Most popular type was for

3 voices, with frequent use of consecutive triads. Words often parodied elevated and sentimental style of madrigal.

**villanelle** (Fr.), song or other vocal piece based on words of poem in *villanelle* form. Normally consists of 3-line stanzas, in which 1st and 3rd lines of opening stanza are repeated alternately as 3rd line of succeeding stanzas.

**Villi, Le** (It., *The Witches*), opera by Puccini (his first), libretto by F. Fontana. First perf. Milan, 1884.

**villota** (It.), form of popular part-song (usually for 4 voices) of N Italian origin current in 16th cent.

**Vinay, Ramón** (1914– ), Chilean tenor, previously baritone. Sang in opera in Latin America, US and Europe. Resumed baritone roles in 1962.

**Vinci, Leonardo** (1690–1730), Italian composer. Made reputation in Naples as composer of *opera buffa* and *opera seria*. Also wrote church music. No relation to artist, Leonardo da Vinci.

**Viñes, Ricardo** (1875–1943), Spanish pianist. Gave first perfs. of several works by Debussy and other 20th-cent. French composers.

**Vingt-quatre Violons du Roi, Les** (Fr., the king's 24 violins), string orchestra maintained by French kings in 17th, 18th cents. Organization was copied by Charles II, who instituted band of '24 violins'.

**Vingt Regards sur l'Enfant Jésus** (Fr., *Twenty contemplations of the child Jesus*), work for piano by Messiaen (1944). Work has 20 movts., and lasts for *c* 2½ hours.

**Vin herbé, Le** (Fr., *The Enchanted Wine*), chamber oratorio for 12 voices, 7 strings and piano by Frank Martin. First perf. Zürich, 1940; extended version presented at Salzburg Festival, 1948. Based on legend of Tristan and Isolde.

**viol** (Fr., *viole*; Ger., *Viole*; It., *viola*; Sp., *vihuela de arco*), family of bowed string instruments, widely used in 16th, 17th cents., and revived in modern times for performance of music of that period. Sizes, tuning and shape varied considerably in 16th cent., but by 17th there was some degree of standardization. Instruments had 6 strings, and 3 sizes normally used in chamber music were tuned as follows: treble viol or discant-viol, D and G on bass clef, middle C, and E, A and D on treble clef; tenor viol, fourth or fifth below treble; bass viol or *viola da gamba,* octave below treble. Back was normally flat and shoulders sloping. Bow was held above palm of hand. Series of gut frets on fingerboard gave clear tone to each stopped note. All were held vertically either between legs or resting on lap, hence generic name for whole family, *viola da gamba* (It., 'leg' viol), later applied exclusively to bass viol. Term *viola da braccio* (It., 'arm' viol) was applied to instruments supported by arm, *ie* violin and viola.

Literature of music for viols is extensive, esp. in England in mid 17th cent. Bass viol in particular was also cultivated as solo instrument, esp. for playing DIVISIONS; for this purpose rather smaller instrument was used. Still smaller bass viol was used for playing 'lyra way', *ie* with variety of tunings to facilitate hand-playing;

problem of constantly using new fingering was solved by writing music in TABLATURE, as for lute. Viols, esp. bass, continued to be used as solo instruments in early 18th cent. Bass viol also had important function as accompanying instrument in 17th cent., being used to play bass line in continuo parts (in association with harpsichord or organ). There was also double-bass viol (It., *violone*), tuned octave below bass, and high treble (Fr., *pardessus de viole*), tuned fourth above treble.

**viola** (It.; Fr., *alto*; Ger., *Bratsche*), orig. generic term for any bowed stringed instrument, but now used exclusively for alto (or tenor) member of violin family. Tuning is C and G on bass clef, and D and A on treble clef. Alto clef is used except in upper register, when treble clef is used to avoid leger lines. Tone differs markedly from violin and cello. Member of orchestra since early 17th cent., though its development in chamber music dates from Haydn's cultivation of string quartet in 18th. As solo instrument received only occasional attention before 20th cent.

**viola alta** (It.), unusually large viola made in 1870s esp. for Wagner Festivals at Bayreuth. Later, 5th string was added, tuned to E (same as violin's top string). *See also* VIOLINO GRANDE, VIOLA POMPOSA.

**viola bastarda** (It.), instrument known in England as LYRA VIOL or viol played 'lyra way' (*see* VIOL).

**viola da braccio** (It.), lit. 'arm' viol; term applied in 16th, 17th cents. to bowed stringed instruments supported by arm, *ie* violin and viola. Hence also *bassa viola da braccia,* cello. By 18th cent., term was applied exclusively to viola.

**viola da gamba** (It.), lit 'leg' viol; term was orig. applied to all members of viol family, but came to be applied exclusively to bass VIOL.

**viola d'amore** (It.; Fr., *viole d'amour*; Ger., *Liebesgeige*), lit. 'love' viol, prob. so called for tender quality of its tone. It is tenor VIOL with 7 instead of 6 strings, normally tuned to chord of D major: D, F and A on bass clef, and D, F, A and D on treble clef. Music is written on alto clef. There are also 7 or 14 sympathetic strings.

**viola da spalla** or **viola de spalla** (It.), lit. 'shoulder viol'. A kind of portable cello, held by shoulder strap, used by itinerant musicians in 17th, 18th cents.

**viola di bordone** (It.), lit. 'drone' viol; alternative name for both VIOLA BASTARDA and BARYTON.

**viola di fagotto** (It.), lit. 'bassoon viol'; alternative name for VIOLA BASTARDA.

**viola pomposa** (It.), name apparently given to 3 different instruments that enjoyed brief existence:

(1) small cello with additional top string. This is prob. violoncello piccolo for which Bach wrote last of his Cello Suites;

(2) viola with additional top string; predecessor of VIOLA ALTA. Seems to be identical with violino pomposa (*see also* VIOLINO GRANDE);

(3) 4-stringed instrument irregularly tuned, lowest note being D below middle C.

**viol d'amour,** open diapason organ stop, similar to VIOLIN DIAPASON.

**viol de gamba,** organ stop imitating string tone.

**viol de gamboys,** early Eng. name for VIOLA DA GAMBA.

**viol d'orchestre,** organ stop similar to VIOL DE GAMBA.

**viole** (Fr.), **Viole** (Ger.), viol.

**violet,** Eng. name occasionally used for VIOLA D'AMORE.

**viole ténor** (Sp.), viola, made in Spain in 1930s, of size proportionate to its pitch as compared with violin. Could be played only in cello position.

**violetta** (It., diminutive of *viola*), (1) in 16th-cent. Italy, name given to early form of violin with 3 strings;

(2) in 18th-cent. Germany, name often given to viola.

**violetta marina** (It.), lit. 'little marine viol'. This rare and obsolete instrument was modified and presumably smaller version of VIOLA D'AMORE.

**violetta piccola** (It.), lit. 'little small violin'; name given by Praetorius as alternative for both violin and kind of small viol.

**violin,** (1) in 17th cent., name of family of bowed stringed instruments (Fr., *violon*; Ger., *Geige*; It., *viola da braccio*; Sp., *vihuela de braço*). Differed from VIOL family in several respects, notably: (a) they have slightly rounded backs and round shoulders, (b) there are normally 4 strings, tuned in fifths, (c) there are no frets, (d) smaller members (violin and viola) are held on arm. Alto (or tenor) violin is now known as VIOLA, and bass violin as cello (abbrev. of VIOLONCELLO). Instrument intermediate between viola and cello existed in late 17th cent. but is now obsolete; often referred to as 'tenor violin', though this is also old Eng. name for viola. Double-bass violin also existed, but double-bass viol was preferred, and from this modern DOUBLE BASS, though it has no frets, is derived.

Ancestry of family is complex. Large number of bowed string instruments of various shapes existed in Middle Ages, and violin family (at first with 3, then 4 strings) evolved from these in 16th cent. From the first they were used for ensemble music, like viols, and when orchestras became necessary for opera in early 17th cent., violin family were preferred because of their more incisive, brilliant tone. From that time they have remained in all essentials the same;

(2) in particular, treble of violin family, to which name 'violin' (Fr., *violon*; Ger., *Violine*; It., *violino*) is now exclusively applied. Standard tuning is G below treble clef, D, A, E. Other tunings were adopted in 17th cent. to facilitate chord-playing (*see* SCORDATURA). Violin was used early in 17th cent. as solo instrument and its capacity for virtuosity explored. Solo sonata and trio sonata for 2 violins and continuo developed side by side. Solo concerto appeared *c* 1700;

(3) smaller violin was used in 17th, 18th cents. (*see* VIOLINO PICCOLO).

**violin diapason,** open diapason organ-stop imitating string tone.

**Violine** (Ger.), violin.

**violino** (It., diminutive of *viola*), (1) name used indiscriminately in 16th cent. for members of viol and violin families;

(2) from 17th cent. onwards, means 'violin', *ie* treble member of violin family.

**violino grande** (It.), large violin, now virtually obsolete, with 5 strings, lowest tuned to C in bass clef, and other 4 as on normal violin. Seems to be identical with one form of VIOLA POMPOSA.

**violino piccolo** (It., Ger., *kleine Discantgeige, Quartgeige*), small violin used in 17th, early 18th cents., tuned perfect fourth or minor third above normal violin.

**violon** (Fr.), (1) name used in 16th cent. for members both of viol and violin families;

(2) in 17th cent., name applied to violin family;

(3) now used exclusively for 'violin', *ie* treble member of violin family.

**violoncello** (It., diminutive of *violone*; Fr., *violoncelle*; Ger., *Violoncell, Violoncello*), bass of violin family. In non-Romance languages normally abbrev. to 'cello'. Orig. known as *bassa viola da braccio*. Now has 4 strings tuned: C below bass clef, G, D, A. Also made with 5 strings in 17th, early 18th cents. – *see* VIOLA POMPOSA (1). Alternative tunings were used for 4-string instrument (*see* SCORDATURA). Music is written in bass clef, except for higher register, where tenor and treble clefs are used to avoid leger lines.

For most of 17th cent. cello was restricted to playing bass line in orchestra and in chamber music (though in latter case bass viol was often preferred). Solo music began to appear at end of 17th cent. and is frequent in 18th in form of concertos, sonatas *etc.* Repertory of more modern concertos is limited.

**violoncello piccolo** (It.), small-sized cello for which Bach wrote obbligato parts in 9 cantatas.

**violon d'amour** (Fr.), lit. 'love violin'. Obsolete instrument, used briefly in 18th cent. Resulted from attempt to provide violin family with equivalent of viola d'amore, albeit at higher pitch. Had 5 playing strings and 6 sympathetic ones.

**violone** (It., augmentative of *viola*), (1) properly, double-bass VIOL (*contrabassa da gamba*);

(2) also applied in 18th cent. to double-bass violin, hence diminutive *violoncello* for bass violin.

*See* DOUBLE BASS.

**violotta,** modern but little used stringed instrument pitched between viola and cello. Tuned octave below violin.

**viol lyra way,** *see* VIOL, LYRA VIOL.

**Viotti, Giovanni Battista** (1755–1824), Italian violinist, composer. Pupil of Pugnani. Toured Europe (1780–2), then lived in Paris, London, and near Hamburg, holding various posts incl. directorship of Paris Opéra (1819–22). Had great reputation as performer, and influence as teacher was far-reaching. Compositions incl. 29 violin concertos and 10 for piano.

**Viozzi, Giulio** (1912– ), Italian composer. Works incl. opera *Allamistakeo,* and threnody for 2 pianos.

**Virdung, Sebastian** (*fl* 15th–16th cents.), German musician. Published important work on musical instruments entitled *Musica getutscht* (Basle, 1511).

**virelai** (Fr.), form of medieval French song, beginning with refrain subsequently repeated after each verse.

**virginal** or **virginals,** member of harpsichord family, first mentioned in early 16th cent. Name is properly applied to oblong (or rectangular) SPINET, but in Tudor and Jacobean period was applied to any instrument of harpsichord type. Clear distinction between harpsichord and virginal was not made till Restoration.

**virtuoso,** performer of uncommon skill and technical mastery. Word is today sometimes used in derogatory sense, implication being that performer who is 'merely' virtuoso, or composer who writes only virtuoso music, may be lacking in feeling and/or intelligence.

**Vishnevskaya, Galina** (1926– ), Russian soprano. Joined Bolshoi Opera in early 1950s, and has also appeared at New York Metropolitan and at Covent Garden. Britten's song cycle, *The Poet's Echo,* and solo soprano part of *A War Requiem* were both written for her. Married to cellist Rostropovich; now lives in West.

**Vision of St Augustine, The,** choral work by Tippett, scored for solo baritone, chorus and orchestra. First perf. London, 1966, with Fischer-Dieskau as soloist.

**Visions fugitives,** set of 20 piano pieces by Prokofiev, op 22 (1915–17), inspired by poetry of Balmont. There is also version for string orchestra by Rudolf Barshai.

**Visitation, The,** opera by Gunther Schuller, libretto by composer. First perf. Hamburg, 1966. Work is based on Kafka's *The Trial,* but action is transferred to Deep South of US, hero being a Black student.

**Vitali, Filippo** (*c* 1590–1953), Italian composer. His *L'Aretusa* (1620) was one of earliest operas perf. in Rome. Also published madrigals, arias for one or more voices with instrumental accompaniment, and church music.

**Vitali, Giovanni Battista** (1632–92), Italian violinist, composer. In service of Duke of Modena. One of most important composers of chamber music in 17th cent. Works incl. trio sonatas, dance movts. for strings, psalms for voices and instruments, operas, and oratorios.

His son, **Tommaso Antonio Vitali** (1663–1745), was also violinist and composer in service of Duke of Modena. Surviving publications incl. 3 sets of trio sonatas. Set of variations above ostinato bass in G minor for violin and continuo has been attrib. to him and published as 'Chaconne'.

**vite** (Fr.), fast, quick.

**Vitoria,** *see* VICTORIA.

**Vitry, Philippe de** (1291–1361), French composer, poet, theorist, diplomat. Became Bishop of Meaux in 1351. His few surviving compositions show him to be master of isorhythmic motet. Title of his treatise *Ars nova* has been adopted as general term for music of 14th cent.

**Vittoria,** *see* VICTORIA.

**vivace** (It.), lively.

**Vivaldi, Antonio** (1675–1741), Italian composer, violinist. Pupil of father and Legrenzi. Ordained as priest (1703) and nicknamed *il prete rosso* (the red-haired priest). For many years taught at music school for girls in Venice. Travelled extensively and was one of most prolific composers of his time. Surviving works incl. concertos for wide variety of solo instruments with orchestra (he was one of first composers to use clarinets), chamber music, secular cantatas, church music, oratorio, and operas. Despite tremendous output, he was by no means a conventional composer, and much of his instrumental work shows a lively and fertile imagination. Since 1950s, there has been enormous revival of interest in Vivaldi's music, esp. his concertos, among which 4 works for violin, collectively known as *The Four Seasons,* have become particularly popular.

**vivo** (It.), lively.

**Vla.,** abbrev. for viola.

**Vlad, Roman** (1919– ), Italian composer, b. Romania. Pupil of Casella. Works incl. ballet *La Dama delle Camelie* (after Dumas), 3 cantatas, symphony, and chamber and film music.

**Vln.,** abbrev. for violin.

**Vltava,** *see* MÁ VLAST.

**vocalise** (Fr.), wordless composition, or passage in composition. Term is often used in connection with vocal exercises, though can apply equally to concert works or sections of opera.

**voce** (It.), voice. *Voce di petto,* CHEST VOICE; *voce di testa,* HEAD VOICE.

**Voces Intimae** (Lat., *Intimate voices*), title given by Sibelius to his D minor string quartet, op 56.

**voces musicales** (Lat.), 'musical notes'. Notes of hexachord, sung to solmization syllables, often used in 16th cent. as *cantus firmus* in vocal and instrumental pieces.

**Vogel, Emil** (1859–1908), German musicologist. Founder and editor of *Jahrbuch der Musikbibliothek Peters* (1894–1900). Published detailed studies of Monteverdi and Gagliano, and *Bibliothek der gedruckten Vokalmusik Italiens aus den Jahren 1500–1700* (1892).

**Vogel, Vladimir** (1896– ), German composer, b. Russia. Resident in Switzerland from 1933. Pupil of Busoni, but more influenced by Schoenberg and Berg. Most important work is 4-hour oratorio *Tyl Klaas* (1945), intended as protest against dictatorship and denial of liberty. Other works incl. large-scale *Epitaffio per Alban Berg* for solo piano (1936), and *Arpiade* (inspired by artist Jean Arp) for soprano, speech chorus and 5 instruments.

**Vogelweide,** *see* MINNESINGER.

**Vogl, Johann Michael** (1768–1840), Austrian baritone. Sang with

Court Opera, his roles incl. Count in Mozart's *Figaro.* Became close friend of Schubert.

**Vogler, Georg Joseph** (1749–1814), German composer, organist, teacher, priest. Held various posts in Germany and Sweden. Pupils incl. Weber and Meyerbeer. Works incl. many operas, and church and instrumental music.

**voice,** (1) sound produced by humans and many animals by vibrating of vocal chords;

(2) technical term used traditionally for individual part or 'strand' in contrapuntal composition (esp. fugue), whether for voices or instruments.

**voice leading** (US; Ger., *Stimmführung*), part-writing.

**Voi, che sapete,** aria sung by Cherubino to Countess in Act 2 of Mozart's *The Marriage of Figaro.*

**voicing,** process of ensuring good and uniform tone quality from set of organ pipes.

**voix céleste** (Fr.), 'heavenly voice'. *See* UNDA MARIS.

**Voix humaine, Le** (Fr., the human voice), opera by Poulenc, libretto by Jean Cocteau. First perf. Paris, 1959. Takes form of long scena for solo soprano and orchestra – voice being that of abandoned woman talking to her lover on telephone.

**volante** (It.), lit. 'flying', *ie* fast and light.

**Volkslied** (Ger.), (1) folk song, in sense of traditional song of unknown authorship;

(2) popular song, whether anon. or by known composer. Their square-cut rhythm and symmetrical structure have had considerable influence on German composers.

**Volles Werk** (Ger.), full organ.

**Volo di Notte** (It., *Night Flight*), opera by Dallapiccola (his first), based on Saint Exupéry's novel *Vol de Nuit,* about early days of flying. First perf. Florence, 1940.

**volta** (It.), 'turn', 'time': (1) *Prima volta* (first time) and *seconda volta* (second time) are used when composition or section of composition is to be repeated with some change in concluding bar(s). Horizontal brackets above stave indicate bars affected: first time performer plays bar(s) marked *prima volta* (or simply '1') and then goes back to beginning, second time he omits those bars and goes straight on to bars marked *seconda volta* (or '2');

(2) lively dance in 6/8 rhythm (Fr., *volte*) in which men swing women high in air; very popular in late 16th, early 17th cents. Also known as *lavolta.*

**volti** (It.), turn over (page). *Volti subito,* turn quickly.

**voluntary,** (1) in general, keyboard piece in free style;

(2) in particular, organ solo played before and after Anglican service.

**von Bülow,** *see* BÜLOW.

**Von Heute auf Morgen** (Ger., *From Day to Day*), opera by Schoenberg, libretto by Max Blonda (pseud. of composer's wife). First perf. Frankfurt, 1930. Schoenberg's first opera using 12-note technique, it is comedy concerning ruses employed by woman to prevent her husband from abandoning her.

**Vorschlag** (Ger.), appoggiatura.

**Vorspiel** (Ger.), prelude.

**Votre Faust** (Fr., *Your Faust*), opera by Henri Pousseur, libretto by composer and M. Butor. Written 1960–7, work is modernization of Goethe's drama, and in each performance, audience is invited to choose between alternative endings.

**Voyevoda, The,** opera by Chaikovsky (his first), libretto by composer and A. Ostrovsky. First perf. Moscow, 1869. Quickly fell from repertoire, and composer later transferred some of material to other works.

**vox angelica, vox coelestis,** *see* UNDA MARIS.

**vox humana** (Lat.), reed organ stop imitating human voice.

**Vulpius, Melchior** (*c* 1570–1615), German composer. Published several vols. of church music for 4 to 8 voices, settings of Lutheran chorale melodies, and *St Matthew Passion*. His own chorale melodies incl. 'Christus der ist mein Leben' and 'Jesu Leiden, Pein und Tod'.

**Vyšehrad,** *see* MÁ VLAST.

**Vyvyan, Jennifer** (1925–74), British soprano. Appeared at Covent Garden, Sadler's Wells and Glyndebourne. Created roles of Governess in Britten's *The Turn of the Screw* and Tytania in his *A Midsummer Night's Dream*.

# W

**Wachet auf** (Ger., 'Sleepers Awake'), title of Bach's cantata no 140 (1731), based on hymn by Philipp Nicolai (1599).

**Waelraut, Hubert** (1517–95), Flemish composer, singer. Compositions, which had great reputation in his day, incl. *chansons*, madrigals and motets.

**Wagenseil, Georg Christoph** (1715–77), Austrian composer. In service of Viennese Court. Numerous works incl. symphonies, concertos, choral and keyboard music, oratorios and operas.

**Wagner, Peter Josef** (1865–1931), German musical historian. First president of International Musicological Society (1927). Principal studies were in field of Gregorian chant.

**Wagner, [Wilhelm] Richard** (1813–83), German composer. Born in Leipzig. Son of civic clerk, who died soon after composer's birth. His mother then married Jewish actor, Ludwig Geyer, who died in 1821. At school he acquired profound interest in drama and in Beethoven's symphonies. Though learnt piano, preferred to study opera scores. Also studied harmony and counterpoint, and by age of 20 had written several orchestral works. He also began to write opera. Became chorusmaster at Würzburg theatre (1833), then conductor at Magdeburg (1835), where he met and married Minna Planer. Moved on to Königsberg theatre, then Riga (1837) and Paris (1839), where lived for 3 years in poverty. During this period, completed *Rienzi* and began *The Flying Dutchman*; both were accepted at Dresden, where he was appointed assistant conductor in 1842. *Tannhäuser* followed in 1845. After abortive revolt in Dresden in 1848, Wagner, having shown liberal sympathies, fled to Zürich, where he started to work out ideas for great political tetralogy, *The Ring*. Meanwhile, friendship with Liszt resulted in production of *Lohengrin* at Weimar (1850). In 1859 completed *Tristan and Isolde* at Lucerne, and in 1860 was allowed to return to Germany. Marital and financial problems were still turbulent, and in 1864 he was being threatened with imprisonment for debt. But Ludwig II of Bavaria, one of his deepest admirers, came to his rescue and invited him to Munich. *Tristan* was produced in Munich in 1865, none too successfully: its importance as one of great turning points in operatic history was not recognized till later. During this period Wagner fell in love with Liszt's daughter Cosima, wife of conductor Hans von Bülow. Ensuing scandal forced Wagner to leave Munich for Switzerland, though *The Mastersingers* was given in Munich in 1868. In spite of more financial problems he planned special festival theatre for his operas at Bayreuth. It opened in 1876 with first performance of *The Ring*. By this time Wagner had married Cosima (Minna having died in 1866). Ill-health interrupted work on last opera *Parsifal* (completed 1882). Died of heart attack in Venice.

Wagner wanted to create new type of dramatic work, in which all parts – music, drama, spectacle – could be united in significant whole – to be called 'music dramas' rather than operas. Works which illustrate, in its different aspects, his theory of operatic construction and philosophy are *The Ring, Tristan, The Mastersingers* and *Parsifal.* Principal points in his theory are that music should not dominate drama, that opera needs emotionally evocative verse and suitable (esp. legendary) subject matter, that operatic conventions must be abandoned, and that orchestra should express everything voice cannot, and should also make use of powerful force of association; above all, symphonic continuity is essential. These principles were most consistently carried out in 4 operas of *The Ring,* in which force of association was maintained by large number of short and reasonably simple thematic fragments, which constantly recur in varying forms. All his mature works exhibit highly developed gift for melody, unusual inventiveness in harmony, and mastery of orchestration which owes little to tradition.

Wrote following operas (words and music):

*Die Feen* (1834, first perf. 1888), *Das Liebesverbot* (after Shakespeare's *Measure for Measure,* 1836), *Rienzi* (1840, first perf. 1842), *The Flying Dutchman* (1841, first perf. 1850), *The Ring of the Nibelung*: (1) *The Rhinegold* (*Das Rheingold,* 1854, first perf. 1869), (2) *The Valkyries* (*Die Walküre,* 1856, first perf. 1870), (3) *Siegfried* (1871, first perf. 1876), (4) *The Twilight of the Gods* (*Götterdämmerung,* 1874, first perf. 1876); *Tristan and Isolde* (1859, first perf. 1865), *The Mastersingers* (1867, first perf. 1868), *Parsifal* (1882).

Other compositions incl. *Faust* overture (1840) and *Siegfried Idyll* (1870) for orchestra.

**Wagner, Siegfried** (1869–1930), German composer, operatic administrator, son of Richard Wagner and Cosima von Bülow. Studied with Humperdinck, and composed operas. Best known for his part in direction of festival theatre at Bayreuth (later controlled by his sons Wieland and Wolfgang).

**Wagner, Wieland** (1917–67), German opera producer, designer, son of Siegfried Wagner and grandson of Richard. With brother **Wolfgang Wagner** (1919– ) controlled artistic and financial welfare of Bayreuth after WWII, ridding it of Nazi associations. His uncluttered designs, dispensing with naturalism in favour of abstraction and symbolism, and with special emphasis on lighting, revolutionized 20th-cent. opera production.

**Wagner tuba,** *see* TUBA.

**wait,** (1) another name for medieval SHAWM;

(2) (Ger., *Stadtpfeifer*), musician, usually wind-player, employed by municipality, so called because original function was to act as watchman and announce hours at night. During 16th cent. their primary purpose changed to that of providing musical entertainment,

and scope was extended to incl. string-players and singers. Term 'waits' is now loosely applied to itinerant musicians who play in streets at Christmas;

(3) piece of music played by waits.

**Walcha, Helmut** (1907– ), German organist. Esp. associated with Bach. Became blind.

**Waldhorn** (Ger.), lit. 'woodland horn', *ie* orchestral horn. Sometimes implies natural (valveless) horn.

**Waldstein Sonata,** Beethoven's piano sonata in C, op 53 (1804), dedicated to Count Waldstein.

**Waldteufel, Emil** (1837–1915), French (Alsatian) composer. Pianist to Empress Eugénie of France. His highly successful waltzes incl. *The Skater's Waltz.*

**Walford Davies,** *see* DAVIES.

**Walker, Ernest** (1870–1949), English composer, pianist, historian, b. India. Wrote *A History of Music in England* (1907), and composed choral and chamber music, and songs.

**Walker & Sons, J.W.,** firm of organ-builders, founded in London by George England (1740) and acquired in 1820 by Joseph W. Walker (d. 1870).

**Walküre, Die,** *see* RING DES NIBELUNGEN.

**Wallace, Ian** (1919– ), English bass-baritone. Made opera debut in 1946, singing at Glyndebourne from 1948. Known esp. in comic roles.

**Wallace, William** (1860–1940), Scottish composer, writer on music. Main sympathies were with Liszt, and he wrote 6 symphonic poems, pioneering form in Britain. First was *The Passing of Beatrice* (inspired by Dante, 1892).

**Wallace, William Vincent** (1812–65), Irish composer. Opera *Maritana* (1845) brought immediate success. Travelled in Australia, New Zealand, India, Mexico and US. Most successful of other operas was *Lurline* (1860). Also wrote violin concerto and piano music. Died in France.

**Waller, Thomas 'Fats'** (1904–43), black American jazz pianist, composer. Performed with enormous exuberance and humour, often singing as well as playing. Numbers incl. *Ain't Misbehavin'* and *Jitterbug Waltz.*

**Wally, La,** opera by Catalani, libretto by Illica (after novel by W. von Hillern). First perf. Milan, 1892. Opera ends with death of heroine, La Wally, and her lover in avalanche. Toscanini named his daughter after heroine.

**Walsh,** firm of London music publishers, founded by John Walsh (d. 1736). Published many of Handel's works.

**Walter, Bruno** (1876–1962), German-born conductor, pianist, composer, writer. Conducting posts incl. Vienna Opera (1901–12, 1936–8), Munich (1913–22), Berlin Städtische Oper (1925–33), Gewandhaus concerts, Leipzig (1930–33), and Vienna Philharmonic (1933–8). When Nazis came to power took French nationality, and later moved to US (naturalized 1946). Excelled in music of Mozart,

Mahler and Bruckner, and in opera (played important part in establishing Salzburg Festival). Composed symphonies, chamber music, and songs.

**Walther** or **Walter, Johann** (1496–1570), German composer, singer, choirmaster. Friend of Luther; played prominent part in establishing music of Reformed Church. Publications incl. first Protestant hymn book, *Geystliche Gesangk-Buchleyn* (1524) and several other collections of church music. Also wrote instrumental music.

**Walther, Johann Gottfried** (1684–1748), German organist, composer, lexicographer. Relative of J.S. Bach, who was godfather to his eldest son. Excelled in composition of chorale preludes.

**Walther, Johann Jakob** (*c* 1650–1717), German violinist, composer. Works for violin incl. imitations of nature and of orchestral instruments.

**Walther von der Vogelweide,** *see* MINNESINGER.

**Walton, William [Turner]** (1902– ), English composer. Largely self-taught. Made reputation with string quartet (performed in Salzburg in 1923) and with *Façade*, series of instrumental pieces played in conjunction with recitation of poems by Edith Sitwell. Reached maturity with viola concerto (1929) and oratorio *Belshazzar's Feast* (1931). His work, even when most successful, gives impression of having been created with effort, though this often gives it extra edge of excitement. Later compositions have been few, and sometimes seem to strive consciously to recreate, not without success, atmosphere of their predecessors. He displays considerable assurance in handling large masses of sounds, as in *Belshazzar's Feast* and 1st symphony, but most characteristic work exploits nostalgic vein, seen at its best in viola concerto. Has occasionally flirted with modern tonality, but in essentials work is in English tradition represented by Elgar. Milestones in his output have been 2 symphonies, opera *Troilus and Cressida* (1954), concertos (for viola, violin, and cello), and orchestral *Variations on a Theme of Hindemith* (1963). Also wrote one-act opera *The Bear* (1967) for Aldeburgh Festival. Knighted 1951.

**waltz** (Fr., *valse*; Ger., *Walzer*; It., *valzer*), dance in triple time, slow or fast, with 1 beat in bar. First appeared in late 18th cent. as development of old DEUTSCHER TANZ. Development of waltzes as dance-form in 19th cent. was due principally to Viennese composers Joseph Lanner and Johann Strauss, followed by Johann Strauss the younger (*The Blue Danube*, 1867) and his brother Joseph.

**Walzer** (Ger.), waltz.

**Wand of Youth, The,** 2 orchestral suites by Elgar, op 1a and 1b. Written as incidental music during composer's childhood; revised and rescored in 1907.

**Wanderer Fantasia,** popular name for *Fantaisie* for piano by Schubert, op 15 (1822). In second section (Adagio) composer uses part of his song 'Der Wanderer', op 4, no 1 (1816). Liszt arranged work for piano and orchestra (first perf. 1851).

**Wanhal, Johann Baptist,** German form of Jan Křtitel Vanhal (1739–1813), Czech composer. Friend of Haydn and Mozart in Vienna. Wrote *c* 100 symphonies, 100 string quartets, 23 Masses, and numerous other instrumental and vocal works. British publishers spelt his name Vanhall.

**War and Peace** (Russ., *Voina i mir*), opera by Prokofiev, libretto by Myra Mendelson (composer's wife) after Tolstoy. First perf. (in concert form) Moscow, 1944; first staged Leningrad (1946). Revised version first perf. Leningrad, 1955.

**Ward, John** (1571–1638), English composer. Wrote madrigals, anthems, fantasias for strings, and keyboard pieces.

**Ward, Robert** (1917– ), American composer, conductor. Pupil of Copland and Hanson. Most famous work is opera *The Crucible* (1961) based on Arthur Miller's play. Other works incl. 4 symphonies, choral music, and pieces for orchestra and band.

**Warlock, Peter,** pseud. of Philip Heseltine (1894–1930), English composer, writer on music. Edited old English music. Compositions incl. song cycle *The Curlew* for tenor, flute, cor anglais and string quartet, *Capriol Suite* for orchestra, choral works, and many songs. Committed suicide.

**Warren, Leonard** (1911–60), American baritone. Made debut in 1939 and subsequently became famous all over world for his Verdi portrayals. Died on stage of New York Metropolitan during performance of *The Force of Destiny.*

**War Requiem, A,** large-scale choral work by Britten. Text combines anti-war poems by Wilfred Owen with Latin Requiem. Composed in 1962 for new Coventry Cathedral.

**washboard,** laundry utensil, made of wood or metal, and played with drumstick or thimbles on fingers. Much used in early jazz bands.

**Wasielewsky, Joseph Wilhelm von** (1822–96), German-Polish violinist, conductor, musical historian. Pupil of Mendelssohn. Led Düsseldorf Orchestra under Schumann, and wrote book on that composer (1858), and several books on violin.

**Water Carrier,** *see* DEUX JOURNÉES.

**Water Music,** orchestral suite by Handel, composed *c* 1715 for royal procession on Thames.

**water organ,** *see* HYDRAULIS.

**Watkins, Michael Blake** (1948– ), English composer. Pupil of Lutyens and Richard Rodney Bennett. Works incl. double concerto for oboe and guitar, concertos for horn and violin, *Dreams* and other orchestral works, brass band and chamber music, and songs.

**Watson, Thomas** (*c* 1557–92), English editor. Edited anthology of Italian madrigals with English words (1590). Most of pieces are by Marenzio; also incl. 2 specially commissioned madrigals by Byrd.

**Watts, Helen** (1927– ), Welsh contralto. Principally known in oratorio, though has also sung in opera.

**Wat Tyler,** opera by Alan Bush, libretto by composer's wife Nancy. First perf. Leipzig, 1953. Work concerns leader of Peasants' Revolt in England in 1381.

**wayte, wait,** old name for hautboy or OBOE.

**Webbe, Samuel** (1740–1816), English composer. Wrote glees, catches, motets, and Masses. His son, **Samuel Webbe** (1770–1843), was pianist, organist, and composer of glees and church music.

**Weber, Ben** (1916– ), American composer. Influenced by Schoenberg and Berg. Works incl. symphony on poems by Blake for baritone and chamber orchestra, ballet *Pool of Darkness*, and chamber and piano music.

**Weber, Bernhard Christian** (1712–58), German organist, composer. His *Well-tempered Clavier,* set of preludes and fugues for organ in all major and minor keys, was once thought to predate Bach's first set (1722), but was actually written more than 20 years later.

**Weber, Carl Maria Ernst von** (1786–1826), German composer, conductor, pianist. Pupil of Michael Haydn. Settled in Vienna (1803), where studied with Vogler. Conductor of Breslau theatre (1804–6), secretary to Duke Ludwig of Württemberg, Stuttgart (1807–10); banished by King of Württemberg in 1810 and moved to Mannheim, then Darmstadt. After several concert tours, appointed conductor at Prague in 1813, and at Dresden Opera in 1816. Most successful work, opera *Der Freischütz,* was produced in Berlin in 1821. In 1826, visited London to produce *Oberon,* written for Covent Garden, and died there soon after first performance.

Weber was virtually the creator of German romantic opera. In its combination of homely and mysterious elements, his *Singspiel* with dialogue, *Der Freischütz*, shows influence of German folklore and countryside. *Euryanthe* (1823), opera with continuous music, recreates atmosphere of medieval chivalry. Weber's piano compositions show fertile imagination and brilliant technical command. His other operas are *Das Waldmädchen* (1800), *Peter Schmoll* (1803), *Silvana* (1810), and *Abu Hassan* (1811). Also composed choral works, 2 symphonies, 2 piano concertos, *Konzertstück* for piano and orchestra, 2 clarinet concertos and clarinet concertino, 4 piano sonatas, and many piano pieces and songs.

**Weber, Gottfried** (1779–1839), German lawyer, composer, theorist. Works incl. church and instrumental music, and songs. Wrote several important works on theory of music and acoustics.

**Weber, Josepha** (1758–1819), Austrian coloratura soprano, eldest of 3 Weber sisters, second cousins of Carl Maria von Weber. Her married names were successively Hofer and Meyer. Mozart wrote for her part of Queen of the Night in *The Magic Flute.* **Aloysia Weber** (1760–1839) was also soprano. Mozart, who had once been in love with her, wrote for her part of Constanze in *Die Entführung aus dem Serail* and several concert arias. Married Joseph Lange in 1790. **Constanze Weber** (1763–1842) married Mozart in 1782; after his death in 1791 she married Georg Nikolaus Nissen (1809), and supervised publication of Nissen's life of Mozart (1828).

**Webern, Anton von** (1883–1945), Austrian composer. Studied composition under Schoenberg, and, with Berg, was Schoenberg's principal disciple. Began career as theatre conductor in Germany and Czechoslovakia, but settled near Vienna after WWI and conducted concerts for Schoenberg's Society for Private Performances and the Workers' Symphony Concerts. However, devoted most of his time to teaching and composition. First published composition, *Passacaglia* (1908), revealed influence of Mahler, and showed no sign of absolute adoption of TWELVE-NOTE SYSTEM which was to characterize his works from then on. His relatively few works, most for small, and often unusual, chamber combinations or voice, reduce music to bare essentials, abandoning traditional harmonic concepts. He concentrated many isolated musical events, ordered by intricate contrapuntal and rhythmic patterns, into extremely brief time spans – his *6 Bagatelles* (1913) for string quartet lasts 3 mins. 37 secs., and *Five Pieces for Orchestra* (1911–13) contains only 76 bars. Later works, *eg Variations* for orchestra (1940), strove for total variation in opposition to traditional developmental techniques. Webern's style was individual, intensely poetic, and expressive. Since his death his music has had growing influence, though while he lived he pursued his goals in almost total isolation. His life was cut short by tragic accident – he was shot by sentry during US occupation of Austria. His works incl. *Das Augenlicht* and Cantatas nos 1 and 2 for chorus and orchestra, 2 songs (settings of Goethe) for chorus and chamber orchestra, 2 symphonies, passacaglia, variations, *Six Pieces* and *Five Pieces* for orchestra, concerto for 9 instruments, 3 works incl. *6 Bagatelles* for string quartet, canons for voice, clarinet and bass clarinet and songs.

**Wechsel** (Ger.), change. *Wechselgesang,* alternating or antiphonal singing. *Wechseldominante, see* SECONDARY DOMINANT.

**Weckerlin, Jean Baptiste Théodore** (1821–1910), French composer, editor, b. Alsace. His opera *L'Organiste dans l'embarras* (1853) was very successful. Published many collections of old French songs.

**Weckmann, Matthias** (1621–74), German organist, composer. Had considerable reputation as organist, working for some time in Denmark. Helped found *Collegium Musicum* in Hamburg, which gave public performances. Compositions incl. church cantatas and keyboard works.

**Wedding, The** (Russ., *Svadebka*), dance cantata by Stravinsky, based on Russian popular texts, scored for chorus, 4 pianos and percussion. Dedicated to Diaghilev and first perf. by Ballets Russes, Paris 1923. French title, *Les Noces,* is inappropriate outside France.

**'Wedge' Fugue,** nickname for Bach's organ fugue in E minor whose opening subject proceeds in gradually widening intervals.

**Weelkes, Thomas** (*c* 1576–1623), English composer. One of most original and inventive of English madrigalists, esp. in works for 6 voices. Also wrote much church music.

**Wegelius, Martin** (1846–1906), Finnish composer, conductor. Became conductor of Finnish Opera in Helsinki (1878), and was founder and director of Conservatory (now Sibelius Academy) in 1882. Pupils incl. Sibelius, Järnefelt and Palmgren.

**Weichsel, Elizabeth,** *see* BILLINGTON.

**Weigl, Joseph** (1766–1846), Austrian composer. Godson of Haydn. Worked as opera conductor in Vienna. Composed *c* 30 operas, ballets, church music, and songs.

**Weihe des Hauses, Die,** *see* CONSECRATION OF THE HOUSE.

**Weihnachtsoratorium,** *see* CHRISTMAS ORATORIO.

**Weihnachtssymphonie,** *see* 'LAMENTATION' SYMPHONY.

**Weill, Kurt** (1900–50), German-born composer. Pupil of Humperdinck and Busoni. Early orchestral music was influenced by Schoenberg, but first major success was *The Threepenny Opera,* modern version of *The Beggar's Opera* written in collaboration with Bertolt Brecht (1928). Work is characterized by fierce social satire, sweet-sour melodies and jazz-orientated accompaniments. Second and more ambitious opera, *Rise and Fall of the City of Mahagonny,* continued in same vein, again with Brecht's collaboration (1930). But this exposure of social corruption, as well as fact that Weill was Jew, provoked increasing opposition from Nazis. In 1933 Weill moved to Paris, where wrote *The Seven Deadly Sins,* and in 1935 settled in US, where his music lost some of its former 'bite'. Later works *eg Down in the Valley* employ contemporary idioms of musical comedy, and compare unfavourably with *Happy End* and *The Lindbergh Flight* (1927–9), 2 'American' works dating from his German years.

**Weinberger, Jaromir** (1896–1967), Czech composer. Settled in US (1938). Best known for opera *Svanda the Bagpiper* (1927), exploiting racy national idiom. Also wrote other operas and orchestral variations and fugue on *Under the Spreading Chestnut Tree.*

**Weiner, Leó** (1885–1960), Hungarian composer. Wrote orchestral and stage works, but best known for chamber music.

**Weingartner, [Paul] Felix** (1863–1942), Austrian conductor, composer. Pupil of Liszt. Succeeded Mahler as conductor of Vienna State Opera in 1907. Later travelled widely and gained international fame for finely-chiselled interpretations of German classics. His compositions, now neglected, incl. operas, symphonies, and choral and chamber works.

**Weinzweig, John Jacob** (1913– ), Canadian composer, conductor, teacher. Best-known for orchestral suite *The Land.*

**Weisgall, Hugo** (1912– ), American composer, conductor, b. Czechoslovakia. Pupil of Sessions. Most important works are operas *eg The Tenor* (1950) and *The Stronger* (after Strindberg, 1952).

**Weiss, Amalie,** *see* JOACHIM, AMALIE.

**Weiss, Sylvius Leopold** (1686–1750), German lutenist, composer. Regarded as finest lutenist of his time. Wrote mostly for lute.

**welcome song,** composition for soloists, chorus and orchestra used in Restoration times to mark return to London of King or other members of royal family. There are examples by Purcell.

**Welitsch, Ljuba** (1913– ), Bulgarian soprano. Famous exponent of such roles as Salome, Donna Anna, Aida and Tosca.

**Wellesley,** *see* MORNINGTON.

**Wellesz, Egon** (1885–1974), Austrian composer, musicologist. Pupil of Schoenberg. Settled in Britain in 1938, becoming research fellow at Oxford. Earlier compositions show strong influence of Schoenberg (*eg* in opera *Alkestio,* 1924), but later music is marked by considerable simplification of harmony and ready acceptance of Romantic idioms. Style of opera *Incognita* (1951) leans towards Mozart and Strauss. Other works incl. ballets, symphonies, and choral and chamber music.

**Wellington's Victory,** also known as *The Battle of Vitoria* or *Battle Symphony,* this short orchestral piece by Beethoven (1813) depicts British victory over Napoleon, and quotes various popular tunes incl. British national anthem.

**Well-Tempered Clavier, The** (Ger., *Wohltemperierte Clavier*), title of 2 sets of preludes and fugues for keyboard by Bach (1722, 1744). Each set consists of 24 preludes and 24 fugues in all major and minor keys. They are clearly designed as practical demonstration of advantage of tuning keyboard instruments in EQUAL TEMPERAMENT.

**Welsh National Opera,** one of Britain's leading opera companies outside London, founded in Cardiff in 1946. Repertory ranges from Mozart to Berg to new Welsh works.

**Welte Photophone,** electronic instrument involving use of photoelectric cell.

**Werckmeister, Andreas** (1645–1706), German organist, theorist. His *Orgelprobe* (1681) and *Musicalische Temperatur* (1691) give detailed instructions for tuning of keyboard instruments.

**Werle, Lars Johan** (1926– ), Swedish composer. Opera *Dreaming about Therèse* (after Zola, 1965) was intended for performance 'in the round', with orchestra surrounding audience and audience surrounding singers. Other works incl. opera *The Journey,* ballet *Zodiac,* and Sinfonia da Camera.

**Wert, Giaches de** (1535–96), Flemish composer. In service of Duke of Mantua for many years. One of most prolific madrigal-composers of 16th cent. Also wrote *canzonette* and motets.

**Werther,** opera by Massenet, libretto by E. Blau, P. Milliet and G. Hartmann (based on Goethe's novel *The Sorrows of Young Werther*). First perf. (in German) Vienna, 1892.

**Wesendonk Songs,** 5 songs for female voice by Wagner based on poems by Mathilde Wesendonk. There are passages in common with *Tristan und Isolde.*

**Wesley, Samuel** (1766–1837), English organist, composer. Son of hymn-writer Charles Wesley. Had written considerable amount of vocal and instrumental music by age of 20, but subsequent career was limited by skull injury. Early British enthusiast for Bach. Best known composition is 8-part motet 'In exitu Israel'.

His son, **Samuel Sebastian Wesley** (1810–76), was organist and composer. Organist at various cathedrals. Compositions, not without individuality, are mostly for church.

**Westrup, Jack Allan** (1904–75), English musicologist, critic, composer. As undergraduate, edited Monteverdi's *Orfeo* and *The Coronation of Poppaea.* Worked as critic for *Daily Telegraph*, then held various academic posts before becoming professor of music at Oxford (1947–71). Chaired editorial board of *New Oxford History of Music,* and edited *Music and Letters* from 1959. Books incl. study of Purcell. Knighted 1961.

**Weyse, Christoph Ernst** (1774–1842), Danish composer, teacher. Works incl. operas, and sonatas and studies for piano. Pupils incl. Gade.

**Whale, The,** dramatic cantata by John Tavener (1968), inspired by story of Jonah and the whale. Scored for mezzosoprano, baritone, speaker, organ and Hammond organ, chorus and orchestra.

**When I am laid in earth,** Dido's lament at end of Purcell's *Dido and Aeneas.*

**Whettam, Graham** (1927– ), English composer. Works incl. opera *The Chef who wanted to rule the world* (1969), concertos, sinfonias and other orchestral works, choral, chamber, brass band, piano and organ music, and songs.

**whiffle,** early English name for FIFE.

**whip,** *see* SLAPSTICK.

**whistle,** general name for any instrument imitating human whistling. *See* TIN WHISTLE.

**White, Robert,** *see* WHYTE.

**whithorn** or **may-horn,** very primitive type of oboe made from bark and wood of willow tree.

**Whittaker, William Gillies** (1876–1944), English conductor, teacher, composer. Lifelong campaigner for works of Bach, many of which he edited for public performance. Also made numerous arrangements of other works (incl. folk songs) for school and domestic use. His own compositions incl. orchestral, choral, chamber and piano music, and songs.

**whittle and dub,** early Eng. name for PIPE AND TABOR.

**whizzer** *see* THUNDERSTICK.

**whole note,** US term for semibreve.

**whole-tone scale,** scale consisting of series of intervals of whole tone. May begin on any note. There is no tonic or any other implicit relationship between notes of series. 2 such scales are possible, notation of which may vary according to convenience: C–D–E–F sharp–G sharp–A sharp–B sharp (or C); and D flat–E flat–F–G–A–B–C sharp (or D flat). Scale starting on D is obviously part of same series as one starting on C, and so on. Debussy and other composers have featured whole-tone scale extensively in their music, both harmonically and melodically.

**Whyte, Ian** (1901–60), Scottish conductor, composer. Pupil of Stanford and Vaughan Williams. Head of Music of B.B.C. Scotland (1931–45), then conductor of B.B.C. Scottish Orchestra (1945–60).

Works, often with Scottish associations, incl. opera *Comala* (after Ossian), ballet *Donald of the Burthens* (incorporating part for bagpipes), symphonies, concertos, symphonic poems, chamber music and many songs.

**Whyte, Robert** (*c* 1535–74), English composer. Works, of high quality, incl. Latin church music, English anthems, and instrumental music.

**Whythorne, Thomas** (1528–96), English composer, teacher. Wrote part-songs and vocal duets. Also wrote autobiography.

**Widdop, Walter** (1892–1949), English tenor. Made debut in 1923, and was later famed for his Wagner portrayals.

**Widor, Charles Marie Jean Albert** (1845–1937), French composer, organist. Organist at St Sulpice, Paris (1870–1934). Works incl. 10 large-scale 'symphonies' for organ, operas, 5 orchestral symphonies (2 with organ), 2 piano concertos, cello concerto, *Une Nuit de Walpurgis* for chorus and orchestra, chamber and piano music, and songs. Also edited Bach's organ works in collaboration with Schweitzer.

**Wieck,** *see* SCHUMANN, CLARA.

**Wieck, Friedrich** (1785–1873), German piano teacher, father-in-law of Schumann. Developed own method of teaching piano and practised it with great success. Pupils incl. Hans von Bülow and his daughter Clara, whose marriage to Schumann he initially opposed with considerable asperity.

**Wiegenlied** (Ger.), cradle song.

**Wieniawski, Henri** or **Henryk** (1835–80), Polish violinist, one of most outstanding of his time. Violinist to Czar (1860–72); later taught at Brussels Conservatoire. Toured widely as soloist with brother Joseph, then with Anton Rubinstein. Composed 2 violin concertos and various other pieces.

**Wigmore Hall,** concert hall in Wigmore Street, London, famous for chamber concerts and recitals. Built as Bechstein Hall in 1901 by the firm of piano-manufacturers, but name changed in 1917.

**Willaert, Adrian** (*c* 1485–1562), Flemish composer. Made his career in Italy. *Maestro di cappella* at St Mark's, Venice (1527–62). One of first composers to write *cori spezzati* (works for 2 antiphonal choirs), which became one of characteristics of Venetian composers. Also one of first composers of typical polyphonic madrigal of mid 16th cent., and one of first to write polyphonic *ricercari* for instrumental ensembles. Also wrote Masses, motets, and chansons.

**Willcocks, David** (1919– ), English conductor, organist. Posts incl. director of music, King's College, Cambridge (1957–73), musical director of Bach Choir from 1960, and director of Royal College of Music from 1973. Knighted 1977.

**Williams, Alberto** (1862–1952), Argentinian composer, pianist, conductor, poet. Pupil of Franck. Works, several influenced by American folk song, incl. 9 symphonies, choral, chamber and piano music, and songs.

**Williams, Grace** (1906–77), Welsh composer. Pupil of Vaughan

Williams and Wellesz. Works incl. opera *The Parlour,* orchestral music, concertos and Welsh folk song arrangements.

**Williamson, Malcolm** (1931– ), Australian composer. Resident in Britain from 1953. Substantial output, in varied but consistently direct idiom, incl. operas *eg Our Man in Havana* and *The Violins of St Jacques,* orchestral, chamber, piano and organ music, and church music in pop song style. Appointed Master of the Queen's Musick, 1975.

**William Tell** (Fr., *Guillaume Tell*), opera by Rossini, libretto by V.J.E. de Jouy and H.L.F. Bis (based on Schiller's drama). First perf. Paris, 1829. Overture remains perennial concert favourite.

**Willis, Henry** (1595–1674), English composer, instrumentalist, singer. Worked in service of Charles I and Charles II, and became professor of music at Oxford in 1656. Wrote *Psalterium Carolinum* in memory of Charles I (1657) and *Cheerful Ayres or Ballads* (1660) and other songs.

**Wilson, John** (1595–1674), English instrumentalist, singer, composer. Musician to Charles I and Charles II; professor at Oxford. Wrote many songs, and *Psalterium Carolinum* in memory of Charles I (1657).

**Wilson, Thomas** (1927– ), Scottish composer. Works incl. operas *The Charcoal Burner* (1968) and *Confessions of a Justified Sinner* (1976), ballet *Embers of Glencoe* (1973), 2 symphonies, and choral, chamber, church and piano music.

**wind band,** ensemble consisting of mixed wind instruments, *ie* both woodwind and brass. Term is sometimes applied to MILITARY BAND.

**wind chimes,** *see* WOOD CHIMES.

**Windgassen, Wolfgang** (1914–74), German tenor. Leading Wagnerian HELDENTENOR of his day. Esp. associated with Bayreuth and Stuttgart opera houses.

**wind instruments,** *see* INSTRUMENTS.

**wind machine** or **aeoliphone** (Fr., *éoliphone*; Ger., *Windmaschine*), instrument consisting of large circular frame covered with silk and rotated by means of a handle, so making silk brush against cardboard or thin wood, thereby imitating sound of wind.

**Winter, Peter von** (1754–1825), German composer. Wrote *c* 30 operas, incl. *Das unterbrochene Opferfest* (1796) and *Das Labirint* (1798), setting of Schikaneder's sequel to *Die Zauberflöte* (set by Mozart, 1791). Also wrote church music, concertos for clarinet and bassoon, and other instrumental works.

**Winterreise, Die** (Ger., *The Winter Journey*), cycle of 24 songs by Schubert, to words by W. Miller on subject of unrequited love.

**Winter Wind Study,** nickname for Chopin's piano study in A minor, op 25 no 11.

**Winter Words,** song cycle by Britten for high voice and piano, based on 8 poems by Thomas Hardy. First perf. by Peter Pears and composer, Leeds, 1953.

**Wirbeltrommel** (Ger.), TENOR DRUM.

**wire brush(es),** thin but stiff wires attached to small handles, used to obtain brushing effects from side drum.

**Wirén, Dag Ivar** (1905– ), Swedish composer. Studied in Paris. Works incl. 5 symphonies, concert overtures, piano and cello concertos, chamber, choral, piano and film music, and songs.

**Wise, Michael** (*c* 1648–87), English organist, composer. Became gentleman of Chapel Royal in 1676. Works incl. anthems, services, songs and catches.

**Wishart, Peter** (1921– ), English composer. Pupil of Nadia Boulanger. Works incl. operas *The Captive* and *Two in a Bush,* 2 violin concertos, and organ and piano music.

**Witch Minuet,** *see* HEXENMENUETT.

**Witt, Jeremias Friedrich** (1771–1837), Austrian composer. His 'Jena' Symphony was once thought to be by Beethoven.

**Wittgenstein, Paul** (1887–1961), Austrian pianist. Lost right arm in WWI. Music specially written for him incl. Ravel's concerto for left hand and works by Strauss and Britten.

**Wohltemperierte Clavier, Das,** *see* WELL TEMPERED CLAVIER.

**Wolf, Hugo** (1860–1903), Austrian composer. Studied at Vienna Conservatorium (1875–7), but was forced to leave after disagreement with director. Made precarious living as teacher and critic. Went insane in 1897 and entered asylum, where he died. Began writing songs in 1876, and for rest of his life alternated between furious spates of composition and periods of inactivity. Showed fanatical admiration for Wagner, whose influence appears in his song accompaniments, which often have character of independent instrumental compositions to which voice-part has been added. This is not because he thought singer superfluous, but because his genius for interpretating mood of music led him to write vocal line which, like Wagner's, is virtually recitative, sung in strict time above accompaniment which ensures continuity and logical development of musical ideas.

Principal compositions:

(1) Songs: *Nachgelassene Lieder,* 12 *Lieder aus der Jugendzeit* (1877–8), *Lieder nach verschieden Dichtern* (incl. settings of poems by Keller, Ibsen, Reinick and Michelangelo, 1877–97), *Mörike-Lieder* (1888), *Eichendorff-Lieder* (1888), *Goethe-Lieder* (1889), *Spanish Songbook* (1890), *Italian* Songbook (1891, 1896);

(2) Operas: *Der Corregidor* (1896);

(3) Choral works: *Christnacht* (1889), *Elfenlied* (1891), *Der Feuerreiter* (1892), *Dem Vaterland* (1898);

(4) Orchestra: symphonic poem *Penthesilea* (1885), *Italian Serenade* (1892);

(5) Chamber music: string quartet (1884), *Italian Serenade* (1887).

**Wolf, Johannes** (1869–1947), German musicologist. Edited complete works of Obrecht, and wrote several books on history of notation.

**Wolff, Albert Louis** (1884–1970), French conductor, composer. Conducted at Opéra-Comique from 1911; conductor of Concerts

Lamoureux (1928–34). Compositions incl. opera *The Blue Bird* (after Maeterlinck, 1919).

**Wolff-Ferrari, Ermanno** (1876–1948), Italian composer. Son of German father and Italian mother. Pupil of Rheinberger. Made reputation as opera composer, exploiting attractive vein of lyricism, and showing particular flair for comedy. Most famous works are *I quattro rusteghi* (1906), *Susanna's Secret* (1909) and *The Jewels of the Madonna* (1911). Also wrote choral, chamber and piano music and songs.

**Wolfrum, Philipp** (1854–1919), German composer, organist. Works incl. choral, chamber and organ music, and songs. Also wrote study of Bach (1906).

**Wolkenstein, Oswald von** (1377–1445), German poet, composer. One of last of MINNESINGER, his songs (some for 2 or 3 voices) have certain affinities with folk song.

**WoO (Werke ohne Opus),** identification tag applied to works of Beethoven without opus numbers.

**Wood, Charles** (1866–1926), Irish organist, composer. Professor of music at Cambridge. Works incl. choral and incidental music, string quartets, and songs *eg* 'Ethiopia saluting the colours'.

**Wood, Henry Joseph** (1869–1944), English conductor. Inaugurated London's promenade concerts in 1895, conducting them till his death. Introduced many new works to British audiences. Also conducted innumerable other symphony concerts and festivals in Britain, Europe and US. Made numerous arrangements of older music. Knighted 1911.

**Wood, Hugh** (1932– ), English composer. Pupil of Hamilton and Seiber. Output, though not prolific, is impressively consistent in quality. Works incl. *Scenes from Comus* (after Milton) for soprano, tenor and orchestra, cello and violin concertos, string quartets, and piano pieces.

**Wood, Thomas** (1892–1950), English composer. Pupil of Stanford. Wrote various choral works, with and without accompaniment.

**wood block,** same as CHINESE BLOCK.

**wood chimes,** also called bamboos or wood chimes. Consist of large number of different-sized hollow bamboo canes suspended together. Played either with hand or wooden stick (or sometimes by wind) and give out dry sound that continues as long as canes remain in motion and so hit each other. Occasionally hard wood is used, giving more brittle sound.

**wood drums,** although various kinds exist all over the world, they are rarely seen in concert halls. The 3 most important types are described. The log drum or wooden gong is large, cylindrical in shape, hollowed out, and has slit running almost whole length of centre. The slit drum is similar but differently shaped, and can attain definite pitch. Wood-plate drums are virtually tom-toms with single head made of wood; they are higher-pitched than other 2 types.

**wooden gong, wooden-headed tom-toms, wood-plate drums,** *see* WOOD DRUMS.

**Wooden Prince, The,** ballet by Bartók, based on scenario by B. Balázs. First perf. Budapest, 1917. Now often perf. as part of triple bill with Bartók's 2 other stage works, *Bluebeard's Castle* and *The Miraculous Mandarin.*

**Woodward, Roger** (1943– ), Australian pianist. Known esp. for performances of new music.

**woodwind instruments,** *see* INSTRUMENTS.

**Wooldridge, Harry Ellis** (1845–1917), British painter, musicologist. Published books on old English music, vols. I and II of *Oxford History of Music,* and edited *The Yattendon Hymnal* and vols. XIV and XVII of Purcell Society.

**Wordsworth, William** (1908– ), English composer. Descendant of Christopher Wordsworth, brother of the poet. Works, reflecting belief in traditional tonality, incl. 6 symphonies, 6 string quartets, and many vocal and instrumental works.

**Worgan, John** (1724–90), English organist, composer. Works incl. oratorios and church, organ and harpsichord music.

**Wozzeck,** opera by Berg, libretto by composer based on Büchner's play *Woyzeck.* First perf. Berlin, 1925. Story concerns German soldier driven to murder and suicide.

**Wranitsky, Paul** (1756–1808), Austrian violinist, composer, conductor. Became conductor at Court Opera, Vienna. Works incl. several successful operas *eg Oberon, König der Elfen* (1789), and instrumental works.

His brother, **Anton Wranitsky** (1761–1820), was violinist and composer. Pupil of Albrechtsberger, Mozart and Haydn. Works incl. symphonies, violin concertos, string quartets and church music.

Anton's daughter, **Karoline Wranitsky** (1790–1872), was soprano. Sang Agathe in first perf. of Weber's *Der Freischütz* (1821).

**Wreckers, The,** opera by Ethel Smyth, libretto (in French) by H. Brewster (after play *Les Naufrageurs*). First perf. (in German version entitled *Strandrecht*) Leipzig, 1906. Plot concerns Cornish community which lives by wrecking.

**wuchtig** (Ger.), weighty, heavy.

**Wunderlich, Fritz** (1930–66), German tenor. Made opera debut in 1954. Known for fine performances of Mozart, Strauss and Mahler.

**Wuorinen, Charles** (1938– ), American composer. Has worked extensively in field of electronic music *eg Time's Encomium* (1969), but has also written symphonies *etc* for conventional forces.

**Wurlitzer organ,** type of UNIT ORGAN at one time much used in cinemas.

**Wurstfagott,** *see* RACKET.

# XYZ

**Xenakis, Iannis** (1922– ), Greek composer, b. Romania. Also architect, mathematician, logician and poet. Pupil of Honegger, Milhaud and Messiaen. As architect, has worked with Le Corbusier. Mathematics has had powerful influence on his music; uses computer to speed work of composition, though actual music is usually scored for conventional instruments of orchestra. Works incl. *Eonta* for piano and 5 brass, and *Atrées* for 10 instruments.

**Xerxes** (It., *Serse*), comic opera by Handel, based on libretto by Minato. Incl. satirical aria 'Ombra mai fù' (in praise of a tree's shade), subsequently solemnized under famous title 'Handel's Largo' – though in fact aria is marked *larghetto*.

**xylophone,** percussion instrument consisting of hardwood bars, laid out like keyboard and set in frame. Nowadays instrument is fitted with tuned metal resonators that help to enrich and sustain tone. They do so only to limited degree, in order not to counteract characteristic hard and bright sound. Tone produced depends on weight and hardness of mallets used by player. Range of instrument varies: large ones have compass of 4 octaves upwards from middle C, but many are limited to 3 octaves and fifth or 3 octaves and tone (lower range being curtailed). *See also* GAMELAN, MARIMBA.

**xylorimba, xylomarimba,** large XYLOPHONE with extended compass down to C in bass stave. Its range of 5 octaves covers those of both xylophone and marimba, hence name.

**Yamash'ta, Stomu** (1947– ), Japanese percussionist, composer. Performs own avant-garde works with extraordinary agility.

**Yancey, Jimmy** (1898–1951), American boogie-woogie pianist, of uncommon sensitivity. Often based style on tango and habanera rhythms, as in *Five o'clock Blues*.

**Yankee Doodle,** song used by British troops to deride American revolutionary troops, and later taken up by revolutionaries themselves. Tune dates from at least 1778, when appeared in Aird's *Selection of Scottish, English, Irish and Foreign Airs*.

**Yeomen of the Guard, The,** comic opera by Gilbert and Sullivan. First perf. London, 1888.

**yodel** (Ger., *Jodel*), form of singing found in Switzerland and Austrian Tyrol, involving alternation between natural voice and falsetto. Music tends to be cheerful, making use of simple dance rhythms.

**Yonge, Nicholas** (d. 1619), *see* MUSICA TRANSALPINA.

**Youll, Henry** (*fl* 16th–17th cents.), English madrigalist. Published vol. of *Canzonets to three voyces* (1608).

**Young, Douglas** (1947– ), English composer. Works incl. ballets

*Pasiphae* and *Charlotte Brontë*, and orchestral, choral and chamber music.

**Young France,** *see* JEUNE FRANCE.

**Young, LaMonte** (1935– ), American composer. Pupil of Stockhausen. Exponent of INDETERMINACY school. Works incl. *Poem for Chairs, Tables and Benches* (1960) and *The Tortoise Droning Selected Pitches from the Holy Numbers for the Two Black Tigers, the Green Tiger and the Hermit* (1964).

**Young, Lester** (1909–59), American jazz tenor saxophonist, clarinettist. Worked with Count Basie's band in 1930s and 1940s, his detached, oblique style foreshadowing 'cool' jazz of 1950s. Esp. associated with jazz singer Billie Holiday.

**Young, William** (d. 1671), English violist, violinist, composer. Published at Innsbruck in 1653 collection of 11 sonatas for strings and continuo – earliest known by English composer. At Restoration became one of king's musicians.

**Young Lord, The** (Ger., *Der junge Lord*), comic opera by Henze, libretto by I. Bachmann (after story by W. Hauff). First perf. Berlin, 1965. Story concerns English aristocrat, idolized by townsfolk of Grunwiesel, who turns out to be ape dressed up as man.

**Young Person's Guide to the Orchestra, The,** variations and fugue on theme from Purcell's *Abdelazer*. Score was commissioned in 1945 by Ministry of Education for film *The Instruments of the Orchestra*.

**Yradier, Sebastián** (1809–65), Spanish composer of popular songs and dances. Most famous song is 'La Paloma' (The Dove); another was adapted by Bizet as 'Habanera' in *Carmen*.

**Ysaÿe, Eugène** (1858–1931), Belgian violinist, composer, conductor. Pupil of Wieniawski and Vieuxtemps. Taught at Brussels Conservatoire (1886–97), and founded and conducted Concerts Ysaÿe in Brussels. Toured widely as soloist and as leader of string quartet, giving premières of many new works. Own output incl. 6 concertos and other pieces for violin. Conducted Cincinnati Symphony Orchestra (1918–22).

**Yun, Isang** (1917– ), Korean composer. Moved to Europe in late 1950s, settling in Berlin in 1964. Kidnapped by South Korean secret agents in 1967, he was sentenced to life imprisonment in his homeland. Released after 2 years, he returned to Germany. Works, mixing eastern and western techniques, incl. *Om mani padme hum*, setting of texts by Buddha for baritone, chorus and orchestra (1964), opera *The Butterfly's Widow* (1968), *Réak* for orchestra (1966) and *Shao Yang Yin* for keyboard (1966).

**Zacconi, Lodovico** (1555–1627), Italian singer, composer, theorist. His *Prattica di musica* (2 vols., 1592, 1619) is one of most comprehensive treatises of its time. Compositions incl. canons and *ricercari* for organ.

**Zachow** or **Zachau, Friedrich Wilhelm** (1663–1712), German organist, composer. Taught Handel. Works incl. church and organ music.

**Zadok the Priest,** first of 4 anthems by Handel for coronation of George II (1727). Still sung at British coronations.

**Zaïde,** opera by Mozart, libretto by J.A. Schachtner. Written in 1779, but left unfinished. First perf. Frankfurt, 1866, with additional material by K. Gollmick and A. André.

**Zaira,** opera by Bellini, libretto by F. Romani (based on Voltaire's tragedy *Zaïre*). First perf. Parma, 1829.

**Zampa,** opera by Hérold, libretto by A. H. J. Mélesville. First perf. Paris, 1831. Story concerns pirate who is dragged to bottom of sea by statue of girl he has betrayed.

**zampogna** (It.), Calabrian BAGPIPE.

**Zandonai, Riccardo** (1883–1944), Italian composer. Wrote operas in traditional style incl. *Francesca da Rimini* (1914) and *Giulietta e Romeo* (after Shakespeare's *Romeo and Juliet,* 1922). Also wrote Requiem and other choral works, concertos for violin and cello, and songs.

**zapateado,** spirited Spanish dance, with 3 beats to bar, in which stamping clogs replace more usual castanets.

**zart** (Ger.), tender. *Zartheit,* tenderness. *Zärtlich,* tenderly.

**Zarlino, Gioseffo** (1517–90), Italian theorist, composer. Pupil of Willaert. Reputation rests on his theoretical works *Institutioni harmoniche* (1558) and *Dimostrationi harmoniche* (1571); subjects treated incl. mathematical basis of music, counterpoint and modes. In 1588 published *Sopplimenti musicali,* partly as reply to attack on his theories by V. Galilei. Surviving compositions incl. 3 motets and spiritual madrigal.

**Zar und Zimmermann,** *see* CZAR AND CARPENTER.

**zarzuela,** characteristically Spanish type of opera with dialogue. Originated in 17th cent., declined in 18th, but revived in 19th.

**Zauberflöte, Die,** *see* MAGIC FLUTE.

**Zaubergeige, Die** (Ger., *The Magic Violin*), opera by Egk, libretto by composer and L. Anderson (after puppet play by Count Pocci). First perf. Frankfurt, 1935; rev. version, Stuttgart, 1954. Written in folk-song style, opera concerns violin whose owner, in return for its magic powers, must renounce love.

**Zauberoper** (Ger.), 'magic opera'; type of opera popular in Vienna in late 18th and early 19th cents. Text tended to be based on fairy-tale subject, usually treated comically and with sumptuous scenic effects. Mozart's *The Magic Flute* is greatest work in form; others incl. Weber's *Oberon.*

**Zazà,** opera by Leoncavallo, libretto by composer (after play by Simon and Berton). First perf. Milan, 1900. Story concerns café singer and her love affairs.

**Zeffirelli, Franco** (1923– ), Italian producer, designer, film director. His opera productions at La Scala, Covent Garden and elsewhere are characterized by meticulously detailed realism.

**Zeitmass** (Ger.), tempo.

**Zeitmasse** (Ger., *Tempi*), work for woodwind quintet by Stockhausen. First perf. (under Boulez) Paris, 1956.

**Zeitoper** (Ger.), 'opera of the times'; type of opera composed in Germany, esp. in 1920s, characterized by social realism. Examples incl. Křenek's *Jonny spielt auf* (1927), and Hindemith's *Hin und Zurück* (*There and back*, 1927) and *Neues vom Tage* (*News of the Day*, 1929).

**Zelenka, Jan Dismas** (1679–1745), Bohemian composer, double bass player. Pupil of Fux. Travelled in Italy, and worked at court at Dresden. Recent resurrection of 6 fine trio sonatas has revealed him to be composer of considerable personality. Also wrote *c* 20 Masses, oratorios, cantatas, motets, and psalms.

**Zelmira,** opera seria by Rossini, libretto by A.L. Tottola (after D. de Belloy's *Zelmire*, 1762). First perf. Naples, 1822.

**Zelter, Carl Friedrich** (1758–1832), German composer, conductor, theorist. Friend of Goethe, many of whose poems he set to music, and Mendelssohn, who was his pupil.

**Zémire et Azor,** opera (*comédie-ballet*) by Grétry, libretto by J.F. Marmontel (after P.C.N. de la Chaussée's comedy *Amour par amour*). First perf. Fontainebleau, 1771. Story is adaptation of *Beauty and the Beast*.

**Zemire und Azor,** (1) opera by Baumgarten, libretto translated by composer and K.E. Schubert from Marmontel's libretto for *Zémire et Azor*. First perf. Breslau, 1776;

(2) opera by Spohr, libretto by J.J. Ihlee (based on Marmontel's libretto for *Zémire et Azor*). First perf. Frankfurt, 1819.

**Zemlinsky, Alexander von** (1872–1942), Austrian composer, conductor. Conducting posts incl. Vienna Opera and Berlin State Opera. Settled in US in 1934. Pupils incl. Schoenberg, who wrote libretto for Zemlinsky's first opera, *Sarema* (1897). Other operas incl. *A Florentine Tragedy* (after Oscar Wilde, 1917) and *Der Zwerg* (after Wilde's *The Birthday of the Infanta*, 1921). Also composed 2 symphonies and other orchestral works, choral, chamber and piano music, and songs.

**Zhizn za Tsara,** alternative Russian title of IVAN SUSSANIN.

**Ziani, Marc' Antonio** (1653–1715), Italian composer. Worked in Vienna from 1700. Wrote many operas, incl. puppet opera *Damira placata* (1680), oratorios and motets.

His uncle, **Pietro Andrea Ziani** (*c* 1620–84), was also composer. Wrote operas, oratorios, church music, and sonatas for instrumental ensemble.

**ziemlich** (Ger.), rather. *Ziemlich langsam,* rather slow.

**zilafone** (It.), XYLOPHONE.

**Zimbel** (Ger.), medieval chime-bell. *See* CYMBALS (1).

**Zimmermann, Bernd Alois** (1918–70), German composer. Pupil of Fortner and Leibowitz. Works incl. multiple opera *The Soldiers,* one of most important and influential works written in Germany since WWII. Also wrote 4 symphonies, violin concerto, and choral works (incl. cantata *In Praise of Stupidity* on texts by Goethe). Committed suicide.

**Zingarelli, Nicola Antonio** (1752–1837), Italian composer. Wrote

35 operas, numerous oratorios and cantatas, and enormous number of Masses, Magnificats and motets.

**zingarese,** *see* ALLA ZINGARESE.

**Zink** (Ger.), CORNETT.

**Zipoli, Domenico** (1688–1726), Italian composer. Published *Sonate d'intavolatura per organo o cimbalo* (2 vols., 1716), part of which was reprinted in England as *A third collection of toccatas, voluntaries and fugues*.

**zither,** flat instrument with up to *c* 40 strings, very popular in Austria and Bavaria. Either played on table or on player's lap, according to size. There are 2 sets of strings both stretched over sound box. Larger group consists of open strings and these serve accompanying purposes. Melodic strings (usually 4 or 5) have fretted finger-board beneath them. They are stopped by thumb of left hand and plucked by plectrum held in right. Fingers on left hand are used to pluck open accompanying strings.

**zither banjo,** small sized BANJO with wire strings.

**Zitti, zitti,** trio for Almaviva, Rosina and Figaro as they make ready to escape through window of Dr Bartolo's house in Act 2 of Rossini's *The Barber of Seville*.

**Zolotoy Petushok,** *see* GOLDEN COCKEREL.

**zoppa,** *see* ALLA ZOPPA.

**Zoroastre,** opera by Rameau, libretto by L. de Cahusac. First perf. Paris, 1749.

**Zugposaune** (Ger.), slide (as opposed to valve) TROMBONE.

**Zugtrompete** (Ger.), slide TRUMPET.

**Zukerman, Pinchas** (1948– ), Israeli violinist, viola-player, conductor. Known both as soloist and in chamber music. Director of English Chamber Orchestra.

**Zukunftsmusik** (Ger.), MUSIC OF THE FUTURE.

**Zumsteeg, Johann Rudolf** (1760–1802), German composer. Famous for composition of *Balladen* (extended solo songs with contrasted sections), which formed model for some of Schubert's earlier works. Also wrote several operas, incl. *Der Geisterinsel* (1798, after Shakespeare's *The Tempest*), incidental music, church cantatas, and 2 cello concertos.

**Zunge** (Ger.), reed.

**zurückhaltend** (Ger.), holding back, *ie* slowing down tempo.

**Zweiunddreissigstel** (Ger.), demisemiquaver.

**Zwischenspiel** (Ger.), interlude, episode (*eg* in fugue or rondo).

**Zwölf** (Ger.), twelve. *Zwölftonmusik,* twelve-note music. *Zwölftonsystem,* twelve-note system.

**Zyklus** (Ger., *Cycle*), piece for solo percussionist by Stockhausen (1959). Music consists of 17 'periods', each of which, according to player's whim, can serve as beginning or end of the piece. Composer later suggested that piece could be performed jointly by 2 players.

**Zymbelstern** (Ger.), percussion stop found in baroque organs.

# SIGNS & SYMBOLS

**Time values of notes and rests**
(Each note has half the value of the preceding note; the note symbol is followed by the equivalent rest symbol.)

breve (rarely used)

semibreve or whole note

minim or half note

*or* crotchet or quarter-note

quaver or eighth-note

semiquaver or sixteenth-note

demisemiquaver or thirty-second note

hemidemisemiquaver or sixty-fourth note

NB: A dot after a note increases its value by a half.

**Clefs in common use** (with position of middle C shown)

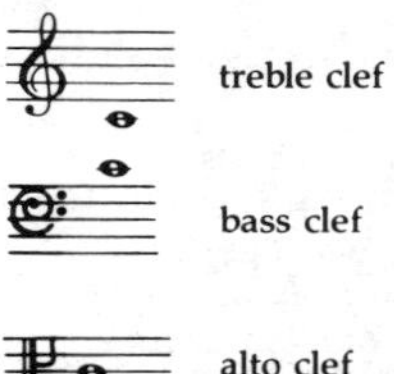


**Accidentals** (*i.e.* signs indicating sharpening or flattening of notes)

♯ sharp – raise note one semitone

| | |
|---|---|
| × | double sharp – raise note one tone |
| ♭ | flat – lower note one semitone |
| ♭♭ | double flat – lower note one tone |
| ♮ | natural – after sharp or flat sign, restore note to normal pitch |

**Time signatures in common use** (giving value and quantity of beats in bar)

Simple duple:

| | |
|---|---|
| 2/2 *or* ¢ | two minim beats |
| 2/4 | two crotchet beats |
| 2/8 | two quaver beats |

Compound duple:

| | |
|---|---|
| 6/4 | two dotted minim beats |
| 6/8 | two dotted crotchet beats |
| 6/16 | two dotted quaver beats |

Simple triple:

| | |
|---|---|
| 3/2 | three minim beats |
| 3/4 | three crotchet beats |
| 3/8 | three quaver beats |

Compound triple:

| | |
|---|---|
| 9/4 | three dotted minim beats |
| 9/8 | three dotted crotchet beats |

$\frac{9}{16}$ three dotted quaver beats

Simple quadruple:

$\frac{4}{2}$ four minim beats

$\frac{4}{4}$ *or* **C** four crotchet beats

$\frac{4}{8}$ four quaver beats

Compound quadruple:

$\frac{12}{4}$ four dotted minim beats

$\frac{12}{8}$ four dotted crotchet beats

$\frac{12}{16}$ four dotted quaver beats

These are the most common time signatures; there are in fact infinite possible combinations.

**Irregular rhythms in common use**

duplet or couplet: in $\frac{3}{4}$ time, two notes to be played in the time of three

triplet: in $\frac{2}{4}$ time, three notes to be played in the time of two

quadruplet: in $\frac{3}{4}$ time, four notes to be played in the time of three

quintuplet: in $\frac{2}{4}$ time, five notes to be played in the time of four

quintuplet: in $\frac{6}{8}$ time, five notes to be played in the time of three

### Ornaments and decorations

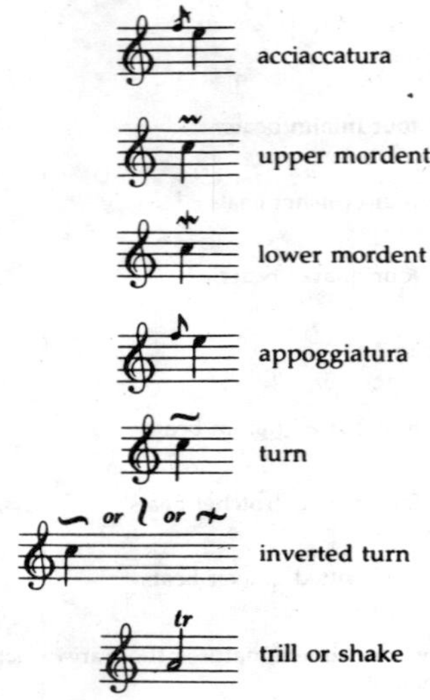


### Dynamics

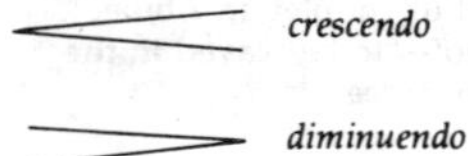


### Curved Lines

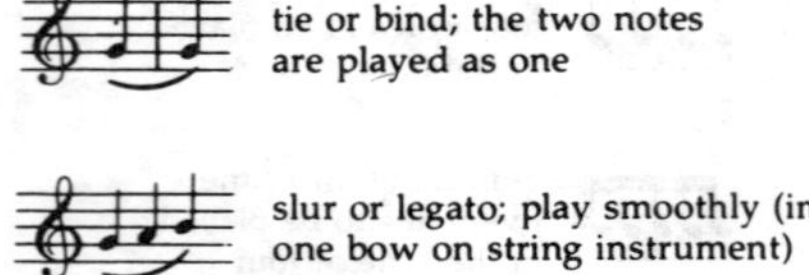


A curved line linking longer passages usually indicates phrasing.

**Staccato marks and signs of accentuation**

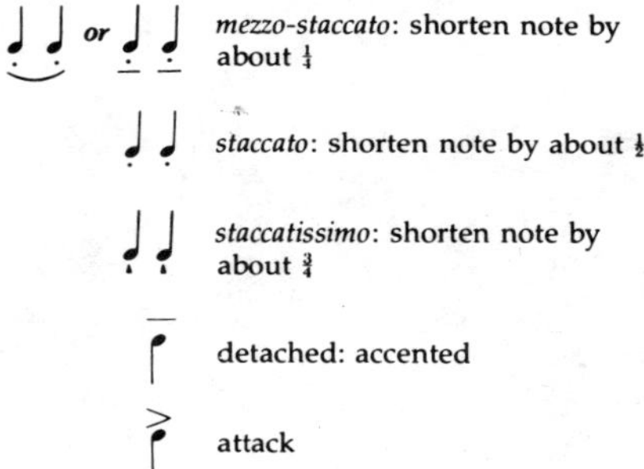


*mezzo-staccato*: shorten note by about ¼

*staccato*: shorten note by about ½

*staccatissimo*: shorten note by about ¾

detached: accented

attack

**Miscellaneous**

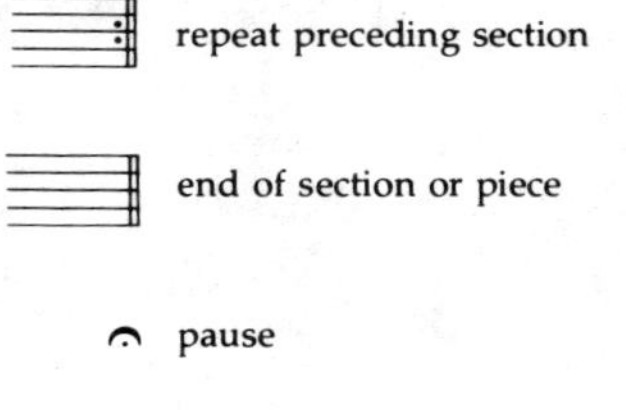

repeat preceding section

end of section or piece

𝄐 pause

8e play an octave above notes written